Handbook of Indian History

Lavanya Vemsani
Editor

Handbook of Indian History

Springer

Editor
Lavanya Vemsani
Department of Social Sciences
Shawnee State University
Portsmouth, OH, USA

School of Historical Studies
Jawaharlal Nehru University
New Delhi, India

ISBN 978-981-97-6206-4 ISBN 978-981-97-6207-1 (eBook)
https://doi.org/10.1007/978-981-97-6207-1

This Springer imprint is published by the registered company Springer Nature Singapore Pte Ltd.
The registered company address is: 152 Beach Road, #21-01/04 Gateway East, Singapore 189721, Singapore

For Aashish and Ramana

Acknowledgments

First of all, I would like to thank my editors at Springer for their support and cooperation throughout the writing and publication process of this book. My thanks are also due to the editorial support team whose support was crucial during the preparation of this book.

I thank my friends for their support throughout the process. My family and friends in New Delhi and Hyderabad supported my research in numerous ways. I thank my colleagues in the Department of Social Sciences at Shawnee State University for their support during my research program in New Delhi as a Fulbright Research Fellow. I also wish to record my thanks to my colleagues at the Center for Historical Studies at Jawaharlal Nehru University for their thought-provoking discussions and support.

I thank our President Dr. Eric Braun for his support throughout the preparation of this book. I thank our Provost Dr. Sunil Ahuja for his support during my research in Delhi as the Fulbright Global Fellow. I would like to thank our associate Provost Dr. Jennifer Pauley for her support and the many interesting discussions. I would like to record my thanks to the Dean of College of Arts and Sciences, Dr. Kimberly Inman. I thank the chair of our department Dr. Chip Poirot, Chair, Department of Social Sciences.

Finally, I would like to thank my husband Venkata R. Vemsani and my son Aashish S. Vemsani for supporting throughout in the process of preparation of this book.

Note of Transliteration

Transliterations are only used sparingly in this book only in connection with linguistic and literary terms. Popular spellings are used throughout the book.

Contents

Editor and Contributors

About the Editor

Lavanya Vemsani is the Board of Trustees Distinguished Professor of History in the Department of Social Sciences at Shawnee State University. Dr. Vemsani is also the Honorary Visiting Professor of history in the School of Historical Studies at Jawaharlal Nehru University and a Fulbright Global Fellow (2021–2022).

She has won a number of academic awards and honors including, Research Professor Award, Distinguished Teaching Award, Shastri Indo-Canada Post Doctoral Research Award, and Best Canadian Ph.D. Dissertation on South Asia 2007 by Canadian Asian Studies Association (CASA) Honorable mention prize.

She is a prolific author and has written well-received academic works including: *Krishna in History, Thought, and Culture: Encyclopedia of the Lord of Many Names*; *Feminine Journeys of the Mahabharata: Hindu Women in History, Text, and Practice*; *Hinduism in Middle India: Narasimha the Lord of the Middle and close to 50 articles.* She is the Editor-in-Chief of *International Journal of Indic Religions* and Associate Editor of *Canadian Journal of History* and *Journal of Indo-Pacific Affairs.*

Her research and teaching interests are interdisciplinary and multifold. She researches and publishes on subjects of ancient history and religions as well as the current history of India. She served as President of the Ohio Academy of History.

Contributors

Bradley Clough (Ph.D., Columbia University) has taught about Asian religions and philosophies for over 30 years, with long-term appointments at Bard College, The American University in Cairo (as the Abdulhadi H. Taher Chair of Comparative Religion), and The University of Montana. Since 2021, he has been a Teaching Faculty member for the Bard College Prison Initiative. His research has focused on meditation and monastic practice in early Indian Buddhism, the history of Sri

Lankan Buddhism, and the religious life of Gandhi. Dr. Clough is the author of the monograph, *Early Indian and Theravāda Buddhism: Soteriological Controversy and Diversity* (Cambria Press, 2012) and co-editor of the volume, *Humanist Perspectives on Sacred Space* (The American University in Cairo Press, 2011). He has published over 20 book chapters and articles, including in such journals as the *Buddhist Studies Review*, the *Journal of the International Association of Buddhist Studies*, the *Journal of Hindu Studies*, and the *Journal of Vaishnava Studies*.

Antoinette DeNapoli is a specialist in South Asian Hinduism with a focus on asceticism, gender, sexuality, embodiment, authority, modernity, and performance. She also conducts ethnographic research on contemporary South Asian Hindu communities centered around the leadership of female gurus and ascetics (*sādhus*), contemporary Hindu feminisms, and contemporary female traditions of devotional asceticism and mysticism in North India. She has recently published a scholarship on sexual abuse and female *sadhus* in Indic Hindu society. Dr. DeNapoli has received fellowships and grants from the American Institute of Indian Studies, Andrew W. Mellon Foundation, American Academy of Religion, Wyoming Institute of Humanities Research, American Philosophical Society, and the Global Religion Research Initiative with the Center for the Study of Religion and Society at the University of Notre Dame. A versatile scholar, Dr. DeNapoli's work draws from multiple and diverse disciplinary traditions and analyzes the forms and dynamics of female agency as accomplished by Hindu female gurus and *sadhus* across power fields. Her first book, *Real Sadhus Sing to God: Gender, Asceticism, and Vernacular Religion in Rajasthan*, was published by Oxford University Press, and her next book entitled, *Female Gurus and Grassroots Feminism: The Modern Struggle for Gender Equality in Hindu Society*, is currently underway with Oxford University Press. She is the editor of and contributor to the anthology entitled, *Gurus, Priestesses, Saints, Mediums, and Yoginis: Holy Women as Influencers in Hindu Culture*, with Dr. June McDaniel, which is forthcoming with *Religions*. Dr. DeNapoli is the John Weatherly Professor of Religion and teaches in the Religion Department of AddRan College of Liberal Arts at Texas Christian University in Fort Worth, Texas.

Michael A. Gollner is a historian of South Asian religions whose research focuses principally on pre-modern and modern Śaiva traditions. He completed his Ph.D. at McGill University in 2021 with a dissertation on the reception history of the *Kāmikāgama*, a scripture which informs many of the practices of major Śaiva temples across South India. He currently lectures in Sanskrit and South Asian religions at McGill University.

Mathieu Gotteland holds a Ph.D. in History of international relations (University Paris I Panthéon-Sorbonne, France). A former Jean Walter-Zellidja fellow (Académie française) and a former Ph.D. fellow of the French Ministry for Defence, he has been awarded by the latter a Prize in Military History (2014).

Justin W. Henry is the Bhagwan Padma Prabhu Endowed Chair (Assistant Professor) in the Department of Religious Studies at the University of South Florida. He has published on aspects of Pali, Sinhala, and Tamil literature in South India and

Sri Lanka, and is the author of *Ravana's Kingdom: The Ramayana and Sri Lankan History from Below* (Oxford University Press, 2023).

Jayendra Joglekar is a Post-Doctoral Fellow at Deccan College Post-Graduate Research Institute (Deemed University), Pune. Jayendra obtained Post-Graduate diploma in Archeology (2013) from Archeological Survey of India (Deemed University), and masters (2011) and Ph.D. (2019) from Deccan College Post-Graduate Research Institute. Jayendra has been involved with archeological research resulting in numerous presentations and publications.

Patrick Felix Krüger studied South Asian art and archaeology and East Asian art history at Freie Universität Berlin, and the history of South Asia at the Humboldt Universität zu Berlin. He received a Ph.D. in Art History of South Asia with a thesis on early modern Jain manuscripts from Freie Universtät Berlin. Specialized on Religion, Art and Culture of Jainism in ancient, medieval and modern India, his research also includes History and Art of Hindu religions; Missionary collections and archives; Religion and Museums. He was visting jun.-professor for South Asian History of Religion at Ruhr-Universität Bochum and interim professor of religious studies at Universität Münster. Since 2016 he is research associate at the Center for Religious Studies (CERES) at Ruhr-Universität Bochum.

Jeffery D. Long is the Carl W. Zeigler Professor of Religion, Philosophy, and Asian Studies at Elizabethtown College, in Pennsylvania, where he has taught since receiving his doctoral degree from the University of Chicago Divinity School in the year 2000. He has authored, among other works, *Hinduism in America: A Convergence of Worlds* (2020), *Jainism: An Introduction* (2009), and, with Michael Long, *Nonviolence in the World's Religions: A Concise Introduction* (2021). In 2021, he received the Ranck Award for Research Excellence from Elizabethtown College, and in 2022, he received an Ahimsa Award from the International Ahimsa Foundation for his work to promote nonviolence through his scholarship. In 2022, he also received the Rajinder and Jyoti Gandhi Award for Excellence in Philosophy, Theology, and Critical Reflection from DANAM (the Dharma Academy of North America) for *Hinduism in America.* He has spoken at a variety of prestigious venues, including three talks at the United Nations. He is the editor of the Lexington Books series *Explorations in Indic Traditions: Ethical, Philosophical, and Theological*

Jyoti Mohan completed her Ph.D. in History from the University of Maryland, College Park, combining her knowledge of Ancient India with the history of European colonization in India. The result, a monograph titled *Claiming India* was published by Sage-Yoda Press. She regularly presents and publishes on French Indian issues at academic conferences and journals. In addition, she is developing several books based on the history of South Asians in the US.

Marie N. Pareja is an Assistant Professor of Art History at Salisbury University, a Consulting Scholar for the University of Pennsylvania, and the Executive Director of the Aegean Bronze Age Study Initiative (ABASI). She also serves as a materials specialist in Bronze Age Aegean plaster for several archaeological teams: Stelida, on the island of Naxos; Sissi, Mochlos, and Gournia, and the South House and Royal Road projects from Knossos, all of which are located on Crete. In 2022, she was invited to co-organize and host the first international workshop on relations between the Indus and Aegean in the Bronze Age at the University of Oxford, and she co-edited the resulting volume, which was published in 2024. Dr. Pareja's most recent work continues exploring the relationships between various regions of Bronze Age Afro-Eurasia through a variety of means, including but not limited to iconography, exchange, and scientific materials analysis.

Rishi Rajpopat earned an MSt in Oriental Studies (Sanskrit focused) with Distinction at the University of Oxford (2017). Having been awarded the Rajiv Gandhi Cambridge Scholarship and Trinity College's MCSC Scholarship, Rishi conducted doctoral research at the University of Cambridge and earned a Ph.D. in Asian and Middle Eastern Studies (Sanskrit focused) in 2022. At Cambridge, Rishi discovered the algorithm that resolves rule conflict in Pāṇini's grammar and therefore runs Pāṇini's derivational machine with remarkable precision – a feat that was covered widely by the global press. In 2022, Rishi won the Gonda Post-Doctoral Fellowship as part of which he conducted Indological research at the International Institute of Asian Studies, Leiden University. Rishi has since been the Academic Editor of the Hinduism section of the St Andrews Encyclopaedia of Theology, School of Divinity, University of St Andrews.

Arjun Rao is an archeologist and Assistant Professor in the Department of History and Archeology of the Central University of Karnataka. Arjun's research focuses on Indian prehistory and landscape archeology, particularly in the semi-arid and tropical savanna regions of Karnataka.

As Principal Investigator, Arjun has led several archeological projects: the Koppa Archeological Research Project (KARP) funded by National Geographic (2017–2018), Rediscovery of Prehistoric Sites of Raichur, Karnataka at the Ancient India and Iran Trust, Cambridge funded by the Nehru Trust for the Indian Collection at the Victoria and Albert Museum (2019–2018 and 2019–2020), Survey and Mapping of the Fortified Settlements of Ancient South Kosala, Chhattisgarh funded by the Luigi and Laura Dallapiccola Foundation (2021–2022), and Stone Tool Economy and Resources Use in Raichur Doab funded by the Indian Council of Historical Research, New Delhi (2022–ongoing). He is Co-Principal Investigator for Nilgiri Archeological Project lead in collaboration with Ghent University, Belgium.

He has delivered talks at professional conferences and seminars in Ireland, United Kingdom, Thailand, and Italy. He has published several research papers in journals of international repute and co-edited a volume on Emperor, Saints, and People (Primus Books, India). Arjun is co-editor-in-chief for the Journal of Archeological Research in India and East Asia Regional Representative for Past Global Changes (PAGES).

Nalini Rao is an Associate Professor in Soka University, California. She holds a Ph.D.in Art History from UCLA and another in Ancient History and Archeology from the University of Mysore, India. Rao's specialization includes South and Southeast Asian Art, Ancient and Modern. Presently she is an Associate Prof. of World Art in Soka University of America, Ca, U.S.A. where she teaches, Indian History, Art and Religion, Ancient and Modern Art, and Architecture, Rao is the author of many books, some of which include, *The Hindu Monastery in South India: Social, Religious and Artistic Traditions* (Harper &Row 2020), (ed.) *Sindhu–Sarasvati Civlilization: New Perspectives Boundaries and Transformations, Lothal: A Glorious Civilization* (Navbharat publications Ahmedabad 2018), *Royal Imagery and Networks of Power at Vijayanagara: A Study of Kingship in South India* (Originals, Delhi 2010), (ed.) *Sangama: Confluence of Art and Culture During the Vijayanagara Period* (Originals, Delhi 2005). *Contours of Modernity: An Exhibition of Contemporary Indian Art* (NR and DB) (G. K. Publications, Bangalore 2005), *Boundaries and Transformations: Masterworks of Indian and South East Asian: Sculptures from the Collection of Dr. and Mrs. William Price* (Amarillo Museum of Art, Amarillo, Texas 1997), Lothal, Belur, and Sravanabelagola. She has published numerous research articles, curated Indian Art exhibits, and organized international conferences. She has produced two videos, (1) Reconstructing the Past, 2011. (2) The Indus Writing and the RigVedic Language, 2009.

She is the Chair of Dr. S. R. Rao Memorial Foundation for Indian Archeology, Art and Culture and Chair, Taksha Center of History and Archeology, Director of Academic Affairs ICHRRF, and Co-editor of South Asia Studies Journal.

Himanshu Prabha Ray is a Research Fellow, Oxford Centre for Hindu Studies, Oxford. She was Anneliese Maier fellowship awardee of Humboldt Foundation from 2014 to 2019. She was the first Chairperson of the National Monuments Authority, Ministry of Culture in New Delhi, India from 2012 to 2015, and former Professor, Centre for Historical Studies, Jawaharlal Nehru University. Her research interests cover Archeology of Religion in Asia, Maritime History, and Archeology of the Indian Ocean. Her recent books include *Coastal Shrines and Transnational Maritime Networks across India and Southeast Asia* (2021), *Archaeology and Buddhism in South Asia* (2018), *Buddhism and Gandhara: An Archaeology of Museum Collections* (ed. 2018), *The Archaeology of Sacred Spaces: The Temple in Western India, 2nd Century BCE to 8th Century CE* (with Susan Verma Mishra, 2017), *The Return of the Buddha: Ancient Symbols for a New Nation* (2014) and *The Archaeology of Seafaring in Ancient South Asia*, (2003). She has jointly edited *The Routledge Handbook of Hindu Temples: Materiality, Social History and Practice*, Routledge, 2023.

Marc Reyes is a Ph.D. candidate in the Department of History at the University of Connecticut. He also is a scholarships and fellowships advisor at Georgia State University's Honors College. A recipient of the Fulbright-Nehru Fellowship, Marc is finishing his doctoral dissertation, a history of India's atomic energy program and its transformation into a nuclear weapons program. In addition to his research and advising, he is a co-founder and editor of *Contingent Magazine*, a historical news magazine for the public.

Herman Tieken studied Sanskrit and Tamil at the Kern Institute of the University of Leiden in The Netherlands, where he later taught Sanskrit. His areas of interest are Kāvya literature in Sanskrit, Prākrit, and Apabhraṃśa, as well as Jaina texts, classical Tamil poetry and the Aśoka inscriptions.

His most recent publication is *The Aśoka Inscriptions. Analysing a Corpus*, Delhi: Primus Books, 2023. He is currently writing short articles on *realia* in Tamil Caṅkam poetry, which are published on his personal website hermantieken.com.

Part I
The Beginnings of Indian Civilization

Chapter 1
Introduction to Handbook of Indian History

Lavanya Vemsani

Abstract This chapter provides the necessary contextual springboard for the Handbook of Indian History.

India is the country with the world's largest population and home to the longest surviving history and lifestyles. Therefore, it is important to understand the history of this unique nation comprehensively through a thorough investigation of broader ideas, themes, and practices. India's role in the Indian Subcontinent during the historical era is immense. Therefore, numerous articles in this book address not only India, but explore its relations to Southeast Asia, West Asia, and Central Asia, including the many nations within the region of Indian Subcontinent.

The Handbook of Indian History examines the expansive history of India in a single volume by focusing on unifying themes of history, while this book also brings forward the new examination of India through its selection of distinct and neglected subjects selected for examination in this volume. The profound examination of special events and impactful personalities of Indian history forms part of the book along with cultural history, including topics of religion, philosophy, and literature as well as science and technology, which provides the intended breadth and depth of knowledge on India. Topics on gender and women's history as well as religious and social history form part of the analysis of a number of chapters throughout the book.

The Handbook of Indian History addresses subjects from the first steps of early Indians to the colonial society and independent India as well as India's international relations.

The Handbook of Indian History is divided into three parts chronologically paying close attention to the subject in each of the three chronological periods under study. Part I is dedicated to the study of subjects of Indian history from the beginning of Indian history to the turn of the first millennium C.E. (390 MYA–1 C.E.). Therefore,

L. Vemsani (✉)
Shawnee State University, Portsmouth, OH 45662, USA
e-mail: lvemsani@shawnee.edu

School of Historical Studies, Jawaharlal Nehru University, New Delhi, India

L. Vemsani (ed.), *Handbook of Indian History*,
https://doi.org/10.1007/978-981-97-6207-1_1

Part I contains articles on India's long history before the turn of the first millennium C.E. Part II contains chapters examining the life and culture of India from the beginning to the end of the first millennium C.E. (1–1000 C.E.). Therefore, Part II includes articles on the historical, cultural, and social development of India during the First Millennium C.E. Part III examines the life and history of India during the second millennium C.E. (1001–2000 C.E.). Therefore, Part III contains articles on the history of India between 1001 C.E. and 2000 C.E. examining the progressive colonization of India. This millennial chronological periodization applied to Indian history in this *Handbook of Indian History* is uniquely suitable to study the long and continuously evolving history of India. Previous divisions of Indian history based on borrowed chronological periodization of history, i.e., ancient, medieval, and modern eras derived from European history are ill-suited to be applied to the history of India. Indian history is different from the history of Europe in that it shows historical development uniquely dependent on the unique circumstances of India amidst its continuous evolution. Indian civilization continues to hold on to its early symbols even though newer cultural traditions are added on to the core of the earlier civilization. There is no complete destruction of older phases of Indian civilization to make way to newer civilizational phases even though there were some course corrections and forced changes to the course of history from time to time. For example, what is considered ancient history across the world is completely different from modern history in many countries across the world. The ancient history, culture, and religion were gradually eclipsed completely across the medieval and modern eras of many nations. However, in the case of India, the symbols of ancient civilization still appear as part of the modern civilization of India. The religions and cultural practices founded in the ancient era of Indian history still continue to dominate the modern history of India. Hence, applying artificial chronological divisions, which depict discontinuation of the previous culture and evolution of a new phase of culture as seen in the case of many countries is not suitable for the purposes of understanding Indian history.

The Handbook of Indian History is conceptualized with a view to illuminate the frequently neglected or less studied aspects of Indian history. Hence, unique subjects such as prehistory, maritime history, gender history, religious history, and colonial history form part of this study.

Part I contains seven chapters including introduction. This chapter *Introduction* provides the necessary introduction, objectives, and background to the present book, *the Handbook of Indian History*. Chapter 2 *The Beginnings of India's History: Archeological and Genetic History* by Lavanya Vemsani utilizes the recently available data to arrive at a comprehensive understanding of the beginnings of Indian history. This chapter traces the history of first Indians and their settlements utilizing archaeological and genetic data. India is postulated to have settlements of 2 major demographic events: The first, during 15 MYA (Million Years Ago) in the form of the first human ancestors also known as archaic humans or hominids (*Homo sapiens*) categorized as Sivapithecene and Ramapithecene (Dryopithecenes) in India. The next larger impactful event is traced to the settlement event of the Anatomically Modern Humans (*Homo sapiens sapiens*) about 170 KYA (Thousand Years Ago). Recent genetic and archeological research shows that these are the only two demographic events that shaped the history of India. However, a new theory, colonial theory introduced in 19th century popularly known as the Aryan invasion/migration was propounded in the twentieth century colonialist histories of India, which proposed a replacement of the original prehistoric settlers of India by neolithic arrivals. However, this third theoretical event merely remains a fictional theoretical proposal due to lack of archaeological and genetic evidence in India. This later migration event (Aryan invasion/migration) has been disproved emphatically by Genetic history, which has already transformed the understanding of Pleistocene human settlements of Anatomically Modern Humans in India, and their contributions to the peopling of the rest of the non-African world, referred to as Foundational event giving the name Founders Zone to India. The legacy of these early prehistoric Founders remains entrenched in the genetic make-up of the current residents of India, as analysis of MtDNA and Y Chromosome heritage of present-day Indians shows, which will improve the understanding of prehistory and shed light on the early human migrations. This chapter together with the other chapters included in this section helps allay the colonialist assumption of Aryan invasions/migrations: Chap. 3 considers the Paleolithic Cultures of India, Chap. 4 considers the Neolithic Cultures of India, and Chap. 5 considers the Bronze Age cultures of India.

Chapter 3 *Palaeolithic Culture of Deccan in the Upper Krishna Basin of India with Special Reference to Recent Studies* by Jayendra Joglekar considers the early peleolithic culture of Peninsular India. Acheulian sites in the Peninsular region of India have attracted academic interest since the early nineteenth century. Previous studies have focused on major centers of Paleolithic culture on the Acheulian sites including Gangapur, Chirki-on-Pravara in the Godavari Basin, Bori, Morgaon in the Bhima Basin, and Yedurwadi in the Krishna Basin, which were discussed briefly in this chapter. However, the main focus of Chap. 3 is examining the new discovery of Acheulian sites in the overlooked Upper Krishna Basin, thus bringing new data into focus disproving the unconvincing reasons previously advanced such as unsuitable raw material (basalt), dense vegetation, and humid environment, etc., were cited for absence of Acheulian record in this region. The present study has successfully brought to light a number of promising Acheulian sites from the Krishna River, Bavdhan nala, and Urmodi River Basins in the Satara district of Maharashtra. The Acheulian assemblages have been collected from varied geomorphic contexts such as coarse channel gravel, cobbly-rubble, breccio-conglomerate, and oligomict conglomerate. The assemblages comprise of >300 artifacts, dominated by cleaver-flakes. Locally available basalt in the form of core stones, boulders, cobbles, and blocks is the exclusive raw material exploited for manufacturing the flake-based artifacts. Chapter 3 shows that the geomorphic contexts and typo-technological study has led to the conclusion that the study area has been occupied by the early hominins at least since the Middle Pleistocene. The present study is the first of its kind which has established the presence of older sediments (at least of Middle Pleistocene) in this region. Therefore, Chap. 3 contributes to tracing the early settlements of India at least to the Middle Pleistocene, thus expanding the scope of the spread of Paleolithic settlements in India. This chapter helps set the course of research included in this volume which helps chart the course of the evolution of Indian civilization from indigenous developments within India.

Chapter 4 *Southern Neolithic Cutlure of India: People, Plants, and Animals* by R. Arjun examine the Neolithic culture of the Indian subcontinent can be broadly categorized into eight geographical zones that flourished during 8000–1200 BCE, specifically focusing on the Neolithic Culture of Southern India. Southern India occupies a major part of the Indian Peninsula, bordering the east and west coasts of India on the Indian Ocean, which is further enhanced by mountain ranges of Western Ghats in the west and Eastern Ghats respectively along the coast. The tract of landscape within these two hill ranges is the Deccan Plateau; the middle and southern part of the plateau has a high density of Neolithic sites of various categories such as the ashmounds, habitation/settlements, stone tool workshop sites, rock art sites, and combination of all these cultural signatures in one site. Such diversity of full-fledged site types and the occurrence of the oldest dates from the region makes the middle-southern part of the Deccan Plateau a core area of the southern Neolithic zone. This chapter takes the reader on each distinct aspect of southern Neolithic culture, ranging from its archaeological studies to detailing their site types, diet, crops, animals, art, tools, ceramics, mortuary practices, and land use patterns.

Chapter 5 *The Indus River Valley and Other Bronze Age Cultures* by Marie N. Pareja serves as a basic introduction to the Bronze Age Indus River Valley Culture (IVC) and other cultures of Bronze Age Afro-Eurasia. This chapter provided an important contextual understanding of the Bronze Age culture of India. This chapter begins with a discussion of the Indus Valley Culture, which serves as a baseline against which other cultures are considered in this chapter. The geographic areas in which each culture lived, as well as key cultural, political, and religious traits, are discussed. When possible, a brief review of the group's early beginnings is also examined. Importantly, this chapter avoids the use the term *civilization* in discussion about the early cultures to describe these different groups, as the word inherently bears biased, colonialist notions. Instead, this chapter discusses people, cultures, groups, and societies that lived in different areas and regions. Other biased terms, such as *advanced* and *sophisticated* are also discarded. This chapter also brings forward new data and presents it in a historically sensitive manner discarding the colonialist tropes throughout the chapter.

Chapter 6 *The Historical Reception of Panini's Sanskrit Grammar* by Rishi Rajpopat adds to the linguistic history of India. The *Ashadhyay* is the world's earliest compendium of linguistics and grammar composed by Pāṇini. It stands out for doing more than merely describing its object language: the *Aṣṭādhyāyī* is a full-fledged machine which helps construct grammatically correct Sanskrit words and sentences through a step-by-step derivation process. In the *Aṣṭādhyāyī*, Pāṇini does not merely give us a general introduction to his work, nor does he discuss the theoretical principles that have been used to construct his *sūtra*s. He conveys whatever has to be said, through his *sūtra*s alone. And this absence of an explicit introductory statement by Pāṇini about the exact nature of his work makes the historical reception of his grammar so interesting: how are we to decide what Pāṇini sought to achieve with his unique grammar and how the commentaries of subsequent traditional scholars have influenced our understanding of Pāṇini's work and motives? This chapter discusses the important aspects of what metarules are and why they play such a pivotal role in scholarly examination of Pāṇini's grammatical framework while also outlining the history of what has come to be called the Pāṇinian grammatical tradition. This chapter also attempts the question that modern scholarship has centered the *Aṣṭādhyāyī* on and whether it can be called a 'machine'. Chapter 6 discusses the problem of rule conflict in the *Aṣṭādhyāyī*. This chapter makes an important contribution to the linguistic history of India.

Chapter 7 *Classical Understanding of Gender in Indian Texts* by Lavanya Vemsani discusses the concept of gender and gender shifting in classical India. Gender is understood through practice and traditional understanding of classical texts. This chapter discusses Amba's transition and journey through two lives along with depictions of temporary gender change in the stories of Arjuna, Bhima, and Shiva. Amba's journey depicted in the Mahabharata brings forward a fresh understanding of gender. Abducted by Bhishma from her own self-choice (svayamvara) ceremony, subsequently rejected by her previously chosen partner, her life turned upside down. Amba vowed to dedicate her life to vanquishing Bhishma. Burning with anger she vows to take revenge on Bhishma in her next life; she is reborn as Shikhandi, initially a female who transitioned later in life into a male, finally killing Bhishma during the Mahabharata war. Amba's unique journey into isolation, asceticism, and life in forest as well as rebirth and gender transition help ascertain the concept of gender in classical India.

Part II of Handbook of India focuses on the history of India from the turn of the First Millennium of the Current Era roughly beginning with considering India's internal history as well as its influence outside of India. Indian history had progressed farther from the days when all aspects of maritime history were neglected. Hence this section begins with examining the maritime history of India on its West Coast while the remaining chapters are dedicated to examining the development of Buddism and its influence on East Asia and other neighbors, history of Jainism, history of Saivism, literary history of Tamil, literary exchanges between India and Srilanka, and history in the Goddess festival. Overall, Part II of the Handbook of India addresses neglected aspects of India's history and India's role in the Indian Ocean world.

Chapter 8 *Sailing Ships and Seafaring Networks: The Indian Ocean and the Maritime Silk Road* by Himanshu Prabha Ray examines the frequently neglected maritime history of India. Traditionally the Indian coasts have been portrayed as inhospitable regions in historical writing, lacking natural harbors and afflicted with a shallow continental shelf and turbulent swells of waves. In addition, colonial historiography has bemoaned the so-called caste system as a major factor in inhibiting travel across the seas. Based on architectural and archaeological evidence and inscriptions, this chapter challenges this long-held notion of Indians being 'inward-looking' and given to agricultural pursuits. Instead, it presents an overview of maritime activity in the period from the second century BCE to the fourteenth century CE from two perspectives: one, the conceptualization of the seas as evident in literary writings and portrayed in temple sculptures. The second relates to the ritual use of sea spaces by analyzing bronze ritual objects recovered from shipwreck sites and discussing these with reference to coastal shrines. The second relates to partnerships and networks established across the Indian Ocean as a result of travels by merchants and trading guilds, Buddhist monks and nuns, musicians, scribes, and a host of others. Thus, this chapter stresses the participation of diverse communities of the Indian subcontinent in vibrant trans-oceanic networks and helps contribute to the understanding of the maritime history of India.

Chapter 9 *Relations Between India and East Asia in Light of Buddhism* by Bradley S. Clough examines historical relations between India and the East Asian countries of China and Japan in light of some of the major interactions that have occurred between Buddhists from these cultures. This chapter contains four parts: Part I provides an introduction to the main doctrinal and practical teachings of the Buddhist tradition, as it arose and developed in India in the last half of the final millennium before the Common Era. Special attention is given to those aspects that made it of universal human appeal, prepared to be transmissible to cultures beyond the borders of its land of origins. Next, the remarkable story of Buddhism's exportation from India, as well as from adjacent regions under strong Indian influence, first into China over the course of the first millennium of the Common Era, and eventually from China to Japan, where Japanese Buddhists too came to regard India as a land of sacred origins, with which they sought meaningful connections. This story will be told in three segments. The first segment, Part II of this chapter, covers the activities of the missionary-minded Buddhist monks of Indian heritage who migrated to China in the earliest centuries CE and engineered the extraordinarily complex, detailed, and challenging work of establishing their religion on foreign soil, primarily by organizing and engaging in the translation of the massive body of Indian Buddhist texts into the Chinese language. The segment will also examine the extraordinary circumstances that led to the creation of a women's monastic order in China, initiated by a cohort of nuns from South Asia. The second segment, Part III of this chapter, will treat the equally impressive endeavors of the dedicated, intrepid Chinese Buddhist monks who, in the centuries following the successful initial implantation of the religion in their own country, journeyed as pilgrims on their own mission to India, to learn and document even more about their chosen spiritual path, as it continued to live and thrive in what they regarded as the sacred terrain of its roots. Finally, in the third segment, Part IV of this chapter investigates the most salient and interesting modern development in the history of interactions between East Asian and South Asian Buddhists. Due to the declining fates of Buddhism in both India and China, not much of historical relevance took place between ancient and modern times. However, in the nineteenth and twentieth centuries, key figures in the Buddhist culture of Japan, where Buddhism had been received from China and Korea 1200 years before and thrived ever since, traveled to India and Sri Lanka, in order to fulfill ambitions quite similar to those of their counterpart Chinese pilgrims from a much earlier era.

Chapter 10 *Shaiva Traditions of Southern India: Tamil Shaivism and Shaiva Siddhanta* by Michael A. Gollner provides an overview of the history of Śaiva traditions of southern India, particularly Tamil Śaivism and Śaiva Siddhānta, beginning with the earliest evidence in Vedic and Tamil Caṅkam sources. The chapter shows how Tamil Śaivism emerged against a background of veneration of the Vedic god

Rudra, the old Tamil cult of Murukaṉ, liṅga worship, and devotional Caṅkam literature of the early 1st millennium. In discussing developments of the sixth to ninth centuries, a broad classification in terms of "lay Śaivism", "ascetic Śaivism", and "Āgamic Śaivism" is provided. Turning to the ninth to fourteenth centuries, there is a survey of Cōḻa-period temple culture and a discussion of major developments in Śaiva literature in Sanskrit and Tamil. A look at developments of the late medieval period shows how the caste-class basis of regional Śaiva monastic institutions changed in these centuries, reflecting an important shift toward non-Brahmin control. Finally, an overview of the origins of the Dravidian movement and neo-Śaivism in the nineteenth and twentieth centuries highlights the role of colonial power dynamics in the construction of Tamil Śaivism and Śaiva Siddhānta today.

Chapter 11 *The Reconstruction of the Early History of Tamil-speaking Southern India* by Herman Tieken discusses the history and culture of Southern India from Tamil sources. Old Tamil Caṅkam poetry contains verses with villagers complaining about their unhappy love lives and poor bards in search of royal patrons who would support them in exchange for poems praising their heroic deeds. The scenes are set in Tamil-speaking southern India from before the appearance of the Pallava dynasty in the 6th and 7th c. On the assumption that the poets describe a contemporary society and in the absence of other material, sources, this corpus of lyrical poetry has become an all-important source for the reconstruction of the history of Tamilnadu and Kerala between the 3rd c. BCE and the arrival of the Pallavas. This chapter argues that the poets did not describe a contemporary society and that Caṅkam poetry was developed only in the 8th c. CE under the *aegis* of the Pandya kings, who wanted to present themselves as the rightful successors of the rulers of that same name of the earlier period and, like them, as patrons of Tamil literature. Therefore, even though this early Tamil literature is an unreliable source for the early history of southern India, it does provide an interesting example of a process taking place around the same time all over the subcontinent, namely the use of the regional languages for fictional literature, which before that was the exclusive domain of Sanskrit. Tamil is not only slightly earlier than the other regional languages but also provides insight into the ideas and successive steps involved in this process of vernacularization. Therefore, this chapter provides a crucial discussion on the sources and history of southern India through an examination of early sources.

Chapter 12 *Jainism in Indian History and Culture* by Patrick Felix Krüger examines the history of Jainism and its role in Indian culture. While the reconstruction of the history of early Jainism is hampered by the lack of reliable sources, the history of medieval and modern Jainism presents the observer with other difficulties. Here it is primarily the severe fragmentation of Jainism into numerous schools and communities as a result of which a common Jain identity among the faithful probably did not exist. The doctrine originally attributed to the Jaina was over time frequently reinterpreted and construed in different ways. Diverging doctrines frequently led to splits and the founding of new directions and schools. These different doctrines and traditions must be taken into account when evaluating the medieval and modern sources; they cannot be interpreted as an expression of a monolithic Jainism, but their validity is often limited to individual groups or communities. This brings into question the concept of Jainism as a unified system of beliefs is therefore, especially for this period, a construction based on Western perceptions and expectations. Therefore, this chapter addresses the evolution of Jainism in its historical development.

Part III Handbook of India examines the colonial era of Indian history during which India was occupied and ruled by invading forces from outside of India by imposing new language and administration. This brought immense changes in the Indian society and culture. This section includes chapters on the history of religion examining the emerging religious conscious of India in a goddess festival and the Vedanta spirituality of Vivekananda. In addition, this section also includes chapters examining colonialism, independence movement of India from outside of India, and India's international relations after Independence.

Chapter 13 *Literary Exchange Between India and Sri Lanka* by Justin W. Henry explores points of contact between India and Sri Lanka with respect to the exchange of religious, poetic, narrative, and philological literature. This chapter examines the initial transmission and translation of canonical and commentarial Pali works in Sri Lanka, the development of Pali literature under the influence of Sanskrit in "the long twelfth century", the prolific and religiously inclusive period of Sinhala literary production during the fifteenth century, concluding with reflections on avenues for future research to enhance our understanding of the influence of Tamil literature on Sinhala.

Chapter 14 *Devotionalism in the Cultural and Social Spheres of India: Popular and Monastic Aspects of Hinduism in History* by Nalini Rao examines the influence of *bhakti* on Hindu monastic organizations and the mode of popularization on Indian monastic system. *Bhakti* as a popular element within Hinduism arose almost at the same time when monasteries emerged and developed; there appears to be an inexplicable relationship between the two. The Hindu monastery is an institution of the ascetic or *sannyasin* who has renounced the world, while *bhakti* is a subjective experience of intense devotion. The two ideologies appear to be in conflict and a conundrum. It raises questions regarding the method and path of bhakti yoga as a means for the popularity of the monastic system. This chapter examines how the ascetic heads redefine, redirect, or re-interpret *bhakti* into the monastic norms of asceticism, teaching, and spirituality. This chapter also addresses the questions of what were the significant changes in doctrine, worship, ritual or imagery within the monastery that attracted the populace? Was it the charisma of the ascetic head (Guru) who weaved the philosophical concepts and *bhakti* poetry or were there other social influences.

Chapter 15 *Hinduism in the New Millennium: History, Tradition, and Practice in a Goddess Festival* by Lavanya Vemsani discusses the cultural change experienced in Indian society due to invading rides of the Islamic rule established in Delhi in the twelfth Century. Focusing on the history and practices associated with the festival of goddesses this chapter contributes to the understanding of the tumultuous history of India at the turn of the Second Millennium of the Current Era.

Chapter 16 *Legacies of Colonial Rule in India: How Race and Caste Continue to Divide Modern India* by Jyoti Mohan examines the use of the word 'race' in the Nineteenth century during the colonial expansion of European powers, to justify and explain why certain nations were able to conquer large parts of the world. In India, French and German Indologists created a hierarchy of races to argue that while India was originally the home of the Indo-European or the so-called Aryan people, explaining away the great cultural achievements of Ancient India as that of others, while its decline was attributed to the racial intermixing over centuries with inferior races. The British harnessed these theories to argue that Indians needed to be governed based on their racial heritage, and created further categories of 'martial' races, and 'criminal' races. They also used the Indian system of social ordering (the caste system) to create concrete, unchangeable categories of hierarchy and power. This chapter looks at the manner in which these colonialist categories were created, and the results of such categories in terms of actual colonial rule. It provides correctives to the colonial studies which justified such divisions and examines the legacy of such categories in contemporary India.

Chapter 17 *Indian Indepentism: Networks Abroad* by Matthieu Gotteland examines the Indian Independence struggles, but from outside of India in both ideas and practice. Foreign events and remote revolutions helped embolden the movement and give impetus to the cause, while inspiration had been found in the—sometimes revisited—history of the West and Asia. Early alliances with anti-British anticolonial parties helped forge from the onset the conscience that the fate of Indian independence was linked to that of oppressed people everywhere. Exposure to foreign ideas and conditions gave shape to a national Indian consciousness shared by Muslims and Hindus, Sikhs, and Bengalis. In Punjab especially, the Ghadr movement is certainly to credit for the widespread rejection of British rule among a population that had been considered a pillar of the empire since the Sepoy Mutiny. Sometimes that also led to rivalries among different sections of activists such as the split between California and the New York Ghadr or the confrontation between M. N. Roy's jihado-communists and Chattopadhyaya's Euramerican parties in Moscow have had the most serious consequences on the overall prospects of success. The claim to transnational identities, based on race, religion or geography, such as pan-aryanism, pan-asianism and pan-islamism, the revisiting of history to claim an equality of rights on the basis of an Indian colonialism or of a superior Indian/Asian civilization were routinely merged and used in the name of furthering the overarching cause of Indian independence. The Indian revolutionaries, pan-jihado-communist networks, or the militaristic nationalists that participated in World War with Japan have participated mightily in the support and provision of this independence movement in India, as well as to the politization of the masses, either through Ghadarite returnees, former jihadists, or simply the publicity given by the British themselves to the numerous trials linked to the activities of political exiles. Through examination of the struggles for India's independence outside this chapter contributes uniquely to the multi-angular understanding of the Indian independence movement.

Chapter 18 *Independent India: Hawkish Neighbors and Few Friends* by Marc Reyes is a close examination of independent India under its first three leaders. All three Prime Ministers dealt with hawkish neighbors and found few friends, both in the decolonizing world and elsewhere. From its 1947 founding, India strived to be an immediate player in global affairs. Its size (a population of 350 million), storied fight for freedom, and later competition with China, attracted the attention of countless people. Because its fight for independence became a global story and foreshadowed the end of British colonialism, Indian leaders like Gandhi and Nehru wanted their nation to handle more than national issues and emerge beyond regional powerhouse; both believed India had a great deal to teach the world and lead it into a freer and more democratic age. The heart of this chapter profiles the first three Indian heads of state and the foreign policy challenges that each encountered. While no Prime Ministers' tenure was the same, all three faced problems with Pakistan and China. All three battled poverty and famine. The three Prime Ministers wrestled with the weight of inheriting the Gandhian mantle and showing that India could offer the world something different; that the violent ways of the past were just that, the past, and that independent India would chart a new path of nonalignment and nonviolence. But all three would have to resort to violence to solve problems. The world may have changed, but how it operated stayed the same.

Chapter 19 *A Living Legacy: The Continuing Influence of Swami Vivekananda in the Western World* by Jeffery D. Long examines the religious changes taking place in India during the turbulent early twentieth century colonial era. This chapter explores the historical background along with the life, and teachings of Swami Vivekananda the impact and continuing influence of Vivekananda in the Western world, which is seen in the existence of Vedanta Societies in just about every major American city, the presence of Hindu themes in the music and lyrics of popular American and British artists, or the teachings of the Jedi master Yoda. Therefore, the imprint of the life and work of Swami Vivekananda forms the central theme of this chapter.

Chapter 20 *How Becoming a Myth Leads to History: A Modern Embodiment of the Goddess Durga as the Female Shankaracharya in Hindu Society* by Antoinette DeNapoli examines Women's access to leadership as monastic heads (i.e., Shankaracharyas) in India has been restricted by enduring patriarchal structures for twelve centuries. Until the female guru named Trikal Bhavanta Saraswati ("Mataji"), who resides in the politically right-leaning northern state of Uttar Pradesh and leads an ascetic women's order she established. the essay illuminates Mataji's performance of personal narrative to rectify gender inequities and restructure power hierarchies, by affirming the normative status of the female ascetic (*sadhu*). A key part of this analysis relates to how she elucidates the feminine symbolism portrayed by the heroic goddess Durga to sanction female *sādhus*' institutional autonomy as a normative right. Through performance, Mataji engenders her identification with the goddess as she acts in myth and in history, empowering women with a localized conception of autonomy as the emanation of Durgā in worldly affairs and the female Śaṅkarācāryā as an incarnation of Durgā. This chapter applies insights drawn from feminist studies, performance studies, and fieldwork observations toward the development of a hermeneutical approach to understanding the roles of religion and gender in Mataji's process of revising perceptions of autonomy as a threat to respectable womanhood.

Chapter 21 *Conclusion.*

India has never completely separated itself from the world stage during any phase of its history. Therefore, each of the chapters included in the Handbook of Indian

History examines important and frequently neglected sections of Indian history while also focusing on the relations, influence, and impact of India beyond the borders with its neighboring nations in the East and West throughout history. The conclusion brings out the contribution of the book to an innovative and comprehensive understanding of Indian history.

Lavanya Vemsani is the Board of Trustees Distinguished Professor of History in the Department of Social Sciences at Shawnee State University. Dr. Vemsani is also the Honorary Visiting Professor in the School of Historical Studies at Jawaharlal Nehru University and Fulbright Global Fellow (2021–2022). She has won a number of academic awards and honors including, Research Professor Award, Distinguished Teaching Award, Shastri Indo-Canada Post Doctoral Research Award, and Best Canadian Ph.D. Dissertation on South Asia 2007 by Canadian Asian Studies Association (CASA) Honorable mention prize. She is a prolific author and has written well-received academic works. Her recent books include: *Krishna in History, Thought, and Culture: Encyclopedia of the Lord of Many Names; Feminine Journeys of the Mahabharata: Hindu Women in History, Text, and Practice; Hinduism in Middle India: Narasimha the Lord of the Middle and over 50 articles.* She the Editor-in-Chief of *International Journal of Indic Religions* and Associate Editor of *Canadian Journal of History* and *Journal of Indo-Pacific Affairs.* Her research and teaching interests are interdisciplinary and multifold. She researches and publishes on subjects of ancient history and religions as well as the current history of India. She served as President of the Ohio Academy of History.

Chapter 2
The Beginnings of India's History: Archeological and Genetic History

Lavanya Vemsani

Abstract While prehistory helps establish the early settlements of humans in India, genetic history helps establish the first human strides. The newly established time clock for MtDNA lineages and Y lineages is one of the most reliable data sources for understanding some of the early migrations and settlements of human groups in India during prehistory. Therefore, the present paper examines the genetic and archeological history of India to help correlate the data from both sources to arrive at a comprehensive understanding of India. This chapter contains two sections in addition to introduction and conclusion. The first section is dedicated to examining the prehistory of India while the second section is dedicated to the examination of the genetic history of India.

Keywords Early Indians · Indian genetic history · Archaeological history · Hominids · Hominins · Pleistocene · East India company · Aryans · Aryan invasion/migration · Siva pithecus · Rama pithecus · Dryopithecus · Attirampakkam · Isampur · Pallavaram · Belum caves · Toba volvanic eruption · Saraswati river · Bagor · Mehregarh · Megalithic culture · Paleolithic culture · Mesolithic culture

2.1 Introduction

The imprint of early Indians is left within the current population of India in the form of genetic data, and their tracks are left in the numerous prehistoric settlements across India.[1] The present chapter examines the established chronology and history

[1] Parts of this chapter are published on my blog manthratalk.blogspot.com. Sections of this chapter might be similar to another version of the chapter which had been included in my upcoming book on Indian history, *Reframing India in World History*.

L. Vemsani (✉)
Shawnee State University, Portsmouth, USA
e-mail: lvemsani@shawnee.edu

School of Historical Studies, Jawaharlal Nehru University, New Delhi, India

L. Vemsani (ed.), *Handbook of Indian History*,
https://doi.org/10.1007/978-981-97-6207-1_2

of MtDNA and Y Chromosomes and correlates the history with the major events in the prehistory of India, to understand the demographic evolution and settlements along with the prehistory of India. Historical India is said to have received 2 major demographic events: the first arrivals and settlements of prehistoric humans about 14 MYA (Million Years Ago) in the form of the first human ancestors also known as Archaic humans or Hominids (*Homo sapiens*). The next larger impactful event is traced to the arrival and settlement event of the Hominins also known as Anatomically Modern Humans (*Homo sapiens sapiens*) during the middle Paleolithic age about 1.9–1.7 MYA. These are the only two demographic events that shaped the history of India. While the imprint of hominids is seen in the early prehistoric settlements of the Paleolithic Era, the evidence of Hominins is noticed in the genetic heritage of the current residents of India. Therefore, India is also considered the Founders Zone since the Hominins of early India are at the root of the genetic heritage of all non-African human populations spread across the world. The oldest non-African genetic heritage is traced to India (Female M and Male C) to be discussed later in this chapter.

2.2 Issues with Previous Narratives of Aryan Occupations: Colonialist Race Theories

Even though archeology and genetic history do not show any evidence of occupations for the period 1900 B.C.E, a new theory popularly known as the Aryan invasion/migration was propounded in the twentieth century proposing the replacement of the earlier prehistoric settlers of India by Aryans, who are said to have become the founders of the population and culture of the Indian Subcontinent. This third theoretical event is said to have replaced or at least partially eclipsed the earlier founders by a new group of people referred to as Aryans in Indian history during the Neolithic phase, who are said to have arrived with the Neolithic package (agriculture, metals, chariot), influencing the indigenous culture of India in a major way. However, evidence is lacking for this premise of third migration into India either in the form of archeology or genetic evidence. The first humans of India Homo Sapiens (Hominids) left their evidence in the prehistory (Paleolithic Era), while the second humans, also known as Anatomically Modern Humans or Homo Sapiens Sapiens (Hominins) left tangible evidence in prehistoric (Upper Paleolithic to the present) as well as genetic history of India, which is still continuing among the Indians in the form of cultural and genetic heritage. The colonialist nature of this theory and its historical evolution has been noted by historians at the beginning of the twenty-first century (Thapar, 1996: 3–29; Bryant, 2001; Bryant and Patton, 2005).

The ancient world is appropriated by modernity in many ways.[2] However, one of the strangest examples of such historical appropriation or rather misappropriation of the ancient world comes from India: The ancient world of the Vedas (Hindu sacred texts) had been appropriated, taken out of context, and misinterpreted to meet the needs of modernity under the British colonizers. Consequently, as modernity was forcefully imposed upon India under the British rule, ancient texts and literature of India were appropriated by colonialist scholars to create historical narratives that suited the colonial rulers by posturing themselves as the superior invaders in the long series of invaders who arrived in India beginning with the mythical Aryans. Max Mueller undertook the translation of the oldest texts of the ancient world, the Vedas, with financial support from the East India Company constructing the myth of the 'race of Aryans' and the 'Aryan Invasion' theory (Thapar, 1996). The British administration used this theory of mythical Aryan invasions to fragment Indian society vertically and horizontally bringing the hitherto unknown racial terms into India. It imposed hierarchy on Indian society by identifying some people of India as the descendants of supposedly invading mythical Aryans. This accomplished the triple purpose: first, it effectively erased the indigenous origins of Indians, Hinduism, and Indian civilization. Second, it divided the society into low and high races or northern and southern races dividing India either vertically or horizontally as they see fit. Third, it also simultaneously normalized the brutal British colonization as another superior race arriving from the north, in the series of invaders similar to Aryans that landed in India supposedly civilizing the masses. Such multiple uses and flexibility in the application of 'Aryan theory' shows its artificial nature, which can be molded to suit any purpose deemed necessary by the powerful rulers. The myth of Aryan race and their invasion/migration into India is the greatest example of appropriation of ancient history and its unforeseen disastrous consequences for the humanity.

This misinterpreted and appropriated ancient world of India wreaked havoc in modern India through imposing fragmentation and segmentation of populations. In addition, this misinterpreted idea of ancient world of India had traveled to the West and resulted in more misinterpretations and imaginary distortions that affected the modernity so as to flame the fans of racism in an unforgettable calamity in the form of the largest humanitarian crisis of the World War II. The Aryan invasion myth, developed from appropriating the ancient world of Vedic India, is so vague and disconnected from reality that it can be retooled and used by anyone in any context, which was exactly what Hitler had done when he infused racist elements into World War II, through his imaginary superior race theories. Appropriation is frowned upon and considered highly inappropriate, but its consequences are not clearly understood. However, here is a glaring example of what types of misfortunes might befall the humanity when such historical appropriations are allowed to spread unchecked without regard for accuracy.

---

[2] An earlier version of this section "Appropriation of Ancient History by Modern World" has been published in the "Head to Head" column of *History Today* (November 2022): 9–10. I thank the editors of the History Today magazine for giving me permission.

The racial classifications of Aryan and non-Aryan races based on the misconstrued notions of the appropriated ancient Indian world were packaged in colonialist textbooks and taught to Indians, which was accepted by Indians educated under the colonialist administration, which was subsequently repackaged and continued to be taught in Indian textbooks even after independence. It is appalling that these constructions are still taught across the world as part of the world history curriculum. The education system has failed to remedy such baseless appropriations of the ancient world by incorporating the Artificial theories of 'Aryan race' and 'invader versus indigenous' deftly designed by the colonialists. Even though, there is a general trend of appropriating ancient literature to create fictional works of art and literature, such appropriations in the subject of history can be calamitous. Aryan superiority theories have caused the deaths of close to 12 million people directly and killed an equal number indirectly. Therefore, these misappropriations need to be countered urgently, especially in view of the disasters it has fueled, and artificial terms like the Aryan race must be banned from use immediately.

Colonial states brought with them the theoretical identity shift, which helped colonial governance, by making them amenable to a group of the general population of the governed, generally a minority, already threatened by the majority. They cling on to this new-found superior identity offered by the colonial rulers, and become part of the exploiters separated from the governed public, by the new theories of identity being popularized by the colonial government. Some of the post-colonial states wrestle with this pseudo-identity for many years, which becomes an irreversible obstacle in their state formation and nationhood. African states such as Yemen, Rwanda, and Sudan, still wrestle with this issue, although India has found some peace, this issue still continues to plague the identity politics in India, conveniently grabbed by two opposing political sections of society- the so-called oppressed and the neoconservatives. Two race theory always involves an indigenous group, and an invader group, although their origins are mired in mystery, this theory has worked in a number of colonial states, sometimes leading to ravaging results in some post-colonial states such as Rwanda (Des Forges, 1995). The invaders are always pale skinned, and come from north, while the indigenous are always dark skinned and come from the south in general. Buying into this theory of dual race origin of Indian population, Indian epics such as *Mahabharata*, and especially *Ramayana* are reinterpreted as representing the struggle between the invaders and the indigenous tribes. The story of Ramayana is interpreted to show that Ravana is the leader of the indigenous tribes, while Rama is shown as the repressing invader. Contradictory evidence of appearances or story is ignored (while Rama is dark skinned, his wife Sita is of dark tan color (the color of the indigenous people), and Ravana is fair skinned and resided on an island off the coast of India raiding the mainland from time to time.

Even though there is no evidence for the theoretical Neolithic migration event (theorized as Aryan invasion/migration) in either archeological or genetic data this theory continues to persist in the narratives of early Indian history. No major outsider led invastions, conquests of settlements, or occupations are noted during the Neolithic era in India in the form of mass burials, proliferation of new weapons, or massive destruction of habitations. No evidence of introduction of a new mode of life or new production was noticed as there were no new abrupt habitations or no new styles of pottery. Continuity is noticed across settlements. Neolithic cultural practices and material evidence such as pottery show continuous evolution rather than abrupt introduction of new culture or material, which disproves emphatically mass arrivals, conquests, or occupations. This emphatic continuity and indigeneity noted in archeology are also supported by genetic history, which has transformed the understanding of Pleistocene human settlements of Anatomically Modern Humans in India, and their contributions to the peopling of the rest of the non-African world, acquiring the epithet of Founders Zone. The legacy of these early prehistoric Founders remains entrenched in the genetic make-up of the current residents of India, therefore, analysis of MtDNA and Y Chromosome heritage of present-day Indians will improve the understanding of prehistory and shed light on the continuous history of India. I first examine the archeological history (also spelled archaeology) of the prehistory of India followed by an examination of the genetic history of India.

2.3 Archeological History of India

Archeological evidence of early human strides is noted in two forms: 1. Human Skeletal evidence and 2. Habitational Settlements and Cultural remains.

2.3.1 Human Skeletal Evidence: Early Hominids and Hominins of India

Due to the long timelapse and the tropical nature of weather in India, it is rare for organic matter to survive the ravages of time to be available to the modern world. However, fragments of early human skeletons appear in prehistoric sites across the world. Skeletal evidence for the Archaic Indian subcontinent is characterized by tropical monsoon climate with characteristic rainfall in Summer (May–June) and Fall (Aug–Sep). Major fluctuations in rainfall are said to have influenced population dynamics during the Pleistocene resulting in a significant shift in the populations of archaic humans (Allchin et al., 1978; Paddayya, 2002; Paddayya 2000; Mishra, 1992). However late Pleistocene and Holocene is characterized by stable weather conditions except for occasional short dry spells recorded in northwestern India and in the formation of the Great Indian Desert or Thar Desert (Kar, 2001). Humans (Homo Sapiens) known as the Pithecines, called by various regional names across the world, as Neandarthals, Australoid, etc., are also noticed in India. A large Pithecine known as Giganto Pithecus and other categories of Pithecines were excavated in the Subcontinent of India by archeologists since the 1800s. Pithecines are known by a variety of names in the Subcontinent such as Siva Pithicus in the Himalayan region and Rama Pithicus in southern and central India. The First Humans/Archaic humans

(Homo sapiens) set foot in India about 15 million years ago (Misra, 2001). Ramapithecus and Sivapithecus identified from the paleontological analysis are two genera of the earliest Higher Primate Subfamily, known as Dryopithecus, which is classed as the genera of Pongid (a term no longer under use). However, this places Indian origins of early humans at an early phase. India is next to Africa in the Human strides of early populations due to the presence of human remains belonging to Dryopithecus. Ramapithecus is the earliest known Hominid some 5 or 6 times older than Pleistocene Hominids (Pilbeam, 1966: 1–2). The remains of Ramapithicus resemble Hominidea and Pongidea equally, leading the scientists to conjecture its early origins. However, the term Pongidea (Great Apes/Higher Primates) is no longer in use as all the primates are classed under Hominidea currently. The other Pithecene noted in India, Sivapithecus also belongs to Dryopethicus. Both Ramapithecus and Sivapithecus are found in early excavations in India putting the early human strides in India at 14–15 Million Years Ago, the beginnings of human origins, pushing it into late Miocene or early Pliocene Era (Pilbeam, 1966: 1–5). Therefore, the human history in India begins with early settlements of Paleolithic culture datable to nearly 14 million Years Ago. More specimens of Dryopithecene are excavated from Hathnora (Sonakia et al. 1985: 612–16) on the northern bank of Narmada earning the name Narmada man for the Hominid skeleton and another from Isampur Karnataka (Paddayya et. al. 2000: 751–2). Dryopithecene (Siva Pithecus and Ramapithecus) settlements are noticed across India through their Paleolithic habitations across India.

2.3.2 *Indian Foundations: Early* **Hominids** *and* **Hominins** *of India*

Humans along with the other great apes (Orangutans, Gorillas, and Chimpanzees) belong to the family of Hominidea, which contains the Great Apes and Lesser Apes along with Human ancestors, since all of them are considered to have evolved from a common ancestor, who lived about 14 MYA. Human ancestor of the Hominidae family, the Hominids gradually evolved and separated from the other Hominids, due to distinct physical characteristics including large brains, voice box (developed vocal cords), and upright posture. Hominid remains in India are variously named after the Gods, such as Sivapithecus in northern reaches of the Himalayas and Ramapithecus in the rest of the Subcontinent (Kennedy, 2000: 1–28). Ramapithecus is the earliest known specimen of the Dryopithecus known from India and East Africa datable to 14 MYA (Pilbeam, 1966: 1–5). This and several varieties of the early *Hominid* fossils were recovered from archeological excavations across India. Two major waves of prehistoric human migrations (Hominid and Hominin) were noted based on the environmental data (Eudald et al., 2010). It is not possible to know how or when the early population migrations might have occurred or if they have happened at all. However, strong evidence of Hominid and Hominin settlements in India establishes very early dating for their arrival in India. Genetic history posits India at the root of all non-African population obtaining India the epithet of Founders Zone. The Hominids of India are dated to as early as Africa to 14 MYA and Hominin arrivals might only date to 74 KYA based on their genetic heritage preserved in the current population of India, however, they might have arrived prior to the Middle Paleolithic era as cultural change can be noticed by the Upper Paleolithic era. Of these, the earliest stone industry along with Hominid skeletal remains is noted in India between 1.9 MYA in Hathnora (Sonakia et al. 1985) and Attirampakkam (Akhilesh, 2018) as well as 1.4 MYA in Isampur (Paddayya et al. 2000). Lower Paleolithic (also spelled Palaeolithic) tool assemblages are found across the Indian Subcontinent, sometimes might contain Hominid fossils along with other animal remains, which indicates that the Lower Paleolithic hominid settlements might have spread across India. Archeologists question the hypothesis of 'Out of Africa' theory based on the evidence of tools, (bifaces and Middle Paleolithic tools) which are coeval with dating of African tools which shows that the African and Indian Hominids might have been developing the tool making skills at the same time (Akhilesh, 2018). However, Lower Paleolithic tools are not always accompanied by hominid fossils in all the Lower Paleolithic settlements but were found sporadically found in a few archeological excavations at these early sites, which might have been due to the short shelf-life of organic matter in temperate climate zone like India. Tools and fossil finds become more frequent in later habitational layers from the Upper Paleolithic era onwards. However, there is a disjunction between the tool assemblage and cultural characteristics noted between the Lower Paleolithic and Middle to Upper Paleolithic, which is attributed to the appearance of Hominins in India during later Paleolithic era, whose genetic traces are represented in genetic ancestry of the current population of India. This indicates that early *Hominid* ancestors were replaced later by the *Hominin*s (Anatomically Modern Humans) during Upper Paleolithic period, whose DNA is most commonly represented in the living populations across the world, although it is not uncommon to find traces of early Hominid DNA rarely. The Middle Paleolithic period could truly be called the transitional phase of the first Human settlements since demographic replacement between Hominids and Hominins might have brought revolutionary changes of civilization.

The prehistory of modern humans in India can be represented in three major establishing events: first, the pioneer arrivals of Hominids and Hominins during the Middle and Upper Paleolithic eras respectively; second, Mesolithic expansion and cultural settlements of Hominins across India and their successive migrations into all of the non-African world including Southeast Asia and the Oceania as well as the Europe, third the Neolithic expansion and regionalization of Early Founders across India. While all of these continuous evolutionary indigenous historical events are well recorded in archeological date and well noted throughout the Indian subcontinent, the Neolithic is pushed into controversy by the introduction of artificial Aryan invasion/ migration theory during the late nineteenth century colonial rule of India. The archeological phases noted above, such as the Paleolithic, Mesolithic, and Neolithic phases are continuous and left sedimentary deposits that could be tracked in archeological sediments as well as genetic markers in the current residents of India. No disjunctions or sudden changes in any of the occupational levels of prehistoric India are noticed at any of excavated archeological prehistoric sites across India. Neolithic settlements across India indicate spread and diversification rather than any sudden destruction or occupation indicating continuous indigenous development and evolution.

2.4 Habitational Settlements and Cultural Remains: Prehistory of India

The prehistory of modern humans in India can be represented in three major establishing events: first, the pioneer colonization of the Middle and Upper Paleolithic, second, Mesolithic expansion and cultural settlements across India and migration into Southeast Asia, as well as Europe, third the Neolithic expansion and regionalization. While showing continuity and gradual evolution all of these historical events are well recorded and well noted on the Indian subcontinent.

However, varieties of Lower Paleolithic phases are noticed in India. If the people of all the cultural phases noted across India might have been the same or not have dominated discussion on the Paleolithic settlements of India.

Although early arrivals of Hominids are noted in Miocene or Pliocene era, during the Pleistocene era (the last great ice age dated between 2.5 MYA (Million Years Ago) to 11.5 KYA (Thousand Years Ago)) Hominins (Anatomically Modern Humans), plants and animals spread through India including all of the Indian Subcontinent and the Southeast Asia as far as the South Pacific.

History is considered to begin with written record. However, the early human journey of prehistory and protohistory leave adequate data in cultural and physical material of early life to enable us to reconstruct the early history of human journey. Immense data is preserved in the subcontinent beginning with the Pleistocene settlements of early humans.

The Paleolithic Age of India is dateable to Paleolithic settlements of early humans is dateable to the middle and late Pleistocene are noted in India from 2.1 MYA to 10 KYA (Chakrabarti, 1999: 53; 74–75). The Paleolithic is divided into three phases Lower Paleolithic Age (2.1 MYA−380 KYA), Middle Paleolithic Age (380 KYA−200 KYA), and Upper Paleolithic Age (200 KYA−15 KYA). Upper Paleolithic lifestyle based on hunter-gatherer food subsistence is still noticed among some of the vanavasi (forest dwellers of India). The Indian Paleolithic Age is important for the discovery of early settlements of humans, both Archaic humans (Hominids also known as Homo Sapiens) and Anatomically Modern Humans (AMA/hominins also known as Homo Sapiens Sapiens) dateable to early periods besides Africa.

The first Paleolithic stone Hand-axe was discovered by Robert Bruce Foote at Pallavaram near Madras in 1863 (Foote, 1916; Chakrabarti, 1979). Soon other discoveries followed at Attirampakkam, and Belum Caves in Kurnool district of Andhra Pradesh, the second largest cave system of India, with a significant amount of cultural artifact pertaining to early human settlements. Belum caves along with numerous other discoveries in Andhra Pradesh played an important role in demonstrating the early life of prehistoric humans (Vemsani, 1999). With these discoveries, the significance of prehistoric settlements to understand the early history of India is established.

Most of the excavated sites of this phase are called after the site of their first discovery. Although stone tools predominate in Paleolithic cultures slight variation and gradual development is noted across technologies in the Paleolithic cultures. Even though there might be some variation most of the Lower Paleolithic showed Chopper/Chopped technology (Northwestern India) and Achuelian technology large bifacials, namely large flake tools such as handaxes and others found across the extent of India, that used large stone tools, which showed a gradual shift toward Levelloise and small flake tools by the Middle Paleolithic period (Paddayya, 1999). Sophisticated stone tool technology, and various advanced hunting techniques are noted in the Upper Paleolithic phase. Archeologists consider the tool and cultural change of the Middle Paleolithic to indicate demographic change indicated by the extinction of Hominids and the settlements of Hominins. The change in stone tool technology along with the cultural changes noted in the Middle Paleolithic Age was attributed to the demographic changes due to the successful settlements of Hominins, who share more common features with the modern humans than the previous Hominids.

Early human habitations of *Hominids* are noted in the Indian Subcontinent beginning as early as 14 MYA while they might have been replaced later by the Hominins (Petraglia and Hannah).[3] Hominids, the Archaic Human beings (*Homo Sapiens*/ commonly) appeared in India in the early Pleistocene fossil record while the anatomically modern human beings (*Homo Sapiens Sapiens*/commonly known as *Hominins*) are noted in the genetic heritage of modern day Indians living in the Indian subcontinent and dates as far back as 74 thousand years ago (KYA). This is the earliest genetic evidence of any non-African genetic history, placing India at the Founders Zone. Even though *Hominins* may have been present in India, since the early Pleistocene Era (2.5–1.4 MYA), since the Middle Paleolithic supports the Hominin settlements, genetic evidence of their occupation and settlement may date to the last stage of Pleistocene Era (73 KYA) due to natural calamities such as the Toba volcano eruption. Recent research has shown that the arrival of Hominins might date earlier models presented at 125,000 Years Ago, since the Middle Paleolithic tool assemblages at Attirampakkam are dateable to about 380,000 Years Ago.[4]

Middle Paleolithic tools (1.4–1 MYA) are more abundant and widespread throughout the region of the Indian Subcontinent, which indicates the range of human settlements not only in India, but the rest of the Indian Subcontinent. The earliest art and artifacts in India are noted abundantly in the Himalayan foothills and the peninsular region of India: noteworthy among them being the Bhimbetka caves of central India (Misra, 1978). Upper Paleolithic (1.2 MYA–55 KYA) tools and fossils appear frequently throughout the Indian subcontinent, and archeologists even claim

[3] Hannah V. A. J and M. D. Petraglia. "Modern Human Origins and the Evolution of Behavior in the Later Pleistocene Record of South Asia." *Current Anthropology* 46:5 pp. S3–S28.

[4] Akhilesh et al., (2018).

continuity between the founders of the Upper Paleolithic culture and the modern residents of the subcontinent. Therefore, the archaic human beings (*Homo Sapiens*) of the Lower and Middle Paleolithic cultures may have been replaced by anatomically modern human beings (*Homo Sapiens Sapiens*) sometime during the Middle Paleolithic period, completely replacing them by the Upper Paleolithic period, which is further corroborated through genetic research. Recent research focusing on DNA has provided the necessary evidence for the late Pleistocene settlements and demographic continuity of early human settlements from Middle Paleolithic onwards and civilizational continuity in India including the rest of the Indian Subcontinent further spreading into Southeast Asia up to Australia by 46 KYA.

2.5 Genetic History of India

It is generally accepted that historians take help from numerous corollary subjects to understand this early phase of history. Similarly, in the case of Indian history data from anthropology, archeology, geography, and geology was utilized formerly. However, excessive reliance on linguistics at the expense of other subjects to devise and impose racial theories misled historical understanding of India as noted in the case of Aryans. Currently, this list is joined by another young subject, the genetic history. Important information from archeology and genetic history will be utilized to present the beginning of history in the Subcontinent of India during the late Pleistocene Era. Before we begin a comprehensive examination of available evidence it is important to discuss some of the colonialist theories based on misinterpretation of the Vedas. Hence, this chapter is dedicated to examining the previous theories of historical origins of Indian civilization followed by a discussion of information from archeological and genetic history research.

Although Upper Paleolithic Age is dated to the late Pleistocene period (1 MYA–55 KYA), the Mitochondrial DNA (MtDNA/female) genetic heritage of India, represented by M clade, dates from about 74 Thousand Years Ago (KYA). Similarly, male genetic heritage Y-DNA (male), represented by C clade, genetic heritage dates from about the same age from 74 Thousand Years Ago (KYA).

Most ancient and ancestral DNA might have been lost due to the Toba volcano with the later populations deriving from small surviving population of the middle region of India. It seems that most of the Pleistocene settlements could be traced only from fossil and archeological artifacts rather than from genetic heritage. One reason put forward to explain this disparity between widespread cultural layers and lack of parallel genetic heritage is the eruption of the Toba volcano in Indonesia about 75 KYA. This eruption had a cataclysmic effect on India and Southeast Asia covering most of the land with a thick layer of ash, which caused the extinction of most of the living population at that time. Hence only a small surviving group of humans remained in the Southern tip of India. From these came the ancestral population of India from 74 Thousand Years Ago (KYA) currently represented in a large section of the population of India, which subsequently also spread to the rest of the world with subsequent evolutions. Therefore, even though the early settlements, tools, and human fossils of Indian Subcontinent date from the early Pleistocene Era and continuous occupation levels are noticed at most of the Prehistoric settlements, DNA heritage is slightly later, one explanation which was explained through the Toba volcano eruption.

2.6 Foundational Zone: Genetic Evidence of Early Humans of India

Tribes of India have become a major focus in the renewed interest in understanding human origin and spread through genetic evidence as they remained outside the fold of mainstream civilizational changes mostly preserving the prehistoric lifestyles. Genetic research establishes that India is home to the three major clades of female genetic heritage MtDNA, M, N, and R that originated in India and spread throughout the rest of the world except Africa. Numerous studies have been published on the genetic profiles of Indians including tribal and caste populations, with very old mitochondrial DNA dated for M clade, while the subsequent mtDNA clades, N and R, have originated within the Indian Subcontinent itself (Palanichamy et al., 2006: 966–78; Thangaraj, 2006: 136–151). The mitochondrial DNA lineage M is the oldest non-African female genetic lineage in the world. All non-African female genetic heritage ultimately traces to this major M clade, while the African female genetic heritage traces to L. Scholars dispute the place of origin of M either in Africa or India, while the most recent studies lean toward placing its origin in India, due to the lack of any ancient and deep-rooted mitochondrial M clades in Africa or West Asia, except for a single, very young M1 clade in Ethiopia. This clade is considered to have been the result of a back migration (Rajkumar et al., 2005: 5–26). Therefore, it could be said that the M clade originated in India and its subclades N and R evolved in situ in India.

India therefore possesses the oldest DNA for M macro haplogroup, dated as far back as 73KA−55KA, while N and R clades are dated to 50KA−70KA.[5] Historians and Archeologist have excavated Paleolithic tools from Toba Volcanic Ash in southern India and the Deccan region which supports the hypothesis for destruction and slow recovery of the population after the calamitous Toba volcanic eruption (Korisettar, 1988). The M haplogroup shows the greatest variation in India with almost 23 lineages arising directly from the M trunk (Rajkumar, 2005: 2–13) associated with the initial peopling of the Indian Subcontinent during Pleistocene settlement and rules out theories of subsequent recolonization events such as the Aryan invasion during the Neolithic period. The Initial mitochondrial DNA pool established in India

[5] Toba volcano in Indonesia erupted 73,000 years ago, covering most of the Indian Ocean region in ash and dark clouds. The genetic evidence therefore, dates from this period onwards, although archaeological evidence of existence of human settlements is dated much farther back in India. Pearce et al. (2014).

upon the initial peopling of India during the Pleistocene has not been replaced but shaped in situ with relatively minor events of gene flow (Metspalu et al., 2005: 1–24). About 60% of Indians trace their matrilineal heritage in M haplogroup regardless of the caste or tribe social groupings, while the remaining derive from the N, and R lines, which evolved from M in India. The remaining 40% trace their genetic heritage from subsequent clades of M and N, and their evolutionary clades. This haplogroup is represented by 58% of the caste and 72% of the tribal populations (Metspalu et al., 2005: 1–25). Successive clades of M Haplogroup and its subclades are represented in populations of Southeast Asia to Australia, which indicates a successive migration of early human groups from India toward Australia (Kaldma, 1999).

The Haplogroups, M2, M3, M4, M5, M6, M18, and M25 are exclusive to India, while all the branches of M haplogroup, M*, C, D, G, E, and Z are observed in other parts of Asia. The subsequent branches of MtDNA, N clade, called haplogroup W is represented by 5% of the population in the North (Gujarat, Punjab, and Kashmir). The R haplogroup is represented by its subclade U, by its Indian specific subbranches of haplogroup U2 (U2i: U2a, U2b, U2c throughout India & U7 in Punjab). These are represented throughout India at 15% among caste and 8% among tribal populations (Metspalu et al., 2005). The recent Rakhigarhi aDNA revealed U2b2, one of the clades originating in India from R, which rules out any outside habitations in India during the neolithic period (Shinde et al., 2019). Although the tribal populations of India are classified variously as n-groid, mongoloid, and australoid based on their physical appearances, they do not show any significant difference in their genetic heritage when compared with the other social groups of India. Hence, it can be assumed that the differences in physical characteristics among native populations of India may be the result of environmental and lifestyle changes rather than genetic changes mediated by population replacement. Uniformly spread continuous branching of mtDNA and Y-DNA across the Indian Subcontinent preclude any assumptions of subsequent population replacement, such as those proposed earlier by the Aryan migration theories. Similar genetic history is represented among the male genetic heritage of India discussed below, which rules out the male derived invasions/migrations. Similar genetic history is noticed among the males of India also, which shows in situ evolution.

2.7 Male Genetic Heritage

The male genetic heritage (Y-DNA) in India is also equally uniform and represents origins in the Indian Subcontinent. The Y-DNA heritage in India is represented by M173, and its successor branch of C (74,000 Years Ago) and its subsequent derivatives R, and M17 (R1a) and is found in high frequencies in India, datable to 56,000 to 36,000 years ago (Karafat et al. 1999; Zhong, 2010). This is the oldest male non-African genetic lineage found outside of Africa. All non-African male lineages trace to this genetic clade C found in India while African genetic heritage traces back to clades A and B. Subsequent clades of these lines, C, F, K, D, L, and R2 are all commonly and widely found in India. MtDNA and Y-DNA lineages in India are much older and more widespread than Europe and Eurasia. In Europe and Eurasia, the Y-genetic heritage of M173 and M17 (R1a) only dates from 33,000 years ago. Similarly, the MtDNA heritage of Europe and Eurasia dates from 40,000 years ago. Hence, it is clear from the genetic evidence that population spread began in India spreading to the rest of the non-African world. It is also clear that apart from the first human migrations into India during the late Pleistocene no subsequent migrations and population replacements occurred in India (Vemsani, 2014).

It is impossible to know how the anatomically modern humans looked 70,000 or 80,000 years ago during their early settlements in India, but it is probable that they might have looked more like the tribal groups rather than the other social groups, since the tribal groups continued to follow the Upper Paleolithic lifestyle of the Pleistocene settlers as hunter-gatherers with intermittent swidden agriculture, unlike the settled settled social groups which changed lifestyles rapidly over the last 5 millennia in India due to quick civilizational progress.

Geographically, India is not a part of the Eurasian landmass, but an appendage to the continent of Asia (Gondwana), surrounded by water on three sides and the tallest mountains of earth (8,800 m at Mount Everest), the Himalayas, on the remaining side with few difficult land passages in the northwest and northeast. The term Indian subcontinent is used to designate this geographical landmass to identify it distinctly from the rest of the Eurasia. Major geographical events, causing climatic changes as well as volcanic eruptions are said to have caused a major population extinction resulting in the extinction of archaic humans and a population bottleneck for the anatomically modern human population of India around 74,000 years ago (Oppenheimer, 2004). Indian subcontinent is characterized by tropical monsoon climate with characteristic rainfall in Summer (May–June) and Fall (Aug-Sep). Major fluctuations in rainfall are said to have influenced population dynamics during the Pleistocene resulting in a significant shift in the populations of archaic humans (Allchin et al., 1978; Paddayya, 2002). However, late Pleistocene and Holocene are characterized by stable weather conditions except for occasional short dry spells recorded in northwestern India which resulted in the formation of the Great Indian Desert or Thar Desert (Dhir and Singhvi, 2012). Thus, India is centrally located from Eurasian continent as well as not completely far off from the African coast or the Southeast Asia and Australia, which was not a great obstacle to travel since the Indian Ocean was shallower and estimated to be at least 15 miles lower in depth during Pleistocene than at present (Oppenheimer, 2004). Therefore, well connected by land and water ways, Indian subcontinent plays a major role in early population migrations and settlements. Therefore, Indian basal mtDNA and Y chromosome lineages are uniquely represented in populations across the world. Therefore, genetic heritage of current Indians represents the continuous in situ evolution from this first Hominin settlers of India refuting any invasions postulated by the colonialist scholars earlier (Vemsani, 2014).

2.8 Civilizational Foundations of India: Cultural and Genetic Continuity from the Upper Paleolithic Phase

Several Upper Paleolithic tools, such as bored stones and grinding slabs are still used by the tribal groups for processing grains. Yanadi (Andhra Pradesh) and other tribal groups used similar fishing tools (bored stones) for fishing well into the late 19th century (Raju, 1988). Microlithic mounted Flake tools formed an important part of the tool assemblage of the Upper Paleolithic, which might have helped the success of hunting expeditions. Continuity has also been noticed in religion and art. At the site of Bagor I and II significant occupational layers and cultural artifacts are noticed (Chakrabarti, 1999: 82, 86; Misra, 1973: 92–110).

At Bagor I, the archeologists found a Goddess temple. The goddess temple is located on circular rubble platform of about 85 cm in diameter upon which was mounted a triangular stone with natural concentric circles (15 cm high, 6.5 cm wide, and 6.5 cm thick) (Chakrabarti 82; Kenoyer 1983). This goddess temple is dated to the last phase of Upper Paleolithic period the upper limit of the date is about 9000 B.C.E (about 11 KYA). Similar temples of goddess are still found currently in the vicinity of Bagor in which worship is offered. This indicates the continuous worship of the goddess over the millennia. Such stones with triangular ellipsoidal laminations in yellowish or reddish brown are found on the nearby Kaimur escarpment, which are placed on similar rubble-built platforms and worshipped as shakti, the representation of numerous forms of goddess. Similar stone icons of goddess installed on stone platforms are focuse of worship throughout present-day India. The present author has seen similar temples in Telugu states of Andhra Pradesh and Telangana. In villages across Andhra Pradesh are found similar shrines associated with goddess worship which are called the Bodrayi/Boddurayi/Nabhirayi (Naval stone). Therefore, the Upper Paleolithic Bagor structure probably represents a prototype of early shrines for goddess worship (grama devata/village goddess) in India. Continuation of goddess worship in a similar manner from 9000 B.C.E. also shows that the human groups who inhabited the Subcontinent during this period continue to inhabit the Subcontinent. Overall, human habitations (Hominids and Hominins) during the Prehistoric era (Paleolithic, Mesolithic, Neolithic era) impressive continuity of human occupations across India. However, rapid transition during the Mesolithic era and quick multiplication of Neolithic habitations across India indicate rapid change brought on by the Hominins/Anatomically Modern Humans, which is also traced with modern Indians through genetic history. But genetic history traces Indians to about 74000 Years Ago (YA) slightly prior to the Mesolithic era, which was attributed to the Toba volcanic eruption. It is established that these Neolithic humans were the ancestors of the current Indians through large occupations spread across India during Neolithic era which do not show any disturbed occupational layers due to war in addition to the continuing genetic heritage. No large genetic change or prehistoric cultural change could be observed in current research. This disproves any Neolithic invasions into India as postulated by the Aryan invasion theories.

2.8.1 *Mesolithic Culture*

The Mesolithic period is not marked by a profusion in the number of settlements and likely doesn't support an increasing population. Few of these Mesolithic sites are excavated (Chakrabarti, 1999: 116), far fewer than the Paleolithic or Neolithic sites. This may also indicate a replacement of archaic humans by the modern humans who then had a favorable environment in which to thrive and multiply gradually. So the upper Paleolithic revolution in the Subcontinent of India is more than a revolution, it also represents a demographic replacement and expansion of settlements. Central Indian rock shelters of this phase also have enormous paintings (Chakrabarti 110–11): scenes of fishing, hunting, social and religious life, as well as foraging for plant food and collecting forest produce such as fruits and honey. This phase shows expanding activities and lifestyles. Mesolithic agriculture might be small but shows rapid change and the beginning of the new adaptions that prevailed in the next phase of civilizational development, the Neolithic era, leaving their permanent imprint on the land and people of India.

Mesolithic tools are primarily based on microliths representing an improvement over the Upper Paleolithic flake-mounted tools. These are tiny tools of 1–5 cm in length, which are hafted on wood or other material to make composite multipurpose tools. The Microlithic tools are used as arrowheads, spearheads, knives, sickles, harpoons, and daggers. Usage of bow and arrow is noticed even though it does not seem common during this period as attested in the numerous paintings in the rock shelters of central India.

2.9 Advancement of the Neolithic Phase in India and Absence of Aryans

Indian Neolithic phase is contemporaneous with Bronze and Chalcolithic cultures and shows multiple varieties across India (Allchin, 1968). Hunting and gathering was replaced by food production resulting in permanent settlements starting at about 12000 YBP (Years Before Present). The Neolithic cultural phase is marked by rapid transition into food production and settled living throughout the Indian Subcontinent. Neolithic culture is dated from 10,000–2000 YBP (Years Before Present).

Domestication of rice, pig, yam, and taro is attributed to Neolithic India, since they are found widely in the wild here prior to Neolithic domestication. Cultivation of rice and other grains such as wheat and barley is noted from the Neolithic period in India. The Neolithic is also characterized by the exploitation of natural minerals: copper mining, and metal use and later in the making of Bronze. Varied Neolithic civilizations are found in India, with typical regional pottery and lifestyles. Southern Neolithic is characterized by ash mounds, and large settlements, while in the Northern Neolithic, the settlements are smaller, and sometimes have pit dwellings as in Kashmir.

A typical feature of the Neolithic culture is that it is spread across the subcontinent, and though there are variations, a commonality exists throughout. As Neolithic people settled and domesticated the locally available plants and animals, they utilized the local resources in an optimal manner. Regional pottery styles emerge. Neolithic phase of culture is therefore not only a revolution where a new lifestyle based on domestication, utilization of wheel, and sedentary life, it is also a lifestyle that emerged in diverse regional styles in Indian Subcontinent. Due to the fixed settlements and sedentary lifestyle of Neolithic phase, regional styles of pottery evolved during this phase.

Mehrgarh (Kacchi plain, Baluchistan) is said to demonstrate the first Neolithic village of settlement of Indian Subcontinent, a precursor to the urbanization in Indus valley (Chakrabarti, 1999: 116–126). The first occupational level of Mehrgarh is dated to 7000 B.C.E. Mehrgarh is at the crossroads of Harappan Civilization and Neolithic culture. It shows the developed Neolithic phase of life, which foreshadows the Indus valley civilization. Decorated pottery and mud kilns are found in excavations, which indicate mass production of wheel-turned and kiln burned pottery. A variety of terracotta figurines with varied hairstyles are also found here. Pipal leaf and humped bull motifs appear on the pottery, which later becomes ubiquitous, during the Indus valley civilization. The humped bull motif commonly found in Indus valley is also commonly found in Shaiva temples across India. The bull Nandi, the dedicated devotee of Shiva, found across India is the sitting bull similar to the humped bull on the Indus valley seals.

2.9.1 Megalithic Culture

Megalithic Culture is widespread in southern India, now constituted by the states of Andhra Pradesh, Telangana, Karnataka, Tamilnadu, Maharashtra, and Kerala (Vemsani, 1999; Chakrabarti, 1999: 234–239). Megalithic culture dates from (3KYA–500 B.C.E.) across India (Chakrabarti, 1999: 237; Murti, 1994). It is marked by large burial complexes sometimes extending in area up to 8 square kilometers consisting of numerous burials, sometimes of many different varieties. Megalithic burials are characterized by the use of large-sized head-stones marking, which can sometimes measure up to the height six meters in length and up to the width of four meters in width. The common types of Megalithic monuments noted in India are: Chambers (constructed with large stone masonry), Cyclocyst (Stone Circles), Pit (pit burial topped by large stone), Menhir (large upright standing stone), and Dolmens (a free standing chamber, consisting of standing stones covered by a capstone). Variety is also noticed in the cultural material recovered from each of these. As noted with Neolithic culture above, Megalithic culture is not uniform and Megalithic and Neolithic phases of life overlap in some regions, such as Karnataka.

A variety of Megalithic monuments are found in India, from Northwestern India (Rajasthan), Northeastern India (Assam) and Southern India (Andhra Pradesh, Karnataka, Kerala and Tamilnadu), Central India (Maharashtra, Chattisgarh and

Madhya Pradesh). A recent discovery of more than a thousand free standing Megaliths in Hire Bekegal near Vijayanagara in Karnataka are impressive, since the free standing tall granite slabs resemble the look of a forest of rocks. Menhirs are also common across South India. A large Menhir as tall as a three-story building stands near the entrance of University of Hyderabad, the alma mater of this author. Megalithic culture thrived across India contemporaneous with the Neolithic culture. It is difficult to know if Megalithic people were cattle herders or nomadic hunter gathers, who marked the burials of their ancestors with Megaliths. Their classification as herders has been most favored by historians, since this may have allowed them a semi-nomadic lifestyle which was necessary for any large group of people to sustain, since large groups could not have survived solely on hunting and food gathering alone. The Megalithic people might have lived a semi-nomadic pastoral life with herding as a major occupation along with some seasonal farming. Places near their farm-settlements might have also served as burial complexes to which they might have returned periodically to offer respect to those buried there. Usage of iron, pottery, and artistic styles indicates a sophisticated life of abundance. Megalithic semi-nomadic people might have co-existed and traded with Neolithic farmers who were their neighbors in some locations in southern India. The Megalithic cultures survive to late 500 B.C.E. in some regions. There does not seem to be a violent ending to the culture as Megalithic settlements continued into later phases. The construction of monuments, however, gradually ceased with the spread of Neolithic and Proto-historic village settlements, which likely indicates the gradual assimilation of the megalithic culture into subsequent cultures.

2.10 Conclusion

Evidence from 14 MYA–2MYA showing evidence of Hominids and Hominins suggests that India played a central role in Eurasian as well as Asian demographic change and cultural movements characteristic of Paleolithic Period onwards. Ancient Humans (*Homo Sapiens/Hominids*) spread across India around 3.8 MYA but were replaced by the Anatomically modern humans (*Homo Sapiens Sapiens/Hominins*) during the Upper Paleolithic period around 1.2 MYA. Mesolithic phase indicates the spread of these anatomically modern humans across India and their successful settlements, and elements of artistic and religious features of Upper Paleolithic era endure in the present-day Indian culture and their genetic continuity is noted among the modern Indians. The next phase marked by the Neolithic and Megalithic cultural phases are marked by the use of a variety of metals, including copper, Iron, and silver in addition to permanent settlements and the most common features of the culture (settled life, metal use, domestication of animals and plants, wheel-turned pottery). Neolithic and Megalithic Cultures also display variety within an overall cultural amalgamation. This seems to stand as a precursor to the later Indian culture and society, which is characterized by variety and pluralistic practice within a unifying cultural matrix. By the end of prehistoric era, India had a secure population spread across the length and breadth of the land, displaying a variety of cultural, and technical adaptations, which supported the continuity and longevity of Indian civilization over the next millennia. No outside (Aryan) invasions/migrations or occupations resulting in demographic or cultural change are noticed in archeological or genetic data of India. Hence, research establishes that India showed continuous occupation and cultural development since the prehistoric foundations.

References

Akhilesh, K., Pappu, S., Rajapara, H., et al. (2018). Early middle Palaeolithic culture in India around 385–172 ka reframes out of Africa models. *Nature, 554*, 97–101. https://doi.org/10.1038/nature25444

Allchin, B., & Allchin, R. (1968). *The birth of Indian civilization.* Penguin Books.

Allchin, B., Goudie, A., & Hegde, K. T. M. (1978). *Prehistory and palaeogeography of the great Indian desert*. Academic Press.

Bryant, E. (2001). *The quest for origins of vedic culture and the Indo-Aryan migration debate.* Oxford University Press.

Bryant, E. F., & Patton, L. L. (2005). *The Indo-Aryan controversy: Evidence and inference in Indian history.* Routledge.

Chakrabarti, D. K. (1979). Robert Bruce Foote and Indian prehistory. *East and West, 29*(1/4), 11–26.

Chakrabarti, D. K. (1999). *Prehistory of India.* Oxford University Press.

Chakrabarti, D. K. (2010 [1999]). *India: An archaeological history.* Oxford University Press.

Dhir, R. P., & Singhvi, A. K. (2012). The Thar desert and its antiquity. *Current Science, 102*(7), 1001–1008.

Eudald, C., Ramos, R. S., Rodríguez, X. P., Mosquera, M., Ollé, A., Vergès, J. M., Martínez-Navarro, B., & de Castro, J. M. B. (2010). Early hominid dispersals: A technological hypothesis for "out of Africa". *Quaternary International, 223–224*, 36–44. ISSN 1040–6182. https://doi.org/10.1016/j.quaint.2010.02.015. (https://www.sciencedirect.com/science/article/pii/S104061821000073X)

Foote, R. B. (1916). *The Foote collection of Indian prehistoric and protohistoric antiquities, notes on their ages and distribution.* Madras Government Museum.

Des Forges, A. (1995). The ideology of genocide. *Issue: A Journal of Opinion, 23*(2), 44–47.

Kaldma, K. et al. (1999). The place of the Indian mitochondrial DNA variants in the global network of maternal lineages and the peopling of the old world. In *Genomic Diversity: Applications in Human Population Genetics* (pp. 135–52).

Karafet, T. M., Mendez, F. L., Meilerman, M. B., Underhill, P. A., Zegura, S. L., & Hammer, M. F. (2008). New binary polymorphisms reshape and increase resolution of the human Y-chromosomal Haplogroup tree. *Genome Research, 18*(5), 830–838.

Kennedy, A. R. K. (2000). *God-apes and fossil men: Paleoanthropology in South Asia.* University of Michigan Press.

Kenoyer, J. M., Clark, J. D., Pal, J. N., & Sharma, G. R. (1983). An upper Palaeolithic shrine in India. *Antiquity, 57*, 88–94.

Korisettar, R., Sheila, M., Rajaguru, S. N., Gogte, V. D., Ganjoo, R. K., Venkatesan, T. R., Tandon, S. K., Somayajulu, B. L. K., & Kale, V. S. (1988). Age of the bori volcanic ash and lower palaeolithic culture of the kukdi valley, Maharashtra. *Bulletin of the Deccan College Research Institute, 47/48*, 135–137. http://www.jstor.org/stable/42930220

Metspalu, M., Kivisild, T., Metspalu, E., Parik, J., Hudjashov, G., Kaldma, K., Serk, P., Karmin, M., Behar, D. M., Gilbert, M. T. P., Endicott, P., Mastana, S., Papiha, S. S., Skorecki, K., Torroni, A., & Villems, R. (2005). Most of the extant mtDNA boundaries in South and Southwest Asia were likely shaped during the initial settlement of Eurasia by anatomically modern humans. *BMC Genetics, 6*, 26–36.

Mishra, S. (1992). The age of the Acheulian in India; new evidence. *Current Anthropology, 33*, 325–328.

Misra, V. N. (1978). The Acheulian industry of rock shelter IIIF-23 at Bhimbetka, central India—a preliminary study. *Australian Archaeology, 8*, 63–106.

Misra, V. N. (1973). Bagor: A mesolithic settlement in northwest India. *World Archaeology, 5*, 92–110.

Misra, V. N. (2001). Prehistoric human colonization of India. *Journal of Biosciences, 26*, 491–531. https://doi.org/10.1007/BF02704749

Murti, U.S. (1994). *Megalithic culture of South India: Socio-economic perspectives.* Ganga Kaveri.

Oppenheimer, S. (2004). *The real eve: Modern man's journey out of Africa.* Caroll & Graf.

Paddayya, K. (1999). New insights into Acheulian: A case study from South India. *Humankind, 1*, 65–71.

Paddayya, K., Jhaldiyal, R., & Petraglia, M. D. (2000). Excavation of an Acheulian workshop at Isampur, Karnataka (India). *Antiquity, 74*, 751–2.

Paddayya, K., Jaldiyal, R., Petraglia, M. D., Ferier, S., & Skinner, A. R. (2002). Recent findings on the Acheulian of the Hunsgi and Baichbal valleys, Karnataka with special reference to Isampur excavation and its dating. *Current Science, 83*(5), 641–649.

Palanichamy, et al. (2006). Phylogeny of mitochondrial DNA macrohalpogroup N in India, based on complete sequencing: Implications for the peopling of Indian subcontinent. *American Journal of Human Genetics, 75*(6), 966–978.

Pearce, N. J. G., Westgate, J. A., Gatti, E., Pattan, J. N., Parthiban, G., & Achyuthan, H. (2014). Individual glass shard trace element analyses confirm that all known Toba tephra reported from India is from the *c*. 75-ka Youngest Toba eruption. *Journal of Quaternary Science, 29*, 729–734. https://doi.org/10.1002/jqs.2741

Pilbeam, D. (1966). Notes on ramapithecus, the earliest known hominid, and dyopithecus. *American Journal of Biological Anthropology, 25*(1), 1–5.

Rajkumar, et al. (2005). Phylogeny and antiquity of M macrohaplogroup inferred from complete mtDNA sequence of Indian specific lineages. *BMC Evolutionary Biology, 5*(6), 5–26.

Raju, D. R. (1988). *Stone age hunter-gatherers: An ethno-archeology of Cuddapah Region.* Deccan College Post-graduate Research Institute.

Shinde, V., Narasimhan, V., Roland, N., Peterson, N., Rai, N., & Reich, D. (2019). An ancient harappan genome lacks ancestry from Steppe patoralists or Iranian farmers. *Cell, 179*(3), 729–735.

Thangaraj, K., Chaubey, G., Singh, V. K., Vanniyarajan, A., Thasneem, I., Reddy, A. G., & Singh, L. (2006). In situ origin of deep rooting lineages of mitochondrial macrohaplogroup 'M' in India. *BMC Genomics, 7*, 136–151.

Thapar, R. (1996). The theory of Aryan race and India: History and politics. *Social Scientist, 24*(1/3), 3–29.

Vemsani, L. (1999). *Settlement patterns of Andhra Pradesh: From prehistory upto protohistory.* Ph.D. thesis. University of Hyderabad.

Vemsani, L. (2014). Genetic evidence disproves Aryan migration/invasion theories: An Examination of small-statured human groups of the Indian Ocean Region. In Rao, N. (Ed.), *Sindhu Saraswathi civilization: A reappraisal.* DK Print World and Nalanda International, 570–594.

Zhong, H., Shi, H., Qi, X. B., et al. (2010). Global distribution of Y-chromosome haplogroup C reveals the prehistoric migration routes of African exodus and early settlement in East Asia. *Journal of Hum Genetics, 55*, 428–435. https://doi.org/10.1038/jhg.2010.40

Chapter 3
Palaeolithic Culture of Deccan in the Upper Krishna Basin of India with Special Reference to Recent Studies

Jayendra Joglekar

Abstract Upland Deccan is a part of the ancient landmass of Peninsular India, consisting of erosional rocky terrain drained by allochthonous and autochthonous rivers. Tectonically the region is relatively stable. All the rivers of this region are presently eroding their beds, consequently exposing the older deposits. Geomorphologically, the landscape is dominated by pediments with inselbergs, tors, and broad box-shaped valleys drained by channels with highly seasonal discharge. The present bedrock channels are ungraded with conspicuous knick points almost up to their confluence with trunk streams. Waterfalls, incised meanders, and deep coalesced potholes are significant erosional features observed in most of the streams. Regolith cover consists of laterites, vertisols, and colluvio-alluvial deposits occurring in foot slopes of pediment scarps and on the banks of bedrock streams. The exposed thickness of colluvio-alluvial deposits rarely exceeds 20 m on both banks of streams and their lateral extent is 1.5–2 km. Acheulian sites in this region have been a part of academic discourse since the early 1950s. Key Acheulian sites such as Gangapur and Chirki-on-Pravara in the Godavari Basin, Bori and Morgaon in the Bhima Basin, and Yedurwadi in the Krishna Basin have been fairly well studied; these will be discussed briefly in this paper. The main focus of this paper is the new discovery of Acheulian sites in the overlooked Upper Krishna Basin. A few unconvincing reasons such as unsuitable raw material, i.e., basalt, dense vegetation, and humid environment were cited for absence of Acheulian record in this region. The present study has successfully brought to light a number of promising Acheulian sites from the Krishna River, Bavdhan *nala,* and Urmodi River basins in the Satara District of Maharashtra. The Acheulian assemblages have been collected from varied geomorphic contexts such as coarse channel gravel, cobbly-rubble, breccio-conglomerate, and oligomict conglomerate. The assemblages comprise of more than 300 artifacts, dominated by cleaver-flakes. Locally available compact vesicular basalt in the form of core stones, boulders, cobbles, and blocks is the exclusive raw material exploited for manufacturing the flake based artifacts. The geomorphic contexts and typo-technological

J. Joglekar (✉)
Department of AIHC and Archeology, Deccan College Post-Graduate and Research Institute (Deemed to be University), Pune 411006, India
e-mail: jayendra2008@gmail.com

L. Vemsani (ed.), *Handbook of Indian History*,
https://doi.org/10.1007/978-981-97-6207-1_3

study have led to the conclusion that the study area has been occupied by the early hominids certainly since the Middle Pleistocene if not earlier. The present study is first of its kind which has established the presence of older sediments (at least of Middle Pleistocene period) associated with Acheulian artifacts in this region.

Keywords Paleolithic culture · Deccan · Krishna river basin · Godavari basin · Acheulian · Attirampakkam · Isampur · Maharashtra · Karnataka · Eastern ghats · Bhima river · Bori · Yedurwadi · Menavali · Atit · Morgoan

3.1 Introduction

The Acheulian culture (Lower Paleolithic culture) was first identified in Europe in 1859, followed by Africa and Asia. However, the oldest evidence has now been convincingly established in Africa around 1.8 MYA (Million Years Ago) (Lepre et al., 2011). The Acheulian technology includes various strategies of core reduction, but the final aim of all these methods is to achieve large-sized flakes (>10 cm) which could be carried for longer distances. The Acheulian sites have more often than not yielded partial reduction sequences with a few exceptions where all the components of the tool manufacturing process have been reported. The Acheulian strategy mostly involves bifacial reduction and large flake based cutting tools. The major tools include handaxes, cleavers, picks, knives, and scrapers made from large flakes. Cores of different types and forms are exploited adopting various reduction techniques in the Acheulian culture. Large/giant-sized boulders, cobbles, blocks, and slabs were selected for the detachment of large flakes. The Acheulian tool making usually involved higher degree of flaking and often small flakes are produced as part of tool trimming or shaping process. These small flakes are part of waste products, but these debitage give important clues for understanding technological details. Although technologically the Acheulian assemblages are quite similar, regional variations have been observed within the tool kits, which could be a result of requirement based tool production or raw material type or form induced.

Rocks of varied kinds and forms have been exploited for making tools by early hominids from the earliest times. Locally available rocks were often exploited for manufacturing tools. In the African context, varieties of igneous rocks, quartz, quartzite, and sandstone were exploited extensively. In Europe, Acheulian artifacts were made from locally available flint, quartzite, and other siliceous material. In Asia, raw materials such as basalt, dolerite, limestone, quartzite, sandstone, granite, siliceous material, etc., were exploited by the Acheulian tool makers. Paleolithic researchers have convincingly established that basalt or other igneous rocks were exploited from the earliest times wherever it was available (for details, see Joglekar et al., 2022).

Acheulian culture is the oldest known hominid culture in peninsular India. While earlier there was a lack of absolute dates; the last three decades have seen a series of dates being published for some well-known sites in peninsular India such as

Attirampakkam and Isampur (both older than 1 MYA) (Paddayya et al., 2002; Pappu et al., 2011). Apart from these, a few relative chronological studies at various sites have also confirmed that the peninsular India was occupied by early hominids in the Early and Middle Pleistocene (Deo and Rajaguru, 2014; Paddayya and Deo, 2017; Deo et al., 2018a, b).

3.2 Upland Deccan

Northern Deccan or Upland Deccan (16° to 20°N; 74° to 76°E) is a part of the ancient landmass of Peninsular India. It consists mostly of erosional rocky upland covering west and south central Maharashtra, and north western Karnataka. Summer monsoon rainfall between June and September is the major source of water. Climatically, the region is labeled as semi-arid, with the annual rainfall varying from 400 to 1000 mm, and is largely covered by dry deciduous to thorny and scrub forests. Morphologically, it is a rolling upland plateau with an average elevation of about 500 m AMSL (Above Mean Sea Level). The plateau has developed over Pre-Cambrian and Cambrian metamorphic rocks such as gneiss, schist, quartzite, and Deccan Trap basalts of the Cretaceous-Eocene age. Northern Deccan is drained by easterly flowing rivers such as the Godavari, Bhima, Krishna, Ghataprabha, and Malaprabha. These rivers have their catchments in the Western Ghats with an average rainfall of > 3000 mm per annum. The main water divides separating these rivers have preserved denudation surfaces that have elevations of 1000, 800, 600–700, and 400–500 m AMSL (Kale and Rajaguru, 1987). Tectonically the region as a whole is relatively stable. The present paper largely will focus on the Krishna Basin within Satara District limits and its implications on Acheulian studies in peninsular India, based on recent findings by the author (Joglekar, 2019, 2022).

It was previously suggested that the basalt rock is not suitable for making stone tools, thus no intensive surveys were carried out in this region in contrast to Kaladgi region and other parts of peninsular India (Pappu, 1974). Robert Bruce Foote (1916) had reported more than 500 sites pertaining to Paleolithic, Neolithic, and Iron Age cultures in peninsular India, except the Deccan trap region. Acheulian studies in the Deccan trap region commenced with the discovery of Lower Paleolithic artifacts during the construction of a dam at Gangapur on Godavari River in Nashik District (Sankalia, 1952). This discovery led to subsequent investigations in the Deccan Upland region resulting in the detection of a number of important Acheulian sites in Pravara, Ghod, Karha, and Krishna basins such as Nevasa (Sankalia, 1956), Chirki-on-Pravara and other localities such as Hathi Well, Barot Garden and Baku Pimpalgaon (Corvinus, 1981, 1983 and other references of Corvinus used therein), Bori (Kale et al., 1986a), Morgaon (IAR 1988–89:64) and Yedurwadi (Kale et al., 1986b) (Fig. 3.1). These findings and further studies (for updated review refer-Deo and Joglekar, 2021) confirmed that early hominids occupied this region at since late Early Pleistocene and continued in Middle Pleistocene (Deo and Rajaguru, 2014; Deo et al., 2018a, b and references used therein). The source region of the Krishna

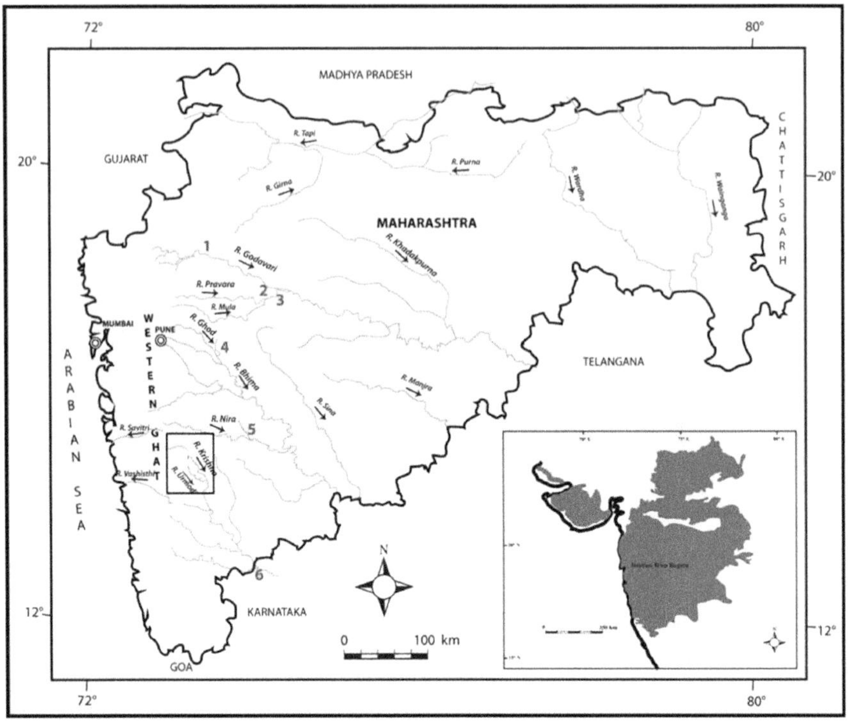

Fig. 3.1 Location of Acheulian sites in the Deccan upland: 1-Gangapur, 2-Nevasa, 3-Chirki-on-Pravara, 4-Bori, 5-Morgaon, 6-Yedurwadi, and rectangular black outline marked area showing the present study area

River had not yielded convincing Acheulian sites, although a small number of stray artifacts were collected from secondary context indicating the potential for further surveys (Pappu, 1974). A few studies related to Quaternary period were carried out by scholars (listed below) in this region. These studies did not yield any rich Acheulian sites suggesting that early hominids occupied this region sparingly, also Early and Middle Pleistocene sediments are not well preserved in this area.

3.3 Acheulian Culture in the Krishna Basin

The Western Ghats form the main source of the Krishna and its tributaries and separate the coastal regions of Konkan and Karwar from the mainland, i.e., the plateau region of Maharashtra and Karnataka. The Ghats slowly give way to transverse offshoots which form the drainage divides and isolated hills and plateaus. To the south/southeast the Nallamalai hills, which are derivative of the Eastern Ghats, form the southern edge of the basin.

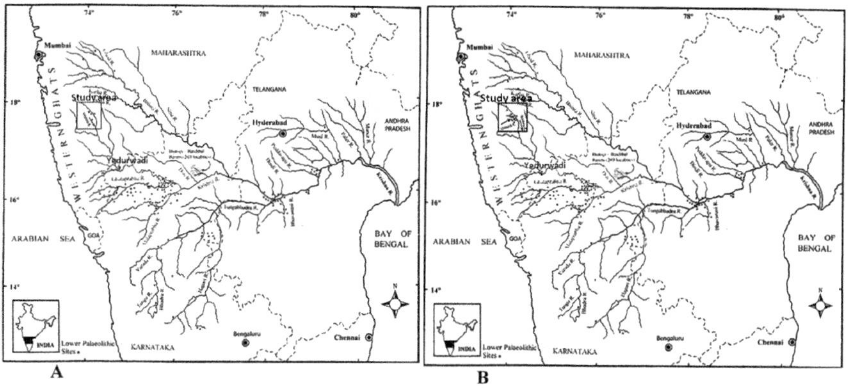

Fig. 3.2 A Acheulian sites in the Krishna Basin: **a** Low number of sites in the study area before 2014, **b** Increased number of sites in the study area discovered during the current work (study area shown by black square) (modified after Jhaldiyal, 2008)

The Krishna Basin has a monsoonal climate and, on the basis of differences in the amount of annual rainfall, temperature, relief, and vegetation, can be separated into wet, intermediate, and semi-arid zones. The tropical evergreen, semi-evergreen, and moist deciduous forests characterize the wet zone where the average annual rainfall is >1250 mm and relief is above 700 m AMSL. Intermediate zone is characterized by the dry deciduous forests where the average annual rainfall is between 750 to 1250 mm AMSL. The thorn and scrub jungle vegetation can be seen in the semi-arid zone, where the rainfall is less than 750 mm AMSL. The greater part of the basin falls in the semi-arid zone. There are different geological formations spread over in the Krishna Basin which will be discussed through the course of this section.

The Krishna Basin as a whole was occupied by the early hominids since the Early Pleistocene period and in subsequent times adjusted to the changing climatic conditions and adapted to varied environments. The basin is further divided into sub-basins. A brief review of Acheulian sites in these basins will be provided here (Fig. 3.2).

3.3.1 The Bhima River Basin

The Bhima originates in the Western Ghats at Bhimashankar in Pune District of Maharashtra. The drainage of the Bhima is separated from the Krishna by the oblique offshoots of the Western Ghats known as Mahadeo Range. Bhima is joined by the Mula-Mutha, the Nira, and the Man as its major left bank tributaries, while the Ghod and the Sina are right bank tributaries. The Bhima River Basin occupies the central portion of the Maharashtra plateau. After flowing for a distance of about 800 km, the Bhima joins the river Krishna near Raichur in Karnataka. The geology of the basin is composed of Eocene–Cretaceous period basaltic rocks commonly known as the Deccan Traps.

The sites of Bori (Kukdi Basin) (Kale et al., 1986a) and Morgaon (Karha Basin) (IAR, 1988–89: 64) are rich Acheulian sites in this basin discovered in the 1980s and subsequently studied by a number of scholars (for details, refer Deo and Rajaguru, 2014; Deo and Joglekar, 2021). Largely all other sporadic Acheulian finds have been reported from secondary fluvial context from the tributaries such as Kukdi, Karha, Nira, Ghod, etc., nothing much can be commented on these finds. Lately, a number of Acheulian localities have been discovered in the Sina River from the loose gravel context (Joglekar, 2023); further studies can yield better results.

3.3.2 The Ghataprabha-Malaprabha Basins

The Ghataprabha and Malaprabha rivers also rise in the Western Ghats. The drainage basins of the Krishna and the Ghataprabha are divided by the Chikodi Range, whilst the Malaprabha range divides the Ghataprabha and the Malaprabha (Pappu and Deo, 1994). Hiranyakeshi and the Markandeya are the major drainages for the Ghataprabha Basin, while the major tributaries of the Malaprabha are the Hire *Halla*, Jaul *Halla*, Beni *Halla*, Sasve *Halla*, Godchi *Halla* and the Chella *Halla*. This is a mixed geological region which is covered by the Deccan Traps, the Kaladagi sedimentary formations, and the Archaeans. The Ghataprabha Basin broadly falls under upper Krishna Basin, while the Malaprabha Basin is a part of the middle Krishna Basin.

Foote (1876, 1916) initially reported Paleolithic sites in these basins. Later on, regional surveys carried out by Joshi (1955), Banerjee (1957), Pappu (1974) Korisettar (1979, 1994), Korisettar and Petraglia (1993), Korisettar et al. (1993), Petraglia et al. (2003) further brought to light a rich complex of Lower, Middle and Upper Paleolithic sites. The geology, drainage features and the Tertiary and Quaternary deposits (which included the laterites, ossiferous deposits, tufa, high level gravels, black and red soils, and alluvium) were probed to comprehend the various processes of landscape evolution, for reconstruction of the paleoclimate and to establish the chronostratigraphy of the prehistoric sites.

The Paleolithic sites in this region were re-classified by Pappu and Deo (1994), based on their different geomorphic contexts, level of usefulness for understanding the Quaternary geomorphic and climatic history of the region as well as the settlement pattern. Majority of the sites in this region are secondary sites, i.e., channel gravel beds or as loose occurrences in the river bed, and few are in stratified alluvial context. The alluvial sites are helpful for the reconstruction of the paleoenvironment and prehistoric cultural chronology, while the river bed sites (find spots) are useful indicators for suggesting the possible presence of primary sites in the surrounding area. Another type of sites includes the cliff section group where artifacts are part of gravel deposits on the river banks ranging from 3 to 7 m above the channel bed. These are semi-primary sites, as the artifacts are not heavily abraded, indicating limited transportation and proximity to their original spot of discard. Apart from these, (1) high level gravels sites which have been found at some places in the middle and lower reaches of the basin; (2) pediment surface sites, where surface of colluvial gravels produced as a result of mass wasting were occupied; and (3) factory sites which occur on the surface, and such assemblages are rich in cores and debitage in fresh condition, while finished tools are present in very low percentages. Though exposed to the surface these sites are fairly undisturbed and are considered as sites in the primary context.

On the basis of geomorphic observations and site distribution patterns, Pappu and Deo (1994) concluded that the lower reaches of the basins were densely occupied by the early hominids, middle reaches were moderately occupied, while the upper reaches having ghats were very sparsely occupied. They argued that rainfall, vegetation, raw material availability, and terrain played an important role for such division and land use pattern. Recent study carried out by Deo et al. (2018a) showed that the site of Anagwadi is of Early Pleistocene period. Lately, a few other aspects of Paleolithic archeology in and around Anagwadi were researched (Baptista et al., 2018; Deo et al., 2018b). Re-investigations were carried out at some Acheulian localities and assemblages from Hiranyakeshi River Basin sites (Joglekar and Deo, 2017a; Salunke et al., 2013).

3.3.3 The Middle Krishna Basin

The middle reaches of Krishna Basin commence when it enters into a gorge near the Jaldurg Falls. Don is the first small tributary joining the Krishna in its middle reaches and then it is joined by a major tributary the Bhima near Raichur. It enters Telangana (state formed in 2014) near the village of Tangadigi in the Mahbubnagar District and forms the northern boundary of the Kurnool District which is a part of Andhra Pradesh. It is further joined by the Tungabhadra at Kudavalli and by the Bhavanasi at Sangameshwaram from its right bank side. A few kilometers downstream the Krishna enters the Srisailam gorge. Southern extent of the Deccan Traps is marked by the middle reaches of the Krishna Basin. The major geological formations found in this region are the Bhima sedimentary formation, the Cuddapah and Kurnool formations, and the Archaeans. Two areas namely the Hunsgi and Baichbal basins, and the Krishna and Tungabhadra doab have yielded fairly rich Acheulian sites in the middle Krishna Basin.

Devapur (Hunsgi) *nullah*, a small tributary of the Krishna has its headwaters in the Hunsgi-Baichbal basins. This basin yielded a very rich concentration of Acheulian sites (Foote, 1876, 1916; Paddayya, 1982, 1987a) along with a number of sites belonging to the Middle Paleolithic, Upper Paleolithic, and Mesolithic phases. Acheulian sites ($n = 203$) yielding artifacts made predominantly from limestone as well as granite-gneiss, dolerite, chert, quartzite, sandstone, shale and schist, and granite-gneiss have been identified. Acheulian artifacts have been recovered from varied contexts which include-within fluvial and colluvial gravels, from the surface of bedrock, calcrete beds, clayey silts, travertine deposits, as well colluvial and fluvial gravels where the assemblage is capped by black and brown silts ranging in thickness from 5 to 200 cm.

Inland parts of the Hunsgi and Baichbal basins were intensively surveyed in order to find primary sites, as the sites occurring in a secondary fluvial context were considered neither good chronological indicators nor constructive for behavioral interpretations (Paddayya, 1978). Sites were categorized as primary and secondary and also modern disturbance processes were documented (Paddayya, 1982). Ethnobotanical survey, the study of present-day climatic conditions, analyses of the geomorphic features, and locating the distribution of water and raw material sources were carried out in order to reconstruct the paleoenvironmental setting in which the Acheulian groups lived. After corroborating all the gathered data which included the distribution of sites across the landscape to the distribution of various resources, a model of dry season aggregation near perennial water sources like springs, and wet season diffusion all over the basin was put forward to elucidate the Acheulian settlement system (Paddayya, 1982). Later on, more work has been undertaken in this area, with the formation process perspective being eminent. Main objective was to understand the variability in the preservation contexts of the Acheulian sites (Paddayya, 1987b, 1987c, 1991; Paddayya and Petraglia, 1993, 1995; Jhaldiyal, 1997, 2006, 2008). Adoption of this approach has led to the detection of a great level of variability in the depositional context of sites on the basis of which the sites have been classified into fluvial, colluvial, sheet wash, and deflationary contexts. Cultural processes were also considered for classification of sites as occupation sites, single episode activity sites, food processing sites, and caches. Many of these sites are associated with fossilized animal remains; few of these have been dated by the Uranium Thorium method (Szabo et al., 1990) and later on by the ESR method (Blackwell et al., 2001; Paddayya et al., 2002).

Krishna-Tungabhadra Doab area has also yielded Acheulian sites in good numbers (Cammiade and Burkitt, 1930; Isaac, 1960; Rao, 1992). Apart from 16 Acheulian sites, numerous later cultural sites have also been reported from this region. Bedrock surfaces, colluvial gravels, and stratified context within the stream laid gravels are the contexts in which artifacts have been found. The archeological record of prehistoric period was recovered from stratified context along the Bhavanasi River (Cammiade and Burkitt, 1930). They classified the assemblages into four series; series 1 being the Acheulian.

Rao (1992) attempted to understand Paleolithic archeology by applying geoarcheological and ethno-archeological methods. Dispersal across the valley during the dry season and aggregation near the river Krishna during wet season was suggested to explain the mobility patterns of the past groups.

3.3.4 The Lower Krishna Basin

Srisailam onwards the Krishna flows through a deep gorge which has eroded the Cuddapah sedimentary formations. Thereafter it enters the Nagarjunakonda Valley (trough like); here the river bed is made of Archaean formations. It meets the Bay of Bengal south of Masulipatnam at Hamsaldivi. Feeders like the Dindi, Peddavagu, Musi, Paler, and Muner meet the Krishna on its left bank. The drainage area includes portions of districts of Hyderabad, Nalgonda, and Krishna to the north and Guntur to the south.

Nalgonda District was explored by Rao (1969), yielding a great number of Acheulian sites along the Dindi, Peddavagu, Paler, Musi, and Muner rivers. Many of these sites were found within stratified fluvial deposits of the rivers or in loose channel gravels within the bed or on the banks. A few sites were classified as open-air factory sites, as the artifacts made from quartzite or sandstone were in unabraded condition, found in cultivated farms generally near the foothills.

The valley of Nagarjunakonda, in the Guntur District, has yielded several Acheulian sites in varied contexts which include as follows: (1) on the surface of disintegrated Archaean rock, (2) on loose surface soil, (3) under a calcareous silt cover fresh and unabraded artifacts were recovered from the surface of calcareous pebble beds overlying the bedrock (Soundara Rajan, 1958; Subramanyam et al., 1975). Valley floor is full of huge deposits of pebble beds which are representative of the mightiness of the river power due to a wet phase that led to the aggradation of the pebbles. Erosional features of high magnitude are almost absent in this region, while fresh artifacts made from quartzite pebbles are seen on the surface of the pebble beds. It was interpreted that the early hominid groups started inhabiting this region during the dry phase.

Area around Srisailam and Krishna District also has yielded quite a few Acheulian sites, but the contexts of the artifacts are not very clear.

3.3.5 The Tungabhadra Basin

The Tunga and Bhadra rivers originate in the Western Ghats from Gangamula at an elevation of about 1198 m AMSL in the Chikmagalur District of Karnataka and unite to form the Tungabhadra. The river flows in a northeasterly direction for about 400 km and joins the Krishna at Kudavalli in Kurnool District in Andhra Pradesh. The main tributaries of the Tungabhadra are Varda, Chinna Hagari, Vedavathi (also known as Hagari in its lower reaches), and Hindri. The river basin consists of varied geological formations which include Archaean rocks like the peninsular gneisses, granites, pegmatites, schists with quartzite, ironstone and manganese horizons, and dolerite dykes.

Largely two contexts have been identified for the Acheulian sites in this river basin which are secondary contexts where artifacts occur in the river bed (Foote, 1916; Subbarao, 1949; IAR 1960–61, 1980–81; Ansari, 1970), while there are some sites reported from surface or within the quartzitic and lateritic gravel beds which occur on the Archaean bedrock (Foote, 1916; Sampat Iyengar 1924; Seshadri, 1955, 1956; Shivarudrappa, 1990; Gururaja Rao, 1990). Foote pioneered research in this region; identified the gravel beds, and termed them as shingle beds. Often these shingle beds yielded Stone Age sites. It was observed that most of the artifacts found on the surface and within the colluvial gravel were in a fresh condition which meant that these had not undergone fluvial transport. It was concluded that the Paleolithic populations occupied the foothill zone of the Copper Mountain and it was due to the surface wash processes that the discarded artifacts and other weathered rock fragments were transported for a short distance and got buried in the colluvial deposits.

In Tumkur District at Kibbanahalli and Biligere, artifacts in similar context were also reported (Sampath Iyengar Seshadri, 1955, 1956; Srinivas, 2014, 2017a, b, c). Artifacts within stratified gravel beds exposed in the rain gullies on the slopes of the Banasandra-Bertahalli hill range were also later on reported.

Several new localities which formed a part of the Kibbanahalli complex were discovered (Gururaja Rao, 1990; Srinivas, 2014, 2017a, b, c). It was concluded that the Kibbanahalli-Biligere Paleolithic site complex was occupied by the Paleolithic groups as it provided an ideal habitat which included the presence of a spring, vicinity of lakes, availability of raw material, away from the fluvial setting, savanna climate with occasional dry–wet phases (Shivarudrappa, 1990).

3.3.6 The Upper Krishna Basin

This region largely is covered by the Deccan trap formation and laterites at higher elevations such as at Panchgani, Mahabaleshwar, Kas, etc. A few (<10) Lower Paleolithic artifacts were reported from sites of Pachwad, Songaon, Limb, and Nisre in the Satara District of western Maharashtra, while more about 90 artifacts were collected from the site at Yedurwadi in Belgavi District of northern Karnataka (Pappu, 1974; Kale et al., 1986b; Kulkarni et al., 2008; Joglekar et al., 2011). The assemblage from Yedurwadi was recently re-examined (Joglekar and Deo, 2019). It has been suggested that the pointed tools and small flakes dominate the assemblage from Yedurwadi while cleavers are in negligible numbers. The assemblage also comprises of variety of small flakes and tools made from cobble/pebble clasts. A quartzite hammerstone is also part of this assemblage which is an exotic item (Joglekar et al., 2011; Joglekar and Deo, 2017a, b).

It is quite evident through this overview that the Krishna Basin, in general, was intensively occupied by the early hominids particularly the middle and lower reaches. As mentioned previously the Deccan trap region of the Krishna Basin has been overlooked by the earlier scholars, and it was concluded that the early hominids sparingly ventured in this region. The site at Yedurwadi is an exception in this region. Apart from Yedurwadi, a few Acheulian artifacts in secondary context have been reported from some sites in the Satara District, hinting potential of the area. The present study area was shortlisted specifically to re-examine the earlier conclusions.

3.4 Quaternary Studies in the Upper Krishna Basin

A few scholars had carried out studies pertaining to Quaternary period and Paleolithic cultures in the Krishna Basin within Satara District. Preliminary survey between Wai and Mahuli yielded only microlithic sites (Malik, 1959). Rajaguru suggested that the exposed colluvio-alluvial deposits (the maximum thickness being 20 m) around Wai, were not older than early Late Pleistocene (<100 KYA) (KYA- Thousand Years Ago). The basal part of the silt unit at Asle on the right bank of Krishna River yielded shells embedded in the thin gravel lenses, dated to 10 KYA by C-14 dating method (Rajaguru, 1970). Quaternary deposits around Wai and Dhom area were studied with a report of the fossilized tusk of *Elephas* sp. along with fresh water shells dated to 33 KYA by C-14 method. These were buried under 10 m thick deposit colluvio-alluvial fill exposed during the foundation trench of Dhom dam (6 km upstream of Menavali) on the river Krishna (Corvinus et al., 1972–1973). This hypothesis was later confirmed, as the calcrete was dated to 75 KYA using Ur-Th method (Joshi and Kale, 1997). Umarjikar (1983) carried out Quaternary geological studies in the Upper Krishna Basin reporting the litho-units from sites such as Menavali (Krishna River), Atit, Valse (both Urmodi River), etc.

Yet, a few Lower Paleolithic/Acheulian artifacts were reported from Pachwad, Songaon, and Limb (Pappu, 1974), and re-investigated reporting one large flake from Pachwad (Kulkarni et al., 2008). Another site at Nisre on the right bank of Koyna River was reported later (Joglekar et al., 2011). Broadly it was concluded that this region had rarely preserved Early and Middle Pleistocene sediments and cultural material. Some other reasons such as (1) focus on sedimentary studies, (2) limited understanding of variation in Acheulian assemblages, (3) impetus on Historical archeology, (4) natural factors such as exfoliation, thermal breakages, and colluvium deposits were rightly pointed for not finding of convincing Acheulian sites in this region (Joglekar, 2019, 2022).

The author carried out intensive field investigations in the Krishna Basin within Satara District, followed by analysis of lithic assemblages. These will be elaborated here.

3.5 Findings in the Upper Krishna Basin

The upper Krishna Basin area was selected for intensive survey as it had indicated the presence of Acheulian culture on a smaller scale. The main aim of the study was to identify Acheulian artifact-bearing localities and contextualize them geomorphologically and archeologically. Reconnaissance of previously known find spots was carried out during the initial stages. These early visits were not fruitful as no artifacts were found from those known spots. Hence, newer spots in the Urmodi River were visited along with two spots in the Bavdhan *nala*, and Menavali on the left bank of

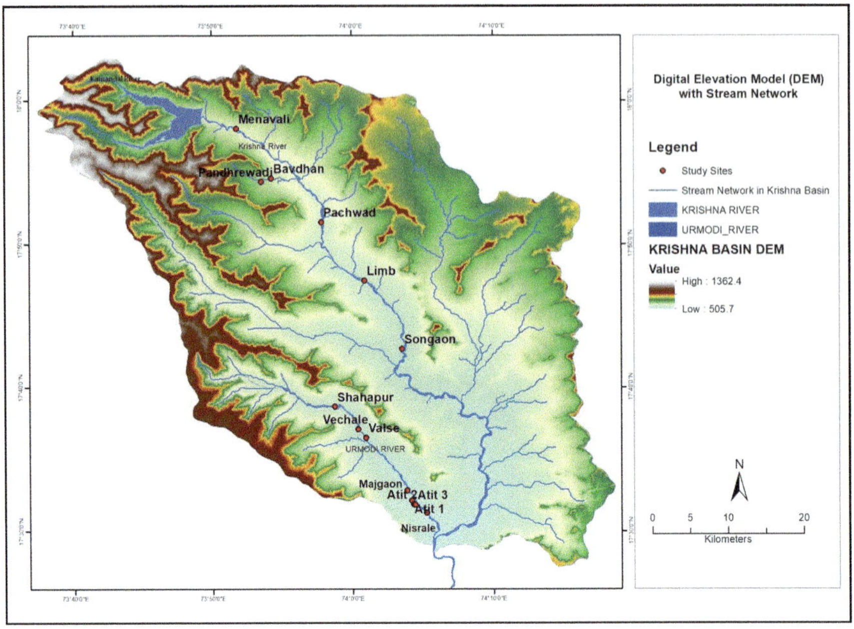

Fig. 3.3 Digital elevation model of the study area and location of the Acheulian sites

Krishna River around 3 km upstream of Wai. These explorations were fairly productive as good numbers of Acheulian artifacts were collected from varied geomorphic contexts from these localities (Fig. 3.3) (Joglekar, 2016, 2018, 2019, 2022; Joglekar and Deo, 2015; Joglekar et al., 2016). The geomorphological observations and lithic assemblages will be elaborated here.

3.5.1 Geomorphological Observations

The main aim was to identify Acheulian artifact-bearing locations in the study area and confirm their geomorphic context. As a result of exhaustive field surveys it was observed that Acheulian artifacts are largely in the secondary context, i.e., from the loose channel gravel from all the sites (Fig. 3.4), while a very few artifacts were collected from cemented gravel/conglomerate (from Menavali and Atit 1) (Fig. 3.5), cobbly-rubble context (from Atit 2) (Fig. 3.6) and weathered relict gravel as observed at Nisre (Fig. 3.7). The recently discovered sites include Menavali on the Krishna River, two localities in the Bavdhan *nala* (Pandhrewadi and Bavdhan), and Shahapur, Vechale, Valse, Majgaon, Atit (1, 2, 3) and Nisrale in the Urmodi River Valley. The Krishna River originates from Mahabaleshwar area about 1371 m AMSL in 18° 1' north latitude and 73° 41' east longitude, about 6 km west of Jor village. Bavdhan *nala* is a southerly tributary (lower order stream) of Krishna River in the Wai taluka

Fig. 3.4 Loose channel gravel commonly observed at all the sites (inset: Acheulian artifact)

of Satara District. The *nala* has its major source of catchment from the Panchgani range of 1293 m AMSL. The Urmodi a right feeder of the Krishna rises near Kas plateau about 1260 m AMSL in Jaoli. The catchment of all these rivers has laterite capping the basalt formation. Thus at all the sites loose gravel comprises of basalt, laterite, and siliceous clasts in varied proportions.

Broadly these sites can be divided into three categories on the basis of their contexts, which are as follows:

The first category consists of the transported secondary sites where the artifacts are associated with fluvial gravels. Majority of artifacts in the present study were collected from this category of sites. The artifacts are found clustered within gravel bars or are part of the channel bed. These are the most disturbed sites where the original site context is unidentified. The original site could have been near the channel bed, as on the channel bank (like Atit 2) from where theartifacts were sorted, washed, and re-deposited in the channel bars. Most of the artifacts recovered from this context have rounded facets and polished surfaces (highly abraded), while a good number of artifacts have sub-angular to sub-rounded facets indicating that they have not been part of long distance transport (slightly to moderately abraded). Seasonality of the river has led to the formation of gravel bars. These bars would not allow for free and easy movement of artifacts in the stream bed (this is also attested by the presence of impact scars and scratches on the artifacts caused as a consequence of clast collision). Geomorphologists too have verified that clasts tend to cluster together when they come in proximity to one another in flowing water which results in the formation of bar deposits (Leopold et al., 1964; Reineck and Singh, 1980). Similar observations

Fig. 3.5 Breccio-conglomerate observed at Atit 1 (inset: Acheulian artifact)

Fig. 3.6 Cobbly-rubble observed at Atit 2 (inset: Acheulian artifact)

Fig. 3.7 General view of the artifact-bearing weathered gravel observed at Nisre

were made for archeological material as well where experimental studies have shown that artifacts tend to accrue wherever there are obstructions in the stream channel in the form of bars, depressions, and meanders (Schick, 1984; Shackley, 1978). Topographical hindrances like closed nature of the valley, low relief, uneven landscape, etc., also would have ensured that the artifacts could not undergo long distance transport from their original area of discard by the seasonal stream processes. These all factors are applicable in the case of the present study area. The total length of the Urmodi River is 88 km, while Bavdhan *nala* is a small stream covering a distance of less than 30 km; similarly, the site at Menavali is located within first 30 km from the origin of the Krishna River. Thus it can be suggested that the artifacts were collected from secondary context but were not transported for longer distances. The artifacts are more abraded due to the flow of water over the artifact-bearing gravel bars, but fairly less rolled attesting the observation. The rivers are competent only to transport finer sediments, thus preserving the large sized artifacts within the gravel bars comprising of coarser litho-clasts.

The second category includes the sites having conglomerate as the artifact-bearing horizon. The artifacts have been part of this conglomerate as a secondary deposit as in the case of Menavali and Atit 1. The artifacts most probably were a part of the weathered bedrock surface elsewhere like at Atit 2. These artifacts over time got assimilated into the gravel, which after cementation turned into a conglomerate. These conglomerates are of different types, in the present study area oligomict and breccio-conglomerate were observed yielding artifacts (classification of conglomerates based on Nichols, 2009). The conglomerates are not commonly observed in the study area, these have been seen as relict features at only few spots. Several artifacts are encrusted with carbonate accretions, suggesting that the assemblages were subjected to continuous cycles of wetting and drying. The discard of artifacts on the fluvial conglomerates provided a surface on which easy movement and transport of artifacts under stream action was restricted and resulted in the local re-working and limited movement of the artifacts. Limited stream action was a result of high bedrock on the banks, low velocity of the flow, and seasonally fed river. The artifacts which get released from the conglomerate become part of the loose gravel as observed at Menavali and Atit 1.

Third category includes only Atit 2 which is most probably closest to the original context. The artifacts collected from this spot are fairly near to their position of discard (fairly less displaced by fluvial process). The capping finer sediment seems to have been partially stripped off by flooding during seasonal rains, resulting in the winnowing away of the very smaller/ micro debitage components of the assemblage. The location is ideal as it is in the vicinity of water source, flora and fauna as food supply, and easily available raw materials. Acheulian localities in the Hunsgi-Baichbal valleys are principal examples of such primary to semi-primary occupations with limited disturbance as far as Krishna Basin is concerned (Jhaldiyal, 2008).

3.5.2 Lithic Assemblages

The stone artifacts were collected from above mentioned sites mostly from secondary context. All the artifacts are made from locally available basalt (coarse grained to fine grained), dominated by medium grained variety. The assemblages are dominated by cleavers/cleaver-flakes (Fig. 3.8), while other important components include large cutting tools (Fig. 3.9), flakes (Fig. 3.10), and cores/flake cores (Fig. 3.11). The Menavali assemblage comprises of 86 artifacts (52 cleaver/cleaver-flakes, 17 flakes, 8 large cutting tools (LCTs), 1 handaxe, 7 cores/flake cores, 1 unfinished tool). Bavdhan *nala* from two localities yielded a total of 57 artifacts (28 cleaver/cleaver-flakes, 17 flakes, 4 LCTs, 3 cores/flake cores, 3 probable anvils, 2 picks). The assemblage from 6 sites in the Urmodi River Valley was studied altogether. It comprised of 175 artifacts (77 cleaver/cleaver-flakes, 60 flakes, 19 LCTs, 7 cores/flake cores, 7 unfinished tools, 1 bolas, 1 handaxe/pick, 2 hammerstones, and 1 spearhead like flake with a tang). The flakes from all these assemblages comprise of side flakes, end flakes, corner flakes, kombewa flakes and flake indeterminate. Two cleavers and a single cleaver-flake were collected from Nisre, while a single large flake was reported from Pachwad; site at Limb yielded four large flakes of Acheulian tradition. Overall the assemblages are dominated by large flakes and also comprised of typical Acheulian artifacts thus it is classified as Large Flake Acheulian (>10 cm) (LFA) artifact assemblage as suggested by Sharon (2010). Although a few small flakes were collected and recorded, these were in negligent numbers. Secondary flake scars on the cores and large flakes suggest that the smaller flakes were mostly part of trimming and thinning process rather than those being used as in the case of Yedurwadi (Joglekar and Deo, 2019). The large flakes were detached from locally available core stones of (>15 cm), boulders, and cobbles of basalt. Exfoliation, i.e., onion peel weathering of basalt has been observed in the study area, core stones are a product of such weathering. These types of core stones are harder as compared to the outer surface of basalt. Core stones have been also exploited at Morgaon for large flake detachment (Mishra et al., 2009).

A variety of large/giant core (>20 cm) exploitation methods were adopted by the early hominids in the Acheulian technology in different regions of the old world (for detailed review, see Sharon, 2007). Although no giant cores are part of the present collected assemblage, yet the exploitation of giant cores is a certainty as the assemblage is large flake based. Cobble opening flake and Victoria West Technique are the most commonly observed methods in the present assemblage with a few specimens of

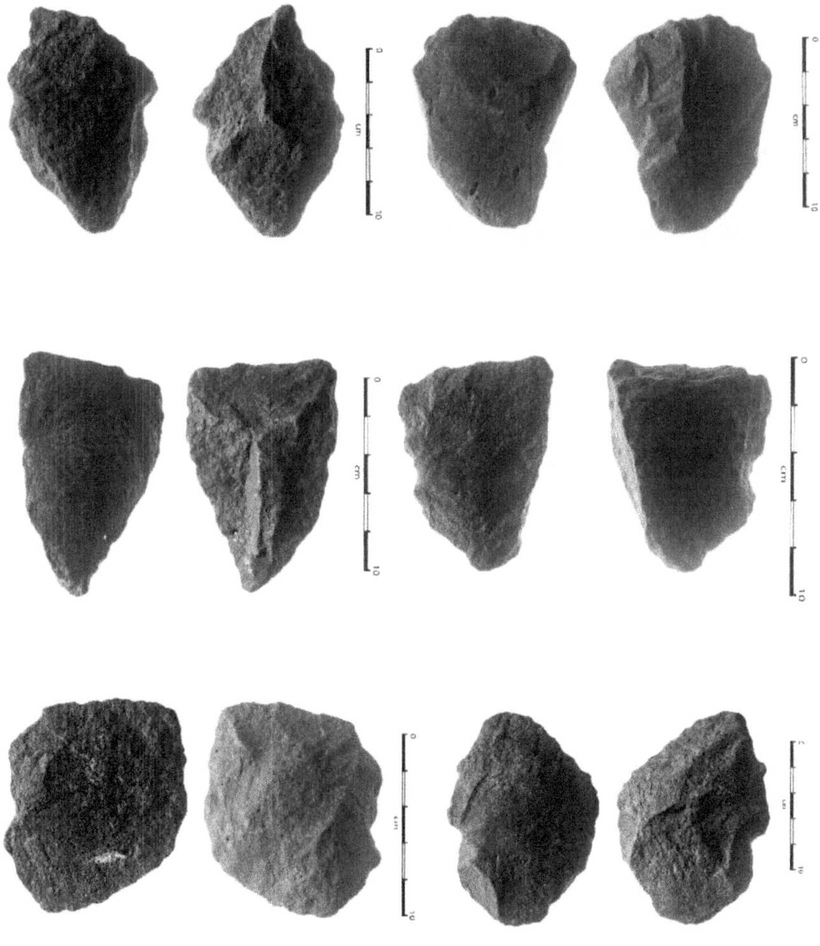

Fig. 3.8 Representative cleavers/cleaver-flakes

Fig. 3.9 Representative LCTs

Fig. 3.10 Representative flakes

other techniques like Kombewa core method, Bifacial core reduction method, Sliced slab method, and Tabelbala-Tachenghit core method were also evidenced. Knapping features such as rounding of the ventral surface, steps, irregular surface, striations/ripples, etc., were observed on some of the artifacts (Joglekar, 2016, 2019, 2022).

The artifacts have a range of patina which is a result of different geomorphic contexts and formation processes (for details, see Joglekar, 2020). The types of patina include Medium light gray (N6), Grayish orange (10YR 7/4), Dark reddish brown (10R 3/4) or Very dusky red (10R 2/2), Grayish black (N2), Dusky green (5G 3/2), and multiple patinations on some artifacts due to their embedded nature within the conglomerates (colors recorded using Munsell Rock color charts, 2009).

A few points have been highlighted after the study of lithic assemblages, these will be summarized here.

1. Locally available raw material in the form of cobbles, blocks, and boulders has been exploited for flake detachments
2. Hard core stones were used as hammers
3. Large/Giant cores ranging from about 20–40 cm were observed but were not collected; were certainly exploited as evidenced through the presence of large flakes

Fig. 3.11 Representative cores/flake cores

4. Victoria West and cobble opening flake are the most commonly observed core reduction techniques
5. Discoid/radial flaking and Levallois core reduction method are absent
6. Side flakes was the most preferred blank type followed by corner flake, and end flake for cleavers/cleaver-flakes

7. A variety of cleavers/cleaver-flakes is the most common artifact, followed by LCTs
8. Minimal secondary flaking on the cleaver-flakes
9. Cleaver/cleaver-flakes have a pointed, rounded, or squarish butt end; parallel, splayed convergent or divergent bit end
10. Pointed tools like handaxe and picks are rare
11. Choppers and chopping tools are totally absent
12. A high number (65%) of artifacts are heavily abraded, about (30%) moderately, and about (5%) are slightly abraded as a reflection of artifacts collected from three categories of sites as mentioned earlier
13. The assemblages from the study area contrast to the assemblage from Yedurwadi which comprises of a few finished tools and is dominated by small flakes which are a product of biface preparation

Variability in the assemblages from sub-humid region (present study area) and semi-arid region (Yedurwadi) could be a result of raw material availability, food availability, and early hominid adaptation to the local environment. The present assemblage is truly large flake dominated but with a few bifacial tools. Although this is a random collection, yet it suggests the Acheulian character of the assemblage with the presence of such a high number of cleavers/cleaver-flakes on large flakes. It also has to be noted that the majority of the artifacts were collected from the channel gravel context, hence it is highly possible that the artifacts were made over thousands of years, but certainly, all belong to Large Flake Acheulian tradition, no artifacts could be classified as Middle or Late Paleolithic on the basis of technological grounds.

Menavali and Atit assemblages have yielded the most variety of artifacts. At these two sites, artifacts have been preserved in conglomerates and cobbly-rubble; these have not been completely fluvially eroded thus preserving the artifacts in a lesser disturbed context. While at other localities the artifacts are often found in fairly transported context, thus only larger artifacts could be recovered.

After considering all the factors, i.e., metrical analysis, typology, technology, context, and preservation condition of the assemblages, it can be suggested that the Acheulian artifacts might be of different phases, some of these might be of early stages while some might be of the evolved stage. Although the stratigraphical development could not be confirmed yet it can be suggested that the thinner artifacts and splayed cleaver-flakes could be of an evolved Acheulian stage. Further studies could throw more light on these aspects.

3.6 Importance and Discussion

The Deccan trap region especially semi-arid areas had yielded a fairly convincing Acheulian record (for detailed review, see Deo and Joglekar, 2021). Yet there were certain areas such as Marathawada, Northern and Southern Maharashtra, and the present study area which had provided scanty evidence of Acheulian culture. This led prehistorians to believe that the early hominids only occupied the Deccan region sparingly (particularly semi-arid regions and areas having dolerite dyke intrusions were occupied) as compared to Kaladgi formation area (Pappu and Deo, 1994), and Hunsgi and Baichbal Valley area having limestone formations (Paddayya, 2007) which was fairly densely occupied. Korisettar (2007) had suggested a model based on various factors which had shown that core area of the Paleolithic occupations were the Purana basins having older geological formations, while areas such as the present study area was marginally occupied by the Paleolithic populations. This research in the upper Krishna Basin calls for reconsideration of this model and encourages further surveys in these marginal regions.

The recent study in this basin, within Satara District, has suggested that the area within the Deccan trap which lacks dolerite dyke intrusions in the vicinity was also occupied by the early hominids. Earlier, Morgaon and Yedurwadi were the only significant sites which had a similar geological situation (no dolerite dyke intrusions nearby), but environmentally both are in semi-arid condition (Mishra et al., 2009; Kale et al., 1986b; Joglekar et al., 2011; Joglekar and Deo, 2019). The present study area falls under sub-humid environmental conditions, suggesting that such areas might have also been occupied by the early hominids; further studies in such heavy precipitation areas are required to confirm this hypothesis. The *terra incognita* areas such as the present study area need to be systematically surveyed. Further study including excavations might give a better picture of the early hominid behavioral pattern and adaptation in sub-humid environment and rocky terrain. The latest study has turned this area into *terra potentia* as far as Acheulian culture is concerned. The loose channel gravel is the most common context for finding Acheulian artifacts in this region. It is certain that the loose gravel was not the original context of these artifacts. Due to the discovery of a large number of Acheulian artifacts in the loose gravels, it is now evident that these gravels are a mixture of older and younger depositions. Further analysis of these gravels in this and other regions is needed to understand and classify these gravels.

The findings of this research could be termed as a culmination of continuous efforts since the 1950s, though earlier efforts yielded only a few find spots, yet they provided some clues for early hominid occupations. The present study has for the first time identified a fairly rich Acheulian complex in sub-humid and rocky terrain in the upper Krishna Basin, and placed this area on the global map of Acheulian occupation complexes. The assemblage from the study area is a rare collection dominated by unifacial cleaver-flakes. The typo-technology of the artifacts and geomorphic contexts suggests that the Acheulian culture flourished in this region certainly in the Middle Pleistocene if not Early Pleistocene. As mentioned earlier, this area was considered almost devoid of any such evidence. The present study has convincingly established possible Middle Pleistocene hominid activity as well as the presence of patches of relict sediments (as observed at Acheulian localities). Although no absolute date is available at this stage, this presents an opportunity for scientists from varied fields such as geo-chemistry, mineralogical analysis, palynological studies, etc., to carry out micro-level studies.

Globally it has been observed that the oldest stone artifacts, i.e., Lomekwian, Oldowan, or Acheulian were made using igneous rocks. Thus, suggesting that the early hominids exploited all types of stones which were locally available. These studies elsewhere in old world indicate that the Deccan Trap region in peninsular India needs to be re-investigated as this area has tremendous potential for understanding the Acheulian culture. The present study is a testament for it and presents a distinctive opportunity to pursue further studies in this challenging and interesting region.

Acknowledgements This paper is dedicated to the Late Prof. S.N. Rajaguru, who has been an eternal guiding light; sadly he passed away in December 2022. The author is thankful to the authorities of the Deccan College PGRI (Deemed to be University), Pune for providing the necessary facilities to carry out this research. The author would like to acknowledge the University Grants Commission (UGC) (JRF) for timely financial support. Prof. Sushama G. Deo, has been a guiding force behind this academic pursuit, I would like to express my gratitude toward her. The author is grateful to Prof. K. Paddayya and Late Dr. R.S. Pappu for their constant encouragement and academic support. I would like to thank to all those who had spared time for field excursions during my doctoral research.

References

Ansari, Z. D. (1970). Pebble tools from Nittur (Mysore state). *Indian Antiquary, 6*(1–4), 1–7.

Banerjee, K. D. (1957). *Middle palaeolithic industries of the Deccan.* Unpublished Ph.D. Thesis, Deccan College, University of Poona.

Baptista, A., Deo, S. G., & Joglekar, J. (2018). Palaeolithic archaeology at and around Anagwadi, dist. Bagalkot, Karnataka with special reference to palaeoenvironment and site context. *Puratattva, 48*, 147–154 + colour plates.

Blackwell, B. A. B., Fevrier, S., Blickstein, J. I. B., Paddayya, K., Petraglia, M. D., Jhaldiyal, R., & Skinner, A. R. (2001). ESR dating of an Acheulian Quarry site at Isampur, India. *Journal of Human Evolution, 40*, A3.

Cammiade, L. A., & Burkitt, M. C. (1930). Fresh light on the stone ages of Southeast India. *Antiquity, 4*, 327–329.

Corvinus, G., Mujumdar, G. G., & Rajaguru, S. N. (1972–73). Some observations on the quaternary of western Maharashtra. *Sonderdruck & us Quarter Bd.*, 23–24, 53–69.

Corvinus, G. (1981). *A survey of Pravara river system in Western Maharashtra, India, Vol. 1: The stratigraphy and geomorphology of the Pravara river system.* Verlag Archaeologica Venatoria; Institut für Urgeschichte der Universität Tübingen.

Corvinus, G. (1983). *A survey of the Pravara river system in western Maharashtra, India, Vol 2: The excavations of the Acheulian site of Chirki-on-Pravara, India.* Verlag Archaeologica Venatoria; Institut für Urgeschichte der Universität Tübingen.

Deo, S. G., Joglekar, J., & Rajaguru, S. N. (2018a). Geomorphic context of two Acheulian sites in semi-arid peninsular India: Inferring palaeoenvironment and chronology. *Quaternary International, 480*, 166–177.

Deo, S. G., Joglekar, J., & Baptista, A. (2018b). Two 'giant cores' from the Acheulian site of Anagwadi, Karnataka: Inferring technological behaviour and site context. *Man and Environment, 43*(2), 1–7.

Deo, S. G., & Joglekar, J., (2021). Re-addressing the lower palaeolithic culture from the Deccan trap region, Peninsular India. In P. Shirvalkar, & E. Prasad (Eds.), *Culture, Continuity and*

Tradition: Disquisitions in Honour of Prof. Vasant Shinde (pp. 47–66+colour plates 253–266). B.R. Publishing Corporation Ltd.

Deo, S. G., & Rajaguru, S. N. (2014). Early pleistocene environment of Acheulian sites in the Deccan upland: A geomorphic approach. In K. Paddayya, & S. G. Deo (Eds.), *Recent Advances in Acheulian Culture Studies in India* (pp. 1–22). ISPQS Monograph No. 6. ISPQS.

Foote, R. B. (1876). The geological features of the South Maharatta country and adjacent districts. *Memoirs of the Geological Survey of India, 12*, 1–268.

Foote, R. B. (1916). *The Foote collection of Indian prehistoric and protohistoric antiquities. Notes on their ages and distribution.* The Commissioner of Museums, Government Museum.

Gururaja Rao, B. K. (1990). A note on the lower and middle palaeolithic industries of Southern Karnataka. In A. Sundara (Ed.), *Archaeology in Karnataka* (pp. 5–7). Directorate of Archaeology and Museums. *Indian Archaeology-A Review*, Archaeological Survey of India

Isaac, N. (1960). *Stone age cultures of Kurnool.* Unpublished Ph.D Thesis, Deccan College, University of Pune.

Jhaldiyal, R. (1997). *Formation processes of the prehistoric sites in the Hunsgi and Baichbal basins, Gulbarga district, Karnataka.* Unpublished Ph.D. Thesis, Deccan College, University of Pune.

Jhaldiyal, R. (2006). *Formation processes of the lower palaeolithic record in the Hunsgi and Baichbal basins, Gulbarga district, Karnataka.* Centre for Archaeological Studies and Training, Eastern India.

Jhaldiyal, R. (2008). Formation processes of the lower palaeolithic record of the Krishna basin-with special reference to the Acheulian sites in the Hunsgi and Baichbal basins, Gulbarga district, Karnataka. In K. Paddayya (Ed.), *Site Formation Processes* (pp. 93–110). Deccan College Post-Graduate and Research Institute.

Joglekar, J. (2016). New light on Acheulian artefacts made on Basalt: A case study of Urmodi river assemblage. *Man and Environment, 41*(2), 18–31.

Joglekar, J. (2020). Types of patina observed on Acheulian artefacts from the Krishna Basin, Upland Deccan, India. *Heritage: A Journal of Multi-Disciplinary Studies in Archaeology, 8*, 144–157.

Joglekar, J. (2023). A study of Acheulian culture in the Sina basin, Upland Maharashtra. *Annals of the Bhandarkar Oriental Research Institute, 100*, 97–118.

Joglekar, J., & Deo, S. G. (2015). Newly discovered Acheulian site at Atit on Urmodi River, Satara District, Maharashtra. *Man and Environment, 40*(1), 14–18.

Joglekar, J., & Deo, S. G. (2017a). On the Acheulian artefacts from Ajra and Madilge, Hiranyakeshi River, Kolhapur District, Maharashtra. *Bulletin of the Deccan College Research Institute, 77–78*, 25–32.

Joglekar, J., Deo, S. G., & Rajaguru, S. N. (2016). Newly discovered Acheulian site at Menavali in the source region of Krishna river, Satara district, Maharashtra. *Heritage: A Journal of Multi-Disciplinary Studies in Archaeology, 4*, 515–530.

Joglekar, J., & Deo, S. G. (2017b). Artefactual evidence of early hominid adaptability in the Deccan trap region of the upper Krishna basin. In S. G. Deo, A. Baptista, & J. Joglekar (Eds.), *Rethinking the Past: A Tribute to Professor V.N. Misra* (pp. 16–24). ISPQS.

Joglekar., & Deo, S. G. (2019). Re-assessment of the lithic assemblage from the Acheulian site at Yedurwadi, Upland Deccan. *History Today, 20*, 1–8+colour plates.

Joglekar, J., Deo, S. G., Rajaguru, S. N., & Mishra, S. (2011). Geoarchaeology of Acheulian sites in the Deccan trap region of the upper Krishna basin with special reference to Acheulian site at Yedurwadi, Karnataka. *Puratattva, 41*, 71–80+colour plates.

Joglekar, J., Deo, S. G., Chimote, M., & Vaddadi, S. (2022). Appraising raw material exploitation patterns of early hominids from Deccan volcanic province, Peninsular India. In S. G. Deo, A. Baptista, & J. Joglekar (Eds.), *Adaptations Across Antiquity: Tracing Quaternary Environments and Prehistoric Cultural Responses in Peninsular India* (pp. 93–112). ISPQS Monograph no. 10, ISPQS.

Joglekar, J. (2018). Recent explorations and discovery of few Acheulian localities in the Urmodi river, Satara district, Maharashtra. In K. Dalal, & R. G. Raghavan (Eds.), *The Proceedings of the Third Workshop on Explorations in Maharashtra 2016* (pp. 72–76). India Study Centre Trust.

Joglekar, J. (2019). *Acheulian studies of the Krishna basin, district Satara, upland western Maharashtra.* Unpublished Ph.D. Thesis, Deccan College Post-Graduate and Research Institute.

Joglekar, J. (2022). Acheulian culture in the Deccan trap region of upper Krishna basin, Peninsular India. In S. G. Deo, A. Baptista, & J. Joglekar (Eds.), *Adaptations Across Antiquity: Tracing Quaternary Environments and Prehistoric Cultural Responses in Peninsular India* (pp. 39–76). ISPQS Monograph no. 10, ISPQS.

Joshi, R. V. (1955). *Pleistocene studies in the Malaprabha basin.* Deccan College and Karnatak University.

Joshi, V. U., & Kale, V. S. (1997). Colluvial deposits in Northwest Deccan, India: Their significance in the interpretation of late quaternary history. *Journal of Quaternary Science, 12*(5), 391–403.

Kale, V. S., Ganjoo, R. K., Rajaguru, S. N., & Ota, S. B. (1986a). Discovery of an Acheulian site at Bori, district Pune. *Bulletin of the Deccan College Research Institute, 45*, 47–49.

Kale, V. S., Ganjoo, R. K., Rajaguru, S. N., & Salahuddin, S. (1986b). A link-channel, occupational site of Acheulian man, upper Krishna valley, Karnataka. *Current Science, 55*(21), 1073–1075.

Kale, V. S., & Rajaguru, S. N. (1987). Late quaternary alluvial history of the Northwestern Deccan upland region. *Nature, 325*, 612–614.

Korisettar, R. (1994). Quaternary alluvial stratigraphy and sedimentation in the upland Deccan region, Western India. *Man and Environment, 19*(1–2), 29–41.

Korisettar, R., & Petraglia, M. D. (1993). Explorations in the Malaprabha valley, Karnataka. *Man and Environment, 18*(1), 43–48.

Korisettar, R., Gogte, V. D., & Petraglia, M. D. (1993). 'Calcareous Tufa' at the site of Banasankari in the Malaprabha valley, Karnataka: Revisited. *Man and Environment, 18*(2), 13–21.

Korisettar, R. (1979). *Prehistory and geomorphology of the middle Krishna, Karnataka.* Unpublished Ph.D. Thesis, Deccan College, University of Poona.

Korisettar, R. (2007). Toward developing a basin model for Palaeolithic settlement of the Indian subcontinent: Geodynamics, monsoon dynamics, habitat diversity and dispersal routes. In M. D. Petraglia, & B. Allchin (Eds.), *The Evolution and History of Human Populations in South Asia(Vertebrate Paleobiology Paleoanthropology Series)* (pp. 69–96). Springer.

Kulkarni, C., Deo, S., & Rajaguru, S. N. (2008). Field studies of quaternary sediments around Wai. *Man and Environment, 33*(2), 32–36.

Leopold, L. B., Wolman, M. G., & Muller, J. P. (1964). *Fluvial processes in geomorphology.* W.H. Freeman and Company.

Lepre, C., Roche, H., Kent, D. V., Sonia Harmand, R. L., Quinn, J. P., Brugal, P. J., Texier, A. L., & Feible, C. (2011). An earlier origin for the Acheulian. *Nature, 477*, 82–85.

Malik, S. C. (1959). *Stone age industries of Bombay and Satara districts.* M.S. University Baroda.

Mishra, S., Deo, S. G., Abbas, R., Naik, S., Shete, G., Agrawal, N., & Rajaguru, S. N. (2009). Excavations at the early Acheulian site of Morgaon, Maharashtra (2000–2007). In K. Paddayya, P. P. Joglekar, K. K. Basa, & R. Sawant (Eds.), *Recent Research Trends in South Asian Archaeology* (pp. 121–137). Deccan College Postgraduate and Research Institute.

Munsell Rock Color Charts. (2009). *Revised edition.* Munsell Color Company, Inc., Baltimore, Maryland 21218.

Nichols, G. (2009). *Sedimentology and stratigraphy* (2nd ed.). A John Wiley & Sons Ltd., Publication.

Paddayya, K. (1978). New research designs and field techniques in the palaeolithic archaeology of India. *World Archaeology, 10*, 94–100.

Paddayya, K. (1982). *The Acheulian culture of the Hunsgi valley (Peninsular India): A settlement system perspective.* Deccan College.

Paddayya, K. (1987a). The stone age cultural systems of the Baichbal valley, Gulbarga District, Karnataka: A preliminary report. *Bulletin of the Deccan College Research Institute, 46*, 77–100.

Paddayya, K. (1987b). The place and study of site formation processes in India. In D.T. Nash, & M. D. Petraglia (Eds.), *Natural Formation Processes and the Archaeological Record* (pp. 74–85). Oxford: BAR International Series 352.

Paddayya, K. (1987c). Excavation of an Acheulian occupation site at Yediyapur, Peninsular India. *Anthropus, 82*, 610–614.

Paddayya, K. (1991). The Acheulian of the Hunsgi-Baichbal valleys, Peninsular India: A processual study. *Quartar, 41*(42), 111–138.

Paddayya, K. (2007). The Acheulian of peninsular India with special reference to the Hunsgi and Baichbal valleys of the Lower Deccan. In M. Petraglia & B. Allchin (Eds.), *The Evolution and History of Human Populations in South Asia* (pp. 97–119). Springer.

Paddayya, K., & Deo, S. G. (2017). *Prehistory of South Asia.* The Mythic Society.

Paddayya, K., Petraglia, M. D. (1995). Natural and cultural formation processes of the Acheulian sites of the Hunsgi and Baichbal Valleys, Karnataka. In S. Wadia, R. Korisettar, & V. S. Kale (Eds.), *Quaternary environments and geoarchaeology of India* (pp. 333–351). Geological Society of India.

Paddayya, K., Blackwell, B. A. B., Jhaldiyal, R., Petraglia, M. D., Fevrier, S., Chaderton, D. A., Blickstein, J. I. B., & Skinner, A. R. (2002). Recent findings on the Acheulian of the Hunsgi and Baichbal valleys, Karnataka, with special reference to the Isampur excavation and its dating. *Current Science, 83*(5), 641–647.

Pappu, R. S., & Deo, S. G. (1994). *Man-Land relationships during palaeolithic times in the Kaladgi basin, Karnataka.* Deccan College.

Pappu, S., Gunnell, Y., Akhilesh, K., Braucher, R., Taieb, M., Demory, F., & Thouveny, N. (2011). Early pleistocene presence of Acheulian hominids in South India. *Science, 331*, 1596–1600+supplementary data.

Pappu, R. S. (1974). *Pleistocene Studies in the upper Krishna Basin.* Deccan College.

Petraglia, M. D., Schuldenrein, J., & Korisettar, R. (2003). Landscapes, activity and the Acheulian to middle palaeolithic transition in the Kaladgi Basin, India. *Journal of Eurasian Prehistory, 1*(2), 3–24.

Rajaguru, S. N. (1970). *Studies in the late pleistocene of the Mula-Mutha.* Unpublished Ph.D Thesis, Deccan College, University of Poona.

Rao, S. N. (1969). *The stone age cultures of Nalgonda district.* Unpublished Ph.D. Thesis, Deccan College, University of Poona.

Rao J. V. P. (1992). *Prehistoric environment and archaeology of the Krishna-Tungabhadra Doab, Andhra Pradesh.* Unpublished Ph.D. Thesis, Deccan College, University of Pune.

Reineck, H. E., & Singh, I. B. (1980). *Depositional sedimentary environments* (2nd ed.). Springer-Verlag.

Salunke, M., Deo, S. G., Rajaguru, S. N., Shinde, S., & Pawar, N. (2013). Field observations of quaternary deposits on the river Hiranyakeshi around Ajra district Kolhapur, Maharashtra. *Bulletin of the Deccan College Research Institute, 72–73*, 99–110.

Sampat, I. (1924). *A palaeolithic settlement and factory in the Mysore state, (paper presented) in the Indian science congress.* Indian Science Congress Association.

Sankalia, H. D. (1956). Animal fossils and palaeolithic industries from the Pravara basin at Nevasa, district Ahmednagar. *Ancient India, 12*, 35–52.

Sankalia, H. D. (1952). *The Godavari palaeolithic industry.* Deccan College Post-Graduate and Research Institute.

Schick, K. (1984). *Processes of palaeolithic site formation: An experimental study.* Unpublished Ph.D. Thesis, University of California.

Seshadri, M. (1955). The palaeolithic industry of Kibbanahalli, Mysore State. *Artibus Asiae, 18*(3/4), 271–287.

Seshadri, M. (1956). *The stone–using cultures of prehistoric and protohistoric Mysore: London.*

Shackley, M. L. (1978). The behaviour of artefacts as sedimentary particles in a fluviatile environment. *Archaeometry, 20*, 55–61.

Sharon, G. (2007). *Acheulian large flake industries: Technology, chronology, and significance.* Archaeopress.

Sharon, G. (2010). Large flake Acheulian. *Quaternary International, 223–224*, 226–233.

Shivarudrappa, T. V. (1990). Environment aspects of early and middle palaeolithic cultures in Southern Karnataka. In A. Sundara (Ed.), *Archaeology in Karnataka* (pp. 23–36). Directorate of Archaeology and Museums.

Soundara Rajan, K. V. (1958). Studies in the stone age of Nagarjunakonda and its neighbourhood. *Ancient India, 14*, 49–113.

Srinivas, A. (2017). Preliminary observations: Palaeolithic investigations at Kibbanahalli, Southern Karnataka. *Man and Environment, 42*(1), 21–35.

Srinivas, A. (2014). Palaeolithic archaeology at Kibbanahalli, Southern Karnataka. *Antiquity, 342.* Project Gallery article. http://antiquity.ac.uk/projgall/srinivas342

Srinivas, A. (2017b). Role of social matrices in the preservation of the archaeological record: A case study of the differential preservation of the archaeological record in the Kibbanahalli Palaeolithic complex, Southern Karnataka, India. In L. Oosterbeek, B. Werlen, & L. Caron (Eds.), *Sustainability and socio-cultural matrices: Transdisciplinary contributions for cultural integrated landscape management* (Vol. III). *Arkeos, 42*, 27–36.

Srinivas, A. (2017c). The missing piece: A review of lower and middle palaeolithic archaeology in Southern Karnataka. *Heritage: Journal of Multidisciplinary Studies in Archaeology, 5*, 715–734.

Subbarao, B. (1949). *Prehistoric and early historic bellary*. Unpublished Ph.D. Thesis, Bombay University.

Subramanyam, R., Banerjee, K. D., Khare, M. D., Rao, B. V., Sarkar, H., Singh, R., Joshi, R. V., Lal, S. B., Rao, V. V., Srinivasan, K. R., & Totadri, K. (1975). *Nagarjunakonda (1954–60), Memoirs of the Archaeological Survey of India* (Vol. 1, No. 7). Archaeological Survey of India.

Szabo, B. S., Mckinney, C., Dalbey, T. S., & Paddayya, K. (1990). On the age of the Acheulian culture of the Hunsgi-Baichbal valleys, Peninsular India. *Bulletin of Deccan College Research Institute, 50*, 317–321.

Umarjikar, S. V. (1983). *Quaternary geology of upper Krishna basin.* Unpublished Ph.D Thesis, University of Poona.

Chapter 4
Southern Neolithic Culture of India: People, Plants, and Animals

R. Arjun

Abstract The Neolithic culture of Indian subcontinent can be broadly categorised into eight geographical zones flourished during 8000–1200 BCE (Baluchistan and Indus basin, Himalayan region, Ganga Basin, North-eastern Himalayas, Eastern India, Northern Gujarat and Rajasthan, Western Deccan (Chalcolithic) and Southern Deccan). Further based on early agricultural origin and crop diversity, these zones are identified into thirteen traditions, and one of them is southern Neolithic (South India) carrying the ashmound tradition spanning across the southern India during 3200–1200 BCE. South India occupies a major part of the Indian Peninsula, bordering offshores of Arabian sea in the west and Bay of Bengal in the east. Further bordered with high hill ranges of Western Ghats in the west and Eastern Ghats in the east. A tract of landscape within these two hill ranges is the Deccan Plateau; the central and southern part of the plateau has high density of Neolithic sites of various categories such as the ashmounds, habitation/settlements, stone tool workshop sites, rock art sites and combination of these cultural signatures in one site (Figs. 4.1 and 4.2). Such diversity of full-fledged site types and the occurrence of the oldest dates from them makes the central-southern part of the Deccan Plateau as core Neolithic zone. This chapter takes the reader on each distinct aspects of southern Neolithic culture, ranging from its archaeological studies to detailing their site types, diet, crops, animals, art, tools, ceramics, mortuary practices and land use patterns.

Keywords Neolithic culture · Peninsular India · Deccan · Ashmounds · Watgal · Utnur · Budihal · Bilamrayanagudda · Sanganakallu-Kupgal · Mesolithic · Raichur Doab · Hallur · Tekkalakota · Ceramics of Neolithic era · Neolithic settlement patterns

---

R. Arjun (✉)
Department of History and Archeology, Central University of Karnataka, Kalaburagi, Karnataka 585367, India
e-mail: arjunrao@cuk.ac.in

L. Vemsani (ed.), *Handbook of Indian History*,
https://doi.org/10.1007/978-981-97-6207-1_4

4.1 Introduction

The Neolithic culture of Indian subcontinent can be broadly categorized into eight geographic zones that flourished during the eighth to first millennium BCE (Baluchistan and Indus basin, Himalayan region, Ganga Basin, North-eastern Himalayas, Eastern India, Northern Gujarat, and Rajasthan, Western Deccan (Chalcolithic) and Southern Deccan). Further based on early agricultural origins and crop diversity, these zones are identified into thirteen traditions (see Korisettar, 2021), and one of them is southern Neolithic (South India) carrying the ashmound tradition spanning across southern India during 3200–1200 BCE. South India occupies a major part of the Indian Peninsula, bordering offshores of Arabian sea in the west and Bay of Bengal in the east. Further bordered with high hill ranges of Western Ghats in the west and Eastern Ghats in the east. A tract of landscape within these ranges is the Deccan Plateau; the central and southern part of the plateau has a high density of Neolithic sites of various categories such as ashmounds, habitation/settlements, stone tool workshop sites, rock art sites, and combination of these cultural signatures in one site (Figs. 4.1 and 4.2). Such diversity of full-fledged site types and the occurrence of the oldest dates from them makes the central-southern part of the Deccan Plateau as a unique Neolithic zone. This chapter takes the reader on each distinct aspect of the southern Neolithic culture, ranging from its archeological studies to detailing their site types, diet, crops, animals, art, tools, ceramics, mortuary practices, and land use patterns.

4.2 Southern Neolithic Studies

The southern Neolithic region is one of the earliest regions to inaugurate the Indian archeological studies, with the discovery of ashmounds in the 1840s by Colonel Mackenzie (Newbold, 1836). Newbold's *Note on the Occurrence of Volcanic Scoria in the Southern Peninsula* (1836) and *On Some Ancient Mounds of Scorious Ashes in Southern India* (1842–1843) initiated the recording of the several ashmounds in Karnataka and excavations were conducted at Kugpal (presently in Ballari district of Karnataka). Taylor (1851, 1853) was next to initiate the studies on ashmounds; while extensively documenting the megaliths of the Shorapur region, he identified the complex megalith on the ashmound surface that instigated him to conclude the ashmounds in mortuary/burial practices. Onward the 1860s to 1890s, the increasing number of Neolithic sites across southern India were explored by Foote (1887a, 1887b, 1895, 1914, 1916). Foote's *Notes on Some Recent Neolithic and Paleolithic finds in the South* (1887a) distinguished the European prehistory with the Indian prehistoric cultural dynamics. *The Prehistoric and Protohistoric Antiquities of India* (1914) *and the Foote's Collection of Indian Prehistoric and Protohistoric Antiquities: Notes on their Ages and Distribution* (1916) established the nature of Neolithic settlements. These works of Foote recorded 252 Neolithic sites out of a total of

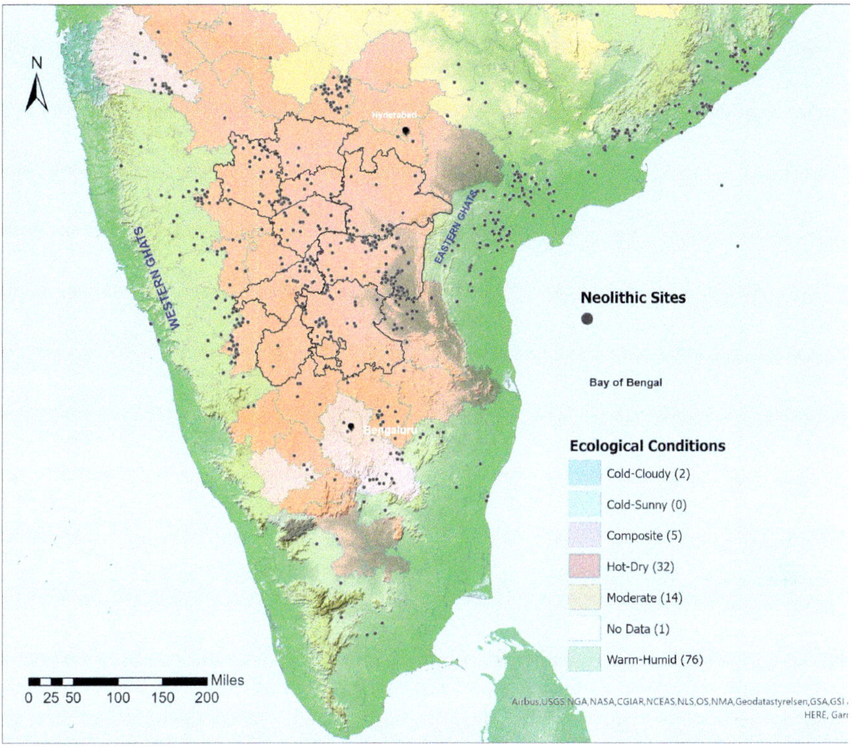

Fig. 4.1 Distribution of Neolithic sites in the southern Indian states of Karnataka, Telangana, Andhra Pradesh, and Tamil Nadu. Red shaded area is Deccan Plateau, semi-arid in condition and the bordered lines are modern districts in Karnataka, Andhra Pradesh, and Telangana indicating the distribution of ashmound sites within the core Neolithic zones

459 prehistoric sites (Korisettar et al., 2002: 153). When the age of the ashmound tradition was debated between the Iron Age and Medieval period origin, Foote rightly pushed the ashmound tradition to the Neolithic period on the occurrences of dolerite tool types and ceramics, and established their source of formation to cow dung. Munn (1934), an engineer working in the gold mines of Raichur Doab began to re-survey ashmound sites alongside the rock art and megalithic sites, and he established geolocational features of the ashmound sites.

The next phase in southern Neolithic studies concentrated on establishing the prehistoric cultural sequence and chronology. The number of settlement sites were excavated, such as the Brahmagiri (Krishna, 1941, Wheeler, 1948), Maski (Thaper, 1957), Kadkal (Yazdani, 1935–1936), Piklihal (Allchin, 1960), Utnur (Allchin, 1961), Palavoy (Rami Reddy, 1976), Budihal (Paddayya, 1991–1992), Tekkalakota (Nagaraja Rao & Malhotra, 1965) and Watgal (Devaraj et al., 1995). The number of PhD researches was presented on the Neolithic archeology (covering Karnataka, Andhra Pradesh, and Tamil Nadu) including but not limited to those from Subbarao (1948), Allchin (1954), Seshadri (1956), Nagaraja Rao (1971), Paddayya (1968),

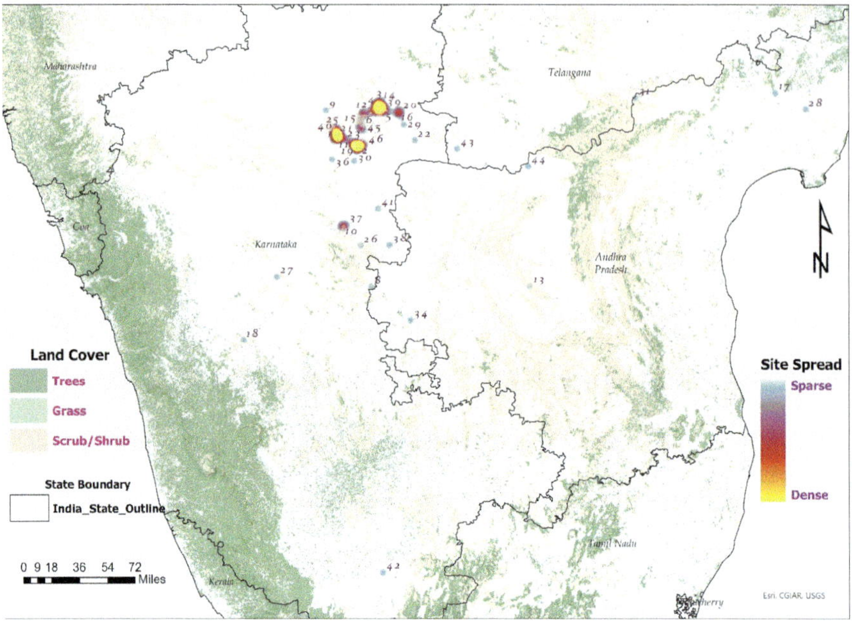

Fig. 4.2 Showing discussed Neolithic sites in this chapter. (1) Advibhavi-Rampura (2) Anandgal (3) Anchesugur (4) Anjal (5) Bairappamaradi site complex (6) Bassapura (7) Bilamrayanagudda (8) Brahmagiri (9) Budihal (10) Bukkasagra (11) Chikka Hesaruru (12) Chinchodi (13) Gandluru (14) Gopalapura (15) Goudur (16) Guntral (17) Guntupalli (18) Hallur (19) Harvapura (20) Hirebooduru (21) Kalapura (22) Kallur (23) Karadkal (24) Kotegal (25) Krishna Bridge (26) Kudutini (27) Kumaranahalli (28) Kunderu (29) Maladkal (30) Maski (31) Nagarjunakonda (32) Navilagudda (33) Nilavanji (34) Palavoy (35) Pamankalluru (36) Piklihal (37) Ramasagara (38) Sangankallu-Kupgal (39) Shambulingeshwaragudda (40) Shilahalli (41) Tekkalakota (42) T-Narasipura (43) Utnur (44) Veerapuram (45) Wandalli (46) Watgal. Sites shown are in the states of Karnataka, Telangana and Andhra Pradesh

Rami Reddy (1976), Narasimhaiah (1980), David Raju (1981), Venkatasubbaiah (1992) and Arjun (2017a).

The archeological studies in the twenty-first century on southern Neolithic is of multi-disciplinary research projects emphasizing on ashmound problems, plant and animal domestication, lithic analysis, obtaining radio carbon dates, landscape, and settlement patterns. With a well-established Neolithic cultural sequence from the sites excavated, the three-phase model developed by (Allchin & Allchin, 1982) was reviewed into a two-phase model (Korisettar et al., 2002). Settlement development and occupational shifts in Sangankallu-Kupgal site complex with radiometric dates, attribute based statistical analysis of the stone tool industry and ceramic variability, identification of crops explained the settlement formations on the hilltop and periodical/sequential shifts from one outcrop to the other (Shipton et al., 2012). Neolithic landscaping at Brahmagiri (Arjun, 2018a, 2022a) and Piklihal (Arjun & Pal, 2023) developed increasing use of rock shelters for socio-political and economic resources and foothill focus in occupational and ashmound formations, this sufficed for a different type in their settlement pattern.

Neolithic rock art is another area of study intermittently developed over the period of southern Neolithic studies. With the recording of rock bruisings (discussed in more detail in the coming section of the chapter), 1890's was the decade of initial phase of Neolithic rock art studies flagged-off with Robert Sewell, Hubert Knox, Robert Bruce Foote, and Fawcett (see Arjun, 2018b, c). Foote (1916) continued to explore several numbers of Neolithic sites; the art and the cultural materials such as the celts led him to identify and associate their cultural affiliations to the Neolithic origin. However, site reporting continued to be often recorded (e.g., Mahadevan, 1941).

Fresh attempts were made to solve the 'ashmound problems' (Fuller, 2006; Fuller et al., 2007; Johansen, 2004; Korisettar et al., 2002; Paddayya, 2019); the formation process of the ashmounds, their dates, and duration, their association with the settlements became increasingly clear. Re-examination of ashmound layers established its multi-layered stratigraphy in the formation of the ashmounds, and the layers were identified as productive in botanical and phytolith samples, and contextualized the topographic and geographic association of the ashmound sites (Rajala et al., 2004). Further, Johansen (2004), and Boivin et al. (2005) made melodramatic projection of ashmounds as monuments of architectural functionality in the startling geolocations. The latest findings on the ashmounds have shifted their focus from large heaped ashmound sites to episodic occurrence of ashmound traditions practiced within the household and settlement levels (Arjun, 2021, 2022a). Thinner sections of vitrified ash (ashmound) layers are identified from the settlements in core southern Neolithic sites, such as the Watgal, Bilamrayanagudda, Brahmagiri, Kotegal, Anandgal, etc. Site-centered studies recording a range of settlement developments and spatial-cultural diversity with the aid of geo-spatial tools are novel attempts made in the landscape archeology (Arjun, 2016, 2017a, b, 2018a, b, c, d, 2021, 2022a; Arjun et al., 2019; Arjun & Jadhav, 2014).

Therefore, three distinct phases can be noticed in the development of southern Neolithic studies. The first phase is the site discovery and recording phase. Ashmound sites and Neolithic sites were explored and studied on the lines of their antiquities. Second phase of studies established the temporal and spatial extents of the southern Neolithic sites and culture features with radio-metric dates and antiquarian remains with several number of sites being excavated. Third phase falls in the last two decades, which have concentrated on the Neolithic subsistence economy with the aid of archeobotany and archeozoology. Site centric studies made key details on the site landscapes, land use strategies, settlement patterns, and geo-spatial analysis examined the spatial composition of the sedentary villages and their continuity into the Iron Age (Arjun, 2017a, 2021, 2022a, b).

4.3 The Ashmounds

One of the unique and earliest cultural features of southern Neolithic is the ashmound sites. Ashmounds are mounds of cow dung, seasonally burned at high temperature, turned to vitrified lumps and ashy material deposits (Fig. 4.3). They were initially called as 'cinder mounds' (Newbold, 1836). Ashmounds are stratified with alternative layers of sediments often mixed with the occurrences of discarded cultural materials such as ceramics, stone tools, and faunal remains. They spatially occupy larger space and expand vertically, as the heaping/accumulation of cow dung and burning practices proceeded over the period of different human generations. Major ashmound sites are concentrated in the north-eastern Karnataka and western Andhra Pradesh. Example are Wandalli, Goudur, Budihal, Utnur, Palavoy, Kudutini (Budikanamma), Kupgal, Palavoy etc. Since the discovery of ashmound in Kudatini (Bellari district in Karnataka) in 1830s (Newbold, 1836: 671), it has been central to several questions on the indented meaning and formation process of the ashmounds, its seasonality in heaping and burning traditions, nature of occupations/settlements associated with ashmounds, their transformation in early to late Neolithic periods, and finding appropriate ethnographic parallels in the modern world to explain the similar process. Overall, few of the 'Ashmound Problems' remain uncertain till date.

Fig. 4.3 Ashmound deposits partially preserved at Watgal

Ashmounds accumulate large quantities of cow dung supplemented by the pastoral communities with their larger cattle herds. Neolithic culture marks developments in agro-pastoral economy, animal domestication came before crop domestication, and remained dominant in southern Neolithic societies (Korisettar et al., 2002: 205–2016). There were interesting and fascinating theories on the formation of ashmounds and their period of occurrence, much of the older views were discarded with systematic studies. On the discovery of ashmounds, their formation was attributed to natural geological processes and volcanic eruption (Newbold, 1843). Rather a peculiar and the rarest type of site, Taylor (1941) in 1840s identified the ashmound in Shorapur Doab surfaced with stone alignments (megaliths) and attributed both the ashmound and stone alignment to the Iron Age. They were also thought to be funeral pyres of the dead soldiers and animals in medieval battles (Sewell, 1899), and as a by-product of industrial activities manufacturing bricks, glass, or gold working. Robert Bruce Foote pointed out that the material of the ashmound is cow dung and was set on fire by accidental incidences (Foote, 1916). He relatively identified ashmounds to be of Neolithic origin based on finding remains of stone tools and ceramics. Later works on Ashmounds began to question the date of their formations, to have occurred in Iron Age, as such large mounds of cow dung were used in the smelting of gold or iron (Rami Reddy, 1976; Sundara, 1970; Woolley, 1939; Yazdani, 1936). Excavations at Palavoy identified the presence of iron objects, slags, and iron age ceramics, which confirmed the Ashmounds to be of Iron Age origin for Rami Reddy (1976). However, the Iron Age materials appeared at the upper levels of the site, and were found to be barren in the proper ashmound levels. Series of excavated ashmound sites such as the Budihal (Paddayya, 1993), Utnur (Allchin, 1961), and Kupgal (Majumdar & Rajaguru, 1966) provided key information on their formations and activities surrounding the ashmound tradition.

Much have been debated on the settlements associated with these ashmounds. The intensity of cultural materials found at the ashmound sites in the subsurface and surface has raised a twofold debate; ashmound sites were seasonal camped sites and the other point of argument is that, ashmounds were centered with the regular sedentary habitations. With the excavations at Budihal, Paddayya (1973) based on the ashmounds were dung discard locations from the cattle pens of nearby villages, and were periodically burned with a ritual cause. Hut floors, hearths, ceramic remains, and other domestic features were unearthed from Budihal. Utnur ashmound also revealed similar kinds of archeological features with well-preserved hoof impression of the cattle on the ashmound, approving them as a cattle pen of a regular pastoral village (Allchin, 1961). The yearlong occupation at Ashmounds sites, is contended by the substantial number of ashmound sites that are devoid of occupational remains (Korisettar et al., 2002). The density and spread of cultural materials at the ashmound sites are meagre, field reconnaissance at the surrounding areas of the major ashmound sites have yield no traces of the existence of settlements. By and large, our focus has been on larger scaled ashmounds. Recent studies are increasingly identifying deposits of ashmound material in the occupational stratigraphy of the Neolithic settlements (Arjun, 2017a, 2021, 2022a). Small section of ashmound occupying the alternative layers of habitational strata, suggests the ashmound activities occurring at the domestic levels in the late Neolithic phase. Example, at Watgal, Brahmagiri, Bilamrayanagudda, Kotekal, etc. The quantum of practice in ashmound formations must have drastically reduced in the Neolithic societies due to the increasing agricultural economy, and much of the cow dung became essentially used as manures in the agricultural fields and fuel for cooking, and the ashmound practice became symbolic in the streets of Neolithic villages.

Calibrated C14 dates available (Fuller et al., 2007) for ashmound sites are quite limited, their activities are dated to 2800–2200 BCE in Utnur, 2200–2300 BCE in Budihal, and 1950–1900 BCE in Sannarachmma (Sangankallu-Kupgal). For a more elaborate and comprehensive information on the southern Neolithic Ashmounds, refer to *Neolithic Cattle Keepers of south India: A Study of the Deccan Ashmounds* (Allchin, 1963) and *Neolithic Ashmounds of the Deccan* (Paddayya, 2019).

4.4 Rock Art

Rock art sites have appeared in several ecological zones of India, dating since the Upper Paleolithic to the present; Neolithic rock art largely overcame the hunting-gathering theme-based content to illustrate site environs linking domesticated animals and humans. The granitic gneissic plateau in the core southern Neolithic zone became a hot spot for rock art production as the Neolithic villages centered at the gneissic hills and its boulders of granite, granodiorite, and dykes offered favorable canvases to draw/bruise images (Arjun, 2017a, b, 2018b). Neolithic rock art artists, though practiced both pictographs (painting with pigments) and petroglyphs (bruising and engravings), yet the trendiest art was the rock bruising (Arjun, 2018c, 2021).

In the words of Robert Bruce Foote (1916:88), *Rock-bruisings would be the best term by which to describe them. They were, I doubt not, produced by hammering the weathered surface of the rock with stones more or less sharp-pointed, a pastime not infrequently indulged in by the herd boys of the present time whom I have sometimes come upon so occupied. It is true they always ran away when I approached, but I examined their rude hammerings carefully and never found the streak of an iron tool on the freshly bruised surface.*

Rock art sites of the southern Neolithic are found in two archeological and geolocational conditions; (a) rock art in the hill cantered full-fledged settlements and (b) rock art on the dyke swarm formations with in non-settlement sites. Neolithic rock art studies developed in two contexts; firstly, studying the content of the neolithic rock art and secondly, association of rock art with occupational features and ascertaining them to Neolithic origin. In the case of multi-period sites, rock bruising continues to be practiced and developed in the Iron Age as well (Arjun, 2017a, 2022b). For example, Piklihal, Bilamrayanagudda, Sanganakallu-Kupgal are multi-period settlement sites with a substantial number of rock bruising; Advibhavi-Rampura, rock bruising appears along the low elevated dyke swarm spreading in 5 km (Arjun, 2022b).

Fig. 4.4 Rock bruised images of cattle facing each other, Bilamrayanagudda

The most common images yet native to southern Neolithic sites is the images of two humped cattle's (*Bos indicus*) facing each other (Fig. 4.4), herd of cattle, herd of deer, anthropomorphs, human figures engaged in sexual appeals, elephants and birds such as the swan, peacock, etc.

The conceptual frameworks so far known on the Neolithic rock art, firstly, explain the stylistic evolution of the humped cattle images which help in relatively ascertaining their temporality falling into early and late Neolithic phases as propounded by Allchin and Allchin (1994–1995). In the second phase of studies, rock art locations at the hill settlements were theoretically attributed on the line of gender and physical abilities in the making of art at the physically challenging locations and the ringing sound on the making of art (Boivin, 2004). Thirdly, the locational analysis of the rock art and a range of allied activities surrounding it established a landmark development in spatial identities (Arjun, 2017a, 2018c).

Allchin and Allchin (1994–1995: 320–322) observed the style and form patterning of the cattle (*Bos indicus*) images in the rock shelters of Piklihal, that contained images of the cattle in red pictographs and several bruised images in different locales. They made the earliest attempt to describe the images into five forms; naturalistic style, exaggerated style, diagrammatic/elliptical style, heavy-bodied style, and crude style. The naturalistic style is aesthetically similar to the anatomy of the cattle with curved projected horns, at Piklihal, such images are found at the ashmound locality. Mannered/exaggerated style of cattle images looks much-sophisticated in art modified with the whole appearance of the cattle. The elliptical style of images shows decreased size of the cattle images with stretched/oval outlined forms, this form of cattle images is much frequently seen in the Neolithic sites. The heavy-bodied style are predominant images with bulky trunk, short stature, and short horns, bruised in the prominent localities on the hill summits. Smaller in size, backward sweeping, upward curving horns, and simple outlined bruising represent the crude style, they are not frequent images found at the sites. Allchin and Allchin (1994–1995) resorted to date rock art aligning on the style forms of the cattle images with similar terracotta figurines of cattle found from the stratigraphic context. Further, they firmly associated the images with the Neolithic settlements and the continuity of similar art production until the early historic period (300 BCE–500 CE). The images of horse and horse riders with metal implements in the panels are associated with the heavy-bodied and crude styled cattle images, assigned to the first millennium BCE and First millennium CE. Later, further rearrangement of the art images and its chronological sequencing continued (see Boivin, 2004; Robinson et al., 2008; Arjun, 2018a, b, c).

Mahadevan (1941) on his geological expeditions in Shorapur Doab, recorded the association of rock art images with sonic production. He identified ringing rocks/lithophones are usually found in the localities linked with the activities concerning the making of rock bruising; Paddayya (1976) recorded a similar association of locations with ringing rocks and images, and assigned them to the Neolithic. Sonic production and the rock bruising locations exhibited their links in the process of making art. Boivin (2004) continued to work on this line at Sanganakallu-Kupgal and advanced the theory of 'Neolithic soundscapes'. Boivin's (2004) gender based physical attributes in the making of rock bruising in the hill summits vaguely demonstrated the 'male athlete' was the artist, who was cable of climbing the hills regularly. Neolithic hill sites are at a relatively low elevated residual/inselberg hills rising 10–50 m from the surrounding plains; they are climbed within a close time range of 5–10 min. These hill formations are relatively steeper (summit) at one end, where the trucking is challenging, whereas on the other parts of the hills are slightly inclined and are conveniently accessible without much efforts invested (Arjun, 2017a, 2018b, c). Latest studies at the site of Advibhavi-Rampura (Arjun, 2022b), low elevated dyke swarm formations stretching 6.5 km, the formations have illustrated a gallery of rock bruising with settlement terraces and ringing rocks up to a continues stretch of 3.5 km. Site like Advibhavi-Rampura suggests the two categories of rock art sites, rock art in settlement sites and rock art at the dyke swarms where rocks are a source for celt workshops with no habitation features viz rock art in non-settlement sites. Several Neolithic sites are being studied in Raichur Doab, the role of ringing rocks appears to be beyond the idea of making sound in the art production; particularly the locales of the cattle images are often found clustered with a range of archeological features; such as the ringing rocks, bedrock mortars, settlement terraces, grinding grooves and water pools on the rocky boulders demonstrate the ringing rocks played its substantial role in the ritual engagements (Arjun, 2017a, 2021). Cattle images are often found with the impact marks on them due to ringing sound, which clearly suggests, sound itself was an 'offering,' and alerted the occupants on the process of rituals and on any domestic activities initiated at the rock art locations and at hill base (Arjun, 2017a, 2021, 2022a, b). Such multiple 'activity complex' became a notable landmark in the Neolithic settlements, leading to the formation of 'social ownerships' in the society, the same must have further continued in the Iron Age.

4.5 Stone Tools

The use of igneous and metamorphic rocks for edge and non-edge tools was clearly distinguished by the neolithic tools makers based on the tool utilities. Much of the Neolithic sites are identified by the finding of the polished axes, and other tools such as the adze, wedges, chisels, and scrappers were all made on diorite and dolerite (Fig. 4.5). The axes have been most regular materials lifted as collections, and being typologically discussed since the time of Foote (1916). Tools equally found significance on the advent of agriculture are rubbers, grinders, querns, pestles, hammers, ring stones, stone disks, and stone balls (like sling balls), all such non-edge tools were generally made on the granite/gneissic verities. Microliths and blade tools were made on the cryptocrystalline rocks such as the chalcedony, chert, and quartz. Such raw materials are gravels generally found on the river banks of Krishna and Bhima. Dykes are intrusive rocks frequently spottable in the granitic hills in this part of the country as swarms.

Microlithic assemblages in South India began to appear since 35 kya (Korisettar & Bora, 2014) and are identifiable in the southern Neolithic sites from c. 8000 BCE (Roberts et al., 2015) at pre-Neolithic levels; microlithic were continued to be in use throughout the Neolithic and Iron Age periods. One of the notable tool types in microlithic assemblages is the lengthy parallel chert blades ranging above 5 cm. Perhaps, it was useful in harvesting crops, Allchin (1960: 95–98) included such assemblages in the Neolithic blade industry (Allchin, 1960: 85). The fluted core technique was a novel practice in the blade production. Two sites which are taken to discussion here are, Watgal (DuFresne et al., 1998) and Sanganakallu-Kupgal (Shipton et al., 2012), giving us much known information on the microlithic assemblage diversity in the pre-Neolithic and Neolithic levels with radio carbon dates.

Watgal excavations (Devaraj et al., 1995) identified a sequence of occupation levels (I, II (A & B), III, and IV). Occupation I (pre 3000 BCE, called Pre-Neolithic), Occupation II (2700–2000 BCE) is Early Neolithic, Occupation III Late Neolithic, and Neolithic-Iron Age transition (c. 2000 BC), Occupation IV (c. 1500 BCE) overlapped with Neolithic-Chalcolithic phase. The radiocarbon dates are available for Occupation II A & B, rest of the levels are undated. The microlithic assemblages from all these levels were statistically studied based on the type-technology and raw material attributes (DuFresne et al., 1998) of Blades, bladelets (lunates), and cylindrical fluted core. The assemblages are largely made on chert throughout the Occupation I to IV, chalcedony substantially appears only in Occupation IIB and declines in the later occupations; in which shoes chert was the most depended raw material for the microliths. The blade length is larger and remains stable throughout Occupation I–III and drops in level IV, which indicates trends in the standardization of blades. Bladelets/lunates are high in numbers during IIA and continue in III and IV with variations in their width dimensions; which reflect changes in their function and were independent of the blade diversity. Chert, chalcedony, quartz, and other materials show a hierarchical use in raw materials throughout all the occupational

Fig. 4.5 Dolerite edge tools from Neolithic assemblages from Raichur Doab. (1) Polished celts/axes, (2) blades and (3) chisel (rarely found)

levels, except chalcedony contending with the chert in Occupation IIB at Watgal. Watgal is located in Raichur District of Karnataka.

Sanganakallu-Kupgal is a complex of four (Sannarachmma, Choudammagudda, Hiregudda and Birappa) hill sites in Ballari district of Karnataka. Among the four hill sites, Hiregudda is the largest one with ashmounds, lithic workshops, rock art, and settlement evidences. Nearly 8,00,000 stone tools assemblages were analyzed and contextualized from these sites tracing their social changes that occurred during 1950–1100 BCE (Shipton et al., 2012). Lithic assemblages can be broadly categorized into microlithic/blade tools, dolerite tools, and non-edge tools. The granitic hills, those like Sanganakallu-Kupgal, generally have the dolerite dyke formations criss-crossing in the landscape, which were a prominent source of rocks for the making of edge/ground tools. Several workshop locales were functioning around the dyke formations and engaged them in the celt productions. The microlithic assemblages predate Neolithic, dated between 9000 BCE–3400 BCE, and there was absence of human activities between 3400 and 1950 BCE. 1950 BCE to 1400 BCE was the period of tremendous settlement developments at these sites, and 1400–1200 BCE marked the transition period from Neolithic to Iron Age. Lithic samples excavated from the Sannarachmma, Choudammagudda, and Hiregudda were categorically studied in pre-ashmound, ashmound, and post-ashmound contexts. At Hiregudda, a circular stone aligned boulders/feature of 7 m in diameter was excavated, it was a dolerite axe making workshop that counted 604,187 flakes and debris. The grooves on the workshop boulders indicated the in-site grounding of axes. Further from the workshop feature, domestic habitation remains such as the pot sherds, animal bones, and post-holes around the circular boulders were found predated to the workshop being active during 1700–1500 BCE and it was abandoned and reoccupied again by 1400 BCE. The dolerite workshop was highly active for a span of 150 years during 1400–1200 BCE.

Analysis of lithic debris from the dolerite workshop (labeled as Area A, Feature 1) led to initiate a detailed study on the manufacturing stages of the axes (Brumm et al., 2007). The source of dolerite tools was the dyke formations on the hilltops of Hiregudda, where the workshop factory was located. They are hard gabbro coarse grained rocks, their petrographic composition is medium grained holocrystalline rock (intergranular in texture), with crystals of plagioclase, augite, biotite, and quartz crystals.

Based on the study of 83,858 artifact samples from Area A, Feature 1, identified three methods in the axe reductions. Namely block-based, slab-based, and flake-based methods (Brumm et al., 2007). Method 1, block-based, consisting five stages, procurement of raw materials, knapping the edges of the block and turning to a rough outlined shape, next flaking on both sides, further bifacial flaking resulted in contouring the tool, and the last stage was pecking uneven surfaces/flake scars and grounded on the bedrock to get a smooth tool surface and sharpen the cutting edge. Method 2 is slab-based approach, consisting of three stages, dolerite slabs are procured, taken to reduce it into desired shape and size by flaking, and lastly pecked the uneven surfaces and grounded on the bedrock. Method 3, flake-based method, firstly dolerite flakes were collected, retouched on both or one side, and then directly grounded on bedrock for grinding. The last stage in the dolerite axe production commonly includes the grinding of tools on the bedrock/rocky boulders. This is a stage of the process where the axes are turned to have a smooth surface, popularly called as polished tools. In this stage of production, two kinds of grooves formed, one is the oval shaped grooves (also called hallows) with shallow depression formed while tool surfaces were grounded, and secondly, long parallel narrow deep grooves, formed due to the axe edge sharpening. The experimental axe production conducted at Hiregudda (Risch et al., 2009) postulate, the tool was placed on the groove and were mechanically pressed and moved up-and-down against, rather than the tool grounded by holding it in the hands.

Recent archeological reconnaissance in Raichur Doab shed light on much precise information on spatially distinguished Neolithic sites patterned for the dolerite axe production (Arjun, 2017a, 2018d, 2021, 2022b). Archeological research projects by the author, *Stone Tool Economy and Resources Use in Raichur Doab* are focusing on the lithic workshop sites and tracing its *Chaîne opératoire*. In the case of Sanganakallu-Kupgal, it is a lithic workshop site at the dolerite dyke formations that exhibit an industrial/factory scale of tool production. However, Neolithic sites are very robust, cautioning classifications with greater attention; (a) Neolithic settlement site with lithic workshops in the non-resource environs, (b) sites in the resource locations for raw material procurement only, (c) specialized lithic workshops which does the grounding of tools only, and (d) Neolithic settlements being on the consumer end. The stone tool workshops in the Neolithic settlement are generally in the form of dolerite flakes and microlithic core assemblages associated with the settlement terraces or generally scattered across the base of the hill sites, e.g., Bilamrayanagudda. Large to small scale dolerite flakes and cores, other flakes often appear as scrappers, suggest the lithic reduction occurred at the site, and boulders on the hill summits were chosen for grounding tools. In Raichur Doab, dyke swarm series are a major intrusive formation in the gneissic landscapes, such formations are partially visible at a range of low elevation of 10–20 m above the surface, and they stretch from 4–7 km in the landscape. One such dyke swarm is, Advibhavi-Rampura (Arjun, 2021), it was intensively studied and recorded with the high density of locations spreading for 5 km, exhibiting a range of features surrounding the rock bruising panels with settlement terraces, grooves/bedrock mortars, and rock gongs. No habitation or lithic workshop were found. The case was similar in another dyke series at Pamankalluru as well. Several Neolithic sites are located close to Advibhavi-Rampura and Pamankalluru dyke formations at 5–10 km radius. Such dyke swarm series are many in Raichur Doab and are a rich source to gather the dolerite blocks for the settlements or lithic workshops. Third category of sites is the occurrence of clusters of prominent and shallow grinding grooves/slicks on the granitic bedrocks in the gneissic hills of Devadurga formations in Raichur Doab. Hundreds of grooves in several clusters were recorded in different sites (Devadurga complex, Nilavanji, and Navilagudda) and found no single flakes or a dolerite tool (see Arjun, 2021, 2018d). This shows rocky sites like these, were meant for only grounding of dolerite tools in axe production stages; celts/axes were knapped and pecked elsewhere, the tool was brought to grounding sites, they grounded the tools and transported it in a much-sophisticated polished forms to settlement sites. Sites like these suggest the trading zones located between the two Neolithic regions such as the Raichur Doab and Shorapur Doab. There is this another category of Neolithic sites with no workshop localities, they remain only at the consumer end, e.g., Brahmagiri (Arjun, 2022a),

Watgal, Tekkalakota, etc. At these sites, we get to find the well-polished, different sized, large to smaller or heavier to lighter dolerite axes (Arjun, 2021).

4.6 Metal Tools and Metallurgy

By the opening of third and second millennium BCE, distinct parts of the Indian subcontinent had witnessed the use of copper and Bronze. E.g., Indus Valley, Ganga Valley, and western Deccan. In southern Indian Neolithic sites seldom small finds of beads, fish hook, rings, miniature axes are reported from the sites such as the Hallur (Nagaraja Rao, 1971), Tekkalakota (Nagaraja Rao & Malhotra, 1965), Gandluru (IAR, 1983–1984), Guntupalli (Rami Reddy, 1968) and Veerapuram (Sastri et al., 1984). Larger objects on copper, antennae-hilted swords were found from Kallur in Raichur Doab (Allchin & Allchin, 1968: 153). This find was similar to the copper hordes of Ganga Valley during the OCP (ochre coloured pottery) phase. Metal tools in the Neolithic sites have generally occurred in the late Neolithic phase, and were often identified as Neolithic-Chalcolithic period in south India (Sundara, 1970) and attempts were made to establish the contact between the southern Neolithic with the Jorwe cultures of western Deccan (Devaraj et al., 1995) connected through the river Bhima (Khaladkar, 2008). In the use of copper/bronze objects, there might have been a low intensity of supply, perhaps from the external contacts within India. However, much more interesting development from recent studies is that, the dates for the use of Iron falling in the Neolithic temporality (3200–1200 BCE). Brahmagiri dated to AMS cal. 2140–1940 BC (Morrison, 2005: 258), iron production at Rampura and Bukkasagara (near Hampi) C14 dated to cal. 1270–1010 BC (Johansen, 2014: 268), and Kumaranahalli dated to 1000 BC (Singhvi et al., 1991). Use of Iron must have emerged in south India on a much vibrant scale, side-lining the other metals such as copper/bronze.

4.7 Ceramics Production and Craft

Ceramics have played a crucial role in the identification of distinct cultures in Indian archeology (often called, ceramics as the 'mother of archeology'). Ceramics marks the functional practices surrounding the kitchen storage and cooking. Southern Neolithic culture is classified into distinct sub-phases considering a range of factors such as the ceramic technology, evolution of sedentary villages, agro-pastoral economy, and lithic technology. In terms of the ceramic technology, southern Neolithic is classified into the 'aceramic' and 'ceramic' phases, the ceramic phase further into lower and upper Neolithic phases. There are invariable differences in the identification of ceramic types, such as typology based or fabric/slip basis, and also on the basis of stratigraphic sequence. For example, Neolithic into Phase A and B at Brahmagiri (Wheeler, 1948), Neolithic into lower and upper at Piklihal (Allchin,

1960), Grey ware, black ware, buff ware, perforated ware, ochre painted ware with incised decorated varieties of handmade types forms the early developments in the early ceramic tradition. These verities are conventionally assigned and limited to lower neolithic phase. Black ware, red ware of slip verities, burnished ware with or without the slip, and rusticated ware (surface rubbed) form the dominant wares in the upper Neolithic Phase. Focusing on the surface treatment of ceramics alone, they fall into four kinds. One is the application of slip, i.e., wet paste usually of red and black shades, and burnishing before firing, secondly, decorating ceramics with motifs through incising, applique (pasting clay motifs on the surface), and fingertip impressed techniques, and thirdly painting with pigment such as the ochre (usually painted on post firing of the pot), and fourthly, rusticating, i.e., rubbing to roughening the surface when pot is leather hard. The black-and-red ware, a much attention seeker ware in Indian Archeology began in its phase in the upper Neolithic levels and marks the transition of Neolithic to Iron Age by 1400–1200 BCE. Thicker profile of clay and coarse sand for handmade pottery in the lower Neolithic, thinner profile with refined clay for wheels made in the upper Neolithic are fundamental distinguishing parameters followed. However, possibilities of partially handmade and wheel turned ceramics production could not be ruled out.

Terracotta figurines in the southern Neolithic were largely of humped cattle animals, birds, human torso kind, round small balls, and beads were made. Beads were made on carnelian and shells as well.

4.8 Diet: Animal Domestication and Pastoralism

The Neolithic economy was based on animal and plant economy, and several debates have taken place on whether which of them emerged first, was it pastoralism or agriculture (see Fuller & Kingwell-Benham, 2018; Mecee, 2018). There has always been less literature found on the animal bones recorded from the southern Neolithic excavations, Mecee (2018) points out at the methodological bias on the recovery of bones from the excavations, as the focus of collection is much on the larger bone remains and least on the smaller ones. Ashmounds and settlement sites are two locational possibilities for recovering the domesticated animal bones for examination. However, caution to be cared in distinguishing the cattle bones in ashmounds and settlements; cattle bones are disarticulated remains in the ashmounds and not of the butchered one, rather of natural death; bone discarded into the ashmound, which is cyclically burned, suggests it enhanced the ritual effectiveness in the ashmound accumulation. Out of domesticated bone assemblages from the Neolithic sites, the cattle (*Bos indicus*) bones are most frequent next to water buffalo (*Bubalus bubalis*) sheep (*Capra ovis*) and goat (*Capra hircus*). Cattle appears very frequently in the Neolithic Rock art than the water buffalo (Fig. 4.6). Though a limited archeozoological studies available from the cluster of sites on river Pennar in Cuddapah (Venkatasubbaiah, 1992; Venkatasubbiaiah et al. 1992), Ballari (Korisettar et al., 2001), Budihal (Paddayya et al., 1995) and Brahmagiri (Pal & Talukdar, 2009) help

Fig. 4.6 Bruised image of water buffalo, and superimposed images of other animals such as the swan and other animals, at Maladkal

in constructing the species diversity of Neolithic domesticated animals and wild fauna in their diet. Among the wild mammals are deer, blackbuck (*Antilope cervicapra*), chital (*Axis axis*) and freshwater resources such as the snail (*Pila globosa*), Mullasc (*Lamettidens* sp.), Mussels (*Parreysia* sp.), tortoise and fish were part of the Neolithic people's diet.

At Budihal, between the settlement area close to the ashmound, Paddayya (1993) identified what he calls as a butchery floor dated to 1900 BCE. About 250 sq.m of the area was prepared, (Deaotare & Kshirsagar, 1993) the butchery floor area was prepared with calcium carbonate, charcoal, potsherds, and bones mixed with water, and rammed the floor. Chopping tools of dolerite, chert, and limestone were lithic accessories for butchering. Much of the bones are of cattle animal, and few sheep, goat, buffalo, and wild animals. Taphonomy study on the bones indicated the use of larger/heavy tools in chopping, splitting, and cutting the animals. The animal bones are found in a cluster at a designated location; therefore the locale could have been a common midden/dump.

The 'ashmound problem' debates have considerably helped in understanding the pastoral economy and spatial configurations of the herding community. While ashmound were mounds made of extensive deposits of cattle dungs, the identification of cattle pens and the pastoralist behavioral pattern came into discussion. Ashmounds basically require a large heap of dung to be supplied from several herds of cattle. At Budihal (Paddayya, 2019) and Utnur (Allchin, 1961) excavations, circular featured cattle pens often enclosed with stone rubbles and thorny bushes were recorded. Pens at Utnur were in larger dimensions, ranging from 200 to 180 feet estimated to occupy about 540–650 animals, the pen was active during 2160 ± 150 BCE with a lifespan of 40–100 years (Allchin, 1961). The settlements invariably surrounded the cattle pens. Among the south Indian cattle herders, such enclosed cattle pens and settlement camps are in practice. Another notable argument surrounding the ashmound formation is the seasonal gathering of herder communities at the ashmound sites with their cattle; they were associated with common rituals/ceremonies and made a short stay (Korisettar et al., 2002). As ashmound thin deposits of layers are of concern from within the habitation deposits, the ashmound related rituals associated with the cattle began to appear at the households or streets of Neolithic villages (Arjun, 2021, 2022a). As of the animal herding is concerned, the fallow landscapes surrounding the ashmound locales must have been favorable for animal grazing and fodder. Such behavioral patterns of the herding communities of the Neolithic period are perhaps associated with the contemporary herders; they migrate along the domesticated stockades on radial or vertical migration patterns and return to their base village in different quarters/seasons of a year.

4.9 Diet: Agriculture and Food Crops

In the last two decades, plant domestication and crop suits of the southern Neolithic were expansively studied and generated with several C14 AMS dates (see Fuller et al., 2007; Korisettar, 2021). The monsoon formations and monsoonal fluctuation in the early Holocene, and the groundwater movements forming perennial networks have altered the vegetation covers and led to form different habitats. Likewise, the weaker monsoonal trends, aridification in the mid and early late Holocene, led to transitions in hunting-gathering economy to crop domestication-based subsistence economy taking the shape of sedentism. Yet in the southern Neolithic, pastoralism seems equally dominant in the agricultural economy for a prolonged period. Fluctuations in the semi-arid climate, monsoonal cycles, and tracing the wild progenitors have been key areas of studies fundamental to the identification of domesticated crops. Southern Neolithic region in the central and southern Deccan plateau is primarily positioned as a rain-shadowed region; severe monsoonal rainfall in the Western Ghats is a primary source for many of the rivers in south India, they activate the major and minor channels and supplement water resource in the hinterlands. The higher altitude of the Western Ghats acts as a barrier to rain bearing clouds moving from Arabian coast in the west to east, it creates the orographic precipitation minimizing the rainfall for the Deccan Plateau. The southern Neolithic agro-pastoralism is largely dominated by the summer monsoon, and depends on minor perennial water networks fed by springs. Emergence of southern Neolithic is of later date origin compared to northern Neolithic regions, but it exhibits an independent origin in agricultural developments, the native crops were in cultivation well before the non-native crops were introduced into their crop suits. Millets remained as a staple crop of the southern Neolithic people. Therefore, the transition from hunter-gathering to herding-cultivating in south India becomes clear (Fuller et al., 2004). Korisettar (2021) categorizes the southern Neolithic agriculture into three sequential traditions; Ashmound Tradition, Kunderu Tradition and Hallur Tradition. Ashmound

Fig. 4.7 Pictograph of plant species in red, from the rock shelter of Maladkal. The plant spices could be leaf of Deccan cycad (*Cycas circinalis*) or a pinnate palm leaf

tradition is the earliest in chronology, active during the third and second millennium BCE, Kunderu and Hallur tradition follows the ashmound tradition during the second millennium BCE and early first millennium BCE. Hallur tradition transits with late Neolithic-Iron Age phases. Perhaps, often attempts were made to illustrate activities such as the ploughing with cattle and plant species (Fig. 4.7) through the rock art in the Neolithic hill sites.

Ashmound tradition represents the phases 2 and 3 of the Neolithic sequence in agriculture, and its plant economy was mainly based on millets. Native crops to ashmound tradition are brown top millet (*Brachiaria ramose*), foxtail millet (*Setaria verticillate*), little millet (*Panicum sumatrense*), kodo millet (*Paspalum scrobiculatum*), mung (*Vigna radiata*), black gram (*Vigna mungo*), horse gram (*macrotyloma uniforum*). Non-native crops included in the crop package are wheat (*Triticum* spp.), barley (*Hordeum vulgare*), flax (*Linum usitatisstnnnn*), rice (*Oryza cr. Sativa*), Hyacinth bean (*Lablab purpureus*), pearl millet (*Pennisetum glaucum*), finger millet (*Eleusine coracana*), and pigeon pea (*Cajanus cf, cajan*). The presence of wheat and barley suggests winter cropping, their importance must have increased in the later Neolithic period.

Kunderu tradition spread around the river Kunderu in the Kurnool-Cuddapah region, which is of a tropical savanna dry climate region with black cotton soil landcover. The Neolithic sites are generally found located on the riverbank and its tributary streams. Hanumantaraopeta, Peddamudiyam, and Balijapple are references to a few sites having archeobotanical records studied (Fuller et al., 2000–2001; Fuller & Korisettar, 2004) and falling at the date range of 1700–1500 BCE (Fuller et al., 2007: 784). This is that Neolithic region which Allchin and Allchin

(1982) described about the occurrence of distinctive painted Patpad ware in the ceramic assemblages. They cultivated Horse gram (*Macrotyloma uniform*), Mung bean (*Vigna radiate*), browntop millet (*Braciaria ramosa*), millet grass, black gram (*Vigna munga* (L.)) pigeon pea (*Cajanus cajan*). Kunderu Neolithic communities did adapt a few ashmound traditional crops, but they were cultivated in completely different settlement systems.

Hallur tradition is based on the findings from Hallur site, located in the upper Tungabhadra region, a transitional zone of Western Ghats and Deccan Plateau. Agricultural landscapes can be in considerate of dry deciduous forest environment and reddish-brown sandy soil landcover. AMS dates locate the main phase of Neolithic developments at Hallur to be between 1660 and 1400 BCE (Fuller et al., 2007). This region is hypothetically understood to be the origin place for agriculture in South India. Pearl/kodo millet (*Paspalum scrobiculatum*), finger millet (*Eleusine coracana*), small quantity of rice (*Oryza sativa*). The cultivated cucurbit such as Cucurbitaceae, *Cucumis cf. prophetarum* L., and gourd (*cf. Luffa cylindrica* (L.) *Roem*) are retrieved. The rarest botanical seed among all the findings is the evidence of cotton (*Gossypium cf. arboreum* L.) cultivation.

4.10 Mortuary Practices

Burial practices in Neolithic are found to be much centered on the infant's death in the settlement areas and at residential floors. Two prominent types of burials from the southern Neolithic are the urn burial, and the extended pit burial for the adults. Another type of burials reported these years are stone covered burials; indicating the pilot stage to megalithic burials of the Iron Age period. The oldest date for burials in South India comes from the Neolithic levels of Watgal during 2700–2300 BCE, here as well, the burial was found covered with stones. Though burials are often found from the Neolithic excavations, the skeletons have not been consistently studied on the lines of osteology/pathological analysis and physical anthropology. 18 out of 21 burials from Brahmagiri were urn burials of infants, 3 from Piklihal, 1 from Utnur, 1 from Nagarjunakonda, 18 from Tekkalakota, 2 from Hallur, 2 from T-Narasipura. 14 burials from Budihal provide somewhat a better biological detail of the skeletons found (Walimbe & Paddayya, 1998–1991). Age estimates based on the cranial and post-cranial remains of the majority of the burials were estimated to belong to infants of less than 2 months of age to 10–12 months. Dental pathology of sub-adult burials suggested their age of death between 8–9 years, and a few between 12–32 months.

4.11 Southern Neolithic Landscapes: Land Use and Settlement Pattern

The Neolithic settlements and physiography have a systematic association in sustaining the lifespan of sedentary villages and agro-pastoral lifeways. Archeological studies have standardized that, the early agricultural communities and the first civilizations of the world were largely based on the perennial rivers. However, for the southern Neolithic population, it seems this was not a compulsion, rather they resorted to hilly landscapes and valleys, began their settlements on the hill-tops which have access to natural springs and depended on the environs of spring fed perennial streams (Arjun, 2017a). In *The Personality of India*, Subbarao (1948), classified the geographical traits with the development of Indian prehistoric cultures into Paleolithic, Mesolithic, and Neolithic. Further, several studies on the man-land relationship viz., a comprehensive association of paleo-ecological and geological formations with the prehistoric cultural zones pictured into the discussion (e.g., Korisettar, 2007; Korisettar et al., 2022; Raju & Venkatasubbaiah, 2002; Paddayya, 1982, 1994; Pappu & Deo, 1994; Shivarudrappa, 1990; Arjun, 2016, 2017a, b, 2022a). Lack of systematic site centric and micro area centric studies have least occurred that enable to understand the site landscape features and land use strategies developed by the sedentary villages.

As discussed earlier, core southern Neolithic sites are concentrated in the granitic gneissic formations covering the modern states of north-eastern Karnataka, north-western Andhra Pradesh, and southwestern Telangana. The core area is considered based on the occurrence of the oldest sites in the ashmound phase dating back to the fourth and third millennium BCE, full-fledged settlement sites in the second millennium BCE, and Neolithic-Iron Age transitional phases in the late second and early first millennium BCE. Raichur Doab is one major geomorphic region with diverse formations of gneiss, schist, dyke swarms (they trend 4–6 km in linear formation) and granodioritic inselbergs/residual hills (Fig. 4.8). Which came to be extensively used by humans during the middle and late Holocene. Population expansion, emergence of high density of sites with intensified perspectives on the land use and resource use developed on the advent of Neolithic culture. Recent archeological and geo-spatial surveys conducted in the Raichur Doab (Arjun, 2017a, 2021, 2022a, b) clearly illustrate the hill based southern Neolithic sites continued to be used over multiple periods ranging from microlithic-Neolithic, Neolithic, Iron Age, and Early History. Which demonstrates robust landmarks formed for distinct activities fitting into social, economic, and ritualistic contexts (Figs. 4.10, 4.11, 4.12 and 4.13). The landscape association of paleolithic communities is mainly in riverine environs, and we can see a pattern trending towards the dry scrub hills in the early Holocene in Raichur Doab (Table 4.1). The interior dry landscapes became quite familiar during the early Holocene hunter-gatherers, by the middle-Holocene sedentary villages made their base for pastoralists and eventually for the farming communities by the third millennium BCE. Once the settlements came to be established as a sedentary village, this marked the beginning of exploring land use patterns. Southern Neolithic settlements are potential sites to understand such innovative developments. Initial phase of hilltop dwellings and their abandonment into the foothill/base need careful re-examination and fresh analysis. Geospatial analysis of the settlements, off sites, and associated features in the Neolithic sites of Raichur Doab, such as at the Bilamrayanagudda, Maladkal, Kotekal, Advibhavi-Rampura demonstrates the rock art locales in the hill summits continued to have an enduring cultural activity with various degrees of activities. Such as the ringing rocks, settlement terraces, bedrock mortars, grinding grooves (of tool edge sharpening and tool grounding types), and further innovation in tapping water runoff near the active springs in the form of modified pools on the bedrocks/boulders (see Table 4.2 and Figs. 4.10, 4.11, 4.12, 4.13). Other activities, such as occupations, workshop activities, burials, and incipient agriculture were concentrated at the hill base. Ashmound formations were mainly buttressed against the hill at the base. Landscape modification by clearing boulders in the foothills for habitation and agriculture cannot be ignored; on the other hand, landscape modifications also did occur on the hill summits and at mid-slopes of the hills in the form of circular terraces (Fig. 4.9). These landmarks must have taken generations to evolve and be recognized, perhaps continued to be happening during the Iron Age too. Their all-time activities are openly focused across the hill summits and their base.

Further, such land use and settlement pattern cannot be normalized with Neolithic sites of the other neighboring region. Piklihal is a multi-period site located 20 km south of Bilamrayanagudda, and was re-explored in mid-2022 (Arjun & Pal, 2023–2024), which suggests a disbursed settlement patterning with multiple habitation locations established in the low elevated closed valleys. Several rock shelters at the base were actively engaged in habitation and rock art production. Ashmound activities were taking place outside the valley. Sanganakallu-Kupgal is a site complex on granitic hills, on which the Neolithic settlements were sequentially shifted from one to other hills spanning during 1600–1200 BCE (Shipton et al., 2012). Brahmagiri is another major Neolithic site located further 100 miles south of the sites discussed above. which demonstrates an entirely straightforward picture. Systematic surveys in the landscapes of Brahmagiri hill (Arjun, 2017b, 2018a, 2022a) where the Neolithic settlements and their activities are limited to spatially larger areas in the hill base, and have left least activities measurable in terms of tangible features. That further testifies, Neolithic rock bruisers preferred dark igneous rocks for the making of art, and the usual older granite/closepet granites for pictographs (Arjun, 2018a, b, c). On the riverine banks beyond the core Neolithic region, e.g., upper Tungabhadra and Kaveri, Hallur (Nagaraja Rao, 1971) and T-Narasipura (Sheshadri, 1968–1989) are located on the alluvial plains and are completely open-air sites. Shows dissention in land use and settlement patterns to above discussions and for more intensive site centric studies.

Table 4.1 Sites distribution based on the geomorphologic-geological context in the western Raichur Doab (After 2017)

Geomorphology	Archeological sites	Number of sites	Nature of sites
Older flood plains	1. Anchesugur	7	Middle Paleolithic, Microlithic/Mesolithic, and Neolithic (no settlements)
	2. Anjal		
	3. Chinchodi		
	4. Gopalapura		
	5. Nilavanji site complex		
	6. Guntral		
	7. Hirebooduru		
Denudational hills	8. Bairappamaradi site complex	2	Microlithic
	9. Shambulingeshwaragudda		
Pediplains	10. Anandgal	14	Multi-period sites: Microlithic/Mesolithic, Neolithic, Iron Age, and Early History
	11. Bassapura		Also continuity from late Medieval to present
	12. Bilamrayanagudda		
	13. Chikka Hesaruru		
	14. Goudur		
	15. Harvapura		
	16. Kalapura		
	17. Kotekal		
	18. Krishna Bridge		
	19. Maladkal		
	20. Navilagudda		
	21. Shilahalli		
	22. Wandalli		
	23. Watgal		
Dyke valley	24. Advi-Rampura	1	Neolithic-Iron Age
Total		24	

Table 4.2 Contextual association of archeological features clustered in the multi-period hill sites of Advi-Rampura, Bilamrayanagudda, Maladkal, and Kotekal

Locality no.	Rock bruisings	Ringing rocks	Water pools	Ax grinding grooves	Bedrock mortars	Settlement terraces
Site: Advi-Rampura Dyke swarm						
A1	■	■	■		■	■
A2	■					
A3	■					
A4	■			■		■
A5	■					
A6					■	■
A7	■	■		■		
A8	■	■				
A9	■					
A10	■	■		■	■	
A11	■					
Site: Bilamrayanagudda						
B1	■	■				
B2	■	■			■	
B3		■				
B4	■					
B5	■			■	■	
B6				■	■	
B7	■					
B8	■	■	■	■	■	■
B9		■	■			
B10	■					
B11	■					
B12		■		■	■	
B13			■		■	
B14	■	■		■		■
B15	■	■				
B16	■	■				
B17	■					
B18	■				■	
B19		■	■	■		
B20			■			
Site: Maladkal						
M1	■	■				
M2	■	■				
M3	■	■		■		
M4	■					■
M5	■	■		■		
M6	■					
M7	■	■				
M8	■		■			
M9	■					
M10	■			■	■	
M11	■	■	■		■	■
M12	■					
M13	■	■				
M14	■			■		
M15	■					
M16	■		■			
M17	■					
M18	■					
M19	■					
M20	■	■				
M21	■					
M22	■					
M23	■					
Site: Kotekal						
K1	■		■	■		
K2	■					
K3	■					
K4	■					
K5	■			■		
K6	■					
K7	■	■				
K8	■	■			■	■
K9	■					
K10				■		
K11	■					
K12	■	■		■		
K13		■				■

Shaded boxes indicated the presence of the features. After Arjun (2017a, 2017b, 2022a, 2022b)

Fig. 4.8 General view of granodiorite hill in Raichur Doab, preferred kind of hill landscape by the southern Neolithic communities

Fig. 4.9 Settlement terrace features in Neolithic hill sites, Kotekal

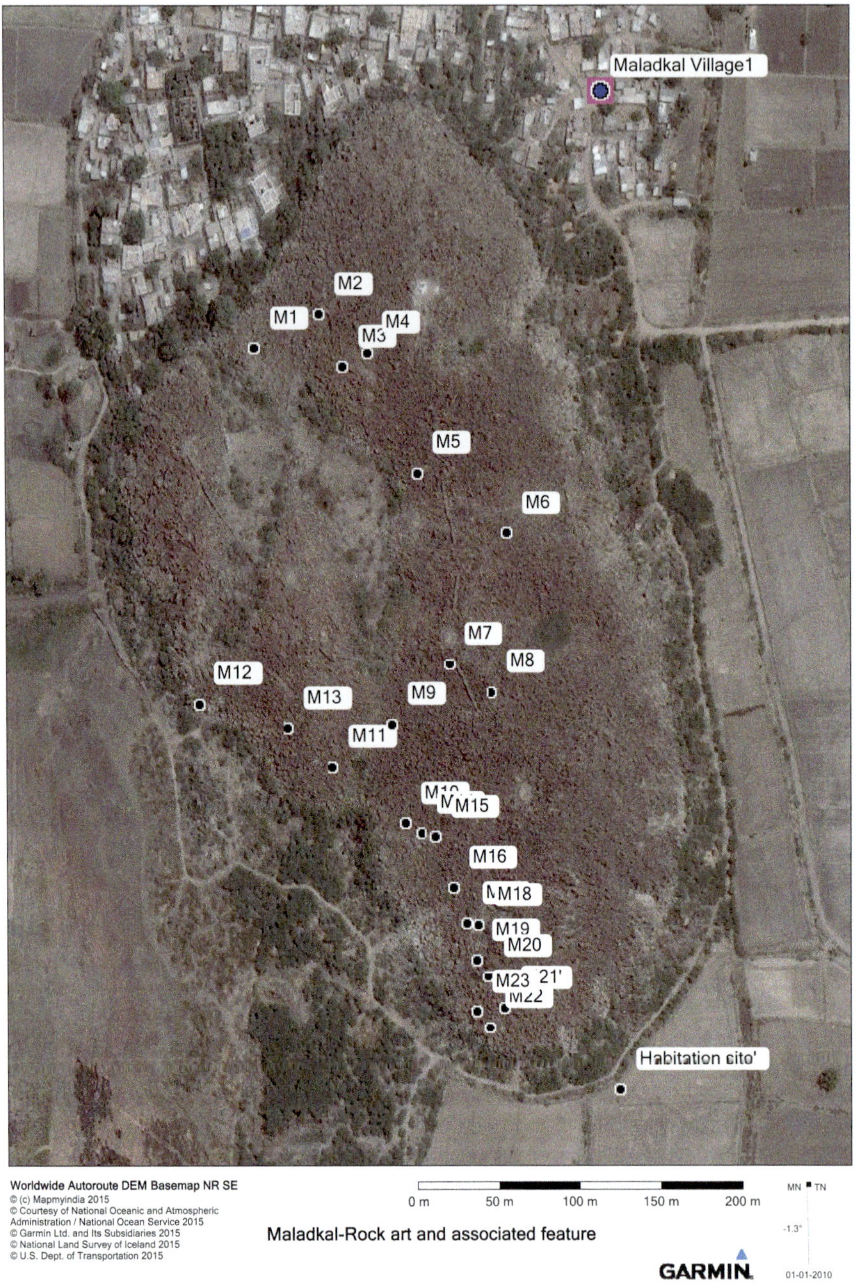

Fig. 4.10 Distribution of clustered archeological features at Maladkal

Fig. 4.11 Distribution of clustered archeological features at Kotekal

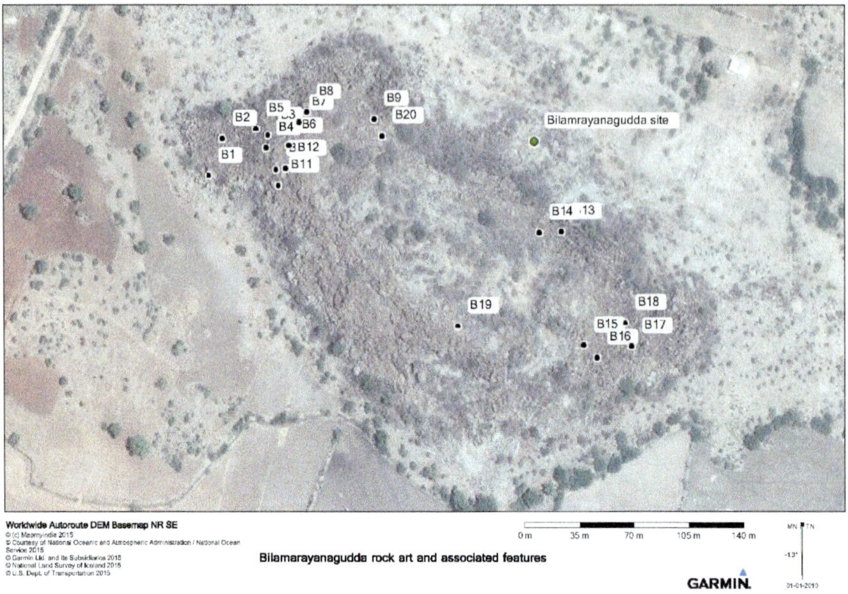

Fig. 4.12 Distribution of clustered archeological features at Bilamrayanagudda

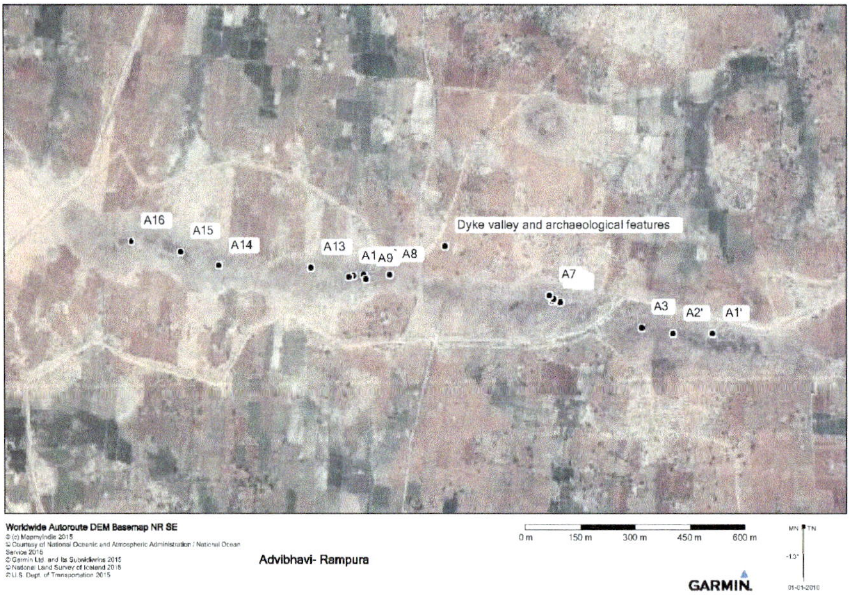

Fig. 4.13 Distribution of clustered archeological features at Advibhavi-Rampura

Acknowledgements This chapter comprehends information and findings drawn from recent archeological research projects of the author in Raichur Doab. Acknowledging the Indian Council of Historical Research (New Delhi)—2015–2017 and 2022–2023 and Nehru Trust for Victoria and Albert Museum (London)—2017–2018 and 2019–2020 for providing research project grants. Figure 4.1 was prepared with the use of site geo-coordinates provided by Dorian-Q-Fuller in 2020 at Institute of Archaeology, University College London, the author acknowledges to his contribution. Thanks to Lavanya Vemsani for inviting me to write on southern Neolithic culture of India and the anonymous reviewers.

References

Allchin, F. R. (1954). *The development of early cultures in the Raichur district of Hyderabad*. Ph.D. Dissertation, University of London.

Allchin, F. R. (1960). *Piklihal excavations*. Andhra Pradesh Government Publications, Archaeological Series No. 1.

Allchin, F. R. (1961). *Utnoor excavations*. Andhra Pradesh Government Publications, Archaeological Series No. 5.

Allchin, F. R. (1963). *Neolithic cattle keepers of South India: A study of the Deccan Ashmounds*. Cambridge University Press.

Allchin, B., & Allchin, F. R. (1968). *The birth of Indian civilization*. Penguin.

Allchin, B., & Allchin, F. R. (1982). *The rise of civilization in India and Pakistan*. Cambridge University Press (also published in 1983 in New Delhi: Select Book Service Syndicate).

Allchin, B., & Allchin, F. R. (1995). Rock art of North Karnataka. *Bulletin of Deccan College Research Institute, 54–5*, 320–322.

Allchin, F. R., & Allchin, B. (1994–95). Rock art of North Karnataka. *Bulletin of the Deccan College Post-Graduate and Research Institute, 54–55*, 313–339.

Arjun, R. (2016). Exploring South Indian iron age Megalithic burial site for its habitational and spatial distribution over the Kaveri landscape at Koppa, Karnataka, India. *Current Science, 110*(12), 2268–2275.

Arjun, R. (2017a). *Landscapes and settlement pattern of Neolithic and iron age cultures of Raichur Doab*. Ph.D. Dissertation, Deccan College Post Graduate and Research Institute.

Arjun, R. (2017b). New approaches towards measuring cupule volume for empirical analysis: An experimental study from Brahmagiri, Southern India. *Current Science, 113*(12), 2335–2341.

Arjun, R. (2018a). Archaeological investigations at the Brahmagiri Rock shelter: Prospecting for its context in South India late prehistory and early history. *Archaeological Research in Asia, 15*, 1–12. https://doi.org/10.1016/j.ara.2016.12.003

Arjun, R. (2018b). Neolithic-iron age rock art in the Northern Maidan of Karnataka: Recent surveys. In R. Korisettar (Ed.), *Beyond stones and more stones* (Vol. 2, pp. 377–400). The Mythic Society.

Arjun, R. (2018c). Rock abrading in South India. In C. Smith (Ed.), *Encyclopaedia of global archaeology*. Springer International Publishing. https://doi.org/10.1007/978-3-319-51726-1_3186-1

Arjun, R. (2018d). Axe grinding grooves in the absence of axes: Neolithic axe trade in Raichur Doab, South India. *Archaeology and Anthropology Open Access, 2*(2), 197–202. https://doi.org/10.31031/AAOA.2018.02.000535

Arjun, R. (2021). Landscapes, land use and settlement pattern of the multi-period sites in the Raichur Doab, South India. *Man and Environment, XLVII*(2), 16–40.

Arjun, R. (2022a). Prehistoric settlement developments in the multi-period sites of South India, Brahmagiri Hill. *L'Anthropologie, 126*(5). https://doi.org/10.1016/j.anthro.2022.103026

Arjun, R. (2022b). Rock Bruisings along the Dyke-Swarms: A gallery of site history in Advibhavi-Rampura, South India. *Boletin APAR, 9*(27), 1355–1364.

Arjun, R. & Jadhav, S. (2014). Labour, industry and production in megalithic period (south Indian Iron Age): nomadic, semi-settled group or settled group?. *Acta Ethnographica Hungarica, 59*(2), 417–421. https://doi.org/10.1556/AEthn.59.2014.2.11

Arjun, R., & Pal, D. (2023–2024). Revisiting Piklihal: Landscape, rock shelters, and potential archaeological researches. *Heritage: Journal of Multidisciplinary Studies in Archaeology.*

Arjun, R., Korisettar, R., Deo, S., Mushrif-Tripathy, V., Naik, S., Jadhav, S., & Mallinathpur, Y. (2019). Koppa Archaeological Research Project (KARP): Exclusive Iron Age landscapes in the Western Ghats, India. *Archaeological Research in Asia, 17*, 173–180. https://doi.org/10.1016/j.ara.2019.01.001

Boivin, N. (2004). Rock art and rock music: Petroglyphs of the South Indian Neolithic. *Antiquity, 78*(2), 38–53.

Boivin, N., Korisetter, R., & Fuller, D. Q. (2005). Further research on the Southern Neolithic and the Ashmound tradition: The Sanganakallu-Kupgal archaeological research project Interim report. *Journal of Interdisciplinary Studies in History and Archaeology, 2*(1), 63–92.

Brumm, A., Boivin, N., Korisettar, R., Koshy, J., & Whittaker, P. (2007). Stone axe technology in Neolithic south India: New evidence from the Sanganakallu-Kupgal Region, mid-eastern Karnataka. *Asian Perspectives, 46*(1), 65–95.

Deotare, B. C., & Kshirsagar, A. A. (1993). Ashmound at Budihal, Karnataka: A chemical approach, Karnataka. *Bulletin of the Deccan College Research Institute, 53*, 39–48.

Devaraj, D. V., Schiffer, J. G., Patil, C. S., & Subrahmanya (1995). The Watgal excavations: An interim report. *Man and Environment, 20*(2), 57–74.

DuFresne, A. S., Shaffer, J. G., Shivashankar, M. L., & Balasubramanya (1998). A preliminary analysis of microblades, blade cores and lunates from Watgal: A Southern Neolithic site. *Man and Environment, 23*(2), 17–44.

Foote, R. B. (1887a). Notes of some recent Neolithic and Palaeolithic finds in South. *Journal of the Asiatic Society of Bengal, LVI*(2), 259–282.

Foote, R. B. (1887b). Notes on prehistoric finds in India. *The Journal of the Anthropological Institute of Great Britain and Ireland, XVI*, 70–75.

Foote, R. B. (1895). The geology of the Bellary district. *Madras Presidency, the Memoirs of the Geological Survey of India, XXV*(1), 1–216.

Foote, R. B. (1914). *Prehistoric and protohistoric antiquities of India.* Government Museum.

Foote, R. B. (1916). *The Foote collection of Indian prehistoric and protohistoric antiquities: Notes on their ages and distribution.* Government Museum.

Fuller, D. Q. (2006). Dung mounds and domesticators: Early cultivation and pastoralism in Karnataka. In C. Jrrige, & V. Lefevre (Eds.), *South Asian archaeology 2001, prehistory* (pp. 117–127). Paris: Editions Recherche sur les Civilisations ADPF.

Fuller, D. Q., & Korisetter, R. (2004). The vegetational context of early agriculture in South India. *Man and Environment, 29*(1), 7–27.

Fuller, D. Q., & Kingwell-Benham, E. (2018). Lost millets and overlooked pulses: Advances in understanding early agricultural developments in South India. In R. Korisettar (Ed.), *Beyond stones and more stones* (Vol. 2, pp. 145–169). The Mythic Society.

Fuller, D. Q., Korisettar, R., & Venkatasubbaiah, P. C. (2001). Southern Neolithic cultivation systems: A reconstruction based on archaeobotanical evidence. *South Asian Studies, 17*, 171–187.

Fuller, D. Q., Korisettar, R., & Venkatasubbaiah. (2000–2001). The beginning of agriculture in the Kunderu river basin: Evidence from Archaeological survey and archaeobotany. *Puratatva, 31*, 1–8.

Fuller, D. Q., Korisettar, R., Venkatasubbaiah, P. C., et al. (2004). Early plant domestications in Southern India: Some preliminary archaeobotanical results. *Vegetation History and Archaeobotony, 13*, 115–129. https://doi.org/10.1007/s00334-004-0036-9

Fuller, D. Q., Boivin, N., & Korisettar, R. (2007). Dating the Neolithic of South India: New radiometric evidence for key social, economic, and ritual transformations. *Antiquity, 81*(313), 755–778.

Indian Archaeology: A Review: 1983-4:3.
Johansen, P. J. (2004). Landscape, monumental architecture and ritual: A reconsideration of the South Indian Ashmounds. *Journal of Anthropological Archaeology, 23*, 309–330.
Johansen, P. G. (2014). Early ironworking in iron age South India: New evidence for the social organization of production from northern Karnataka. *Journal of Field Archaeology, 39*(3), 256–275.
Khaladkar, V. (2008). Archaeological investigations in Middle Bhima Basin, Maharashtra: A preliminary report. *Puratatva, 38*, 25–38.
Korisettar, R. (2007). Toward developing a basin model for Palaeolithic settlement of the Indian subcontinent: Geodynamics, monsoon dynamics, habitat diversity and dispersal routes. In M. D. Petraglia & B. Allchin (Eds.), *The evolution and history of human populations in South Asia* (pp. 69–96). Springer.
Korisettar, R. (2021). Ancient agriculture in the Indian subcontinent: The archaeobotanical evidence. In D. Hollander & T. Howe (Ed.), *Comparative agricultural history a companion to ancient agriculture* (pp. 577–610). Wiley.
Korisettar, R., & Bora, J. (2014). Jwalapuram. In D. K. Chakrabarti & M. Lal (Eds.), *History of India: Protohistoric foundations* (pp. 423–437). Vivekananda International Foundation and Aryan Books International.
Korisettar, R., Joglekar, P. P., Fuller, D. Q., & Venkatasubbaiah, P. C. (2001). Archaeological re-investigation and archaeozoology of seven Southern Neolithic sites in Karnataka and Andhra Pradesh. *Man and Environment, 26*(2), 47–66.
Korisettar, R., Venkatasubbaiah, P. C., & Fuller, D. Q. (2002). Brahmagiri and beyond: The archaeology of the Southern Neolithic. In S. Settar & R. Korisettar (Eds.), *Indian archaeology in retrospect prehistory archaeology of South Asia* (Vol. I, pp. 151–356). Manohar and Indian Council of Historical Research.
Korisettar, R., Janardhana, B., Hegde, R., Arjun, R., & Kunneriath, M. (2022). Palaeolithic occurrences in the Malnad Borderlands, Karnataka: Implications for the Palaeolithic archaeology of the Western Dharwar Craton, South India. *Puratattva, 51*(2021), 39–69.
Krishna, M. H. (1941). Chitaldurga district the Brahmagiri site. *Directorate of Archaeology and Museums in Karnataka, 1940*, 63–74.
Mahadevan, C. (1941). Geology of the south and south-western parts of Surapur Taluk of Gulbarga District. *Journal of Hyderabad Geological Survey, 4*(1), 102–161.
Majumdar, G. G., & Rajguru, S. N. (1966). *Ashmound excavations at Kupgal*. Deccan College.
Mecee, S. (2018). Neolithic-Megalithic zooarchaeology of Southern India. In R. Korisettar (Ed.), *Beyond stones and more stones* (Vol. 2, pp. 127–144). The Mythic Society.
Morrison, K. D. (2005). Brahmagiri revisited a re-analysis of the South Indian sequence (pp. 251–261). In C. Jarrige & V. LeFevre (Eds.), *South Asian archaeology*. Recherche sur les Civilisations, ADPF.
Munn, L. (1934). Prehistoric and protohistoric finds. *Journal of Geological Society, II*(1), 121–135.
Nagaraja Rao, M. S. (1971). *Protohistoric cultures of the Tungabhadra Valley: A report on Hallur Excavation*. Dharwad.
Nagaraja Rao, M. S., & Malhotra, K. C. (1965). *The stone age hill dwellers of Tekkalakota*. Deccan College.
Narasimhaiah, B. (1980). *Neolithic and megalithic cultures of Tamil Nadu*. Suddeep Prakashan.
Newbold, T. J. (1836). Note on the occurrence of volcanic scoria in the Southern Peninsula. *Journal of the Asiatic Society of Bombay*, 670–671.
Newbold, T. J. (1843). On some ancient mounds of scorious ashes in Southern India. *Journal of Royal Asiatic Society (London), 7*, 129–136.
Paddayya, K. (1976). Cup-marks in the Shorapur Doab (South India). *Man, 2*, 35–38.
Paddayya, K. (1968). *Pre- and protohistoric investigations in Shorapur Doab*. Ph.D. Thesis, University of Poona.
Paddayya, K. (1973). Prehistoric culture sequence in Shorapur Doab, Gulbarga District. In A. V. Narasimha Murty (Ed.), *Archaeology of Karnataka* (pp. 23–30). University of Mysore.

Paddayya, K. (1982). *The Acheulian culture of the Hunsgi Valley (Peninsular India): A settlement system perspective.* Deccan College.

Paddayya, K. (1991–92). The ashmounds of South India: Fresh evidence and possible explanation. *Bulletin of the Deccan College Post-Graduate Research Institute, 51–52*, 573–626.

Paddayya, K. (1993). Ashmound investigation at Budihal, Gulbarga District, Karnataka. *Man and Environment, XVIII*(1), 57–87.

Paddayya, K. (1994). Investigation of man-environment relationship in Indian archaeology: Some theoretical considerations. *Man and Environment, XIX*(1–2), 1–28.

Paddayya, K. (2019). *Neolithic ashmounds of the Deccan: Their place in the archaeology of peninsular India.* Aryan Book International.

Paddayya, K., Thomas, P. K., & Joglekar, P. P. (1995). A Neolithic animal butchering floor from Budihal, Gulbarga District, Karnataka. *Man and Environment, 20*(2), 23–31.

Pal, T. K., & Talukder, B. (2009). Animal remains from Brahmagiri archaeological site (Karnataka) and their relevance to the ancient Civilization. *Memoirs, 21*(3), 1–31.

Pappu, R. S., & Deo, S. G. (1994). *Man-land relationships during Palaeolithic times in the Kaladgi Basin, Karnataka.* Deccan College, Pune.

Rajala, U., Madella, M., & Korisettar, R. (2004). Surveying ashmounds—integrated data collection for the establishment of site life cycles in Southern Deccan (India). Beyond the artifact. Digital interpretation of the past. In *Proceedings of the computer applications and quantitative methods in archaeology conference*, Prato, Italy, 13–17 April 2004, Budapest.

Raju, D. (1981). Early settlement patterns in Cuddapah District, Andhra Pradesh: A palaeoanthropological study. Ph.D. Dissertation. Pune: Deccan College Post Graduate and Research Institute.

Raju, D. R., & Venkatasubbaiah, P. C. (2002). The archaeology of the upper Palaeolithic phase in India. In S. Setter & R. Korisettar (Eds.), *Indian archaeology in retrospect: Prehistory, archaeology of South Asia* (pp. 85–110). Indian Council of Historical Research and Manohar Publishers.

Rami Reddy, V. (1968). *Pre- and proto history of South-Western Andhra Pradesh.* Ph.D. Thesis, University of Poona.

Rami Reddy, V. (1976). *The prehistoric and protohistoric culture of Palavoy, South India, with special reference to the Ashmound Problem.* Government of Andhra Pradesh.

Risch, R., Boivin, N., Petraglia, M., Gomez-Gras, D., Korisettar, R., & Fuller, D. (2009). The prehistoric axe factory at Sanganakallu-Kupgal (Bellary District), Southern India. *Internet Archaeology, 26*. https://doi.org/10.11141/ia.26.26

Roberts, P., Boivin, N., Petraglia, M. D., Masser, P., Meece, S., Weisskopf, A., Silva, F., Korisettar, R., & Fuller, D. Q. (2015). Local diversity in settlement, demography and subsistence across the Southern Indian Neolithic-iron age transition: Site growth and abandonment at Sanganakallu-Kupgal. *Archaeological and Anthropological Sciences, 8*(3), 575–599.

Robinson, D. W., Korisettar, R., & Koshy, J. (2008). Metanarratives and the (re) invention of the Neolithic: A case study in rock art from Birappa and Hireguddu hill, South Central India. *Journal of Social Archaeology, 8*(3), 355–379.

Sastri, T. V. G., Katuri Bai, M., & Varaprasad Rao, J. (Eds.) (1984). Veerapuram a type site for cultural study in the Krishna Valley. Birla Archaeological and Cultural Research Institute.

Seshadri, M. (1956). *Stone using cultures of prehistoric and protohistoric cultures of Mysore.* University of Mysore.

Seshadri, M. (1968–1969). A Neolithic burial from T. Narasipur. *Puratatva, 2*, 55–56.

Sewell, R. (1899). The Cinder-Mounds of Bellary. *Journal of the Royal Asiatic Society, 51*, 1–16.

Shipton, C., Petraglia, M., Koshy, J., Bora, J., Brumm, A., Boivin, N., Korisettar, R., Risch, R., & Fuller, D. Q. (2012). Lithic technology and social transformations in the South Indian Neolithic: The evidence from Sanganakallu-Kupgal. *Journal of Anthropological Archaeology, 31*, 156–173.

Shivarudrappa, T. V. (1990). Environment aspects of early and middle Palaeolithic cultures in Southern Karnataka. In A. Sundara (Ed.), *Archaeology in Karnataka* (pp. 23–40). Directorate of Archaeology and Museums in Karnataka.

Singhvi, A. K., Agarawal, D. P., & Nambi, K. S. V. (1991). Thermoluminescence dating: an update on application Indian Archaeology (pp. 173–180). In S. R. Rao (Eds.), *Recent advances in marine archaeology*. National Institute of Oceanography.
Subbarao, B. (1948). *The stone age cultures of Bellary*. Deccan College, Pune.
Sundara, A. (1970). Brahmagiriya eradu tamra vastualu (two copper objects from Brahmagiri). *Manavika Karnataka, 1*(1), 179–184.
Taylor, M. (1851). Ancient remains at the village of Jewargi near Ferozabad on the Bhima. *Journal of Bombay Branch of the Royal Asiatic Society, III*, 179–193.
Taylor, M. (1853). Notices on Cromlechs, Carias and other ancient Scythe-druidical remains in the principality of Shorapur. *Journal of Bombay Branch of the Royal Asiatic Society, 4*(XVII), 380–429.
Taylor, M. (1941). Megalithic tombs and other ancient remains in the Deccan (Collected papers edited by G. Yazdani). Hyderabad State.
Thaper, B. K. (1957). Maski-1954: A Chalcolithic site of the Southern Deccan. *Ancient India, 13*, 114.
Venkatasubbaiah, P. C. (1992). *Protohistoric investigations in Central Pennar Basin, Cuddapah, Andhra Pradesh*. Ph.D. Dissertation, Deccan College.
Venkatasubbiaiah P. C., Pawankar, S. J., & Joglekar, P. P. (1992). Neolithic Faunal remains from the Central Pennar Basin, Cuddapah District, Andhra Pradesh. *Man and Environment 17*(1), 55–59.
Walimbe, S. R., & Paddayya, K. (1998–1999). Human skeletal remains from the Neolithic Ashmound Site of Budihal, Karnataka. *Bulletin of the Deccan College Post-Graduate and Research Institute, 58/59*, 11–47.
Wheeler, R. E. M. (1948). Brahmagiri and Chandravalli 1947: Megalithic and other Cultures in the Chitaldrug District, Mysore State. *Ancient India, IV*, 81–321.
Woolley, L. (1939). *A report on the work of the Archaeological Survey of India*. Government of India.
Yazdani, G. (1935–1936). *Notes on a survey of Neolithic Sites*. Annual Report of the Archaeological Department of H.E.H. the Nizam's Dominions—Appendix A, 20.

Chapter 5
The Indus River Valley and Other Bronze Age Cultures

Marie N. Pareja

Abstract The Bronze Age Indus River Valley Culture is among the earliest in Afro-Eurasia, together with Mesopotamia and Egypt. This chapter is dedicated not only to providing a general understanding of the Bronze Age and the cultural foundations from which later periods grow but also to highlighting the distinctly unique elements of this period in the Indus River Valley. After an introduction to this region, each area's geographic boundaries, brief history, religion, and culture (including select architecture, art, and artifacts) are reviewed. These various peoples are included in this discussion to foster a deeper understanding of both individual groups and neighboring regions by facilitating comparative methodologies and discussions. This knowledge then serves as a foundation for a more nuanced understanding of inter-connectivity: the different peoples and cultures of Bronze Age Afro-Eurasia are much more communicative and integrated with one another, whether directly or via down-the-line trade, than most people anticipate.

Keywords Indus · Bronze age · Archeology · Afro-Eurasian · Exchange · Trade

5.1 Introduction

This chapter serves as a basic introduction to the Bronze Age Indus River Valley Culture (IVC) and other cultures of Bronze Age Afro-Eurasia. The IVC will be discussed first and serve as a baseline against other cultures that may be considered. The geographic areas in which each culture lived, as well as key cultural, political, and religious traits, are discussed. When possible, a brief review of the group's early beginnings is also provided.

Importantly, the term *civilization* will not be used to describe these different groups, as the word inherently bears biased, colonialist notions. Instead, this chapter

M. N. Pareja (✉)
Salisbury University, Salisbury, MD, USA
e-mail: mncummings@salisbury.edu

Consulting Scholar, University of Pennsylvania, Philadelphia, USA

L. Vemsani (ed.), *Handbook of Indian History*,
https://doi.org/10.1007/978-981-97-6207-1_5

discusses people, cultures, groups, and societies that lived in different areas and regions. Other biased terms, such as *advanced*, *primitive*, and *sophisticated* are also discarded.

5.2 What is the Bronze Age?

Defining the Bronze Age is deceptively simple. It is generally considered the time during which a culture (or cultures) began smelting copper and tin to create bronze (ca. 3300–1200 BCE; Kristiansen & Larsson, 2005: 32–33). Falling between the Stone and Iron Ages, this is a time when many tools and implements were first and then continually made from this new, more resilient alloy. The absolute dates of the Bronze Age differ according to region: some areas began using bronze earlier or later than others, while some regions also abandoned it in favor of iron comparably earlier or later than other cultures (Fig. 5.1a, b). Because of this, dates for the Bronze Age are slightly different in different regions depending on the area of Afro-Eurasia being discussed.

Many of the earliest settlements from this period are in areas that exhibit continuous habitation, meaning that a group of people continued to live in one place from one period to the next. It is perhaps of little surprise that such areas are most frequently located along rivers' floodplains: the Tigris and Euphrates Rivers for Mesopotamia; the Indus River (Sindhu River) and its tributaries for the Indus River Valley cultures; the Nile for Ancient Egypt; and the Yellow and Yang Tze Rivers in China. In these regions, where seasonal or annual flooding inundated the riverbanks with nutrient-rich silt that naturally supported agricultural practices, settlements also took root that would develop into the expansive—sometimes palatial (palace-based)—structures that are found throughout the Bronze Age Afro-Eurasian world.

5.3 Indus Valley

Located in Punjab, Pakistan, the Indus River Valley is one of the earliest cultures to begin using bronze, together with Mesopotamia and Ancient Egypt, and the people who live in the regions between them (Coningham & Young, 2015: 18; Fig. 5.2). From at least 3300 BCE through 1700 BCE, the Bronze Age Indus was host to sprawling cities and bustling trade ports, many of which were located along or near major waterways: the banks of the Indus River, a system of rivers from Ghaggar-Hakra (fed by monsoons, which create seasonal rivers in eastern Pakistan), and along the coast line of the Arabian Sea (Wright, 2009: 1–7). The Indus Valley culture stretched from Pakistan into northeastern Afghanistan and western India.

Harappa is the earliest site recorded by the 1861 Archeological Survey in India (Wright, 2009: 2). Because it was the first publicized, widely known site, many scholars began referring to the broader Indus Valley culture as Harappan. Shortly

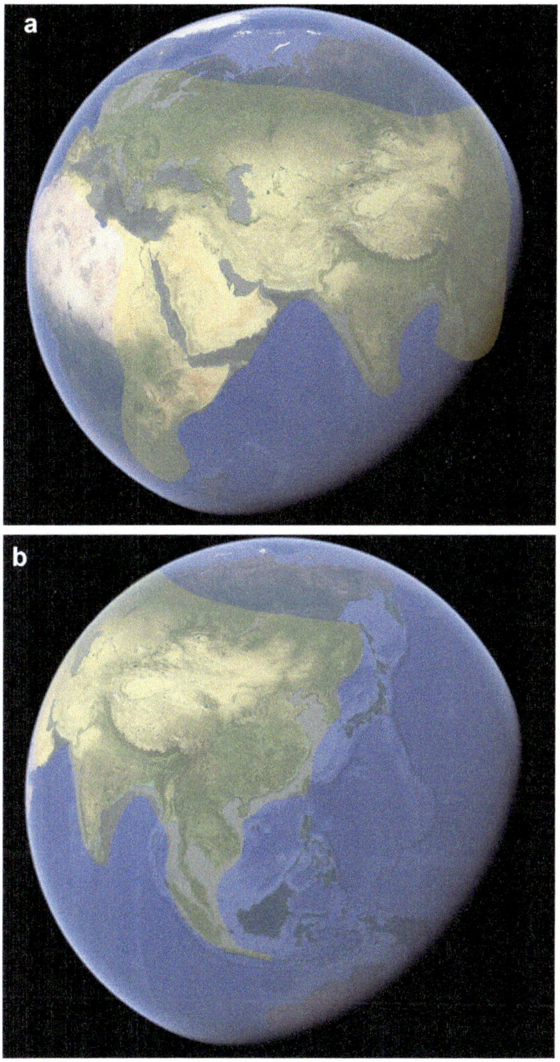

Fig. 5.1 **a**, **b** Map with Bronze Age areas highlighted throughout Afro-Eurasia. Image by Marie N. Pareja after Google Earth

thereafter, the site of Mohenjo-Daro was discovered, and Harappan became a term to identify both different chronological phases (or time periods) for these groups and the broader region during the Bronze Age. These phases can be divided into pre-, early, mature, late, and post-Harappan periods. The region that serves as the chronological term's namesake encompasses several sites in addition to Harappa. The area known as Harappa encompasses the areas from Haryana and Punjab, through Sindh and Rajasthan, and throughout Gujarat. Additional nearby sites outside of this

Fig. 5.2 Map with Indus River Valley culture highlighted. Image by Marie N. Pareja after Google Earth

immediate range can also be associated with Harappa, but it may be best to consider these as hinterland, somewhat synonymous with the modern concept of outlying rural areas. Although plenty of Harappan sites preserve archeological evidence for habitation and settlement in early periods, these groups reached their height during the Mature Harappan phase (ca. 2700–1900 BCE). At this point, the population at the site of Harappa ranged from 30,000–60,000 individuals, and the broader culture may have grown to anywhere from 1 to 5 million people (Dyson, 2018: 29). Five major urban centers have been identified to date including Harappa, Mohenjo-Daro, Dholavira, Ganeriwala, and Rakhigarhi. This chapter will focus primarily on the site of Harappa, with some finds from Mohenjo-Daro, as well as the Early Harappan site of Mehrgarh.

During the Early Harappan phase (ca. 3300–2600 BCE), farmers began to move into and settle in the river valley. While some scholars argue these farmers originally moved from Elam, the eastern and oldest region of Mesopotamia, others maintain that these people already knew about different farming techniques and brought that knowledge into the river valleys with them. Perhaps surprisingly, the people who lived along rivers did not develop irrigation, as the seasonal monsoons and summer floods took care of such matters until the climate became dryer. This shift may have inspired the shift from several smaller cities to considerably larger urban centers (Brooke,

2014: 296). Although some evidence for earlier cities survives, many Bronze Age sites' earliest roots may date to this period.

Mehrgarh, in Pakistan, is a well documented Early Harappan site that dates to the Neolithic period (ca. 7000–2000 BCE; Parpola, 2015: 17). Located on the Kacci Plain in Pakistan, the site sprawls over six mounds. The earliest portion of the site was a small farming village—the earliest known in Pakistan—and some have argued that the surviving evidence from this area shows concerted influence from Neolithic Near-Eastern groups, based on food remnants including domesticated wheat (Gangal & Sarson, 2014: 5).

The Mature Harappan phase (ca. 2800–1900 BCE) is considered the apex of Indus Valley culture. The period saw extended urban planning of baked brick houses, baths, and other (often non-domestic) structures, as well as extensive drainage and water supply systems (Maisels, 2003: 216). These large, sprawling settlements were clearly and carefully planned, rather than organically spreading outward from an older central portion of the city. This may be due in part to many different sub-cultures or ethnic groups that worked and lived together: different elements of architecture and city planning from different cultures are visible at the largest settlements, such as Harappa and Mohenjo-Daro.

Several innovations make their first appearances in these sprawling urban centers. Indus Script, the writing system employed by the inhabitants of the Indus Valley that dates to the 3rd millennium BCE, remains undeciphered. The writing appears to be based on the use of seals and the creation of impressions into a clay or wax surface as opposed to ink-based script applied on top of a paper-like or leather surface. Characters most often appear inscribed on the surfaces of small beads or other lightweight, portable items, and they may belong to either a syllabic or alphabetic writing system. Nevertheless, over 100 Bronze Age Indus archeological sites have been excavated (as of 2023) to provide ample material culture from which to learn about these people (Joshi & Parpola, 1987: xvii–xx; Meadow and Kenoyer 2010: xliv–lviii; Wells, 1999: 17).

Additionally, houses had access to clean, potable water from wells (Madella & Lancelotti, 2022: 119–131). Larger single houses often appear with a dedicated well, and multiple smaller houses often share one between them. Once this water was dirtied (from bathing or other activities), the wastewater was poured into covered drains that ran underground along the exterior of streets, which carried the sullied water away. Such systems were present in contemporary regions (Mesopotamia, Egypt, and so on), but nowhere else were they as extensive or integrated into the settlement structure.

Harappan houses feature differentiated living quarters. The domestic structures are separate from other sections of the settlement (commercial areas, for instance), and the houses themselves are subdivided into different living spaces. Additionally, the houses feature flat roofs that were likely also used for a variety of activities. Other features that showcase Harappan settlement innovation include granaries, dockyards, and massive defensive walls that probably protected people from both floods and perhaps physical conflicts.

The political structure during this period remains largely unknown (Green, 2022: 163). Although some artworks are named for positions of rulership or power (such as the Priest King), scholars do not yet know whether a king, queen, family, or counsel ruled these centers, or whether no one entity ruled them at all. Considering the relatively low concentration of wealth across the site, this society may have been relatively egalitarian (there was not centralized rulership, but everyone shared an equal responsibility for the society; Green, 2020: 153–202). Nevertheless, the presence of standard weights and measures, public facilities, and the grid-patterns of settlements indicate that some form of central authority existed, however distinct they may have been from today's notions of such a position. Notably, the civic planning and town layout of Mohenjo-Daro and Harappa are acutely distinct from one another, as a comparison of the site plans illustrates.

The standardization of certain cultural elements belies not only local organization, but also exchange. For instance, Harappan weights are largely consistent throughout the Indus, with the rare exception of a secondary, rarely occurring, also standard alternate system. This second system is characteristic of a distant region: Mesopotamia. By identifying the Mesopotamian standard in the Indus, and the Indus standard in Elam and Susa (in the greater Mesopotamian area), scholars conclude that the two regions must have been trading relatively regularly with one another (Ialongo et al., 2021: 2).

Additionally, temples or palaces are not readily identifiable from architectural remains or from imagery found on artifacts (Kenoyer, 2008: 719). Nevertheless, fortified structures have been identified, which may function as temples, palaces, or administrative centers. Workshops, however, appear often dedicated to particular types of manufacture that may have varied by neighborhood, including but not limited to glass-like faience beads, shell adornments and small containers, stylized statues of humans and animals made from various stones and metals, and steatite seals that show inscriptions, animals, plants, and people (Kenoyer, 1997: 263–276; Ratnagar, 2004). Artisans and craftspeople also fashioned vessels and figurines (cows, bears, monkeys, dogs, and others) from clay. Finally, one of the most frequently exported items from Chanhudaro, Dholavira, and Mohenjo-Daro are etched and elongated biconical cylinder beads made from carnelian (Kenoyer, 1997: 270–283). The unique process of drilling used for these beads allows for the identification of carnelian beads in such far-flung areas as China, Egypt, and the Aegean.

Notably, some scholars think that some of the earliest roots of Hinduism may stretch back to this or the Late Harappan periods (Parpola, 2015). Some seal imagery shows fantastic hybrid creatures, one of which is nicknamed the unicorn, by virtue of the single horn that extends from the forehead of a bovid-like animal (Fig. 5.3). Such images may suggest belief in a hybrid, mythological creature. Although unicorns are not unique to the Indus Valley, another figure that often appears on seals is generically referred to as The Master of Animals (Fig. 5.4). This figure appears with wild animals, often seated with legs crossed while wearing a large hat or headdress. Some scholars suggest that this could be an early representation of a proto-Shiva, or an early version of Shiva that became the Hindu god of balance, nature, creation,

Fig. 5.3 Unicorn Seal, Mohenjo-Daro. White fired glazed steatite. MNP 50.192. Image courtesy of the National Museum, Karachi

and destruction. Notably, some of these seals created in the Indus River Valley have been identified and recovered in Mesopotamia.

In Harappan art, human figures occur alone and together with animals. The depicted animals are usually wild, although sometimes they may be tamed or domesticated, such as zebu, or humped cattle. Such depictions often occur together with geometric motifs, and they survive on seals, on pottery, or as clay, bronze, or stone figurines. The Dancing Girl, a stylized bronze figurine found at Mohenjo-Daro, shows a nude young woman with one hand on her hip, long hair bound behind her, and she wears a necklace, bracelets, and armbands. Although the figurine is named for dancing, thanks to the British archeologists who initially discovered the object, more recent finds suggest that she instead carries an offering that was not preserved and is now lost. She is not, in fact, dancing. In contrast to the artistic style of the Dancing Girl, a more formal style can be seen in other figures, such as the Priest King sculpture. This small piece shows the torso and head of a male figure with loose hair, a fillet around his head, an armband, and a robe that wraps over one shoulder and under the opposite arm. The robe is decorated with repeated tri-lobed motifs. Without the ability to decipher Indus Script—and without any text explicitly identifying the person after whom the piece was made—it is almost impossible to determine who or what office/position this bust might represent. Nevertheless, the geometric patterns

Fig. 5.4 Master Impression from Mohenjo-Daro. Object 420. Image courtesy of the National Museum in Delhi

on the figure's clothing and jewelry, the careful carving and polishing of the stone, and the relatively small size of the object can all serve to provide additional information about life in the Indus River Valley.

By the end of the Late Harappan Period, migrating populations from the Steppe Region in the north settled and mixed with local Indus communities (Wiener, 2018: 9–10). These northern people were originally thought to have brought the Vedic texts (earliest writings in Hinduism) to the Indus (Parpola, 2015). Such beliefs and traditions almost certainly could have subtly shifted and mingled with those of the people who already inhabited the Indus River Valley, and so it remains possible that modern Hinduism may bear traces of the mysterious ideologies from the Bronze Age Indus. It remains unclear how much influence, if any, earlier Indus culture and beliefs had on these stories.

Then, after a couple hundred years, many Bronze Age settlements were abandoned. A series of factors served as catalysts, including the drying up of some major tributaries, a generally more arid climate, and likely relative social and economic instability. No evidence survives for an invading group—no mass-graves are identified from this period, and the known human remains do not feature any marked increase of battle-related trauma or cause of death. The Sea Peoples who plagued the Late Bronze Age Mediterranean do not appear to have harassed settlements along

Indus shorelines. Nevertheless, with this abandonment at the end of the mature period comes the transition from Bronze to Iron Age in the Indus River Valley.

5.4 Other Bronze Age Cultures

5.4.1 Mesopotamia

The ancient Greeks named the land between and around the Tigris and Euphrates Rivers Mesopotamia, which translates to English as "land between the rivers" (McIntosh, 2005: 3–6; Fig. 5.5). This region sits within the northern portion of the Fertile Crescent. It is often heralded as the birthplace of civilization, as some of the earliest settlements that show evidence of irrigation, agriculture, animal husbandry, trade, metalwork, masonry, and pottery occur in northern Mesopotamia, well before the Bronze Age begins (ca. 6500–3700 BCE; Stein, 1994: 35–37). For discussion at hand, Bronze Age Mesopotamia broadly includes present-day Iraq and areas of present-day Iran, Kuwait, Syria, and parts of Turkey.

Fig. 5.5 Map with the broader Mesopotamian region highlighted. Image by Marie N. Pareja after Google Earth

Sumer is a southern Mesopotamian region with evidence of bronze working as early as the 6th and 5th millennia BCE (Crawford, 2004: 5–27). The word Sumer is a name given to this southern population by those from eastern Mesopotamia, the Akkadians. Sumerian city-states formed a large part of the foundation for the modern understanding of Mesopotamian religion and culture in many ways, although the area was later conquered by the Akkadians (ca. 2270 BCE). Once the Akkadians united Mesopotamia under a single ruler and language, reforms for standardization swept the region (Liverani, 1993: 1–10). From weights and measures to law codes and mathematics, subsequent rulers strove to implement a single unifying standard across Mesopotamia. This may have been due in part to the quickly expanding trade networks for which the region often served as intermediary for overland and maritime exchange, a lynchpin among Africa, Asia, and Europe. These connections fluctuate in strength throughout the rest of the Bronze Age, together with changes in rulership through the Akkadian, Babylonian, and Assyrian periods (to name only a few) in the Middle and Late periods.

The first known form of writing, called cuneiform, emerged during the early phases of the Bronze Age in Mesopotamia (Glassner & Heron, 2003: 1–17). The characters are formed by impressing a stylus into a wax or clay surface, to create impressions in the soft surface. Although the writing system began as a series of pictographs, it became increasingly abstracted through time, until the symbols no longer resembled the images, syllables, or sounds they represented. The epic tale of *Gilgameš* was first recorded in cuneiform from its original mode of communication: oral tradition.

Mesopotamian society was highly stratified (had many layers, or separate groups with different degrees of personal independence), with a king and priestly class wielding the most power and influence over the rest of society. The perceived world order is clearly depicted on a vessel known as the Warka Vase (Winter, 1983: 2–27; Fig. 5.6a and b). The flowing water pictured at the bottom of the vessel supports the growth of plants, which feed the quadrupeds in the register (or horizontal space for imagery) above the river scene. Above a blank register, enslaved people or workers carry containers full of offerings (or taxes?). Above a second blank register, a female figure (probably the goddess Inanna) accepts offerings from a male figure, probably the king or priest. Missing from the scenes on the Warka Vase are the priestly class, ranks of merchants and traders, artisans, and common folk (Wiggerman et al., 1995: 1859–1868). Critically, the relationship between the ruler and the deity is represented. In Mesopotamia, rulers functioned as intermediaries between the people and the divine. If the god(s) was displeased by the king's performance, they would punish the people with plague, drought, and conflict, and if the deities were appeased by the ruler, they would reward people with abundance, health, and general success.

Cities were often constructed around a massive central ziggurat, a platform on top of which a small shrine or temple was located (McMahon, 2016: 321; Fig. 5.7). Due to their organic nature, the shrines themselves decomposed and no longer exist, but the eroded remains of ziggurats are still identifiable. The Ziggurat at Ur is the best-preserved of these types of structures, and it has been heavily reconstructed. Palaces

a b

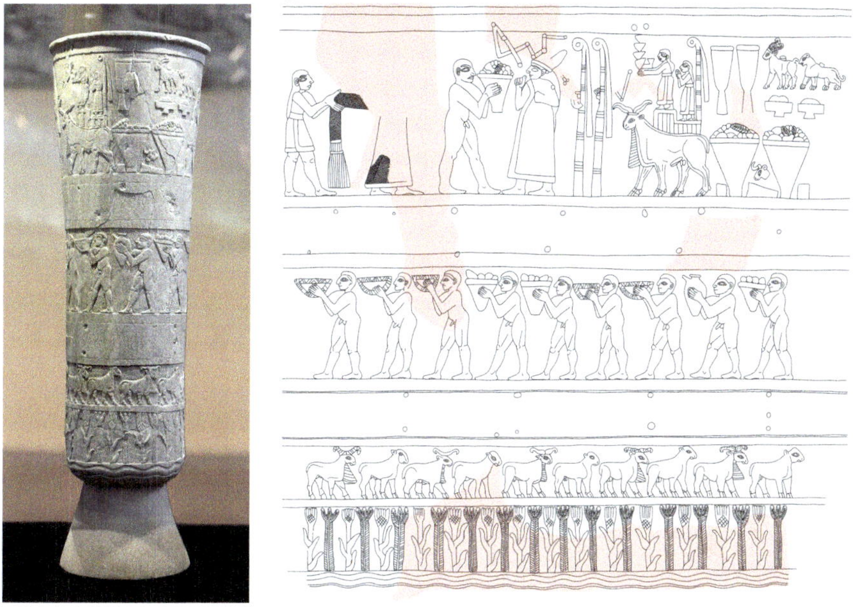

Fig. 5.6 **a** Warka Vase. IM19606. Image courtesy of The Iraq Museum **b** Warka Vase. Line drawing by Marie N. Pareja adapted from Iraq Museum Object Number IM19606

for the local rulers were typically located beside the ziggurat at the center of the settlement with large-scale defensive walls around the perimeter of the settlement.

Each city-state had a patron deity, for whom the largest temple and several annual feast days and festivals would be dedicated (Schneider, 2011: 117–124). The

Fig. 5.7 Ziggurat at Ur. Photo: Joseph Dean Cummings

Mesopotamians were polytheistic, meaning they believed in and worshipped multiple deities. They followed a vast pantheon of gods who embodied natural forces, such as water and storm clouds, as well as abstract concepts, such as death, the crossing of boundaries, and duality. Perhaps the most popular of these deities, Inanna (later Ištar or Astarte) was one of the earliest occurring deities whose worship survived into the 1800s CE. Notably, although most Mesopotamians followed the same general religion, regional variations existed, so that the worship of a deity in one town may be in some ways different from the worship of that same god in a different location. These practices and beliefs appear to stand at odds with the evidence that survives from one of Mesopotamia's eastern trade partners, the Indus.

5.4.2 East Africa

Although little is known about the broader African continent during the Bronze Age, east Africa is host to multiple cultures in distinct regions, among which were Punt, Nubia, and Ancient Egypt (Fig. 5.8). Egyptians lived along the Nile River, and Nubians lived along and between the river's southern tributaries. The land of Punt, while attested in historical records, has not yet been positively identified. Although it is currently thought to be located in the areas of modern-day Somalia, Djibouti, Ethiopia, Eritrea, and Sudan, some scholars think that Punt may have existed in the Horn of Africa and areas of Southern Arabia (Meeks, 2012: 53–55). Each of these regions was inhabited from at least the Pleistocene onward and during the Neolithic period, and yet the most extensive archeological excavations and studies of these prehistoric periods remain focused on Egypt.

The Predynastic period was one of settlement and growth, and it spans from the end of the Neolithic period to the beginning of the Early Bronze Age (5500–3150 BCE; Van de Mieroop, 2021: 31–49). Although relatively little evidence survives from this phase, ample pottery, combs, bracelets, beads, small statues, cosmetic palettes, and stone and metal objects are among the most common surviving artifacts. The presence of obsidian (from Ethiopia), few pieces of lapis lazuli (from northeastern Afghanistan), and shifting artistic styles and images indicate early exchange with Mesopotamia. Using the Nile River not only for agriculture but also trade, Predynastic Egyptians also traded with Nubians, as well as oases-dwelling groups in the western desert. With the surplus of goods and extended trade networks, a class of elites and eventually royals emerged, which are identified by their grave goods and funerary treatments, as well as larger dwellings stocked with valuable items. This is also the period in which hieroglyphics, the Egyptian form of writing, first emerged. Hieroglyphics would become a sacred form of text, limited to the priestly class, while merchants later used Demotic. Because writing was established so early in Egypt, used to document people, events, and administration, and because these documents survive exceptionally well due to the arid climate, significantly more is known about Ancient Egypt than many other Bronze Age cultures.

Fig. 5.8 Map with Egypt, Nubia, and Areas that May Be Punt. Image by Marie N. Pareja after Google Earth

The rest of Ancient Egyptian history is dynastic, meaning that different royal families ruled for generations before another family rose to power. These dynasties are grouped according to larger trends in Ancient Egypt. The Early Dynastic Period (3150–2686 BCE) began just before one king, Narmer, unified upper and lower Egypt as one kingdom (Fig. 5.9). This event marks a period of rapid growth: the population of Egypt grew (and therefore the labor force), and wealth increased, leading to even more trade. The first large-scale tombs, called mastabas, were constructed, and the political structure was solidified.

The Old Kingdom Period (2686–2181 BCE) is a continued phase of wealth accumulation and expansion (Van de Mieroop, 2021: 55–74). The royal family ordered the construction of the Great Pyramids at Giza. This massive expenditure of wealth and manpower would never again be seen in the history of Ancient Egypt. A group of scribes and scholars emerged who, although they were central to administrative proceedings of the great empire, ranked just below the priestly class. To manage distant areas of Egypt, the region was split into smaller states, called nomes, for which a nomarch (similar to a governor) was appointed to run their territory, collect taxes, and report back to the king. The grand expense of extended building projects and a prolonged, intense draught brought the Old Kingdom Period to an end and

Fig. 5.9 Narmer Palette front and back. Object Number JE32169. Image courtesy of The Cairo Museum

heralded the First Intermediate Period (2181–2055 BCE), a period of destabilization, uncertainty, and conflict. Nomarchs rebelled, seeking power and calling themselves kings in an attempt to establish their own dynastic rule and again unify Egypt. King Mentuhotep II reunified Egypt, and the Middle Kingdom began.

The Middle Kingdom (2134–1690 BCE) is a period of local peace and stability for Egyptians, who also at this time conquered the northern areas of Nubia (Van de Mieroop, 2021: 97–121). Again Egypt flourished, with increased population and focus on the arts and religion. During this period, the building of large stone pyramids was abandoned for the construction of smaller, mudbrick and sand pyramids that have hardly survived through today. Amenemhat III, the last ruler of the Middle Kingdom, allowed an influx of Canaanites to the Nile Delta region to contribute labor for his building campaigns. These people would soon rise to power and seize the delta and areas along the northeastern Egyptian coast, calling themselves the Hyksos, and signaling the onset of the Second Intermediate Period (1674–1549 BCE). Again, Egypt is in disarray: the new Hyksos rulers demanded taxes, in the form of tribute, from the Egyptian king (Van de Mieroop, 2021: 126–143). The foreigners brought horses, chariots, and the composite bow to Egypt, which became instrumental in the eventual chasing of the Hyksos from Egypt by Ahmose I. Not only did he run them out of Egypt, but he chased them back to their capital city, which he raided and sacked before returning, victorious, to rule Egypt.

The New Kingdom (1549–1069 BCE) is yet another period of widespread peace and prosperity (Van de Mieroop, 2021: 151–256). Egypt re-forges strong relationships with neighboring areas, from the Levant (the area west of Mesopotamia to the Mediterranean coast) into Mesopotamia and reinforces their southern boundaries with Nubia. It was during this period that rulers adopted the title of pharaoh. Hatshepsut, the female pharaoh about whom the most is currently known, ruled for almost 20 years, and she was instrumental in expanding the kingdom's wealth, diplomacy, and trade. Notably, most female pharaohs ruled when their husband dies before the successor to the throne comes of age, and so there are currently only six female pharaohs known from throughout the thousands of years of Ancient Egyptian history.

Akhenaten, ruling a few generations later, tried to overthrow the traditional, polytheistic religious system in Egypt in favor of his single solar deity, Aten, who he claimed was his father (Montserrat 2014). He and his wife Nefertiti outlawed the old ways, constructed a new capital of Egypt, and changed the artistic style during his reign, and yet his son, Tutankhamun (commonly referred to as King Tut), rose to power and all but eradicated his father's legacy, returning Egypt to its long-held traditions. During this period, the funerary structures of rulers also change: they are now buried in the Valley of the Kings, in deep shafts cut into the rocky mountainside (Wilkinson & Weeks, 2016). The New Kingdom ended with invasion by the Libyans, raiding by the Sea Peoples, and civil unrest. Although the history of Ancient Egypt continues, the end of the New Kingdom also marks the end of the Bronze Age.

Aside from the short worship of Aten in the 18th Dynasty, Ancient Egypt maintains a long-lived tradition of polytheism (Teeter, 2011). Deities are most often represented with human bodies and animal heads, although some may also be represented as entirely animal, such as Thoth, who may appear as a baboon. Like Mesopotamian deities, many of these entities represent elements of nature or abstract concepts. Egyptian life is governed by a concept called *ma'at*, or divine order and justice. Perhaps surprisingly, *ma'at* does not entail what is good or bad, but only what serves to reinforce order and keep chaos at bay. One of the tenants of *ma'at* is that people live according to the ways of the gods. Such a concept reinforces the rule of the elites and societal structure, but it also bears other implications: like the gods, the King and queen were siblings and married to one another.

Although temples are devoted to a singular deity, as in Mesopotamia, many of the kings of Ancient Egypt contributed to the building of a single, great temple complex outside of Thebes, called Karnak, which predominantly used to worship the god Amun (Ikram, 2009, 47–68). Kings were often worshipped after their death, for a while as mere mortals, but after a few generations, it seems their status as an ancestor shifted to that of a (lesser?) god. This had changed by the New Kingdom, when pharaohs were more strictly considered the living divine.

While many aspects of life and religion in Mesopotamia and Egypt are similar, the Bronze Age Aegean remains markedly different.

5.4.3 Aegean

The Aegean Sea defines the broader Aegean, which is located in the eastern Mediterranean Sea and includes the island of Crete, the Cycladic Islands, and the Greek

Mainland, the three principal regions into which the Aegean is divided (Cline, 2010; Fig. 5.10). When considered more generally, the Aegean may also sometimes include the coastlines and major port cities of the eastern Mediterranean, including Anatolia (modern-day Türkiye), the Levant, Cyprus, and the remaining groups of Greek islands (Dodecanese, Sporades, and the Saronic Islands). As such, this region is unique by virtue of its many geographical areas that rely on insoluble geographic delineations: island coastlines. While other Bronze Age cultures engage in terrestrial warfare, battling over flexible sociopolitical boundaries (meaning there are no hard, immovable geological boundaries to indicate the limits of a group's domain, such as coastlines, rivers, or mountain peaks), the Aegean is made up of different landscapes, some too small for such boundaries and some too large to go without them, sometimes separated from one another by the sea itself.

During the Paleolithic period, people already inhabited the Aegean Islands, whether as Homo neanderthalensis or Homo sapiens, although relatively little is currently known about them (Carter et al. 2019; Strasser et al. 2018). Later, during the Neolithic period, people migrated from Anatolia westward, through the Balkans and into Mainland Greece, as well as into and through the Aegean islands, venturing from one to the next (Tomkins, 2010: 31–45). Some settled in the Cyclades and others continued on to Crete. Perhaps because of their status as islanders, the Minoans

Fig. 5.10 Map of the Aegean. Image by Marie N. Pareja after Google Earth

(those who lived on Crete) and Cycladic people (those who lived in the Cyclades) are often considered together as one large group, but the subtle diversity among each of these island cultures remains constant through time.

These early groups maintained limited exchange with areas farther east with the onset of the Early Bronze Age (3200–2160 BCE), as is evident by the survival of imported goods and materials, such as lapis lazuli, carnelian, gold, and ivory, among others (Pareja, 2023a and b). Most settlements were located at some distance from the main coastlines, in easily defensible positions. With the onset of a particularly arid period, the Aegean appears to have temporarily ceased trade with neighboring regions.

Throughout the Middle Bronze Age (ca. 2160–1600 BCE), several phases of palatial building and expansion occurred at major sites across Crete and throughout the islands (Rehak, 2008; Younger, 2008). During the middle of this period, a catastrophic event took place—whether an earthquake, conflict, or something else remains unknown—and destroyed many of the largest of these palatial structures. In the following period, they were rebuilt and in many ways redesigned, culminating in large-scale administrative structures that feature drainage systems, storage magazines, shrines, central courtyards, reception and/or performance spaces, and living quarters. Knossos, located along the north central coastline of Crete, is perhaps the best known of these sites. Such constructions were not unique to Crete, however, as both the Cycladic Islands and Mainland built similar structures that were adapted to the local landscapes.

Although the Aegean people surely brought previous religious beliefs and practices with them from Anatolia, these likely changed and shifted over time and with exposure to other cultural groups (such as the Egyptians, for instance), ultimately becoming uniquely Aegean (Rehak, 2008: 165–180). Ample imagery survives that might contain clues about Aegean religion: wall paintings, seals, and figurines made from a variety of materials might show goddesses, priestesses, queens, or other important women, but their precise identities remain mysterious (Fig. 5.11). No central male ruler or deity is evident in any of the surviving imagery or artifacts. Aegean beliefs remain largely unknown due in part to the inability to translate contemporary scripts (Steele, 2017). Cretan Hieroglyphic and Linear A are scripts that both appeared during the Middle Bronze Age on Crete. Linear B, another script that was used later and predominantly by Mainland Greek groups, has been translated and is considered the precursor of the Greek language known today. Linear B was an administrative language, mostly used to document the movement of goods and people from one place to another, and as such is not used to record stories, events, or myths. If Aegean rulership is connected to religion, as in contemporary groups in Mesopotamia, Egypt, and the regions between, then one might conclude that religious imagery might speak to political matters and vice-versa. This too remains uncertain.

By the beginning of the Late Bronze Age (ca. 1600–1100 BCE), the island cultures were at their height and deeply enmeshed in local, regional, and vast, far-flung networks of exchange. There appears to be no evidence for large-scale warfare in or among the islands, which seems unique when compared to neighboring regions that value battle and conquest. It is at this cultural apex that cataclysm strikes: the

Fig. 5.11 Line Drawing of The Master Impression from Khania, Crete. Image courtesy of the CMS Heidelberg

eruption of the volcano at Thera. The eruption was massive—larger than the eruption of Vesuvius, but similar in that it too preserved the nearby town under a layer of ash. This town is called Akrotiri.

Akrotiri is particularly well preserved by ash, lending a unique facet to the study of Aegean prehistory (Doumas, 1992). Up to three stories of some buildings survive, and some of the best-preserved wall paintings from the Bronze Age adorn the interiors of many of these structures (Fig. 5.12). Such paintings provide invaluable insight into life during this period that would otherwise be long lost. Additionally, the voids in the ash left behind by decomposed organic materials, such as wood and ivory, served as molds and were filled with plaster, so that archeologists could learn what such objects (tables, chairs, stools, beds, and so on) looked like and how they might have been built. Critically, no evidence survives of humans caught in the eruption—unlike the people at Pompeii, the citizens of Akrotiri appear to have left with their most valuable items well before the city was buried in ash.

The resulting destruction from this eruption almost certainly caused the demise of the Cycladic and Minoan societies. The sky would have been darkened with ash for extended periods, which would have affected crops and livestock. Creatures governed by circadian rhythms (such as insects, frogs, and other pests) may have swarmed. Iron-rich ash may have affected various sources of fresh water. A tsunami affected closer islands, including Crete, as well as the distant shores of Anatolia and perhaps Egypt. In the wake of such destruction, the Mycenaean Mainland rose to prominence (Dimova & Raykova, 2017: 22–26).

In the middle and later phases of the Late Bronze Age, the Mycenaean Mainland thrived (Hooker, 2014). Major sites include Pylos, Tiryns, and Mycenae, and these

Fig. 5.12 Monkeys Wall Painting from Akrotiri, Thera. Courtesy of the Akrotiri Archive

groups perpetuated many of the sociocultural behaviors and structures of the Aegean islanders. Mainlanders adapted practices and structures to suit local tastes, geographies, and sociopolitical landscapes. For instance, palatial administrative complexes were located in highly defensible locations and often enclosed by a large defensive wall. When possible, these cities included access (sometimes via seemingly secret passageways) to fresh water sources. The subjects of wall paintings and other forms of art seem to shift away from the natural world and toward the very human concerns of hunting and battle. Nevertheless, Mycenaeans appear to assume and maintain the trade connections from earlier periods, as indicated by an influx of valuable raw materials and commodities from distant regions. Although the core identity of the Mainland remains Aegean, the cultural attitude is significantly distinct from that of the earlier island people.

The Aegean Bronze Age ended with nearly complete systems collapse. A multitude of factors, not least of which were overpopulation, economic and political decline, and repeated raids by the Sea Peoples contributed to the fall of Mycenaean Greek society (Middleton 2020). Ultimately, Greece would have to survive a dark age before it could begin to rebuild.

5.4.4 Asia

This section focuses on the central, eastern, and southern areas of Asia, as the western portion is discussed in the Indus and Mesopotamian sections (Fig. 5.13). The different cultures spread across the rest of the continent began using bronze at different times, and it is worth noting that "Bronze Age" is not a term conventionally used to discuss prehistory in this part of the world. This section focuses on China but includes minimal additional information about Thailand, Burma, Korea, and Japan.

The earliest bronze objects appear in Burma as early as 3500 BCE (Moore & Pauk, 2001: 43–44) and as part of the Majiayao culture in China from 2900–2740 BCE (Bai, 2003: 157–163). Later evidence survives from sites nearby the Yellow River and its tributaries, especially to the south, where the Erlitou culture flourished (ca. 1900–1500 BCE). The people at Erlitou built large palaces that presumably required some form of organization and administration. They also maintained workshops devoted to the smelting of bronze. The earliest dings, or bronze ritual vessels, survive from this period, as well as bronze bells, tools, utilitarian vessels, weapons, and plaques

Fig. 5.13 Map of central, eastern, and southern areas of Asia. Image by Marie N. Pareja after Google Earth

with animal faces. Such a broad variety of products, together with nuanced technological knowledge, attests to the presence of skilled, large-scale bronze production and working well before the Shang Dynasty.

Some scholars argue that bronze smelting and working was an independent development for eastern Asia, first appearing during the Shang Dynasty (1766–1122 BCE; Liu, 2005: 231–235). Others maintain that this knowledge was likely shared by people from western Asia, first in Xinjiang and then the Yellow River Valley and the areas around its tributaries. This latter situation is more likely, particularly given the simultaneous appearance of wheeled wagons (or chariots) and the domesticated horse with bronze (Romgard, 2008: 18–20). Unlike the almost ubiquitous use of bronze elsewhere, in China, the metal was regarded as a special material for ritual art, much like jade, although some tools were also crafted from it (predominantly adzes and spear points; Hung, 1995: 11–15).

Although the Shang Dynasty coincides with the Late Bronze Age in Mesopotamia, the Indus, Egypt, and the Aegean, this period is often treated as an Early Bronze Age in central and eastern Asia, due to the roughly contemporary first appearances of bronze in several other areas (Thorp, 2005). The metal appeared in Thailand as early as 2100 BCE (Hamilton, 2001, 8); and both the technology and material were imported together into far southeastern Asian areas and Korea by 1000 BCE (Eckert et al. 1990: 9; Higham et al., 2011: 228–233, 272–273). Finally, the metal is introduced to Japan in approximately 300 BCE (Teramae, 2017: 189–190).

The earliest writing, however, appears as glyphs on Chinese oracle bones, which are objects used for divination (Wilkinson 2022, 1278). Such bones were mostly turtle shells and animal scapulae that were etched or carved with writing. First appearing during the Shang Dynasty, these items provide valuable insight into economics, religious practices, arts, medicine, and politics.

The Shang Dynasty was centralized at the royal palace of Yinxu, which served more of an administrative function than a residential one (Fairbank & Goldman, 2006: 33). Several storage pits were located just outside of palace walls, and smaller living quarters, presumably for servants, were also found nearby. Although many of the graves had been looted throughout time, one undisturbed burial was discovered that held Lady Fu Hao and her grave goods, among which were jade hair combs and figurines, ivory and bone hair pins, bronze vessels and weapons, and several clay vessels (Thorpe 1981: 424–245). Oracle bones with information about her life, conquests (both military and otherwise), and engagement in religious activities were also recovered from her tomb.

A large part of religion in Asia is devoted to ancestor veneration, also known as ancestor worship. Ancestors, ghosts, spirits, and gods are part of nature and ever present as opposed to supernatural entities, like the Egyptian gods. Ritual celebrations and offerings focus on deified ancestors and family lineages, and people often provide offerings of food and items to feed and otherwise support these ancestors. The king, acting also as high priest, often led divination ceremonies and sacrifices (Ebrey, Walthall, & Palais, 2006: 14). Sacrifices were made by the king for the royal ancestors, the high god (Di), and powerful nature entities, such as the sun or a particularly large mountain (Keightley, 2002: 56–113). Ancestor veneration and sacrifice can be practiced on their own, or together with other philosophies and beliefs, such as divination.

Due in large part to fragmentary archeological and historical records, relatively little is known about the early of bronzeworking technologies to different cultures throughout central, eastern, and southern Asia. Although most surviving evidence may indicate that the Bronze Age occurred relatively late—when compared with the regions previously discussed—select finds suggest that this chronological difference may not be accurate. Such is also the case for the cultures in Western and Northern Europe.

5.4.5 Western and Northern Europe

The Bronze Age emerges in successively later periods the farther one travels from Mesopotamia. As in the eastern and southern reaches of Asia, the western and northern areas of Europe began smelting and using bronze in slightly later periods (ca. 2100–700 BCE) than their central European neighbors (ca. 2300–1100 BCE). Britain, being one of the last groups to adopt bronze technologies in Afro-Eurasia, is explored here.

The Bronze Age in Britain (ca. 2300–800 BCE) arrived on the heels of the Neolithic period, although several practices from the earlier phase continued, such as the building and modification of megalithic henges (Pearson, 2021: 43–67). Stonehenge and Avebury Henges are examples of such structures. Simultaneously, agriculture became more widely adopted. It is worth noting that Britain is not host to any significant river valley culture, as most of these groups occur farther south, in warmer climates.

The earliest culture to use bronze in was the Bell Beaker culture, who are known for their distinctively bell-shaped drinking cups (Brodie, 1997: 297–303). The use of this cup shape was not limited to the British Isles, however, and appears contemporarily in the areas known in modern-day as Spain, northwestern Africa, Germany, and all the areas between. By the end of the Bell Beaker culture (1800 BCE), these regions were engaging in long-distance exchange networks that facilitated the introduction of a number of new materials and technologies (Cunliffe & Koch, 2010: 27–30). For instance, archery and new types of adornment first appear during the Bell Beaker culture, together with the importation of new cultural and religious notions of power, hierarchy, and wealth. Local elites answer to regional elites, who rule over larger areas. The highly regionalized nature of this culture is evident not only in physical location, but also in the different expressions of culture, wealth, and identity (Fokkens and Nicolis 2012: 200). Perhaps it is better to understand this trend as a unification of several different and widely dispersed cultures than the imposition of one large, homogenous group of people.

In the south of Britain, the Wessex culture emerged after the Bell Beaker culture (2000–1400 BCE). The local climate became considerably wetter, and people moved into valleys, where livestock cultivation became easier and steadily increased. Many of the barrows and tombs that are dug shallowly into the ground and constructed in such a way that the resulting mound often becomes a noticeable part of the natural landscape, resembling a hill, date to this period. Stonehenge also dates to this period, although only its later phases. These tombs, with their cremated (or, less frequently, interred) inhabitants, boast items and materials from across the Bronze Age world, including Mycenaean daggers, gold, and beads; amber from the Baltic region; and glass beads from Egypt and Mesopotamia (Horn and Kristianson 2018: 53). Between the large-scale exchange and the megalithic building projects, the presence of some form of administration and social organization is expected, although at present, remains largely unknown.

The Deverel-Rimbury culture (1400–1100 BCE) continued in much the same way as the Wessex Culture, and they are known primarily for extracting tin from Cornwall and copper from the Great Orme Mine in northern Wales. Evidence for the export and use of this tin appears in the Aegean—particularly from the site of Mochlos, Crete—as tin ingots from Cornwall (Berger et al., 2019).

At the end of the Deverel-Rimbury culture, the western and northern areas of Europe experience the fallout from the late Bronze Age collapse affecting the Aegean, Levant, Anatolia, and other Mediterranean and eastern areas. Some scholars argue that a cultural disruption around 1100 BCE indicates a breakdown in the far-reaching trade with the southern and eastern groups most affected by the collapse. Still others maintain that an influx of people over the next 500 years up-ended traditional practices and social norms (possibly invasion, although migration is more likely), leading to a relatively unstable final phase of the Bronze Age in Britain (Patterson et al. 2021: 590–591).

5.5 Interconnections

Although each of the sections above addresses cultures separately, with minimal discussion of trade and exchange, it is critical to understand that particularly between 2500 and 1100 BCE, Africa, Asia, and Europe were highly connected with one another via expansive networks. Although the majority of evidence for such interconnection discussed here is based on the movement of raw materials, a variety of other types of information moved with the goods (and the people who moved them), including knowledge, beliefs, and traditions (Pareja and Arnott forthcoming, 2024). This final section is intended to help the reader create a more holistic, integrated understanding of the Bronze Age than traditional textbooks allow. The following is a sampling of some of the most recent evidence for such connections. It is subdivided into three groups: textual documentation, iconographic studies, and scientific analysis.

5.5.1 Texts

Mesopotamian texts from the second millennium BCE contain references to the Indus River Valley cultures. Such passages are particularly well known between 2334–2124 BCE, and they indicate both contact and familiarity with the Indus and the regions between (Buck, 2019: 169; Glassner, 1996: 235–238; Potts, 1993: 379–402). Some of these inscriptions indicate that Mesopotamians desired carnelian and lapis lazuli from the Indus traders. Evidence even survives for a translator, Shu-ilishu, who can aid in communication between Indus and Mesopotamian languages (Louvre Museum AO 22,310). Perhaps the need for a translator is surprising, considering that a village of people from the Indus—probably artisans or craftspeople—was found in Mesopotamia (Parpola et al., 1977: 136–37; Vermaak, 2008: 454).

Finally, the Indus (called Meluhha in Mesopotamian texts) is directly named or indirectly referenced in multiple myths from throughout Bronze Age Mesopotamia. For instance, shiploads of precious cargo from the Indus are mentioned in the mythical tale of Enki and Ninhursaga (Michalowski, 2011: 257, n. 28). In *Curse of Agade*, various exotic animals are listed together in groups, among which are monkeys, elephants, and water buffalo, which may have been grouped together due to their importation together from the Indus (Boehmer, 1974: 1–19; Cooper, 1983: 51, line 21; Dunham, 1985: 236; Kenoyer, 1998: 84–98; Pareja, 2021, 52–53; Çakirlar & Ikram, 2016: 168–70, 176–78).

5.5.2 Iconography

A number of particular motifs are identified from Early Bronze Age Crete as imports from Egypt. Some of these motifs, such as scarabs, the Egyptian hippopotamus goddess Taweret, monkeys, and other mythical hybrid creatures (to name only a few), were also imported to the Levant and Mesopotamia during the Early Bronze Age (Sahoglou, 2005). Among this broad collection of imagery, some designs seem to have a steady, traceable westward movement through time, from the Indus through Mesopotamia, the Levant, Anatolia, and sometimes Egypt, to the Mediterranean and perhaps beyond (Pareja et al., 2019; Pareja, 2023a and b; 2024). Notably, many of these motifs occur together with foreign raw materials and crafting technologies (Aruz, 2003: 241–245; pers. comm. Ludvik, 4–5 December 2022).

Stylistic emulation and overlap between these areas—beyond direct importation—betrays a familiarity with other cultures' imagery. Examples of this include Aegean-like styles in Egypt, the Levant, and Anatolia (particularly pottery); the Aegean-style wall paintings from Tel Dab^{c}a in Egypt (Bietak & Marinatos, 1995; Morgan, 1988; 2004); Egyptian-like styles, patterns, and imported objects found on Crete (Aston, 2015: 9–10; Cline, 1994; Dothan et al., 2000: 1); and Egyptian objects found at the Temple of the Obelisks in Byblos, in Mesopotamia (Tufnell & Ward,

1966), among many others. Most of the items that show this close degree of connection are small, highly portable, and often indicate identity. A multitude of artistic styles, subjects, and compositions connect each of these regions to one another and those farther beyond (Pareja, 2017: 113–118; 122–123; 2021, 43–56, 60–61).

5.5.3 Analysis

Organic residue analysis from a vessel found at a tomb near Meggido (in Canaan, which is part of the Levant), was performed to learn the ancient contents of the vessel. Analysis revealed an unexpected ingredient: vanillin (Linares et al., 2019: 77). Until this point, the earliest users of vanilla (or plants bearing the compound vanillin) appeared to be the pre-contact Aztec people, living in Central America (Bythrow, 2005: 129). The discovery of this residue inside a vessel from the Levant not only rewrites botanic history but also indicates that this area was involved in the exchange with eastern Africa, the Indus, or more likely, areas of southeastern Asia (Görg, 1984: 219–224; Linares et al., 2019: 81–82).

Another analytical study was performed on several human remains from Meggido and Tel Erani in the Levant (Scott et al., 2020). Some individuals' dental calculus (hardened tartar on the teeth) bore evidence of bananas, turmeric, ginger, and soy—tropical plants indigenous to southeastern Asia. This single find indicates a connection between cultures at the heart of the earliest phases of the Bronze Age and cultures that are currently thought to have learned about bronze much later. Perhaps southeastern Asian cultures did not want to adopt the use of bronze in such early periods, or more likely, archeologists simply have not yet discovered evidence of bronze's presence there yet.

Although carnelian deposits are known from various Afro-Eurasian areas, the stone varies on color and patterning based on the location from which it comes (Groman-Yaroslavski & Mayer, 2015: 86; Ludvik et al., 2015: 7–15). The techniques and methods for the cutting and shaping of beads are also regionally specific (as are subsequent alterations), so that stylistic aspects may be considered clear indications of origin and/or places to or through which the objects traveled (Chakrabarti, 1993: 266). Indus-style carnelian beads are currently known as far east as Guangzhou in southeastern China (Zhao, 2014: 177–78), and as far west as the island of Aegina during the Early Bronze Age (Aruz, 2003: 239–250). Although they have not yet been analyzed, some of the carnelian beads from the Bell Beaker Culture (and later cultures) may have originally been shaped in the Indus River Valley. Currently, the regions with the greatest concentrations of these beads are Mesopotamia and the Levant (pers. comm. Ludvik, 4–5 December 2022).

Isotopic analysis of tin from a few objects found at Aegean island sites indicates an original source in the Indus River Valley (Weeks, 1999: 2–7). Nevertheless, some objects from Crete indicate the use of tin sources from Cornwall, as stated above. Countless other raw materials were also exchanged from the Indus to the Aegean and further westward from the Neolithic through the Bronze Age, including but not limited to amber, amethyst, chalcedony, gold, ivory, and a variety of other metals (Chapin & Pareja, 2020, 2021: 126; Colburn, 2008: 210–12; Hughes-Brock, 2011: 101–08; Loze, 2011: 59–62; Ratnagar, 2004: 106–211).

5.6 Conclusions

The Indus Valley cultures were in many ways similar to other groups throughout Bronze Age Afro-Eurasia, and yet they appear strikingly different in others. Generally speaking, and despite the varied dates of the Bronze Age in different parts of Afro-Eurasia, a few patterns are recognizable. First, cultures are largely settled and participate in agriculture, which in many cases shows evidence of cultivating or adopting similar products during the earlier Neolithic period. From these humble roots, sprawling cities blossomed. Often, groups within these larger cultures possess some form of writing—whether they can be translated today or not—and practice different beliefs or religions. Sometimes the religious leader is also the political leader, although in the case of the potentially egalitarian IVC, this remains unknown. People contribute to and abide by standardized guidelines that dictate social order and organization. Often, religion and belief reinforce social structure.

Finally, cultures trade for materials from distant locations, and both the Indus and Mesopotamia seem to have functioned as major hubs for exchange—they were instrumental in the facilitation of exchange between and amongst the various cultures in Afro-Eurasia. This last commonality continuously sheds more light on what life in the Bronze Age was truly like, especially because it is now becoming clear that each group is considerably more interconnected with the others than previously thought. With the severing of these connections, however, many regions entered a period of considerable decline before reemerging in the Iron Age.

References

Aruz, J. (Ed.). (2003). *The Art of the First Cities: The Third Millennium B.C. from the Mediterranean to the Indus*. Metropolitan Museum of Art.

Aston, D. A. (2015). A copy of a copy of a copy, or an imitation Kamares-Ware vessel from Tell el-Dab'a, in A. Jiménez-Serrano and C. von Pilgrim (eds.) *From the Delta to the Cataract. Studies dedicated to Mohamed el-Bialy. Culture and History of the Ancient Near East* 76: 1–11. Brill. https://doi.org/10.1163/9789004293458_002.

Bai, Y. (2003). A Discussion on Early metals and the Origins of Bronze Casting in China. *Chinese Archaeology, 3*(1), 157–165.

Berger, D. J.S. Soles, A.R. Giumlia-Mair, G. Brügmann, E. Galili, N. Lockhoff, & Pernicka, E. (2019). Isotope systematics and chemical composition of tin ingots from Mochlos (Crete) and other Late Bronze Age sites in the Eastern mediterranean Sea: An ultimate key to tin provenance? *PLOS ONE.*

Bietak, M., & Marinatos, N. (1995). The Minoan Wall paintings from Avaris, Ägypten und Levante/ Egypt and the. *Levant, 5*, 49–62.

Boehmer, R. M. (1974). Das Auftreten des Wasserbüffels in Mesopotamien in historischer Zeit und seine sumerische Bezeichnung. *Zeitschrift Für Assyriologie und Vorderasiatische Archäologie, 64*(1), 1–19. https://doi.org/10.1515/zava.1974.64.1.1

Brodie, N. (1997). New perspectives on the Bell-beaker Culture. *Oxford Journal of Archaeology, 16*(3), 297–314.

Brooke, J. L. (2014). *Climate Change and the Course of Global History: A Rough Journey.* Cambridge University Press.

Buck, M. E. (2019). *The Amorite Dynasty of Ugarit: Historical Implications of Linguistic and Archaeological Parallels.* Brill.

Bythrow, J. D. (2005). Vanilla as a medicinal plant. *Siminars in Integrattive Medicine, 3,* 129–131.

Carter, T., Contreras, D. A., Holcomb, J., Mihailović, D. D., Karkanas, P., Guérin, G., Taffin, N., Athanasoulis, D., & Lahaye, C. (2019). Earliest occupation of the Central Aegean (Naxos), Greece: Implications for hominin and Homosapiens' behavior and dispersals. *Science Advances 5,* 1–9.

Chakrabarti, D. K. (1993). Long-barrel cylinder beads and the issue of pre-Sargonic contact between the Harappan civilization and Mesopotamia, In Possehl G. (Ed.). *Harappan Civilization: A Recent Perspective*: 265–70. Warminster: Aris & Phillips.

Chang, K. C. (1982). *Studies of Shang Archaeology.* Yale University Press.

Çakirlar, C., & Ikram, S. (2016). 'When elephants battle, the grass suffers.' Power, ivory, and the Syrian Elephant. *Levant* 48.2: 167–83.

Chapin, A. P., & Pareja, M. N. (2020). Peacock or Poppycock: Exotic Animal Imagery in Bronze Age Crete and the Cyclades, in R. Laffineur and T.G. Palaima (Eds.) *NEOTEROS: Studies in Bronze Age Aegean Art and Archaeology in Honor of Professor John G. Younger on the Occasion of his Retirement (Aegaeum 44)*: 215–26. University of Texas, Austin.

Chapin, A. P., & Pareja, M. N. (2021). Betwixt and Beyond the Boundaries: An Ecosocial Model of Animal-Human Relations in Minoan and Cycladic Animal Art, In Laffineur R. & Palaima T. G. (Eds.). *ZOIA: Animal-Human Interactions in the Aegean Middle and Late Bronze Age (Aegaeum 45)*: 125–34. University of Texas, Austin.

Cline, E., (Ed.). (2010). *The Oxford Handbook of the Bronze Age Aegean,* Oxford University Press.

Cline, E. (1994). *Sailing the Wine Dark Sea.* Archaeopress.

Colburn, C. S. (2008). Exotica and the Early Minoan elite: Eastern imports in Prepalatial Crete. *American Journal of Archaeology, 112*(2), 203–224.

Coningham, R. & Young R. (2015). *The Archaeology of South Asia: From the Indus to Asoka, c. 6500 BCE–200 CE,* Cambridge University Press.

Cooper, J. S. (1983). *The Curse of Agade.* Johns Hopkins University Press.

Crawford, H. J. (2004). *Sumer and the Sumerians.* Cambridge University Press.

Cunliffe, B, & Koch, T., (Eds.). (2010). Chapter One: Celtization from the West, *Celtic From the West: Alternative Perspectives from Archaeology, Genetics, Language, and Literature,* Oxbow: 27–31.

Dimova, L. R., & Raykova,. (2017). Tsunami Radiation Pattern in the Eastern Mediterranean. *Journal of Physical Technology, 1*(2), 22–27.

Dothan, T., Zuckerman, S., & Goren, Y. (2000). Kamares Ware at Hazor. *Israel Exploration Journal, 50*(1–2), 1–15.

Doumas, C. (1992). *The Wall Paintings of Thera.*

Dunham, S. (1985). The monkey in the middle. *Zeitschrift Für Assyriologie und Vorderasiatische Archäologie, 75*(2), 234–264.

Dyson, T. (2018). *A Population History of India: From the First Modern People to the Present Day.* Oxford University Press.

Eckert, C. J., Ki-Baik, L., Young Ick, L., Robinson, M., & Wagner, E. W. (1990). *Korea, Old and New: A History.*

Ebrey, P. B., Walthall, A., & Palais, J. B. (2006). *East Asia: A Cultural, Social, and Political History,* Houghton Mifflin.

Fairbank, J. K., & Goldman, M. (2006). *China: A New History.* Harvard University Press.

Fokkens, H., & Nicolis, F. (Eds.). (2012). *Background to Beakers: Inquiries in Regional Cultural Backgrounds of the Bell Beaker Complex*, Sidestone.
Gangal, K. G. R., & Sarson, A. S. (2014). The Near-Eastern Roots of the Neolithic in South Asia. *PLoS ONE, 9*(5), 1–6.
Glassner, J. -J. (1996). Dilmun, magan and meluhha: observations on language, toponymy, anthroponymy, and theonymy. In Reade J. (ed.) *The Indian Ocean in Antiquity*. Routledge: New York.
Glassner, J.-J., & Heron, D. M. (2003). *The Invention of Cuneiform: Writing in Sumer*. Johns Hopkins University Press.
Görg, M. (1984). Oils from Abroad [in German]. *Studien Altägyptischen Kultur, 11*, 219–226.
Green, A. S. (2022). Of revenue without rulers: public goods in the egalitarian cities of the indus civilization. *Frontiers in Political Science, 4*, 150–168.
Green, A. S. (2020). Killing the Priest-King: addressing egalitarianism in the indus civilization. *Journal of Archaeological Research, 29*(2), 153–202.
Groman-Yaroslavski, I., & Mayer, D.E.B.-Y. (2015). Lapidary technology revealed by functional analysis of carnelian beads from the Early Neolithic site of Nahal Hemar Cave, southern Levant. *Journal of Archaeological Science, 58*, 77–88.
Hamilton, E. (2001). Bronze from ban chiang, Thailand: a view from the laboratory. *Expedition, 43*, 7–8.
Higham, C., Higham, T., Ciarla, R., Douka, K., Kijngam, A., & Rispoli, F. (2011). The origins of the Bronze age of Southeast Asia. *Journal of World Prehistory, 24*(4), 227–274.
Hooker, J. (2014). *Mycenaean Greece*. Routledge.
Horn, C., & Kristiansen, K., (Eds.). (2018). *Warfare in Bronze Age Society*, Camrbidge University Press.
Hughes-Brock, H. (2011). Exotic Materials and Objects Sent to—and from?—the Bronze Age Aegean. Some recent work and some observations, In Vianello, A. (ed.). *Exotica in the Prehistoric Mediterranean*: 99–114. Oxbow Books: Oxford, UK.
Hung, W. (1995). *Monumentality in Early Chinese Art and Architecture*. Stanford University Press.
Ialongo, N. R., & Hermann, & Rahmstorf, L. (2021). Bronze Age weight systems as a measure of market integration in Western Eurasia. *PNAS, 118*(27), 1–9.
Ikram, S. (2009). *Ancient Egypt: An Introduction*. Cambridge University Press.
Joshi, J. P. & Parpola, A. (Eds.). (1987). *Corpus of Indus Seals and Inscriptions I: Collections in India*, Helsinki.
Keightley, D. N. (2002). *The Ancestral Landscape: Time, Space, and Community in Late Shang China, ca. 1200–1045 B.C.*, University of California Press.
Kenoyer, J. M. (2008). Indus Civilization. In Pearshall, D. M. (Ed.). *Encyclopedia of Archaeology*: 715–733. Academic Press, New York.
Kenoyer, J. M. (1998). *Ancient Cities of the Indus Valley Civilization*. Oxford University Press and American Institute of Pakistan Studies.
Kenoyer, J. M. (1997). Trade and technology of the indus valley: new insights from Harappa. *Pakistan, World Archaeology, 29*(2), 262–280.
Kristiansen, K., & Larsson, T. B. (2005). *The Rise of Bronze Age Society*. Cambridge University Press.
Lawler, A. (2008). Indus Collapse: The End or the beginning of an Asian Culture? *Science, 320*(5881), 1281–1283.
Linares, V., Adams, M. J., Cradic, M. S., Finkelstein, I., Lipschits, O., Martin, M. A. S., Neumann, R., Stockhammer, P. W., & Gadot, Y. (2019). First evidence for vanillin in the old world: Its use as a mortuary offering in Middle Bronze Canaan. *Journal of Archaeological Science: Reports, 25*, 77–84.
Liu, L. (2005). *The Chinese Neolithic: Trajectories to Early States*. Cambridge University Press.
Liverani, M. (1993). Akkad: An Introduction, In Liverani, M. (Ed.). *Akkad: The First World Empire: Structure, Ideology, Traditions*, New Haven: 1–10.

Loze, I. (2011). Neolithic Amber Processing and Exchange on the Eastern Coast of the Baltic Sea. In Vianello, A. (Ed.), *Exotica in the Prehistoric Mediterranean* (pp. 59–62). Oxbow Books.

Ludvik, G., Kenoyer, J. M., Pieniażek, M., & Aylward, W. (2015). New perspectives on stone bead technology at Bronze Age Troy. *Anatolian Studies, 65*, 1–18.

Madella, M., & Lancelotti, C. (2022). Archaeobotanical perspectives on water supply and water management in the indus valley civilization, In Rost, S., (ed.). *Irrigation in Early States: New Directions, 13*, 113–136.

Maisels, C. K. (2003). *Early Civilizations of the Old World: The Formative Histories of Egypt, the Levant, Mesopotamia, India and China*, Routledge.

McIntosh, J. R. (2005). *Ancient Mesopotamia: New Perspectives*, ABC-CLIO.

McMahon, A. (2016). Reframing the Ziggurat, in Bille, M., & Sorensen, T.F. (Eds.). *Elements of Architecture: Assembling Archaeology, Atmosphere, and the Performance of Building Spaces*: 321–340.

Meadow, R.H., & Kenoyer, J.M., (Eds.). (2010). *Corpus of Indus Seals and Inscriptions. Volume 3: New material, untraced objects, and collections outside India and Pakistan. Part 1: Mohenjo-daro and Harappa*, Helsinki.

Meeks, D. (2012). *Locating Punt* (pp. 53–80). UCL Press.

Michalowski, P. (2011). *The correspondence of the Kings of Ur: an epistolary history of an ancient Mesopotamian kingdom.* Winona Lake: Eisenbrauns.

Middleton, G.D., (Ed.) *Collapse and Transformation: The Late Bronze Age to Early Iron Age in the Aegean*, Oxbow Books.

Montserrat, D. (2014). *Akhenaten: History, Fantasy, and Ancient Egypt*. Routledge.

Moore, E., & Pauk, P. (2001). Nyaung-gan: a preliminary note on a Bronze age cemetery near mandalay, Myanmar (Burma). *Asian Perspectives, 40*(1), 35–47.

Morgan, L. (1988). *The Miniature Wall Paintings of Thera: A Study in Aegean Culture and Iconography*. Cambridge University Press.

Pareja, M. N. (2024). Potnia's Participants: Considering the Gala, Assinnu, and Kurgarrû in an Aegean Context. *Arts, 13*(20), 1–27.

Pareja, M. N. (2023a). Global Interfaces and the Earliest Evidence for Afro-Eurasian Exchange, In Franicevic, B., & Pareja, M. N. (Eds.). *Imperial Horizons of the Silk Roads: Archaeological Case Studies*, Archaeopress.

Pareja, M. N. (2023b). Polyvalent power and bronze age ideologies, In Franicevic, B., & Pareja, M.N. eds., *Imperial Horizons of the Silk Roads: Archaeological Case Studies*, Archaeopress.

Pareja, M. N. (2021). The Minoan Monkey: Ties between the Aegean and Indus River Valley via Mesopotamia, In Recht, L., & Zeman-Wisniewska, K. (Eds.). *Animal Iconography in the Archaeological Record*: 42–70. Equinox Publishing.

Pareja, M. N. (2019). Reconstructing Cult Practices through Secondary Sources, in *The Proceedings of the 12th International Congress of Cretan Studies, Heraklion, 21–25 September 2016:* 21–25. Herakleion.

Pareja, M. N. (2017). *Monkey and Ape Iconography in Aegean Art*. Uppsala.

Pareja, M.N., & Arnott, R., (Eds.). Forthcoming 2024. *There and Back Again: Indus-Aegean Relations in the Bronze Age*, Archaeopress.

Pareja, M.N., McKinney, T., Mayhew, J.A., Setchell, J.M., Nash, S.D., & Heaton R. (2019). A New Identification of the monkeys depicted in a Bronze Age Wall Painting from Akrotiri, Thera. *Primates (Online First)*.

Parpola, A. (2015). *The Roots of Hinduism: The Early Aryans and the Indus Civilization.* Oxford University Press.

Parpola, S., Parpola, A., & Brunswig, R. H., Jr. (1977). The Meluhha village: Evidence of acculturation of Harappan traders in late third millennium Mesopotamia. *Journal of the Economic and Social History of the Orient, 20*(2), 129–165.

Patterson, N., Isakov, M., Booth, T., Büster, L., et al. (2022). Large-scale migration into Britain during the Middle to Late Bronze Age. *Nature, 601*, 588–594.

Pearson, M. P. 2021. *Bronze Age Britain*, Batsford Books.

Płoszaj, T., Chaubey, G., Jędrychowska-Dańska, K., Tomczyk, J., & Witas, H. W. (2013). MtDNA from the Early Bronze Age to the Roman Period Suggests a Genetic Link between the Indian Subcontinent and Mesopotamian Cradle of Civilization. *PLoS ONE, 8*(9), 1–9.
Potts, T. F. (1993). Patterns of Trade in third-millennium BC Mesopotamia and Iran. *World Archaeology*: Taylor and Francis.
Ratnagar, S. (2004). *Trading Encounters: From the Euphrates to the Indus in the Bronze Age* (2nd Ed.), Oxford University Press.
Rehak, P. (2008). Minoan Culture: Religion, Burial Customs, Administration, In Shelmerdine, S., (Ed.). *The Cambridge Companion to the Aegean Bronze Age*, Cambridge University Press: 165–185.
Romgard, J. (2008). Questions of ancient human settlements in xinjiang and the early silk road trade, with an overview of the silk road research institutions and scholars in Beijing, Gansu, and Xinjiang, *Sino-Platonic Papers* 185, University of Pennsylvania Press.
Şahoğlu, V. (2005). The Anatolian trade network and the Izmir region during the Early Bronze Age. *Oxford Journal of Archaeology, 24*(4), 339–361.
Schneider, T. J. (2011). *An Introduction to Ancient Mesopotamian Religion*, Eerdmans Publishing Company.
Scott, A., Power, R. C., Altmann-Wendling, V., Artzy, M., Martin, M. A. S., Eisenmann, S., Hagan, R., Salazar-García, D. C., Salmon, Y., Yegorov, D., Milevski, I., Finkelstein, I., Stockhammer, P. W., & Warinner, C. (2020). Exotic foods reveal contact between South Asia and the Near East during the second millennium BCE. *PNAS*. https://doi.org/10.1073/pnas.2014956117.
Steele, P. (2017). *The Aegean Writing Systems: Understanding Relations Between Scripts*, Oxbow Books.
Stein, G. (1994). Economy, Ritual, and Power in 'Ubaid Mesopotamia. In Stein, G., Rothman M. S. (Eds.), *Chiefdoms and Early States in the Near East: The Organizational Dynamics of Complexity* (pp. 35–46). Prehistory Press.
Strasser, T. F., Murray, S. C., van der Geer, A., Kolb, C., & Ruprecht Jr, L. A. (2018). Palaeolithic cave art from Crete, Greece. *Journal of Archaeological Science: Reports 18*, 100–108.
Teeter, E. (2011). *Religion and Ritual in Ancient Egypt*. Cambridge University Press.
Teramae, N. (2017). *Bunmei ni kōshita Yayoi no hitobito (The Yayoi people who resisted civilization)*, Yoshikawa Kobunkan. In Japanese.
Thorp, R. L. (2005). *China in the Early Bronze Age: Shang Civilization*, University of Pennsylvania Press.
Tomkins, P. (2010). Neolithic Antecedents. The Origins of the Aegean Bronze Age, In Cline, E., (Ed.). *The Oxford Handbook of the Aegean Bronze Age*, University of Oxford Press: 31–49.
Tufnell, O., & Ward, W. A. (1966). Relations between Byblos, Egypt, and Mesopotamia at the end of the third millennium BC. A study of the Montet Jar. *Syria, 43*, 165–241.
Van de Mieroop, M. (2021). *A History of Ancient Egypt*. John Wiley and Sons.
Vermaak, P. S. (2008). Guabba, the Meluhhan village in Mesopotamia. *Journal for Semitics, 17*(2), 553–570.
Weeks, L. (1999). Lead isotope analyzes from Tell Abraq, United Arab Emirates: New data regarding the 'tin problem' in Western Asia. *Antiquity, 73*(279), 49–64.
Wells, B. (1999). *An Introduction to Indus Writing*. Early Sites Research Society Monograph Series II.
Wiener, M.H. (2018). *The Collapse of Civilizations*, Belfer Center for Science and International Affairs. Harvard Kennedy School Paper.
Wiggermann, F. A. M., Sasson, J. M., & Baines, J. (1995). Theologies. *Priests, and Worship in Ancient Mesopotamia, Civilizations of the Ancient near East, 3*(3), 1857–1870.
Wilkinson, T. (2022). *Chinese History: A New Manual,* Harvard University Asia Center.
Wilkinson, R.H., & Weeks, K.R., (Eds.). (2016). *The Oxford Handbook of the Valley of the Kings*, Oxford University Press.
Winter, I. (1983). *The Warka Vase: Structure of Art and Structure of Society in Early Urban Mesopotamia*. American Oriental Society.

Wright, R. (2009). *The Ancient Indus: Urbanism, Economy, and Society*. Cambridge University Press.

Younger, J.G. (2008). The material culture of neopalatial crete, In Shelmerdine, S., (Ed.). *The Cambridge Companion to the Aegean Bronze Age*, Cambridge University Press: 140–164.

Zhao, D. (2014). Study on the etched carnelian beads unearthed in China. *Chinese Archaeology, 14*, 176–181.

Chapter 6
The Historical Reception of Panini's Sanskrit Grammar

Rishi Rajpopat

Abstract The *Aṣṭādhyāyī* is a comprehensive grammar of the Sanskrit language as known to its author Pāṇini. It stands out for doing more than merely describing its object language: the *Aṣṭādhyāyī* is a full-fledged machine which helps construct grammatically correct Sanskrit words and sentences through a step-by-step derivation process. In the *Aṣṭādhyāyī*, Pāṇini does not give us a general introduction to his work, nor does he discuss the theoretical principles that have been used to construct his *sūtra*s. He conveys whatever has to be said, through his *sūtra*s alone. And this absence of an explicit statement by Pāṇini about the exact nature of his work makes the historical reception of his grammar so interesting: how are we to decide what Pāṇini sought to achieve with his unique grammar and how the commentaries of subsequent traditional scholars have influenced our understanding of Pāṇini's work and motives? In this paper, I first dwell on why it is challenging to interpret the *Aṣṭādhyāyī* and discuss the interpretative developments that likely followed its composition within a couple of centuries. I then explain what metarules are and why they play such a pivotal role in our decipherment of Pāṇini's grammatical framework while also outlining the history of what has come to be called the Pāṇinian grammatical tradition. Next, I discuss how modern scholarship has received the *Aṣṭādhyāyī* and whether it can be called a 'machine'. Thereafter, I summarize the problem of rule conflict in the *Aṣṭādhyāyī*, underscore the key findings of my doctoral thesis, and explain my work in a philosophical context—broaching issues surrounding the epistemology and the ontology of this discipline. Finally, I offer a succinct intellectual history of the Pāṇinian grammatical tradition focusing on the one metarule that Pāṇini has taught us to deal with rule conflict.

R. Rajpopat (✉)
University of St Andrews, St Andrews, Scotland, UK
e-mail: rishirajpopat@gmail.com

L. Vemsani (ed.), *Handbook of Indian History*,
https://doi.org/10.1007/978-981-97-6207-1_6

6.1 Introduction

Panini[1] composed the *Astadhyayi* around 350 BC (Cardona, 1976: 267–268) in North-Western South Asia.[2] The *Astadhyayi* is a collection of *asta(n)* 'eight' *adhyaya*s 'books', hence the name *Asta-adhyay(a)-i*. Each book of the *Astadhyayi* has four *pada*s 'chapters' that are made up of *sutra*s 'rules'. In all, the *Astadhyayi* comprises about 4000 rules.

The *Astadhyayi* is a comprehensive grammar of the Sanskrit language as known to its author Panini. It stands out for doing more than merely describing its object language: the *Astadhyayi* is a full-fledged machine which helps construct grammatically correct Sanskrit words and sentences through a step-by-step derivation process. In the *Astadhyayi*, Panini does not give us a general introduction to his work, nor does he discuss the theoretical principles that have been used to construct his *sutra*s. He conveys whatever has to be said, through his *sutra*s alone.

And this absence of an explicit statement by Panini about the exact nature of his work makes the historical reception of his grammar so interesting: how are we to decide what Panini sought to achieve with his unique grammar and how the commentaries of subsequent traditional scholars have influenced our understanding of Panini's work and motives?

In this paper, I first dwell on why it is challenging to interpret the *Astadhyayi* and discuss the interpretative developments that likely followed its composition within a couple of centuries. I then explain what metarules are and why they play such a pivotal role in our decipherment of Panini's grammatical framework while also outlining the history of what has come to be called the Paninian grammatical tradition. Next, I discuss how modern scholarship has received the *Astadhyayi* and whether it can be called a 'machine'. Thereafter, I summarize the problem of rule conflict in the *Astadhyayi*, underscore the key findings of my doctoral thesis, and explain my work in a philosophical context—broaching issues surrounding the epistemology and the ontology of this discipline. Finally, I offer a succinct intellectual history of the Paninian grammatical tradition focusing on the one metarule that Panini has taught us to deal with rule conflict.

---

[1] In this paper, to avoid diacritics, I have used popular spellings for certain frequently used Sanskrit words, personal names, texts, places, etc. Since this article has been written for the benefit of historians, I have tried to omit, to the extent possible, technical details which are not central to the arguments I make. There are many disagreements about the dates, and what I mention here are the dates agreed upon by much recent scholarship.

[2] I say 'composed' and not 'wrote' because scholars disagree on whether he used the aid of writing to create his grammar. In recent times, Vergiani (2020) has present strong arguments in favor of the proposition that Panini did use written means to put together his magnum opus. Writing or not, it is known that, just as happened with the Vedas, the *Astadhyayi* too was orally transmitted from one generation to the next.

6.2 Challenges in Understanding the Astadhyayi

To truly understand the *Astadhyayi*, one needs to familiarize oneself with the methodology used by Panini to compose and arrange rules in his work. Panini's style is not entirely self-evident, and one faces challenges at multiple levels when attempting to unravel the enigma that is the *Astadhyayi*. Firstly, it is not easy to determine the exact meaning of Panini's rules because the *sutra* style in which they are composed is very concise and compact. Much information is often packed into a few words, thereby making it considerably difficult to comprehend their exact purpose.

Secondly, to make sense of any given rule, it is essential to take into account the contents of the preceding rules. This is because Panini uses a device called *anuvrtti* 'continuation into the following rules' to economically express his observations: to understand the complete and correct meaning of a rule, certain words from preceding *sutra*s may need to be borrowed into that rule by *anuvrtti*. But there is no universal convention as to which terms are supposed to or can become 'continued' into a certain rule.

Thirdly, even after the meaning of the rule has been understood, it does not become patently obvious how to use it. This is because Panini's rules are placed together on the basis of topical and functional categories, and not according to the derivations in which they participate. Thus, one cannot easily ascertain the order in which rules apply or select the step at which they become applicable.

Fourthly, after one has come to a conclusion about where to apply a given rule, one is often faced with situations in which two (or more) rules become applicable at the same step. This is called 'rule conflict'. How should we decide which one of these two (or more) rules should be applied at that step? A rule taught by Panini, namely 1.4.2 *vipratiṣedhe paraṁ kāryam*, which we will study later in this article, addresses this issue. However, given the way it has been understood by traditional scholars, it seems unable to give the right answer when applied to certain cases of conflict.

We can conclude that the *Astadhyayi* is a very sophisticated grammar, and that to operate its grammatical machine, we have to understand it at multiple levels. What would an early grammarian or linguist have done in order to interpret the *Astadhyayi* independently? With negligible access to any commentary on the text, and with limited or no guidance of a teacher well-versed in the *Astadhyayi*, a scholar would have taken notes for himself in order to comprehend, analyze and corroborate the teachings of the *Astadhyayi*. He would have started by paraphrasing the contents of the *Astadhyayi* to establish what they exactly mean, both independently and in the context of the preceding rules.

To ensure that he had understood such a complex grammar correctly, or to confirm that the grammar accurately describes the structure of the language, a scholar would have tried to verify the validity and accuracy of different rules against spoken language or attested literature. He would have gradually developed his own ideas about where rules should apply, and how derivations should proceed. He would have noticed how rules interact among themselves and would have come up with ways to classify and deal with such interactions. He would also have suggested certain changes to these rules to make them more precise, to help them better characterize their object language, and/or to help them function more consistently with other rules within the Paninian system.

This is presumably what happened in the Indian grammatical tradition when Katyayana understood the meanings and functions of Paninian rules on the basis of his independent study of the *Astadhyayi*.[3] Then as a teacher, he also taught them to his pupils—using his notes on the *Astadhyayi* as pedagogical aid. His students taught the *Astadhyayi* to their students using Katyayana's work and also commented on Katyayana's writings, thereby sharing their own opinions, interpretations, and analyzes with their students and readers. Successive generations participated in this process of knowledge processing, production, and transmission, thereby giving birth to the Paninian grammatical tradition.

The texts of the Paninian grammatical tradition have played a dominant role in influencing and shaping our understanding of, and opinions about the *Astadhyayi*. They also give us significant insights into the evolution of different ideas in the Paninian tradition. Below I introduce the texts that I shall refer to in the rest of the article and briefly discuss the history of the Paninian tradition with special reference to 'metarules', which, as the name suggests, help us understand the 'eta' aspects, i.e., the overall functioning of Panini's grammar.

6.3 Metarules in the Paninian Grammatical Tradition

Early grammatical thought in the Indian subcontinent, as represented by the works called *Pratisakhya*s, was intended to assist the recitation of Vedas by explaining the pronunciation of accents and dissolution of *sandhi*s. Their objective was merely descriptive, that is, to make grammatical observations and offer clarifications where necessary. But a number of independent and full-fledged grammars emerged subsequently which sought to 'derive' language rather than simply 'describe' it: they built mechanistic systems which perform various operations on bases and affixes in order to produce correct word forms and, using these fully derived words, to construct meaningful sentences.

While Panini himself mentions many of his predecessors in his *sutra*s, his work, the *Astadhyayi*, remains the oldest surviving derivational grammar of Sanskrit. Composing such a grammar required Panini to meticulously design every aspect of the derivational procedure, which explains why Panini made significant efforts in formulating his *paribhasa sutra*s 'metarules'. These metarules play a pivotal role in the correct interpretation and application of *vidhi sutra*s 'operation rules' at every

[3] I think that there was a break in the transmission of the *Astadhyayi* between Panini and Katyayana, since Katyayana seems to be in the process of understanding the *Astadhyayi* without much help from anyone else. To the extent possible, I will dwell on this topic later in this article.

step of the derivation, thereby ensuring that the derivational machine produces the grammatically correct output.

Given the *Astadhyayi*'s remarkable exhaustiveness and accuracy, it is not surprising that Katyayana, around 250 BC (Cardona, 1976: 267–268), undertook a systematic analysis of what must have been for him, just like it is for us, an unprecedented and extraordinary treatise. Katyayana recorded his thoughts and findings in the form of *varttika*s, which are short statements seeking to explain, examine, criticize, and sometimes integrate Panini's rules with additions. Without overlooking the more specific and individual aspects of the grammar, Katyayana sought to develop a broad perspective about the functioning of the *Astadhyayi* as an integrated machine. This involved interpreting the metarules of Panini's grammar, providing examples and counterexamples to determine their verity, and composing new metarules to help the Paninian system run even more smoothly.

Around 150 BC, Patanjali wrote the *Mahabhasya*, which is a commentary on Katyayana's *varttika*s.[4] It records the arguments and counterarguments that must have transpired between Patanjali and his pupils about the contents of the *varttika*s. Patanjali too approached the *Astadhyayi* with his independent perspective about its derivational system, and skilfully wove Katyayana's *varttika*s into his own presentation of and narrative about the Paninian machine. In doing so, he both established his independent interpretation of Panini's and Katyayana's metarules and wrote new metarules to afford us greater clarity about the *Astadhyayi*'s derivational procedure.

In the course of time, some Paniniyas[5] took it upon themselves to compile and comment on all such metarules from Patanjali's *Mahabhasya*. They also came up with new metarules to fill the knowledge gaps that they thought existed in the tradition. They came to be known as *paribhasakara*s 'authors of *paribhasa*s', and the literature composed by them, as *paribhasa* literature. *Paribhasa* texts have been written over many centuries—from around (or soon after) Patanjali's time, if not before him, to the eighteenth century (Abhyankar, 1967: 12). Among the *paribhasa* texts of the Paninian tradition, the most popularly studied, quoted, and commented upon in modern times is the relatively recent *Paribhasendusekhara* of Nagesa Bhatta, which was written in the eighteenth century.

A rich tradition of *paribhasa* literature has long existed in other schools of Sanskrit grammar too (e.g., *Katantra, Haima, Candra*).[6] Both Paninian and non-Paninian *paribhasakara*s were especially interested in certain topics, for example, rule conflict. In Nagesa's work, the section containing *paribhasa*s 38–70 deals exclusively with rule conflict and is thus called *badhabija* (Abhyankar, 1967: 12). Similarly, in the *Katantra* system, *paribhasa sutra*s are actually divided into *balabala sutra*s 'metarules dealing with comparison of rule strength' and others which do

[4] The two major commentaries on the *Mahabhasya* are the *Pradipa* of Kaiyata and the *Uddyota* of Nagesa.

[5] This term is used to refer to any traditional scholar who has directly or indirectly commented on or written about Panini's grammar.

[6] K. V. Abhyankar has edited and compiled many Paninian and non-Paninian *paribhasa* treatises in his *Paribhasasamgraha* (1967).

not deal with this topic (Abhyankar, 1967: 3). A significant exchange of ideas took place between Paninian and non-Paninian traditions due to mutual borrowing of *paribhasas*, including, especially, those on rule conflict.

Circa seventh century AD, Jayaditya and Vamana wrote the *Kasika*, which consists of *vrttis* on each rule. A *vrtti* paraphrases the rule, underscores metarules that help us correctly apply that rule, gives examples of its application, and justifies the existence of each word of that rule. *Vrttis* borrow a significant proportion of their contents from Patanjali's *Mahabhasya*. They are unique in that they do not comprise new metarules, yet by quoting some metarules from Patanjali's *Mahabhasya* and ignoring others, they present an evolved perspective about the mechanistic aspects of Paninian derivations—often quite different from Patanjali's.

Lastly, let us talk about *kaumudi* texts, which explicitly envision the *Astadhyayi* as a grammatical machine. The *kaumudi* tradition which began in the fifteenth century with Ramacandra's *Prakriyakaumudi*, reorders the *sutras* of the *Astadhyayi* to reflect their derivational roles: in any *Kaumudi* text, a rule is introduced when the first derivation involving it is taught. The *Kaumudi* texts first introduce *samjna sutras* 'rules that give certain items specific terminological designations' and *paribhasa sutras* 'metarules', then teach *sandhi* 'phonological combination' rules, then introduce nominal and verbal inflections in the order in which forms appear in paradigms, and then teach derivatives and compounds. The most celebrated text in this genre is Bhattoji Diksita's *Siddhantakaumudi* written in the seventeenth century. By reordering the *Astadhyayi*'s rules, the *Kaumudi* not only gives us a glimpse of how Panini's derivational mechanism actually works, but also tells us which metarules apply where, and how these metarules enable us to perform derivations uniformly.

Even though the traditional texts discussed above broadly agree on most derivational technicalities, they present different perspectives on the nature and characteristics of the machine.

6.4 Modern Perspectives on the Functioning of the *Astadhyayi*

Before we explore how modern scholarship perceives the *Astadhyayi*, let us very briefly consider what the tradition, and more specifically Katyayana and Patanjali say, about the meaning and purpose of *vyakarana* 'grammar'. In vt. 14 of the *Paspasahnika*,[7] Katyayana says: *lakṣyalakṣaṇe vyākaraṇam* 'grammar (stands for the combination of) *lakṣya*, i.e., words (and sentences)' and *lakṣaṇa* 'rules'. This is true of any grammar, not just the *Astadhyayi*. But does the *Astadhyayi* have certain mechanistic properties which set it apart from conventional grammars? Below we will look at modern perspectives on this topic. According to Patanjali (Mbh I.1.14), *vyakarana* serves the following purposes: *rakṣohāgamalaghvasandehāḥ* "*rakṣā* 'protection of

[7] Mbh I.12.15. Note that Mbh I.12.15 stands for Volume I of *Mahabhasya* edited by Kielhorn, page number 12, line number 15.

the Vedas', *ūha* 'adapting inflected forms in Vedic mantras as required during rituals', *āgama* 'following Vedic injunctions', *laghu* 'brevity, i.e., ease of learning the language', and *asandeha* 'resolution of doubts'". These certainly are some of the factors that must have motivated Panini to write his grammar. But was Panini also aiming to build a somewhat mechanistic model for deriving Sanskrit words (and subsequently, sentences)? Let us look at what modern scholarship tells us about topics like rule conflict and order of rule application in Paninian derivations, and therefore, about the status of the *Astadhyayi* as a 'machine'.

Let us start by looking at Bronkhorst's work on this topic. Bronkhorst (2004) shows that Patanjali prefers a linear reading of the *Astadhyayi*, that is, Patanjali believes that in order to decide which rule should apply at any step in a derivation, one need not know the outcomes of previous or following steps. He says, "It is clear from the above that Patanjali tries both to avoid looking back and looking ahead in explaining grammatical derivations" (Bronkhorst, 2004: 37). He writes: "According to the traditional view, decisions concerning the continuation of a grammatical derivation at any particular point are taken on the basis of the situation at hand. More specifically, no information about the earlier or later phases of the derivation is required to make a correct decision at any stage". Bronkhorst states that he is unconvinced by Patanjali's evidence suggesting that the *Astadhyayi* functions linearly. He thinks that Panini did not intend for the *Astadhyayi* to be approached linearly, and attempts to establish that at least for some derivations, the knowledge of the derivation's history and/or its future course is essential to select the right rule at a given step (Bronkhorst, 2004: 6).

One of the reasons Bronkhorst thinks looking ahead into the derivation is required is to determine the order in which two rules should apply with respect to each other (Bronkhorst, 2004: 16–17). Roodbergen has a different opinion on this subject (Roodbergen, 1991: 313). He recommends some changes to the traditional order in which certain processes occur. So, while Roodbergen does believe in reading the *Astadhyayi* linearly, he disagrees, to some extent, with the tradition's order of rule application. And he thinks that this topic is not related to rule conflict and its resolution: 'This ordering principle has nothing to do with a feeding relation between rules in which the application of one rule is made dependent on the effect of the application of another rule. It has nothing to do either, with the question of conflict of rules. To solve a conflict, other principles apply…'.

Scholars working on rule conflict have peripherally addressed the topic of linearity. Cardona says that 'the derivational prehistory of a form is pertinent to the operations which apply to it' (Cardona, 1970: 41). Joshi and Kiparsky think that it is important to look ahead into a derivation. They propose the extended *siddha* principle which they claim governs Paninian derivations and which 'scans entire candidate derivations…' (Joshi & Kiparsky, 2005: 7) thanks to its 'global (trans-derivational) "lookahead" condition on derivations' '…and chooses the one in which *siddha*-relations (bleeding and feeding)[8] are maximized'. So, both Cardona and Joshi & Kiparsky, do not support an exclusively linear reading of the *Astadhyayi*.

According to Houben, 'a comparison between Panini's grammar and "a machine" may be useful in demonstrating some of the features and procedures it incorporates, but the comparison has now and then been carried too far' (Houben, 2003: 50). He continues: 'in fact, in the practice of Paniniyas through the ages up to the present, no-one can ever have produced a correct form through Panini's system that was not already his starting point, or among his starting options ... the system is therefore not well characterized as "synthetic", even if synthetic procedures are central and most visible; rather the system is to be called "reconstitutive"—which implies the presence of a user, a preliminary statement, and the application of both analytic and synthetic procedures to the words in it ... aiming at the best possible, *saṁskr̥ta* form of his preliminary statement' (Houben, 2003: 53). He attributes the reception of Paninian grammar as a machine to Bhattoji Diksita's *Siddhantakaumudi* and Nagesa's *Paribhasendusekhara*: 'in order to provide the desired solid authoritative basis to Sanskrit grammar it was moreover necessary to posit it as a closed system of rules and metarules—something it had never been in a true sense of this term for around two millennia, although Katyayana's and Patanjali's investigations on selected *sutra*s had prepared the ground for such an approach. The culmination in this trend came only a few generations later with Nagesa Bhatta's *Paribhasendusekhara*...' (Houben, 2015: 6).

Let us summarize what we have surveyed so far. Houben is not in favor of perceiving the *Astadhyayi* as a derivational machine, thereby also implicitly dismissing both the concept of linearity and consistent conflict resolution procedures. Roodbergen believes that the *Astadhyayi* is a derivational machine, and proposes his own version of a linear reading of the *Astadhyayi*. Roodbergen also argues that the order of rule application and resolution of rule conflict are not related or associated with each other. Bronkhorst claims that the existence of *paribhasa* 38 of the *Paribhasendusekhara*, which creates a hierarchy of conflict resolution tools (in addition to Patanjali's statements), indicates that the tradition prefers a linear reading of the *Astadhyayi*. In doing so, Bronkhorst establishes a correlation between consistent rule conflict resolution procedures and a linear reading of the *Astadhyayi*. Bronkhorst rejects the linear approach. On the other hand, Joshi & Kiparsky, and Cardona seem to think that their rejection of a strictly linear reading of the *Astadhyayi* does not substantially undermine the mechanistic prowess of the Paninian system and devote much of their scholarly attention to solving rule conflict.

We have seen what the existing literature on the subject says about the functioning of the *Astadhyayi*. But to fully understand the reception of the *Astadhyayi* as a grammatical machine, we have to focus on the topic rule conflict, which as stated before, can broadly be described as the situation in which two or more rules become simultaneously applicable at any given step of a Paninian derivation, leaving us

[8] The contents in brackets have been added by me. Rule A bleeds rule B if B, which was applicable before the application of A, is no longer applicable after the application of A. A feeds B, if B, which was not applicable before the application of A, becomes applicable after the application of A.

wondering which one of these rules should be applied at that step. Let me explain why.

When we think of a machine, we think of an apparatus which, upon being fed a certain input, follows a predetermined procedure consistently and delivers the desired output—whatever that might be. Therefore, if Panini's grammar has to pass muster as a machine, it must be able to resolve conflicts using the same algorithm every time it constructs a word, while also being able to supply grammatically correct forms as outputs at the end of the derivation. At each step, decision-making should rely exclusively on the algorithm, and not on what is likely to happen next or what happened earlier. We have discussed this above in the context of linearity (the absence of 'looking back' and 'looking ahead' into the derivation), so I will not belabor this point.

Before we delve into the topic of rule conflict, let me make my position clear. In my doctoral thesis (Rajpopat, 2022), I have concluded that Panini did intend for the *Astadhyayi* to be interpreted linearly and as a closed grammatical machine. I will expound on this, to the extent possible, later in this article. But first, let us examine what Panini says about rule conflict and how traditional scholarship has interpreted his instruction(s).

6.5 Panini and the Paniniyas on Rule Conflict

Panini has taught us only one metarule, namely 1.4.2 *vipratiṣedhe paraṁ kāryam*, to tackle the issue of rule conflict. The tradition interprets it as follows: 'In the event of a conflict between two rules of equal strength (in Sanskrit: *tulyabala*), the rule that comes later in the serial order of the *Astadhyayi* must be chosen'. What does equal strength mean though? Before we look at how the traditional answers this question, note that Panini has not mentioned any such thing as equal—or unequal—strength in his grammar, and this concept is clearly a post-Paninian invention.

Coming back to the question, which pairs of rules should be called *tulyabala* 'of equal strength'? The tradition's answer is: 'those pairs which are not of unequal strength'. This begs the question: how do we define 'pairs of unequal strength'? The tradition answers this question by inventing multiple new concepts (such as *nitya-anitya*, *antaranga-bahiranga*, *niravakasa-savakasa*) of which we find absolutely no mention in Panini's *Astadhyayi*. The tradition says that:

(1) if one rule is *nitya* ('applicable both before and after the application of the other rule') and the other *anitya* ('not applicable after the application of the other rule'), then the *nitya* rule is stronger (and thus wins). Since these two rules are not equally strong, the conflict between them cannot be resolved using 1.4.2, which deals only with conflicts between rules of equal strength.
(2) if one rule is *antaranga* (defined in a complex way; means 'relatively internal') and the other *bahiranga* (defined in a complex way; 'means relatively external'), then the *antaranga* rule is stronger (and thus wins). Since these two rules are

not equally strong, the conflict between them cannot be resolved using 1.4.2, which deals only with conflicts between rules of equal strength.

(3) if one rule is *niravakasa* (does not apply in any other derivation) and the other *savakasa* (applies in at least one other derivation), then the *niravakasa* rule is stronger and thus wins. Since these two rules are not equally strong, the conflict between them cannot be resolved using 1.4.2, which deals only with conflicts between rules of equal strength.

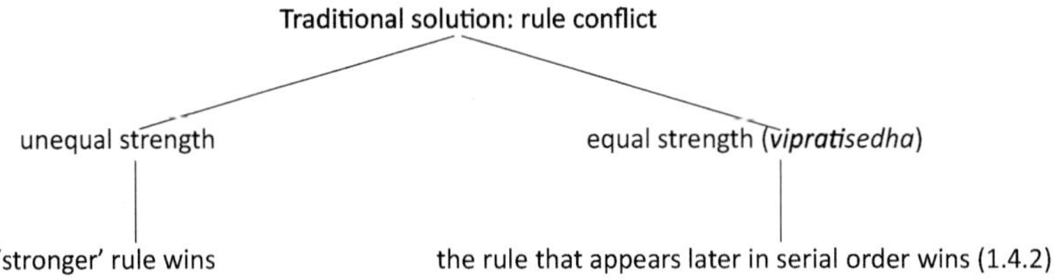

We will not delve into the details. It should suffice to mention that the tradition has also created a hierarchy of preferences for the aforementioned tools. However, these arrangements too often fail to ensure the derivation of grammatically correct forms. Thus, the tradition has written numerous additional metarules to add exceptions to, qualify, restrict, or extrapolate the scope of the aforementioned statements. In sum, this has culminated into a complex system of norms and exceptions which is incredibly difficult to use or navigate.

Below, I present an abridged version of how I think the current method of solving rule conflict has gradually evolved. Having realized that treating all rule conflicts as *vipratisedha* and applying 1.4.2 uniformly to every instance of such a conflict gives the grammatically incorrect form in many cases, the Paniniyas:

(1) claimed that they found *jnapaka*s 'hints or clues' in Panini's *sutra*s which authorized them to devise new tools like *nitya*, *antaranga*, *niravakasa*, etc., for the purpose of solving rule conflicts;
(2) restricted the jurisdiction of rule 1.4.2 by declaring that *vipratisedha* implies only *tulyabala* conflicts, i.e., conflicts between two equally strong rules; and
(3) declared that rule pairs like *nitya-anitya*, *antaranga-bahiranga*, and *niravakasa-savakasa* were to be called *atulyabala* 'not equally strong'.

This allowed them to exclude the *atulyabala* 'not equally strong' rule pairs, namely *nitya-anitya, antaranga-bahiranga,* etc., from the jurisdiction of 1.4.2, thereby containing the problems caused by their interpretation of 1.4.2 to a smaller number of cases.

However, as stated above, these post-Paninian tools are not without flaws, to compensate for which umpteen other metarules have been written by Paniniyas. Many of these metarules address very specific cases[9] or even single examples of

[9] For example, consider Pbh 52 of the *Paribhasendusekhara*, *antaraṅgān api vidhīn bahiraṅgo lug bādhate* 'A *bahiranga* rule teaching *LUK* deletion defeats an *antaranga* rule [in case of conflict]', which is an exception of Pbh 50 *antaraṅge bahirangam asiddham* 'An *antaranga* rule treats a *bahiranga* rule as suspended.'.

conflict, thereby defeating the entire purpose of writing metarules, which is to arrive at broad generalizations that can govern the application of and interactions within the whole body of rules. And even after this, the Paniniyas are not able to solve every case of conflict correctly: every time they falter, they find one tortuous explanation or the other to justify that 'exception'.

I do not accept this interpretation of the Paninian system. However, I do not think that all the metarules taught by the Paniniyas should be rejected. Many post-Paninian metarules accurately capture how the Paninian machine functions and thus are of great importance to us. They are mostly descriptive in nature and make insightful observations about the *Astadhyayi*. However, we also find post-Paninian metarules that teach us tools for rule conflict resolution, such as *nitya* and *antaranga*, which Panini would certainly not have left unstated if he actually wanted to teach them, and which impose post-Paninian ideas onto the *Astadhyayi*. Thus, the validity of this set of metarules is questionable.

6.6 Philosophy of the Discipline

The traditional system of performing Paninian derivations is wrought with intractable problems, some of which I have underscored above. Let us now consider two broad questions that have to do with the philosophy of Paninian linguistics as a discipline in its own right.

The first question that we ought to consider is: what should constitute the epistemological foundation of any inquiry into Panini's derivational system? Should we accept the answers, explanations, and logical frameworks, offered by Panini's *sutras*, Katyayana's *varttikas*, Patanjali's *bhasya*, the *Kasikavrtti*, *paribhasa* literature, etc., as the tradition does, or should we rely exclusively on those offered by Panini's *sutras* and treat the rest merely as supplementary and confirmatory sources of information—as I prefer to do? Put differently, can so many distinct sources of information, all written with different goals and centuries apart, and which often contradict each other, contribute toward the running of the same grammatical machine? I think not.

Another important question that ought to be asked is: is it acceptable to modify Panini's ontological infrastructure—as the tradition does by introducing new categories like *nitya*, *antaranga*, *niravakasa*, *purvavipratisedha*, etc.? If there are no qualitative or quantitative limits on the introduction of such post-Paninian categories—as is the case within the Paninian tradition—what yardstick can be employed to ascertain the correctness of our understanding of Panini's grammar? In fact, how can we ever establish the truth while taking such creative liberties? As I will discuss below, I try to rely solely on Panini's own concepts and categories and choose not to take the sorts of liberties that the tradition does in this respect.

In my doctoral thesis, to get instructions about dealing with rule conflict, I try to rely, as much as possible, upon 'internal metarules', that is, those metarules which Panini has taught in his work, setting aside any 'external metarules', that is, those metarules that are not found in the *Astadhyayi*, such as *nitya*, *antaranga*, post-Paninian *paribhasas* from various texts, etc. In my thesis, I have come up with my own interpretation of the rule 1.4.2 *vipratiṣedhe paraṁ kāryam* and, using that, I have reinterpreted Panini's derivational mechanism. I have attempted to show that Panini's grammatical machine is self-sufficient, that is, its own (internal) metarules, are able to run it with remarkable perfection, and that no external metarules are able or required to aid this process.

6.7 My Interpretation of the Paninian System

As stated above, in my doctoral thesis, I offer a completely new interpretation of Panini's rule 1.4.2 *vipratiṣedhe paraṁ kāryam*, and thereby a novel method of resolving rule conflicts in Panini's grammar—one which allows us to perceive it as a machine.

We have seen that the tradition interprets 1.4.2 as follows: in the event of a conflict between two rules of equal strength (in Sanskrit: *tulyabala*), the rule that comes later in the serial order of the *Astadhyayi* must be chosen. Here, the operative phrase is '*paraṁ kāryam*'. One meaning of *para* in Sanskrit is 'that which comes after (the other)'. However, one is bound to ask: in what context? The tradition assumes that *paraṁ kāryam* means 'that rule which comes after the other in the serial order of Panini's rules.' However, in my thesis, I argue that it means 'that operation which comes after the other going from left to right' (i.e., 'the rule applicable to the right-hand-side item'; see diagram below). I supply ample philological evidence to support my claims: I show that in every other rule of his grammar, when Panini uses the term *para* for technical purposes, he means 'that which comes after the other going from left to right'. Similarly, I show that when he uses *pūrva*, which is the antonym of *para*, in a technical way, he means, 'that which comes before the other going from left to right'. I interpret the term *vipratiṣedha* as any rule conflict wherein two rules are simultaneously applicable to two different items respectively, one to the left and the other to its relative right. In my thesis, I also explain the possible reason behind the tradition's misunderstanding of the term *para* in 1.4.2, but we will not discuss those details here.

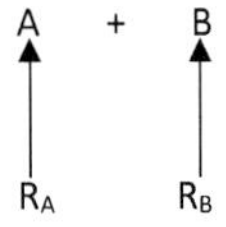

On the other hand, I argue that when two rules are simultaneously applicable to the same item (see diagram below), the rule that is more specific constitutes the exception and defeats the general rule. Although Panini does not say anything explicit about this, I argue that he does not do so for good reason: the general-exception framework is inherent to the *sutra* style of textual composition in classical Indian traditions including *vyakarana, nyaya, mimamsa,* etc. so it is not surprising that Panini did not deem it necessary to make any statement to that effect. I provide derivational evidence to support all the aforementioned claims and show that Panini's grammar is self-sufficient and does actually function like a linguistic machine.

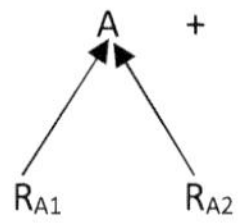

6.8 A Summary of Post-Paninian Ideas on 1.4.2

Through the *varttikas* of Katyayana, who as stated above, was the first known scholar to comment on Panini's grammar, we know that he interprets *para* in 1.4.2 *vipratiṣedhe paraṁ kāryam* as 'the rule which comes later in the *Astadhyayi's* serial order'. And this is not the only incorrect conclusion drawn by Katyayana about Panini's grammar.

But I think that it is unwarranted to look for 'correct' statements in the *varttikas*. This is because, in my opinion, Katyayana's *varttikas* are often a medium for him to share all kinds of thoughts with fellow grammarians—not just the 'correct' ones. Very often, we find him use *na vā* 'or rather not' and *ca* 'and' in a series of consecutive *varttikas* to discuss alternative or even contradicting possibilities and explanations.

This style of discussing multiple possibilities without striving to always be correct, is very much akin to Patanjali's style, which also involves a discussion about the pros and cons of various perspectives. In both Katyayana's and Patanjali's work, we find no rigidity or urgency to establish the truth. Instead, their work is characterized by curiosity and a willingness to critically examine a motley of ideas.

Coming back to the topic of *para*, although the aforementioned interpretation of *para* taught by Katyayana has been fully endorsed and internalized by the later tradition, most traditional and modern scholars have almost entirely overlooked a very important idea about *para* that we find in a *varttika* on 6.1.158 *anudāttaṁ padam ekavarjam.* Katyayana says, in vt. 12 (Mbh III.100.12): *śāstra-paravipratiṣedhāniyamād vā śabdaparavipratiṣedhāt siddham* '[in the event of *vipratiṣedha* between two operations] because it has not been [explicitly] mandated that *paratva* of rules [alone should be used to resolve] *vipratiṣedha,* alternatively *paratva* of sounds [may also be used to] accomplish [the task of resolving] *vipratiṣedha*'. In other words, here, Katyayana suggests that alongside inferring that the rule that is *para,* i.e., that comes later in the serial order of the *Astadhyayi* wins, we may also infer that the operation that is applicable to the *para,* i.e., right hand side (henceforth RHS) sound or group of sounds wins.

This shows that Katyayana was either exposed to or himself thought about the possibility that *para* in 1.4.2 could stand for the RHS operation. If he had chosen to further develop this line of thought, this idea could potentially have reached its logical conclusion, namely the correct interpretation of 1.4.2. One could argue that, by choosing to focus on and subsequently by accepting the wrong interpretation from among the two possible interpretations of *para* discussed in the aforementioned *varttika*, Katyayana completely changed the developmental trajectory of the Paninian tradition. Katyayana's successors too failed to recognize the sheer potential of this *varttika*, and thus the key to the *Astadhyayi*'s algorithm remained before everyone's eyes and yet hidden from everyone's mind.

One key repercussion of Katyayana's belief that *para* in 1.4.2 stands for 'the rule that comes later in the *Astadhyayi*'s serial order' must have been that he likely got numerous incorrect forms at the end of derivations where he solved conflicts using his interpretation of 1.4.2. Perhaps it is to avoid these undesirable outcomes—wherever possible—that he decided to reduce the jurisdiction of 1.4.2, as I have already highlighted above. For example, in vt. 1 on 1.4.2, he defines *vipratiṣedha* in a way that allows him to exclude *niravakasa-savakasa* pairs from the jurisdiction of 1.4.2: *dvau prasaṅgāv anyārthāv ekasmin sa vipratiṣedhaḥ* (1) (Mbh I.304.10–305.3) '[When] two rules [which are] applicable elsewhere [become applicable] to the same place, this [is called] *vipratiṣedha*'. We have already looked at this earlier so we will not discuss this in detail here.

But even after making such changes, solving conflicts using 1.4.2 led to an incorrect answer at the end of the derivation. Thus, Katyayana wrote what are called the *purvavipratisiddha varttika*s. By using the expression '*purvavipratisiddha*', Katyayana points out that instead of the rule that comes later in the Astadhyayi's serial order, which should win as per his interpretation of 1.4.2 *vipratiṣedhe paraṁ kāryam*, it is the rule that comes earlier in the *Astadhyayi*'s serial order that emerges victorious.

Commenting on most *purvavipratisiddha varttika*s, Patanjali says that they are not required at all. He gives various reasons for this, of which the following one is used by him on multiple occasions. On vt. 10 on 7.1.96 stated above, he says: *na vaktavyaḥ. iṣṭavācī paraśabdaḥ. vipratiṣedhe paraṁ yad iṣṭaṁ tad bhavati* '[This] should not be said. The word *para* means desirable. In [the event of] *vipratiṣedha*, the *para*, i.e., desirable [rule] applies.' It is evident that in this context Patanjali tries to defend 1.4.2 against Katyayana's criticism. In fact, this is anything but an isolated instance: scholars like Goldstücker (1861: 119–121) and Weber (1872: 297–298) were among the earliest modern scholars to argue that Katyayana was severely critical of Panini's *sutra*s, and that Patanjali invested significant effort in countering such negative remarks. While many scholars, starting with Kielhorn, have presented rebuttals to this, even Kielhorn (1876: 50) cannot deny "that Patanjali has refuted some of the (i.e., Katyayana's)[10] objections, that he has rejected some of the additional rules of Katyayana".

I would argue that by hurrying to dismiss Katyayana's *purvavipratisiddha varttika*s using a rather feeble argument, namely that *para* means desirable, Patanjali missed the opportunity to discover the truth of 1.4.2. Instead, if he had accepted Katyayana's statement as valid and had pondered over the cause of this phenomenon, he could possibly have realized that Katyayana's interpretation of *para* itself was

[10] The contents in round brackets have been added by me to Kielhorn's quote.

incorrect, and that it was this misinterpretation which had led him to write the *purvavipratisiddha varttika*s. This would certainly have been a far superior defense of Panini's rule 1.4.2 against Katyayana's criticism than the one mounted by Patanjali.

The relationships between concepts like *tulyabala*, *vipratisedha*, *nitya*, *antaranga*, *para*, etc. were fully and concretely established by the twelfth century. Alongside the metarules teaching of these tools, dozens of metarules teaching exceptions to these tools were also written by later scholars. On this account, given its unwieldy and complicated nature, the traditional solution completely fails the Occam's razor test. Additionally, the flexibility of ideas, free thinking, and willingness to consider a wide variety of possibilities and alternatives, which, as stated earlier, are so characteristic of the early tradition, i.e., Katyayana's and Patanjali's work, came to be replaced by a willing acceptance of rigid, ossified, established, and widely-accepted 'facts' and 'truths' in the later tradition—in particular, in *paribhasa* literature. It is noteworthy that many of these metarules are *anitya* 'not always, i.e., consistently applicable' by the tradition's own admission!

Here, one may ask: why do the *Kasika* and the *paribhasa* texts not question the correctness of Katyayana's interpretation of the term *para* in 1.4.2? I think the first broad reason is that, along with Panini, who composed the foundational treatise of the tradition, Katyayana and Patanjali too came to be worshiped in the tradition, which might have made it almost unthinkable for subsequent scholars to disagree with Katyayana or Patanjali over such fundamental aspects of the grammar as the meaning of *para* in 1.4.2.[11] It must be noted that even though the *Kasika* does present an alternative viewpoint to that of the *Mahabhasya* on many occasions, it completely embraces Patanjali's ideas on this subject. Secondly, even among the three *muni*s, Patanjali's word superseded Katyayana's and Katyayana's word superseded Panini's, right from the time of Kaiyaṭa, who famously stated: *yathottaraṁ hi munitrayasya prāmāṇyam* 'Among the three *muni*s, the authority of later *muni* supersedes that of his predecessor(s)'.[12] Thus, Patanjali became the most important person in the tradition, surpassing Panini himself, whose work he had set out to expound on. So, hypothetically speaking, even if a traditional scholar had discovered that Patanjali had misinterpreted *para* in 1.4.2, he would have preferred Patanjali's interpretation to what Panini actually intended to say in all likelihood!

One would have expected the tradition to start paying ever closer attention to the topic of rule conflict with the writing of the *Kaumudi* texts, the main goal of which was to teach students how to perform derivations. To achieve this goal, the *Kaumudi* texts took the radical decision to reorder the rules of the *Astadhyayi* so that a rule would be taught in the *Kaumudi* only when it applied at some step in a certain derivation. However, unfortunately, these texts did not challenge the existing interpretation of *para* in 1.4.2 and, like previous texts, performed derivations using the traditional tools for conflict resolution. In fact, not only did the *Kaumudi* texts fail to discover the correct meaning of 1.4.2, but they also unwittingly ensured that coming generations would not decipher the same.

[11] Deshpande (1998, 2019) discusses this topic in great detail.

[12] See *Pradīpa* on *Mahabhasya* on 1.1.29.

They did this by shifting the focus of the tradition from the comprehensive functioning of the Paninian machine to the many individual products of the machine, namely, individual derivations of various forms. Over time, students of the *Kaumudi* got so familiar with these derivations that now, they do not have to and, consequently, do not, stop at most steps of the derivation to ask themselves: which rules are applicable at this step? Which of these rules should I apply? And why? And if pupils do apply conflict resolution tools of their own accord and end up getting the wrong form, they are not encouraged by their teachers to ask why. Instead, they are advised to consult the *Kaumudi* texts to 'correct' themselves, i.e., to memorize the explanation offered by their authors.

This chain of accepting what previous scholars have said was finally broken by many modern Indologists, including Houben (2003), who asked if Panini's grammar is meant to function like a machine at all, and Bronkhorst (2004) who questioned the 'linearity' of Paninian derivations. Others have tried to make changes in some parts of the traditional conflict resolution mechanism.

Even though none of these scholars have been able to offer a radically different interpretation of 1.4.2, their willingness to ask questions, propose new ideas, and challenge the traditional method of conflict resolution inspired me to do the same, eventually leading me to the interpretation of 1.4.2 I have presented in my doctoral thesis.

I remain hopeful that my doctoral work will open doors for further exploration of Panini's brilliantly devised grammatical system and continue the long tradition of critical thinking and spirited, informed debate among scholars of the Indian grammatical tradition.

6.9 Conclusion

In this paper, I have shown that we face multiple challenges in understanding not just individual rules taught by Panini but also the functioning of his grammar as a whole. I have argued that contrary to established belief, Katyayana, the first known author to comment on this grammar, too may have faced some of these very challenges that we do. Having discussed both traditional and modern interpretations of one of Panini's key rules—which significantly impacts the workings of his grammar—I have argued for a completely new interpretation of this rule, and therefore, of Panini's grammatical system. I have drawn attention to the fact that the philosophical underpinnings of this discipline have a substantial bearing on the outcomes of our research endeavors. I hope to have demonstrated through these discussions that studying the reception and interpretation of Panini's grammar over the centuries affords us brilliant insights into our rich and fascinating intellectual past.

References

Primary Sources

Astadhyayi (Panini): Dīkṣita, P. (ed.). (2010). *MaharṣiPaninipraṇītaḥ Astadhyayisutrapāṭhaḥ.* Saṁskr̥ta Bhāratī.

Kasikavr̥tti(Jayāditya & Vāmana): Sharma, A., & Deshpande, K. (eds.). (1996). *Kasika: A commentary on Panini's grammar (Part 1 and 2).* Sanskrit Academy, Osmania University.

Laghusiddhāntakaumudi (Varadarājācārya): *Laghusiddhāntakaumudi.* Gītāpresa Gorakhapura.

Mahabhasya (Patanjali):

(1) Kielhorn, F. (ed.). (1880–1885). *The Vyākaraṇa-Mahabhasya of Patanjali* (Vols. I–III). Government Central Book Depot.

(2) Śāstrī, B., et al. (eds.). (1987–1988). *VyākaraṇaMahabhasya with Bhāṣyapradīpa and Bhāṣyapradīpoddyota* (Vols. 1–6). Caukhambā Saṁskr̥ta Pratiṣṭhāna [Reprint of Nirṇaya Sāgara Press Edition].

Paribhasendusekhara (Nagesa): Abhyankar, K.V. (ed.). (1962). *The Paribhasendusekhara of NāgojīBhatta (with the commentary Tattvādarśa of MM. Vasudev Shastri Abhyankar) Part I.* Bhandarkar Oriental Research Institute.

Pradīpa (Kaiyaṭa): see *Mahabhasya* (2).

Siddhāntakaumudi (Bhattoji Diksita): *Vaiyākaraṇa-siddhāntakaumudi with Bālamanoramā and Tattvabodhinī, 4 vols.* (2006). Motilal Banarsidass.

Uddyota (Nagesa): see *Mahabhasya* (2).

Secondary Sources

Abhyankar, K. V. (ed.). (1967). *Paribhasasaṁgraha (a collection of original works on Vyākaraṇa Paribhasas).* Bhandarkar Oriental Research Institute.

Bronkhorst, J. (2004). *From Panini to Patanjali: The search for linearity.* Bhandarkar Oriental Research Institute.

Cardona, G. (1970). Some principles of Panini's grammar. *Journal of Indian Philosophy, 1*(1), 40–74.

Cardona, G. (1976). *Panini: A survey of research.* Mouton.

Deshpande, M. (1998). Evolution of the notion of authority (Prāmāṇya) in the Paninian tradition. *Histoire Epistemologie Language, 20*(1), 5–28.

Deshpande, M. (2019). *From Panini to Patanjali and beyond: Development of Religious Motifs in Sanskrit Grammar (26th J. Gonda Lecture 2018).* Royal Netherlands Academy of Arts and Sciences.

Goldstücker, T. (1861). *Panini: His Place in Sanskrit Literature.* N. Trübner and Co.

Houben, J. (2003). Three myths in Modern Paninian studies. *Asiatische Studien/Études Asiatiques, 57*(1), 121–179.

Houben, J. (2015). Paninian grammar of living Sanskrit: Features and principles of the Prakriyā Sarvasva of Nārāyaṇa-Bhatta of Melputtūr. *Bulletin D'études Indiennes, 32*, 149–170.

Joshi, S. D., & Kiparsky, P. (2005). The extended Siddha-principle. *Annals of the Bhandarkar Oriental Research Institute, 86*, 1–26.

Kielhorn, F. (1876). *Katyayana and Patanjali: Their relation to each other, and to Panini* [Printed at The Education Society's Press, Byculla].

Rajpopat, R. A. (2022). *Panini we trust: Discovering the algorithm for rule conflict resolution in the Astadhyayi.* Ph.D., thesis, University of Cambridge. https://doi.org/10.17863/CAM.80099

Roodbergen, J. A. F. (1991). Time for a little something. In M. Deshpande, & S. Bhate (Eds.), *Paninian studies: Professor S. D. Joshi felicitation volume* (pp. 293–322). University of Michigan Press.

Vergiani, V. (2020). Panini's Astadhyayi: A turning point in Indian intellectual history. *Rivista Degli Studi Orientali, XCII*(3–4), 11–35.

Weber, A. (1872). Das Mahabhasya Des Patanjali. *Indische Studien, 13*(2–3), 293–496.

Chapter 7
Classical Understanding of Gender in Indian Texts

Lavanya Vemsani

Abstract Gender is understood through practice and traditional understanding of classical texts. Amba's journey depicted in the Mahabharata brings forward a fresh understanding of gender. Abducted by Bhishma from her own self-choice (svayamvara) ceremony, subsequently rejected by her previously chosen partner, her life turned upside down. Amba vowed to dedicate her life to vanquishing Bhishma. Burning with anger she vows to take revenge on Bhishma in her next life; she is reborn as Shikhandi finally killing him in the Mahabharata war. Her journey into isolation, asceticism, and forest as well as rebirth and gender change help ascertain the uniqueness of feminine heroics in ancient India. Gender is entangled in a web of social, political, and economic relationships rather than individual preference, which is generally steered on the basis of hegemony.

Historically, gender is entangled in a web of social, political, and economic relationships rather than individual preference, which is generally steered on the basis of hegemony. It is only during the modern era that academic studies began focusing on concepts and practices associated with gender and sexuality, even though ancient lore preserves valuable information on gender. Recent scholarship has closely studied the multiple masculinities (Connell, 1987, 1995) which has laid down the basic concepts of sociology of gender.[1] However, this left out large swaths of the population out of the gender studies as the femininities and the other genders in between such as the transgender, bisexual, or others (LGBTQ +) are scarcely studied. Femininities, hegemonic or not have been studied in the last decade (Schippers, 2007:

[1] An earlier version of this chapter had been published in my book *Feminine Journeys of the Mahabharata* (Vemsani, Lavanya. 2022. "Amba's Journey Through Multiple Lives and Genders." *Feminine Journeys of the Mahabharata*. SpringerNature/Palgrave McMillan, 2022: 175–193). I thank my editors and publisher SpringerNature for giving me permission to include a revised version of the chapter here.

L. Vemsani (✉)
Shawnee State University, Portsmouth, OH, USA
e-mail: lvemsani@shawnee.edu

School of Historical Studies, Jawaharlal Nehru University, New Delhi, India

L. Vemsani (ed.), *Handbook of Indian History*,
https://doi.org/10.1007/978-981-97-6207-1_7

85–102). Similarly, work on the non-binary genders has also begun in earnest in the last two decades marking one of the important developments of twenty-first century (Anderson, 2002; Connell, 1992). Sterotypical views on feminities gave rise to predominant regional steriotypes of gender identities. The hyper sexualization of Asian women is so prevalent that stereotypical articles are published about their work ethic labeling them as 'being like men'. Even more complex is the concept of transnational sexuality such as Latina or Asian-American women (Pyke & Johnson, 2003: 33–53) are rarely studied. Especially Asian women are hyper sexualized in the West and labeled that they are 'like men.' Even the Chronicle of Higher Education, one of the news and discussion outlets of Higher Education in America has published an article indicting Asian women academics for their higher exceptional research output as being 'like men'. Black women faced similarly derogatory labeling (Hill Collins, 1990). While being 'like a woman' (Martin, 1998: 1249–1273) in the case of a man is seen as objectionable and less productive similar aspects in women are considered productive and even thought to be more desirable. However, a close study of classical and early understanding of gender is necessary to gain a comprehensive understanding of gender. Therefore, within the modern scholarly examination of multiple perspectives on gender, it is important to examine the concepts of classical thought on gender from all available sources. I examine the story of Amba, who lived as a woman in two lives before transitioning into becoming a man. Concepts of gender are complex and expressed in numerous stories of the life of gods and heroes of Classical India. Amba's journey from one gender to the other is difficult and excruciating to the point that she burned herself in her first life to be reborn and transition to another gender. Classical Hindu lore preserved in the Mahabharata[2] brings forward numerous aspects of gender prevalent in ancient India. This chapter analyzes classical accounts of gender preserved in the Mahabharata composed between the fourth century B.C.E to the third century C.E. representing the largest compendium of literature in the world.

Concept of gender seems fluid in the classical stories of gender which abound in classical literature of India including the Mahabharata. Hindu God Vishnu is depicted as changing his gender to female during the world changing event of Samudra Manthana (churning of the Milk Ocean) to extract Amrita as described in the Mahabharata (Adiparva. Astikaparva Section XVIII) and other puranas including the Vishnupurana (Vishnupurana. Ch. IX: 70).[3] One of the protagonists of the Mahabharata, Arjuna, also underwent gender change due to a curse and lived in a temporary state of gender neutral state (gender disporia) losing his masculinity for a year during the exile of the Pandavas in the court of Virata in the Matsya Kingdom (Mahabharata.

[2] The following translations of the Mahabharata are cited in this chapter. Translation of the Vulgate text of the Mahabharata refers to Ganguli Kisari Mohan/P.C. Roy. 2004 [1883–1896]. Mahabharata. Vol. 1–4. New Delhi: Munshiram Manoharlal. References to this text of the Mahabharata are cited as Mahabharata. Translation of the Critical Edition of the Mahabharata refers to the Van Buitenen. J. A. B. 1973–1978. Mahabharata (Mbh). Vol. 1–3. Chicago: University of Chicago Press. References to this text of the Mahabharata are abbreviated as Mbh.

[3] The Vishnu Purana, translated by Horace Hayman Wilson, [1840], hosted online at sacred-texts.com.

Aranya Parva. Virataparva). However, the textual evidence only indicates gender dysphoria, but doesn't indicate if he experienced a feminine state. The second of the five Pandava brothers, Bhima cross-dresses as a female when Draupadi feared sexual molestation due to the advances of Kichaka while they were in exile at the court of Virata in Matsya Kingdom (Mahabharata. Virataparva Section XXII). Dressed as a female Bhima enters the bedchamber overpowering Kichaka and killing him there. Therefore, the heroes of the Mahabharata, Arjuna, and Bhima, flout the norms of masculinity as noted here. While Arjuna lived in a neutral state of gender losing his sexuality as a male, Bhima undertook cross-dressing as a woman to accomplish the task of vanquishing Kichaka who approached Draupadi with evil intent. God Shiva is represented as Ardhanarishwara (Half-female and half-male) symbolizing the universe as a blend of masculine (purusha) and feminine (prakriti) energies (shakti) of the universe (Kramrisch 1981; Yadav, 2000). Lord Shiva emblemizes the body, soul, and mind complexity, which is a blend of male and female sensitivities regardless of the gender expression. However, I selected the story of Amba for my examination of gender in classical India, since, Amba goes through multiple genders and forms going through not one but two lives, living a successful life fulfilling her objectives.

Amba is unique in every aspect of womanhood. Reborn as Shikhandi in her next life, she is realized as a male, and her life becomes even more unique as a transgender male later. She traversed through two lives, two worlds, two physical forms, and two genders to avenge the iniquitous action inflicted on her by Bhishma, the one blessed with ending his life at his own choice. Amba's appearance in the next life finally pushed him to the edge to realize the debacles of his life and wish for death.

All stages of Amba's life depict her journey through two genders, during her first life as Amba, a preparation, and during her second life next as Shikhandi, undergoing the gender transition moving from one gender to the other. Therefore, I examine both of her lives together here dividing the journey of Amba's two lives into five stages for convenience of examination. Amba faced disappointment in her first life not due to her actions, but because of the actions of other men, especially, Bhishma. The first stage of her life depicts her initial vendetta perpetrating her abduction and unexpected turn of events. The second stage is refusal and rejection of the marriage proposal offered to her and its consequences. This results in her loss of desired marriage with chosen groom and subsequently life. The Third stage is her journey through asceticism. The fourth stage is rebirth as Shikhandi and her gender transition to a male. The fifth and final stage is Shikhandi's participation in the Mahabharata war resulting in the defeat and death of Bhishma, thus fulfilling the passionate desire of Shikhandi as Amba in the past life. Shikhandi's emergence from Amba is wrought with immense struggles.

Significance of Amba is noticed in the Mahabharata as Amba's journey finds mention in the list of major events as well as separate sections of the book dedicated to her story in the Udyogaparva (Ambopakhyana) of the Mahabharata (Ganguly. Mahabharata. 18; 25;). Part of her story is also narrated by Bhishma as an answer to Duryodhana's questioning of Bhishma for not killing her. Amba's story is narrated twice in the Mahabharata which shows the special emphasis placed on the narrative.

The story of Amba also demonstrated the differences between the attitudes of older generation of men and younger generation of men in the Mahabharata toward the gender change of Shikhandi from male to female. This is in direct contrast to the reaction of women including his wife, who all seem to have been accepting of her change to male. While Bhishma was unaccepting of Shikhandi's gender change considering her as a woman until the end of his life, that did not concern other young heroes such as Arjuna, Krishan, and even Duryodhana. To all his faults this is the only aspect Duryodhana's attitude that aligns with his rival Arjuna. Duryodhana asked Bhishma why he did not kill Shikhandi as he was bewildered by the actions of Bhishma during the war. However, the world of Western Indology had not been as accepting of the gender change of Shikhandi considering her femininity even though the text of Mahabharata doesn't support that assumption. In fact, one of the scholars has remarked about the final war remarking that it was almost as if "Arjuna shot his arrow at Bhishma hiding behind his grandmother" alluding to the transitioned male Shikhandi's previous life as Amba, a woman and elder sister of Arjuna's grandmother Ambalika (Doniger, 1997; Goldman, 1993). Modern scholars have displayed patriarchal dominance and utter disregard for the gender sensitivity of the transitioned person. This displays complete insensitivity without regard for the gender sensitivities of a transitioned person not even found in the classical work of Ancient India, the Mahabharata, set to writing almost two thousand years ago.

Although Amba's story is unique among all those myriads of stories of feminine divinity in the Mahabharata no full length study of her life has yet been undertaken, which in itself demonstrates the complexity of the subject. However, cryptic studies of Amba's life are common in numerous works in connection with examining female goddesses considering the epithets of goddess as the term Amba alternatively appears as a generic term representing the Goddess. Incidentally, the names of the three princesses of the Mahabharata (Amba, Ambika, Ambalika) noted in this story also appear in other contexts in connection with the names of goddess together with the list of numerous other names of the goddess (Coburn, 1984:99–106). Amba simply is a designation for mother in Sanskrit (Goldman, 1978:336), which is commonly attached to names of goddesses to designate the nurturing benevolent nature of goddesses, but in her life, Amba defies all these categorizations by standing up for her will. Scholars have also treated the subject of feminine accounts with superficial assumptions. Appearance of the names, Amba, Ambika, and Ambalika anywhere in any context is connected to the three sisters of the Mahabharata treated as if it was a puzzle to be solved rather than treating their story, especially Amba's story, as a deep contextual account related to life in ancient India. Scholars (Biardeau, 2002; Jamison, 1996) connected the appearance of the names of Amba, Ambika, and Ambalika in the hymns of Asvamedha yagna to the story of the Mahabharata without direct link or any internal textual evidence, which led another scholar (Hiltebeitel, 2011:211) to remark that those previous scholars have found key pieces to solve the puzzle which the 'Mahabharata composers have intentionally left out' (Vemsani, 2022:7).

Amba is the feminine protagonist, too confusing and concerning for many who impose certain categorizations on the feminine heroic, hence, her story is ignored from scholarly studies. Surprisingly, if her story was studied at all her story was studied, it is only examined partially, to probe into her sexuality and gender concerns narrowly. Therefore, most of the scholarly works focused on studying Bhishma in his various activities as match maker (Allen, 2007:176–188) or his role as a father figure by applying Freudian psychoanalytical theory (Goldman, 1978; Fitzerald, 2007:189–207). This is also a patriarchal tendency. Such overemphasis on the sexuality of feminine heroics minimizes their sacrifice and presents them as bizarre personalities. Few studies also considered other perspectives such as considering Bhishma's service to his father as selfless service and sacrifice (Karve, 1969). Among these early studies focus always on examining Bhishma, rather than Amba, through application of Freudian psychoanalytic theory, and almost a lone voice considers it inappropriate to apply Freudian psychoanalytical theory to all father and son conflicts (Sax, 2002: 79–80). While Bhishma attracted numerous studies, strangely none of them even ventured a partial study of Amba; they only included her story when it was possible to implicate her as an incompetent outlier as in the case of the death of Bhishma. Such gross negligence of the study of Amba the only gender fluid hero in the Mahabharata indicates the prevalence of male attitudes toward the feminine in the Western Academia, especially concerning Indology in particular.

Stage 1. The Initial Vendetta: Amba is Bereft of Her Choice

When the king of Kashi announced svayamvara (bridegroom choice/self-choice) for the three princesses renowned for their charm, numerous princes arrived in Kashi. While Kashiraja has announced the svayamvara in preparation for the wedding of his three daughters, unbeknownst to him, other plans for their marriages were being orchestrated elsewhere (Mahabharata. Book1. Sambhavaparva. Section. CII). Amba is the eldest of the three daughters of king of Kashi. In the meanwhile, in Hastina, Satyavati, the matriarch of the Kuru dynasty, summoned Bhishma and consulted with him on the prospect of marrying the Kashi princesses to her son, Vichitravirya. Bhishma planned accordingly, knowing that young Vichitravirya might be averse to attending the svayamvara. However, as Bhishma took matters into his hand not everything went as planned. Bhishma stormed the assembly hall and abducted the princesses of Kashi from their Svayamvara. The king of Kashi as well as other princes assembled there were shocked and vehemently opposed this heinous act of Bhishma and attacked him with their respective forces.

Salva, king of Saubya, confronted Bhishma directly. Bhishma used aindra weapon and overpowered Salva. Having defeated all the opposition including the king of Kashi and Salva and other princes, Bhishma continued with his journey back to Hastinapura along with the three abducted princesses, Amba, Ambika, and Ambalika. As they reached Hastinapura, the Kaurava matriarch Satyavati began preparations for the wedding of the three abducted princesses with her son, Vicitravirya.

Concerned with these developments Amba approached Bhishma and said, "At heart, I had chosen the king of Saubha for my husband. He had, in his heart, accepted me for his wife. This was also approved by my father. At the svayamvara ceremony also I would have chosen him as my lord. Thou art conversant with all the dictates of virtue, knowing all this, do as thou likest" (Section CII). Upon hearing Amba's request, Bhishma consulted with his councilors and brahmins there; he made arrangements for Amba to go to Kashi and marry Salva according to her wishes. These events show the will power and strong nature of Amba. Abducted and taken to an alien state surrounded by numerous strangers making arrangements for her wedding, Amba still found her courage to express choice. Her strength becomes even more clear in the face of her timid sisters, who remained quiet. Amba is not only strong enough to choose her mate and fall in love, but she is also brave enough to express her will to strangers, to stand up for her wishes. The audacity of Amba becomes even more stark when compared with her sisters, Ambika and Ambalika, who remained quiet for fear of censure, even though they faced similar fate of being married forcefully (Vemsani, 2022: 23–43).

Having said that she had already decided to marry Salva, the ruler of Saubya, to whom she had given her heart she hoped for her marriage to be arranged with him. However, Bhishma realizing his error, allowed her to return to her home. Amba hoped she could fulfill her choice with Bhishma's help. Bhishma sent her to Saubya kingdom to marry Salva rather than arranging her marriage as he considered that he was the one responsible for her debacles. However, a rude reaction awaited her from her paramour Salva, who rejected her proposal for marriage. She is left as a rejected or lest woman. It might have been received differently if Bhishma were to take the initiative to arrange her wedding instead of sending her alone to Salva's kingdom. Amba learns from Salva that he no longer desired to marry her as Amba was taken from the Svayamvara by Bhishma, who won the war against Salva as well as the attending princes and her father, which was akin to a legitimate marriage, regardless of whether Bhishma married them or married them off to his brother's son Vicitravirya. Amba is left forsaken as the male chivalry dictated that a woman taken by another man is his, regardless of the circumstances of such action. In this situation Amba was left precarious and without much recourse to help. Amba came back to Hastinapura with the demand that Bhishma should marry her as he was responsible for taking her away from the svayamvara. Bhishma expressed his inability to marry her as Bhishma took the vow of celibacy previously (see Vemsani, 2022: 23–43 for more information of Bhisma's vow). Thus, once abducted, twice rejected (by Bhishma and Salva), Amba was deeply dejected initially. Her dejection gradually turned into anger. However, she was right in her anger toward Bhishma who pushed her into this precarious situation leaving her no option for marriage and a happy life that she desired for herself. Even though she did not find fault with Salva there seems to be some misjudgment on the part of Salva. The Mahabharata identified him as a reincarnation of a daitya (demon) known as Ajaka (Mahabharata. Book 1. Adiparva. Adisambhavaparva. Section LXVII). Depicted as an incarnation of a demon Salva is on the darker side of creation.

Even though Salva considered that he followed male chivalry in rejecting Amba, it is obvious that he was acting under the dark nature, associated with demons, the *tamasa*, clouded vision. Although Amba is utterly frustrated and finds no further aspiration to go on with her life, instead of ending her life then and there, she devoted the rest of her life carrying out austerities to kill Bhishma, who she considered was the cause of her miseries. From here onwards her journey proceeds with her anger burning within her crystallizing in her desire to vanquish Bhishma. Her journey reads like a science-fiction story rather than a historical story from here onwards. In her struggle to achieve her goal, she goes through numerous difficulties but never gave up. She undergoes strict asceticism, strange forms such as part river and part human simultaneously, while she becomes dual gendered with male and female aspects in her next life. The second part of Amba's life goes to tremendous upheaval, which shows her immense mental and physical strength that prepared her for her next life in which she goes through gender transition and accomplishes her goal of killing Bhishma.

Stage 2. Refusal and Rejection Leads to Asceticism: Path to Gender Transition

Amba's dual gender is clear and unassumingly mentioned in the Mahabharata (Mahabharata. Book.5 Udyogaparva. Section L) in the words of Sanjaya as spoken to Dhritarashtra:

> while living of yore as the daughter of the king of Kasi, had practiced the austerest penances; she, who, O bull of the Bharata race, desiring even in a subsequent life to compass the destruction of Bhishma, took her birth as the daughter of Panchala, and accidentally became afterward a male; who, O tiger among men, is conversant with the merits and demerits of both sexes; that invincible prince of the Panchala who encountered the Kalingas in battle, with what Sikhandin skilled in every weapon, will the Pandavas fight against you. She whom a yaksha, for Bhishma's destruction, metamorphosed into a male, with that formidable bowman will the Pandavas fight against you.

Pushed into a corner of no escape Amba left completely dejected and walked into the forests on the edge of the kingdom by nightfall. There, she met some sages, who after listening to her story they took pity on her and advised her to return to her father, but she refused. Sages then contemplated on ways to help Amba. It is important to note here that Amba meets her maternal grandfather, Hotravahana, accidentally who happened to pass by that forest incidentally that night. This is one of the commonly noted themes in a number of classical stories of female protagonists that members of maternal household of the feminine heroines offer to help and support in times of calamitous distress, which is also previously noticed in the stories of Damayanti (Vemsani, 2022: 111–137). Maternal relatives frequently help and support by giving direction to their quest. Here, meeting her maternal grandfather is phenomenal for Amba as this brings the necessary direction for her quest. Amba's dejection turns into a blazing quest that leads her to undertake the unimaginably impassioned journey transitioning through two physical forms, two lives, and two genders until she finds closure in the death of Bhishma. Her transformation from a helpless woman, who is dejected upon being deprived of her choice of life to a strong woman willing to take any risks to avenge for the deeds that threw her into the clutches of misfortune is long and arduous.

Amba's travel from victim to victor begins with this chance meeting of her grandfather in the forest. Hotravahana introduced Amba to Parashurama (Mahabharata. Udyogaparva. CLXXXIX; CLXXXI). Amba sought the help of Parashurama and Hotravahana narrated the story of Amba's debacles following the wreckage of her svayamvara by Bhishma. Parashurama vowed to avenge her pain declaring war on

Bhishma (Mahabharata. Udyogaparava. CLXXXIX). Parashurama (Gail, 1977) an incarnation of Vishnu, son of sage Jamadagni, killed his mother Renuka on the orders of his father. Parashurama is also known to have vanquished all the Kshatriyas (warrior class) from the Earth. Parashurama known for matricide and kshatracide (Mahabharata. Book 7. Dronaparva. Section LXX) is a blend of contradictions (Biardeau, 1976). It is only natural that he is allied with Amba; In fact, he is the only person sympathetic to her cause to readily agree to support her cause in addition to her grandfather.

However, his war with Bhishma only ended in a draw as Parashurama failed to bring Bhishma to compromise. Bhishma was granted a special boon by his father Shantanu when he took the vow of complete Brahmacharya for life. According to this special boon, he got a death-choice, so he could choose to end his life according to his choice, but none can kill him. Hence, Parashurama could not vanquish him in battle. Thereafter, Parashurama advised Amba to seek protection from Bhishma and compromise, saying: "O damsel, in the very sight of all these persons, I have fought according to the best of my power and displayed my prowess! By using even the very best of weapons I have not been able to obtain any advantage over Bhishma, that foremost of all wielders of weapons! I have exerted now to the best of my power and might. O beautiful lady, go withersoever thou wishest! What other business of thine can I accomplish? Seek the protection of Bhishma himself! Thou hast no other refuge now! Shooting mighty weapons Bhishma hath vanquished me!". This angered Amba even further as she sought to seek her own revenge. She has resolved in her mind as she informed river goddess Ganga later: "I am practicing the severest penances for the destruction of Bhishma. I wander over the earth, O goddess, so that I may slay that king! In everything I do, O goddess, even this is the great end of my vows!" (CLXXXIX). The most difficult objective of Amba was to kill Bhishma who cannot be killed by anyone, which seems like an impossible objective, but Amba accomplished it in her second life. Goddess Ganga did not take pity on Amba but rather cursed her in anger as she found out the objective of Amba's penances was to kill her son Bhishma. Ganga's motherhood dominated all other aspects of her pure divine personality (see Chap. 10, Vemsani, 2022: 193–209 for detailed discussion on Ganga) as she cursed Ganga to become a river rather than blessing her with success. The solidarity of womanhood fails here as the motherhood dominates.

As unfair as this curse is for Amba, as luck would have it, this curse, in fact, turns into a boon as part of her manifested into a river at Vatsabhumi, while another part of her remained as Amba and she continued her austere penances. Thus, Amba remains part woman in half of her body and part of her body becomes a natural being, a waterbody, regarded as a river goddess. However, her appearance as part river is symbolic of the fluid nature of gender and the next stage of her life as a transitioning female in the next life. Therefore, due to her austerities, within a single life, even being burned with anguish Amba attained multiple manifestations possible only to the divine (Mahabharata. Udyogaparva. (Book 5. Section. CLXXXIX).

Goddess Ganga might have wished to cool Amba's anger by turning her into a river. However, Amba's anger is so deep that even Ganga's curse hadn't been able to turn her into a river fully. Merely, half of her body turned into a river while the upper portion of her body remained intact as she continued her penances without caring for the transformation in her body. The details of the last part of her journey before she decided to self-immolate are discussed below.

Stage 3. Journey Through Austerities

This is the most crucial step of her journey through wilderness and austerities, two of the aspects of life that she might have never thought that she would endure in her life. Amba lived in the sacred groves of Ganga and Yamuna rivers. Initially, Amba performed her severe austerities such as, standing on one foot and standing in the river Yamuna while abstaining from food, in solitude for dozens of years, as described by Bhishma, "that maiden, entering a cluster of retreats practiced austerities, that were beyond human powers (of endurance). Without food, emaciated, dry, with matted-locks and begrimed with filth, for six months she lived on air only, and stood unmoved like a street-post. And that lady, possessed of wealth of asceticism, foregoing all food in consequence of the fast she kept, passed a whole year after this, standing in the waters of the Yamuna. Endued with great wrath, she passed the next whole year standing on her front toes and having eaten only one fallen leaf (of a tree). And thus, for twelve years, she made the heavens hot by her austerities. And though dissuaded by her relatives, she could not by any means be weaned off (from that course of action)". (Section. CLXXXIX).

However, even though Amba tried to approach the kings and sages of the Bharata, her efforts remained futile to mobilize support for her cause. As Amba continued her penances even though half of her body was turned into river, the sages residing in Vatsabhumi came to inquire her about the cause of her penances. Even though, they sympathized with her, knowing the invincibility of Bhishma, they hesitated to help her. God Shiva appeared at that time while she was surrounded by many sages and offered her a boon. She asked for a boon to defeat Bhishma and god Shiva blessed her, saying: "Thou shalt slay him", (Section CXC). To this, Amba wondered and said again to Shiva, "How can it happen, O god, that being a woman I shall yet be able to achieve victory in battle. O lord of Uma, as a woman, my heart is quite stilled. Thou hast, however, promised me, O lord of creatures, the defeat of Bhishma. O lord, having the bull for thy mount, act in such a way that promise of thine may become true, that encountering Bhishma, the son of Santanu, in battle I may be able to slay him" (Section CXC). To this, Shiva assured her unequivocally that his blessing will become true in her next life explaining that, "The words I have uttered cannot be false. O blessed lady, true they will be. Thou shalt slay Bhishma, and even obtain manhood. Thou shalt also remember all the incidents (of this life) even when thou shalt obtain a new body. Born in the race of Drupada, thou shalt become a Maharatha. Quick in the use of weapons and a fierce warrior, thou shalt be well-skilled in battle. O blessed lady, all that I have said will be true. Thou shalt become a man at the expiration of sometime (from thy birth)!" (Section CXC). It seems as though Shiva took pity on her partly for her condition of living as half human and half river and partly for the reason that it was the result of a curse meted out to her by Goddess Ganga, his other wife (Vemsani, 2022:193–209). In this episode, it is important to note that Shiva the lord of the universe represented as Ardhanarishvara (half-woman form) gave this unique boon in which lets one born as a female change to a male later in life.

However, these divine boons did not immediately manifest into fulfilling Amba's wish to vanquish Bhishma. Thus, finding hope to fulfill her goal of avenging Bhishma in her next life Amba decided to end her life. On the banks of Yamuna, she collected wood and arranged her funeral pyre; she set herself ablaze on that funeral pyre thus ending her life saying, 'for Bhishma's destruction,' (Section CXC). Even at the time of ending her life, she resolved to announce her goal, which shows her commitment to her goal even in death. Thus, blessed by Shiva to take revenge on Bhishma in her next life giving up her life at an appropriate time Amba was reborn as Shikhandi to Drupada. Although Drupada is an unassuming personality in the Mahabharata, his children are completely overpowering and connected to fire in symbolism. Fire is represented in the life and personality of his children. Amba, born as Shikhandi, holds her anger as a burning cider in her, while her siblings Draupadi and Drushtadyumna are born from the sacrificial fire (Vemsani, 2022: 71–95).

A southern recension of the story also connects Amba to Kartikeya, son of Shiva, although classical evidence is lacking. It is noted in a twentieth century composition from southern India that Kartikeya presented Amba with an everlasting garland of lotus flowers telling her that anyone wearing that garland would cause the death of Bhishma.[4] This aspect of Shikhandi wearing garland is also commonly noted in Telugu literature and films.[5]

Amba's death wish finally came to fruition in her next life, when she took rebirth as Shikhandi, as the child of Drupada. Amba remembered her past life and her vengeance for Bhishma patiently waiting for an appropriate time to take revenge on Bhishma.

Section 4. Rebirth and Transition: Female to Male

This second birth of Amba is crucial to the story of Mahabharata in addition to Draupadi, which is clearly narrated in the Mahabharata. King of Pancala, Drupada, and his wife, Prishata, worshiped Shiva desiring a son. However, Shiva blessed them with a daughter saying that, "Thou shalt have a child who will be a female and male" (Section CXCI). Drupada prayed to god Shiva begging for merely a son. However, Shiva said, "This is Destiny's decree. It will not be otherwise" (Section CXCI).

Amba is reborn to Drupada and his wife Prishata as a girl child. Therefore, the king and queen decided to raise their daughter as a son naming him as Shikhandi, remembering the instruction of Shiva, while hoping that the child would one day become male according to the instructions of Shiva. However, keeping the sex of the child as a secret they raised her as a male child (Section CXCI). Hence, born girl and raised boy, Amba is a gender fluid child apparent since her birth. King Drupada had Shikhandi taught fine arts, literary skills, as well as archery and training in using many types of weapons (Section CXCII).

---

[4] Rajagopalachari, Raja. 1951. Mahabharata. Bombay: Bharatiya Vidya Bhavan. P.22.

[5] Telugu film, *Dana Veera Shura Karna*, depicts Shikhandi wearing garland of lotus flowers even on the battle field.

As the child grew to be an adult, Shikhandi's parents arranged for the wedding, still concealing her sex of being a female, since they assumed that she would turn into a male soon after marriage. They married her to the daughter of Hiranyavarma, the king of Dasarnakas. The fact of her gender comes out soon after the marriage as the daughter of Hiranyavarma learns it and informs her father. Hiranyavarma was enraged and sent an envoy to Drupada with stern warning at what he perceived as a grave case of dishonesty by concealing the true gender of Shikhandi (Section CXCII). Drupada consulted with his wife Prishata upon the threat of impeding war following the message of Hiranyavarma. They called an urgent meeting of the ministerial council. At the meeting of the Counsels and others, Prishata conceded to the fact that she concealed the gender of Shikhandi by raising her daughter as a son on the instructions of God Shiva and sought their advice. She added that she hoped to see her daughter Shikhandi turn into a man as per the blessings of Shiva that stated, "Born a daughter, she will become a son" (Section CXCIV). While her parents are conversing in this manner, Shikhandi was filled with desperation thinking that she was the cause of their misery and decided to leave her family thinking of giving up her life. Shikhandi then reached into a dense forest haunted by a Yaksha, Sthunakarna. There finding a mansion, Shikhandi entered it, and abstaining from food in her preparation for death, she became emaciated. Taking pity on Shikhandi, the Yaksha, Sthunakarna, enquired the reasons for her condition, saying, "For what object is this endeavor of thine? I will accomplish it, tell me without delay" (Section CXCIV). Shikhandi informed the Yaksha in detail about the story of birth, marriage, and impending war that his father Drupada may have to fight with Dasarnakas due to the issue of Shikhandi's concealed gender. She requested yaksha for help urging, "O Yaksha, save me, my mother, and my father! Indeed, thou hast already pledged thyself to relieve my distress! Through thy grace, O Yaksha, I would become a perfect man!" (CXCIV). The yaksha taking pity on Shikhandi agreed to exchange his sex with her, but imposed a condition saying, "For a certain period I will give thee my manhood. Thou must, however, come back to me in due time. Pledge thyself to do so!" (CXCV). Thus, having agreed to Yaksha's condition they exchanged their sex. Shikhandi became a man while yaksha became a woman. Shikhandi reached home and informed his parents of his becoming a man. His parents were elated with happiness and sent a message to the king of Dasarnakas, Hiranyavarma, immediately. Hiranyavarma sent some women to ascertain that Shikhandi was in fact a man. Once, the women confirmed the fact of his gender and informed him that Shikhandi was in fact a man. Hence, hearing that Hiranyavarma felt very happy, rebuked his daughter for misunderstanding her husband and sent her to Pancala with appropriate gifts apologizing for the misconstrued declaration of war earlier. This episode shows that the secret of Shikhandi's gender is leaked to the general public only after his transition. This also shows that his gender change is wholeheartedly accepted by the women, and his wife's family, which also shows the general acceptance of the public for his gender change.

While in this way the difficulties began subsiding for Shikhandi difficulties were merely beginning for the yaksha in the forest. During this time, Kubera, the chief of Yakshas, visited the forest resting at the mansion of Sthunakarna. However, Kubera was puzzled as Sthunakarna did not appear in person to Kubera, which seemed disrespectful to the visiting entourage of yakshas. Therefore, Kubeara enquired about Sthunakarna and dispatched other yakshas to find him. When the yaksha Sthunakarna was brought to him, he appeared as a woman rather than a man that he was. When inquired for details he informed the story of his sex exchange with Shikhandi. This angered Kubera. He gave a curse to the yaksha that he will remain female forever losing his gender to Shikhandi, saying: "O thou of wicked understanding, her femininity,–since, O wicked wretch, thou hast done what hath never been done by anybody,–therefore from this day, thou shalt remain a woman and she shall remain a man" (Section CXCV). However, all took pity on Sthunakarna and yakshas pleaded with Kubera not to curse him forever, but limit the curse. With that Kubera said, "After Sikhandin's death" (Section CXCV). Fortunately, this turned out to be a boon for Shikhandi, allowing her to remain the remainder of her life as a male. He remained a male and accomplished the goal of killing Bhishma in the Mahabharata war. This is one strange tale of transgendered male in ancient India. Even though the central aspect of the narrative here is the gender transition of Shikhandi from female to male, the story also includes the gender change of Yaksha from male to female. Hence, the story provides an inclusive assertion of male and female gender change. However, as noticed in the modern culture, the female to male transition was accepted more openly than the male to female transition. The gender transition of Yaksha was seen as a foolish act and he was dismissed from his role as guardian of the forests.

Even after Shikhandi changed her gender to become a man, she continued to be treated as a woman, and a representative of her past life, Amba. The change between the genders of Shikhandi (feminine) and Shikhandin (male) remains confusing throughout the depiction of her story in the Mahabharata. As far as the true story of Shikhandi in the Mahabharata is concerned she is male, even though it was assumed for part of the life. Although born a female Shikhandi is raised as a male child and eventually turns a male, but her mind remained feminine rooted in the memory of his past life, Amba. Outsiders like Bhishma have never accepted her as a man, since she was originally born female. This is the reason Bhishma refused to fight Shikhandi on the battlefield, as he previously vowed not to fight women. Bhishma told Duryodhana that "this is my vow, known over all the world, viz., that I will not, O son of Kuru's race, shoot weapons upon a woman, or one that was a woman before or one bearing a feminine name, or one whose form resembleth a woman's. I will not, for this reason, slay Sikhandin. Even this, O sire, is the story that I have ascertained of Sikhandin's birth. I will not, therefore, slay him in battle even if he approacheth me with weapon in hand. If Bhishma slayeth a woman the righteous will all speak ill of him. I will not, therefore, slay him even if I behold him waiting for battle!" (Section CXCV). The ingrained resistance to accepting the gender change of Shikhandi is seen only in Bhishma and no one else in the Mahabharata. He received widespread acceptance. However, Bhishma's adamant behavior against accepting the gender change of Shikhandi seems to be innocuous and shows the remaining attitudes of an earlier society, as Bhishma represents a society prevalent two generations ago.

The resistance of Bhishma to accept Shikhandi as a male, but stubbornly consider him as female, despite the fact that she changed her gender to become male, seems to be the text's way of preserving the vendetta and anguish of her past life intact. This aspect of unacceptable gender change from female to male is also interpreted as society's resistance to accept women assuming authority (Custodi, 2007) under any circumstances, unlike a male's sex change to female. However, the lack of any stories to that effect might indicate the opposite. The only story available to that effect of male undergoing a gender change to female, for only a short period of time that too as a disguise, not open transformation, was Arjuna during his incognito exile. Bhima dons female costume to trick Kichaka and kill him subsequently. However, in the case of Arjuna, nobody knew about this change, since he was under incognito; they only found out about it once he transformed out of it at the end of his incognito exile. There is no way to know if the general society knew about his gender change while he was living in that state, as a female dance teacher Brihannala, if the reaction might have been different and he might have faced even more censure or acceptance. However, gender perspectives are not always completely dichotomous. Short duration disguises are acceptable, especially under excruciating circumstances. Females donning male disguises to get away from enemy territories as well as males donning female costumes under similar circumstances is known and acceptable. Any temporary disguise or change is not considered a true change of personality or sex. Therefore, I think in the case of Arjuna and Bhima, the disguise of the feminine they assumed is more readily acceptable. Similarly, disguises as male and female during theatrical performances are also common and not taken seriously. Males performing theatrical parts dressed as a female is not uncommon. Kuchipudi dance tradition of Andhra Pradesh and Ramaleela performances are some of the common examples of this cross-dressing theater traditions. Females performing male theatrical parts is also not uncommon. Indian perspectives of gender in classical India are more fluid than in modern India. Colonial and alien administrations brought changes to the perspectives on gender through legislative enactments and education.[6] However, in classical Indian tradition, the personhood is understood as a combination of male and female sensitivities. Hence, short-term transgressions and disguises are not censured with any strict concern for decorum. Therefore, short-term gender dysporia of Arjuna and singular event of cross-dressing by Bhima could not be compared with the complete and permanent gender transformation of Amba.

However, it is difficult to know what might have been the reaction of the general public in understanding gender norms with regard to female transformation to male is difficult to know in the absence of any stories to that effect. However, in the story of Yaksha Stunakarna his female appearance was not too severely censured, but he lost his job of guarding the forest for the frivolous nature of his act of agreeing to gender change without giving due thought to the process of gender change or its consequences. However, a complete lack of stories may indicate suppression rather than support.

However, Amba lived as a male for all her life in her second life as Shikhandi. Amba reborn as a female child Shikhandi, due to the fact of her being raised as a male

[6] https://blogs.lse.ac.uk/gender/2019/06/17/hijras-and-the-legacy-of-british-colonial-rule-in-india/ India stuck down the Colonial Era legal code discriminating against the transgendered in 2014.

child, is trained in martial arts and well versed in combat and defense techniques, even though his transition to male gender occurred later in life. As he transitioned into male Shikhandi later, it helped her to finally realizing her wish of vanquishing Bhishma. On the 10th day of Mahabharata war when Shikhandi rode alongside Arjuna, the invincible Bhishma conceded defeat, willingly shot by the arrows of Arjuna and Shikhandi. Even though Bhishma vowed not to fight a woman, he did not give up without a fight as it took a whole day of fierce battle to bring down Bhishma. Mahabharata (Udyogaparva. Bhishma kanda. Section CXX) described the fierce battle between Shikandin and Bhishma. When Shikhandin shot Bhishma he thought: "Sikhandin, however, that foremost of car-warriors, protected in the battle by the diadem-decked (Arjuna), pierced Bhishma, in that encounter, with ten shafts after the latter's bow had been cut off. And he struck Bhishma's charioteer with other shafts, and cut off the latter's standard with one shaft. Then the son of Ganga took up another bow that was tougher. That even was cut off by Phalguni with three sharp shafts". Bhishma was hurt and lost his bow, he then thought, "For two reasons, however, I will not fight with the Pandavas, viz., their unslayableness, and the femininity of Sikhandin". It is clear here that Shikhandi cut the bow of Bhishma through firing ten shafts at him, and he was the only reason that Bhishma stopped fighting for fear of being killed by a (wo)man unable to escape his preconceived assumptions. Thus an impossible task is achieved by Shikhandi. Amba as Shikhandi took a fierce vow of accomplishing the impossible task of killing Bhishma who could not be otherwise killed.

The war continued to get fierce until finally, "(Arjuna), excited with rage and placing Sikhandin to the fore, approached Bhishma (nearer) and once more cut off his bow. And then piercing Bhishma with ten arrows, he cut off the latter's standard with one. And striking Bhishma's chariot with ten arrows, Arjuna caused him to tremble. The son of Ganga then took up another bow that was stronger. Within, however, the twinkling of an eye, as soon, in fact, as it was taken up, Arjuna cut that bow also into three fragments with three broad-headed shafts. And thus the son of Pandu cut off in that battle even all the bows of Bhishma. After that, Bhishma the son of Santanu, no longer desired to battle with Arjuna. The latter, however, then pierced him with five and twenty arrows" (Section CXX).

Thus, Bhishma became completely overpowered, but still continued to fight. Pierced all over with arrows, his body touched not the ground, laid on a bed of arrows. "At that moment, O bull of Bharata's race, a divine nature took possession of that great bowman laying there on a bed of arrows. The clouds poured a (cool) shower (over him) and the Earth trembled. While falling he had marked that the Sun was then in the southern solstice. That hero, therefore, permitted not his senses to depart, thinking of that (inauspicious) season (of death)" (Section CXX). Hence, Bhishma laying there on the battlefield waited for the arrival of the northern declension of the sun until his last breath. The Mahabharata notes that Bhishma laid there on the battlefield of Kurukshetra for 58 days, a long time, considering the sad and sorrowful events taking place there around him.

Bhishma might have had a very miserable final few days since lying there on the battlefield he might have watched all his near and dear kin and soldiers fall on the battlefield. He might have also watched the sorrow of their families collecting their dead bodies from the battlefield for last rites. That is certainly a miserable end to a great hero.

For Shikhandi that was the best outcome even though it took two lives and a gender transformation to achieve her goal. She defeated Bhishma, while relegating him to spend his miserable final days on the battlefield steeped in sorrow with no one to care for him. This final episode of Bhishma's life more than made up for Amba's anguish from Shikhandi's past life.

It seems that the question of whose arrow finally resulted in killing Bhishma appears futile, since the appearance of Shikhandi spelled doom to Bhishma, which was the goal of Amba reborn as Shikhandi. As expressed by Bhishma, Shikhandi is unmistakably the main cause of the death of Bhishma. It is a well-known fact that if Shinkandi had not fought on that chariot ahead of Arjuna Bhishma would have never dropped his bow to be defeated and killed. However, scholars have interpreted this episode as not successful for Shikhandi. They also derogatorily described it in the case of Arjuna, by remarking that the fact of defeating Bhishma was, 'accomplished by Arjuna by hiding' (Doniger, 1997; Goldman, 1993) behind his grandmother indicating the relationship of Shikhandi in his past life as Amba. These interpretations inadvertently attribute the success to Arjuna and not Shikhandi, by invoking Amba as grandmother, to whose credit it was to be attributed. This discredits the life goal of Amba and negates her gender transition. This demonstrates still prevailing attitudes towards gender status in present society. This misses the central aspect of the story of Amba and her journey. Her issue was not becoming male, but seeing Bhishma, the unassailable one, fall to the ground to die, which is accomplished by the shafts of Shikhandi that day as it was Shikhandi who shot Bhishma first with ten arrows and overpowered him, which later permitted Arjuna to shoot him precisely, even though not finally killing him as Bhishma desired to die during the northern course of the Sun. Arjuna helped Amba/Shikhadi achieve her goal of seeing Bhishma die, but not the other way around. Attributing the killing of Bhishma to Arjuna belittles the efforts of humongous efforts of Amba spanning two lifetimes. What is important to note in the narrative of Amba is that none of the participants (Arjuna, Duryodhana, etc.) or narrators (Sanjaya) paid any attention to the issue of Shikhandi's gender change but accepted him as a male. However, the dominant patriarchal attitudes of gender in Western Indology are revealed in the manner the story of Shikhandi is treated: first refusing to accept her as male and second refusing to assign credit for his immensely significant task, instead choosing to credit Arjuna by attributing it to him.

As far as the text and central notion of the Mahabharata are considered based on internal textual evidence, Shikhandi is the final vanquisher of Bhishma, and a male. Ganga did not blame Arjuna for the killing of Bhishma; she is unequivocal in her condemnation of Shikhandi. Ganga noted this during her lament when the Pandavas reached Ganga, the sacred river as well as the mother of Bhishma, to immerse the ashes of Bhishma, she rose up and said:

> He could not be vanquished by even Rama of Jamadagni's race with his celestial weapons of great energy. Alas, that hero has been slain by Sikhandin. Ye kings, without doubt, my heart is made of adamant, for it does not break even at the disappearance of that son from my

> sight! At the Self choice at Kasi, he vanquished on a single car the assembled Kshatriyas and ravished the three princesses (for his step-brother Vichitravirya)! There was no one on earth that equalled him in might. Alas, my heart does not break upon hearing the slaughter of that son of mine by Sikhandin! (Mahabharata. Book 13. Anusasana Parva (Section. CLXVIII).

Bhishma's mother Ganga makes it a point to note here that her son is 'slain by Shikhandin' duely acknowledging that he could not be previously killed by Rama Jamadagni, the most fiercest warrior. The reasons are well-known. Arjuna could not have vanquished Bhishma, if it was not for Shikhandi, whoover powered Bhishma by breaking his bow with ten shafts. Therefore, whatever finer points the episode may contain it is clear that the end of Bhishma is brought on by Shikhandi, satisfying her vows from a previous life. I don't think Ganga is mistaken in considering Shikandi as the vanquisher of Bhishma.

Shikhandi's (previously Amba) goal is to vanquish Bhishma, but not concerned about her gender. Whether she lives as a male or female is not a major concern for her as that of killing Bhishma. With her goal accomplished Amba's struggles as well as her commitment to her next life as Shikhandi concludes. As someone committed to her goal against all odds Amba showed unwavering commitment and veracity to accomplish her goal. Amba therefore is a successful feminine leader of the Mahabharata. Her journey is unique and her passage through two genders and two lives is a fantastic feat.

7.1 Conclusion

Examination of the female and male lives of Amba illuminates unique perspectives on the classical understanding of gender, making her the most unique feminine leader of the classical era. Her journey through two lives and genders is strewn with the most difficult conditions. However, she passed through all trials and tribulations to emerge a winner. An underlying aspect of the story is the forceful abduction and planned marriage of Amba, which goes wrong. Amba burned her life with asceticism and anger as her dreams of wedding and life were shattered.

Amba defies all known categorizations with regard to gender. Perhaps, this is one of the reasons she continues to be ignored in most of the studies focusing on the examination of male heroics or divinities as well as feminine divine. Amba's first life as a woman and her later rebirth as Shikhandi is emblematic of the difficult life many gender fluid females/males or gender-transitional males/females face in society. However, Amba prevailed against all odds finally achieving her goals of winning lasting fame as the most unique female hero who also lived as a male hero thus appearing special among all the myriads of feminine characters of the Mahabharata. The story of Amba reborn as Shikhandi stands unique as no parallel tales of such gender transition from female to male or from one life to another are noted in classical tales. Amba's story also shows that historical society might have been more open to gender fluidity and gender disguise under emergency, duress, or lighthearted activities such as theater but not real life. Absolute silence or direct misinterpretation on this subject area from the Western academia may indicate suppression of gender rather than support for gender fluidity or gender transition.

References

Allen, N. (2007). Bhishma as Matchmaker. In B. Simon & B. Black (Eds.), *Gender and Narrative in the Mahabharata* (pp. 176–189). Routledge.

Anderson, E. (2002). Openly gay athletes: contesting hegemonic masculinity in a homiphobic environment. *Gender and Society, 16*(6), 860–877.

Biardeau, Madeleine. (1976). "Parasurama". 1976. *Études de Mythologie Hindoue (IV): Bhakti et avatāra, Bulletin de l'École française d'Extrême-Orient*, École française d'Extrême-Orient 63: 182–191, context: 111–263.

Biardeau. (2002). *Le Mahabharata. Un récit fondateur du brahmanisme et son interpretation.* Seuill: Philosophie ginirale Sc.Human.

Coburn, Thomas, B. (1984). *Devi Mahatmya: The Crystallization of the Goddess Tradition.* Delhi: Motilal Banarsidass.

Connell, R. W. (1987). *Gender and Power: Society, the Person, ad Sexual Politics.* Polity.

Connell, R. W. (1992). A very straight gay: masculinity, homosexual experience, and the dynamics of gender. *American Sociological Review, 57*(6), 735–751.

Connell, R. W. (1995). *Masculinities.* University of California Press.

Custodi, A. (2007). 'Show You are a Man': Transsexuality and Gender Bending in the Characters of Aruna/Brihannada and Amba/Shikhadin(i). In B. Simon & B. Black (Eds.), *Gender and Narrative in the Mahabharata* (pp. 208–230). Routledge.

Doniger. (1997). Myths of transsexual masquarades in ancient India. In *India and Beyond: Aspects of Literature, Meaning, Ritual, and Thought*, ed. Dick van der Meji. Kegan Paul International: London/New York.

Fitzgerald, J. (2007). Bhishma Beyond Freud, The Fall of the Sky: Bhishma in the Mahabharata. In S. Brodbeck & B. Black (Eds.), *Gender and Narrative in the Mahabharata* (pp. 189–207). Routledge.

Gail, A. (1977). *Parasurama: Brahmane und Krieger*. Otto Harrosowitz.

Goldman. (1978). Fathers, Sons, and Gurus: Oedipal Conflict in the Sanskrit Epics. *Journal of Indian Philosophy, 6*, 325–393.

Goldman. (1993). Transsexualism, gender, and anxiety in traditional India. *Journal of the American Oriental Society, 113*(3), 374–401.

Hill Collins, P. (1990). *Black Feminist Thought: Knowledge, Consciousness, and the Politics of Empowerment*. HarperCollins.

Hiltebeitel, A. (2011). *Dharma: Its Early History in Law, Religion and Narrative.* Oxford University Press.

Jamison, S. W. (1996). *Sacrificed Wife/Sacrificer's Wife: Women, Ritual and Hospitality in Ancient India.* Oxford University Press.

Karve, Iravati. (1969). *Yuganta.* Poona: Deshmukh Prakashan.

Kramrisch, S. (1994). *The Presence of Shiva.* Princeton University Press.

Martin, P. Y. (1998). Why can't a man be more like a woman? reflections on connell's masculinities. *Gender and Society, 12*(4), 472–474.

Pyke, K. D., & Johnson, D. L. (2003). *Power at Play: Sports and the Problem of Masculinity.* Beacon.

Sax, William. (2002). Dancing the Self: Personhood and Performance in the Pandav Lila. Oxford University Press.

Schippers, M. (2007). Recovering the feminine other: masculinity, femininity, and gender hegemony. *Theoretical Sociology, 36*, 85–102.

Vemsani, Lavanya. (2022). Feminine Journeys of the Mahabharata: Hindu Women in History, Text, and Practice. *SpringerNature/Palgrave McMillan.*
Yadav, Neeta. (2000). *Ardhanarishvara in Art and Literature.* D.K. Printworld.

Part II
India Beyond the Borders

Chapter 8
Sailing Ships and Seafaring Networks: The Indian Ocean and the Maritime Silk Road

Himanshu Prabha Ray

Abstract Based on architectural and archeological evidence and inscriptions, this chapter challenges this long-held notion of Indians being 'inward-looking' and given to agricultural pursuits. Instead, it presents an overview of maritime activity in the period from second century BCE to fourteenth century CE from two perspectives: one, the conceptualization of the seas as evident in literary writings and portrayed in temple sculptures. The second relates to the ritual use of sea spaces by analyzing bronze ritual objects recovered from shipwreck sites and discussing these with reference to coastal shrines. It highlights partnerships and networks established across the Indian Ocean as a result of travels by merchants and trading guilds, Buddhist monks and nuns, musicians, scribes, and a host of others. Thus, this chapter stresses the participation of diverse communities of the Indian subcontinent in vibrant trans-oceanic networks and helps contribute to the understanding of maritime history of India.

Keywords Indian Ocean · Maritime Silk Roads · Archaeology of Indian seafaring · Sanganakallu · Kalpavriksha · Kamadhenu · Dhanvantari · Nagarjunakonda · Vishnu · Aihole · Alampur · Krishnagiri hills · Kanheri · Belitung Shipwreck · Famen temple · Mogao caves · Bharhut stupa · Borobudur · Indonesia · Sumatra and Java · Cirebon shipwreck · Krawang shipwreck · Mahavamsa · Srivijaya empire · Nagapattinam · Singapore

Temples and religious shrines are a striking aspect of the Indian coastline extending from the Gulf of Kachchh south to Kerala and along the east coast up north to the Ganga delta in Bengal (Ray, 2021: 136–165). Often located near fishing villages and the hamlets of sailing communities, these shrines were an integral part of the maritime cultural landscape of the region. This paper is an attempt to focus on archeological finds, such as ritual bronzes from shipwreck and other sites to underscore the ritual use of sea spaces by diverse communities who sailed across the Indian Ocean. This would

H. P. Ray (✉)
Research Fellow, Oxford Center for Hindu Studies, Oxford, UK
e-mail: rayhimanshuprabha@gmail.com

L. Vemsani (ed.), *Handbook of Indian History*,
https://doi.org/10.1007/978-981-97-6207-1_8

bring into the conversation not only the utilization of sites and shrines as centers of social integration but would also weave in data from portable ritual objects, such as bronze icons, clay votive tablets, and so on. But two issues need to be explained: one, how is the perception of the coastal shrine as envisaged in this paper to be reconciled with the notion of the Maritime Silk Road as accepted by UNESCO? Following this is the second sub-theme, viz. that of the conceptualization of the ocean in Indic literature and sculpture, especially as it was adapted and accepted across the Bay of Bengal in Southeast Asia.

To return to the Maritime Silk Road. The UNESCO website defines it as follows: "The early Middle Ages saw an expansion of this network, as sailors from the Arabian Peninsula forged new trading routes across the Arabian Sea and into the Indian Ocean. Indeed, maritime trading links were established between Arabia and China from as early as the eighth century CE".[1] In his 2016 paper, Singaporean scholar Kwa Chong Guan traced the beginnings of the term "Maritime Silk Road", focused on trade in silk connecting Han China and Rome, to the German geographer Ferdinand Freiherr von Richthofen (1833–1905) (Kwa, 2016: 1–2). By appropriating an idea and using it to further current geo-political interests the People's Republic of China has sought to mythologize the past. Kwa continues that the same is also true for India which launched Project Mausam in 2014. As explained on the website of the Ministry of Culture, Government of India: by focusing "on monsoon patterns, cultural routes, and maritime landscapes, Project 'Mausam' is examining key processes and phenomena that link different parts of the Indian Ocean littoral as well as those that connect the coastal centers to their hinterlands".[2] The reasons for this Kwa suggests lie in both India and China viewing Southeast Asia as a passive recipient of cultural influences rather than an active partner. One of the points that Kwa misses is that the terms South and Southeast Asia did not get defined until the twentieth century and were largely based on the geo-strategic interests of European colonial governments (Noor, 2018: 301–323). Colonial interventions brought about a radical transformation in the scale and magnitude of intra-Asian connectivity that had been in existence since the early centuries of the Common Era. These early connections were fluid; they involved religious scholars, pilgrims, merchants, adventurers, craftspeople, and sailors and more importantly were managed by Asians themselves. In contrast, the militarized objective of the colonial project by the British, the French and the Dutch was to conquer and hold territory far removed from its home base, as well as to dominate economic interactions in the region.

Elsewhere, I have suggested that labeling trans-oceanic connectivity simply as 'trade' between present political entities or nation states is a restrictive point of view, as it limits the understanding of maritime mobility only to trade activity and excludes other reasons for traffic across the seas, such as travel by local fishing and sailing communities; religious scholars in search of knowledge; adventurers; musicians, and the list goes on (Ray, 2019: 39–61). In my 2003 publication *The Archaeology*

[1] https://en.unesco.org/silkroad/about-silk-roads#:~:text=The%20early%20Middle%20Ages%20saw,as%20the%208th%20century%20CE. Accessed on 30th March 2024.

[2] https://indiaculture.gov.in/project-mausam accessed on 31st March 2024.

of Seafaring in Ancient South Asia, I have also examined the popular misconception that trade in the ancient period was largely restricted to luxuries or prestige items exchanged as gifts between empires or states, or through trading expeditions mediated and controlled by the state (Ray, 2003). On the contrary, a regular sailing and maritime network was sustained historically in the Indian Ocean by traffic in timber, cloth, metal, food items, dried fish, salt, and so on. The commodities involved in the Indian Ocean trade may be divided into various broad categories such as aromatics, medicines, dyes, and spices; foodstuffs, wood, and textiles; gems and ornaments; metals; and plant and animal products. These categories find mention in a range of textual sources from the first-century CE Greek text, the *Periplus Maris Erythraei* (Casson, 1989: 39–44) to the eleventh to thirteenth-century Geniza documents written in Judeo-Arabic script (Goitein & Friedman, 2008), as also Chinese and Arab accounts.

The Indian Ocean developed a unique coastal subsistence pattern in the fourth and third millennium BCE, while the earliest boat finds date to 5000 BCE. There is evidence for the spread of crops and plants in the second millennium BCE. The movement of these perishable items was the result of travel by small-scale fishing and sailing groups across the region. Archeological wood charcoal from the Neolithic site of Sanganakallu in the Bellary district of Karnataka in south India has produced a few specimens of what has been identified as true sandalwood (*Santalum album*) from levels dating to 1400–1300 BCE (Asouti & Fuller, 2008: 134). Sandalwood probably originally occurred in the wild in the driest parts of Indonesia, such as eastern Java and the Lesser Sundas.

Based on architectural and archeological evidence and inscriptions, this paper presents an overview of maritime activity in the period from the second century BCE to the fourteenth century CE with a focus on peninsular India from two perspectives: one, the conceptualization and attempted control of the seas as evident in textual accounts and sculptural representations. The second relates to partnerships and networks established across the Indian Ocean through travels by merchants and trading guilds, religious functionaries, musicians, scribes, and a host of others. Thus, the paper stresses the participation of diverse communities of the Indian subcontinent in vibrant trans-oceanic networks and investigates their presence in the archeological record.

The Conceptualisation of the Waters

The churning of the ocean by the gods and the demons to retrieve the treasures that lie beneath the waters is an ancient legend that appears in the epics such as the *Mahabharata* and the *Puranas*. The fourteen treasures included Kamadhenu, the cow of plenty; Kalpavriksha, the wish-fulfilling tree; but also, Lakshmi, the goddess of wealth; Vishnu's conch shell; and Dhanvantari, the physician of the gods. More importantly, the waters produced nectar, the drink of immortality that led to a conflict between the gods and the demons, which was finally won by the former. The narrative highlights the tremendous wealth associated with the ocean in cultural memory and the aspiration to attain immortality. It has been interpreted from a variety of perspectives by scholars ranging from a theological point of view to an allegory of human consciousness that could be controlled through Yogic practices. Joanna Williams presents a more mundane interpretation of the story as referring to the use of natural resources, especially the waters (Williams, 1992: 145–155). This is nowhere more explicitly represented than in the inscribed conch shell (*turbinella pyrum*) from temple site 29 at Nagarjunakonda in coastal Andhra. The 3rd— 4th century legend on the conch reads *bhagavato aṭhabujasāmisa* or eight-armed deity, a reference to the god Vishnu. Symbols of an eight spoked chakra on pillar, and ax with banner on pillar, raised side by side on a rectangular pedestal, are engraved beside the inscription.[3]

Srinivas Reddy reads the story of the churning of the ocean as a reflection of an Indic perspective on the unity of the Ocean (Reddy, 2020). The story appears prominently in visual depictions on temples from the 7th to the 13th century, such as in the rock-cut caves at Badami in north Karnataka; the Virupaksa temple at Aihole; and the 10th century Papanasam temple at Alampur, 200 kms from Hyderabad in Mahboobnagar district. The well-known representations of the Churning of the Ocean in the temples of Cambodia and especially Angkor have drawn global appreciation (Bhattacharya, 1959: 121–134).

The conceptualization of the seas is by no means limited to the Sanskrit Epics and Puranas. Varied conceptions of the ocean are to be found in the early Tamil poems, such as *Purananuru*, an anthology of four hundred poems in Old Tamil. The references in the poems include analogies such as rivers flowing into the ocean, armies like the vast ocean (Hart & Heifetz, 1999: 189), clouds collecting water from the ocean, and so on. Some of these are detailed below:

May you live long, with your days and your years increasing more.

Than the water of the great ocean dense with waves, than the sand in that ocean, than the drops of the rain in the trailing,

Lofty clouds! (Hart & Heifetz, 1999: 125).

As if I were someone dumb and blind.

Whose boat has overturned on a rain-swept night and his heart.

is swollen with intolerable suffering and he sinks without hope.

into the ocean…. (Hart & Heifetz, 1999: 148).

The possibility of shipwreck and sinking without hope in the waters was a danger faced by those who ventured out to sea and figures in Buddhist texts as well.

If one happens to fall into the dreadful ocean, the abode of Nagas, marine monsters and demons, he has but to think of Avalokitesvara, and he shall never sink down in the king of waters..... (*Saddharmapuṇḍarīka Sūtra*, 24, 6).

This was not merely an empty promise of protection from the danger of shipwreck described in the texts, but the scene was also sculpted prominently in the rock-cut Buddhist caves at Kanheri near the present city of Mumbai. At the time that the one hundred and four rock-cut caves were carved in the Krishnagiri hill, the site was located on Salsette island which was the largest religious center along the west coast of India. Kanheri contains an elaborate representation of the litany of Avalokiteshvara in Cave 90. The litany scene depicts the Bodhisattva, with Tara

[3] 'Early Inscriptions of Andhradesa' no. 22, http://hisoma.huma-num.fr/exist/apps/EIAD/works/?start=21 (accessed on 9 October 2018).

as his companion, saving the devotee from ten dangers, including from shipwreck. Three Pahlavi inscriptions in Cave 90 record visits of Parsis to the site in the 11th century (Gokhale, 1991). How are these conceptualizations of the waters and the ocean represented in the archeological record? In this paper, I focus on bronze ritual objects from shipwreck sites and discuss these with reference to coastal shrines.

Cargoes, Commodities, and Rituals[4]

There has been a phenomenal increase in the number of shipwreck sites discovered in Southeast Asian waters. While only two sites were documented prior to 1974, more than a hundred have been reported since then (with an average of four or five sites discovered every year) (Brown, 2004: 43). Most of these date to the period after the 13th century. Prominently displayed in the Asian Civilizations Museum in Singapore in the gallery labeled 'Trade and the Maritime Silk Routes' is the Tang shipwreck, which "traces the ancient routes of Singapore's maritime trading heritage" as stated in the Gallery write-up.

The Tang shipwreck of the ACM is also known as the Belitung shipwreck since it was found off the Belitung Island in Indonesia's territorial waters by local fishermen in 1998. In accordance with Indonesian law, a commercial salvage company was tasked with the job of salvaging the wreck and the company recovered approximately 60,000 objects from the seabed. "After extensive conservation and a major marketing campaign, some 53, 227 of these objects were sold to Singapore in 2004 for USD$32 million. Upon receiving the objects, Singapore re-branded them as the Tang Shipwreck Collection, emphasizing in no uncertain terms the wreck's Chinese connections and, in the process, erasing Indonesia's". Two other wrecks and their cargoes are of interest here. These include the Intan and the Cirebon shipwrecks.[5]

The ninth-century Belitung shipwreck carried a large cargo of Chinese ceramics, gold artifacts of imperial quality, silver and lead ingots, aromatic resin, star anise from China, and a well-made wooden box. The gold dishes recovered from the Belitung wreck are extraordinary, as also is the presence of Buddhist emblems on them, such as the swastika on the gold dishes (Miksic, 2014: 115–119). John Miksic suggests that the shipwreck's location shows that its intended route was not through the Straits of Melaka. Instead, the ship's location is on a known and popular route from the South China Sea to Java. He proposes that the cargo was full of gifts for kings and might have been Chinese imperial presents sent in response to a Javanese mission to China (Miksic, 2013: 70).

In contrast, Derek Heng argues that the practice of presenting gifts of gold to foreign rulers was rare and only four have been documented in Chinese records. Instead, he notes that the archeological record shows that Tang gold objects have only been recovered in three specific contexts: from China's imperial tombs; as

---

[4] This section was first presented at the Asian Civilizations Museum conference on 'China and the Maritime Silk Road: Shipwrecks, ports and products', 21 to 23 August 2020. I am thankful to Dr. Stephen Murphy, then Curator of ACM for the invitation.

[5] Natali Pearson, Wrecked? Belitung, Indonesia and the politics of maritime heritage, https://indonesiaatmelbourne.unimelb.edu.au/wrecked-belitung-indonesia-and-the-politics-of-maritime-heritage/ accessed on 2nd April 2024.

reliquary objects in Buddhist monastic sites like that of Famen Temple in Shaanxi province and the Mogao Caves at Dunhuang; and at foreign royal sites, like the royal tombs of Nara, Japan (Heng, 2017: 153). The reference to their enshrinement in Buddhist temples is significant for this paper, as is the fact that the swastika motif on the gold dishes is not found commonly in the Tang design repertoire. In addition to the gold dishes, Buddhist symbols such as the swastika and stupas are also represented on ceramics, as is the sea monster called *Makara* (Heng, 2019: 25), which is a familiar motif in Buddhist sculptural representations at sites in India and elsewhere. Perhaps the earliest representation of a seafarer in distress is to be seen on a medallion on a railing bar from the second- or first-century BCE stupa at Bharhut in central India, which shows a gigantic sea monster threatening to swallow a boat. An inscription reads: "Vasugupta rescued by Mahadeva from the belly of the monster (*timitimimgula*)" (Cunningham, 1879: pl 34).[6] A similar scene also occurs on Borobudur, the ninth-century Buddhist temple in central Java, which is well-known for its sculptural exuberance and representations of eleven boats and ships.

The Intan wreck is assigned to the tenth-century and was excavated off the coast of south-eastern Sumatra (Flecker, 2002; Mathers & Flecker, 1997). This ship, which carried an assortment of Chinese, Middle Eastern, and Southeast Asian goods, appears to have been en route from Sumatra to Java. The Intan finds include Chinese ceramics; Indian and/or Southeast Asian Buddhist objects, such as vajra, stupika molds, bells, and images of Buddhist deities; gold jewelry; Middle Eastern glass; and a range of metal items, including bronze, lead, silver, iron, and tin goods–some 13,500 artifacts altogether. Eighty silver ingots with Chinese characters were found in the excavations. It has been suggested that the ship was of Indonesian origin and, as Miksic wrote, "did its main business there" (Miksic, 2013: 88).

Other shipwrecks dated to the tenth-century in Indonesia include the Cirebon and Krawang shipwrecks. The Cirebon shipwreck was discovered on the north-western Java coast in 2003 and was commercially excavated (Liebner, 2014). The ship is estimated to have carried a cargo of 300 tons, including large quantities of Chinese ceramics, and also ceramics from the Persian Gulf. Horst Liebner noted that, "at least 87% of all individually registered ceramic objects are unadorned, green-glazed bowls and dishes, and that the majority of these divides into only half-a-dozen different types" (Liebner, 2014: 148). Ritual objects on board the vessel included a piece of gold sheet with a Buddhist mantra (Art.148341), a small amulet mold and a number of beads with short invocations of Buddhist and Islamic faith. The *dharani* inscribed on the gold sheet has been translated as follows:

Homage to the Triad of Jewels! Homage to noble Avalokiteśvara, the Bodhisattva, the great being, of great compassion. [The mantra is] like this: Om, … of the wind …, goddess who have the luster of …, you bear …. (Griffiths, 2014: 157).

Arlo Griffiths proposes that the gold foil may have been worn as an amulet for protection against dangers encountered at sea.

A careful analysis of the ritual objects has led Liebner to suggest that the ship carried several Buddhist practitioners on board. These ritual objects included a

[6] The panel now in the Bharat Kala Bhavan Museum, Varanasi.

female image (Art.112537) identified as the goddess Tara or Vajraraga, and, as Horst describes, a "*vajra*-sceptre, Art.27178, a bell without handle, Art.151406, and a number of figurines" (Liebner, 2014: 196). He goes on to note, "Of the latter, Art.30509 could represent the 'mythical leonine creature, of Indian origin, called *vyala* ("bad, wicked")', here possible worked into a *kuṇḍikā*", then lists more of the cargo, "two probable alms-bowls; a number of (lion-feet) tripod stands; the more elaborated bronze lamps (or censers) and lamp holders"; and ends with a description of heavy bronze objects, which were perhaps pedestals and bronze mirrors (Liebner, 2014: 196–97).[7] Another group of ritual objects includes what are termed "stupikas", which are essentially small metallic versions of the clay votive offerings common in both India and insular Southeast Asia (Liebner, 2014: 199–200). Liebner explained, "Among comparable objects retrieved from the approximately contemporary Karawang wreck is a distinctly stūpika-shaped cone that has the lower sections of its hole filled with a metal-like material" (Liebner, 2014: 199). Finally, a small object formed of two joined cylinders was identified as a portable reliquary. A similar object was found in the Intan wreck, and it has been suggested that it is a reliquary containing small fragments of rock crystal. The presence of Buddhist ritual objects as part of the cargo in shipwreck sites is undeniable. It is also evident that perhaps a majority of these were in demand in the Indonesian archipelago. The finds of reliquaries from shipwrecks supports Peter Skilling's contention that, "the early monks and nuns did not travel empty-handed. They carried relics and wherever they went stupas were set up. With the relics traveled ideas, rituals, practices, technologies and material culture" (Skilling, 2005: 276; Sen-Gupta, 2002).

In addition to the relics themselves, other connections, such as the visual language of the stupas that housed the relics were also significant. Anne Blackburn has noted, "The relic monuments in which they were placed, and the temple complexes within which these were created, also copied elements from exemplary temple centers in the Indic Buddhist heartland" (Blackburn, 2010: 318). A second link that relics established was with kings and royalty, especially in Buddhist countries such as Sri Lanka. The *Mahāvaṃsa,* for example, vividly portrays the protective powers of relics in revitalizing a newly built city. It would be erroneous to assume that relics comprised solely teeth or hair of the Buddha. At the Khin Ba mound in Myanmar, there is an example of gold leaves inscribed with verses from the Pali Canon being enshrined inside a silver reliquary and placed inside the stupa in the sixth century. This was by no means an exception as there are several instances of the *pratītyasamutpāda* verse being placed inside stupas, including in Sumatra (Griffiths, 2011). Other examples include bronze images of the Buddha and the bodhisattvas found in stupa deposits, such as at Sopara, on the west coast of India, and Nagapattinam, on the Tamil coast, dated to the eighth or ninth-century. The case for religious travel across the Bay of Bengal is supported by the Buddhagupta inscription found near the remains of a Buddhist temple in Seberang Perai in Malaysia in 1835–also the ninth- and tenth-century bronze images found during archeological excavations of a temple site in

[7] Liebner quotes from a listing of the secondary cargo on a webpage of the Musée royal de Mariemont, Brussels, in the passage.

Bujang Valley, Kedah. The Buddhagupta inscription with a stupa with multiple *chhatras* (umbrellas) on a slab of schist 66-cm high and 8- to 9-cm wide was subsequently transferred to the Indian Museum, Kolkata, and has been discussed in detail (Ray, 2021). In the next section, I discuss some of the coastal shrines in Sumatra, which were contemporary to the finds of ritual objects from shipwreck sites in Indonesian waters.

Coastal Architecture: Anchoring the Coasts

In secondary sources, the Indonesian archipelago and the Malay Peninsula have often been termed sacred locales of the "Buddhist cosmopolis" or "Esoteric Buddhism" from the seventh through thirteenth-century (Acri, 2016: 17). These formulations have been based on biographies of Buddhist masters who traveled between India and China (Sundberg and Giebek, 2011), archeological finds of portable objects such as bronzes and unbaked clay sealings, and use of Siddhamatrka script, which originated in Nalanda in eastern India and spread to Indonesia and Thailand. Other writings view these exchanges as a part of diplomatic and economic exchanges of Srivijayan kings across the seas, with Nagapattinam, a small town on the Tamil coast, erroneously labeled a port (Sen, 2003). Singularly missing in these writings are discussions of religious architecture located within its cultural context and its interactions with other sites in the region and across the seas.

The coastal sites that need to be brought into the discussion are those on the island of Sumatra, including Barus, Kota Cina, Padang Lawas, and Muara Jambi. In 1873 the famous Lobu Tua Tamil inscription, comprising 26 lines and dated to 1088, was discovered in the Barus area on the west coast of Sumatra. It deals with the payment of taxes by ships calling at Barus to the local representative of the south Indian merchant guild Ayyavole (Subbarayalu, 1998). A second inscription is bilingual, with Old-Malay in the Old Javanese script on top and a Tamil language and script record at the bottom. It is inscribed on a pillar decorated with the head of Ganesha on top and mentions offerings for the merit of a king named Pāduka Śrī mahārāja, who is said to have reigned from 1213 to 1265. Further evidence for the presence of workers from the Tamil region is provided by an inscribed gold ring found in Lobu Tua with a Sanskrit inscription dated to the tenth-century. The inscription has been read as "In the darkness, I have chosen to work" and identified as belonging to a Tamil miner working in the gold mines of Sumatra (Perret and Surachman, 2011). Another important find is a stone discovered in 1990 in the vicinity of Banda Aceh, at the northern tip of Sumatra, which bears a Tamil inscription dating from the very end of the thirteenth-century. The inscription refers to activities related to gold trade and the occurrence of the word *mandapam* could refer to the foundation of a temple or to a donation to a temple, which was a common practice at the time among merchant groups (Wisseman Christie, 1998: 258–59).

The archeological complex at Muara Jambi lies 30 km downstream from the present city of Jambi on the Batanghari River (Tjoa-Bonatz et al. 2009). It consists of eight large Hindu/ Buddhist temples and more than thirty structures dated to the ninth to fourteenth century. Candi Gumpung is the largest temple at the site. During reconstruction of the candi in the 1980s, eleven holes in the base of the temple foot were found to contain ritual deposits comprising cups made of gold, silver, and bronze; small gold plates, some without inscriptions; gold lotus flowers; semi-precious stones; crushed lead plates; and also a box containing gemstones and twenty-one inscribed gold plates with names of Tantric deities. Boechari described these plates as affiliated with the Vajradhatu mandala (Boechari, 1985). Other images found at the site include a makara and a headless female figurine identified as Prajnaparamita. Other finds from Muara Jambi include a nandi, fragments of images of the Buddha, Chinese, and Thai ceramics, and several objects of gold, silver, and bronze. A bronze gong found at the site has a date of 1231 (Salmon, 2008). A unique feature of the Muara Jambi archeological site is architectural images inscribed on terracotta bricks. It has been suggested that these drawings represent the diverse domestic architecture that existed in the region, though their exact purpose remains unclear.

It is also important to highlight the diversity and complexity in Buddhism that existed in Sumatra from the seventh to the fourteenth century. In the lower Musi River clay and bronze stupikas have been found with the Sanskrit *pratītyasamutpādagāthā*, often called the *ye dharma* verse. Dredging in the river led to the recovery of bronze images of the Buddha, bronze bases of three images comparable to an image of Lokeśvara discovered in the Padang Lawas region (Griffiths, 2011: 151), stamps used to print Buddhist texts, mirrors and bells with vajra handles, and metal votive objects inscribed with mantras. According to John Miksic, "A number of other sites with classic statues are found along the middle course of the Batanghari: Tanah Periuk, Teluk Kuali, Betung Berdarah, and Marem River", and these have been dated to the ninth or tenth-century. Finds of Chinese ceramics from Jambi date to a later period, from the eleventh to thirteenth-century (Miksic, 2012: 47).

Muara Jambi is not the only site with Buddhist remains in Sumatra, as is evident from the remains of twenty-six temples and temple complexes scattered at Padang Lawas near the Panai River. The earliest dated object from Gunungtua in the Padang Lawas region is an image of Avalokitesvara with two female deities, inscribed with the date of 1039 and a Malay word. Other inscribed images use both Tamil and Sumatran languages and scripts. Recent archeological excavations date the temples to the tenth to fourteenth century; statuary from the site includes images of the Buddha, miniature stupas, *chhatras*, and the vajra motif (Perret et. al., 2007). Inscribed gold plaques with Sanskrit inscriptions in the Nagari script have been found in ritual deposits at the site.

Many of the bronze images found at Padang Lawas bear similarities to those from eastern and south India (D. Perret, updated inventory, nr. 156, 168, 229) dating from the ninth to eleventh or twelfth century. In addition, there are two stone images of the seated Buddha, possibly imported from south India (Edwards McKinnon, 1977: 22). A small stupa-shaped bronze reliquary found in Borobudur (Borobudur 1977 # 29, p. 115) bears resemblance to one found at Nagapattinam (Ramachandran, 2014). Another cast image of the Buddha in the teaching mudra recovered from Candi Bahal III, one of the temples at Padang Lawas, bears a close resemblance to images from Nalanda dated to the tenth-century. Also interesting is the stupa-shaped reliquary with several *chhatras* (nr. 170) recorded in the same inventory. Thus, the images present heterogenous styles that point to analogies with different geographical regions in India.

The site of Muara Takus was explored and surveyed by W. P. Groenveld in 1880, and excavations have been conducted there periodically since. The research on the Muara Takus archeological site was carried out in 1983, and two zones were demarcated. It resulted in mapping of the ancient embankment remnants, the Mahligai Temple compound, and other ancient structures in Zone 1.[8]

Another important site in north Sumatra is that of Kota Cina, which is a part of the suburbs of the present-day city of Medan. The site has been known since the nineteenth century and archeological excavations since the 1970s have uncovered remains of eight religious structures made of brick, including Shiva temples and Buddhist stupas, as well as stone sculptures, Hindu and Buddhist images, hundreds of kilograms of earthenware, stoneware, and porcelain shards, metal artifacts, glass, stone beads, and kilograms of organic remains, dating to between the end of the eleventh century and the beginning of the fourteenth (Perret et al., 2013). From 2011 to 2017, several brick-built religious structures have been identified and a rich hoard of images was discovered from Buluh Cina, about 7 km inland from Kota Cina. The most significant is a slightly damaged bronze standing Buddha image, 38.5 cm in height, made by hollow casting, a technique well-known in south India, as well as a miniature bronze of Ganesha (Edwards McKinnon 2018).

Digging for sand during road construction in the 1980s at Paya Pasir yielded remains of twenty-five pieces of wood of various sizes and shapes, including planks showing traces of dowelling and lashing, parts of keels, part of a wooden anchor, and a paddle. Two types of vessels built according to the Southeast Asian lashed-lug construction technique were identified: a medium-sized vessel, 15–25 m in length, and a larger type (Manguin, 1989, pp. 205–9). In 2012 a boat framing wooden member was discovered at Kota Cina (in KC7), which was dated by means of AMS radiocarbon dating to the bracket mid-twelfth to mid-thirteenth-century (Perret et al., 2016: 8).

Two images of the seated Buddha in *dhyana* mudra, made of granite and ranging in height from 62 to 86 cm, were chance discoveries from the site. Other finds include a four-armed, headless standing Vishnu, lower part of a female deity, stone lingas, and a small granite pillar base. The images show similarities with those from the Nagapattinam area. Four bronze images from the site include two of the Buddha and one of Parvati, while other bronze finds are circular disks, a lamp, and bells. Gold was used for pendants and an imitation dinar from the twelfth century (Perret et al., 2013).

A key artifact in Singapore's National Collection, the Singapore Stone, was formerly located at the mouth of the Singapore River, before the British destroyed it with dynamite in 1843 (Miksic, 1985, pp. 13, 40, 41). Researcher Iain Sinclair, a contributor to Miksic's book identified "kesariva" in the inscriptions found on parts of the Singapore Stone. He said it could be part of the word "parakesarivarman"—a

[8] Muara Takus Compound Site, UNESCO Tentative Lists [https://whc.unesco.org/en/tentativelists/5464/], accessed 10 August 2020.

title used by several kings of the Chola dynasty, a Tamil dynasty of southern India and one of the longest-ruling in history (ninth–thirteenth century). The finding suggests a Tamil presence in the Strait of Singapore dating back 1,000 years (Mahizhnan and Gopal 2019).

The thirteenth-century Karimun Besar inscription, etched into the hill on the northern coast of Karimun Besar, one of the Riau islands located to the southwest of Singapore, records the visit of a holy man, "the glorious Gautamaśrī, Mahāyānist pundit of Gaur", identified with Bengal in eastern India (Sinclair, 2018).

This brief overview of bronze Buddhist relics found in shipwreck sites and coastal sites located in the Indonesian archipelago and the Malay Peninsula opens up possibilities for further research involving not only finds from shipwreck sites, but also encompassing data from coastal shrines. Coastal regions have participated historically in the Indian Ocean network, which in several cases are characterized by local traditions of boat building and navigation, architectural features, as well as narratives of the central experience of trans- locality of maritime communities. In the absence of maps and nautical charts, coastal architecture provided orientation to sailing ships and hence defined the sailing world in the ancient period. The coastal shrines had inter-linkages with traveling groups that moved both across the sea, as well as on routes into the interior, and this is also reflected in the ritual objects found in cargoes at shipwreck sites. Thus, emphasis on the long-distance maritime networks needs to be balanced with an understanding of the local context of coastal shrines and regional connections. This balance is critical for a holistic understanding of objects recovered from shipwreck sites.

References

Acri, A. ed. (2016). *Esoteric Buddhism in Mediaeval Maritime Asia: Networks of Masters, Icons, Texts*. Singapore.

Asouti, E., & Fuller, D. Q. (2008). *Trees and Woodlands of South India. Archaeological Perspectives*. Walnut Creek.

Bautze-Picron, C. (2014). Buddhist images from the Padang Lawas region and the South Asia connection in *History of Padang Lawas. II. Societies of Padang Lawas (mid-9th–13th century CE)*. Cahiers d'Archipel 43, edited by Daniel Perret, Paris, pp. 107–10.

Bhattacharyya, A. K. (1959). The Theme of churning of the Ocean in Indian and Khmer Art. *Arts Asiatiques, 6*(2), 121–134.

Blackburn, Anne. (2010). *Locations of Buddhism: Colonialism and Modernity in Sri Lanka*. Chicago.

Boechari. (1985). Ritual deposits of Candi Gumpung (Muara Jambi) in *SPAFA, Final Report on the Consultative Workshop on Archaeological and Environmental Studies of Srivijaya* (IW2b), 16–30 Sept: 229–72.

Brown, Roxanna M. (2004). History of shipwreck excavation in Southeast Asia. In *The Belitung Wreck: Sunken Treasures from Tang China,* New Zealand: 42–55. [http://nsc.iseas.edu.sg/documents/belitung/The%20Belitung%20Wreck/02_brown_040to055.pdf].

Casson, L. (1989). *The periplus maris erythraei: text with introduction, translation, and commentary*. Princeton University Press.

Christie, J. W. (1998). The medieval Tamil-Language inscriptions in Southeast Asia and China. *Journal of Southeast Asian Studies, 29*(2), 239–268.

Cunningham, Alexander. (1879). *The Stupa at Bharhut.* London.

Flecker, Michael (2002). *The Archaeological Excavation of the Tenth Century Intan Shipwreck.* BAR International Series 1047. Oxford.

Goitein, S. D. F. & Friedman, M. A. (2008). *India Traders of the Middle Ages: Documents from the Cairo Geniza*, Leiden: Brill.

Gokhale, Shobhana (1991). *Kanheri Inscriptions* (Pune Deccan College Post Graduate and Research Institute.

Griffiths, A. (2011). Inscriptions of Sumatra: Further data on the epigraphy of the Musi and Batang Hari Rivers Basins. *Archipel, 81*, 139–175.

Griffiths, A. (2014). Written traces of the buddhist past: Mantras and dhāraṇīs in Indonesian inscriptions. *Bulletin of the School of Oriental and African Studies, 77*(1), 137–194.

Hart, G. L., & Heifetz, H. (1999). *The Four Hundred Songs of War and Wisdom: An Anthology of Poems from Classical Tamil: The Purananuru.* Columbia University Press.

Heng, G. (2019). An Ordinary Ship and its stories of early globalism: World travel, mass production, and art in the Global Middle Ages.". *Journal of Medieval Worlds, 1*(1), 11–54.

Heng, Derek. (2017). The Tang Shipwreck and the nature of China's maritime trade during the late Tang period" in Singapore: 142–59.

Kwa, Chong Guan. (2016). The maritime silk road: The history of an idea". Nalanda-Sriwijaya Centre Working Paper, 23. October.

Liebner, H. H. (2014). *The Siren of Cirebon: A tenth-century trading vessel lost in the Java Sea.* University of Leeds.

Manguin, P.-Y. (1989). The Trading Ships of Insular Southeast Asia: New evidence from Indonesian archaeological sites, In: Proceedings, Pertemuan Ilmiah Arkeologi V, Yogyakarta 1989—[Jakarta]: Ikatan Ahli Arkeologi Indonesia, vol. I 200–22

Mathers, W. M. & Flecker, Michael eds. (1997). *Archaeological Report: Archaeological Recovery of the Java Sea Wreck.* Annapolis, Maryland.

Mahizhnan, Arun & Gopal, Nalina eds. (2019) *From Sojourners to Settlers—Tamils in Southeast Asia and Singapore.* Singapore.

McKinnon, E. E. (1977). Research at Kota Cina: A Sung-Yuan period trading site in eastern Sumatra. *Archipel, 14*, 19–32.

McKinnon, Edwards, E. (2018). An early Buddha image from Buluh Cina Plantation, Deli Serdang Regency, North Sumatra. *NSC Highlights* 7 (Dec 2017–Feb 2018): 8–9.

Miksic John N. Miksic, (1985). *Archaeological Research on the 'Forbidden Hill' of Singapore: Excavations at Fort Canning, 1984.* Singapore: National Museum.

Miksic, John N. (2012). "Riverbeds of Sumatra: The latest target of treasure hunters". *International Institute for Asian Studies Newsletter* 59 (Spring).

Miksic, John N. (2013). *Singapore and the Silk Road of the Sea*, 1300–1800. Singapore.

Miksic, John N. (2014). "The Srivijaya Empire and its maritime aspects". In *The World in the Viking Age*, edited by Søren M. Sindbæk and Athen Trakadas (Roskilde): 115–19.

Noor, Farish A. (2018) An Imperial Divorce: The Division of South and Southeast Asia in Colonial Discourse of the Nineteenth Century, Shyam Saran edited, *Cultural and Civilisational Links between India and Southeast Asia*, Palgrave Macmillan: 301 – 323.

Pearson, M. N. (2003). *The Indian Ocean.* London and New York.

Perret, D., Surachman, H., Koestoro, L. P., & Susetyo. Sukawati,. (2007). Le program archéologique francoindonésien sur Padang Lawas (Sumatra Nord). Réflexions préliminaires. *Archipel, 74*, 45–82.

Perret, D., Surachman, H., Soedewo, E., Oetomo, R. W., & Mudjiono. (2013). The French-Indonesian archaeological project in Kota Cina (North Sumatra): Preliminary results and prospects. *Archipel, 86*, 73–111.

Perret, D., Surachman, H., Oetomo, R. W., Nasoichah, C., Sutrisna, D., & Mudjiono. (2016). The French-Indonesian archaeological project in Kota Cina (North Sumatra): The 2014–2015 excavations. *Archipel, 91*, 3–26.

Perret, Daniel & Surachman. Heddy (2011) South Asia and the Tapanuli area (North-West Sumatra): Ninth–Fourteenth Centuries CE. In: *Early Interactions Between South and Southeast Asia: Reflections on Cross-Cultural Exchange,* edited by Pierre-Yves Manguin, A. Mani, and Geoff Wade, Singapore and New Delhi: 161–76.

Ramachandran, T. N. (1965) *The Nagapattinam and other Buddhist Bronzes in the Madras Museum.* Madras.

Ray, H. P. (2003). *The Archaeology of Seafaring in Ancient South Asia.*

Ray, Himanshu Prabha, (2019). 'Project Mausam'. India's Transnational Initiative: Revisiting UNESCO's World Heritage Convention, Burkhard Schnepel and Tansen Sen edited, Travelling Pasts: *The Politics of Cultural Heritage in the Indian Ocean World,* Brill: Leiden: 39 - 61.

Ray. Himanshu Prabha,. (2021). *Coastal Shrines and Transnational Maritime Networks across India and Southeast Asia.* Routledge.

Reddy, Srinivas Seven Seas and an Ocean of Wisdom: An Indian Episteme for the Indian Ocean, Himanshu Prabha Ray edited, (2020) *The Archaeology of Knowledge Traditions of the Indian Ocean World*, Routledge.

Salmon. Claudine,. (2008). The Chinese origin of the Muara Jambi gong as evidenced by a new archaeological find. *Archipel, 76*, 7–14.

Sen, Tansen. (2003). *Buddhism, Diplomacy, and Trade: The Religious Realignment of Sino-Indian Buddhism, 600–1400.* Honolulu.

Sen-Gupta, A. (2002). Portable Buddhist shrines. *Arts of Asia, 32*(4), 42–61.

Sinclair, Iain. (2018). New light on the Karimun Besar inscription (Prasasti Pasir Panjang) and the Learned Man from Gaur. *NSC Highlights* 11 (Dec 2018–Feb 2019): 16–17.

Skilling, Peter. (2005). Cutting across categories: The ideology of relics in Buddhism. *ARIRIAB* (*Annual Report of the International Research Institute for Advanced Buddhology at Soka University for the Academic Year 2004*) VIII: 269–322.

Subbarayalu, Y. (1998). The Tamil merchant-guild Iinscription at Barus: A rediscovery. In *Le site de Lobu Tua. I: Etudes et documents. Histoire de Barus.* Cahier d'Archipel 30, edited by C. Guillot, Paris: 25–33.

Sundberg, J., & Giebel, R. (2011). The life of the Tang court monk Vajrabodhi as chronicled by Lü Xiang 呂向: South Indian and Śrī Laṅkān antecedents to the arrival of the Buddhist Vajrayāna in 8th century Java and China. *Pacific World: Journal of the Institute of Buddhist Studies (third Series), 13*, 129–222.

Tjoa-Bonatz, Mai Lin, Neidel, J. David & Widiatmoko, Agus (2009). Early architectural images from Muara Jambi on Sumatra, Indonesia. *Asian Perspectives 48*, 1 (Spring): 32–55.

Williams, Joanna. (1992). The Churning of the Ocean of Milk— Myth, Image and Ecology, *India International Centre Quarterly*, Spring—Summer, *19*, 1–2: 145–55.

Chapter 9
Relations Between India and East Asia in Light of Buddhism

Bradley S. Clough

Abstract This chapter will examine historical relations between India and the East Asian countries of China and Japan in light of some of the major interactions that have occurred between Buddhists from these cultures. Our investigation is organized into four parts. Part I will provide introduction to the main doctrinal and practical teachings of the Buddhist tradition, as it arose and developed in India in the last half of the final millennium before the Common Era. Special attention will be given to those aspects that made it of universal human appeal, prepared to be transmissible to cultures beyond the borders of its land of origins. Next, we will turn to the remarkable story of Buddhism's exportation from India, as well as from adjacent regions under strong Indian influence, first into China over the course of the first millennium of the Common Era, and eventually from China to Japan, where Japanese Buddhists too came to regard India as a land of sacred origins, with which they sought meaningful connections. This story will be told in three segments. The first segment, Part II of this chapter, will cover the activities of the missionary-minded Buddhist monks of Indian heritage who migrated to China in the earliest centuries CE and engineered the extraordinarily complex, detailed, and challenging work of establishing their religion on foreign soil, primarily by organizing and engaging in the translation of the massive body of Indian Buddhist texts into the Chinese language. The segment will also examine the extraordinary circumstances that led to the creation of a women's monastic order in China, initiated by a cohort of nuns from South Asia. The second segment, Part III of this chapter, will treat the equally impressive endeavors of the dedicated, intrepid Chinese Buddhist monks who, in the centuries following the successful initial implantation of the religion in their own country, journeyed as pilgrims on their own mission to India, to learn and document even more about their chosen spiritual path, as it continued to live and thrive in what they regarded as the sacred terrain of its roots. Finally, in the third segment, Part IV of this chapter, we will investigate the most salient and interesting modern development in the history of interactions between East Asian and South Asian Buddhists. Due to the declining fates of Buddhism in both India and China, not much of historical relevance took place between ancient and modern times. However, in the nineteenth and twentieth

B. S. Clough (✉)
Bard College, Annandale, NY, USA
e-mail: bclough@bard.edu

L. Vemsani (ed.), *Handbook of Indian History*,
https://doi.org/10.1007/978-981-97-6207-1_9

centuries, key figures in the Buddhist culture of Japan, where Buddhism had been received from China and Korea 1200 years before and thrived ever since, traveled to India and Sri Lanka, in order to fulfill ambitions quite similar to those of their counterpart Chinese pilgrims from a much earlier era.

Keywords Chinese Buddhism · Japanese Buddhism · Intercultural history · Global Buddhism · Siddhartha Gautama · Upanishads · Samsara · Shravakayana · Mahayana · Ashoka · Dipavamsa · Moggaliputtatissa · Gandhara · Takshashila · Gandhara · Kushan · Bamiyan · Kashgar · Dunhuang · Kumarajiva · Amitabha sutra · Sukhavati sutra · Vimalakirtinirdesha · Faxian · Xuanzang · Yijing · Nalanda · Shilabhadra · Kanauj · Bodhisena · Todaiji

9.1 Introduction

In the case of a civilization with as long, rich, and influential a history as India's, it is hardly surprising that a prominent dimension in that history would be intercultural in scope. Considering not only Indian but also global intercultural history, certainly one of the most fascinating and noteworthy chapters is that of South Asia's relations with the major East Asian countries of China and Japan, as significantly facilitated by the spread of the Buddhist religion from the subcontinent to these lands. In pre-modern times especially, it was largely in this realm of religious—rather than political—activity that we find most of the important interchanges between these cultures taking place.

This chapter promises to examine the history of Indian relations with China and Japan in light of Buddhism, with a focus on this history's most impactful episodes and persons. To orient the reader, Part I will provide an introduction to the main doctrinal and practical teachings of the Buddhist tradition, as it arose and developed in India in the last half of the final millennium BCE. Special attention will be given to those aspects that made the religion of universal human appeal, preparing it to be transmissible to cultures beyond the borders of its land of origins.

Next, we will turn to the remarkable story of Buddhism's exportation from India, as well as from adjacent regions under strong Indian influence, first into China over the course of the first millennium CE, and eventually from China to Japan, where Japanese Buddhists too came to regard India as a land of sacred origins, with which they sought meaningful connections. This story will be told in three segments. The first segment, Part II of this chapter, will cover the activities of the missionary-minded Buddhist monks[1] of Indian heritage who migrated to China in the earliest centuries CE and engineered the extraordinarily complex, detailed, and challenging work of

[1] The Buddhist community or Sangha [*saṃgha*] has been comprised of two wings, lay and monastic. Within the monastic wing there are nuns or bhikshunis [*bhikṣuṇī*], as well as monks or bhikshus [*bhikṣu*]. When we are referring to only male members of the Sangha is this chapter, we will use the word "monk(s)." This will be frequent, because most of the activities we will document were exclusively carried out by them. On those occasions when we are referring exclusively to female

establishing their religion on foreign soil, primarily by organizing and engaging in the translation of the massive body of Indian Buddhist texts into the Chinese language. The segment will also examine the extraordinary circumstances that led to the creation of a women's monastic order in China, initiated by a cohort of nuns from South Asia. The second segment, Part III of this chapter, will treat the equally impressive endeavors of the dedicated, intrepid Chinese Buddhist monks who, in the centuries following the successful initial implantation of the religion in their own country, journeyed as pilgrims on their own mission to India, to learn and document even more about their chosen spiritual path, as it continued to live and thrive in what they regarded as the sacred terrain of its roots. Finally, in the third segment, Part IV of this chapter, we will investigate the most salient and interesting modern development in the history of interactions between East Asian and South Asian Buddhists. Due to the declining fates of Buddhism in both India and China, not much of historical relevance took place between the first millennium and modern times. However, in the nineteenth and twentieth centuries, key figures in the Buddhist culture of Japan, where Buddhism had been received from China and Korea 1200 years before and thrived ever since, traveled to India and Sri Lanka, in order to fulfill ambitions quite similar to those of their counterpart Chinese pilgrims from a much earlier era.

9.2 The Buddhist Religion and Its Transmissibility Across Cultures

Buddhism is the religion founded by the historical figure known as Siddhartha [Siddhārtha] Gautama, who lived sometime around the 5th–fourth centuries BCE in the Ganga River basin region of India. Based upon the central event at the core of Buddhism, which is the spiritually liberating awakening that he is said to have experienced at the culmination of his practice, his followers ever since have referred to him as the Buddha or "Awakened One". Tradition holds that he achieved this awakening at age 35, after which he spent the remaining 45 years of this life spreading the teaching, known as the Dharma, of what he had realized and forming a small but growing community, known as the Sangha, of monastic and lay adherents.

In an era when Buddhism began, a revolutionary religious movement was afoot in the Ganga River basin that was seminal in establishing a worldview that would become commonly shared by all spiritual traditions that developed in India. This movement, which included those teachers and disciples who would compose the foundational Hindu Upanishads [*Upaniṣad*], as well as the followers of the leader Mahavira [Mahāvīra] who would form the Jain religion, was comprised of individuals and communities who had chosen to renounce societal and familial ties and adopt ascetic ways of life, in order to pursue, in a very rigorous fashion, the goal of liberation from worldly suffering. According to the worldview commonly held among these

members of the Sangha, we will use the word "nun(s)." At other times, when we are referring collectively to both male and female cenobites, we will use the word "monastic(s).".

renouncers, life was a constantly repeating cycle (samsara [*saṁsāra*]: "that which flows around"; bhavachakra [*bhavacakra*]: "cyclical existence"[2]) of birth and death. The driving force behind repeated existence or rebirth in this world was karma or "action". As a doctrine of moral cause and effect, the law of karma dictated that the conditions of a person's present life and subsequent rebirths were determined by the nature of the actions committed by that person. In short, positive actions that were beneficial to others resulted in good and bettering living conditions in this and future lifetimes for the individual committing them, and negative actions that were harmful to others resulted in bad and worsening conditions in the future. In response to the human dilemma thus conceived—that we are bound by our actions to live in an endless cycle of existence, where even in the best of conditions we are subject to repeatedly experience inevitably unpleasant conditions like sickness, old age, and death—these renouncers maintained that a state of complete, eternal liberation from the afflictions of samsara was real and achievable, and thus devoted their lives to developing and pursuing spiritual disciplines designed to bring that goal (termed variously in different traditions: Hindu: moksha [*mokṣa*]; Jain: *kaivalya*; Buddhist: nirvana [*nirvāṇa*]) about.

The essence of the Buddha's particular Dharma is found in a formula he taught while wandering and preaching in his environs, called the "4 Noble Truths". The first of these shows that Buddhism, like other major traditions that have become global religions over history, is primarily concerned with addressing the problem of human suffering and offering a way of living that leads to its transcendence. Specifically, the First Noble Truth maintains that all conditions of human life are characterized by a deep and pervasive sense of duhkha [*duḥkha*], typically translated as "suffering", but more literally meaning "dissatisfaction".

The Second Noble Truth identifies the *cause* of duhkha, which is intense desire or craving for the things of this world as sources of lasting pleasure, satisfaction, and happiness. Such craving leads us to an addictive clinging or attachment to worldly things. Underlying craving and attachment is a fundamental ignorance or delusion about the nature of reality.

The Second Noble Truth's assessment of the human condition stems from one of the key insights that the Buddha realized during his liberative spiritual awakening, which was that all existing things in the world, whether animate beings or inanimate objects, are basically insubstantial and impermanent. To use Buddhist terminology, all things are shunya [*śūnya*], meaning "empty" of substantial existence, or anatman [*anatman*], meaning "without self"—"self" in the sense of a permanent core essence. Gaining this wisdom into the true nature of things, the Buddha concluded that we suffer because we ignorantly crave lasting pleasure from people, experiences, and things that by their very nature can't provide such enduring satisfaction. When we intensely desire everlasting happiness from things which are too fleeting to be reliable sources of ongoing satisfaction, we suffer. Due to deluded expectations that our happiness lies in lasting pleasant experiences, we are bound to be dissatisfied every time that they inevitably turn out not to persist. The solution to the problem of

[2] All Indian terms in this chapter, unless otherwise noted, are given in the Sanskrit language.

suffering would then be to give up its cause, attachment to the ephemeral things of the world. This liberation from attachment to things can be achieved by anyone, by gaining access to the same meditative insight that the Buddha had about the impermanence of things, which instills the wisdom that there is no reason to crave for and cling to anything.

The Third Noble Truth reasons that if persistent suffering arises from the cause of deluded craving and attachment, then a lasting *cessation* of suffering can be realized once that cause is eradicated. The Buddhist term for this eternal freedom is nirvana, which means the "extinguishing" of suffering. The term "bodhi", referring to the experience of "awakening" to the truth that frees one from suffering, is often synonymous. The Third Noble simply asserts that just as there is the reality of persistent suffering in the bondage of samsara, due to passionate attachment based in ignorance, there is also the reality of everlasting freedom and bliss in nirvana, due to dispassionate detachment based on wisdom.

This leads us to the Fourth Noble Truth, which lays out the path of practical discipline that leads to the extinguishing of suffering that is nirvana. Although there is some variation in the path structures of the two major forms of Buddhism that originated in India and would predominate in different parts of Asia once the religion spread beyond the subcontinent, with the Shravakayana [Śrāvakayāna] ("Disciples' Vehicle") form that would flourish in Southeast Asia describing its path in terms of 8 practices (the "Noble Eightfold Path") and the Mahayana [Mahāyāna] ("Great Vehicle") form that would thrive in Central and East Asia (including China and Japan) describing its path in terms of 6 practices (the "Path of 6 Perfections"), what these paths hold in common is most significant.[3] These forms of Buddhism agree that the three essential areas of religious training are: (1) morality; (2) meditation; and (3) wisdom.

As indicated above, the realization of wisdom, the understanding of "things as they really are", as Buddhist texts put it, is a primary goal of the path. With respect to practically achieving this goal, meditation or cultivation of the mind is foremost in importance. If the mind ignorantly sees worldly things as permanent and thus the sources of lasting satisfaction in life, the consequent craving and attachment that arise in the mind will lead to suffering. However, if one can retrain the mind through meditation, to wisely understand things as impermanent ("without self" or "empty" in Buddhist terms), the consequent dispassion and detachment that arise from this mental reorientation will lead to the freedom and contentment of nirvana.

Two meditation techniques are employed in the Buddhist practice of the path, one following upon the other. In order to engage in the quintessential kind of Buddhist mental cultivation, known as "insight meditation", a practitioner must first prepare the mind with what is called "tranquility meditation". The idea is that before one can skillfully use the mind to arrive at a liberating wisdom into the true nature of

[3] In India, the Shravakayana was divided into approximately 18 schools. One of them, the Theravada [Theravāda] or "Teaching of the Elders," is the school that would predominate in Sri Lanka and Southeast Asia. The Mahayana, a slightly later developing reform movement, saw itself as a superior form, and thus typically labeled Shravakayana schools with the pejorative label Hinayana [Hinayāna] or "Lesser Vehicle".

reality, which is what is accomplished in insight meditation, one must first stabilize, pacify, and focus the mind for prolonged periods of time, which is what tranquility meditation accomplishes. Once the ability to maintain a calm and concentrated mind is strong, one initiates insight meditation, which employs the technique known as "mindfulness". Mindfulness practice involves undistracted observation of life in the process. It applies unadorned, nonjudgmental, and nonreactive attention to the flux of one's own everchanging physical, emotional, and mental states, as well as to the objects of the outside world that are perceivable to the mind through the senses. By repeatedly practicing mindfulness, one deeply ingrains the understanding that everything within and without oneself is subject to change. This internalized realization of the impermanent nature of things leads the practitioner to no longer crave and become attached to things, and thus reach nirvanic freedom from them.

This liberating insight into the impermanent nature of things also has important implications for the other key practical dimension of the Buddhist path, morality, because it forcefully impacts how one sees oneself and others, and thus how one should treat and interact with others. When one realizes that one's very own person is (like everything else) "empty" or "without self" in any unchanging, enduring sense, one sees that the notion of humans as individuals existing separately and independently from each other is delusional. Instead of seeing oneself and others as separate individuals, one realizes that in truth, we exist in profoundly dependent and interconnected ways with each other.

When the delusion of separate individuality is seen through and there is recognition instead of the interdependence of all things, the Buddhist practitioner understands that each person's actions can affect the living conditions of everyone else in the world, and vice-versa, that everyone else's actions can impact one's own life situation. And with the realization that every being's actions have universal consequences and thus all beings' fates are intertwined, comes a crucial kind of moral imperative for Buddhists: the best, most skillful way to live in this world is with great compassion and generosity toward all.

When one examines Buddhist discourse on morality, these two principles of compassion and generosity stand out. As discussed so far here, their importance in the Buddhist scheme of things stems from meditative insight, the kind that the Buddha experienced during his great awakening, which in turn informed the content of the Dharma he taught thereafter. This insight has been available as well to the small minority of monastics within historical Buddhist communities who both possessed a high degree of intense personal drive and were afforded the lengthy amounts of free time necessary to engage in serious, fruitful meditation practice. However, for the vast majority of Buddhist lay followers especially, those whose busy work and family lives make meditation practice close to impossible to pursue, the preeminent principles of compassion and generosity are taught as root moral foundations of the Buddhist path, as the indispensable centerpieces of the Buddhist life from its very onset. Compassion and generosity are related to another fundamental Buddhist ethical precept, ahimsa [*ahiṃsā*] or nonviolence, but move beyond avoidance of harm to others to include active relief of others' suffering and promotion of others' wellbeing.

In the Shravakayana and Mahayana forms of Buddhism, both of which Indian missionaries brought to East Asia, compassion is regarded as the essential complement to wisdom in the ideal religious life. But in the Mahayana forms that would eventually predominate in China and Japan, compassion, in the sense of selflessly caring for others' welfare above one's own, becomes the paramount quality in the person of its path's ideal adherent, the bodhisattva ("being intent upon awakening").[4] Dedicating oneself to compassionate work for the benefit of others is at the core of the vow that all Mahayana adherents take as motivation for their practice, because of the conviction that it above all else will lead to the awakening of all beings, both self and others. Ultimately, working for the benefit of others means showing them the way out of samsara, that is, the way to awakening, by instructing them in the Dharma and modeling for them its moral and meditative way of life. But of equal importance, and what necessarily must come first, is working for the benefit of others by actively relieving their suffering.

In helping to remove the suffering of others, no type of activity is more important than giving or generosity. In Mahayana practice, generosity is the very first of the six "perfections" or ideal virtues that comprise the path of the bodhisattva. One reason why it is so instrumental is that just as compassion serves as an effective antidote to hatred, one of the main causes of suffering according to the Buddha, generosity works well to counteract selfish craving for material possessions and pleasures, which as we've seen is another major source of suffering. In this way, generosity has a positive spiritual impact on the donor. But how it can help others is always regarded as the nobler motivation.

Generosity also functions as *the* key connecting link between the monastic and lay wings of the Sangha. Monastics give instruction in the Dharma, which is regarded as the most valuable gift possible, because it directly furthers its recipients along the path to awakening. Lay people reciprocate by providing material support, especially in the form of clothing and regular almsfood, for the mostly possessionless monastics. Taking care of the monks' material needs enables them to devote most of their time to their own practice in pursuit of awakening. These and other acts of generosity are primary generators of what Buddhists call "merit", the store of wholesome karma that promises to bear positive, beneficial fruits for the giver in this and future lifetimes. But again, it is regarded as most valuable in terms of what it can do to aid others. Once merit is earned, it too can be given away for others' benefit. Sharing one's merit with others less fortunate is one of the most strongly encouraged forms of generosity in Buddhist societies.

With an overview of the main dimensions of Buddhism now in place, we can turn to the question of how a religion so grounded in a specifically Indian worldview—presupposing ideas like samsara, karma, and nirvaṇa—could also be of universal appeal and thus so transmissible to other cultures, such as the East Asian ones of China and Japan.

---

[4] In Mahayana Buddhism, the term bodhisattva refers to both human aspirants to the goal of awakening or Buddhahood and divine figures who utilize extraordinary powers to assist and protect their human devotees.

First, in comparison with other major missionary-oriented religions that have spread widely around the world, namely Christianity and Islam, Buddhism has been decidedly less exclusivist and more tolerant with respect to indigenous traditions it encounters when introducing itself to new cultures. In such situations, Buddhism has tended not to forbid the worship of native deities, accepting them rather as newly converted protectors of the Dharma. Furthermore, it has been more flexible and accommodating with respect to more worldly matters. While Buddhism has seen itself as religiously superior in terms of spiritual truth and efficacy, in other areas of human societal life—particularly economic, social, and political ones—it has usually been content not to interfere, leaving them to be addressed by native traditions. Here examples of other major religions, such as Hinduism and Confucianism are germane. It is hard to imagine the ethical program of Hinduism, tied so closely as it is to the situational contingencies of India's unique social system, wherein moral expectations for people often differ according to their particular caste affiliation, being transportable outside of that country, and historically this has proven to be largely so. Similarly, Confucianism, based as it is so firmly in distinctly Chinese political notions, such as the "mandate of Heaven", wherein a ruler can only maintain his divinely given right to govern when citizens' obedience to laws is reciprocated with paternalistic care, has only been capable of flourishing in East Asian countries within the greater Chinese sphere of cultural influence, which accept the notion that cosmic spiritual harmony is contingent upon human social cooperation.

By contrast, Buddhism has shown itself to have greater translatability outside of its land origins than the more culturally specific traditions discussed just above. Looking at the two main domains of Buddhist practice, in the realm of ethics it is more universalist in the moral standards it applies to all persons, regardless of economic, social, or political status, and in its system of meditation, it is more concerned with treating individual psychological traits that are commonly shared by all human beings, irrespective of the given social categories and norms of any particular society.

Turning to meditation first, Buddhism's clear orientation toward the inner world of the individual psyche as the locus of where suffering is both created and transcended, gives the religion much of its universal relevance and applicability, for people's characteristic emotional and psychological states are the same everywhere, differing not from culture to culture. The mental attitudes that Buddhism treats as the causes of suffering are common to the human condition: Craving sensual pleasures and wishing pleasant feelings to never cease, as well as aversion to sensorial pain and wishing unpleasant feelings never to arise, are part of shared human experience. It is hardly untypical for people to feel hatred and enmity toward beings and forces that they perceive to be separate from and antagonistic toward themselves. And it is not unusual for individuals to draw false conclusions about the nature of the world based on mere appearances or be ignorant of how things work beneath the surface of reality, and to suffer as a result. Likewise, the states of mind that the Buddhist program of meditative cultivation promotes as the pathways to the transcendence of suffering—detachment and equanimity to eliminate and replace craving and aversion, compassion and loving-kindness as antidotes for hatred and enmity, and wisdom or insight into the true nature of reality to treat delusion and ignorance—are also available to any and all human minds willing to undergo the rigorous training necessary to develop them fully. Finding lasting sources of contentment and joy in peace, love, and understanding is universal too.

But as discussed, meditation, especially in pre-modern Buddhist times, was largely practiced within the relatively rarefied monastic contexts. So, to see what has been even more universally appealing about Buddhism, we must turn to the moral aspects of the Dharma that apply to all participants—laypersons and monastics alike—across the tradition.

One key to understanding Buddhist morality's universal appeal and transmissibility is how centrally it is framed in terms of its practicality and the benefit it confers upon those who apply it in their lives. We can see this especially in the way Buddhism conceives of personal conduct, wherein an individual's actions are considered "good" not only because they are virtuous or wholesome in an ethical sense, but also because they are useful, with the results stemming from them being beneficial to the actor's future existential condition. This is best captured in the concept of kushala [*kuśala*], an adjectival term that is applied both to good moral actions like nonviolence, honesty, and generosity that are motivated by wholesome intentions like loving-kindness and clearmindedness, and to the fortunate future karmic consequences that result from them. Kushala simultaneously has the connotations of: (1) "good", "virtuous", or "wholesome"; (2) "skillful" or "useful"; and (3) "fortunate", "salutary", or "meritorious".

So, for people operating within a Buddhist worldview, actions that are morally "good" aren't just so in some abstract or metaphysical ethical sense, they are also good in the very practical sense that they help you navigate life's difficulties more skillfully and bring fortune to your future life conditions, according to the law of karma. To be good is a useful, beneficial thing to be. And to be clear, it isn't just material life circumstances that one is positively affecting with one's good behavior. With every good thought, word, or deed, a person is also improving mental conditioning, orienting the mind toward states of greater positivity. This is how the law of karma works within an individual's mental world: For every action—mental, verbal, or physical—that a person intentionally takes, a corresponding tendency or habit (samskara [*saṁskāra*]) is formed in the mind. So, every time someone acts with generosity and compassion, for example, the more the actor's mind will become more habitualized toward such giving, loving states in the future, as well as toward the contentment and happiness that stem from seeing the positive results such motivated actions have.

Such benefits aren't limited to the actor in a merely self-serving way. Treating others with love, kindness, and generosity also practically benefits those on the receiving end of such moral action. A telling example of this is found in the central act of exchange within historical Buddhist communities discussed earlier—the monastics giving Dharma instruction and the layfolk reciprocating by providing their teachers with the basic necessities of life, food and clothing especially. For the lay people, giving daily food to monastics doesn't just karmically improve their own circumstances and strengthen their own mental frames of mind, it is salutary for the recipients as well, assuaging their physical hunger and the psychological stress that comes from lack of nutrition, and freeing them up to devote their time and energy most fully to practical spiritual exercises like meditation. So, in this way, doing good in the Buddhist scheme of things very practically benefits both self and others. This is surely a great source of Buddhism's universal appeal and a major reason why it's been so transmissible across cultures.

9.3 The Importation of Indian Buddhism to China: The Translation of the Buddhist Canon into Chinese and the Creation of the Nuns' Order

As much as the Buddhist orientation toward individual training of the mind and its emphasis on universalist ethics made the religion eminently transmissible across cultures, the historically extraordinary exportation of this religion from India to China that we will document would not likely have occurred without a clear and explicit directive from its founder, stating that the mission to spread it abroad was central to and consistent with the principles of his Dharma. In the section of the early Indian Buddhist scriptures devoted to the Buddha's formation and development of his monastic community, we find this telling set of instructions, delivered to an assembly of the first 60 monks to join his Sangha:

> Go forth wandering, o monks, for the benefit of the many, for the happiness of many, out of compassion for the world, and for the welfare, benefit, and happiness of humans and gods. Let not two of you travel in the same direction. Meaningfully and articulately expound the Dharma that is beautiful in the beginning, beautiful in the middle, and beautiful in the end. Reveal the holy life that is completely realized and wholly pure. There are beings with little dust in their eyes who are going to ruin because they are not hearing the Dharma, but understanding the Dharma, they will flourish.[5]

It is one thing for Buddhist teaching to be of broad doctrinal and practical appeal in theory, but without the religion's founder issuing such an explicit directive—so clearly imbued with that universalistic spirit of compassion and drive for liberating wisdom that we've discussed—for its monastic representatives to actively take up missionizing as a key part of their way of life, it's unlikely that Buddhism would have spread as remarkably widely as it would, far beyond India's borders to almost every corner of Asian continent, including the Eastern lands of China and Japan that are our concern here.

History also tells us that for those religions that fulfilled their project to spread expansively across cultures, another key to success was the support of imperial political power which could greatly strengthen their missionary project. For Buddhism in its Indian place of origin, this necessary development came during the Maurya Empire

[5] This passage is found in two places in the canon of ancient Buddhist texts preserved in the Pāli language: Vinaya I, 20–21 and Saṃyutta Nikāya 1. 105–106.

in the reign, from 268–232 BCE, of its mightiest ruler, Ashoka [Aśoka]. In the immediate aftermath of conquering almost the whole subcontinent, King Ashoka converted to Buddhism and devoted much effort to facilitating its influence throughout India and beyond. Profoundly disillusioned with the violence he was responsible for in his military campaigns, Ashoka found much solace in Buddhism's peaceful ethics. In the many rock and pillar edicts and inscriptions that he famously had erected throughout his empire, as well as in the work of governmental ministers he appointed to oversee and enforce his policies, Ashoka vigorously promoted what he called the "victory of Dharma" over that of harmful warfare. For the most part, this "Dharma" that he publicly advanced was not the particular Buddhist Dharma that he seems to have adopted in his personal life, but rather a more general kind of moral righteousness that embraced concerns for social welfare, religious tolerance, and ethical principles of truth and nonviolence commonly shared by Hindus, Jains, Buddhists, and members of other currently prominent spiritual movements alike. However, there is also evidence that he took active measures to promote the health of the monastic community and increase its sphere of influence. Prior to Ashoka, Buddhism was not well-established much beyond the region known as the Madhyadesha [*Madhyadeśa*], the greater Ganges River basin area of northeastern India. According to the historical chronicle the *Dipavamsa* [*Dīpavaṃsa*], composed in Sri Lanka around the fourth century CE, Ashoka convened an important monastic council during his reign and under the leadership of the monk he appointed to head it, Moggaliputtatissa, one of its main outcomes was the dispatching of Buddhist missions to nine new regions. Some of these lands, Sri Lanka (Pali [Pāli]: *Tambapaṇṇi*) and lower Burma (Pali: *Suvannabhumi* [*Suvaṇṇabhūmi*]), were beyond India, while others were within it, in specific areas to the west (parts of modern-day Sindh [Pakistan], Gujarat, and Maharashtra), south (northern Karnataka and Mahishamandala [Mahiṣamaṇḍala], a district below the Vindhya mountains), and north (Kashmir-Gandhara [Kashmira-Gandhāra] and the Himalayas) of Madhyadesha.[6]

Before proceeding further in our narrative, it is important to pause here and make a note about the kind of sources we often rely upon to tell the story of Indian Buddhism's eventual spread to East Asia, and the historical reliability of these sources. These sources frequently deal with personages to whom Buddhist traditions ascribe great holiness or saintliness, and as such must be regarded as "hagiographical" ones, which typically embellish the accounts of revered figures by adding layers of legend to them, to the point where difficulties arise in discerning what events in their lives have actual historicity to them. In such cases, we must seek as much as possible independent corroboration of events in other, alternative sources which are comparatively free of hagiographical motivations and content.

Buddhist accounts of King Ashoka are among the most hagiographically elaborate ones, and so here is a case where independent confirmation of evidence must be found. With respect to the *Dipavamsa*'s chronicling of the nine missions initiated by Ashoka, there is much other evidence found, both in his own edicts about where

[6] *Dīpavaṃsa* 8.1–13.

he sent religious envoys and in inscriptions made by monks and royal patrons in the regions themselves, that verify the historicity of these missions (Hazra, p. 39).

Of these various Indic cultural areas named in this account of Ashoka's nine missions, the one that bears most significance for how Buddhism spread to China, is that of the northwestern area of Kashmir-Gandhara. Gandhara, located in the Swat and Peshawar valleys (of today's northern Pakistan and southeastern Afghanistan), was a cosmopolitan place at the crossroads of the various trade routes, known collectively as the "Silk Road", that ran back and forth between Europe, the Middle East, India, Central Asia, and China. As merchants from all these areas moved through Gandhara, it became a place of rich cultural exchange. Gandhāra's capital of Takshashila [Takṣaśilā] (known in the West by its Greek name, Taxila), flourished as a center for Buddhist as well as Hindu learning, especially between the first and fifth centuries CE, the crucial period of Indian Buddhism's importation to China (Buswell and Lopez, entries on "Gandhāra" and "Takṣaśilā", p. 311 and p. 892, respectively).

From this vital area of the Indian northwest, the religion was carried to the Central Asian territories of Bactria, Parthia, Sogdia, Khotan, and Kucha, which in turn became prominent Buddhist centers and the launching grounds from which monks introduced the Dharma to China (Ch'en, p. 18). These developments intensified during the next major dynasty in India following the Mauryas under Ashoka, the Kushan [Kuṣāṇa] Empire (30–375 CE), which was centered in Gandhara. Led by kings of Scythian (Chinese: Yuehzhi) heritage,[7] the Kushaṇ Empire, extending into the Central Asian territories mentioned above, also provided major patronage to Buddhism in the early centuries CE. Under the auspices of the Kushaṇ monarch King Kanishka [Kaniṣka], whom Buddhist tradition holds in esteem second only to Ashoka, an important council was held in Kashmir, where all available scriptural manuscripts were gathered and a project of composing commentaries on them was initiated, and thus the Dharma became even more firmly established in this pivotal transit zone in northwest India (Ch'en, p. 18).

For travelers venturing the long and difficult overland trip from India to China, like the Buddhist lay merchants and monastic pilgrims who did so in first exporting their religion in the early centuries CE, northwest India was the usual starting point. From there, they would initially journey to Bamiyan (in today's Afghanistan), then across the Hindu Kush mountains to Balkh, and from Balkh over the Pamir range to Kashgar. Kashgar, with its numerous Buddhist monasteries, was a welcome resting place for voyagers exhausted by the arduous climbs over treacherous alpine passes. From Kashgar, they had the choice of two major international trade highways—both part of the famous Silk Road referred to above—that ran through oases towns along the northern and southern rims of the imposing Taklamakan Desert. The centers at Kucha on the northern route and Khotan on the southern route were by far the most important. The two arteries eventually converged in the northwest Chinese frontier city of Dunhuang, which developed into the most important locale in Buddhist history. To provide havens for road-weary monks, caves were dug out if its hills, and

[7] The Scythians or Yuehzhi had their origins in northwest China. Subsequently, nomadic wanderings brought them eventually to India via Central Asia.

in these grottoes scholars from all over the known Buddhist world gathered to hold religious discussions and debates, translate sacred scriptures, and create Buddhist art (Ch'en, pp. 17–18).

Whereas these land routes appear to be the most commonly used passages for the transmission of Buddhism from India to China, especially in the early half of the first millennium CE when Indian and Central Asian monks were carrying out the project, it was also possible to make the voyage via sea routes (Lancaster, *passim*), with the major points of departure on the Bay of Bengal being Kaveripattanam at the mouth of the Cauvery River and Tamralipti at the mouth of the Ganga. Ships would either follow the coastline around the Malay Peninsula until arriving in Tomkin or Canton, or sail to these south China ports after stopping over in Java. Ocean travel was the preferred way for Chinese Buddhist pilgrim-monks to come to India, especially in the latter half of the first millennium, when Chinese power was no longer dominant in Central Asia (Ch'en, p. 20).

Legends abound in the Chinese sources about how Buddhism was first introduced to their country, all of which greatly simplify the complex processes involved in the religion's transmission,[8] but the most reliable historical records indicate that Indian and Central Asian traders formed the crucial first wave of its importation at the beginning of the Common Era (Mitchell and Jacoby, pp. 223–24). There is evidence of merchant Buddhist communities in the Han Dynasty (207 BCE–220 CE) capital of Luoyang around the first century CE (Hanson, p. 155). This information fits very well with what we know about the social makeup of the laity within Buddhist communities since their very inception in India. From his very first efforts to win followers, the Buddha focused on cities rather than rural settings, for there he found members of the merchant classes who could provide essential financial support (Hanson, *ibid*). From the urban lay merchants' side, there appears to have always been an elective affinity between their work ethic, according to which intensive labor and investment bears future profit, and the pragmatic Buddhist notion we've discussed of good, skillful karma creating merit, which can be seen as a kind of spiritual currency that could be laid up in treasury to secure a better future rebirth.

Of course, the activities of mendicant monks coming along the trade routes from India and Central Asia in the close wake of these merchants—activities like the translation of Buddhist texts from Indic languages to Chinese, the most important project of the missions and our central focus hereafter—were possible only because of great lay participation, for after all nothing practical could be accomplished without the food that sustained and the cloth that protected the monks as they went about their essential work (Carrithers, p. 84).

Before we document the fascinating history of translation of texts, one of the richest chapters in the story of Sino-Indian relations in light of Buddhism, we must briefly outline the conditions in the late Han period that opened the door for the introduction of this foreign religion. Chinese culture has always looked askance at the importation of anything that comes from outside of its own civilization; outside

[8] Ch'en, pp. 29–40 has a helpful summary of these entertaining but historically unedifying tales.

people and customs were typically labeled "barbarian" (*yi*), so conditions would've had to have been rather unusual.

Competition on the religious front was the main obstacle to Buddhism's establishment, and here it faced great resistance from the two major native traditions with ancient roots, Confucianism and Daoism. Confucianism stood as the strongest opponent, due to both its central principles and its status within the political power structure. Confucian principles center on realizing social and cosmic peace through harmonious human relations, which are established by loyalty to family and, by extension, to the ruling government. Thus Confucians stood forcefully against the renunciatory ethic of Buddhist monasticism, which they saw as socially parasitic and damaging to the fabric of family and society. Furthermore, Confucianism in this era had the full support of governmental power behind it, for the teachings of its classic texts had been adopted as the official ideology of the Han imperial regime. While Daoism did not possess such sanctioning by the state, it nevertheless enjoyed widespread popular appeal, due to its emphasis on individual freedom and peaceful living, achieved through harmonizing oneself with the great forces of nature. By the late Han era, the main goal of Daoism had become physical immortality, realized by the ingestion of elixirs, and in this regard Daoists found Buddhism, with its focus on the impermanence of life and detachment from bodily desires, disappointing and lacking.

Despite these substantial challenges to Buddhism, the door to its establishment was opened by the end of the Han era, when its ruling classes descended into violent factionalism and oppression of the peasant masses, which led to the government's collapse and the discrediting of the Confucian teachings and institutions with which the regime had been so closely associated.[9] Daoism remained popular, but many Chinese saw Buddhism, with its similar emphasis on simple, unadorned living, as a worthy complement to it (Mitchell and Jacoby, p. 224). Moved by the striking images of the Buddha brought by monks, they incorporated him as a divine member of the growing pantheon of Daoist deities, and in time a significant portion of the country's influential gentry class of Daoist-oriented intellectuals became deeply impressed by the sophistication of Buddhism's philosophical ideas and the effectiveness of its meditation techniques, which they also saw as compatible with their religion (Wright, p. 32).

Once there were such breaches into which Indian Buddhism could step, the millennium-long, complex process of its acculturation into Chinese civilization could begin, as it did in the politically tumultuous period of the "Six Dynasties" (220–589 CE) following the Han. Our focus will be on the richest and most fascinating aspect of this process, with respect to the history of Sino-Indian relations: the great collaborative project of translating Buddhist canonical literature—most often from Sanskrit, but from other Buddhist Prakrit languages as well—into Chinese.

[9] See Chapter One, titled "Han China," of Arthur F. Wright, *Buddhism in Chinese History* (Stanford: Stanford University Press, 1971), for a cogent and more detailed treatment of the religious and political developments of this period. My brief description here is indebted to Wright's work.

For the Central Asian and Indian scholar-monks who brought their scriptures to this land now bristling with enthusiasm for spiritual teachings of this new religion and their earnest, newly ordained Chinese partners, many challenges arose in their translation work, beginning with the profound dissimilarities between Sanskrit and classical Chinese, both languages with long literary traditions stretching back at least to the second millennium BCE. Sanskrit, belonging to the Indo-European family of languages, has a phonetic alphabet, while Chinese, belonging to the Sino-Tibetan linguistic group, is written in logographic characters. Sanskrit words are usually polysyllabic, while Chinese words are largely monosyllabic. Sanskrit is a highly inflected language, wherein nouns have many cases and verbs have many tenses and persons, while Chinese is uninflected, with nouns having one case and verbs having one tense (Hanson, p. 161). Sanskrit has a formal and very elaborate grammatical system, while Chinese has no systematized grammar. In terms of styles of writing, Indian literature has a tendency to be discursive and abstract, with a penchant for elaborate, flowery metaphors, while Chinese literature prefers terse expression and concrete imagery, with metaphors drawn from familiar nature (Wright, p. 33).

Furthermore, profound conceptual gulfs also existed between Indian and Chinese cultures. Indian religious traditions had developed a sophisticated science of psychological analysis, while Chinese traditions at this historical juncture had shown little interest in analyzing the individual human personality in component parts. Concepts of time and space were also quite different, with the Chinese conceiving of both as finite and measuring time in terms of lifetimes, generations, and political periods, and the Indians imagining time and space to be infinite and thinking of time according to grand cosmic eons rather than limited units of earthy existence (Wright, pp. 33–34).

Lastly, the spiritual orientations of Indian and Chinese religions were disparate. Whereas Chinese religions have been said to be "traditions of immanence", emphasizing harmonization with earthly realities, Indian ones have been said to be "traditions of transcendence", emphasizing emancipation from worldly conditions.

In their efforts to bridge such deep cultural gaps, deal with the overwhelming number of completely novel terms used in Indian Buddhist texts, and begin to make things somehow intelligible to the Chinese, the early translation teams in the second and third centuries developed and used a system of "matching concepts" (Chinese: *geyi*) that sought to directly relate Buddhism to the Chinese thought system seen as most closely resembling it, which, as noted above, was Daoism. To give some examples: nirvana, the term for goal of freedom from suffering, was translated with the Daoist term *wuwei* (literally "non-action"), connoting spontaneous, natural action; *arhat*, the term for a noble disciple who had achieved nirvana, was equated with the personage of the perfect Daoist sage, *zhenren*; *dao*, the key Chinese term for a spiritual "way" of life, was used not only for Dharma, but for bodhi ("awakening") and *yoga* (spiritual "discipline" or "union") as well; and *xiao xun*, the very specific Confucian term for "filial piety", was equated with the Sanskrit shila [*śīla*], meaning "morality/ethics/virtue" in quite a broad sense (Wright, p. 36). While certainly some correspondence can be found between these terms, they are imprecise at best, and resulted in at least as much confusion as edification when they were regularly applied in the translation process.

Another problem in the earliest centuries of translation was that very few Indian monks knew Chinese well, and likewise Chinese monks with significant Sanskrit training were rare (Ch'en, p. 365). Instead of language knowledge, the main criterion was deemed to be a doctrinal insight into the meaning of a text. This emphasis on exegetical skills remained central throughout the history of translation in China (Zacchetti, p. 140). At this stage, translation usually involved just two scholars working together, perhaps a few more. The prevailing technique in the third and fourth centuries was to have a foreign (Indian or Central Asian) monk try to explain the Indian text as best he could in his limited contemporary oral Chinese, and then a Chinese monk would endeavor to write it down as best he heard, in classical Chinese. The reciting monk, knowing little classical written Chinese, would have almost no idea of what had been recorded, and thus had no ability to compare the new rendering with the original text, to check for accuracy. Likewise, the recording monk could not check his written words with the original, lacking knowledge of its Indian language. The serious flaws in such a technique are obvious, with the potential for misunderstanding being present throughout the process (Ch'en, pp. 365–366).

Another potential source of difficulty between Indian and Chinese approaches was differing positions on what constitutes an authoritative "text". Chinese culture, with a very long history of writing, regarded the written word as authentic and authoritative, whereas in ancient India, oral transmission of texts and preservation of them through memorization were the standards. However, records show that the initially skeptical Chinese soon came to trust the Indian scholars and their methods, once it was shown that they were consistently capable of recalling even very lengthy sutras (Ch'en, p. 366).[10]

Another point of contention had to do with what form of translation was superior—direct, literal ones that honored faithfulness to the precise wording of the original, or more free, semantic ones that took discursive departures from the literal text in order to explain its meaning more fully. The latter type also favored beauty in style, so as to render a text more readable (Ch'en, p. 369). The influential Chinese scholar Dao'an (312–385) took important steps to effectively settle this issue. While criticizing free, semantic translations on the grounds that they permitted too much subjective interpolation that could compromise the pristine original words of the Buddha himself, he also allowed that translations must make the profound truths of the original texts understandable to even the common layperson. Dao'an went as far as to create concrete guidelines in this regard, articulating specific points where translators should adhere to the exact reproduction of the Sanskrit original and points where they should be allowed to deviate from the primary text for the sake of edification. Dao'an's rules had a lasting impact on translation tradition (Zurcher, p. 203).

[10] In Buddhism, the term "sutra" [sūtra]" refers to texts containing the original sermons of the Buddha. The other main form of Indian Buddhist scripture is the commentary on a sutra. There are many Indic terms for commentaries, but in the Sino-Indian context, shastra [śāstra] was the most commonly used one.

We will return to this and other related issues later when we turn to discuss the figure of Kumarajiva [Kumārajīva], the great genius scholar-monk of Indian heritage who revolutionized the art of translation. But returning now to our historical discussion of how translation collaborators worked together, we find that the process improved somewhat in the late fourth century, when the size of teams increased somewhat to at least three members, with separate roles for the transmitter who recited the original text (usually from memory, as discussed above), the interpreter who orally translated the text, and the scribe, who wrote that translation down (Zacchetti, p. 138). Sometimes there would be a fourth participant, who would write down the Sanskrit text, after it had been recited and before it had been translated (Ch'en, p. 366). The key development here in the creation of translations with greater accuracy was of course the presence of a translator who knew both Sanskrit and Chinese well.

Among those important monks with dual knowledge of Sanskrit and Chinese were several Indians, with the key pioneer in this regard being a scholar-monk of Indo-Scythian heritage from Gandhara, known as Lokakshema [Lokakṣema].[11] Arriving in the Han capital of Luoyang around 167, he collaborated for the next 30 years with another Indian monk[12] and three Chinese laymen to produce the first renderings of essential sutras from the Mahayana, the form of Buddhism that the Chinese would come to accept as supreme. For this work, Lokakshema is regarded as the father of Mahayana Buddhism in China, which is no small distinction. Another important Indian figure who directly translated texts from Sanskrit to Chinese was a Kashmiri named Sanghadeva [Saṅghadeva], who traveled widely and was a major presence at several major Chinese Buddhist sites throughout the late fourth century. His introduction of the genre of Buddhist scholastic philosophy, known as Abhidharma, through both his translations of essential texts and oral teachings delivered around the country, contributed much to the Chinese understanding of the finer technical points of Buddhist thought.[13] In the biographical entry on him in the earliest Chinese scriptural catalog, Sanghadeva is celebrated as a jovial man of extraordinary talent, who nevertheless always remained modest, courteously adapting to the various customs of the different regions he visited. He was widely known for delivering the most lucid explanations of the inner meanings of the texts he translated, which accounts say totaled over a million words, and his lectures were famous among the Chinese monks who flocked to hear them.[14]

Chinese Buddhist biographical accounts of the most eminent monks in their history document, with much specificity and detail, the significant contributions of many Indian monks to the transmission process. While each merits investigation,

---

[11] His Sanskrit name is a tentative reconstruction from the names the Chinese knew him by, Loujiaqian or Loujiachan (Zurcher, p. 35).

[12] Known only by his Chinese name, Zhu Shuofo (Zhu was the ethnikon used in Chinese to indicate a person from India).

[13] See Zurcher, pp. 202–204, 211, 230, and 246 for treatment of Sanghadeva's work.

[14] See Saroj Kumar Chaudhuri's translation of Sengyou's early sixth century work, the *Chu Sanzang Jiji ("Collection of the Records of the Translation of the Tripiṭaka)*, in his *Lives of Early Buddhist Monks: The Oldest Extant Biographies of Indian and Central Asian Monks* (New Delhi: Abha Prakashan, 2008), pp. 92–95.

the clear giant of them all was a genius monk of Indo-Kuchean heritage, Kumarajiva (344–413), the scholar-monk who, through his combined mastery of both the Chinese language and the breadth and depth of Indian Buddhist teachings, set new standards in the art of translation. Kumarajiva came to be held in such high esteem by the Chinese that he was named National Preceptor (*Guoshi*) (Ch'en, p. 83). In the truly collaborative work he did with Chinese Buddhists, seen in the prominent roles he assigned to them on his groundbreaking translation team and the fruitful correspondences he carried out with influential Chinese devotees, he represents the very best that came from Sino-Indian religious relations. Considering all of these accomplishments, it can be said that Kumarajiva stands out as the individual most singly responsible for the successful transference of Indian Buddhism to China.

Kumarajiva's father, Kumarayana [Kumārayāna], was a brahmin who served in a series of prestigious ministerial posts in India, before renouncing the world and wandering north across the Pamir mountains to the Central Asian oasis kingdom of Kucha, which as noted earlier was an important Buddhist center along the Silk Road.[15] The King of Kucha, impressed by Kumarayana's abandonment of power and privilege, appointed him to the high position of "guru of the nation", and married him to his intelligent sister, a Kuchean princess. The two conceived a child, upon which various signs and omens appeared, indicating that their baby would become an exceedingly handsome, talented, bright young man. But his mother longed to ordain as a Buddhist nun, and under her guidance young Kumarajiva, at age 7, took novice ordination as a monk as well. Receiving excessive amounts of alms because of her status as the king's sister, his mother became disillusioned and fled Kucha for Kasmir with her son, now age 9, in tow. There his reputation as a precocious learner only increased, as he studied and mastered all the canonical texts of the Sarvastivada [Sarvāstivāda] branch of the Shravakayana under Bandhudatta, a famous Kashmiri master. At the palace of the king of Kashmir, Kumarajiva defeated non-Buddhist opponents in debate and consequently was assigned disciples of his own to train. When he reached age 12, his mother set out to return to Kucha. Along the way, they stopped for a long sojourn in Kashgar, another great Silk Road center of Buddhism, where Kumarajiva first pursued the study of the Hindu Vedas and the panchavidya [*pañcavidyā*] or "five sciences" of Indian tradition: grammar, logic, medicine, arts, and metaphysics. He continued his Buddhist education under several other masters at Kucha, learning the literature of monastic practice (Vinaya) from the Kashmiri Buddhayashas [Buddhayaśas], and most notably investigating the Mahayana under the tutelage of Suryasoma [Sūryasoma] and converting to it as a result. All the while, he committed every Buddhist text he read to memory and gained growing notoriety as a teacher who could clearly expound up the deepest meaning of any scripture he referred to. Finally returning to Kucha at age 20, he underwent full ordination as a monk, continued his Vinaya studies under the Indian master Vimalaksha [Vimalākṣa], and devoted the next 20 years to rigorous work with the sutras and shastras of the

[15] The following account is based on Kumarajiva's biography in the *Chu Sanzang Jiji*, Chaudhuri, pp. 96–109.

Madhyamaka school, the foremost school of philosophy emphasizing the central Mahayana doctrine of *shunyata* [*śūnyatā*] or "emptiness".

During this period, he became renowned as the greatest scholar in the entire Kuchean Sangha of 10,000 monks strong, and from Kucha, his fame spread throughout the Buddhist world, China included. In 379, the Qin Dynasty's Emperor Fu Jian sent a delegation to bring him to the capital Chang'an. However, upon arriving at Kucha, the army's general, Lu Guang [Lü Guang], rebelled against the Qin ruler and took him as a hostage, after which he was held in Liangzhou, near Dunhuang, for the next 18 years (Keown and Prebish, entry on "Kumārajīva", pp. 464–65). While Kumarajiva's captivity was surely a great hardship for him, where the celibate monk was subject to indignities such as being forced to sire children, in the hopes that he would father equally gifted offspring, it also ironically turned out to be quite fortuitous, for during this long period he was able to learn colloquial and classical Chinese fluently and familiarize himself with other aspects of Chinese culture as well.

When the Qin Dynasty finally regained power, and reconquered Liangzhou in 401, Kumarajiva was finally brought to Chang'an. One of the great innovations, established just a few decades earlier by the aforementioned Buddhist leader Dao'an, who played a part in bringing Kumarajiva to the Qin capital, was the creation of translation bureaus (Chinese: *yijing yuan*) comprised of as many as hundreds of learned Buddhists (Ch'en, p. 367). With the one that was formed under and led by Kumarajiva, who is said to have had over 800 collaborators in his projects (Keown and Prebish, p. 465), these large-scale teams became the norm in this era, producing reliable, high quality renderings of the scriptures that would remain the standard versions over the long course of history. As mentioned earlier, thorough, careful exegesis of the texts had always been the guiding principle of the work. Now, assemblies with hundreds of participants regularly gathered, to engage in rigorous debate and analysis, before the actual task of translation was initiated (Zaccetti, p. 140). This kind of collaborative project, which brought together many of the greatest Indian and Central Asian pandits, steeped in the study of the original works, with the best, most dedicated minds in China—native monks and laymen now quite learned themselves, after four centuries of exposure to the Dharma—is surely one of the crowning achievements in the history of Sino-Indian relations.

Beginning with Kumarajiva's project, translation bureaus were royally patronized and furnished with spacious quarters, either at an imperial court or a famous temple.[16] As for the composition of the committees themselves, the way they were constituted from Dao'an and Kumarajiva's time on allowed for much improved work, with the Indian and Central Asian monks becoming better acquainted with Chinese and the Chinese Buddhists acquiring sounder knowledge about Indian teachings and better fluency in Indic languages. An account left by Kumarajiva's close associate, Sengrui, reveals something of the impressively thorough methodical approach taken by the master. Holding the original in hand, Kumarajiva would read it and comment upon its meaning twice over, taking great pains to arrive at the most precise phrasing to

[16] Kumārajīva's committee is known to have had two such venues in Chang'an, at Ximing Pavillion and Xiaoyao Garden (Ch'en, p. 367).

explain it. Based on his previous memorization of the text, he could discern if any passages were missing, and if so would endeavor to obtain another copy to verify his suspicion and fill in the lacunae. After this, the entire assembly would further discuss possible meanings and also assess the literary quality of the Chinese, as it had been written down by a native scribe. Then Kumarajiva would re-check things by comparing the new Chinese translation in progress with the original, to see how well the versions accorded with each other. Only after all of this would a final rendering be essayed (Ch'en, pp. 367–68).

In assessing the greatness of the work produced by Kumarajiva and his translation bureau, John McRae, a leading scholar of Chinese Buddhism, identified four key qualities (McRae, entry on "Kumārajīva" [Buswell, p. 442]). The first quality is the sheer volume of the work. The Kumarajiva project produced no less than 74 works totaling 384 fascicles or scrolls, including many major Mahayana scriptures that had not been adequately translated before. Several of these were of importance to Mahayana Buddhists of all varieties, such as the seminal "Perfection of Wisdom" sutras, key works on meditation practice, and the Lotus Sutra, the root text of the influential "Heavenly Terrace" (Chinese: *Tiantai*; Japanese: *Tendai*) school of philosophy and beyond that, the single most popular book in all of East Asian Buddhism (McRae, *ibid*).

The second quality is the richness and variety of the work (McRae, *ibid*). With respect to its richness, the Kumarajiva team's output included the entire core of the texts associated with the Madhyamaka school of philosophy, including the three treatises associated with its Indian founders, Nagarjuna [Nāgārjuna] and Aryadeva [Āryadeva]. Accordingly, the Chinese version of Madhyamaka is known as the "Three Treatises School" (*San lun song*) and Kumarajiva is rightfully regarded as its founder (McRae, *ibid*). But Kumarajiva was no mere sectarian; he and his associates demonstrated a great catholicity of interest in their work that addressed the wide variety of disparate traditions of thought and practice within Chinese Mahayana, including the two schools that would emerge as the most popular and influential throughout East Asia. Their translations of the *Amitabha* [*Amitābha*] and *Sukhavativyuha* [*Sukhāvativyūha*] sutras provided the Pure Land School (Jingtu zong) with their foundational scriptures, and likewise their translation of texts like the Perfection of Wisdom sutras and the related *Vimalakirtinirdesha* [*Vimālakīrtinirdeśa*] *Sutra* ("Sermon on Vimalakirti's Teachings") did the same for the Meditation (Chinese: Chan; Japanese: Zen) School. Furthermore, the Kumarajiva bureau's translations contained much more than doctrinal exposition. Within their texts, we find songs and poetry, legends and stories, literary styles and motifs, and a vast repertoire of religious images (McRae, *ibid*).

The third quality is the readability and fluency of the work (McRae, *ibid*). With respect to rendering the Indian originals with greater precise faithfulness, the Kumarajiva project's work had far greater accuracy than previous renderings (McRae, *ibid*). However, he firmly believed that strictly literal translations were inevitably flawed, because it was impossible to capture the original's flavor in a new language. Accordingly, he maintained that clear communication of the texts' ideas and meanings was always paramount. If emendations were needed to achieve this aim, then so be it (Ch'en, p. 371). Indeed, a distinguishing characteristic of his team's translations is the often-lengthy interpolated glosses composed by Kumarajiva himself, inserted whenever the meaning of a specific Sanskrit term couldn't be adequately conveyed by a single-word or short-phrased Chinese equivalent (Keown and Prebish, p. 465). Once articulated, Kumārajīva's decided preference for semantic over literal rendering became the undisputed standard for Chinese translations thereafter (Ch'en, p. 372). As for style, the Kumarajiva translations are also renowned for their elegance and floridity. Zurcher attributes their stylistic and literary beauty to the collaborative spirit that Kumarajiva instilled in his team, brought about by his insistence that the Chinese redactors involved play a central role and have the last say on how his translations should appear in their finalized form (Zurcher, p. 69).

Taking these first three qualities that McRae identified into consideration, it is no surprise that the Kumarajiva bureau's translations not only immediately became the preferred versions to use by Chinese Buddhists, but with few exceptions have remained so throughout history, up to the present, even as newer, more literally precise ones have continually come along since (Keown and Prebish, p. 465).

The legacy of Kumārajīva and his work is the fourth and final quality of greatness (McRae, p. 442). He is said to have had thousands of Chinese disciples throughout the Qin Empire who benefitted greatly from receiving his teachings (Zurcher, p. 227). Among them, many are famously influential in subsequent Chinese Buddhist history, including an inner circle of four—namely Daosheng, Sengzhao, Daorong, and the aforementioned Sengrui—whose future impact was so deep that they are known collectively as the "Four Sages" (Buswell and Lopez, entry on "Kumārajīva", p. 453). It is also well recognized that his work did much to clarify many of the fine points of philosophy that had been most confusing to Chinese Buddhist aspirants in previous generations who, as noted, were often left to find imprecise if not completely misleading equivalent concepts drawn from native Confucian and Daoist traditions, which operated on conceptual suppositions quite alien to Indian Buddhist ones. Establishing clearer understandings of the difficult Mahayana teaching of emptiness, stemming from Kumarajiva's edifying elucidations of the Perfection of Wisdom and Madhyamaka literature, was perhaps his greatest contribution in this regard.

On the subject of Kumarajiva's legacy and his special contributions to a greater understanding of Buddhist philosophy, there is one other aspect of his life that epitomizes the remarkable relations that were established between the Indians and Chinese in light of Buddhism. Even while ensconced in his difficult, time-consuming work in the northern capital of Chang'an, he managed to keep up long-term, detailed correspondences with earnest Buddhist devotees from among the Chinese gentry in the far-flung south. Of these, perhaps the most noteworthy is the series of 18 letters he exchanged from 405–409 CE (Zurcher, p. 226) with Dao'an's most gifted disciple, one Huiyuan. The letters explore a wide range of the finer points of Mahāyāna philosophy upon which Huiyuan sought edification. Here we cannot do more than offer a summary of them, so as to show something of their importance. Among the crucial matters treated were those dealing with various Buddhist practical paths to awakening: What distinguishes the training and realizations of the arhat and "solitary Buddha" (*pratyekeka-buddha*) figures of the Shravakayana from the bodhisattva ideal of the Mahayana, and where do bodhisattvas stand in relation to Buddhas? How does one practice meditative visualization of Buddhas, and to what end? Other discussions were more philosophical or theological in nature: How can Buddhas be immanent and transcendent beings at the same time? How does one reconcile Buddhist texts which present things like nirvaṇa as permanent with those that teach the emptiness of all experiences? How is nirvaṇa experienceable, or how are concentration and memory possible, if mind is nothing but a series of momentary mental events? How does one reconcile emptiness with our Daoist belief in the immortal Spirit? (Zurcher, pp. 227–29).

Besides the content of Kumarajiva and Huiyuan's exchanges, which includes explanations from the Indian pandit not found in any other source (Zurcher, p. 227), their tone also reveals interesting things about the challenges of communication between such Indian and Chinese Buddhists, often so different in their cultural sensibilities yet so compatible in their religious concerns. In reading the letters,[17] one finds the two at cross-purposes at times, with the Chinese correspondent's insistences on concrete answers and examples at odds with the Indian scholar's predilections to respond in abstract discourse and cite passages from scholastic sources. At the same time, it is striking to see their mutual efforts to find true connections across the cultural divides. Huiyuan's words are filled with humility and reverence for his Indian teacher. He joyously welcomes the master's arrival in China and at times when Kumarajiva expresses frustration with life and work in a foreign land, passionately pleads with him to stay. For his part, Kumarajiva's missives frequently pass along pious encouragements to his student as he struggles in his study and practice, as well as offer sincere apologies to him for perceived failures to communicate more directly and fully.

Besides Kumarajiva's team, there were several others who made significant contributions to the grand endeavor that was the translation of Buddhist texts from Indic languages to Chinese. According to the records of the scholar-monk Zhisheng, by the mid-seventh century, the size of the canon of scriptures translated was around 2280 texts totaling approximately 7000 scrolls (Wu, "The Chinese Buddhist Canon Through the Ages" [Wu and Chia, p. 42, fn 4]!!! This surely makes the collaborative project we have covered one of the most extraordinary achievements in human history.

So far, the interactions between Indian missionaries and aspiring Chinese Buddhists have been treated with respect to male actors only, which might give the impression that women were not involved in these religious developments. This is far from the case. There were of course both Chinese Buddhist laymen and laywomen, and on the monastic level, many Chinese women desired to become nuns. While there is no evidence of either lay or monastic females being among the missions to China in the early centuries of Buddhism's importation, Indian and Central Asian missionary monks were certainly willing to conduct initiation ceremonies for nuns. However, a significant legal problem arose. Monastic literature (Vinaya), which included the *pratimoksha* [*prātimokṣa*] or list of rules for conduct in cenobitic communities, was

[17] See Zurcher, pp. 246–249, for substantial translations of some of the letters.

the last canonical genre to be adequately translated. When it finally was, in the fifth century, it became clear to all involved that whereas monks could legitimately ordain nuns at the *shramanerika* [*śrāmanerikā*] or "novice" level, for women to become officially full-fledged nuns (*bhikshuni*), a quorum of such bhikshuṇis must also be present along with a quorum of monks, to conduct a proper *upasampada* [*upasaṃpadā*] or higher ordination ritual (Heirman, pp. 63–64). The lack of any bhikshunis in China to help lead the higher ordination process created quite a crisis in the Buddhist community, most acutely of course among the aspiring nuns themselves.

The way the situation was remedied constitutes another extraordinary episode in the history of South and East Asian Buddhist relations. Quickly after the problem was recognized, it was arranged for the required quorum of bhikshuṇis to be transported on the long, dangerous sea journey from Sri Lanka (called in Chinese texts the "Land of the Lion", based on the ethnic term "Sinhala") to China, to carry out the necessary ritual.[18] In 429, the first of two cohorts of Sri Lankan nuns, led by the Elder nun Devasara [Devasārā], arrived in China, and immediately took to learning Chinese, so that they could conduct the ceremony in the soon-to-be initiates' native language (Rongzi, 2002a, p. 103). After the second cohort arrived in 433, creating the required quorum, an *upasaṃpada*, led by the Indian Vinaya master Sanghavarman [Saṃghavarman], was held in 434 at the Nanlin Monastery in Jianye (modern Nanjing). There, 300 women became the very first fully ordained nuns in Chinese history (Rongzi, 2002a, p. 104).

The main Chinese source that documents this story, Baochang's sixth century work, *Biqiuni zhuan* ("Biographies of Buddhist Nuns"), contains many wonderful stories about determined Chinese women overcoming great gender prejudices to become serious monastics. Jingjian, joyously illumined upon her initial exposure to the Dharma, was taken under the wing of the kindly Kashmiri preceptor Jnanagiri [Jñānagiri], who led her to become China's first *shramanerika*, ordained by another Indian monk, Dharmagupta, in the early fourth century. Described in the text as elegant, moderate, and upright, Jingjian went on to organize the first Chinese community of novice nuns, at her Bamboo Grove Nunnery (Rongzi, 2002a, pp. 71–73). Sengguo, the first of the 300 to be fully ordained at Jianye in 434, was reportedly so dedicated that she began following Vinaya rules as a child. Senguo died an early and mysterious death at age 34, but even at a young age, she had become such an accomplished meditator that all the local skeptics had come to revere her (Rongzi, 2002a, pp. 103–04). Baoxian (400–477) took to the renunciatory life as a teenager, following the death of her mother. Recognized by a series of emperors as highly learned in both meditation practice and monastic conduct, she rose up the ranks to the level of being appointed, by imperial decree, Director of Capital Nuns at age 66. At this time, ordination had become something of a novelty among the capital's women, whose conduct at the nunneries had become quite lax. Under Baoxian's

[18] Sri Lankan or Sinhalese Buddhism can be seen as a continuation of the Indian tradition, in that chronicles report that King Ashoka's son and daughter, Mahinda and Sanghamitta [Saṅghamittā], brought the Dharma to the country, respectively initiating the monks' and nuns' lineages there.

strict but compassionate leadership, proper discipline was quickly restored within the order (Rongzi, 2002a, pp. 110–112).

9.4 Chinese Pilgrims' Accounts: What They Reveal About India and Sino-Indian Relations

After Kumarajiva, substantial translation endeavors would continue, often facilitated by other outstanding Indian scholar-monks, such as Paramartha [Paramārtha] (499–569) from Ujjain, who in China did for other important Indian Buddhist systems—namely the Yogachara [Yogācāra] ("Meditation Practice")[19] and Tathagatagarbha [Tathāgatagarbha] ("Buddha Nature") schools—what Kumarajiva did for the Madhyamaka school (Daniel Boucher, entry on "Paramārtha", [Buswell, pp. 630–631]). Such efforts served well to set up Chinese Buddhism for its periods of greatest flourishing—the Sui (581–618), Tang (618–906), and Song (960–1279).[20] In these eras, however, a significant change with respect to the actors who initiated the process of cultural transmission took place. Heretofore, we have seen that it was the missionizing monks coming to China out of India and Central Asia who gave developments their impetus. Hereafter, we find the direction of momentum largely reversing, with the lead mostly taken by intrepid Chinese pilgrim-monks voyaging from their country to India. Perceiving India to be not only the holy ground of the Dharma's origin, but also the only place where the Dharma was still fully preserved in pristine textual form and practiced with complete authenticity, scores of pilgrims embarked upon the arduous journey to the "Western Regions (*Xiyu*)", one of their terms for India. There they could witness Buddhist life as it was truly intended to be, sit directly at the feet of India's supreme masters to learn, and retrieve those missing scriptures deemed essential to a full and valid national integration of Buddhism back in their homeland. Their pilgrimages and the substantial written accounts they composed about them will be the subject of this section.

There were hundreds of Chinese Buddhist pilgrims who ventured the incredibly arduous journey from China through Central Asia to India, across treacherous mountain and desert terrain, from the 4th through eleventh centuries.[21]

[19] Chinese: She lun.

[20] Translation projects continued in these periods as well, though on a much smaller scale, with far fewer members. The great interest in Buddhism under these dynasties, when under certain regimes it became the official state religion, meant that the committees came under the strict control of the imperial courts, who were extremely selective about both the foreign and native composition of the translation teams. See Zacchetti, pp. 140–141.

[21] The work that documents the largest number of these was composed by one of the most preeminent pilgrims, Yijing (636–713), in his *Da Tang Xifu qiufa gaoseng zhuan* ("Biographies of Eminent Monks Who Visited India in Search of the Dharma during the Great Tang Dynasty"). There is an English translation of this: Latika Lahiri, *Chinese Monks in India: Biography of Eminent Monks who went to the Western World in Search of the Law during the Great T'ang Dynasty* (Delhi: Motilal Banarsidass Publishers, 1986).

Among these, three figures stand out, primarily because they composed the lengthiest, most detailed travelogs about what they experienced in India which, given the aforementioned Chinese notion that all outside civilizations are "barbarian", they rather amazingly considered to be the center of the world both geographically and spiritually, because of Buddhism's roots there (Felt, accessed at: https://escholarship.org/content/qt695817kw/qt695817kw_noSplash_a7e60d02943b851982b5a262d071313a.pdf?t=mutn9t). It was Chinese Buddhist pilgrims who conceived the surprising notion of India as a sophisticated and advanced civilization at least on par with their own civilization, an idea that continued to persist in the country for centuries, especially within Buddhist circles (Sen, 2003b, p. 27). The three outstanding figures are: (1) Faxian (337–422), who traveled to India from 399 to 413, and composed the *Faxian zhuan*, ("Record of Buddhist Kingdoms"); (2) Xuanzang (602–664), who traveled to India from 629 to 647, and composed the *Da Tang xiyu ji*, ("Great Tang Dynasty Record of the Western Regions"; and (3) Yijing (635–713), who traveled to India from 671 to 695, and composed the *Nanhai Jigui Neifa zhuan*, ("The Record of Buddhism as Practiced in India, Sent Home from the Southern Seas"). The records of Faxian, Xuanzang, and Yijing are some of the most valuable documents we possess on the history and culture of Indian Buddhism in particular and all of Indian culture more broadly from the 4th to seventh centuries, because of the richness in which they describe Buddhist practices and institutions, as well as many other aspects of subcontinental life: the environment, language and literature, economics, society, and politics. As sources providing insight into cross-cultural perceptions and interactions between Indians and the Chinese, they are unsurpassed as well (Sen, 2003b p. 24). In the following discussion, we will summarize the contributions of Faxian and Yijing, and then examine the life and work of Xuanzang more fully, for he is the greatest of the Chinese Indophiles, who also had the biggest impact on Chinese culture upon his return home, with what he brought back from India and instilled there.

Faxian departed the capital at Chang'an in 399 at age 62. By the time he returned 14 years later, by precarious sea voyage to the Chinese coast via Southeast Asia, he had traversed the precarious Taklamakan Desert, visited all the major sites in India where the Buddha practiced and taught, and touched down for a substantial stay in Sri Lanka as well. The opening passages of his *Record of Buddhist Kingdoms* tell us that his main purpose was to retrieve a full version of the Vinaya canon, which he believed had been incompletely and inadequately translated in China. This indicates that greater practical guidance was a major need felt among Chinese monks, to complement the doctrinal teachings that had been the focus of translation work to date.

One of the most fascinating aspects of Faxian's writings is his references to multiethnic societies in Central Asia that combined Chinese and Indian cultural characteristics. He reports that in the kingdom of Shanshan (on the northeastern end of the Taklamakan, commonly known as Loulan), the people dressed like Han Chinese but otherwise followed Indian customs. Speaking of the Central Asian domains he reached to the west of there, he says that whereas the commonfolk spoke whatever language was indigenous to a particular area (presumably either a Persian or

Sinitic dialect), the monks of these Buddhist lands always read Sanskrit and Prakrit scriptures and spoke only Indic languages (Rongzi, 2002b, pp. 163–164).

In terms of living Buddhist practice in India, perhaps Faxian's most interesting ethnographic descriptions are of the veneration of relics. His accounting of such rituals contributed enormously to the growth of this becoming a major form of Buddhist worship back in China, triggering great demand there for bodily remains and other objects associated with the life of the Buddha, as well as the establishment of special networks of exchange, through which Buddhist doctrines and ceremonial items circulated between South and East Asia (Sen, 2003b, p. 26). Such networks also fostered relationships of mutual benefit between Buddhist monks and itinerant merchants, wherein monks often traveled on merchant caravans and ships, while Buddhist monasteries provided accommodations and health care for long-distance commercial travelers on the trade routes, who would reciprocate the hospitality with donations to the Sangha.[22]

In Faxian's work, we also see the expression of the Chinese pilgrims' novel perception that their homeland was a spiritual hinterland compared to the holy ground upon which the Buddha himself walked in India. He describes Daozheng, a monk who accompanied him, being so moved by the sacred Buddhist destinations in India and the intensity of practice at its monastic centers that he vowed to stay there and never to be reborn in a borderland like China, where discipline was so comparatively lax, until his attainment of Buddhahood (Ronzi, 2002b, p. 203).

Unlike Faxian and especially Xuanzang, Yijing showed almost no interest in documenting social and political conditions, or any other non-Buddhist matters, in his account of his time spent in India. Like Faxian, his primary focus was the monastic life. This shows that contrary to impressions one might get from just considering the translation agendas of Kumarajiva and company (who did translate Vinaya works too, by the way), monks' concerns were at least as much about practical discipline as they were about philosophical and scholastic issues. Yijing's text covers 40 particular monastic activities as they were carried out in the Indian institutions he visited—ranging from the taking of meals and the wearing of robes to the conducting of ordination ceremonies and how matters of disease and death are handled—with an eye toward correcting the "errors" repeated in Chinese practice of the Vinaya, by showing how they went against the original intent of the Buddha and the principles he represented (Sen, 2003b, pp. 31–32). Some of the most intriguing sections of Yijing's text are about the application of the medical arts, a central part of Buddhist monastic life across cultures that sometimes go underrecognized. He discusses how medical treatments must accord with Buddhist principles of moderation and nonviolence: nothing should be given that increases bodily sloth or passion, and remedies must not contain any harmful, potentially poisonous, ingredients.

As much as Yijing emphasized that Chinese monastics must adhere to original Indian standards for the Buddhist way of life to be followed authentically, it is noteworthy that he offered compromises as well, where obvious cultural differences

[22] Sen, ibid. For a full treatment of this phenomenon, see Sen, *Buddhism, Diplomacy, and Trade: The Realignment of Sino-Indian Relations, 600–1400* (Honolulu: University of Hawai'I Press, 2003).

existed that required negotiation (Sen, 2003, p. 32). Whereas the original Vinaya refers to Indian eating customs, where the right hand or a spoon was used, in China chopsticks should be permissible, since their allowance wouldn't violate any moral principle and their prohibition might unnecessarily cause people to laugh or complain about the Dharma (Takakusu, p. 90). Likewise, in the field of medicine, herbs that were found in China but not India may be used, as long as they were wholly beneficial (Takakusu, pp. 128–129). For the same reason, effective techniques that were employed in China but not found in India, like acupuncture, could be employed without reservation. Here, in an interesting reversal of the typical Chinese pilgrims' attitude that India was the greater civilization, Yijing effused on the vast superiority of China's medical culture to India's, a fact he claimed was well known among his Indian comrades (Takakusu, p. 136).

In the copiously detailed record composed by Xuanzang about his own 18-year journey to India, we find the great scholar-pilgrim sharing many of the same Buddhistic interests as Faxian and Yijing. He was keen to visit all the hallowed sites of the religion's glorious past and sure to document fully how the Vinaya was being followed in contemporary India. Indeed, some of his account's most fascinating sections are about life at the grand, sprawling monastic complexes at Nalanda [Nālandā] in Bihar and Takṣashila in Gandhara, which in their multifaceted curricula stand as the world history's first true universities. He also supplemented Faxian's descriptions of Central Asian kingdoms well, adding more about the marked Indic cultural influences upon them, largely due to Buddhism's pervasive influence. However, the parts of his text that deal with matters beyond the exclusive scope of Buddhism—his informative treatments of geography, climate, natural environment, commerce and economics, legal systems, language and literature, science and mathematics, cosmology, social structures and norms, cuisine, civil administration, and politics—are where his contributions to our understanding of Indian history are most uniquely valuable. Along with his relationships with monks at Takṣashila and Nalanda, it is in his interactions with Indian monarchs that we find the richest insights into the nature of Sino-Indian relations in the seventh century. We will highlight aspects of these cross-cultural encounters in the following treatment of Xuanzang's life and work.

Born into an important family of scholar-officials serving the Sui Dynasty, Xuanzang was a highly intelligent child dedicated to learning the Confucian tradition that had given his ancestors their prestige and power. But after his father died when he was 9, he turned to Buddhism out of grief, following in the footsteps of an older brother which led him to a monastery in Luoyang, where he studied the Dharma for the next five years and was ordained at the unusually young age of 13 (Kinnard, p. 93). Described in his biography[23] as a precocious and ambitious student, Xuanzang was particularly enamored with Yogachara philosophy and sought out China's

[23] Huili and Shi Yancong, *Da Tang da ci en si Sanzangfashi zhuan.* The English translation I employ is Li Rongzi, *A Biography of the Tripiṭaka Master of the Great Ci'en Monastery of the Great Tang Dynasty* (Berkeley: Numata Center for Buddhist Translation and Research, 1995).

best scholars in this tradition, only to conclude that its essential scriptures were either poorly translated or entirely missing (Sponberg [Jones, p. 9861]).

Thus he set out for the Western Regions in 629, with the aim of studying Sanskrit and original Buddhist texts under India's renowned masters, and retrieving as many scriptures as possible and bringing them back to China, so that they could be translated for the first time or retranslated with better accuracy. Xuanzang did so in flagrant disregard of a strict nationwide prohibition, issued by the current Tang Dynasty emperor Taizong, against traveling outside of China to "barbarian" lands. Sen theorizes that the illegal nature of his mission motivated Xuanzang to arrange the impressive audiences he gained with monarchs in Central Asia and India, under the reasoning that these connections would make his travels and ultimate return to China free of bureaucratic intrusions, and that Emperor Taizong would appreciate the powerful diplomatic relationships established (Sen, 2003b, p. 29). The most intimate and fruitful of these relationships was with the mighty King Harshavardana [Harṣavardhana] (Harsha for short; Xuanzang refers to him as Shiladitya [Śīlāditya]), ruler of the large Pushyabhuti [Puṣyabhūti] Empire in northern India for over four decades (606–647).

The most detailed of the many accounts Xuanzang gave of the Indian towns and kingdoms he visited is that of Kanauj (referred to by Xuanzang as Kankyakubja [Kanyākubja]), the capital of Harsha's empire. When Xuanzang reached there sometime in 637 or 638, Harsha was at the height of his rule, his domain extending from northwestern Bengal in the east to the river Beas in Punjab to the west (Sen, 2003, p. 30). While scholars debate whether Harsha's personal religious allegiance was to Hinduism or Buddhism, what is historically most important was his public patronage of both religions—the policy of many Indian rulers since Ashoka—which brought great peace and prosperity to northern India during his reign. Unsurprisingly, Xuanzang praised Harsha most for his support of Buddhism, found in acts like his banning of animal slaughter and sacrifices and his sponsoring of many projects to build monasteries, stupas [stūpas] or Buddhist reliquaries, and highway hospices for travelers and the poor (Rongxi, 1996, pp. 125–128). Still, in his reporting of Harsha's organization of other events, like multireligious festivals and annual conferences that brought together scholars of various philosophical stripes, where he bestowed charitable alms upon all participants, Xuanzang also evidences the Indian monarch's considerable ecumenicism (Rongxi, ibid, pp. 130 and 138).

In another intriguing episode, Harsha informs Xuanzang that he is familiar with the reign of a compassionate ruler in China. Overjoyed, Xuanzang responds by detailing how China's current economic prosperity and civil harmony are the result of Taizong's policies of reducing taxation and mitigating criminal punishments. As for the emperor's moral and educational influence, Xuanzang continues, they are beyond measure. Equally delighted, Harsha replies, "Excellent! The people of your land must have performed good deeds in order to have such a saintly lord (Rongxi, ibid, p. 146)".

Sen's research has shown how this meeting between Xuanzang and Harṣa led to the establishment of diplomatic relations between Kanauj and the Tang court, and how the Chinese pilgrim's role in it was officially acknowledged by the Tang court. Upon returning to China, Xuanzang in fact continued to actively promote religious and diplomatic exchanges between the two empires. Sen speculates that Xuanzang's motivation to promote such relations was likely related to the fact that major Buddhist pilgrimage sites and his beloved university at Nalanda were part of Harsha's domain. Cordial relations between the two courts would've facilitated meaningful Buddhist exchanges between Tang China and northern India.[24]

Regarding Buddhist contacts, Xuanzang visited dozens of monasteries, learning Sanskrit, gathering copies of the key texts, and studying various aspects of the Dharma with teachers at each step along the way. His most important sojourns in this respect were the two years he spent studying both Shravakayana and Mahayana scriptures at the great complex at Takshashila, where he found over 5,000 monks housed in 100 monasteries, followed by an additional two years of work in Bihar under the tutelage of India's preeminent Yogachara scholar, the 106 year old Shilabhadra [Śīlabhadra], at the Buddhist world's foremost university, Nalanda, where he also immersed himself in the "five sciences" and the Vedas, along with other Buddhist philosophical systems (Kinnard, p. 94).

As for Xuanzang's religious relationships with the abbot Shilabhadra and other monks at Nalanda, his more historically reliable travelog has much less content than his more hagiographically embellished biography, composed by devotees of his. However, there is one interesting episode in the travelog that reveals much about intercultural sensibilities. While at Nalanda, Xuanzang had turned down repeated requests from an important regional king, Bhaskaravarman [Bhāskaravarman], for an audience, on the grounds that the ruler was Hindu. As his mentor, Shilabhadra informs him that although the ruler is a heretic, it is only because of family tradition, and points out that any kindly intentioned invitation should be honored. He goes on to advise Xuanzang that if he truly wishes to accord with the Buddha's compassionate spirit and make good on his bodhisattva vow to liberate all beings, he should relinquish foolish national and religious pride and make the long journey to Bhaskaravarman's court. After all, he might convert the tolerant monarch to the Dharma, which of course would have far-reaching benefits for many. Xuanzang sees the great wisdom in this and complies. At their meeting, Bhaskarvarman generously sings the praises of China's moral traditions, and the two end up traveling together up to Kanauj, to participate in an almsgiving ceremony being convened there by King Harsha himself (Rongzi, 1996, pp. 264–266)!

In the biography, one of the most remarkable things to emerge about Xuanzang's religious activities in India is the widespread fame he apparently achieved there for his prodigious learning. If the accounts from this hagiography are to be fully believed, it seems that his intellectual reputation was so great that he was chosen from among all the brilliant scholars at Nalanda to represent the university in a highly publicized debate with Hindu and Jain philosophers at Kanauj in 642, held under the auspices of Harsha. This of course would have required great skill in Sanskrit as well as whatever current spoken Indian language the contestants had agreed upon, not to mention an understanding of his opponents' various positions. Xuanzang's eventual victory in

[24] For Sen's full treatment of relations between the Pushyabhuti and Tang empires, see Chap. 1 of his *Buddhism, Diplomacy, and Trade*.

this debate is presented in the biography as the apogee of his career in India (Buswell and Lopez, entry on "Xuanzang", p. 1015).

Upon his eventual return to China in 647, Xuanzang became a national hero for his religious and political accomplishments. Named "Jewel of the Empire" by the imperial court, he came to wield unmatched power and influence over the entire Chinese Buddhist community. He was also honored with the highest title of *sanzang fashi*, "Master of the Tripitaka [Tripiṭaka]"[25] by emperors Taizong and Gaozang, under whose lavish sponsorship a major translation bureau was set up under Xuanzang's directorship, at the five-story Great Wild Goose Pagoda in Chang'an. The project drew the best scholars from all over China and Korea, among whom Xuanzang worked closely with over 60 major collaborators to produce 76 translations out of the body of the 657 scriptures that he brought back from India. Totaling 1347 fascicles or scrolls, the Xuanzang team's output was four times the size of Kumarajiva's project (Mayer, [Buswell, p. 909]). As Director, he took on an amazing range of tasks, supervising the legions of disciples transcribing the texts, clarifying their meaning, compiling the new translations, polishing their style, and certifying their syntax and meaning (Buswell and Lopez, "Xuangzang", p. 1015). As for the quality of Xuanzang's work, his mastery of both Sanskrit and Chinese is regarded as unsurpassed in Chinese history. Many hold that he was a superior stylist as well, with his translations reading more smoothly than most previous versions (Ch'en, pp. 368–369). Xuanzang and his team are given particular credit for developing an etymologically precise set of Chinese equivalents for Sanskrit technical terms that became the unquestioned standard for all subsequent translation work (Buswell, and Lopez, "Xuanzang", p. 1015). In terms of form, his more conservative approach stood at odds with that of Kumarajiva, with the former favoring rigorous philological accuracy over the latter's emphasis on semantic elaboration. On the whole, Kumarajiva's translations are more often preferred for their greater readability, but in some cases, Xuanzang's renderings are the most used ones in the Chinese canon. His versions of treatises in the traditions of Abhidharma, Buddhist logic, and Yogachara especially are what have most secured his place as a giant in the history of the Dharma's transmission to China (Mayer, p. 909).

9.5 Indo-Japanese Relations in Light of Interactions Between Buddhists in Japan and South Asia

The history of relations between Buddhists in Japan and India, compared with what transpired between them in China and India, is comparatively slight. One main reason for that is that Japan, which began receiving Buddhism from Korea and China around the sixth century CE, has always seen China as its main outside source of civilization. For those Japanese who began embracing Buddhism in the early centuries of its transmission from the East Asian mainland, the religion was by and large a Chinese,

---

[25] "Tripitaka" is the general term for the Buddhist canon.

not Indian, cultural phenomenon. There was of course a growing awareness over time that this religion had its origins and many of its most major developments in India, but by the era that the Dharma took serious hold throughout Japan, the Heian period (794–1185), the presence of Buddhism had begun to diminish greatly in the subcontinent. This chapter is not the place to treat Buddhism's decline in India in depth, but in short, the main contributing factors were that popular Buddhism was largely absorbed into a revitalized Hindu tradition from the eighth century on, and the basis of Buddhist operations that remained in the wake of this, its monastic institutions, found themselves to be easy targets at the hands of antagonistic invading military forces from Islamic lands, who began their eventual conquest of much of India in the ninth and tenth centuries. Somewhat similar factors led to a corresponding major decline of the Dharma in China, where from the Song period on, resurgent native Confucian and Daoist traditions effectively marginalized Buddhist influences to a significant extent.

There were other factors involved. When it came to eager Japanese Buddhist pilgrims seeking greater immersion in the Dharma in the lands of its greatest establishment, sea travel between Japan and China was hazardous enough. Still many persisted, and for most passage to China was enough, for the major schools of the religion that they practiced, Pure Land and Zen, were really indigenous Chinese forms not found at all in India. There were indeed those who longed to study and practice in India, but travel there was nearly impossible. The pilgrimage records of Faxian, Xuanzang, and Yijing, very well known to Japanese as well as Chinese readers, instilled in potential voyagers a hearty fear of the dangerous rigors of the journey.[26] There are occasional indications that a few Japanese did find their way to India, but there are no prominent examples on record (Morrell, p. 180). As for missionizing Indian Buddhists venturing to Japan, the exception that proves the rule that cases of the reverse voyage were equally rare, is documentation in Japanese sources of the presence of the south Indian figure Bodhisena (Japanese: Bodaisenna, 704–760)—also known there as Baramon Sojo [Baroman Sōjō] or the "Brahmin High Monk"—who officiated over a magnificent ceremony dedicating the world's largest Buddha image, the Daibutsu, at one of Japan's most vital Buddhist temples, Todaiji [Tōdaiji], in 752, and remained there as an influential teacher of Sanskrit and philosophy until his death (Tamura, pp. 44 and 47).

There were no missions or official relations between India and Japan in premodern times (Rambelli, p. 260). However, India's importance grew enormously within Japanese Buddhism from Heian times up to the nineteenth century. Fabio

[26] Robert E. Morrell, "Passage to India Denied: Zeami's Kasuga Ryūjin," *Monumenta Nipponica* Vol. 37 No. 2 (Summer 1982), pp. 179–180. This article mostly treats the fascinating story of the ambitious Pure Land priest Myoe Shonin [Myōe Shōnin] (1173–1232), who planned to lead a small cohort of disciples to India. Using the Chinese pilgrims' accounts, he calculated that once reaching Chang'an, the trip to India's great Buddhist sites would take 1600 days! Undeterred, the party stuck to their agenda, only to be stymied in the end by a vision from Myoe's patron deity prohibiting it, due to all buddhas and bodhisattvas already existing in Japan, in the form of local spirits (*kami*). This was followed soon after by the priest's fatal illness. These events are immortalized in a play by the great Noh dramatist Zeami.

Rambelli asserts that because of, as much as despite, the lack of direct contact between the countries, the *idea* of India as the very center of the world and universe flourished in the Japanese Buddhist *imagination* (my emphases) (Rambelli, p. 259). The image of India's centrality stemmed from cosmological descriptions found commonly in Buddhist scriptures, of Mt. Sumeru, mythically located in the Himalayas, as the axis of the whole universe, and of the center of the entire human world being in India (Japanese: *Tenjiku*), on the Jambudvipa [Jambudvīpa] continent to Sumeru's south (Rambelli, p. 261). With no references to Japan at all in their holy texts, Buddhists there were forced to develop some conception of their country's place in their religious scheme of things. The notion that grew to occupy powerful prominence throughout medieval times was that Japan, in the face of Buddhism's great decline in both India and China, had now become the ultimate preserve of Indian Buddhist wisdom. In effect, on this basis, Japan had become the new India, the "real" India (Rambelli, p. 262). Rambelli documents all sorts of concrete ways that Japan, under the influence of this idea, was thus "Indianized", importing distinctively Indian elements taken from Buddhist texts into its literature, politics, social structures, and occupational concerns. On the religious front, legends developed about great Indian Buddhist patriarchs visiting Japan to implant the Dharma and important Japanese Buddhist leaders being reincarnations of Indian masters. Tales were even told about India's sacred landscape transporting itself onto Japanese soil by air or sea! These holy sites in turn became represented in objects of sacred art, like the maṇḍalas used in meditative visualization practices (Rambelli, pp. 262–264). Also in art, the great saints of Indian Buddhism were portrayed with distinctly East Asia features. Likewise, India's holy sites were depicted with markedly Japanese geographical features (Rambelli, p. 269).

In recent modern centuries, challenges arose that diminished the status of Buddhism in Japan, brought about by nineteenth century changes like the opening of Japanese society to the West, which introduced increasingly bold Christian missionizing, and the reascent of the native Shinto tradition as it became the official state religion under the Meiji Restoration. In response, Buddhist leaders sought measures to revive their religion. One kind of measure, built upon the belief we've discussed that Japanese Buddhism was the highest efflorescence of the original Indian tradition, was that as representatives of a true world religion, they must reach out to make contacts around the globe, with of course no international connections being more important than those with the lands of the Dharma's South Asian origins.

No scholar has treated nineteenth and twentieth century exchanges between Japanese and South Asian Buddhism more fully than Richard M. Jaffe, especially in his book, *Seeking Śākyamuni: South Asia in the Formation of Modern Japanese Buddhism.* Among the several different Japanese–South Asian Buddhist interactions covered by Jaffe, one of the most impactful episodes is the story of the cleric Kitabatake Doryu [Dōryū], the first Japanese Buddhist to visit the site of Shakyamuni [Śākyamuni] Buddha's awakening, the Mahabodhi [Mahābodhi] Temple in Bodhgaya, India. In the footsteps of the great Chinese pilgrims, Kitabatake composed popular travelogs of his stays at sacred South Asian Buddhist locales, inspiring waves of Japanese monks to journey to South Asia themselves. Many of these monks then joined forces with Buddhists in India and Sri Lanka to oppose the current religious colonization efforts zealously pursued by European Christians in the region (Jaffe, Chap. 1).

Another fascinating relationship is that of the Zen monk Shaku Soen and the American Theosophist and Sri Lankan Buddhist revival leader, Henry Steele Olcott, who collaborated to create a new form of Japanese Buddhism that was self-consciously centered on the Indian founder Shakyamuni Buddha himself (Jaffe, pp. 44–49). Jaffe discusses other similar efforts to reform Japanese Buddhism into a "pure Buddhism" focused on Shakyamuni and his original teachings, which these Mahayanists surprisingly identified with the Theravada tradition as preserved in Sri Lanka. (Jaffe, pp. 58 and 92).

Regarding developments that trended in the reverse direction, Jaffe chronicles the story of two Sri Lankan monks, Kheminda Thera and Soma Thera, who spent years in Japan working with scholars there to produce a translation of an important Theravada practice manual that had long been lost in the original Pali language and survived only in a Chinese version (Jaffe, Chap. 5).

9.6 Conclusion

There are many other instances of the rich exchanges between modern Japanese and South Asian Buddhists that we cannot cover. Likewise, this chapter cannot capture all the noteworthy personages and activities that have made the interchanges between South and East Asian Buddhists some of the most remarkable examples of cross-cultural relations in human history.[27] It is very much hoped that the representative developments highlighted here have brought a greater understanding of this history.

References

Boucher, D. (2004). Paramārtha. In R. E. Buswell (Ed.), *Encyclopedia of Buddhism*. Thomson Gale.

Buswell, R. E. (Ed.). (2004). *Encyclopedia of Buddhism*. Thomson Gale.

Buswell, R. E., & Lopez, D. S. (eds.). (2014). *The Princeton dictionary of Buddhism*. Princeton University Press.

Carrithers, M. (1983). *The Buddha*. Oxford University Press.

Chaudhuri, S. K., tr. (2008). *Lives of early Buddhist Monks: The oldest extant biographies of Indian and Central Asian Monks*. Abha Prakashan.

Ch'en, K. (1972). *Buddhism in China: A historical survey*. Princeton University Press.

[27] For example, we have not mentioned perhaps the most famous of Indian patriarchs credited with bringing the religion to China, Bodhidharma, the colorfully portrayed founder associated with the foundation of Chan/Zen Buddhism. While the stories about Bodhidharma are marvelous, edifying expressions of Zen principles, they belong almost entirely to the realm of the legendary, and so have been omitted in this historical treatment.

Felt, D. J. (2010). De-centering the Middle Kingdom: The argument for Indian centrality within Chinese discourses from the 3rd to 7th Centuries. Paper given at Beyond Borders: Selected Proceedings of the 2010 Ancient Borderlands International Graduate Student Conference. Accessed from https://escholarship.org/content/qt695817kw/qt695817kw_noSplash_a7e60d02943b851982b5a262d071313a.pdf?t=mutn9t

Hanson, V. (2000). *The open empire: A history of China.* W.W. Norton and Company.

Hazra, K. L. (1982). *History of Theravāda Buddhism in South–East Asia, with special reference to India and Ceylon.* Munshiram Manoharlal Publishers.

Heirman, A. (2010). Fifth Century Chinese Nuns: An Exemplary Case. *Buddhist Studies Review, 27*(1), 61–76.

Jaffe, R. M., & Śākyamuni, S. (2019). *South Asia in the formation of modern Japanese Buddhism.* University of Chicago Press.

Jones, L. (ed.). (2005). *Encyclopedia of religion.* Thomson Gale.

Kinnard, J. N. (2006). *The emergence of Buddhism.* Greenwood Press.

Kumājīva. In R. E. Buswell, & D. S. Lopez (Eds.), *The Princeton dictionary of Buddhism.* Princeton University Press.

Kumārajīva. In D. Keown, & C. S. Prebish (Eds.), *Encyclopedia of Buddhism.* Routledge.

Lahiri, La., tr. (1986). *Chinese Monks in India: Biography of Eminent Monks who went to the Western World in search of the law during the Great T'ang Dynasty.* Motilal Banarsidass Publishers.

Lancaster, L. (2022). *The Buddhist Maritime Silk Road.* Fo Guang Cultural Enterprise Co., Ltd.

Mayer, A. L. (2004). Xuanzang. In R. E. Buswell (Ed.), *Encyclopedia of Buddhism.* Thomson Gale.

McRae, J. (2004). Kumārajīva. In R. E. Buswell (Ed.), *Encyclopedia of Buddhism.* Thomson Gale.

Mitchell, D. W., & Jacoby, S. H. (2014). *Buddhism: Introducing the Buddhist experience.* Oxford University Press.

Morrell, R. E. (1982, Summer). Passage to India denied: Zeami's Kasuga Ryūjin. *Monumenta Nipponica, 37*(2), 179–200.

Oldenberg, H. (ed.). (1879–1883). *The Vinaya Piṭakam.* The Pali Text Society.

Oldenberg, H. (ed. and tr.). (1879). *The Dīpavaṃsa: An ancient Buddhist historical record.* Williams and Norgate.

Rambelli, F. (2015). The Idea of India (Tenjiku) in pre-modern Japan: Issues of signification and representation in the Buddhist translation of cultures. IN T. Sen (Ed.), *Buddhism across cultures: Networks of material, intellectual, and cultural exchange* (pp. 259–290). ISEAS-Yosef Ishak Institute.

Rongzi, L., tr. (1995). *A biography of the Tripiṭaka Master of the Great Ci'en Monastery of the Great Tang Dynasty.* Numata Center for Buddhist Translation and Research.

Rongxi, L., tr. (1996). *The Great Tang Dynasty record of the Western Regions.* Numata Center for Buddhist Translation and Research.

Rongzi, L., tr. (2002a). Biographies of Buddhist Nuns. In M. Sengaku (Ed.), *Lives of great Monks and Nuns* (pp. 67–154). Numata Center for Buddhist Translation and Research.

Rongzi, L., tr. (2002b). The journey of the Eminent Monk Faxian. In M. Sengaku (Ed.), *Lives of the Great Monks and Nuns* (pp. 155–214). Numata Center for Buddhist Translation and Research.

Sen, T. (2003a). *Buddhism, diplomacy, and trade: The realignment of Sino-Indian relations, 600–1400.* University of Hawai'i Press.

Sen, T. (2003b, Winter). The travel records of Chinese Pilgrims Faxian, Xuanzang, and Yijing: Sources for cross-cultural encounters between ancient China and Ancient India. *Education About Asia, 11*(3) (Winter 2003), 24–33.

Sponberg, A. (2005). Xuanzang. In L. Jones (Ed.), *Encyclopedia of religion.* Detroit: Thomson Gale.

Takakusu, J., tr. (1998). *A record of the Buddhist religion as practiced in India and the Malaya Archipelago.* Munshiram Manoharlal Publishers.

Tamura, Y. (2000). *Japanese Buddhism: A cultural history.* Kosei Publishing Company.

Wu, J. (2016). The Chinese Buddhist Canon through the ages. In J. Wu & L. Chia (Eds.), *Spreading Buddha's word in East Asia: The formation and transformation of the Chinese Buddhist Canon*. Columbia University Press.

Wu, J., & Chia, L. (Eds.). (2016). *Spreading Buddha's word in East Asia: The formation and transformation of the Chinese Buddhist Canon*. Columbia University Press.

Xuanzang. In R. E. Buswell, & D. S. Lopez (Eds.), *The Princeton dictionary of Buddhism*. Princeton University Press.

Zacchetti, S. (1996). Dharmagupta's unfinished translation of the Diamond-Cleaver (Vajracchedikā-Prajñāpāramitā-Sūtra). *T'uong Pao, LXXXII*, 137–152.

Zurcher, E. (1959). *The Buddhist conquest of China: The spread and adaptation of Buddhism in early Medieval China*. E. J. Brill.

Chapter 10
Shaiva Traditions of Southern India: Tamil Shaivism and Shaiva Siddhanta

Michael A. Gollner

Abstract This chapter provides an overview of the history of Shaiva traditions of southern India, particularly Tamil Shaivism and Shaiva Siddhanta, beginning with the earliest evidence in Vedic and Tamil Sangam sources. The chapter shows how Tamil Shaivism emerged against a historical background of veneration of the Vedic god Rudra, the old Tamil cult of Murugan, pan-Indic *liṅga* worship, and devotional Sangam literature of the early 1st millennium. In discussing developments of the 6th to 9th centuries, we differentiate between three broad classifications of Shaivism, namely "lay Shaivism", "ascetic Shaivism", and "Agamic Shaivism". Turning to the 9th to 14th centuries, we survey Chola-period temple culture and discuss major developments in Shaiva literature in Sanskrit and Tamil. A look at developments of the late medieval period shows how the caste-class basis of regional Shaiva monastic institutions changes after the 14th century with an important shift toward non-Brahmin control. Finally, an overview of the origins of the Dravidian movement and neo-Shaivism in the 19th and 20th centuries highlights the role of colonial power dynamics in the construction of Tamil Shaivism and Shaiva Siddhanta today.

Keywords Shiva · Southern India · Linga · Shivabhakti · Murugan · Vedic · Sangam · Rudra · Upanishads · Mahabhashya · Mahabharata · Pallava · Pandya · Appar · Sambandar · Nayanars · Mahabalipuram · Agamas · Shaiva Tantras · Pashupata · Chola · Kamikagama · Chidambaram · Periyapuranam · Matha

The Shaiva traditions of southern India can be traced back to the emergence of Shiva as a major god in the Vedic period (ca. 1500–500 BCE). While the earliest evidence for the veneration of Shiva comes from northern India,[1] developments from the closing centuries of the first millennium BCE—such as *liṅga* worship and the old

[1] For a discussion of northern Indian elements in the earliest Tamil literary sources, see Hart (1975, 50–81).

M. A. Gollner (✉)
McGill University, Montreal, Canada
e-mail: m.a.gollner@gmail.com

L. Vemsani (ed.), *Handbook of Indian History*,
https://doi.org/10.1007/978-981-97-6207-1_10

Tamil cult of Murugan—combine with evolving conceptions of Shiva in Vedic and early post-Vedic sources, giving rise to an efflorescence of Shaiva devotion (*śivabhakti*) in the Tamil South beginning in around the 6th century CE. Tamil Shaivism thus emerges as a principal feature of the southern Indian religious landscape. At around the same time, in northern India, Shaiva Siddhanta—an originally esoteric, initiation-based form of Shaivism—takes shape as a cultural force itself, spreading across the subcontinent and beyond to parts of Southeast Asia. These two Shaiva traditions come to influence each other profoundly in the Tamil South, particularly from the 12th century onward in the context of a series of far-reaching cultural, social, and political transformations.

Although the Shaiva traditions of southern India enjoy a rich history, the construction of Tamil Shaivism since the 19th century as a monolithic Hindu sectarian tradition with Shaiva Siddhanta re-conceived as an originally Tamil development is also, crucially, the result of the colonial encounter. As such, modern Tamil Shaivism carries with it traces of a Dravidian nationalist historiography (Ramaswamy, 1997, 25–44; Vaithees, 2015, 23–60), which has been profoundly influential in shaping popular understandings of the development of Shaivism in Tamilnadu since the late 19th century.[2] In the final section of this chapter, we will look at this aspect of Tamil Shaivism more closely. The rest of the chapter is structured in five parts that examine key historical, conceptual, and theological developments from the earliest period down to the present day.

10.1 Ancient Origins: Up to the 6th Century CE

We can trace the origins of Shaivism in southern India back to three primary sets of sources: (i) references to Rudra and Shiva in Vedic and early post-Vedic sources; (ii) early evidence of *liṅga* worship; and (iii) references to Murugan and Shiva in Tamil Sangam (*caṅkam*, "academy") literature. In discussing these sources, I am excluding from serious consideration the so-called "proto-Shiva" seal (no. 420) of the Indus civilization. As the work of Doris Srinivasan (1975, 1983), Alf Hiltebeitel (1978), and Asko Parpola (2015) has shown (convincingly, I believe), the Indus civilization figure, despite certain notable iconographic traits, is most likely not a form of Shiva.[3] In discussing the three other sets of sources, I begin with the earliest.

[2] Cf. Vaithees (2015, 288–315).

[3] Although Parpola (2015) draws attention to apparent continuities between the Indus civilization and later classical Hinduism, he suggests the Indus figure may have more in common with later forms of Brahma (194) and Varuna (181).

10.1.1 References to Rudra and Shiva in Vedic and Early Post-Vedic Sources

Several iconographic and mythological features associated with Shiva make their first appearance in the earliest portions of the Vedas, the "family books" of the *Ṛgveda-Samhitā*.[4] These iconographic and mythological features, however, are originally associated with the deity Rudra (lit. the "howler" or "roarer"), a wrathful and destructive storm god who also elicits appeals for his benevolence and healing powers. The pronounced duality between Rudra's hostile and benign characteristics has been taken as an indication of his possible non-Vedic origins, although some (e.g., Srinivasan 1983) have argued against such a view. The identification of Rudra with Shiva, common in post-Vedic sources, is a secondary development, as no references to Shiva as such are found in the oldest parts of the Vedas. One of the earliest occurrences of the word Shiva (lit. "auspicious") in this connection is adjectival, used as a qualifier for a form of Rudra. Thus in the *Taittirīya-Saṃhitā* of the Black Yajur Veda, in the opening of the *Śatarudrīya* ("The Hundred [Aspects] of Rudra") litany, Rudra is characterized as having two bodily forms: one auspicious (*śiva*) and one terrifying (*ghora*).[5] It is only in the later books of the Vedas, such as the *Śvetāśvatara Upaniṣad* (ca. 4th century BCE, though perhaps later[6]), that the theonym Shiva comes to be employed more commonly.[7] By the late-Vedic period, references to Rudra/Shiva display many of the traits associated with mature forms of Shiva. And in early post-Vedic sources, such as the *Mahābhāṣya* of the grammarian Patañjali (2nd BCE) and the two Epics, we find several early references to images, devotees, and myths of Shiva.[8]

10.1.2 Early Evidence of *Liṅga* Worship

Evidence of *liṅga* worship appears in the historical record in the final centuries before the common era. One of the earliest examples is the Guḍimallam *liṅga*, a markedly phallic-looking *liṅga* with a representation of Rudra/Shiva on the front, dated to between the third and first centuries BCE and located in modern-day Andhra Pradesh.[9] A number of other *liṅga*s dated to approximately the same time period have also been found in Mathura to the north, indicating that *liṅga* worship was widespread at this time (von Mitterwallner, 1984, 12–31). Notably—and somewhat

---

[4] See, for instance, *Ṛgveda-Samhitā* (2.33, 6.49, 6.59).

[5] *Tasyaite tanuvau ghorānyā śivānyā* (*Taittirīya-Saṃhitā*, 5.7.3.4). "He has these two bodies: one that is frightful; another that is auspicious."

[6] See Oberlies (1988, 35–62); Bisschop (2009, 741–54).

[7] Cf. Bisschop (2009, 742).

[8] See, for instance, *Mahābhāṣya* (5.3.99, 5.2.76); *Rāmāyaṇa* (1.33–36, 1.23.11–14); *Mahābhārata* (3.39–41, 10.7).

[9] For a discussion of the Guḍimallam *liṅga*, see von Mitterwallner (1984, 12–31).

curiously given the preponderance of material evidence—we find only scattered references to *liṅga* worship in textual sources from this period. One such reference is the Tilottamā myth of the Mahabharata, discussed by Bakker (2002), which features a form of Shiva as a "post" (*sthānu*) that is clearly suggestive of a *liṅga*. Bakker hypothesizes that the relative dearth of references to *liṅga* worship in textual sources from the turn of the millennium compared to material sources may be due to the "different sections of society to which these sources pertain" and that "the brahmanical elite … frowned on liṅga worship" (404–5). In Tamilnadu, a pre-existing tradition of memorial stones (*naṭukal*s) erected for the eminent dead appears to have converged with *liṅga* worship at some early stage, whereby *liṅga*s rather than stones came to be set up for the deceased.[10]

10.1.3 Tamil Sangam References to Murugan and Shiva

Another pre-existing tradition in Tamilnadu that contributes to developing conceptions of Shiva is the old cult of Murugan, particularly through the association of Murugan with Shiva's mythological son Skanda, also known as Karttikeya or Subrahmanya. References to Murugan can be found in the oldest Tamil Sangam literature (ca. 300 BCE to 300 CE). As Fred Clothey (1978, 23–43; 2012) has pointed out, the Murugan of early Tamil Sangam works differs somewhat from later conceptions of Murugan. In early Sangam works, Murugan shares a number of similarities with evolving conceptions of Rudra/Shiva, such as an association with mountains, malevolent forces, illness, healing, and a dual nature characterized by anger and benevolence. In a later stage of development, Murugan comes to be identified with warriors and chieftains and the cult of *naṭukal*s set up for dead warriors. It is in this later stage, in the early centuries CE, where the now well-known association of Murugan with Skanda coalesces, no doubt due to the connection they both share with war. Yet parallels between Murugan and Shiva have persisted as Françoise L'Hernault (1984) has observed: "[Murugan] as a supreme deity is but a variant of Śiva himself" (270). We find other early references to Shiva in Sangam literature from the beginning of the common era, such as the *Puṟanāṉūṟu*.[11] These references share notable continuities with the Tamil Shaiva poems of the 6th to ninth centuries, with comparable eulogies that praise Shiva's iconographic features and mythological feats.

[10] This is discussed by Hart (1975, 25–26).

[11] See, for instance, *Puṟanāṉūṟu* (1, 6, 55, 56, 166).

10.2 Shaivism During the Pallava and Pandya Dynasties: 6th to 9th Centuries

The centuries between the end of the Sangam period in ca. 300 CE and the rise of the Pallava and Pandya dynasties in the 6th century are generally regarded as a "dark age" in southern Indian history. Little is known of the Kalabhra dynasty that ruled the South during this interregnum. What we do know is that Buddhism and Jainism flourished in these centuries and that the Pallavas of Kanchipuram and Pandyas of Madurai, both credited with ending the Kalabhra age, patronized and presumably adhered to Jainism early on.[12] In due course, however, rulers of both dynasties converted to Shaivism. In the case of the Pallavas, King Mahendravarman I (590–630) reportedly converted from Jainism to Shaivism through the influence of the Shaiva poet Appar (alias Nāvukkaracar; ca. 570–650) (Nilakanta Sastri, 1988, 382–83). A similar story is recorded for the Pandyas, whose ruler Neṭumāṟaṉ (ca. seventh century) is said to have converted to Shaivism after witnessing the Shaiva poet Sambandar (alias Ñāṉacampantar; ca. 7th century) defeat a group of Jain monks in a debate.[13] These two Shaiva poets and a third by the name of Sundarar (alias Cuntaramūrti; ca. 7th–8th century) would emerge as the vanguard of Tamil Shaivism and the crest of a new wave of devotional (*bhakti*) poetry that would sweep across the subcontinent for over a millennium.[14]

The 6th to 9th centuries, then, are when Tamil Shaivism emerged in earnest. The works of Appar, Sambandar, and Sundarar are supplemented by compositions of sixty additional Shaiva poets—Nayanars (*nāyaṉār*s; lit. "leaders")—whose works were collected as part of the *Tirumuṟai* corpus between the 11th and 13th centuries (Peterson, 1989, 12–18; Prentiss, 1999, 110–13). These developments in Shaiva bhakti poetry are mirrored on the Vaishnava side by the poetry of the Alvars (*āḻvār*s; lit. "those who are immersed [in god]"). In studies of the Bhakti movement, the ethos of devotionalism is generally traced back to the *Bhagavad Gītā* or late devotional *Upaniṣad*s.[15] But there are other important threads of influence, particularly from southern India, as the Nayanars' and Alvars' works display considerably greater continuities in poetic form and content with late-Sangam literature than with the philosophical speculation and dialogical structure of the *Bhagavad Gītā* and *Upaniṣad*s.

Expressions of Tamil Shaivism from the 6th to 9th centuries extend beyond poetic literature into other domains of art and culture. The Pallava king Mahendravarman,

[12] Cf. Nilakanta Sastri (1988, 131, 135); Peterson (1989, 20–21).

[13] Some uncertainty persists about the precise identity of Neṭumāṟaṉ. According to Nilakanta Sastri (1988, 383), the monarch in question is either Māṟavarman Avaniśūlāmani (590–620) or Arikēcari Māṟavarman (650–700).

[14] Much has been written about the Bhakti movement. See, for instance, Ramanujan (1973, 39–40) and Hawley (2015, 2–4).

[15] See, for instance, Biardeau (1989, 89–90); Prentiss (1999, 17–24).

mentioned above, is notable for his early patronage of Hindu rock-cut architecture.[16] A 7th-century cave temple in Maṇṭakapaṭṭu dedicated to Brahma, Shiva, and Vishnu carries an inscription with a reference to Mahendravarman claiming the temple was the first of its kind to be built in the region.[17] The famous monuments at Mamallapuram (Mahabalipuram), including the cave temples (*maṇṭapa*s), monolithic temples (*ratha*s), and bas-relief sculptures, were carved under the patronage of Mahendravarman's son Māmalla Narasiṃha I (r. 630–668) and later descendants of the Pallava line (Nilakanta Sastri, 1988, 413–14). Among the most important Shaiva temples from this period are the Shore Temple in Mamallapuram and Kailasanathar Temple in Kanchipuram, which herald the later grand-scale of royal Chola temple design.

Up until now, in discussing Tamil Shaivism, we have been speaking of what can be generally characterized as "lay Shaivism". This must be distinguished from two other broad traditions of Shaivism that developed in the early and mid-first millennium CE, originally in northern India, and that came to play an important role in the development of Tamil Shaivism from the 6th century onward. These other traditions can be classified as (i) Agamic Shaivism (also known as Mantramārga or Tantric Shaivism), which includes the Shaiva Siddhanta tradition; and (ii) ascetic Shaivism (also known as Atimārga Shaivism), which includes the Pāśupata Shaiva tradition. Before discussing these two traditions, I would first like to sketch the contours of lay Shaivism in somewhat more detail.

10.2.1 Lay Shaivism

In recent scholarship, discussions of lay Shaivism have primarily centered on Sanskrit textual sources, predominantly from northern India, such as the *Skandapurāṇa* and *Śivadharma* corpus.[18] Comparatively little attention has focused on southern Indian sources of lay Shaivism, among which the poetry of the Nayanars may be included. One reason for lack of focus on southern sources is that research into lay Shaivism as an independent tradition is still in its early stages (De Simini and Kiss 2021b, vii–xi). In addition, scholars of lay Shaivism have thus far been predominantly Sanskrit scholars, not Tamil scholars. Nevertheless, it is clear that northern Indian lay Shaiva sources share a certain fundamental similarity with the Nayanars' poems in their predominantly devotional ethos.

Aside from poetry, another major expression of lay Shaivism from the 6th to 9th centuries is temple worship. While temple practices have long been assumed to be

[16] Although the focus here is on royal patronage, it should be noted that most patronage in this period was not by royalty and that agency for developments and innovations in art and architecture throughout the medieval period lies less with royal donors and more with wealthy non-royal patrons (cf., Heitzman 1997, 18–19). See also Kaimal (1996, 33–36); Orr (2007, 123).

[17] See Gopinatha Rao (1923–24, 14–17); Nilakanta Sastri (1988, 412).

[18] See, for instance, Bisschop (2006; 2018); Bakker (2014; 2022); De Simini (2016a; 2016b); Sanderson (2019); Mirnig (2019); De Simini and Kiss (2021a; 2021b).

an aspect of the Shaiva Siddhanta tradition, this assumption has been called into question by the work of European scholars beginning in the early 1990s (Brunner, 1990a, 1990b, 1998; Goodall, 1998, 2013, 2015Sanderson 2009).[19] At the present state of research, it is reasonably clear that public Shaiva temple cults were generally within the purview of lay Shaivism—at least until about the12th century. We see evidence of this in the iconographic schemes of deities installed in Shaiva temples and shrines built before the 12th century—schemes that are demonstrably at odds with prescriptions for worship in pre-12th century Shaiva Siddhanta textual sources (Brunner, 1990a; Sanderson, 2019, 6).

10.2.2 Agamic Shaivism

The tradition of Agamic (or Tantric) Shaivism, of which Shaiva Siddhanta is the mainstream form, emerged in around the 6th–7th century, although parts of the earliest known text of this tradition—the *Niśvāsatattvasaṃhitā*—may be dated to the mid-5th century.[20] The primary scriptures of the tradition are constituted by what I call an "ideal canon" of twenty-eight Agamas or Tantras.[21] I use the term "ideal canon" since it is an open question whether these works all actually existed as historical texts; although some works may have been lost, others may have only ever existed as "mythical texts" (Goodall et al., 2015, 31).

In its early, classical phase (7th–12th centuries), Shaiva Siddhanta espouses a form of ontological dualism where souls (*paśu*) and the lord Shiva (*pati*) are held to be eternally and ontologically distinct.[22] Yet the feature of Shaiva Siddhanta (and of Agamic Shaivism more broadly) that distinguishes it most from other forms of Shaivism is its emphasis on a salvific form of ritual initiation (*dīkṣā*), regarded as a prerequisite for liberation. In early Agamic Shaivism and Shaiva Siddhanta, devotion played a commensurately negligible role. This is fundamentally different from the ethos of lay Shaivism. For early Shaiva Siddhanta exegetes, devotion was no substitute for the doctrinal view that what tied an individual soul (*paśu*) to the world of repeated rebirths was a tenacious fetter (*pāśa*), a subtle Impurity (*mala*), held to be a material substance (*dravya*), which could only be removed by means of ritual initiation.[23] What enabled Agamic Shaivism to rise to a position of dominance during

[19] This is discussed in more detail in Gollner (2021, 14–16, 91–99).

[20] For a discussion of this dating, see Goodall, Sanderson, and Isaacson (2015, 19–73).

[21] The terms "Agama" and "Tantra" are lexically synonymous; both terms were used interchangeably in the medieval period to denote the same genre of scripture.

[22] For an accessible overview of Shaiva Siddhanta, see Davis (1991), although the historiographical treatment of "temple Hinduism" in this work is now somewhat dated.

[23] As Sanderson (1992) has pointed out, "this Impurity (*malam*), though it is imperceptible, is a material substance (*dravyam*). Because it is a substance, only action (*vyāpāraḥ*) can remove it; and the only action capable of removing it is that of the rituals of initiation and their sequel taught by Śiva in his Tantric scriptures" (285). In other words, devotion was not viewed as sufficient to free one from this bondage.

the latter half of the first millennium was the tradition's success in forging relationships with powerful patrons, including royalty and wealthy elites, who established temples or provided for them, thereby benefitting lay and priestly communities.[24] Major endowments to temples for their operations and renovations, in turn, served as concrete markers of the power, influence, and wealth of those patrons—to say nothing of the benefits they believed would accrue to them in their lives and afterlives.[25]

10.2.3 Ascetic Shaivism

Between the earliest references to the worship of Shiva in the final centuries BCE and the emergence of Agamic Shaivism in the 5th–6th century CE, another major Shaiva tradition emerged that would have great importance in the Tamil South. By "ascetic Shaivism", I refer specifically to the Pāśupata tradition and Pañcārtha system of Kauṇḍinya. As Acharya (2011) has pointed out, the Pāśupatas represent the oldest sectarian branch of Shaivism, although the tradition no longer exists as such (458–59). Despite its antiquity, the Pāśupata tradition emerged in the early centuries CE against a cultural background where the worship of Shiva was already well-established (Bakker, 2021, 5). In Bakker's view, the Pāśupata tradition was successful in accommodating the existing Shaiva base by providing a "doctrinal superstructure" that encompassed and shaped a variety of "local modes of worship and conduct" (5–6). But we should not imagine this was some broadly inclusive tradition, as Pāśupata Shaivism was open only to Brahman men already invested with the sacred thread (Sanderson, 2006, 147–48).

The doctrines of the Pāśupata tradition are replete with pentads, which speaks to a peculiar fondness Pāśupatas had for the number five (Acharya, 2011). The name of the school's doctrinal system, Pañcārtha, refers to its five main theological principles: *kāraṇa* ("cause"), *kārya* ("effect"), *vidhi* ("prescribed rules"), *yoga* ("union"), and *duḥkhānta* ("end of suffering") (Bisschop, 2014, 28). The main practice of the Pāśupatas consisted of a five-stage observance (*vrata*). In the first stage, the ascetic would bathe routinely in ashes, sleep in ashes, and live in a temple worshiping Shiva through song, dance, and laughter. In the second stage, he was to leave the temple, abandon his sectarian identity, and behave in anti-social and provocative ways so as to court ridicule and abuse from passers-by. The rationale for this was that the ascetic's bad karma would transfer to the passer-by, whose good karma would transfer to the ascetic. In the third stage, the ascetic was to retire to a cave or secluded place and act like a bull or wild animal while worshiping Shiva through the recitation of mantras. The fourth stage involved dwelling in a cremation ground and living off

[24] On the elite clientele of Agamic Shaivism, including its focus on the consecration of royal palaces and the establishment of Shiva's forms in temples across the subcontinent and beyond, see Sanderson (2009, 254–82). On wealthy temple patrons as sponsors of the construction of Shaiva temples and the consecration of Shiva's forms, see Brunner (1998, iii–iv).

[25] Cf. Sanderson (2019, 6–7, 23n).

of whatever he could find there until death. The final stage consisted of union with Shiva (Acharya, 2011, 460–62).

Despite the antinomian elements of Pāśupata practice, the tradition was remarkably widespread, extending across the subcontinent and into parts of Southeast Asia (Acharya, 2011, 464). It was also a tradition with considerable internal diversity, including multiple sub-traditions—such as the Lākulas, Kāpālikas, and Kālāmukhas—attested to in different regions and over many centuries. In southern India, we find evidence of the Pāśupatas from the seventh century onward. An early and notable reference to the tradition is found in the play *Mattavilāsa Prahāsana* authored by the Pallava monarch Mahendravarman, mentioned above.

10.3 Shaivism Under Chola and Later Pandya Rule: 9th to 14th Centuries

The rise of Chola power in the 9th century overlaps with the decline of the Pallava and Pandya dynasties in the same period, although the Pandyas would regain supremacy of much of the South in the 13th century. In many respects, the 9th to 14th centuries represent an expansion of the patronage that Tamil Shaivism received in previous centuries. The period witnesses major developments in Shaiva temple culture and literature, both in Tamil and Sanskrit, and an emerging synthesis between Tamil Shaivism and Shaiva Siddhanta.

10.3.1 Temple Culture During the Chola Period

In her analysis of Chola-period temple culture, Leslie Orr (2007) observes "a rather remarkable continuity with pre-Chola patterns of temple worship" adding that "several novel features of temple culture" appear in this period (122). One such feature that Orr discusses is the incorporation of Tamil Shaiva hymns in temple liturgies, a development that we find recorded in temple inscriptions as early as the ninth century but with increasing frequency in the tenth century. The practice is not detailed in any contemporaneous Shaiva ritual manual that we know of, but we find a reference to the performance of liturgical hymns in Dravidian and other languages in the *Kāmikāgama*,[26] although this is largely a post-12th century text.[27] Orr also observes

[26] *Tadūrdhvaṃ gauḍabhāṣādyair gānaṃ dhūpāntam ācaret | ūrdhvaṃ drāviḍabhāṣāṅgaṃ gānaṃ nṛttayutaṃ tu vā* (*Kāmikāgama, Pūrvabhāga* 4.437 cd–438ab). "After that, [the ritualist] should perform songs in [regional] languages such as Bengali (*gauḍabhāṣādi*) until the end of the incense [offering]; or optionally, next, [he may perform] songs in Dravidian dialects (*drāviḍabhāṣāṅgaṃ*) accompanied by dancing."

[27] For a discussion of the *Kāmikāgama*'s date, see below.

that it is in this period that we find the earliest bronze images of Tamil Shaiva poet-saints and the earliest inscriptional references to their worship (2007, 122). Such images are commonly found in Shaiva temples today, and rituals for the worship of poet-saint images can be readily observed across Tamilnadu. References to this practice are also detailed in the *Kāmikāgama*.[28]

Another novel feature of Chola-period temple culture is the considerably grander scale of architectural design relative to earlier precedents. However, this feature primarily applies to the three royal temples whose construction was sponsored by Chola kings: the Brihadisvara Temple in Thanjavur by Rajaraja I (r. 985–1014), the Brihadisvara Temple in Gangaikonda Cholapuram by Rajendra I (r. 1014–44), and the Airavatesvara Temple in Darasuram by Rajaraja II (r. 1150–73). Nevertheless, many pre-existing temples were expanded or underwent significant renovations during Chola times, predominantly through the sponsorship of wealthy patrons—not Chola rulers (Kaimal, 1996, 33–66; Branfoot, 2013, 32–36).

10.3.2 Shaiva Literature in Sanskrit

The extent of the circulation of Shaiva literature in Sanskrit throughout Tamil country during the first millennium is shrouded by the fact that palm-leaf manuscripts from so long ago do not survive in the harsh climatic conditions of the region. Although an abundance of Sanskrit Shaiva sources from first-millennium northern India can be found in archives across Tamilnadu today, it is rarely clear when these works were first transmitted in the South. To ascertain dates of transmission and reception, we must rely on southern Indian authors with known dates whose works survive.

The earliest known Shaiva author writing in Sanskrit from southern India was a certain Rāmanātha (late-11th century) (Goodall, 2014, 179). As Goodall (2014) has pointed out, Rāmanātha was a pontiff of a *matha* associated with the pan-Indian Goḷakī monastic network in an area known as Puṣpavana, thought to be in or near modern-day Thiruvarur (177–83). In the concluding section of Rāmanātha's ritual manual, *Naṭarājapaddhati*, he gives an account of his background, noting that his antecedents were from the northeast (Gauḍadeśa) (187–88). From this ritual manual and another surviving work, *Siddhantadipikā*, we can glean that other Sanskrit Shaiva Siddhanta literature was also in circulation in the South at this time, including the influential *Somaśambhupaddhati* (alias *Karmakāṇḍakramāvali*), which Rāmanātha appears to have drawn on in writing his ritual manual.

About a half-century after Rāmanātha, the next important name in Sanskrit Shaiva literature from Tamilnadu is Aghoraśiva (mid-12th century). Like Rāmanātha, Aghoraśiva was associated with the Goḷakī monastic network and also traced his background to the northeast, although he was primarily based in Chidambaram.[29] One of the most influential works of Aghoraśiva is his eponymous ritual manual,

[28] *śivabhaktapratiṣṭhāvidhipaṭala* (*Kāmikāgama, Uttarabhāga* 66).

[29] Cf. Davis (1986–92, 367–78); Goodall (1998, xiii–xvii).

the *Aghoraśivapaddhati* (alias *Kriyākramadyotikā*). Other major works include his commentaries on Rāmakaṇṭha's *Nādakārikā*, Bhojadeva's *Tattvaprakāśikā*, Śrīkaṇṭha's *Ratnatrayaparīkṣā*, three works of Sadyojyotiḥ (i.e., *Tattvasaṃgraha*, *Tattvatrayanirṇaya*, and *Bhogakārikā*), and the *Mṛgendrapaddhati*, a ritual manual based on the *Mṛgendrāgama*. Several other works are attributed to Aghoraśiva, but not all appear to be by the same 12th-century author (Goodall, 1998, xiii–xiv).

Writing at approximately the same time as Aghoraśiva and based in Chidambaram as well, at least for a time, was his co-religionist Jñānaśiva (alias Jñānaśambhu). At some point, Jñānaśiva moved north to Varanasi.[30] Although not quite as prolific as Aghoraśiva, Jñānaśiva nevertheless wrote two important works, a ritual manual entitled *Jñānaratnāvalī* and the liturgical hymn *Śivapūjāstava*. Both works shed important light on developments in Shaiva Siddhanta in this period. The influence of Jñānaśiva's works is attested to by citations in later sources and a detailed 13th-14th-century commentary (*vyākhyā*) on the *Śivapūjāstava*.

Also writing in this period is Trilocanaśiva, a disciple of both Aghoraśiva and Jñānaśiva (Goodall, 2000). Trilocanaśiva's background is given in the introduction to his commentary on the *Somaśambhupaddhati*, where he identifies himself as a member of the lineage of teachers of the Āmardaka monastery, connected with the Goḷakī network.[31] Of the works attributed to Trilocanaśiva, it is unclear whether all were composed by the same person; among those that are believed to be by the well-known 12th-century author are the *Siddhāntasārāvalī*, *Prāyaścittasamuccaya*, *Dhyānaratnāvalī*, and *Somaśambhupaddhatiṭīkā* (Sathyanarayanan et al., 2012, xxii–xxiii). In his oeuvre, Trilocanaśiva follows the teachings of his gurus closely, and his work represents the final stage of what we may call the "classical" phase of Shaiva Siddhanta, characterized by a dualist ontology and a ritual focus on individual worship (*ātmārthapūjā*) with little or no reference to public temple-based worship (*parārthapūjā*).

10.3.2.1 South Indian Temple Agamas

Beginning in around the 12th century, a new wave of Shaiva scriptures makes its appearance in the Tamil South, taking as its principal focus the rituals and practices of public Shaiva temples. Goodall (2018) has described this new wave of scriptures in the following terms:

> The 'South Indian Temple Āgamas' that began to be composed in the 12th century are quite different from the liberation-centered early scriptures of the Śaivasiddhānta, for their purpose appears rather to prescribe every detail of the social and religious life of large Cōḻa-period and post-Cōḻa temples in such a way as to justify the entitlement of certain castes (mainly Śaivabrāhmaṇas/Ādiśaivas) to certain rôles in ritual and thereby naturally to certain privileges. (Goodall, 2018, 106)

[30] For accounts of Jñānaśiva's life and oeuvre, see Goodall (2000, 209–12; 2004, cx–cxi).

[31] As Goodall (2015) has pointed out, "Āmardaka … is both Ur-lineage and Śaiva monastery" (18).

The distinction between early "liberation-centered" Agamas and post-12th century "temple Agamas" is thus an important one, for Agamas are still often assumed *in toto* to be scriptures focused on temple-based practices—which is really only true of the latter group of post-12th works.

One of the most important of these temple Agamas is the *Kāmikāgama* (or *Kāmika* for short), mentioned above. The title of the work, *Kāmika*, can be traced back to the 5th–6th century. Yet the *Kāmika* in its present form is the result of multiple stages of composition and redaction. Some portions of the text are borrowed from 6th–8th-century sources, such as the *Śivadharmottara*, *Svacchandatantra*, and *Mataṅgapārameśvarāgama*. But most of the work appears to have been composed after the 12th century, with the recension that formed the basis of modern print editions being perhaps only finalized in the 18th or nineteenth century.[32] As I have demonstrated elsewhere (Gollner, 2021, 53–59), the chapters on daily ritual (*Pūrvabhāga*, 4–5) draw significantly on lay Shaiva precedents.

We find evidence of the proliferation of South Indian Temple Agamas in the 13th–14th century in a detailed commentary (*vyākhyā*) on Jñānaśiva's *Śivapūjāstava*. The commentary is one of the first sources to cite a substantial number of verses attributed to the *Kāmika* that are found in the printed version of the text today. Moreover, the commentary cites the *Acintyāgama*, *Kāraṇāgama*, *Makuṭāgama*, and *Suprabhedāgama*—all of which were also recast as temple Agamas in or after the 12th century. Additional temple Agamas continued to be composed and redacted in subsequent centuries. In fact, the strategy of recasting or rewriting Shaiva Agamas to authorize and reflect novel Shaiva practices can be observed in the Virashaiva tradition as well, where new Virashaiva-inflected Agamas were composed from the 12th century onward also using old titles drawn from the original list of twenty-eight.[33]

10.3.3 Shaiva Literature in Tamil

On the Tamil side, the 9th to 14th centuries mark a major watershed in the development of South Indian Shaiva literature. While devotional Tamil hymns began to be incorporated into temple liturgies from the 9th century, the compilation and canonization of the *Tirumuṟai* and *Tēvāram* occurred somewhat later, in the 11th–13th centuries. This process appears to have taken place in several stages, although accounts of the process include semi-mythological elements, which makes it difficult to separate fact from fiction. Briefly, according to the *Tirumuṟaikaṇṭapurāṇam* (14th century?),[34] a Chola king named Rajaraja Apayakulacēkaraṉ, moved by piety after hearing the singing of bhakti hymns, requests a young Brahman, Nampi Āṇṭār

[32] See Gollner (2021); see also Goodall (2018, 133–36).

[33] See Sanderson (2014, 84–85); see also Gollner (2021, 158–74).

[34] This work is attributed to Umāpati Civācāriyar; however, as Goodall (2004, cxv–cxvi) has pointed out, there appear to be at least three different authors with the name Umāpati.

Nampi, to propagate the poems of the Nayanars throughout Tamil country.[35] Acting on the king's request, as the story goes, Nampi discovers a cache of Tamil manuscripts in a storehouse of the Chidambaram Nataraja temple (Prentiss, 2001, 10). The cache is collected and constituted as the *Tēvāram*, the first seven volumes of what would later become the twelve-volume *Tirumuṟai* (Dorai Rangaswamy, 27–35). According to the legend, additional works were also found in this Chidambaram storehouse and incorporated as volumes eight to eleven of the *Tirumuṟai*. The twelfth and final volume of the *Tirumuṟai*, the *Tiruttoṇṭarpurāṇam* (alias *Periyapurāṇam*), composed in the 12th century by Cēkkiḻār, narrates the lives and legends of the sixty-three Nayanars. This work was added to the *Tirumuṟai* at a later stage, although it is not clear precisely when.[36]

The 12th–14th centuries also mark the earliest extensive use of Tamil for Shaiva Siddhanta theology. Before the 12th century, we find only a smattering of references in Tamil sources to Agamic concepts (e.g., *tattuvam*, *ākamam*, *pācam*, etc.). The earliest substantive Tamil engagement with Shaiva Siddhanta theology comes from the 12th to 14th centuries, particularly the corpus of fourteen texts known as the *Meykaṇṭacāttiram*s, a locus classicus for the synthesis of devotional Tamil Shaivism with Shaiva Siddhanta. The *Meykaṇṭacāttiram*s mark a departure from the classical dualism of Shaiva Siddhanta and a shift toward a form of non-dualism congruent with influential developments occurring contemporaneously in Vedantic thought.

10.3.3.1 The Tamil Shaiva Siddhanta Synthesis

Named after the theologian Meykaṇṭatēvar (alias Meykaṇṭār; ca. early 13th century), whose work, *Civañāṉapōtam*, is foundational for most of the other works in the collection, the *Meykaṇṭacāttiram*s include two earlier, 12th-century works, the *Tirukkaḷiṟṟuppaṭiyār* and *Tiruvuntiyār*.[37] In the *Tirukkaḷiṟṟuppaṭiyār*, we find expressions of a non-dualist outlook in the context of a devotional discourse on union with Shiva. Throughout the work, the author weaves in references to the Nayanars and their devotional exploits alongside elements drawn from Agamic Shaivism, although the work appears intended as a discourse for lay Shaivites.

The *Civañāṉapōtam*, for its part, is structured as a commentary on twelve foundational verses held to be excerpts from the Sanskrit *Rauravāgama*.[38] While the corresponding verses have not been located in any known manuscript of the *Rauravāgama*, there is a Sanskrit version of the *Civañāṉapōtam* (= *Śivajñānabodha*), which

---

[35] This king has been variously identified as Aditya I, Rajaraja I, and Kulottunga I. See Dorai Rangaswamy (1990, 22–23); Prentiss (2001, 20).

[36] Cf. Prentiss (1999, 144–45).

[37] The dating of the *Civañāṉapōtam* to the thirteenth century is based on inscriptional references to Meykaṇṭār (Zvelebil 1995, 435). The *Tiruvuntiyār*, ascribed to Tiruviyalūr Uyyavantatēva, and the *Tirukkaḷiṟṟuppaṭiyār*, ascribed to Tirukkaṭavūr Uyyavantatēva, are traditionally dated to 1148 and 1178 CE, respectively (668, 702).

[38] See also Ganesan (2003, xix). Despite the traditional attribution of the twelve verses to the *Rauravāgama*, some have argued that the verses were not originally in Sanskrit but in Tamil.

includes only the root verses in Sanskrit, without Meykaṇṭār's commentary.[39] Several of the authors of sub-commentaries on the *Civañāṉapōtam*, such as Śivāgrayogin, Vedajñāna II, and Jñānaprakāśa, also wrote commentaries on the Sanskrit version of the text, and regarded it as originally part of the *Rauravāgama*.[40] The profusion of commentaries and sub-commentaries on these twelve verses in Tamil and Sanskrit highlights their importance for both linguistic expressions of Shaiva Siddhanta and points to an overarching unity in the tradition above linguistic difference.

What made these twelve verses so important? As I have argued elsewhere, they provided a basis for a synthesis between classical Shaiva Siddhanta dualism and an emergent non-dualism, which accommodated new, more inclusive forms of initiation, a devotion-based soteriology, and a rapprochement with Vedanta (Gollner, 2021, 142–58). By the 14th century, it seems, non-dualism and Vedanta had come to exert a considerable influence on Shaiva Siddhanta. This influence can be gauged by the assertion of one of the most prominent voices of the tradition in the fourteenth century, Umāpati Civācāriyār, author of the *Civappirakācam* (and of at least seven other major Tamil works[41]), that Shaiva Siddhanta is the "essence of Vedanta" (*vētāntat teḷivām*).[42] This view is also echoed in contemporaneous Sanskrit sources, notably in the *Śivapūjāstavavyākhyā* (13th–14th) in a citation attributed to the *Kāmika*: "[Shaiva] Siddhanta is the essence of the Veda".[43] And a similar assertion is found in a ca. 14th-century commentary on the Sanskrit *Śivajñānabodha* in a citation that is again attributed to the *Kāmika*: "There is no difference between [Shaiva] Siddhanta and Vedanta".[44] These last two examples are noteworthy, for they not only show that the *Kāmika* had been recast by this time to reflect the emergent Vedantic congruency of Shaiva Siddhanta, but that the *Kāmika* was also cited as an authority for the tradition's Vedantic stance.

But what are we to make of these claims that Shaiva Siddhanta was "essentially" a Vedantic tradition? Particularly when we know that Shaiva Siddhanta was not a Vedantic tradition, no less in the 14th century than it is now. It suggests that Vedanta was a more influential current in the 14th century than has thus far been assumed, and that this was something with which Shaiva Siddhanta exegetes had to contend.

---

[39] According to Ganesan (2011, 523), the earliest known commentary on the Sanskrit *Śivajñānabodha* is by Sadāśiva Śivācārya (fourteenth century?).

[40] This is discussed in Gollner (2021, 150).

[41] As discussed above, there are multiple authors with the name Umāpati. The Umāpati Civācāriyār credited with authoring the *Civappirakācam* is also held to have authored seven other *Meykaṇṭacāttiram* works: *Tiruvaruṭpayaṉ*, *Viṉāveṇpā*, *Caṅkaṟpanirākaraṇam*, *Pōṟṟippakṟoṭai*, *Neñcuviṭutūtu*, *Koṭikkavi*, and *Uṇmaineṟiviḷakkam*.

[42] *Civappirakācam*, *pāyiram*, 7: *vētāntat teḷivām caiva cittānta[m]*.

[43] *"siddhāntaṃ vedasāraṃ hi" iti kāmike* (*Śivapūjāstavavyākhyā*, 65).

[44] *Kāmike – "siddhānte naiva vedānte viśeṣaḥ ko 'pi vidyate"* (*Śivajñānabodhavṛtti*, 43). This commentary (*vṛtti*) on the *Śivajñānabodha* is attributed to Sadāśiva Śivācārya, mentioned in a footnote above. For a discussion of this passage, see Goodall (2006, 99, 109–10).

10.4 Developments in the Late Medieval Period, 14th to 18th Centuries

The 14th to 18th centuries mark major changes in South Indian polity. Following the end of the Chola dynasty in the 13th century and the Later Pandyas in the 14th century, the next three hundred years see the rise and fall of the Vijayanagara dynasty, the Nayaka dynasty, and the establishment of Maratha rule in the 17th century. In the context of these seismic political shifts, we can observe a consolidation and institutionalization of the Tamil Shaiva Siddhanta synthesis that began in previous centuries. We see this through inscriptional references to the Meykaṇṭār lineage in connection with monastic institutions, *mathas* (*maṭhas*, Skt.; *maṭams*, Ta.), starting in the 14th century. And from the 16th century, new Shaiva institutional networks emerge that come to wield considerable cultural and economic power from their central bases in the Kaveri basin.

10.4.1 Institutional Developments: Shaiva *Mathas*

Although Shaiva monastic institutions have existed in the Tamil South since Pallava times, their association with Meykaṇṭār and his school represents a new development in the 14th century. The earliest evidence of this is an inscription from the late 14th century, which records a gift of land to an individual connected with the Meykaṇṭār lineage (ARE 1909/665 = SII 26.716). Another inscription from the 15th century mentions a certain "Maraijñānasambandar of the lineage of Meykaṇḍa-Santāna", said to have composed a Purāṇa, for which he was rewarded by local temple authorities in the form of a land grant (ARE 1935–36/180). While inscriptions that refer to *maṭha* lineages in connection with Meykaṇṭar are few and far between (Orr, forthcoming), we can see a marked increase in the proportion of people belonging to non-Brahman caste-classes in connection with Shaiva monastic institutions leading up to the 14th century (Karashima et al., 2010, 217–34). This is significant, as before the 12th century individuals associated with *mathas* are predominantly Brahmans. But in subsequent centuries, particularly from the 16th century onward as the avowedly non-Brahman, Vellalar lineages of Tiruvāvaṭuturai and Tarumapuram *ātīṉams* emerge as vital centers of Shaivism claiming affiliation to Meykaṇṭār's school, we can observe a major shift in the caste-class constitution of Shaiva institutional networks across southern India.

The organizational structure of Shaiva monastic institutions is a topic that has received relatively little scholarly attention. Apart from the work of Kathleen Koppedrayer (1990), accounts of how these institutions were organized and structured historically are scarce. As Koppedrayer has shown, Shaiva *mathas* often functioned as administrative centers of temples or temple endowments, which explains why *mathas* were typically situated in proximity to temples. At the same time, *mathas* were also often part of larger monastic networks, such as the Goḷakī network, mentioned above, or Tiruvāvaṭuturai or Tarumapuram *ātīṉam*s from the 16th century onward. As such, *matha*s were (and to some extent still are) important economic endpoints that operated as trustees of local temple resources, including land and wealth, with their administration ultimately overseen by central nodes in the network (Koppedrayer 1990, 18–19). At least this is how Tiruvāvaṭuturai *ātīṉam* appears to have operated historically. The term "*ātīṉam*" in this context refers to the governing node of the network. As British District Officer F. R. Hemingway observed some time ago, the term designates "central mutts [*matha*s] exercising control and supervision over subordinate mutts and other institutions such as temples".[45] To what extent this organizational structure is representative of earlier Shaiva *matha*s is not yet clear.

Over the course of the 16th to 18th centuries, the *ātīṉam*s of the Kaveri basin with their branch *matha*s and temples spread far and wide became the pre-eminent seats of Shaivism in the Tamil South. There were also several other important institutional Shaiva lineages and groups, such as the Kāmakoṭi *matha* in Kanchipuram associated with the Shankaracharyas, the Kukai (*Guhā*, Skt.) *matha* in Chidambaram, which was an institutional base for the prolific Tamil and Sanskrit Shaiva authors Vedajñāna I (Maṟaiñāṉa Campantar) and Vedajñāna II (Maṟaiñāṉa Tēcikar), and many other *matha*s, some of which were aligned (or co-aligned) with Virashaivism.[46] But the consolidation of institutional control, wealth, and power among the non-Brahman *ātīṉam*s of the Kaveri basin was of a greater order of magnitude than the other Tamil Shaiva institutions of the day. And with this wealth and power, it seems there was some anxiety about the legal rights of non-Brahman monastics to administer these institutions and associated endowments. This is discernible in a proliferation of texts advocating for the legitimacy of non-Brahman Vellalars as monastics or renunciants (*saṃnyāsin*s). To contextualize this development, it is important to note that Brahmanical law only recognized the three upper caste-classes as eligible for the rite of renunciation; non-Brahman Vellalars, categorized as Shudras—the fourth, lowest caste-class—were thus not viewed as legitimate renunciants or monastics in the eyes of Brahmanical law, and there were important financial and administrative implications to this.[47] Examples of counter arguments to the Brahmanic position are found in the *Śaivasaṃnyāsapaddhati* (16th century) written by Śivāgrayogin (i.e., Śivāgrayogīndra Jñānaśivācārya), second pontiff of Cūriyaṉārkōyil *ātīṉam*, and the *Varṇāśramacandrikā*, written by an anonymous author affiliated with Tarumapuram *ātīṉam* in the 17th century. Ultimately, the holdings of Shaiva *ātīṉam*s and temples were appropriated by the British East India Company in the early 19th century, although they were transferred back a few decades later following pressure from Christian societies in India and England about the Company profiting from religious practices they considered questionable.[48]

[45] Madras District Gazetteers: Tanjore (Madras, 1906), 232; cited in Koppedrayer (1990, 12).

[46] On the Kukai *matha*, see Trento (2021, 101–44); see also Gollner (2021, 186). On *matha*s in Tamil country aligned with Virashaivism, see Raman (2022, 200–32).

[47] This is discussed in more detail in Gollner (2021, 178–81).

[48] Cf. Presler (1987, 15–27).

10.5 Modernity and Neo-Shaivism, 18th Century to the Present

The passing of the East India Company Act and the establishment of Company rule in 1784 brought far-reaching changes to southern India, not the least of which was the progressive expansion of the Company's territories and policies. The attempt to bring Shaiva *matha*s, temples, and lands under Company control was mentioned above. The overturning of this policy in response to Christian missionary pressure speaks to the increasing power of Christian groups in shaping and influencing religious and cultural developments in the 19th century. Related to this, the work of Trautmann (1999) and Ravindiran/Vaithees (2000, 2015), among others, has shed valuable light on the role of "missionary orientalism" in catalyzing the Dravidian movement. As they have shown, Robert Caldwell's *A Comparative Grammar of the Dravidian or South Indian Family of Languages* (1856) had a far-reaching influence in fomenting a divide between Brahmans and non-Brahman caste-classes. Caldwell's motivation appears to have been to speed the conversion of non-Brahmans to Christianity. To this end, his critique of Brahmanism in his *Comparative Grammar* intended to show "that Brahmanism was alien to the Dravidians" and a "pernicious influence" on Tamil culture (Ravindiran, 2000, 57).

Leaving aside the question of the historical veracity of Caldwell's claims, we can observe a legitimate cause for grievance on the part of non-Brahmans in the mid-19th century who were disproportionately excluded from the power structures of the colonial regime. As Pandian (2007) has shown, approximately half of the high-paying jobs in the Madras administration at that time were held by Brahmans, who constituted about only three percent of the local population. By the turn of the 20th century, this exclusion was mirrored by a political disenfranchisement from participation in the emergent Indian National Congress. At the same time, another source of grievance stemmed from the activities of Christian missionaries who publicly disparaged Hindu beliefs in order to gain converts. While the critiques of missionaries were not targeted at non-Brahmans specifically as much as at Hindus in general, this was an important factor in the rise of what has come to be called Neo-Shaivism and its alliance with Dravidian ideology.[49]

One of the key figures linking Dravidian ideology with Neo-Shaivism was the Scottish-Canadian Methodist George Uglow Pope. Having translated a number of classic Tamil works, including the *Tirukkuṟaḷ* and *Tiruvācakam*, in his introduction to the latter, he made the following bold declaration:

> The *Çaiva Siddhānta* system is the most elaborate, influential, and undoubtedly the most intrinsically valuable of all the religions of India. It is peculiarly the South Indian, and Tamil, religion … Çaivism is the old prehistoric religion of South India, essentially existing from pre-Āryan times, and holds sway over the hearts of the Tamil people … Its text-books (probably its sources) exist in Tamil only, and in high Tamil verse … (Classical Tamil is very little studied, yet this key alone can unlock the hearts of probably ten million of the most intelligent and progressive of the Hindu races). (Pope, 1900, lxxiv)

[49] Cf. Ramaswamy (1997 25–26), Vaithees (2015, 20–28).

Like Caldwell, Pope had a tremendous influence on the developing Dravidian movement and its revisionist historiography. The legacy of this influence is discernible today in the fact that statues of both men were erected in Chennai under DMK rule in the 1960s.

Several prominent figures associated with Neo-Shaivism have been discussed in the scholarly literature. One of the earliest is Arumuka Navalar (1822–1879) of Jaffna, Sri Lanka, whose prolific print output and activities in Shaivite revival and reform made him a fixture in Madras and Chidambaram. Four other notable figures based in Madras and associated with this revival were Somasundara Nayakar (1846–1901), P. Sundaram Pillai (1855–1897), J. M. Nallaswami Pillai (1864–1920), and Maraimalai Adigal (1876–1950). Of these, Nayakar is known for his "inclusivist" approach that advocated for the uplift of Ādiśaiva Brahman temple priests alongside non-Brahmans more broadly.[50] In a different vein from Nayakar, Sundaram Pillai and Nallaswami Pillai wrote in English, promoting Shaivism for a largely European orientalist audience. But arguably the most important figure in the Neo-Shaivite revival was Maraimalai Adigal. As Vaithees (2015, 61) has observed, it is with "Maraimalai Adigal, that the ideas generated by figures such as Caldwell, Pope, Somasundara Nayakar, Sundaram Pillai, and Nallaswami Pillai finally find their most elaborate and powerful expression". Moreover, unlike Sundaram Pillai and Nallaswami Pillai, Adigal wrote and lectured extensively in Tamil, cultivating a wide audience across the Tamil South. In his later years, Adigal became increasingly unorthodox and anti-Brahmanical, leading him to spearhead the Pure Tamil Movement in the late 1910s, which sought to expunge non-Tamil loan words (particularly Sanskrit words) from the language.

The rise of the Dravidian movement into the realm of political power in the early 20th century overlapped with the beginnings of the Pure Tamil Movement and contributed to the propagation and entrenchment of the revisionist historiography promoted by Adigal and others. Many books on southern Indian religions from the early 20th century—and a number from the latter half of the twentieth century—include claims regarding the ostensible Tamil origins of Shaivism and Shaiva Siddhanta. To some extent, we can understand this as an expression of national myth-making: in the early 20th century, Brahmanic, missionary, and colonial hegemony were real pressures against which Dravidianists fought for a sense of emancipation. Although the preceding pages have shown that Shaivism and Shaiva Siddhanta were not the originally Tamil traditions that Dravidianist historiographers made them out to be, we also saw that these traditions did become distinctly southern Indian through their formative and enduring transformations in the Tamil South.

Abbreviations

ARE Annual Reports on (Indian) Epigraphy

[50] Cf. Vaithees (2015, 38–51).

BORI	Bhandarkar Oriental Research Institute
EFEO	École Française d'Extrême-Orient
IFI	Institut Français d'Indologie
IFP	Institut Français de Pondichéry
SIAA	South Indian Archakar Association
SII	South Indian Inscriptions

References

Primary Sources

Annual reports on (indian) epigraphy. Delhi: Manager of Publications, 1887 ff.

Civañāṉapōtam of Meykaṇṭatēvar in *Meykaṇṭacāttiram: mūlamum uraiyum.* Ceṉṉai: Kāñci Nākaliṅka Mutaliyār, 1897.

Civappirakācam of Umāpati Civācāriyār in *Meykaṇṭacāttiram mūlamum uraiyum.* Ceṉṉai: Kāñci Nākaliṅka Mutaliyār, 1897.

Kāmikāgama, pūrvabhāga. *Kāmikāgamaḥ pūrvabhāgaḥ.* Published by Ce. Svāmināthaśivācārya (= C. Svāminātha Gurukkal). Ceṉṉai: SIAA, 1975.

Kāmikāgama, uttarabhāga. *Kāmikāgamaḥ uttarabhāgaḥ.* Published by Ce. Svāmināthaśivācārya (= C. Svāminātha Gurukkal). Ceṉṉai: SIAA, 1988.

Mahābhārata. *The Mahābhārata for the First Time Critically Edited.* Edited by V. S. Sukthankar and S. K. Belvalkar. 19 vols. Puṇe: BORI, 1927–1959.

Puṟanāṉūṟu. *Puṟanāṉūṟu mūlamum uraiyum.* Edited by U. V. Cāminātaiyar. Vē. Tā. Jūbili Accukkūṭam. Ceṉṉai, [1894,] rev ed. 1935.

Rāmāyaṇa of Vālmīki. *The Vālmīki-Rāmāyaṇa.* Edited by G. H. Bhatt, P. L. Vaidya, P. C. Divanji, D. R. Mankad, G. C. Jhala, Umakant Premanand Shah. 7 vols. Baroda: Oriental Institute, 1960–1975.

Rauravāgama. Edited by N. R. Bhatt. 3 Vols. Publications de l'IFI No.18. Pondichéry: IFI, 1961, 1972, 1988.

Rigveda-saṃhitā. *Ṛgveda-saṃhitā: Rig Veda in 4 Volumes (Sanskrit Text, English Translation and Notes).* Edited by Ravi Prakash Arya and K. L. Joshi. Translated by H. H. Wilson. Varanasi Indica Books, 2002.

Sivajñānabodha with the commentary (-laghuṭikā) of Śivāgrayogin. *Śivajñānabodha with the Laghuṭīkā of Śivāgrayogī.* Edited and translated by T. Ganesan. Ceṉṉai: Śrī Aghoraśivācārya Trust, 2003.

Sivapūjāstava of Jñānaśiva with the commentary (-vyākhyā) of an anonymous author. *Śivapūjāstavaḥ savyākhyaḥ jñānaśambhuśivaviracitaḥ.* Edited by K. M. Subrahmaṇyaśāstrin. Devakoṭṭai, 1935.

South indian inscriptions. 34 vols. Delhi: Director-General, Archaeological Survey of India, 1891–2015.

Taittirīya-samhitā. *Kṛṣṇayajurvedīya Taittirīya-saṃhitā.* Edited by Rangasami Laksminarayana Kashyap. Bengaluru: Sri Aurobindo Kapali Sastry Institute of Vedic Culture, 2003.

Vyākaraṇa-mahābhāṣya (mahābhāṣya) of Patañjali. Edited by Franz Kielhorn; rev. ed. K. V. Abhyankar. Puṇe: BORI, 1996.

Secondary Sources

Acharya, D. (2011). Pāśupatas. In K. A. Jacobsen, H. Basu, A. Malinar, V. Narayanan (Eds.) *Brill's encyclopedia of Hinduism* (Vol. 3, pp. 458–66). Leiden: Brill.

Ambalavanar, D. N. (2006). *Arumuga Navalar and the construction of a caiva public in Colonial Jaffna*. Cambridge, MA: Harvard University, PhD Dissertation.

Bakker, H. T. (2002). Sources for reconstructing ancient forms of Śiva worship. In F. Grimal (Ed.) *Les Sources et le temps. Sources and time: A colloquium, Pondicherry, 11–13 January 1997* (pp. 397–412). Pondicherry: IFP/EFO.

Bakker, H. T. (2014). *The World of the Skandapurāṇa: Northern India in the Sixth and Seventh Centuries*. Leiden: Brill.

Bakker, H. T. (2021). Diversity and organisation in early Śaivism. In F. De Simini & C. Kiss (Eds.), *Śivadharmāmṛta: Essays on the Śivadharma and its Network* (pp. 1–17). UniorPress.

Biardeau, M. (1989). *Hinduism: The anthropology of a civilization*, trans. Richard Nice. Delhi: Oxford University Press.

Bisschop, P. C. (2006). *Early Śaivism and the Skandapurāṇa: Sects and Centres*. Groningen: Forsten.

Bisschop, P. C. (2009). Śiva. In K. A. Jacobsen, H. Basu, A. Malinar, V. Narayanan (Eds.) *Brill's encyclopedia of hinduism* (Vol. 1, pp. 741–54). Leiden: Brill.

Bisschop, P. C. (2014). Pañcārtha Before Kauṇḍinya. *Journal of Indian Philosophy, 42*(1), 27–37.

Bisschop, P. C. (2018). *Universal Śaivism: The appeasement of all gods and powers in the Śāntyadhyāya of the Śivadharmaśāstra*. Leiden: Brill.

Branfoot, C. (2013). Remaking the past: Tamil sacred landscape and temple renovations. *Bulletin of the School of Oriental and African Studies, 76*(1), 21–47.

Brunner, H. (1980–81). "Le Śaiva Siddhānta, 'essence' du Veda (l'Étude d'un fragment du Kāmikāgama)." *Indologica Taurinensia* 8–9:51–66.

Brunner, H. (1990a). L'image Divine Dans Le Culte Āgamique De Śiva. Rapport Entre L'image Mentale Et Le Support Du Culte. In A. Padoux & B. Bäumer (Eds.) *L'image Divine. Culte Et Méditation Dans L'hindouisme* (pp. 9–29). Paris: Editions du CNRS.

Brunner, H. (1990b). Ātmārthapūjā Versus Parārthapūjā in the Śaiva Tradition. In *The Sanskrit tradition and tantrism* (pp. 4–23). Leiden: Brill.

Brunner, H. (1998). Introduction. In *Somaśambhupaddhati, Quatrième partie, Rituels optionnels: pratiṣṭhā*, i–lxv. Pondicherry: Institut Français d'Indologie.

Clothey, F. (1978). *The many faces of Murukaṉ: The history and meaning of a South Indian God*. Mouton Publishers.

Clothey, F. (2012). Murukaṉ (Skanda, Kārttikeya, Subrahmaṇya). In K. A. Jacobsen, H. Basu, A. Malinar, V. Narayanan (Eds.) *Brill's encyclopedia of hinduism*. Brill Online. Leiden: Brill Online.

Davis, R. H. (1986–92). Aghoraśiva's background. *Journal of Oriental Research Madras (Dr. S.S. Janaki Felicitation Volume), 56*(62):367–78.

Davis, R. H. (1991). *Ritual in an oscillating universe: Worshipping Śiva in Medieval India*. Princeton University Press.

De Simini, F. (2016a). *Of Gods and books: Ritual and knowledge transmission in the manuscript cultures of premodern India*. Berlin: De Gruyter.

De Simini, F. (2016b). Śivadharma manuscripts from Nepal and the making of a Śaiva corpus. In M. Friedrich & C. Schwarke (Eds.) *One volume libraries: Composite and multiple text manuscripts* (pp. 233–286). Berlin: De Gruyter.

De Simini, F., & Csaba, K. (Eds.) (2021a). *Śivadharmāmṛta: Essays on the Śivadharma and its Network*, eds. Florinda De Simini and Csaba Kiss. Napoli: UniorPress

De Simini, F., & Csaba, K. (Eds.) (2021b). On how we got here. In *Śivadharmāmṛta: Essays on the Śivadharma and its Network*, eds. Florinda De Simini and Csaba Kiss, vii–xv. Napoli: UniorPress.

Dorai Rangaswamy, M. A. (1990). [1958]. *The religion and philosophy of Tēvāram with special reference to Nampi Ārūrar (Sundarar).* Madras: University of Madras. (Pagination follows 1990 edition.)

Ganesan, T. (2003). Schools of Śaivasiddhānta. In *Śivajñānabodha with the Laghuṭīkā of Śivāgrayogī*, ed. and trans. T. Ganesan, vii–xxvi. Chennai: Śrī Aghoraśivācārya Trust.

Ganesan, T. (2009). *Two Śaiva teachers of the sixteenth century: Nigamajñāna i and his disciple Nigamajñāna II*. Pondicherry: IFP.

Ganesan, T. (2011). Śaiva Siddhānta. In K. A. Jacobsen, H. Basu, A. Malinar, V. Narayanan (Eds.) *Brill's encyclopedia of Hinduism* (Vol. 3, pp. 514–531). Leiden: Brill.

Gollner, M. A. (2021). *The descent of scripture: A history of the Kāmikāgama.* Montreal: McGill University, PhD dissertation.

Goodall, D. (1998). *Bhaṭṭarāmakaṇṭhaviracitā kiraṇavṛttiḥ. Bhaṭṭa Rāmakaṇṭha's commentary on the Kiraṇatantra*, Vol. 1: chapters 1–6. Pondicherry: IFP/EFEO.

Goodall, D. (2000). Problems of name and lineage: Relationships between South Indian Authors of the Śaiva Siddhānta. *Journal of the Royal Asiatic Society, Series 3, 10*(2), 205–216.

Goodall, D. (2004). Introduction. In *The Parākhyatantra: A scripture of the Śaiva Siddhānta*, ed. and trans. Dominic Goodall, xxxv–xciv. Pondicherry: IFP/EFEO.

Goodall, D. (2006). Initiation et délivrance selon le Śaiva Siddhānta. In *Rites hindous, transferts et transformations*, eds. Gérard Colas and Gilles Tarabout, 93–116. Paris: Éditions de l'École des Hautes Études en Sciences Sociales, 2006.

Goodall, D. (2013). "parārthapūjā" in *Tāntrikābhidhānakośa III*, eds. Dominic Goodall and Marion Rastelli, 399–400. Vienna: Verlag der Österreichischen Akademie der Wissenschaften.

Goodall, D. (2014). Saiddhāntika paddhatis I. On Rāmanātha, the Earliest Southern Author of the Śaivasiddhānta of Whom Works Survive, and on Eleventh-century Revisions of the Somaśambhupaddhati. In *Cracow indological studies, 16*, 169–201.

Goodall, D. (2015). Introduction. In *Śaiva rites of expiation: A first edition and translation of Trilocanaśiva's Twelfth-century Prāyaścittasamuccaya (with a transcription of Hṛdayaśiva's Prāyaścittasamuccaya)*, ed. and trans. R. Sathyanarayanan (pp. 15–63). Pondicherry: IFP/EFEO.

Goodall, D. (2018). Rudragaṇikās: Courtesans in Śiva's Temple? Some Hitherto Neglected Sanskrit sources. *Cracow Indological Studies, 20*(1), 91–143.

Goodall, D., Sanderson, A., & Isaacson, H. (2015). *The Niśvāsatattvasaṃhitā: The Earliest Surviving Śaiva Tantra* (Vol. 1). IFP/EFEO/Universität Hamburg.

Gopinatha Rao, T. A. (1923–24). *Epigraphia Indica* (Vol. 17), H. Krishna Sastri (Ed.). New Delhi: Archaeological Survey of India.

Hart, G. (1975). *The poems of ancient tamil: Their Milieu and their Sanskrit counterparts.* Oxford University Press.

Heitzman, J. (1997). *Gifts of power: Lordship in an early Indian State.* Oxford University Press.

Hiltebeitel, A. (1978). The Indus Valley 'Proto-Śiva', reexamined through reflections on the goddess, the buffalo, and the symbolism of vāhanas. *Anthropos, 73*(5–6), 767–797.

Kaimal, P. (1996). Early Cōḻa Kings and 'Early Cōḻa Temples': Art and the evolution of kingship. *Artibus Asiae, 56*(1/2), 33–66.

Karashima, N., Subbarayalu, Y., & Shanmugam, P. (2010). *Maṭhas* and medieval religious movements in Tamil Nadu: An epigraphical study. *Indian Historical Review, 37*(2), 217–234.

Koppedrayer, K. I. (1990). The sacred presence of the guru: The 'Velala' Lineages of Thiruvavaduthurai, Dharmapuram, and Tiruppanantal." Hamilton, ON: McMaster University, PhD dissertation.

L'Hernault, F. (1984). Subrahmaṇya as supreme deity. In M. W. Meister (Ed.) *Discourses on Śiva: Proceedings of a symposium on the nature of religious imagery* (pp. 257–270). Philadelphia: University of Pennsylvania Press.

Mirnig, N. (2019). 'Rudras on Earth' on the eve of the Tantric Age: The Śivadharmaśāstra and the making of Śaiva lay and initiatory communities. In N. Mirnig, M. Rastelli, & V. Eltschinger (Eds.), *Tantric communities in context* (pp. 471–510). Verlag der Österreichische Akademie der Wissenschaften.

Nilakanta Sastri, K. A. (1988). [1955]. *A history of South India from prehistoric times to the fall of Vijayanagar*. New Delhi: Oxford University Press. (Pagination follows 1988 edition.)

Oberlies, T. (1988). Die Śvetāśvatara-Upaniṣad: Eine Studie ihrer Gotteslehre. *Wiener Zeitschrift Für Die Kunde Südasiens, 32*, 35–62.

Orr, L. C. (2007). Cholas, Pandyas, and 'Imperial Temple Culture' in Medieval Tamilnadu. In A. Hardy (Ed.), *The temple in South Asia* (pp. 109–130). British Academy.

Orr, L. C. forthcoming. Maṭhas in the history of southernmost India: Temple, guru, god and patron in the thirteenth to seventeenth centuries. In C. Simmons & S. P. Taylor (Eds.) *Beyond the monastery: The entangled institutional history of the South Asian Maṭha*. New York: Oxford University Press.

Parpola, A. (2015). *The roots of hinduism: The early Aryans and the Indus civilization*. Oxford University Press.

Peterson, I. V. (1989). *Poems to Śiva: The Hymns of the Tamil Saints*. Princeton University Press.

Pope, G. U. (1900). *The Tiruvāçakam or 'Sacred Utterances' of the Tamil Poet, Saint, and Sage Maṇikka-vāçagar*. Clarendon Press.

Prentiss, K. P. (1999). *The embodiment of Bhakti*. Oxford University Press.

Prentiss, K. P. (2001). On the making of a canon: Historicity and experience in the Tamil Śiva-bhakti canon. *International Journal of Hindu Studies, 5*(1), 1–26.

Presler, F. (1987). *Religion under bureaucracy: Policy and administration for Hindu temples in South India*. Cambridge University Press.

Raman, S. (2022). *The transformation of tamil religion: Ramalinga Swamigal (1923–1874) and Modern Dravidian Sainthood*. London and New York: Routledge.

Ramanujan, A. K. (1973). *Speaking of Śiva*. Penguin.

Ramaswamy, S. (1997). *Passions of the tongue: Language devotion in Tamil India, 1891–1970*. University of California Press.

Ravindiran, V. (2000). Discourses of empowerment: Missionary orientalism in the development of Dravidian Nationalism. In T. Brook & A. Schmid (Eds.), *Nation Work: Asian Elites and National Identities* (pp. 51–82). University of Michigan Press.

Sanderson, A. (1992). The Doctrine of the Mālinīvijayottaratantra. In T. Goudriaan (Ed.) *Ritual and speculation in early tantrism. Studies in Honor of André Padoux* (pp. 281–312). Albany: State University of New York Press.

Sanderson, A. (2006). The Lākulas: New evidence of a system intermediate between Pāñcārthika Pāśupatism and Āgamic Śaivism. *The Indian Philosophical Annual, 24*, 143–217.

Sanderson, A. (2013). The impact of inscriptions on the interpretation of early Śaiva literature. *Indo-Iranian Journal, 56*(3–4), 211–244.

Sanderson, A. (2014). The Śaiva literature. *Journal of Indological Studies, 24–25*, 1–113.

Sanderson, A. (2019). How public was Śaivism? In N. Mirnig, M. Rastelli, & V. Eltschinger (Eds.) *Tantric communities in context*. Vienna: Österreichische Akademie der Wissenschaften.

Sathyanarayanan Sarma, R., & Sarma, S. A. S. (2012). Introduction. In R. Sathyanarayanan Sarma & S. A. S. Sarma (Eds.) *Dhyānaratnāvalī of Trilocanaśiva*, xix–xxxvii. Karaikkal: Srimath Srikanta Sivacharya Research Institute, 2012.

Srinivasan, D. M. (1975). The so-called Proto-Śiva seal from Mohenjo Daro: An iconological assessment. *Archives of Asian Art, 29*, 47–58.

Trautmann, T. (1999). Inventing the history of South India. In D. Ali (Ed.), *Invoking the past: The uses of history in South Asia* (pp. 36–54). Oxford University Press.

Trento, M. (2021). Translating the Dharma of Śiva in sixteenth-century Chidambaram: Maṟaiñāṉa Campantar's Civatarumōttaram With a preliminary list of the surviving manuscripts. In F. De Simini & C. Kiss (Eds.), *Śivadharmāmṛta: Essays on the Śivadharma and its Network* (pp. 101–144). UniorPress.

Trento, M. (1983). Vedic Rudra-Śiva. *Journal of the American Oriental Society, 103*(3), 543–556.

Vaithees, R. V. (2015). *Religion, Caste, and Nation in South India: Maraimalai Adigal, the Neo Saivite Movement, and Tamil Nationalism 1876–1950*. Oxford University Press.

von Mitterwallner, G. (1984). Evolution of the Liṅga. In M. W. Meister (Ed.) *Discourses on Śiva: Proceedings of a symposium on the nature of religious imagery* (pp. 12–31). Philadelphia: University of Pennsylvania Press.
Zvelebil, K. (1995). *Lexicon of Tamil literature*. Leiden: Brill.

Chapter 11
The Reconstruction of the Early History of Tamil-Speaking Southern India

Herman Tieken

Abstract In Old Tamil Sangam poetry we hear villagers complaining about their unhappy love lives and poor bards in search of royal patrons who would support them in exchange for poems praising their heroic deeds. The scenes are set in Tamil-speaking southern India from before the appearance of the Pallava dynasty in the sixth and seventh centuries. On the assumption that the poets describe a contemporary society and in the absence of few other, material, sources, this corpus of lyrical poetry has become an all-important source for the reconstruction of the history of Tamilnadu and Kerala between the 3rd c. BCE and the arrival of the Pallavas. It will be argued, though, that the poets did not describe a contemporary society and that Sangam poetry was developed only in the 8th c. CE under the *aegis* of the Pandya kings. These later Pandyas presented themselves as rightful successors of the rulers of that same name of the earlier period and as carrying on a literary tradition that we are made to believe goes back to these earlier rulers. In Sangam poetry, we have to do with fiction, fiction about life in the countryside, and fiction about the past. While it is an unreliable source for the early history of Southern India, it does provide an interesting example of a process taking place around the same time all over the subcontinent, namely the use of the regional languages for fictional literature, which before that was the exclusive domain of Sanskrit. Tamil is not only slightly earlier than the other regional languages but also provides insight into the ideas and successive steps involved in this process of vernacularization.

Keywords Sangam (poetry) · Vernacularization · Bhakti (poetry) · Cheras · Cholas · Pandyas · Pallavas · Sanskrit · Bardic poetry (otherwise: bards) · Sattasai · Kamasutra · Vishnu · Shiva · Krishna · Murugan

---

The Reconstruction of the Early History of Tamil-speaking Southern India.
—Herman Tieken

H. Tieken (✉)
University of Leiden, Leiden, The Netherlands
e-mail: H.J.H.Tieken@hum.leidenuniv.nl

L. Vemsani (ed.), *Handbook of Indian History*,
https://doi.org/10.1007/978-981-97-6207-1_11

11.1 Introduction[1]

In the absence of much other, material, evidence, the reconstruction of the Early Historic period of present-day Tamilnadu and Kerala from approximately the 3rd c. BCE to the arrival of the Pallava dynasty in the 6th and 7th c. CE is to a large extent based on the most unlikely of sources, namely a collection of lyrical poems. In one set of poems, we hear village people complaining about their love lives, in the other poems bards praising kings. The latter scenes are historical but at the same time one-sided, as they picture a heroic age seen through the eyes of the bardic poet, who is also the main beneficiary of the successful warrior-king.

The poems describe a world from before the Pallavas, with the arrival of whom Tamilnadu experienced a complete transformation as a result of the massive importation of northern Indian culture with stone temples and sculpture, and Sanskrit literature. This is a world alien to that depicted in the poems, which is local and regional, and much less sophisticated and cosmopolitan. At the same time, these poems are dated in the period they describe, reporting events as they happen, and evincing a direct, personal relation between the bards and kings in question (Shulman, 2016: 81). After their rediscovery they have become widely available through printed editions between the last decade of the 19th c. and the first two of the 20th (Rajesh, 2014), and have since then been liberally used to flesh out the period before the arrival of the Pallavas. As according to a medieval source the poems are the work of members of an academy they are known as Sangam poetry (Tamil *cankam*, from Sanskrit *sangham*, "community"). And so is the period they depict, which as the Sangam Period has come to occupy a virtually inviolable position in the Southern Indian historical canon. As a result, archeological discoveries that have subsequently been made are treated in the most selective way. In doing so, the inevitable conclusion that the scenes described in the poems cannot belong to such an early period is constantly postponed and made to wait for further textual study or field work. In reconstructing the early history of the deep south of India we should therefore be much more careful and restrict ourselves in the first place to the available material evidence. At this stage, it is impossible to offer a fully worked-out version of the history-without-Sangam. Instead, I will deal with the way the different sources are used (or ignored) and how against all odds one tends to stick to the position originally taken in, which indirectly tells us much about the present political situation in this southernmost corner of India. Furthermore, as with all this, the date of the poems is still open, an attempt will be made to situate them in the proper historical setting. After all, we are dealing with an important moment in history, one at which it was decided to use a regional language as a literary idiom, a domain that in India up to that time had been reserved for Sanskrit. In the following therefore much attention will be paid to literary matters, which include investigations into the relationship between the Tamil poems and certain literary genres (the term genre is used very loosely here)

[1] Many of the Sangam poems and other text passages discussed in this chapter have been dealt with in more detail before in Tieken (2001) and following publications, including Khoroche and Tieken (2009).

of northern Indian Sanskrit literature. The selections the Tamil poets made from among the available genres will provide information from within about a process eventually seen all over India, one by which upcoming regional powers strove to assert themselves politically as well as culturally (Pollock, 2006 and Tieken, 2008a). I will start, though, with what remains of what we know about the extreme south of India in the pre-Pallava period if we ignore Sangam poetry. This is directly followed by an outline of the history of the remainder of the first millennium, which saw the revival, well-documented this time by textual (inscriptions) as well as material sources (temples), of the dynasties of the earlier period.

11.2 History Without Sangam

In his inscriptions Ashoka, king of Magadha (middle of 3rd c. BCE), provides a list of people living to the south of his realm, namely the Codas and Pandiyas, a Kelalaputta and a Satiyaputta, the latter two evidently kings or heads of lineages, and the River Tambapanni (present-day Tamraparni, flowing into the Gulf of Bengal off Thoothukudi). In the first three names, we may recognize the Cholas, Pandyas, and Cheras, the main dynasties of Sangam poetry (Chera, Tamil Cera, also Ceralar, showing the palatalization of *k* before *e*). As we will see, the first three make their reappearance from the 8th c. CE onwards, if they had ever been away. This time with veritable imperial ambitions, temples, inscriptions, and literary texts. Evidence of their presence in the earlier period is restricted. It consists, for instance, of square punch-marked coins, showing their emblems, a tiger, fish, and bow and arrow respectively, some of which also bear inscriptions in the ancient Brahmi script. Thus, we have one coin that reads "the great Valuti", Valuti being a title peculiar to the Pandyas, and two that read "Irumporai" and "Makkotai" respectively, titles donned by the Cheras in the poems as well as by the later Cheras (Krishnamurthy, 1997). Some of these titles are also met with in the Tamil-Brahmi inscriptions which, as a group, are dated between roughly the 2nd c. BCE and 4th CE (Mahadevan, 2003). The inscriptions are found on the in- and outside of natural caves and mention the donors who have turned these caves into suitable shelters for wandering monks, mainly Jain monks. Besides traders (oil and salt merchants, toddy-sellers) and craftsmen (ironmongers), the donors include Chera kings (Irumporai) and a person bearing the royal title Valuti. Interestingly, one donation was made by what seems to be of the village council (Tieken, 2007: 510), and in two inscriptions the donors identify themselves as members of a *nikama*, from Sanskrit *nigama*, which in later inscriptions serves as a term for a merchant guild (Mahadevan, 2003: nos. 3 and 6).

While contemporary evidence of how trade was organized is rare, in the period under consideration Southern India was actively involved in trade with the Roman world.[2] Thus, the *Periplus Maris Erythraei*, or *The Circumnavigation of the*

[2] Much of the following information on the trade between South India and the Roman world and the "Muziris Papyrus" has been drawn from Tomber (2008) and Chakravarti (2006, 2015).

Erythrean Sea (mid 1st c. CE), written by an anonymous Greek-Egyptian trader from Alexandria, mentions the harbor of Muziris on the present-day western Kerala coast. The goods traded were pepper, pearls, ivory and gemstones, and nard and malabathrum, the latter two, plants used for making ointments or perfume. The availability of these items in coastal Muziris testifies to widespread internal trade. Thus, while pepper was grown in the Western Ghats, which forms Muziris' immediate hinterland, gemstones came from the other side of the Ghats Mountain Range, more exactly from the Coimbatore region in Tamilnadu, accessible through the Palghat Gap. Furthermore, nard, a flowering plant of the honeysuckle family, grows in India in the Himalayas in the far north at an altitude of between 3000 to 5000 m. An interesting piece of evidence for the trade between Roman Egypt and Muziris is formed by the fragmentary "Muziris papyrus", which contains a contract involving a loan between a merchant and a financier for the voyage from Alexandria to Muziris and back. The papyrus dates from around 150 CE, and the contract was most likely drawn up in Alexandria. It also describes the cargo of a ship called Hermapollon—it is unclear if this is the same ship for which the loan was made—and specifies the import taxes to be paid at the eastern border of the Roman empire amounting to one quarter of the goods *in natura*. The total cargo of the Hermapollon came to 250 tons. Due to the fragmentary nature of the papyrus, of the five types of goods mentioned only two can be identified, namely 167 tusks, half a ton of ivory pieces, and 80 boxes of nard.

Attempts to find Muziris, which makes its appearance in Sangam poetry as Muciri, have of late been concentrated on Pattanam, north of Kochi. Excavations have yielded some brick architecture, a wooden wharf, a boat, amphorae and Italian earthenware. The amphorae suggest that wine made up an important part of the export from the West. In the vicinity, no fewer than four hoards have been found with Roman coins up to Emperor Trajanus (r. 98–117 CE). The greatest concentration of Roman coin hoards are, however, found in the Coimbatore area. The coins date from the 1st to the later half of the 4th c. CE. Coimbatore was situated on an inland route connecting the west and east coasts. However, the east coast had international harbors of its own. So far, two of them have been properly excavated, namely Arikamedu south of Pondicherry and Alagankulam on the Gulf of Mannar. In Arikamedu archeologists have identified two distinct areas, one an industrial sector with workshops for bead and bangle making, already occupied before the sea trade, and the other sector having fragments of a wall, possibly a quay. The Roman pottery and amphorae which have been found belong to the period between the 1st c. BCE and the 2nd c. CE, but also include a handle from the 5th c. Among the finds are also products made locally but inspired by Hellenistic or Roman examples. Coins are comparatively rare. Excavations at the other site, Alagankulam, have among other objects yielded imported amphorae and coins from the late 1st c. BCE to the 4th CE.

Roman trade with India seems to have started in the first century. BCE. However, from the end of the 2nd c. CE onwards material evidence at the sites mentioned above, such as western pottery, amphorae, and Roman coins became increasingly more rare, with an occasional object or coin from the 4th or 5th c. As we will see later, however, in India the memory of trade with the Roman world was still alive several centuries later.

Apart from the rare fragments of brick constructions mentioned above, there are no remnants of architectural constructions or sculptures in stone from the Sangam period. This changed radically in the 6th and 7th c., which saw the arrival of the Pallavas from Andhra into Tamilnadu (Francis, 2013–2017). Under this dynasty, the first stone temples were built, dedicated to the northern Indian gods Shiva and Vishnu and embellished with reliefs depicting the feats attributed to these gods in Sanskrit mythological literature. In their temple building project, the Pallavas seem to have been inspired by their contemporaries from the northern, Deccan part of peninsular India. Their most famous temples are found at Mahabalipuram on the beach south of Chennai, with examples of excavated cave temples with decorated pillars and wall sculptures side by side with free-standing temples, which were hewn out of a single, large piece of rock. The site is also famous for its open-air rock relief of 96 by 43 feet on two large boulders depicting the myth of the descent of the Ganges. The Kailasanatha temple in the Pallava capital of Kanchipuram, in its turn, is a constructed temple, raised with stones cut to size and roofed over with stoneslabs. It seems as if the Pallavas wanted to show off their knowledge of temple architecture, for in an inscription found in the rock-cut temple in Mandagapattu the king, who built this temple for Brahma, Shiva and Vishnu "without using any brick, wood, metal or mortar", calls himself "the one with a playful mind".[3]

The Pallavas also had inscriptions engraved in both stone and on copper plates, laying down in writing the donations they made to these temples or to settlements of learned brahmins, however, not after first having presented their credentials in an extensive genealogy which through a number of figures from the Sanskrit epic, the *Mahabharata*, goes back to northern India's "first" god, Brahma. While the technical details of the donations are in the local Tamil language, the first, genealogical, part, with its many references to Sanskrit epic and mythological literature, is in Sanskrit. To the division of labor between Sanskrit and Tamil, I will come back below. Besides duly enumerating the heroic feats performed by the kings, these genealogies also mention the sacrifices they performed, in particular the extensive, and expensive, Vedic Horse Sacrifice. All these innovations show the growing influence of the learned brahmin at the Pallava court and in society at large, as this figure alone possessed knowledge of the Sanskrit language and the Vedic sacrifices.

In the course of the 9th c. the Pallavas gradually disappeared from the scene. Their place is taken by the Cholas, who had their capital in Tanjavur. The 8th c. has already seen the rise of the Pandyas further south, around Madurai. As the names adopted by them show, these dynasties presented themselves as heirs of the earlier Pandyas and Cholas and, indeed, in their inscriptions, they pay lipservice to the political constellation described in Sangam poetry, in which, as we will see, the

---

[3] Mahalingam (1988: no. 27). Note that with bricks, wood, metal and mortar the king is not referring to building materials used before in Tamilnadu. There is no archeological evidence of these building materials there, except for bricks, but these were used in the 1st and 2nd c., not in the immediately following centuries.

Tamil-speaking world was ruled by the three crowned heads (*mu-ventar*, *mum-muti*, *mu(m)* is Tamil for "three"), the Pandyas, Cholas, and Cheras. The royal Chola inscriptions are bilingual, showing the same division of labor between Sanskrit and Tamil as seen in those of the Pallavas. The Cholas were great temple builders—one of their most impressive examples is the Brihadeeshvara temple in Tanjavur—and during their reign, the finest examples of bronze images were produced, among which those of the dancing Shiva. As for the Pandyas, there are strikingly few temples built by the royal family itself. At the same time, the realm must already have been dotted with temples, as becomes clear from the many inscriptions recording donations made by their subordinates for, for instance, keeping temple lamps burning. To the Pandya inscriptions, especially those of the royal family, I will come back later. Around 800 CE the third ancient dynasty, the Cheras, made its comeback as well, namely along the west coast in present-day Kerala (Veluthat, 2009: 249–276).

11.3 The Early Tamil Literary Corpus

As indicated, the early history of the southern tip of peninsular India before the arrival of the Pallavas has almost in its entirety been written on the basis of information gleaned from Sangam poetry.[4] It consists of a set of eight anthologies of poems and a treatise on the language and poetics, which according to a legend preserved in a medieval commentary on a poetical treatise, Iraiyanar's *Akapporul* (*Treatise on Love Poetry*), were the work of an academy, established by the Pandyas at their royal seat in Madurai (Buck & Paramasivam, 1997 and Tieken, 2010a).

The poems of the *Eight Anthologies* (*Ettuttokai*, *ettu* is Tamil for "eight") fall apart into two genres, namely poems about love (labeled *Akam*, or "interior") and poems about heroism (*Puram*, or "exterior"). Of the eight anthologies, six deal with love. Of these, four consist of short poems of 3 to 6 lines each in the *Ainkurunuru* (*Five Hundred Short Poems*), of 4 to 8 lines in the *Kuruntokai* (*Collection of Short Poems*), of 8 to 13 lines in the *Narrinai* (*Good-Type Poems*), and of 13 to 31 lines in the *Akananuru* (*Four Hundred Poems on Love*). The other two contain dramatic scenes made up of narrative stanzas framing songs. The titles, *Paripatal* (*Pari Songs*) and *Kalittokai* (*Collection of Kali Songs*), refer to metrical patterns, *pari* and *kali* respectively. The two remaining anthologies, the *Purananuru* (*The Four Hundred on War*) and *Patirruppattu* (*The Ten Times Ten Poems*), deal with war and heroism. These eight collections are accompanied by a work on grammar and poetics, titled *Tolkappiyam* (*Traditional Poetry*). Modern scholarship, however, has added a tenth to these nine texts, the *Pattuppattu* (*The Ten Songs*), a collection of 10 long poems of between 103 and 782 lines each.

[4] An overview of early Tamil literature is provided by, for instance, Zvelebil (1973) and Marr (1985). The same information may be found in studies devoted to specific aspects of Tamil literature (Hart, 1975; Wilden, 2006) or translations (Ramanujan, 1967, 1985, Hart, 1979, 2015 and Hart & Heifetz, 1999).

In the modern text editions, the poems are accompanied by colophons and commentaries. Old commentaries are rare, most of the commentaries that we have, were written by the modern editors. The colophons mention the poets, the persons who are speaking in the poems, and the circumstances under which they do so. A typical colophon of a love poems reads like this: "The poet Kapilar presents what a girl or a woman deserted by her lover said when evening approached". The colophons of the heroic poems are more elaborate, as can be seen in the following example: "This is the song of the bard Kalattalaiyar praising the Chera king Peruñceralatan, who, ashamed of the back wound he received in the battle against the Chola king Karikal Peruvalattan, faced north, to commit suicide by fasting to death". It is unfortunately not clear at what stage in the transmission this type of information has been added to the poems. The entire corpus comprises 2381 poems in various meters of various levels of complexity, ascribed to approximately 473 poets (102 poems are anonymous). Of these 473, 77 composed both love and heroic poems, which agrees with the tradition that the corpus is the work of a collective or academy.

For more material on the period concerned historians also consulted two so-called satellite texts, the *Cilappatikaram* (*The Tale of an Anklet*, Parthasarathy, 1993) and the *Manimekalai* (*The Renunciation of Manimekalai*, Monius, 2001). These two epic poems, which are set in the same world as the Sangam poems but are at the same time believed to be later, are dated somewhere between the end of the Sangam poems and the Pallava dynasty, if, that is to say, the last Sangam poems do indeed date from before the arrival of the Pallavas. As will be shown, this is not self-evident as some of the poems mention aspects of northern Indian culture, which had not been there yet before the Pallavas. To deal with this anomaly some texts are placed at the very end of the period, as close as possible before the Pallavas without actually touching them (Wilden, 2014: 6–26). One such supposedly late text would be the *Paripatal*. However, the poet of one of the poems of this collection is mentioned in the *Akananuru*, which is, however, claimed to be one of the earliest texts (Tieken, 2008b: 597). This particular anomaly is explained away by suggesting that the poem in question must be a later interpolation in the latter text. Instead, the real problem is the early, pre-Pallava date assigned to the corpus in its entirety.

The study of the Sangam corpus is marked, or rather, marred, by two firm convictions. The first is that the poems were composed in the period which they describe, which is pre-Pallava, as this dynasty does not play a role in the poems. The second is that the Tamil poems are unique; we would be dealing with a literature that had originated independently of that of Sanskrit. In fact, if Sangam poetry did indeed have its origin in the 3rd c. BCE, it would be older than Sanskrit literature, as the use of Sanskrit for fiction does not go back further than the 1st c. CE. Both convictions are interdependent, in the sense that the later the poems the less likely it is that they had not been influenced by contemporary Sanskrit literature. I will start, though, by looking into the supposed uniqueness of the Tamil tradition, first going through the Akam poems, next through the Puram poems, to give an idea of the kind of poetry we are dealing with and of the historical information that may be found in it.

11.4 The Poems on Life in the Village

The term "love poetry" generally used for the poems in the *Ainkurunuru, Kuruntokai, Narrinai,* and *Akananuru* is inadequate. "Village poetry" seems to be a more apposite descriptor. The poems depict various village types struggling to make a living and doomed to unhappy, frustrating love lives. Below a few examples will be given of the great variety of awkward situations the villagers find themselves in.[5] For instance, the simple peasant has to employ his daughter in the fields to chase away birds, where the innocent girl may be accosted, and seduced, by young men who happen to come along. In the following fragment from *Kuruntokai* 223, we hear how the girl regrets her mistake, realizing she has shattered her parents' ambitions to marry her to a "good" party:

But he waylaid me,
to help me scaring parrots
gave me a slingshot and rattles,
and a skirt of young leaves
which he said looked good
on me,
and with his lies
he took the rare innocence
that mother had saved for me.
And now I am like this.

(Adapted from Ramanujan, 1967: 70)

Once married the situation does not improve. Most of the time the husband is away from home. In *Kuruntokai* 124 he passes through an inhospitable jungle. However, his hardships are nothing compared to the grief of his wife at home:

You say that the wasteland
you have to pass through
is absence itself:
wide spaces where sometimes
salt merchants have gathered for a while
and gone, *omai* trees that stand
like ghost towns once busy with living.
But tell me really,
do you think that home will be sweet
for the ones you leave behind?

(Ramanujan, 1967: 56)

[5] For more examples, see Tieken (2001: 11–53).

The husband's travels are not undertaken for pleasure but to support the family and fulfill the obligations incumbent on him as a householder. Thus, in *Narrinai* 284 we overhear a man saying that while his heart tells him to return to his beloved wife, reason tells him "not to hurry, as unfinished work brings poverty, dullness, and shame". In *Akananuru* 173 a woman is consoled with the words "Men who stay at home with their wives are not able to keep their family from ruin. Therefore your husband decided to leave and gather wealth". In *Kuruntokai* 12 we read that the jungle he is going through is infested by bands of robbers "with bent bow in the ready, whetting the points of their arrows" (Ramanujan, 1967: 24). It is also dotted with so-called hero stones that commemorate heroes fallen in the defense of their villages against cattle raids. These simple monuments add to the picture of a jungle dangerous for travelers. What makes things even worse is that the heroes in the stones are worshiped with rather primitive rituals that involve alcohol and animal sacrifices, as seen in the following fragment from *Akananuru* 35:

> To worship the god in a stone erected because of a hero's resolute strength,
> they put a peacock feather on it, beat the *tuti* drum, and sacrifice
> palm wine and sheep.
>
> (Hart, 2015: 43)

In the above poem, no priest is mentioned. If a priest was involved, most probably it was the same one operating in the village. Thus, when a young girl suffering from love sickness has lost her beauty her mother calls in the local Velan priest to determine the cause of the illness. This priest has dedicated his life to Murugan, the god with the spear (*vel*). Therefore, his diagnosis is always the same: the girl is possessed by this handsome young god from the mountains. To exorcize the girl's possession the priest dances, working himself into a trance. See the following fragment from *Akananuru* 98:

> In a large pandal decorated for the dance,
> the Velan will put on palmyra leaves and *katampu*,
> and, dancing to the sweet rhythmic beat,
> he will cry out the great name of the god in a frenzy
> as he graces the wide floor, and like a puppet
> dancing for a skilled puppeteer, he will sway and swing.
>
> (Hart, 2015: 109-110).

Ironically, the diagnosis is a blessing: the girl is freed from the odium of having a secret love affair and therefore the parents can continue the search for a suitable husband for their daughter. But what if the cure does not work and the girl's body does not regain its original brightness, which of course it doesn't? Therefore, the girl is from the very beginning worried that her mother will spend the little money they have on the "useless" Velan, who makes things only worse. In the following fragment from *Akananuru* 292 the girl tells her friend that the priest's séance won't help her:

Tell me what I should do, friend.
Mother doesn't know what troubles me and pours out her money,
fearful and confused. But I, I will feel even more ashamed
if the useless Velan has them kill a lamb
that, denied its mother's milk, eats shoots
and then dances his frienzied dance
while the garland on his chest bobs up and down.
I don't know what to do. Even though he [the girl's lover] sees how I suffer
and my bright bangles grow loose, he doesn't marry me.

(Hart, 2015: 297)

Besides these petty farmers, traders,and fishermen every village also has its own family belonging to the landed gentry, who live in "a large 'palace' set in the midst of small huts" (*Narrinai* 169). This family can afford a wet-nurse for their daughter, whom they spoil with delicious food and who, in her turn, spoils her pet-myna, a speaking bird, with sweet milk. However, in agreement with the general drift of the poetry this idyll is disrupted by the daughter running away with a poor fellow rather than marrying her parents' choice. The person speaking in *Akananuru* 369 is the girl's wet-nurse. First, this woman describes the desolate state of the house after the girl's elopement: her myna bird refuses to speak and to drink the sweet milk, her friends look glum, the flowerpots are empty, and the goddess painted on the wall are no longer presented with offerings. Next, the wet-nurse regrets that she had not realized what was going on in the girl's mind when on her wedding day she refused to have her hair done. After her family had decorated their house, so that it looked as new and resembled Urantai, the capital of the Cholas, only in this late stage of the preparations, it became clear that the girl did not agree with the marriage candidate selected by her parents as she ran away with her lover. The wet-nurse suffers at the thought that the little girl is doomed for the rest of her life to live in this poor boy's house, a hut thatched with grass, which has only one pole in the front yard with only one cow tied to it, in a small village without any luxury.

While the scenes of the poems take place in small villages or the countryside, occasionally we get glimpses of another, more fascinating world, namely that of the king and the city. As to the king, it should be emphasized that he is not a main character in the poems. He is the leader of military expeditions, which are one of the causes for the husband's absence from home. Thus, in *Ainkurunuru* 447 the soldiers are looking forward to the end of the campaign: "May we be released from our work for the king, so that we will see again the bright foreheads of our wives", and in 466 the soldier's wife anxiously waits for his return: "I know for certain that he will come back immediately after he has finished the important task entrusted to him by the king and has received permission to leave". The references to cities are likewise marginal and found mainly in comparisons. Thus, in *Akananuru* 369, summarized above, the house decorated for the wedding is compared to the Chola capital, Urantai. In other poems, houses are compared to Vañci or Madurai, the capitals of the Cheras and Pandyas respectively. The city is a symbol of beauty and richness, as, for instance, in *Akananuru* 396: "Leave me, but first give me back my beauty, which was like Vañci", in 237 of the same collection: "Even if your lover were to acquire Urantai, he would not forsake the fluid oozing from between your white teeth" or in *Narrinai* 234: "If you are considering a price to pay for her, Urantai and Vañci both together will be too small". These cities functioned as commercial centers. For instance, the port mentioned in *Akananuru* 227 had a busy market: "He who left, leaving behind a gossip (about our love) as loud as the noise in the market in the port with beautiful houses on the beach". The capital mentioned in *Narrinai* 295 was an international port: "My youth, confined to the house, will grow ripe like the jars of wine [from Rome] in the port of our lord, where ships come with cargoes from many different countries".

11.5 The Village Poetry's Counterpart in Northern Indian Sanskrit Literature

Sangam poetry has been studied in almost complete isolation. It was dated too early to look for possible counterparts in Sanskrit literature. This is to be regretted as precisely on this point there appears to be much to gain. Admittedly, the northern Indian texts concerned do not belong to the commonly known genres but are found among the largely under-studied so-called minor literary types of Kavya literature. Kavya is a literature written in Sanskrit, originally the language of the learned, scholarly treatises, which had next ventured upon fictional literature, including play texts. (On how Sanskrit absorbed all kinds of literary activities, see Tieken, 2014). The court scenes in plays naturally figure characters, like queens and servants, who, as women and low-class characters, could not be made to speak a learned language like Sanskrit. In the play texts, they speak a so-called Prakrit, that is, an imitation in Sanskrit of the spoken language (e.g., Sanskrit *ukta*, "which was said", becomes *utta*). These Prakrits have within Kavya literature produced a literature of their own, consisting of texts featuring women or low-class characters. As we will see, the counterparts to the Sangam texts are to be found among this category of texts. Thus, the Tamil-speaking villagers in the Akam poem belong to the same category of people as the Prakrit speaking farmers in Hala's *Sattasai* (*The Seven Hundred*). As I will argue below, the implicit identification in Sangam poetry of Tamil with Prakrit plays a decisive role in dating the Tamil poetic tradition.

The Tamil village poems have a counterpart in Hala's *Sattasai*, a Prakrit text of 700 short poems in which villagers complain about their love lives. The link between the two is obvious and has been made before by G.L. Hart, who, however, did not go much further than collecting similar themes and figures of speech and ended up with a highly convoluted scenario, according to which both the Tamil and Prakrit poems continued a common megalithic Deccan tradition (Hart, 1975). As I have argued before (Tieken, 2001: 54–80; see also Khoroche & Tieken, 2009), and will argue here again, the *Sattasai* poems do not go back to a megalithic Deccan culture but were inspired by a much later Sanskrit treatise on love and sex, namely the *Kamasutra.* This is made clear in poem 2:

> Shame on those who cannot appreciate
> This ambrosial Prakrit poetry
> But pore instead
> Over treatises on love.
>
> (Khoroche & Tieken, 2009: 15)

The poor, inexperienced, and luckless lovers in the poems are implicitly set off against the "hero" of the *Kamasutra*, the *nagaraka*, or the ever successful lover from the town (*nagara*). Take poem 324:

> When he fell asleep,
> Exhausted after a day of dragging the plow through thick mud,
> His wife,
> Angry at missing the pleasure of love,
> Cursed the rainy season.
>
> (Khoroche & Tieken, 2009: 164)

The pun of the poem lies in the contrast it offers to the circumstances of the "townsman" of the *Kamasutra*, a well-to-do man who does not have to work to make a living and can devote himself entirely to the pursuit of love. Language is also part of the pun. One of the accomplishments of the townsman is his knowledge of the Sanskrit language, through which he has access to a vast corpus of literary and scholarly texts, including the *Kamasutra.* The villagers in the *Sattasai* are made to speak a Prakrit dialect, in this particular case an approximation of the language of the countryside of present-day Maharashtra.

Some of the poems of the *Sattasai* revolve around situations dealt with in the *Kamasutra.* A case in point is 158 about a newly wed couple:

> He was embarrassed
> But I laughed and gave him a hug
> When he groped for the knot
> Of my skirt and found it
> Already undone.
>
> (Khoroche & Tieken, 2009: 59-60)

This scene may be compared with the chapter in the *Kamasutra* entitled "Winning a Virgin's Trust", which explains how the husband should win over his inexperienced wife by going through a series of small steps, beginning by gently taking her on his lap and ending by loosening the knot of her skirt. However, what the *Kamasutra* presents here is just one of many possible scenarios. Moreover, the above poem shows its uselessness in real life, in which rather than relying on such a list of steps one should be able to make an exact assessment of the situation one is in, on pain of making a complete fool of oneself.

Each figure, the inexperienced lover from the village in the poems and the successful lover from the town in the *Kamasutra*, is to some extent a caricature: the idealized *nagaraka* is even more unreal than the villager. The point is the contrast, which is deliberately exaggerated. It seems very likely that the *Sattasai* and the *Kamasutra* originated in the same milieu and at about the same period. The *Sattasai* has been dated to the 1st c. CE. This date, which has been based on references found in the text itself and which are part of the fictional world created in it, will now have to be moved forward to sometime after the third century, which is the earliest possible date of the *Kamasutra.* A date *ante quem* for the *Sattasai* is provided by Bana's *Harshacarita*, a biography of King Harsha, from the 7th c., in which it is mentioned.

All this also casts a new light on the question of the origin and date of the Tamil village poems, depending on who borrowed from whom—in the light of what follows a scenario involving independent origination may be ignored. Before going into that question, I want to turn to the two other Akam collections, the *Paripatal* and *Kalittokai*, which, as will be shown, have exact parallels in northern Indian Kavya literature as well, which, like the *Sattasai*, are typical Prakrit texts. Furthermore, in these two cases, the identifications are supported by the Tamil tradition itself.

11.6 The Paripatal

The poems of the *Paripatal* and *Kalittokai* are much longer than those dealt with so far. The shortest *Paripatal* poem counts 73 lines, and the longer ones are 130 lines or more. A typical poem from these two collections consists of several independent stanzas with different meters, which coincide with switches in speakers and in songs and narration. The *Paripatal*, discussed here first, is a collection of 22 poems (Gros, 1968). They deal with religious festivals connected with the god Murugan (8 poems), the River Vaiyai (8 poems), and Mal or Mayon, Tamil names of the gods Vishnu and Krishna (6 poems). To give an idea of the contents and complex structures of the poems, below a synopsis of poem no. 8 is given.

The scene is a festival dedicated to God Murugan residing on Mount Parankundram. In the first 35 lines, this mountain is praised. Next, the focus switches to the nearby town of Kutal (*alias* Madurai, the Pandya capital, so-called after northern Indian town Mathura) with an exchange taking place there between a husband, a wife, and a confidante (36–89). The first "speaker" is the husband, who praises Mount Parankundram, which is said to grant faithfulness. Next, we hear his wife accusing him of having seen another woman. The husband denies this, swearing "by the gardens on the sweet, sanded bank of the Vaiyai, the cool woods on the slopes of the Parankundram, and the seers". The wife's confidante, however, doubts the husband's sincerity and warns him that if he does not abide by his oaths the spear of the god of Parankundram, that is, Murugan, will kill him. The husband asks how she can doubt a man who is constantly praising that mountain, offering flowers to it, bringing offerings, and singing songs of praise. The exchange ends with the confidante warning the husband again.

After this follows a long passage (90–123) describing various people worshiping Parankundram in the hope that this mountain will make their marriages happy again. The poem ends with a blessing of Parankundram: "May, even if the sky remains dry, the richness of waterfalls forever be with you, o cool Parankundram!" The poem presents people at the festival in a dramatic way, by putting them on stage as it were. A clear example is the passage 36–66, which is an actual sketch of quarreling lovers.

The eight poems on the Vaiyai river are set at another festival, during which young and old, and men and women, throw offerings into the river, swollen after the first rains. The festival includes water games in which both sexes participate, which gives occasion to all kinds of jealous scenes between lovers. Thus, in one poem we overhear an angry altercation between a man and his mistress. In another, people are quoted who are looking on at the water games from the high river banks.

Of the six poems describing festivals in honor of Mal/Mayon, the "Dark One", five (1–4 and 13) deal with Vishnu, the great god of northern Indian mythology, and one (15) with Krishna-the-god, the ally of the Pandavas, one of the two warring parties in the Indian epic poem, the *Mahabharata*—not the young cowherd Krishna, dancing with the cowherd girls (see below). In the poem Krishna is accompanied by his elder brother Balarama, forming a "pair of great fame" (15. 66; see also 15. 13, 19 and 28). The men and women praising these gods have no scores to settle in their love lives, as they do in the other poems: we have to do with pure praise poetry. The poems do not only betray a detailed knowledge of Sanskrit mythology developed around Vishnu and Krishna, which is rooted in the Vedic tradition – Vishnu is called the "essence of the Vedas" (3. 66; see also 1. 13, 3. 14, 4. 65)—but also assign an important role to the brahmins, the custodians of this tradition. Thus, in the Vaiyai poems, the people of Kutal gather on the banks of the river, when after a dry period the water level starts rising again. They bring offerings and swim in the river, as a result of which its water loses its purity and startles and confuses the brahmins, who are obsessed with (ritual) purity. It is, however, the very same brahmins who start the festival (6. 43–45 and 11. 78 respectively). Even Murugan, evidently the village god *par excellence*, is touched by the brahmin brush and represents a mixture of a local, terrestrial god and a transcendent deity. He resides on a local mountain and in heaven and earth, and he has a village priest, the above-mentioned Velan, but at the same time abides by the *dharma* of the twice-born brahmins (5. 15 and 12. 3, and 14. 27–28 respectively). Moreover, he is married to the daughter of Indra of the northern Indian pantheon as well as, to the former's grief, to Valli, a girl from the mountains (9. 7–10).

To these poems of the *Paripatal*, I will return below. It may be noted already here, however, that the detailed knowledge of the mythology of Vishnu and Krishna and the role assigned to the brahmins seen here is incompatible with a pre-Pallava text. It is the reason why some scholars place this collection at the very end of the Sangam period, just before the arrival of the Pallavas.

In the *Paripatal* the festival has been turned into a dramatic scene, which is named after the songs sung during a festival: in poem 11, line 137 *paripatal* is used as a technical term for such songs. This development is not unique to Tamil literature but has taken place in Sanskrit literature as well, which knows of various minor dramatic scenes, such as the *carcari* and *hallisaka*, which are set at festivals. Unfortunately, the northern Indian evidence is relatively late and incomplete. What we do have are definitions in the tenth-century commentary by Abhinavagupta on the *Natyashastra*, a treatise (*shastra*) on drama (*natya*) of the 4th or 5th c., and in Bhoja's *Shringaraprakasha* (*Explanation of Erotic Love*) an encyclopedic handbook on everything literary, from the 11th c., and some early fragments like a festival song in King Harsha's play *Ratnavali* (7th c.). All later and complete examples are texts by Jaina authors, who used the genre for religious purposes. All examples, old as well as late, are in Apabhramsha, which is a Prakrit, but slightly farther removed from Sanskrit than the Prakrit of the *Sattasai* and therefore a degree more vulgar. This is in accordance with the nature of the songs, which were sung by common people on the streets.[6]

11.7 The Kalittokai

The *Kalittokai* is the third collection of Akam poetry having Prakrit counterparts in the Indian Kavya literary tradition. Like the *Paripatal* poems, those of the *Kalittokai* are made up of several autonomous stanzas. In the *Kalittokai* poems, the centerpiece is formed by a set of songs, which are introduced and concluded by stanzas describing the circumstances under which these songs were sung. The topic of the poems is unhappy love, the protagonists are jealous lovers or estranged married couples.

The *Kalittokai* is a collection of altogether 150 poems. The poems show considerable variation in the alternation of songs and descriptive or narrative stanzas. A typical poem is 44. In it, we meet a girl acting as a go-between between her friend and her friend's lover. The latter is apparently in no hurry to ask the girl's parents for their daughter's hand. However, the girl is afraid that if she complains her friends might take the lover to task too rudely.

In the opening stanza, the go-between tells the boy that the girl will bring great prosperity to his house. After that we get three short stanzas in a different meter, evidently meant to be sung, in which the go-between reports how the girl hides her frustration in front of others (to paraphrase):

> Even if her grief is great, my friend hides your lack of grace from me, for she is afraid that if I hear about it, I will upbraid you in front of others.
>
> Even if this great illness is overpowering her, my friend hides your lack of grace from the village, for she is afraid that if they hear about it the villagers will chase you away.

---

[6] For a more detailed discussion of the *Paripatal* poems as minor dramatic scenes set at festivals and their counterparts in the northern Indian literary tradition, see Tieken (2001: 170–182). The literary effect created by Apabhramsha is dealt with in Tieken (2008a).

Even if she suffers from a killing illness, my friend hides your lack of grace from her companions, for she is afraid that they will tell others about your lack of virtues.

These three stanzas are followed by the short phrase "like this", which underlines their separate status. After that, the meter changes once more, with the go-between addressing the young man:

Thinking of the terrible things such as these, which could happen to you, she protects you with such rare virtue. But let us go to her quickly to alleviate her suffering.

In the following fragment from another poem, 55, a girl comments on the flattering words with which a boy tried to seduce her:

He stopped me.
Came close,
to look closer
at my brow, my hands, my eyes,
my walk, my speech,
and said, searching
for metaphors:
"Amazed, it grows small, but it isn't the crescent.
Unspotted, it isn't the moon.
Like bamboo, yet it isn't on a hill.
Lotuses, yet there's no pool.
Walk mincing, yet no peacock.
The words languish, yet you're not a parrot".
and so on.
On and on he praised my parts
with words gentle and sly.

(Ramanujan, 1985: 197-198)

Though a study of the formal features of the *Kalittokai* poems is still lacking, even a quick look shows that the pattern seen in 44 is the most common one. Consisting of songs embedded in stanzas outlining the dramatic context, they immediately bring to mind the *Gitagovinda* (*Govinda in Song*, Bengal, late 13th c. Govinda is another name of Krishna). A typical *Gitagovinda* poem like the 9th consists of 8 songs sung by Krishna's wife Radha. They are introduced by a stanza in which a friend of Radha describes to Krishna the circumstances under which the songs were sung. Peculiar to the *Gitagovinda* is that instead of by words "like this" or "and so on" the songs are concluded by an envoy which assigns them to a certain Jayadeva. With this the poem is, however, not finished. After the songs and the envoy follow several more verses in which the friend addresses Krishna again, urging him to act (Stoler Miller, 1977: 88–89).

In the *Tolkappiyam*, a treatise on the language and literary properties of Sangam poetry, the *Kalittokai*, together with the *Paripatal*, is classified as drama. The *Gitagovinda* calls itself a dance drama as well. For a possible origin of the *Kalittokai* and *Gitagovinda* poems this sets us upon the trail of the so-called *lasya*s, small-scale dramatic scenes or miniature plays including dance, music, and songs. In the absence of complete early examples of this genre, for information on its form and content we have to fall back on the definitions supplied in the *Natyashastra* and Bhoja's *Shringaraprakasha*, already briefly referred to above. The situations cover a wide range of erotic situations, for instance, about a woman deserted by her lover, her body hot from the fire of love, a woman who remains devoted to her lover though he has offended her, and a lover's tryst which has gone wrong. A *lasya* is performed by one female actor only. The role of the man who in one of the *lasya*s tries to appease the woman with "soft words" is played by this female actor. This is presumably also the case in the so-called "dialogue *lasya*", which consists of angry recriminations by the woman, alternating with soothing words uttered by the man. Like the *Kalittokai* and *Gitagovinda* poems, the *lasya*s are composed of a number of stanzas in different meters, among which are meters to be sung (arias) and meters to be recited (recitativo).

As will be pointed out below, the identification of the *Kalittokai* poems as *lasya*s seems to be supported by the criteria used in the compilation of this anthology. Before that, it should be noted that if the *Gitagovinda* poems are *lasya*s as well, they present a special development. For one thing, in the *Gitagovinda* the number of songs is fixed; it is always eight. Furthermore, the songs are "signed", their author being identified as Jayadeva. Interestingly, these pieces of texts of eight songs *plus* an envoy of the *Gitagovinda* seem to represent a literary genre in itself, of which another example may be found in Tamil Bhakti poetry, which consists of nine or ten songs likewise followed by an envoy mentioning when they were sung by whom (Tieken, 2001: 152–170 and 222–225, and 2003a and 2010b). To the Tamil Bhakti poems, I will briefly come back below. The second innovation concerns the use of Sanskrit in the *Gitagovinda*. In most poems, the person "speaking" is a woman. In Sanskrit drama the female roles do not normally speak Sanskrit but a Prakrit. An early example of a *lasya* song, or *lasya* type song, in Kalidasa's *Malavikagnimitra* (5th c.) is indeed in Prakrit. In the Sanskrit *Gitagovinda*, however, we seem to be dealing with a "translation" of an original Prakrit genre into Sanskrit, of which Bengal in the 13th c. provides other examples. This development in Bengal has unfortunately not been properly investigated yet.

11.8 The So-Called Kuravai Poems in the Kalittokai

The lack of early, complete examples of *lasya*s and festival scenes in the style of northern Indian tradition, which renders the identifications of the genres of the *Kalittokai* and *Paripatal* strictly speaking uncertain, is made up for by a "mistake" in the compilation of the *Kalittokai*. As indicated above, the *Kalittokai* is a collection of small-scale dramatic scenes each of which is performed by one female actress who on her own takes care of the various roles in the scene. The poems can be identified as *lasya*s. However, the so-called *kuravai* poems, 101–108, of the *Kalittokai* fall out of tune. They depict a festival involving a bull-baiting contest in which cowherd boys, eagerly watched by the girls of the village, subdue fierce bulls. The prize is the hand of the village headman's daughter. The bull fight is followed by the *kuravai* dance in which the boys and girls dance, praise god, and express the hope that the Pandya king of the realm may prosper. This dance has given the poems their name. In depicting a festival, the poems belong to the same type as the *Paripatal* poems. The question then is why they have been included in the *Kalittokai* instead of the *Paripatal*. The answer may be found in Bhoja's *Shringaraprakasha*, in which the bull-baiting scene has by accident been classified together with the *lasya*s instead of the festival scenes.

The bull-baiting poems correspond to the so-called *goshthi*, a minor dramatic scene in which the young cowherd Krishna conquers the demon-bull Arishta. The *goshthi* forms a pair with the *hallisaka*, in which cowgirls dance in a circle around the victorious Krishna. In Bhoja's *Shringaraprakasha* both *lasya*s and festival scenes have been lumped together in one list of twelve small-scale dramatic scenes, which the author has next divided into two distinct categories on the basis of the number of actors involved. Some, like the *lasya*, have only one actress on stage, others, like the festival scenes, feature a number of actors of both sexes. However, in the case of the *goshthi* and *hallisaka* Bhoja seems to have been led astray by the definitions received from an earlier source. The central character in both scenes is Krishna, who is the only man amidst a host of cowgirls. (This Krishna is to be kept apart from Krishna, one of the main characters in the *Mahabharata* epos.) The relevant phrase describing Krishna seems to have been mistaken by Bhoja as referring to the number of actors on stage. Conformingly, he placed the *goshthi* and *hallisaka* in the same category as the *lasya*s instead of the festival scenes.

This agreement between the Sanskrit and Tamil traditions confirms the identifications of the *Kalittokai* poems as *lasya*s and those of the *Paripatal* as festival scenes. Furthermore, we have to do with a mistake, which, rather than by the poets, was made by the author of that scholarly treatise in which the twelve minor dramatic scenes were brought together in a single list. While we cannot be certain if it was Bhoja himself (11th c.) who made the mistake or if it was made in one of the sources used by him, it was made relatively late. Consequently, the anthologization of the *pari* and *kali* poems must have been carried out relatively late, most probably only after the arrival of the Pallavas.[7]

11.9 The Puram Poems

The Akam poems describe small villages in the countryside. The people speaking in the poems are anonymous men and women, rather than individuals they represent typical village types living typical village lives. By contrast, the Puram poems are historical in the sense that in them we meet historical kings. The Puram poems

[7] For a more detailed discussion of the way the *kuravai* poems have come to be identified as examples of *lasya*s, see Tieken (2001: 186–190).

describe a period during which Tamilnadu was dominated by, and divided between, the Pandyas, Cholas, and Cheras. These three were continuously at war with each other and with some minor kings occupying the interstices. The ambition of each of them was to unite the three kingdoms under one rule. Thus, of a Pandya, it is said that he could not bear to share the Tamil land with the Chola and Chera kings (*Purananuru* 58). The three kingdoms are often defined linguistically as the land where Tamil is spoken. In *Purananuru* 35 a king is praised as follows: "Among the three kings who own the cool Tamil-speaking world you alone deserve to be called 'king'". Other than in the case of the Akam poems, Sanskrit Kavya literature does not have something like the Puram poems. As we will see, for depictions of the world of the three kingdoms we have instead to turn to the Pandya inscriptions of the 8th and 9th c., which evoke the very same past as that described in the poems.

The scenes in the Puram poems belong to a time and age that attached great importance to heroic values. The protagonists are kings and warriors, their wives and mothers, and bards singing these heroes' praises. In *Purananuru* 59, for instance, we hear a bard speaking to a king addressed as Valuti, a title belonging to the Pandya dynasty:

> Valuti! Your beauty glows, as befits you! Your strong
> arms reach to your knees and a necklace hangs down low
> upon your handsome chest! You know, at your own free will,
> how to show your grace! You do not take lies for truth!
> You are, great being, like the sun that rises from the ocean,
> never relenting in your burning ferocity
> toward your enemies, but you are like the moon to men like me!
>
> (Hart & Heifetz, 1999: 46)

For more detailed information about the bard and the king we have to turn to the colophon, with informs us that the bard was a certain Cittalai Cattanar from Madurai and the king, the Pandya Nanmaran killed at Cittiramatam. What we see here, accounts for all poems and colophons: in the poems the kings, if not by a personal pronoun, are referred by a dynastic title, in the colophons they are provided with names and other personal details including the wars they have fought and in which they were killed. The king in the above poem is praised as handsome, smart, and ferocious in battle, but in the very last line, he is reminded of his duty to support bards. In other poems, bards are directing poor colleagues to a liberal patron who might alleviate their distress, as in the following fragment from *Purananuru* 155:

> To your side withering away with hunger you, a bard, press
> your small curving *yal* [harp] and briefly, with a few choice words, you ask
> where are those caring people, alert to relieve your suffering?
> Listen to me now! ...
> ....turn toward the chest crossed
> With a cool garland of the master of great
> Konkanam Mountain, he whose fame glows, and then the dishes

blossom with food!

(Hart & Heifetz, 1999: 98)

It is generally assumed that the bards speaking *in* these two poems are also the poets *of* the poems. However, this does not work in the following three poems in which the persons who are made to speak in the poems and occupy the same position as the bards in the two above poems, are people not known for their poetical skills. Thus, in *Purananuru* 74 we hear what a king said to himself when he was treated disrespectfully by his captors:

A child born dead,
a child born nothing but a mass of flesh –
my ancestors still thought it was human
and never failed to cut it with the sword.
Has a man sprung from them on this earth
to sit
and suffer like a dog,
in chains,
to beg for the grace of a drink of water from his enemies
to calm the fire in his stomach
that he can no longer bear?

(Hart, 1979: 154)

In *Purananuru* 86 the speaker is "just" a mother:

You stand and hold the post of my small house,
and you ask, "Where is your son?"
Wherever my son is, I do not know.
This is the womb that carried him,
like a stone cave
lived in by a tiger and now abandoned.
It is on the battlefield that you will find him;

(Hart, 1979: 159)

and in *Purananuru* 255 it is a wife desperately trying to drag her husband's dead body into the shade:

I would cry out for help, but I am afraid of tigers.
I would embrace you, but I cannot lift your broad chest.
May evil Death, who made you suffer so,
shiver as I do.
Take my wrist, thick with bangles,
and we will reach the shade of the mountain.
Come, walk, it is very near.

(Hart, 1979: 195)

As said, the king and the women in these three poems are not known for their poetic skills. If the bards in the first two poems are, instead, professional poets, their poems are not of the type associated with bards. The latter composed their praise songs on the spot standing before the king, producing short sentences full of stock phrases or formulae (Kailasapathy, 1968). The poems do contain stock phrases and formulae, but consist of extremely long sentences and highly convoluted syntactic constructions. Most poems, the short as well as long ones, consist of one or two sentences, which rather than on the spot composition, suggests a slow and careful process of composition making use of writing. Some of the poems are veritable grammatical puzzles which are hard to solve in one quick reading session. Therefore, George L. Hart concluded that the poems we now have are not the work of poor, illiterate bards but of learned poets, producing imitations of such performers (Hart, 1975: 147–158). The learned poets as it were put on stage a certain bard addressing a certain king or a woman speaking to her husband while she drags his dead body away from the battle field.[8] It is, incidentally, a moot question if the colophons had been part of the task set to the poets ("compose a poem in which a young girl complains to a friend about her lover", "compose a poem in which a bard praises that King X who was later killed in battle Y") or were added later to provide a setting. It should be noted that the names of the kings, though convincing names for kings, are found only in the context of Sangam poetry. Whatever is the case, like the king and the women in the last three poems, the bards are characters considered typical of a society, or time, which attached great importance to heroic values, in the same way as the farmers and their tribulations serve to color in the pictures of a typical village.

11.10 The Anachronisms

In Hart's view, the learned poets composed, or rather wrote, the poems in the first two centuries CE. The bards, the predecessors of the learned poets, would belong to a much earlier period, namely that of the Deccan megalithic culture, which, again according to Hart, had simultaneously fed the village poems of the *Sattasai*, dealt with above. The learned poets would produce imitations of the *extempore* compositions of those earlier bards. On closer consideration, though, they are poor imitations which fail to offer a consistent picture of an early bardic society. The society painted in the poem is both primitive and advanced, and the more advanced aspects belong to a period after the arrival of the Pallavas.

To begin with those aspects pointing to an early date, the society is as yet free from social divisions on the basis of castes, which were at the time already well-entrenched in northern India. They do not use or mention the term *varna*, "caste". This is not to

[8] Shulman argues instead that the poets composed poems about events they would have personally witnessed only a few days before. In this connection he mentions the "immediacy and freshness" of the poems, and the "vivid description(s)" and "the sparseness of lines" (Shulman, 2016: 80–81). The only thing these qualities would show, though, is that we have to do with good poets possessing a great imagination and empathy.

say that there was no social stratification. The poems distinguish several low-status groups, among whom leather-workers, washermen, fishermen, undertakers, bards, drum players, and musicians, contact with whom is anxiously avoided (Hart, 1987). Furthermore, in the poems, there is no evidence that the king exercized any form of control over agriculture or had developed any system of revenue collection, whether on agricultural products, craft products, or trade goods. And though there are coins from the period under consideration, economic transactions were not yet monetized. Thirdly, in contradistinction to the Tamil-Brahmi inscriptions (see above), the poems do not refer to any organizations like guilds, that facilitated trade or craft industry (Champakalakshmi, 1999: 26–27). They mention only individual traders like the salt merchant goading his oxen which pull his heavily overloaded wagon in *Purananuru* 60 (Hart & Heifetz, 1999: 46–47) or the bangle maker in *Akananuru* 24 (Tieken, 2020: 294–295).

This picture of an archaic society is rudely disturbed by descriptions of things belonging to a more advanced culture. An example is the description of stone or brick city walls in, among other poems, *Purananuru* 343, of which there is no archeological evidence for such an early period:

> Would our large town have suffered less if the girl's father, saying that she will not marry someone unworthy of her, had not permitted the ladders, raised by those who had come [for his daughter] to climb over the walls—our town within the walls of which vultures are taking a rest after a day's hard work and the streets are blocked by layers [of bricks or stones] broken off from these same walls?[9]

When we turn to religious practices a similar mixed picture emerges. They range from the antics of the local Velan priest, called in to treat a young girl's love sickness and bull fights in which young men compete for the hand of the village headman's daughter to festivals taking place in the neighborhood of the capital city of the Pandyas dedicated to the great Indian gods Vishnu and Krishna. To this may be added the numerous descriptions of Vedic sacrifices. Thus, besides sacrifices comprising libations of alcoholic beverages, the killing of a young goat, and possession of a local quack-priest, all performed on behalf of villagers, there are Vedic sacrifices organized by kings and supervised by learned brahmins. These brahmins are renowned for their knowledge of the Four Vedas, and it is in this capacity that they direct the performances of complex Vedic sacrifices. The poems show a strikingly detailed knowledge of these sacrifices. Thus, in *Purananuru* 400 we read about a sacrificial site, where the posts, that is, the *yupa*s to which the sacrificial victims are tied, are attended by learned brahmins; poem 224 of the same collection describes the Vedic altar, which according to the Vedic scriptures has the form of a falcon:

> The king had a Vedic sacrifice performed, which offered a feastmeal for the vultures who ate the victim that was tied to the high sacrificial post (*yupa*) on the altar made of many layers of bricks and has the shape of a falcon;
>
> (Tieken, 2020: 292)

---

[9] *Purananuru* 343 and other descriptions of city walls are dealt with in Tieken (2020: 290–293). Anticipating the conclusions drawn below, the descriptions of fortresses may have been borrowed from Kavya literature or else the Sanskrit epics (see Kaul, 2010 and Schlingloff, 2014).

and in poem 2 we read of mountain slopes where under the glow of the three fires brahmins offer ghee in accordance with the complex rules of their rites. The three fires mentioned here are the *garhapatyagni*, or the fire kept burning by the householder, the *ahavaniya* fire in which the oblations are poured, and the *dakshinagni*, the fire placed in the south of the sacrificial arena, meant to protect the sacrifice from the evil forces coming from that direction. While all this concerns visible aspects of the Vedic sacrifices, in *Purananuru* 166 we come across elements that belong to the extensive scholastic tradition that had developed around the Vedas and Vedic sacrifice. In this poem, we hear not only of the Four Vedas, that is, the *Rig-*, *Yajur-*, *Sama-* and *Atharvaveda*, but also of the Six Vedangas, treatises auxiliary to the Vedas, dealing with, for instance, their grammar and meters, and of the twenty-one sacrifices, that is, the seven *somayajña*s, the seven *haviryajña*s, and the seven *pakayajña*s. These twenty-one sacrifices are part of a comprehensive rubrication of Vedic ritual in the *Karmantasutra* appended to the *Baudhayana Shrautasutra* (24.4)[10]:

> You who are descended from men renowned
> for their superb learning, men who
> performed to perfection all twenty-one
> kinds of sacrifice, who confirmed
> the truth, never thinking it false,
> who understood lies that resembled truth,
> thus defeating those who would contend
> with the one ancient work of six sections
> and four divisions.
>
> (Hart & Heifetz, 1999: 107-108)

As to the function of these descriptions of Vedic sacrifices, the sacrifices were occasions for laying on feasts involving great expenses in the form of food for the guests and fees for the priests. By praising the king as an organizer of Vedic sacrifices the poet praises him for his liberality, at the same time presenting himself as a worthy recipient of the king's support. For all we know, these descriptions show that the Puram poems cannot be pre-Pallava, and this would also apply for the Akam poems, which were composed by the same set of poets. Take *Purananuru* 166 cited above, it is ascribed to Mulankilar from Avur, who, besides composing altogether eight Puram poems, is also credited with three Akam poems depicting simple villagers.

Given such intrusions from a much later period into scenes purported to describe a society from before the Pallavas, it cannot be maintained that the poems were written long before the arrival of the Pallavas in Tamilnadu. Below, before an attempt is made to establish more exactly when the Tamil literary tradition may have started, the main arguments put forward in support of an early date of Sangam poetry will be dealt with briefly.

---

[10] For this information I am most grateful to Timothy Lubin; for details, see Lubin (2016).

11.11 Evidence Forwarded for an Early Date of Sangam Poetry

In the poems, the Tamil-speaking lands are divided between the Pandyas, Cholas, and Cheras. The same three dynasties are mentioned in the inscriptions of the early Indian emperor Ashoka (ca. 250 BCE). Therefore, the Sangam poetic tradition is claimed to go back to the 3rd c. BCE, if not further back. However, the same three dynasties make their appearance again from the 8th c. CE onwards and have probably never been away entirely between the 3rd c. BCE and the 8th CE. Yet another piece of evidence advanced are the references in the poems to trade with the Roman world, which archeological evidence shows, had its apogee between the 1st c. BCE and the 2nd CE. It is unlikely, however, that after the fall of Rome the Arabian middlemen stopped trading with India as well. In this connection it should be noted that the people coming from the west, in the poems called *yavanas*, that is, Ionian Greeks, appear to be wearing Arabian clothes (Tieken, 2003b). Furthermore, trade with Rome was still remembered by the seventh century poet Dandin in his *Dashakumaracarita* (*The Adventures of the Ten Young Men*, Onians, 2005: 411–413). The same applies to the hero stones mentioned in the poems (see above): in Tamilnadu no specimens are found older than the fourth or fifth century. What is more, they were still being raised and worshiped as late as the seventeenth century (Rajan, 2000: 23).

The Tamil-Brahmi inscription from Pugalur from the second century CE provides a list of three generations of the kings that would correspond to the three generations of Chera kings mentioned in the *Patirruppattu*. The inscription is said to provide the "sheet anchor" in establishing an early date for Sangam poetry (Wilden, 2002: 124 and Mahadevan, 2003: 117). but is actually a hoax, as the two lists do not agree at all, as can be seen below:

Pugalur inscription	*Patirruppattu*
Ko Atan Cel Irumporai	Celvak katunko Valiy Atan
Perunkatunkon	Peruñceral Irumporai
Katunkon Ilankatunko	Ilañceral Irumporai

Apart from that, if they had agreed, what would it prove for the date of the poems? For we do not date the fifth century poet Kalidasa in the 2nd to 1st c. BCE because his historical play *Malavikagnimitra* has been situated in that period (Tieken, 2008b: 591–592).

As indicated, the end of the Sangam period is taken to coincide with the rise of the Pallava dynasty in the sixth and seventh centuries CE as this dynasty is absent in the poems. It is uncertain, however, if the Pallavas are absent as there are a few references to people occupying that part of Tamilnadu that exactly overlaps that of the Pallava. One of these peoples's names is based on Tamil *tontai*, a plant name like Sanskrit *pallava*. An additional argument is the rareness of Sanskrit loan words, which language was introduced into Tamilnadu by the Pallavas. However, contrary to the poems, the *Tolkappiyam*, which is generally believed to be contemporary to, and by some even older than the poems, abounds in Sanskrit loan translations and is in both its grammatical and poetical parts highly indebted to the Sanskrit tradition (Burnell, 1875: 8–20, Scharfe, 1973 and Tieken, 2013). In fact, the rareness of Sanskrit loanwords may be compared with the absence of the Pallavas in the poems: apparently, they did not fit into the scene, or the time, the poems intended to evoke, which was Southern India from before the arrival of the Pallavas. (For the supposedly archaic nature of the language of the poems, see below.) However, another aspect of Sanskrit culture, the Vedic sacrifices, slipped through the maze: in painting a picture of the king as a liberal patron one could not do without or think of something else.

11.12 Sangam Poetry and the Pandyas

When all is said and done, none of the above-mentioned phenomena points incontrovertibly to a pre-Pallava date. Rather we look for that in the period after the Pallavas, for the period described in the poems was not their past. Furthermore, as can be gathered from their donative inscriptions, they were not involved in the development of Tamil as a literary language: the literary, or fictional, part of the inscriptions, consisting of the dynastic history, was composed in Sanskrit, Tamil was used for the administrative winding up of the donations. Who else then was interested in the particular period evoked in the poems and in the development of Tamil as a literary language? For that, we have to turn to the Pandyas of the eighth century. By adopting their dynastic names, the Pandyas, Cholas, and Cheras presented themselves as heirs to these dynasties (or peoples) that lived in Tamilnadu already in the centuries before the beginning of the common era. But the Pandyas of the eighth century were the first to do so. In their inscriptions, they refer to the old political constellation of the three kingdoms, which they claim to have revived. To add drama to this claim, in their inscriptions, the Pandyas introduced a "dark period" of unspecified length, during which the earlier Pandya rule had been held in abeyance (Gillet, 2014). One of their kings is said to have renovated the capitals of the three earlier dynasties. Another king claims to have defeated the other two dynasties and to have "deleted" the words "common rule" from the country, yet another to have abolished "common ownership", all expressions and phrases—and ambitions—common in the Sangam poems (Tieken, 2001: 131–134).

The heroic poems would thus make perfect sense as historical fiction patronized by the Pandyas of the 8th to 10th c. For Akam poetry we arrive, albeit via a different route, at the very same Pandyas. For that, it may first be noted that besides a deep interest in the early history of Tamilnadu, the Pandyas evinced a great interest in Tamil as well. In their inscriptions they claim to have turned Tamil into a literary language besides Sanskrit, to have commissioned a grammar of Tamil and a Tamil translation of the Sanskrit *Mahabharata* epic, and to have established a *cankam*, or academy, in their capital Kutal, present-day Madurai, to support Tamil literature, a feat also mentioned in a much later legend already referred to above.

As indicated, in the Pallava donative inscriptions there is a clear division of labor between Sanskrit and Tamil. Sanskrit is used in describing the genealogy of the present king, going back to gods and heroes from the *Mahabharata.* This mythological part is followed by a list of the present king's immediate, historical, ancestors. After this mythological-historical part, mostly in verse and called *prashasti*, or "praise-poem", the text switches to Tamil for the practical matters of the donations made in the grant. The Pandya inscriptions from Velvikkudi (ca. 770) and Dalavaypuram (ca. 910), however, have two *prashasti*s, one in Sanskrit, which is followed by one in Tamil (Krishnan, 2002: no. 7, pp. 5–15, and no. 61, pp. 72–83). The Sanskrit *prashasti* provides the Pandyas with a genealogy firmly based on Sanskrit mythology. By contrast, the Tamil *prashasti* is a piece of purely local history, enumerating the ancestors of the present king and adding details concerning the battles he had fought with his neighbors. The novelty of the Tamil *prashasti* cannot be sufficiently emphasized. We seem to be dealing with a once-only experiment, as the later Cholas, with minor alterations, reverted to the Pallava model again. As in the Pallava inscriptions, in those of the Pandyas there is a division of labor between Sanskrit and Tamil, but this time not that of a literary and an administrative language, but between two literary languages. As literary languages Sanskrit and Tamil are related hierachically: Sanskrit for the transcendent world of Indian gods and Tamil for local history (and local people and local gods). In the Pandya inscriptions, Tamil is to Sanskrit while in Kavya literature Prakrit is to Sanskrit.[11]

The Pandyas were the first to show an interest in the world depicted in Sangam poetry and they were the first to use Tamil for literature. It is therefore not unlikely to assume that Sangam poetry was invented by the very same poets who composed the inscriptions for the Pandyas between the eighth and tenth centuries. As shown above, the Akam Sangam texts have exact counterparts in Indian Kavya literature. As the northern Indian examples are all older than the Tamil ones, we may safely assume that Tamil was the borrower. The Prakrit status of the Tamil language appears to have determined the selection of texts to be adapted, which, as shown above, are all Prakrit texts.

[11] One of the arguments advanced in favour of the pre-Pallava date of Sangam poetry is the archaic nature of the language. At first sight it does indeed look archaic, but this does not say anything about its absolute date, and rather than archaic it may better be called peculiar (Tieken, 2004). As I have suggested elsewhere, the relationship between the poetic language and the language of the Tamil inscriptions of the Pallavas and the Pandyas of the 8th to 10th c. resembles that between Prakrit and Apabhramsha, and classical Sanskrit (see p. xiv of the preface to the second edition of *Kāvya in South India. Old Tamil Caṅkam Poetry.* Delhi, 2017).

As we will see, Tamil as a Prakrit fits with the role of Tamil as a literary language in Sangam poetry.

11.13 The Pattuppattu

If in Sangam poetry the genres (village poetry, festival and minor dramatic scenes, and local history) were indeed selected in accordance with the function of the language, Tamil being a kind of Prakrit, in the *Pattuppattu* the genre seems to have been adapted, or better, regionalized, in accordance with the language (Tieken, 2001: 196–200). The *Pattuppattu* is a collection of ten long poems, ranging between 103 and 782 lines. The poems combine Akam as well as Puram themes. In five of the ten poems, we listen in on a bard pointing another bard the way to a liberal royal patron. In one of these poems, the *Tirumurukarruppatai*, or *Guide to Murukan̲*, the faithful are directed to the shrines of God Murugan (Filliozat, 1973). As indicated, the *Pattuppattu* is not mentioned in the traditional list of Sangam works. On closer consideration, it does indeed not belong there. For instance, the setting has shifted from the village to the city and typical Akam scenes have been transplanted from the village to the capital city. Thus, two poems depict a queen pining away in her large, seven-storied palace waiting for her husband, the king, to come home again. Another difference concerns the role of the Pallavas in the *Pattuppattu.* Sangam poetry evokes a period in which Tamilnadu was ruled by the Pandyas, Cholas, and Cheras, who also functioned as sponsors of Tamil poetry. The Pallavas do not play a role in these poems. One of the *Pattuppattu* poems, however, the *Perumpanarruppatai, The Guide for Bards playing the Large Harp*, is in its entirety dedicated to a Pallava king, who, like the Pandyas, Cholas and Cheras, is praised as a patron of Tamil poetry. And a third difference is the extraordinary length of the *Pattuppattu* poems. The Tamil Akam poems and their northern Indian counterparts dealt with so far consist of autonomous stanzas, either one or, as in *Kalittokai* and *Paripatal,* a string of them. But even in the latter case, each stanza is a complete unit in itself, grammatically self-contained. In the Sanskrit tradition, we speak of *Muktaka*, or “isolated” poetry. In Tamil, the stanza can be blown up from 3 to 4 lines in the *Ainkurunuru* to 30 or even more in the *Akananuru.* The length of the *Pattuppattu* poems, between 103 and 786 lines, has been generally taken as the outcome of this very same process of expansion. However, a closer look at one of the causes of the length of the poems may suggest that another mechanism is at work here. One of the causes is long descriptive passages. For instance, lines 238–326 of the *Maturaikkanci, The Good Counsel at Madurai*, provide detailed descriptions of the five types of landscape that in the Akam poems form the backgrounds of the different stages in people’s love lives: e.g., clandestine love affairs are set in the hills and mountains and those describing the husband’s travels in an inhospitable jungle infested by bands of robbers. In the one poem dedicated to a god, namely Murugan, to which poem I will come back below, 98 lines are dedicated to similar descriptions of the landscape, 15 lines to Murugan’s six faces, and 11 to this god’s arms. Another example is the passages in which kings, and Murugan, are described limb by limb from head to foot. Such long descriptive passages are not found in the shorter poems as they would go against their lyrical spirit. On the other hand, they are a regular feature of Sanskrit Mahakavyas, long epic texts dealing with gods and kings. The Mahakavyas abound in elaborate descriptive passages, including descriptions of kings and gods from head to feet, or from feet to head. These passages are made up by long strings of stanzas, which, however, are not autonomous units but are grammatically dependent on the very first or the very last one in the series which contains either the main verb or the grammatical subject. Most likely the *Pattuppattu* poems are adaptations of this Mahakavya, which besides the occurrence of the well-organized descriptive passages would also explain the appearance of gods and kings in them. However, in Sanskrit Mahakavyas, to which may be added plays, the kings are mythic kings, like Dushyanta in the Kalidasa's play *Shakuntala* (5th c.) and so are the gods, such as Shiva in this same author's epic poem *Kumarasambhava*. However, on the way from the short Akam and Puram poems to Mahakavya, *Pattuppattu* seems to have got stuck somewhere half-way, being interested in typically terrestrial and local life. Thus, while as said, the scene of the action in the shorter poems is Southern India ruled by the Pandyas, Cholas, and Cheras, the *Pattuppattu* does describe a wider area, but it did not go much further than adding the Pallavas, just another local dynasty. And it does feature a god, but only a typically South Indian god, Murugan, and describes the five holy places in the Tamil-speaking world in which this god resides even though early evidence places worship of Murugan in northern and northwestern India (Mann, 2011). In this connection, it is to be noted that Mahakavya is in origin a Sanskrit genre. It may be argued that the regionalization of the genre seen in *Pattuppattu* is actually the direct consequence of the Prakrit function of the Tamil language.

The story of Sangam poetry does not end with the Pandyas. Thus, there is evidence that the corpus as we now have it, is a version produced by the Cheras. The story of Tamil as a literary language does not end with the Pandyas either: in the 10th c., under the Chola dynasty, it became a language fit for the great Indian gods Vishnu and Shiva.

11.14 From Pandyas to Cheras

In the light of the late date of the Sangam literary tradition, the internal chronology of the various texts, which as indicated has been treated in singularly stepmotherly way so far, will have to be investigated anew and more systematically. Here, however, I restrict myself to when and where the corpus as a whole—with the grammar *Tolkappiyam* but without the *Pattuppattu*—acquired its final form. Sangam poetry reflects mainly Pandya interests. For instance, the *Paripatal* describes festivals in and around this dynasty's capital, Kutal, *alias* Madurai. The bull-baiting festival in *Kalittokai* concludes with praising the Pandya king. The historical situation alluded to in *Purananuru*, in which Tamilnadu is ruled by the three dynasties, should be considered in the light of the Pandyas' ambition to unite the territories of the three dynasties under one rule. One text, however, falls out of tune, namely the *Patirruppattu*, which deals exclusively with the Cheras of Kerala. It is not clear for what purpose the Pandyas would have supported the composition of this text. Most likely *Patirruppattu* is a Chera text. If so, its inclusion in the list of Sangam texts would suggest that the corpus as we now have it has not come down directly from the Pandyas but through the Cheras.

There is indeed evidence of the importation of Pandya culture into Chera country, or Kerala. The legendary account of Sangam literature as the work of an academy, referred to above, tells how through a long line of teachers the text and commentary had arrived from Madurai in the harbour town Muciri on the west coast. Other evidence is supplied by the epic poem *Cilappatikaram*, which tells how the cult of the goddess Pattini moved from Madurai to the Chera country.[12] Unfortunately, this development is difficult to date exactly, mainly due to lack of early literary sources from Kerala, delimiting the area and describing the language and literature. The earliest sources are the *Keralotpatti*, *The Origins of Kerala*, and the *Lilatilakam*, *The Diadem of Poetry*, dated to the twelfth and fourteenth centuries respectively (Freeman, 2003).

11.15 From the Language of Villagers to that of the Gods

Though the village god Murugan in the *Paripatal* has traits of a transcendent deity and the festival on the banks of the Vaiyai river is organized by brahmins, the setting is explicitly Tamilnadu: Murugan resides on Mountain Parankundram near the Pandya capital Kutal. The festive crowd depicted in the poem is on its way from Kutal to the Parankundram, in which mountain also the Vaiyai river rises (*Paripatal* 19. 15 and 6. 59 respectively). However, in contrast to Murugan, northern Indian Vishnu is not assigned a particular local site. In *Paripatal* 4, 66–70 he is said to reside in the branches of a tree, in *katampu* trees, in islands in the middle of a river, in the mountains, in these and many other places; he resides in simply everything. In contrast to Vishnu, his avatar Krishna does have a mountain of his own, namely Irunkundram, "Black Mountain", *alias* Malirunkundram (*irun* means "black", *mal* "black" as well as "large") or Tiruccolaimalirunkundram, "the (Large) Black Mountain with the Sacred Garden". In fact, the whole point of the poem seems to be to provide this god with a mountain, the names of which are mentioned no fewer than eight times. Moreover, the third name, found in lines 22–23, is the object of a technical, grammatical explanation: "Malirunkundram, preceded in a compound by the words *tiru*, 'sacred', and *colai*, 'garden'". However, the poem does not provide any information on the basis of which the mountain can be identified. By giving Krishna his mountain he is presented as a god like Murugan, but for all we know Irunkundram is a mythical mountain invented for the occasion. In this respect, this Krishna, the epic one, differs from the Krishna in the *kuravai* poems in the *Kalittokai*. The latter, another of Vishnu's avatars, is a young cowherd god who dances with the girls of his village. As a member of the cowherd community, he could, at least in poetry, easily

[12] On the *Patirruppattu* and *Cilappatikaram* as "Chera" texts and the date of the latter text, see Tieken (2001: 201–210). The *Cilappatikaram* is on extremely shaky grounds dated between the fourth and fifth centuries, but would also be post-Sangam. It is, however, either the one or the other.

be inserted, or accommodated into what must have been an existing cult popular in that community (Thurston & Rangachari, 1909: 43 ff.). Moreover, this Krishna is made part of the Pandya landscape, for after the dance the girls praise god, "so that this world accepts the royal command of the Southern king", that is, the Pandya king (Hardy, 1983: 188–189).

The cowherd Krishna underlines the position of Vishnu and epic Krishna as coming from outside Tamilnadu without a fixed abode in the Southern Indian landscape. Curiously, that other great Indian god, Shiva, is ignored altogether, though at the time he must have had his temples. Thus, in *Purananuru* 6 a king is admonished "to circumambulate the temple of the god with the three eyes [Shiva] whom the brahmins worship". In devotional Bhakti poetry, which in time follows closely up on Sangam, the picture is changed radically. Murugan has completely dropped out of the picture. The gods of Bhakti poetry are Shiva and Vishnu-Krishna. Furthermore, while in the *Paripatal* the latter pair had no fixed abode in the Tamil-speaking area, in the Bhakti poems the devotees make a virtual pilgrimage along all the shrines of these two gods. Thus, the 30th decade of the devotee and poet Cuntaramurtti is dedicated to Shiva residing in Karuppariyalur in Tanjavur District, as can be seen in the following fragment from the first poem of the decade:

Exulting,
we close our eyes,
we place him joyfully in our thoughts
and won't let go –
our god of the jasmine shrine
in Karuppariyalur
where peacocks dance
and cuckoos call in the budding mango-groves.

(Shulman, 1990: 182)

The 31st decade is one long list of shrines, all located in the Southern Arcot District, and the 32nd is dedicated to Shiva in Tirukkotikkulakar. The great Indian gods have been brought down to earth in the Tamil-speaking world. Moreover, though a local language, Tamil has become the language of, and for the gods. It is the gods who sing Tamil songs through their devotees, as in the following fragment of a poem of the Vaishnava saint Nammalvar:

My lord
who swept me away forever
into joy that day,
made me over into himself
and sang in Tamil
his own songs
through me.

(Ramanujan, 1981: 85)

What we have here is an example of a regional language which has finally managed to become Sanskrit's equal. But with Bhakti poetry we have arrived at the 9th c. at the earliest.[13]

11.16 Some Concluding Remarks

The study of Tamil as a literary language has suffered greatly from the political climate in Tamilnadu. The end of the nineteenth century, when Sangam poetry became known for the first time to a wider audience through printed editions, was a time of strong nationalist, anti-brahmin sentiments. It was also a time when scholars went purposely in search of old Tamil texts to bolster up their language pride. Sangam proved their claim that Tamil had a literary tradition of its own, older and independent of the Indian Sanskrit tradition of these much-maligned brahmins. The exceptional position of Tamil—for instance, literary Telegu texts do not date from before the 11th c. and are adaptations of Sanskrit texts—rather than leading to a critical examination of the evidence, has instead given food to the notion that among all Indian languages, Tamil is special. A provisional culminating point of this idea is the intensive campaign for UNESCO recognition of Tamil as a classical language, which was successful in 2004.[14] Both in India and abroad academic careers have been built on the basis of Sangam poetry, in literary and historical studies as well as sociology and anthropology, and, not to forget, politics. It is therefore vain to think that a frontal attack as undertaken here, and has been undertaken by me before, will make scholars change their minds. What might be useful though, in particular for the new generation of scholars, is to make them wary of some ingrained habits. One is to explain away anomalies so as to make them agree with an early date of Sangam poetry. This tendency has become almost second nature, so that we hardly notice it. Take the following observation by the historian R.N. Nandi: "Toward the close of the Sangam period [he refers to the *Patirruppattu*, which he dates to the 7th c.] we also hear of sluices and shutters used in tanks for controlled drainage of fields". In the absence of archeological evidence, he concludes that "[a]ll this would *anticipate* the great expansion of agriculture during the closing centuries of the first millennium" (my italics) (Nandi, 2000: 89, Tieken, 2003c: 277–278). Another historian, R. Champakalakshmi, draws attention to irrigation works mentioned in one of the *Pattuppattu* poems. The absence of archeological evidence would be only a temporary situation: "archeological corroboration is *at the moment* non-existent" (my italics) (Champakalakshmi, 1999: 94 and p. 141, n. 7).

[13] The date of Bhakti poetry, its relationship to Sangam poetry – it presents itself as an heir of Sangam poetry, it characterizes its language as "Sangam Tamil" and uses a format met with in the *Kalittokai* (and the *Gitagovinda*) – its link to temple worship and the role of the saint-poet, is dealt with in Tieken (2001: 213–228).

[14] For the political climate at the end of the nineteenth and the beginning of the twentieth centuries, see Irschick (1969). For the passions and madness involved in it all, see Ramaswamy (1997, 2004), and Tieken (2010a).

Often the reader is sneakily made to be reasonable and join the category of "serious scholars". For instance, those scholars who date Sangam poetry in the 10th c. BCE—they are there—and those who date it between the 6th c. BCE and the 10th CE, are by F. Gros *en bloc* set against discussions among serious scholars (*discussions sérieuses*), who agree on a date between the second and fourth centuries CE (Gros, 1968: IV-V). Zvelebil's treatment of the so-called Gajabahu synchronism is of the same kind. This synchronism is, after the Pugalur inscription discussed, and rejected, above, the second "sheet anchor" in dating Sangam poetry (Zvelebil, 1973: 37). In the *Cilappatikaram*, *The Tale of an Anklet*, we read about the Chera king Cenkuttuvan, who established the cult of the Goddess Kannaki-Pattini in his capital Vañci. One of the kings who are invited to worship the goddess is "Gajabahu, the king of sea-girt Ilankai (Sri Lanka)". Cenkuttuvan is also the ruler praised in poems 41–50 of the *Patirruppattu*. The reference to Gajabahu in the *Cilappatikaram* is in the first place used to date the latter epic. Gajabahu, known from the Buddhist chronicles *Dipavamsa* and *Mahavamsa*, is dated in the 2nd c. CE, which would make the epic contemporaneous with the bulk of the Sangam corpus. This scenario is, however, ruled out by Zvelebil: according to him, the *Cilappatikaram* cannot have been composed before the 5th-6th c. (Zvelebil, 1973: 174–175). At the other end of the spectrum, there is Obeyesekere, who draws attention to the fact that Gajabahu had lived on after the 2nd c. to become a typical Sinhala culture hero immortalized in chronicles from the sixteenth and seventeenth centuries. According to Obeyesekere Gajabahu in the *Cilappatikaram* is this mythic figure, caught somewhere half-way between king and cultural hero (Obeyesekere, 1984: 361–380). To Zvelebil's taste, all this would be much too late to have any relevance for the attempts to date both the *Cilappatikaram* and Sangam poetry. His solution is a supposedly more reasonable approach, a middle position between two awkward positions: "The third possibility—and this is what, *according to my conviction*, is the correct approach—is to accept the Gajabahu synchronism *with reservations*: the text of the *Cilappatikaram* refers to Gajabahu and Cenkuttuvan as contemporaries, and though the *Cilappatikaram* was most probably composed (much?) later than the events it deals with, the reference to the contemporaneity of the two kings is based on a *valid* historical tradition (my italics)".[15] In this way, the early date of Cenkuttuvan, the *Patirruppattu*, and Sangam poetry are rescued.

Zvelebil dates Cenkuttuvan and the poems praising this king accordingly in the 2nd c. (more precisely in ca. 180 CE) (Zvelebil, 1992: 114). Above, we have seen that the historian Nandi dated the same collection in the 7th c. The same lack of consensus is found in establishing the beginning of the Sangam literary tradition, and with that the beginning of the Sangam period. Some place it in the 3rd c. BCE on the basis of the mention of the Pandyas, Cholas and Cheras in the Ashoka inscriptions, others, like Zvelebil, and without further explanation, in the 1st c. BCE (Zvelebil, 1992: 114). More recently Wilden places it in the beginning of the 1st c. CE. Every author

[15] Zvelebil (1992: 113). In a footnote Zvelebil contrasts this "valid historical tradition" against Obeyesekere's "admirable and thought-provoking *magnum opus*", in which "myth-making, myth-makers and myth-consumers have too much place".

seems to pick his own dates at his or her convenience, or, as admitted by Wilden: "[t]he coincidence between the start of the literary tradition and the beginning of the Christian era must be regarded as a mere 'date of convenience'" (Wilden, 2014: 7). This lack of consensus – and discussion – is due to these scholars' unwillingness to acknowledge the leads provided by archeology, the poets' knowledge of Vedic sacrifice and the language policy met within the inscriptions of the Pandyas of the eighth-ninth centuries. By taking recourse to explanations of the above type, scholars abundantly show they have no arguments.

References

Anne E. Monius. (2001). *Imagining a Place for Buddhism. Literary Culture and Religious Community in Tamil-Speaking South India.* Oxford.

Burnell, A. C. (1875). *On the Aindra School of Sanskrit Grammarians: Their Place in the Sanskrit and Subordinate Literatures.* Mangalore.

Chakravarti. (2015). id. Examining the Hinterland and Foreland of the Port of Muziris in the Wider Perspective of the Subcontinent's Long-Distance Networks, In: Mathew, K. S. (ed.), *Imperial Rome, Indian Ocean Region and Muziris*, New Delhi, pp. 307–338 (reprinted in Chakravarti 2021, 133–164).

Chakravarti. (2021). id., *The Pull Towards the Coast and Other Essays. The Indian Ocean History and the Subcontinent before 1500 CE*, Delhi.

Champakalakshmi, R. (1999). *Trade, Ideology and Urbanization. South India 300 BC to AD 1300.* Delhi.

David, C., Buck, & Paramasivam, K. (1997). *The Study of Stolen Love. A Translation of* Kaḷaviyal eṉṟa Iṟaiyaṉār Akapporuḷ *with Commentary by Nakkīraṉār.* Atlanta.

Dieter Schlingloff. (2014). *Fortified Cities of Ancient India: A Comparative Study.* London.

Eugene F. Irschick. (1969). *Politics and Social Conflict in South India. The Non-Brahmin Movement and Tamil Separatism, 1916–1929.* Berkeley and Los Angeles.

Eva Wilden. (2002). Towards an internal chronology of old tamil Caṅkam literature. Or How to Trace the Laws of a Poetic Universe". *Wiener Zeitschrift für die Kunde Südasiens, 46*(2002), 105–133.

Francis 2013–2017: Emmanuel Francis, *Le discourse royal dans l'Inde du Sud ancienne. Inscriptions et monuments pallava (IVème- IXème siècles).* Tome I: Introduction et sources, Tome II: Mythes dynastiques et panégyriques. Louvain.

François Gros. (1968). *Le* Paripāṭal. *Texte tamoul.* Pondichéry

Friedhelm Hardy. (1983). *Viraha-Bhakti. The early history of Krsna devotion in South India.* Oxford.

Gananath Obeyesekere. (1987) *The Cult of the Goddess Pattini.* Delhi.

George L. Hart III. (1975) *The Poems of Ancient Tamil. Their Milieu and their Sanskrit Counterparts.* Berkeley.

George L. Hart., & Hank Heifetz. (1999). *The Four Hundred Songs of War and Wisdom.* New York.

Hart. (1979). id., *Poets of the Tamil Anthologies. Ancient Poems of Love and War.* Princeton.

Hart. (1987). Id, Early evidence of caste in South India. In P. Hockings (Ed.), *Dimensions of Social Life: Essays in Honour of David G* (pp. 467–492). Mandelbaum.

Hart. (2015). id., *The Four Hundred Songs of Love. An Anthology of Poems from Classical Tamil. The* Akanāṉūṟu. Pondichéry.

Hartmut Scharfe. (1973). *Tolkāppiyam* Studies. In: *German Scholars on India.* Varanasi, 268–278.

Herman Tieken, (2001). *Kāvya in South India. Old Tamil Caṅkam Poetry.* Groningen. (Reprinted with a new preface with Manohar, Delhi 2017).

Iravatham Mahadevan. (2003). *Early Tamil Epigraphy from the Earliest Times to the Sixth Century A.D.* Chennai and Cambridge, Massachusetts.
Jean Filliozat. (1973). *Un Texte de la religion kaumāra. Le* Tirumurukāṟṟuppaṭai. Pondichéry.
John Ralston Marr. (1985). *The Eight Anthologies. A Study in Early Tamil Literature.* Madras.
Kailasapathy, K. (1968). *Tamil Heroic Poetry.* Oxford.
Kamil Veith Zvelebil. (1973). *The Smile of Murugan. On Tamil Literature of South India.* Leiden.
Kesavan Veluthat (2009). Medieval Kerala. State and Society. In: Kesavan Veluthat, *The Early Medieval in South India.* Delhi 2009, 249–276.
Krishnamurthy, R. (1997). *Sangam Age Tamil Coins*, Madras.
Krishnan, K. G. (2002). *Inscriptions of the Early Pāṇḍiyas. c. 300 B.C. to 984 A.D.* New Delhi.
Mahalingam, T. V. (1988). *Inscriptions of the Pallavas.* Delhi.
Mann, Richard. (2011). *The Rise of Mahāsena: The Transformation of Skanda-Kārttikeya in North India from the Kuṣaṇa to Gupta Empires.*Leiden: Brill.
Miller, S. (1977). *Barbara Stoler Miller.* Love Songs of the Dark Lord. Jayadeva's Gītagovinda.
Nandi, R. N. (2000). *State Formation, Agrarian Growth and Social Change in Feudal South India c. AD 600–1200*, Delhi.
Onians,. (2005). *Isabelle Onians.* What Ten Young Men Did.
Parthasarathy, R. (1993). *The Tale of an Anklet. An Epic of South India. The* Cilappatikāram *of Iḷaṅkō Aṭikaḷ.* New York.
Peter Khoroche and Herman Tieken. (2009). *Poems of Life and Love in Ancient India. Hāla's* Sattasaī. Albany.
Rajan, K. (2000). *South Indian Memorial Stones.* Thanjavur.
Rajesh, V. (2014). *Manuscripts, Memory and History. Classical Tamil Literature in Colonial India.* New Delhi.
Ramanujan, A. K. (1967). *The Interior Landscape: Love Poems from a Classical Tamil Anthology.* Bloomington.
Ramanujan. (1981). id., *Hymns for the Drowning. Poems for Viṣṇu by Nammāḻvār.* Princeton.
Ramanujan. (1985). id. *Poems of Love and War from the Eight Anthologies and the Ten Long Poems of Classical Tamil.* New York.
Ramaswamy (2004). ead., *Fabulous Geographies, Catastrophic Histories. The Lost Land of Lemuria.* Berkeley.
Ranabir Chakravarti. (2006). On Board the Hermapollon. Transporting Gangetic Nard from Muziris. In: Martin Brandtner and Shishir Kumar Panda (eds), *Interrogating Indian History for Professor Hermann Kulke*, New Delhi, 119–137 (reprinted in Chakravarti 2021, 116–132).
Rich Freeman. (2003). Genre and society. The literary culture of Premodern Kerala. In: Sheldon Pollock (ed.), *Literary Cultures in History. Reconstructions from South Asia.* Berkeley, 437–500.
Roberta Tomber. (2008). Indo-Roman Trade. From Pots to Pepper.
Sheldon Pollock. (2006). *The Language of the Gods in the World of Men. Sanskrit, Culture, and Power in Premodern India.* Berkeley.
Shonaleeka Kaul. (2010). *Imagining the Urban. Sanskrit and the City in Early India.* Ranikhet.
Shulman. (1990). *David Dean Shulman.* Songs of the Harsh Devotee. The Tēvāram of Cuntaramūrttināyaṉār.
Shulman. (2016): id., *Tamil. A Biography.* Cambridge, Massachusetts.
Sumathi Ramaswamy, (1997). *Passions of the Tongue. Language Devotion in Tamil India, 1891–1970.* Berkeley.
Thurston, E., & Rangachari, K. (1909). *Castes and Tribes of Southern India. V.* Madras.
Tieken. (2003a). id., The Genre of Jayadeva's *Gītagovinda. Cracow Indological Studies* IV-V (2002/2003), 587–608.
Tieken. (2003b). id., The Yavanas' Clothes in Old Tamil Literature. *Indo-Iranian Journal, 46/3*(2003), 261–273.
Tieken. (2003c). id., Old tamil Caṅkam literature and the So-called Caṅkam period. *The Indian Economic and Social History Review, XL/3*(2003), 247–278.

Tieken. (2004). id., The nature of the language of Caṅkam poetry. In: Jean-Luc Chevillard & Eva Wilden (eds.), *South-Indian Horizons. Felicitation Volume for François Gros on the Occasion of His 70th Birthday*. Pondichéry, 365–387.

Tieken. (2007). Id, Review mahadevan 2003. *Zeitschrift der Deutschen Morgenländischen Gesellschaft, 157*(2), 507–511.

Tieken. (2008a). id., The process of Vernacularization in South Asia. *Journal of the Economic and Social History of the Orient. 51/1*(2008), 338–383.

Tieken. (2008b). id., A propos three recent publications on the question of the dating of old tamil Caṅkam poetry. *Asiatische Studien/Études Asiatiques, LXII/2*(2008), 575–605.

Tieken. (2010a). id., Blaming the Brahmins. Texts lost and found in Tamil literary history. *Studies in History, 26/2*(2010), 227–243.

Tieken (2010b). id., Songs accompanied by So-called *bhaṇitā*s in dramatic texts. In: Karin Steiner and Heidrun Brückner (eds), *Indisches Theater: Text, Theorie, Praxis.* Wiesbaden: 63–75.

Tieken. (2012). id. On a recent translation of classical Tamil love poetry. *Asiatische Studien/Études Asiatiques, LXVI/3*(2012), 811–832.

Tieken. (2013). id. Early tamil poetics between *Nāṭyaśāstra* and Rāgamālā". In: Whitney Cox and Vincenzo Vergiano (eds), *Bilingual Discourse and Cross-Cultural Fertilisation: Sanskrit and Tamil in Medieval India.* Pondichéry, 69–91.

Tieken. (2014). id. On beginnings: introductions and prefaces in *Kāvya*". In: Yigal Bronner, David Shulman, Gary Tubb (eds), *Innovations and Turning Points. Towards a History of* Kāvya *Literature.* Oxford, 86–108.

Tieken. (2020): id., Translating tamil Caṅkam poetry: Taking stock. *Orientalistische Literaturzeitung, 115/4–5*(2020), 287–303.

Timothy Lubin. (2016). Baudhāyanīya contributions to smārta Hinduism. In: Jan E. M. Houben, Julieta Rotaru & Michael Witzel (eds), *Vedic Śākhās: Past, Present, Future. Proceedings of the Fifth International Vedic Workshop, Bucharest 2011*, Harvard Oriental Series, Opera Minora 9, Cambridge, Massachusetts, pp. 591–606.

Valérie Gillet. (2014). The dark period: myth or reality?. *The Indian Economic and Social History Review* 51/3 (2014), 283–302.

Wilden. (2006). id., *Literary Techniques in Old Tamil Caṅkam Poetry. The* Kuṟuntokai. Wiesbaden.

Wilden. (2014). id., *Manuscript, Print and Memory. Relics of the Caṅkam in Tamilnadu.* Berlin.

Zvelebil. (1992). id., *Companion Studies to the History of Tamil Literature. Handbuch der Orientalistik. Zweite Abteilung. Indien.* Leiden.

Chapter 12
Jainism in Indian History and Culture

Patrick Felix Krüger

Abstract Jainism is a religion based on an ascetic doctrine of salvation which, according to tradition, emerged in north-eastern India around the middle of the first millennium BCE. At its center is the worship of the Jinas, a series of twenty-four mythical proclaimers or innovators of a doctrine of salvation presented as eternal, which offers redemption from the cycle of rebirths through the practice of strict asceticism and absolute non-violence. Since its foundation, Jainism has undergone numerous changes. Its development in ancient times was characterized by a consolidation of community structures, which included the formation of a lay class. During the Indian Middle Ages, Jainism flourished above all in the area of the present-day union states of Gujarat and Rajasthan as well as in Karnataka. While ancient Jainism was characterized by the ascetic lifestyle of the wandering monks, medieval Jainism was shaped by the growing influence of the laity and the emerging system of temple-based worship. Early modern Jainism is primarily characterized by reform movements and a split into numerous directions and schools. In the 19th century, the encounter with Western culture followed and in the 20th century, Jain diaspora communities emerged in Africa, Europe and North America. Around 4 million people worldwide describe themselves as followers of Jainism today.

Keywords Jina · Vardhamana Mahavira · Svetambara · Digambara · Acharangasutra · Kalpasutra · Kharavela · Udayagiri · Kandagiri · Yapaniya · Karnataka · Rajasthan · Gujarat · Ujjain · Mathura · Hemachandra · Kumarapala · Ala ud-Din Khilji · Sittanavasal · Rashtrakuta · Ellora · Sravanabelgola · Mahabharata · Harivamsapurana · Kalpasutra · Gaccha

Jainism is literally the doctrine of the Jinas ('victors') or the faith and religion of their followers. The honorary title Jina is used in Jain tradition to refer to a series of mythical saviors who attained omniscience through the strictest asceticism and, following on from this, proclaimed a doctrine of salvation which is intended to free the human

P. F. Krüger (✉)
Ruhr-Universitat Bochum, Bochum, Germany
e-mail: Patrick.krueger@rub.de

L. Vemsani (ed.), *Handbook of Indian History*,
https://doi.org/10.1007/978-981-97-6207-1_12

soul from the sordid cycle of eternal rebirth. In order to attain eternal liberation, man must follow the step-by-step 'path of salvation' *(mokṣamarga)* pointed out by the Jinas. According to Jain understanding, this path has existed since eternal times, but was forgotten in the Dark Ages and proclaimed anew in each era by twenty-four successively appearing Jinas. Special veneration is given to the last Jina of the present age, the Jina Vardhamana Mahavira (Vardhāmana Mahāvīra). He is said to have lived around the middle of the 1st millennium B.C.E.[1]

The life and teachings of Mahavira and his predecessors are described in Jain literature, but there are no reliable historical sources to verify these descriptions. Nevertheless, Mahavira is often mentioned in academic historiography as the historical founder of Jainism (Gombrich, 2006: 18; Armstrong, 2006: 240ff.) or as the reformer of an older ascetic tradition (Schubring, 1962: 29; Jain, 1991: 12), which is said to have been founded by his predecessor Parshva (Pārśva) (Saxena, 2021: 56).[2] His predecessors, in turn, are usually interpreted as mythical figures. Today, the followers of the Jinas call themselves Jains, a modern term derived from the older Sanskrit term *jaina* ('belonging to the Jina'), which gave rise to the English term Jainism in the nineteenth century. The original names of the followers of the doctrine proclaimed by the Jinas have not been handed down. The term Jaina as a designation of religious affiliation dates back to the seventh century.[3]

Due to the scarcity of sources, it is difficult to trace the formation and early development of Jainism. Written and archeological sources are lacking especially for the time Jainism supposedly emerged. In order to reconstruct the circumstances that might have led to the founding of Jainism to some extent, research must therefore draw on the literary tradition as a substitute. The resulting picture is incomplete and characterized by a vagueness which arises from the fact that tradition is closely interwoven with myths and legends.

Thus, while the reconstruction of the history of early Jainism is hampered by the lack of reliable sources, the history of medieval and modern Jainism presents the observer with other difficulties. Here it is primarily the severe fragmentation of Jainism into numerous schools and communities (see Jain, 1975), as a result of which a common Jain identity among the faithful probably did not exist. The doctrine originally attributed to the Jina was over time frequently reinterpreted and construed in different ways. Diverging doctrines often led to splits and the founding

---

[1] According to Shvetambara calculation Mahavira was born in 599 B.C.E. and died 527 B.C.E. at the age of 72 years. This calculation is based on a statement at the end of the Jina legend in the Kalpasutra, claiming that 980 or 993 years had passed since the death of Mahavira. Contrary to Shvetambara tradition, the Digambaras date the salvation of Mahavira to 510 B.C.E.

[2] The Kalpasutra (§ 169) narrates that Parshva attained salvation 250 before Mahavira. In addition, Buddhist literature contains hints to disciples of Parshva in the lifetime of the Buddha (Mette 2010: 205).

[3] The Prakrit word *jaiṇa* was already used in the Shvetambara canon (for example Aupapatikasutra (Aupapātikasūtra) Sects. 42, 48 and 49), its original meaning being 'quick '(<Skt. *javina*, see Leumann 1966: 119); it was wrongly translated as Skt. *jayana* 'victorious' by the commentators of the texts. This sankritisation was taken up first by Jinabhadra in the seventh century and later also by Hemacandra (Mette 2010: 201).

of new directions and schools. These different doctrines and traditions must be taken into account when evaluating the medieval and modern sources; they cannot be interpreted as an expression of a monolithic Jainism, but their validity is often limited to individual groups or communities. The concept of Jainism as a unified system of beliefs is therefore, especially for this period, a construction based on Western perceptions and expectations. This also raises the question, which continues to the present-day, whether a cohesive Jain community can be assumed at all (see Sangave, 1980; Carrithers & Humphrey, 1991).

Jainism was a religion of the urban population from its inception. It spread rapidly through the urban centers of northern India, appealing primarily to members of the merchant guilds through its promise of salvation based on merit transfer. Members of Jain communities were prohibited by lay vows from engaging in most craft activities especially from farming, so most families lived by trade and money lending. The spread of Jainism, especially among those families who had achieved wealth and prosperity through long-distance trade, continues to characterize the laity to the present-day and led Weber (1921: 203) to classify Jainism as a *"merchant sect"*. The trade relations of the families converted to Jainism favored the spread of Jainism along the trade routes as far as southern India already in antiquity.

In the past, several attempts have been made to periodize the history of Jainism, but none of these attempts has been generally accepted.[4] For the following presentation, the tripartite periodization proposed by Williams (1983: xxi) was used, according to which history can be roughly divided into antiquity, the Middle Ages, and modern times. This structure is supplemented here by an account of the modern and contemporary period.

12.1 Antiquity (C. 500 B.C.E. –500 C.E.)

After its formation, the development of Jainism in antiquity as a whole is characterized by the missionary spread of the doctrine as well as a consolidation of the community structures, which first and foremost included the formation of a lay community. The division into the two main branches of Shvetambara *(śvetāmbara)* and Digambara also occurred during this period. On the literary level, the Shvetambara canon was formed by the middle of the 1st millennium C.E., and numerous commentaries were written on the texts it contained. The earliest Jina images were produced around the turn of the millennium in the Mathura region. This marks the beginning of Jain art and materiality, allowing the history of Jainism to be traced archeologically as well.

[4] Since Jainism as a whole does not represent a real unity, a division into epochs is difficult and depends on the sources used, for example literature or art. There are also major differences between the development of Jainism in northern and southern India. The discourse and the different proposals of a periodization are described by Flügel 2018: 123f.).

According to Jain tradition, Jainism begins with the Jina Mahavira, who is preceded by a series of mythical predecessors. A narrative of the life of the Jina Mahavira from his birth to salvation was written comparatively late and was probably created under the influence of the Buddha legend. This is suggested by the strong similarities in the life paths of both religious founders. Like the Buddhists, the Jains attribute the founding of their religion to a prince who gave up rulership and wealth, renounced the world, and finally, after years of strict asceticism, found a path to salvation.[5] The necessity of a founder legend is attributed to the fact that the Jain missionaries saw themselves at a disadvantage compared to their Buddhist competitors, since the latter had a story about the life of their founder (Mette, 2010: 243). The oldest tradition about the life of Mahavira is found in the canonical literature of the Shvetambaras and consists only of individual set pieces and short episodes, scattered over various works. Some of these episodes were later incorporated into the Jina legend, the earliest known version of which is contained in the Acharangasutra (Ācārāṅgasūtra) and depicts the life and work of Mahavira from birth to the attainment of all-encompassing knowledge. Later versions of the Jina legend, such as the particularly widespread Kalpasutra (Kalpasūtra) or the biography of the Jina written by Hemacandra in the twelfth century, also recounted in greater or lesser detail the lives of the twenty-four Jinas who, according to legend, promoted the Jain doctrine in earlier times and are therefore regarded as Mahavira's predecessors.[6]

However, the lack of historical evidence about the existence of Jina could also suggest that a single founder figure did not exist, and it is therefore conceivable that Jainism did not originate from an individual founder figure. More realistic than the founding of a religion by a single person is a historically contingent accumulation and condensation of religious ideas around a core of ideological, ritual, and organizational elements (Flügel, 2018: 128) that were only attributed to a founder figure at a later date. Undisputed is the veneration that the Jina Mahavira receives from the faithful. Their imagination is fed by a wealth of legends and stories about the life and work of Mahavira. It seems reasonable, therefore, to begin by understanding Mahavira less as a historical figure than as a literary figure who appears in various ways within Jain writing. In instructional literature, Mahavira is primarily a spiritual teacher, whereas legends and narratives turn him into a saint who is increasingly deified over time.

The teachings attributed to the Jina developed in a time of social upheaval and growing social inequality (Jain, 2010 [1]: 271f.), brought about by the so-called

---

[5] The pronounced parallels between the Jina legend and the life story of the Buddha raise the question whether the description of Mahavira contains a historical nucleus at all or whether it is entirely fictitious.

[6] It is uncertain when the idea of a series of twenty-four saviors emerged, because the development cannot be traced in Jain literature. The Ajivika *(ājīvika)* also cultivated the concept of a series of twenty-four mythical predecessors of the founder of the order (Basham 2009: 27). The Buddhist work 'Connected Discourses' (Saṃyuttanikāya) mentions the antediluvian Buddhas, and the 'Collection of Long Discourses' (Dīghanikāya) mentions six Buddhas who preceded the 'historical' Buddha Siddhartha Gautama, but only the last three belong to the present world age. The late-canonical 'Buddha Chronicle' (Buddhavaṃśa) eventually expands the number of predecessors to twenty-four.

'second urbanization' (see Sawant & Shete, 2016). The Vedic sacrificial system, which according to the view of the time stabilized the world order, had lost its power as an instrument of contingency management in parts of the population. Instead, itinerant preachers roamed the countryside, proclaiming their doctrines of salvation and gathering followers around them. Instead of ritual sacrifice, their path to salvation was characterized by renunciation and asceticism. Whether the figure of Jina Mahavira goes back to one of these itinerant preachers or, as already explained, is a later invention of Jain literature can no longer be decided. Some sources report that Mahavira, apart from Bihar, also roamed parts of southern and western Bengal on his wanderings, but in essence, like the Buddha, he did not move beyond the boundaries of this region. Neither Buddhist nor Jain sources report a meeting of the two religious leaders. Mahavira's teachings spread throughout the most diverse social strata. Inscriptions from the Mathura region prove that donations in the first centuries of our time were also made by women (Quintanilla, 2000: 89) and that they thus actively participated in religious life.

The Jain doctrine spread beyond the borders of Bihar, first westward to the region around Mathura and southward to the area of present-day Orissa.[7] In addition to the wealthy lay followers, the Jain missionaries seem to have increasingly enjoyed the support and goodwill of princes and kings. The fact that individual rulers themselves converted to Jainism was repeatedly claimed by Jains, but it could rarely be proven and seems rather unlikely in view of the entanglement of ancient Indian royalty with Brahmanical rites.[8] It is more likely that some ancient Indian princes and kings promoted the ascetic reform movements in order to limit the at times overwhelming influence of the Brahmins.

One exception may have been Kharavela, who ruled over the kingdom of Kalinga *(kaliṅga)* in present-day Orissa in the first century B.C.E. and in whose kingdom Jain communities may have existed at a fairly early date. Evidence for this is an inscription in the 'elephant cave' (*hāthīgumphā*) at Udayagiri, which shows him to be a peaceful ruler, a patron of monks and religion, who had temples repaired and recognized members of all faiths (Jayaswal and Banerji, 1929). This was quite in keeping with the idea of a Jain ruler primarily committed to charity toward his subjects. In fact, the inscription also tells of his numerous campaigns of conquest. This also corresponded with the ancient Indian ideal of the 'world ruler' *(cakravartin)*, who follows the commandment to conquer the regions of the world (Kulke & Rothermund, 1998: 95). By the Jainas, Kharavela is considered a follower of their doctrine, possibly even by birth and not by conversion. However, contemporary sources that unequivocally confirm the king's affiliation with Jainism have not been discovered until today.

---

[7] The Singhalese Island Chronicles report that Jain monks lived on the island before the arrival of Buddhist missionaries (Rahula 1956: 43); from a historical perspective, this seems rather improbable.

[8] For example, Candragupta Maurya and his grandson Ashoka probably promoted Jainism as well as Buddhism. The Jain tradition also names several early rulers, such as Shrenika (Śreṇika) and his son Kunika (Kūṇika) (Shah 2004: 57f), who have been handed down in Buddhist sources as Bimbisara (Bimbisāra) and Ajatashatru (Ajātaśatru), where they are regarded as promoters of Buddhism.

The cave complexes of Udayagiri and Khandagiri are today considered to be the oldest architectural complex of Jainism. The two-story cave complex consists of adjoining small cells where the monks and nuns presumably spent the rainy season. Whether this developed into a permanent presence of monks and nuns for a short period of time, like in Buddhism, where comparable caves were established as early monastery complexes, cannot be proven. The literary tradition of the Jains does not mention any monastic structures.[9] During the rainy season, wandering was interrupted, and the monks and nuns sought protective 'places of refuge' (*upāśraya*). Initially, these were probably not more than sheltered campsites. These places were frequented visited by lay followers to provide the monks and nuns with food in fulfillment of their religious duties. Instead of the campsites, in later times, structures were built, which on rocky terrain could also take the shape of cave complexes like Udayagiri and Khandagiri. Such structures were donated by laypeople and visited by the lay community. Presumably to increase the value of an endowment, but also to enhance the significance of the ascetics' abode, a cave complex was artistically designed. In Udayagiri and Khandagiri, above the entrances to the individual cells on the arches of the outer facade are extensive stone reliefs, the pictorial content of which has not yet been clearly identified and thus could not be assigned with certainty to the Jain tradition. There are no images of the Jinas, but this can be explained by the early period of construction of the complex. The cave complex is dated to the second century B.C.E. and thus was built sometime before the creation of the first Jina images. The intricately carved reliefs indicate rich endowments, which provided temporary housing for Jain monks and religious merit for the donor.

By the turn of the first century at the latest, Jainism spread to the Mathura area. The place developed into a hub of important trade routes in the centuries around the beginning of the Common Era, and the Jain doctrine spread rapidly. For several centuries, Mathura thus became an important center of Jainism. By this time, as can be seen from the inscriptions from this period, a lay class had already emerged, which supplied the order of wandering ascetics and was instructed in Jain doctrine by the monks. As an expression of lay piety, the first stone sculptural images of the Jina were created at this time, which presumably served as models for the Buddha images that emerged a little later (Quintanilla, 2007: 250; DeCaroli 2015: 151).

The archeological findings suggest that since the first century C.E. the worship of cult images of the Jina emerged; they were produced in large numbers by the workshops in this region. The exact circumstances that led to the first figural representation of the Jina are unclear. However, the invention of the stone cult image illustrates in several respects the transformation of Jainism, which since its founding developed from the doctrine of salvation of a group of wandering ascetics into a fixed religious system with its own ritual culture. The oldest images of the Jina are found

[9] The Jain ascetics were not allowed to stay in one place for a long time except during the rainy season. The older texts limit the permitted stay in a village to one day and in a city to five days. This strict rule was not changed until the Middle Ages; since then, itinerant ascetics have been allowed to stay in a village for several days and in a town for up to two months. This probably met the needs of the lay communities, who demanded a longer stay of their spiritual teachers in order to be instructed comprehensively in religion and doctrine.

on stone votive tablets (*āyāgapaṭa,* Fig. 12.1), which were made around the turn of the era and were apparently the object of a lay cult (see Quintanilla, 2000).[10] About a century later, three-dimensional cult images of the Jina were produced, showing the founder of the religion in a sitting or standing posture (Fig. 12.2). Whether the Jina image was originally intended as a cult image is disputed. More likely is its initial use for commemoration and as a visible symbol of the Jain doctrine of salvation (Cort, 2010: 127.), the suggestive power of which was to promote the formation of the lay order under the image of the founder.[11] Nevertheless, a cultic system apparently developed around the Jina image quite early. Jainism developed in this way from the audible doctrine of salvation of the wandering monks to a visible religion. Although this visibility was already given by the monks and nuns before, they could only be worshiped by offering them food because of their strict vows.

The places where the stone cult images of the Jina were placed are not known. However, the good state of preservation suggests that they were protected from the weather in shrines or smaller temples. Remains of accessible buildings that can be attributed to Jainism have not been found so far. However, other religious traditions demonstrably had temple buildings in the Mathura area (Härtel, 1993: 64ff.). Like the Buddhists, the Jains apparently also used the Stupa *(stūpa)* as a religious building. In Mathura, toward the end of the nineteenth century, the foundations of a Stupa were uncovered, which has been interpreted as a Jain structure (see Smith, 1969). However, unlike in Buddhism, in Jainism Stupas were built solely to commemorate the Jina and his teachings and do not contain any relics. The inscriptions affixed to some objects provide information about the donors, most of whom were members of the lay class.

Since its foundation, Jainism has been subject to constant change and has had to adapt to social and political changes. That this did not always take place without conflict is evidenced by the numerous schisms in the community, among which the so-called 'great schism', which split the order into the denominations of the white-robed Shvetambaras and the Digambaras, who are walking in the nude, represents one of the most lasting events in Jain history.[12] The timing of the great schism is disputed, but Jain tradition places it in the reign of Chandragupta Maurya (r. 322–298 B.C.E.), with Shvetambaras and Digambaras each citing different reasons for

---

[10] The surviving texts do not contain any references to the use of such votive tablets, but the image on a contemporary tympanum from Kankali Tila allows us to draw some conclusions (Quintanilla 2007: Fig. 222). The image shows two people standing with offerings in a posture of veneration in front of two votive tablets decorated with flowers and placed horizontally on pedestals.

[11] What is most remarkable here is that, apart from a few stylistic changes, the Jina image was not subjected to any significant further development, but instead was fully developed at this early stage. The Jina image is not a portrait of the Jina according to the descriptions in the literature, but an ideal depiction of the human body, designed not according to the natural specifications of anatomy, but without the modeling of musculature or bone structure, an image of spiritual beauty, shaped according to fixed measurements and proportions.

[12] The 'great schism' was preceded by a total of eight other divisions of the church, with the disintegration of the early church beginning, according to tradition, with the heresy of Jamali, a disciple of Mahavira.

Fig. 12.1 Stone votive tablet *(āyāgapaṭa)* with the image of a Jina, Mathurā, first century (National Museum, New Delhi)

the separation.[13] In the Jain tradition as well as in parts of historical research, the split of the community is usually seen as a theological event, the cause of which lay in a controversy over the interpretation of the strictness of asceticism. Moderate groups and advocates of a stricter interpretation were opposed to each other, the latter deriving the particularly strict form of asceticism from the traditions about the life and work of Mahavira, to whom a tightening of the rule of the order was

[13] In the Digambara tradition, the 'great schism' dates back to a famine that is said to have raged for over twelve years in Magadha in the fourth century B.C.E. To escape starvation, half of the Jain community migrated south under the leadership of their leader Bhadrabahu, while the remaining monks stayed behind in Magadha under the leadership of his disciple Sthulabhadra. Due to the consequences of the famine, these monks were no longer able to fully observe the rule of the order imposed on them, they changed their customs, and in the end, they also preserved the holy scriptures only incompletely. The tradition of the Shvetambaras, on the other hand, connects the division of the community to Shivabhuti, who 609 years after Mahavira's death in Rathavirapura in northern India tried to enforce a doctrine, which was considered heretical. According to this doctrine, the custom of absolute lack of possessions, including the monks' going naked as introduced by Mahavira was to be reintroduced as a binding rule.

Fig. 12.2 Stone stele with four Jinas, Mathurā region, c. first or second century (Government Museum, Mathura)

attributed and who, sometimes after his ordination, even discarded the monk's robe and henceforth went naked.

It is possible that it was actually a conflict of this kind within the community that led to a split. However, from a historical perspective, it is more likely that the split was a result of the decline of Jainism in Mathura during the reign of the Gupta dynasty (ca. 320–460). In the fourth century, a renewal of Hindu traditions began; Brahmanical schools became competitors to Jainism and the previously dominant Buddhism. The Vaishnavas, in particular, benefited from this development, so that the worship of the god Krishna gained strong influence. That this affected Jainism is evident from the myths surrounding the Jina Arishtanemi (Ariṣṭanemi), which probably arose during this period. According to legend, Arishtanemi was related to the Hindu god Krishna and clearly superior to him in strength. He combines Jain and Brahman mythology. In this way, an attempt was made to subordinate the Brahmanical doctrine to the Jain one. The rise of Brahmanism caused the decline of Jainism, which is most conspicuous in the decreasing number of inscriptions and archeological traces of the Jains. At the same time, Jain inscriptions and archeological remains are increasing in the Mysore region.

Presumably, tensions between Jains and followers of Hindu traditions led to an exodus of Jain communities to the south and west, which later, when both sides had already become estranged, was reinterpreted as the legend of the great schism (Ohira, 1994: 481). This is supported, among others, by the fact that the archeological material from the period before Gupta rule contains no evidence of a division of the community. Iconography also shows no evidence of a difference between Digambaras and Shvetambaras before the fifth century. Therefore, the legends surrounding the division of the community probably arose at a later date. There is no record of Jainism in South India until the beginning of the Gupta rule, but at that point in time the formation of the two Jain centers in Karnataka and Gujarat began, which exist to this day.

The founding of the Yapaniya *(yāpanīya)* community can be seen as a kind of unification attempt between the hostile main currents (Upadhye, 1933, 1975). This group, first mentioned in an inscription in Karnataka in the fifth century, attempted to unite the positions of the Digambaras and the Shvetambaras by introducing a balanced middle way. The Yapaniya movement was most prevalent in the south Indian area and disappeared in the fourteenth century, probably by merging with the Digambaras. Individual Digambara communities have survived to the present-day, especially in Rajasthan, while the majority of Jains in northern India today belong to the Shvetambaras. In southern India, on the other hand, the Digambaras dominated from earliest times. After the final separation, Shvetambaras and Digambaras apparently coexisted in relative peace for a while. Since the eighth or ninth century, both directions have developed a partly independent iconography; cult images of the Digambaras at this point can usually be clearly distinguished from those of the Shvetambaras.[14]

Jainism has produced an extensive literature, the older works of which were mostly written by learned monks., The monks in ancient India used the rainy season to work on the writings, as they interrupted their migration during these months. A safe dating of the oldest writings is not possible according to today's knowledge, but it is considered unlikely that the surviving texts go back further than the third century B.C.E.

From the philological point of view, the older literature of the Jains is divided into canonical and the post-canonical literature. The canonical literature was written in Prakrit[15]; it deals primarily with the monastic rule and the related questions of ethics and the right way of life. Some of the oldest Jain writings belong to this group. In addition, a narrative literature developed quite early, which includes legends as well as hagiographies and conversion stories, occasionally picking up motifs from contemporary Buddhist and Brahman literature. These works explain the rather theoretical deliberations on ethics and monastic discipline in a more accessible way.

[14] In figurative art, the Jina has since been depicted with a loin cloth. In seated figures, a pleated garment tip in front of the feet served as a feature to distinguish the figure from the unclothed cult images of the Digambaras. This feature to distinguish Digambara and Shvetambara cult images may have developed after a dispute between the two groups over dominance on the holy place of Mount Girnar in the eighth or ninth century (Shah, 1951: 6).

[15] The language of the early works of the Shvetambara are the Middle Indian Prakrit languages. Presumably, the use of the language used in everyday life in the early days of Jainism was a means to support its spread. It was only around the middle of the first millennium C.E., when the former folk dialects had long since ceased to be understood by the population, that they were replaced by Sanskrit as a literary language. The Digambaras, on the other hand, began using ancient Indian Sanskrit for their literature much earlier, as it was considered a kind of 'scholarly language' and was no longer understandable to the people.

Post-canonical or non-canonical literature is characterized by its thematic diversity and includes, first of all, commentaries on canonical literature. Until the seventh century, these commentaries were written in Prakrit, from the eighth century onwards in Sanskrit. The post-canonical literature of the Middle Ages and the early modern period is increasingly addressed to lay followers. For example, rules of conduct for the faithful are now written down, and devotional books emerge to support worship practices. In addition, novels, dramas, and works of poetry are produced on a larger scale.

This categorization into a canonical and a post-canonical literature of the Jains, which is still used in philological research today, may seem simplistic and unsatisfactory at first glance, since it basically only discerns an 'original' and more or less 'authentic' tradition and its later commentary and further reception. At the same time, the focus is only on the literary tradition of the Shvetambaras. This division, however, on the one hand reflects the philological orientation of Jainism studies, which over a long period of time concentrated on the ancient and medieval India, and on the other hand represents the concept, widespread especially in the nineteenth century, of a canonical collection of sacred scriptures being a standard and a fundamental prerequisite of every so-called 'high religions', to which Jainism was also counted.

Depending on the count, the canon consists of 45 to 50 separate books (see Kapadia, 1941). At the same time, later Jain literature contains various lists giving the titles of those scriptures that are considered authoritative and thus canonical.[16] The Jain canon as a self-contained whole is in this sense primarily a Western projection (see Bruhn, 1987 and Folkert, 1993). At the same time, however, the literature classified as canonical is, on the whole, the oldest surviving textual stratum, even if this does not apply equally to each individual book of the canon, and some very old works are also to be found in the post-canonical literature. In terms of its genesis, the canon is the result of a very long development. According to present knowledge, the systematic compilation of the Jain doctrine began at a fairly early date. However, none of the surviving Jain texts can be attributed with certainty to the founder of the order, Mahavira himself, or to any of his disciples.

The authority of the canonical tradition is relatively undisputed, at least within the Shvetambara communities. The final version of the canon was determined by councils convened by the Shvetambara communities, which probably took place in the fifth century in Vallabhi and Mathura; here, the decision was made to reorganize and write down all the scriptures that had been transmitted orally until then. This canon is not recognized by the Digambaras, who did not attend the council. In their tradition, the original sacred writings are believed to have been lost before the Vallabhi and Mathura councils, and the canon written down there is thus considered spurious. The lost canon is replaced among the Digambaras by a collection of various later writings distributed among the four subject groups of cosmology, world history, philosophy,

[16] These lists, which date back to the thirteenth century, differ in the number of works listed, in the titles mentioned, and in their order (Bruhn, 1987: 101). The canonical writings recorded in these lists, on the other hand, were written several centuries earlier, namely in a period from around 200 B.C.E. to about 400 C.E. Thus, there is a rather old collection of sacred writings, but counting and compilation are partly inconsistent.

and ethics, usually referred to as the secondary canon. From a philological point of view, however, it is not a completely independent tradition. Instead, the Digambara canon is dependent on the canonical tradition of the Shvetambaras. Independently of this secondary canon, however, the works of the Digambaras also contain lists in which the writings of the lost canon are listed, albeit with clear deviations from the lists of the canonical writings of the Shvetambaras.

12.2 Middle Ages (C. 500–1400)

During the Indian Middle Ages, Jainism flourished especially in northwestern India (Gujarat and Rajasthan) and southwestern India (Karnataka), but at the same time, it was subject to profound changes and underwent reforms that led to a transformation of the religious and cultural ideas of the followers as well as the monks and nuns.[17] Whereas ancient Jainism was determined by the ascetic lifestyle of itinerant monks, medieval Jainism is characterized by the growing influence of the laity and the emerging system of temple worship. This coincided with a stronger subdivision of the Jain community into different groups and subgroups (Flügel, 2018: 147ff.).

After the decline of Jainism in Mathura, archeological evidence suggests a spread of Jainism in the coastal regions of Gujarat since the sixth century. When the Jain doctrine was first spread in Gujarat is unknown. It is possible that the first missionary attempts started from Ujjain. The city of Ujjain, located southwest of Mathura, is the center of the Malwa region in the present-day union state of Madhya Pradesh, and is considered a site of early Jain religiosity and scholarship. As early as pre-Christian times, Ujjain is said to have been visited by numerous Jain teachers and saints (Jain, 2010 [2]: 430), and in Shvetambara literature, the place is associated with the reign of the mythical king Gardabhilla, who was driven out by the Jain monk Kalaka with the help of foreign armies.[18] A Jain legend also reports that Samprati, a grandson of Ashoka, led a congregation of 5,000 ascetics from Ujjain to the holy mountain Shatrunjaya in the southeast of the Kathiawar peninsula to missionize Gujarat (Jain, 1963: 10). Again, this cannot be historically substantiated, but it shows that the Jain communities in Gujarat sought to convey the idea of a long-standing tradition of Jainism in the area.

The presence of Jain communities in Gujarat at least since the sixth century is attested to by the bronze cult images of a hoard find discovered around 1950 in Akota, a western suburb of Vadodara. Inscriptions were attached to some of the bronze cult images, which, although they rarely contain an exact date, can be dated

[17] Williams (1983: xx) argues that Jainism developed from a philosophy to a religion only with the introduction of lay rituals in the Middle Ages.

[18] This legend has been handed down in the 'Story of the Jain monk Kalaka' (Kālakācāryakathā), a tale that probably emerged in the late tenth century and has been transmitted in several versions (Brown, 1933). However, neither the ruler Gardabbilla nor the foreign conquerors known as the Sahi *(sāhi)* can be safely identified with any historical agents. Attempts to identify the Sahi or Saka attack with the advance of the Indo-Scythians *(śaka)* in the first century B.C.E. proved fruitless.

paleographically. Accordingly, the oldest piece of the hoard found was made in the period around 550 C.E. (Shah, 1959: 29).

Jain literature names Gujarat, and in particular the Kathiawar peninsula, as an important center of faith early on, where according to one tradition a council in the fifth century decided on the form and composition of the canon of the Shvetambaras (Dundas, 2002: 22). Above all, Gujarat's geographical location, with its ports that formed important intersections on the trade routes to southern Arabia and East Africa, favored the economic boom of the merchant families living there. The growing prosperity of the Jain communities was evidenced primarily by a growing number of donations, which were to a large extent provided by wealthy citizens in addition to royal patronage. In this way, a multitude of temples with attached libraries as well as pilgrim hostels came into being, which provided safe accommodation for the wandering ascetics on their otherwise perilous journeys. In the construction of temples, the Jains also received royal support. For example, Mularaja I, the founder of the Solanki dynasty, who ruled during the last third of the tenth century and was himself a follower of Shaivism, supported the foundation of numerous Jain temples (von Glasenapp, 1964: 48). There is no record of Jain temples in Gujarat for the period before the tenth century (Singh, 1982: 183). After this point in time, due to the increasing prosperity of the Jain communities, the number of newly built temples grew rapidly. The emerging concept in the Middle Ages of coming closer to salvation not only by practicing asceticism, but also by donating to a temple, changed Jainism permanently. To increase wealth and prosperity for the benefit of the community became the duty of the layman.[19]

Probably the greatest contribution to the cultural upswing of the Jain culture of western India, however, was made by the learned monk Hemacandra (1088–1172), who was born in Dhandhuka as the son of a merchant and joined the order of the Shvetambaras as a child. In the course of his life, he composed numerous writings on various subjects and received the honorary title of 'omniscient in the present age' (*kalikālasarvajña*) due to his extensive knowledge. His best-known works are the 'Yoga Treatise' (Yogaśāstra), a kind of dogmatic guide to the Jain doctrine of salvation, addressed especially to the laity (Qvarnström, 2002), and the 'Life Stories of Sixty-three Extraordinary Men' (*Triṣaṣṭiśalākā-puruṣacaritra*), which includes, among other topics, the biographical legends surrounding the lives and work of the twenty-four Jinas (Johnson 1931–62). According to tradition, Hemacandra even succeeded in converting the ruler Kumarapala to Jainism, whereupon the latter began to transform his kingdom into a Jain model state and thus promoted the development of Gujarat into the center of the Shvetambaras (Jain, 2010 [2]: 495).[20] Traditional

---

[19] Medieval literature contains guidance on the 'right conduct of Jain laypeople' *(śrāvakācāra).* This includes increasing wealth as long as it is done in accordance with Jain ethics and not through theft, treachery, or violence (cf. Williams, 1983: 260).

[20] It is questionable whether the rulers referred to as Jains in the tradition actually became followers of Jainism. What is certain is that numerous rulers supported Jainism through donations. That they saw themselves as members of the Jain community, on the other hand, can hardly be proven from a historical perspective and is rather uncertain.

sources also claim that Hemacandra composed the 'Yoga Treatise' for this ruler as a guide for lay Jain followers.

The significance of Jainism as a formative cultural force in Gujarat can be historically traced only to the reign of the Solanki princes Siddharaja and his successor Kumarapala, whose reign was in the twelfth century (Majumdar 1965: 207). However, the growing importance of Jainism during this period came less from the itinerant ascetics than primarily from the lay communities. Their members were forbidden by lay vows to engage in most craft activities, especially agriculture, thus many families earned their living from trade and money lending. The geographical location of Gujarat, whose ports formed important intersections on the trade routes to southern Arabia and East Africa, favored the economic upswing of those families in particular who engaged in long-distance trade. The large donations and endowments were, unlike similar acts involving different Hindu cults, not supported primarily by kings and princes, but mostly by wealthy communities or rich individual citizens. It should also be emphasized here that there is no reliably documented case where a ruler who supported the founding of Jain institutions like temples or libraries actually converted to Jainism.

Jain ascetic doctrine originally knew no temple worship, but lay Jain communities seem to have rapidly adopted the concept originally introduced by the Hindus. Indian temple worship emerged at about the same time within Jainism and within Hindu religions. It is therefore not surprising that the architecture and structure of both temple traditions are very similar. The temple structure common in northern India consists of a vestibule (*maṇḍapa*), through which the worshiper enters the building, and the sanctuary (*garbhagṛha*), in which the cult image of the Jina or a deity is placed. In larger temples, there is an inner shrine within the sanctuary that can be circumambulated. As a rule, the worshipers do not enter the sanctuary itself; the performance of the rituals, especially in West Indian temples, is mostly the responsibility of temple priests employed by the community that runs the temple; these usually belong to the Hindu tradition of Vaishnavism.

At the same time, however, the growing prosperity and the numerous temple foundations led to lasting changes within the Jain monastic order. Some writings of the canonical literature of the Shvetambaras already list so large a number of items as permitted possessions of monks and nuns (Schubring, 1962: 256–262) that it is almost inconceivable how permanent wandering was possible with such large baggage. As mentioned before, according to the monastic rule their members were expected to wander except for the rainy season and were not allowed to stay in one place for long; particularly the sojourn in villages and towns was only allowed for a very limited period. The establishment of more and more Jain temples, however, favored an increasingly sedentary lifestyle for members of the order. Some monks even seem to have abandoned itinerant asceticism altogether, and from the twelfth century onward, disputes arose in Gujarat between 'temple-dwelling monks' *(caityavāsins)*, who had procured lodgings near Jain temples or even lived in the temples, and the non-sedentary 'forest-dwelling monks' *(vanavāsins)*, who refused to stay in one place for long periods (Cort, 1991: 657). The temple-dwelling way of life was at odds with the original rule of the order. Possibly the prosperity of the lay communities had spurred this development, because the offspring of the ascetic order in this period was probably also recruited from members of wealthy families, who were interested in the prestige of the ascetic state, but not in its deprivations.

The spiritual leadership of the community was the responsibility of the ascetics, but since the Middle Ages, the organizational leadership was taken over by particularly deserving laymen. Within some Shvetambara communities, the office of Yati (*yati* loosely translated 'cleric') was created to lead the communities and temples. These were monks or spiritually advanced lay persons, who were less strictly bound by the vows or interpreted them as they saw fit. From a historical perspective, the Yatis probably go back to the temple-dwelling monks. Some Yatis established families and lived in prosperous circumstances. In addition to managing the community, they kept libraries and performed rituals in the temples or taught the faithful for a fee. Their reputation within the communities was ambivalent. On the one hand, the Yatis were respected because of their influence and occasionally feared because of their attributed magical powers; at the same time, the faithful showed them a certain disdain, since some of them came from families of little repute and did not adhere to the strict rules of monastic discipline.

Among the Digambaras, the tradition of the Bhattaraka (*bhaṭṭāraka* 'venerables') arose at about the same time. The Bhattaraka were similarly responsible for organizational duties within Jain communities and institutions. As a kind of clerical authority, they administered endowments, directed the libraries attached to the temples, and organized the training of disciples and ascetics or presided over initiation ceremonies. Their office, like that of the Yatis, may have evolved from the medieval temple-dwelling monks. Institutionally, the Bhattaraka stand, in a sense, between the lay state and the monastic community and are, in a sense, considered domesticated Digambara monks who were permitted to wear clothing (Jain, 2017: 65). In this sense, they are partially bound to abide by monastic rules, but are allowed to use means of transportation and acquire property. In the Middle Ages, 36 Bhattaraka seats existed in all parts of India; only a fraction of them have survived.

Over the centuries, the development of Jainism was continuously influenced by its confrontation with other religious doctrines. Buddhism, which had been the strongest competitor of the Jain communities in ancient times, was first replaced by Hindu traditions and, since the eighth century in northwestern India, increasingly by Islam, which both inspired and threatened the Jain religion.

Since ancient times, the inhabitants of India's west coast maintained close trade relations with the Arab world. The Arab historian and geographer al-Masudi (895–957), who visited northwestern India around 926, also reports of ten thousand Arab traders who settled on India's west coast with the permission of the local princes and married women from local families (Barbier de Meynard, 1965: 85f.). During this period, the relationship of the Jain population, whose wealth depended to a large extent on long-distance trade, was characterized on the one hand by a kind of peaceful coexistence with their Muslim business partners, who were allowed to live in India according to their own laws and could practice their religion without restriction, but on the other hand also by the forays of Islamic conquerors from Central Asia, who repeatedly passed through the region and left major destruction in their wake. It can be assumed, however, that the Jains knew how to distinguish between such Muslim invaders and their business partners of the same faith, because trade relations with Arabia hardly seemed to suffer.

The Muslim conquest of northern India took place over several centuries and, according to tradition, was accompanied by looting. In Gujarat, above all the campaigns of Ala ud-Din Khalji between 1297 and 1298 take a prominent place in the collective memory of the Jains, because many Jain temples were demolished and their stone cult images destroyed. Whether the destruction was really as devastating as the writings claim, is doubted by present-day scholars.[21] During these years, undoubtedly the influence of Jainism on Gujarat's religious culture declined. Many communities were initially severely weakened after Muslim looting and pillaging, in which many Jains lost their lives; in addition, members of the communities were lost due to their conversion to Islam. Historical evidence of the conversion of larger Jain groups to Islam is particularly well documented for the area further south around Bijapur, where the Arab missionary Pir Mahabir Khamdayat had been working since 1304.

While the libraries attached to the temples were sometimes housed in secret underground vaults where the manuscripts could be kept safe from the grasp of Muslim looters, the bronze cult images were often buried or hidden in the foundations of the temples. Some of these hoards were not retrieved by their owners, fell into oblivion, and were rediscovered only more recently during excavations; for example, the finds of Lilva-Deva, Vasantgarh, and Hansi (Shah, 1952–53, Shah, 1955–56, Handa, 2022), as well as the aforementioned hoard of Akota. In response to the destruction, movable objects such as bronze figurines and manuscripts, which could be hidden in case of danger, were increasingly donated instead of temples from the thirteenth century onward. The donors were mostly wealthy citizens and minor officials, while temple construction was financed primarily by donations from the ruling families.

Since the seventh century bronze cult images were produced in large numbers and were part of the ritual equipment of most Jain households in Western India. The figural program of these altarpieces was gradually expanded, with subsidiary figures initially grouped around the main figure. Later, the figures were arranged vertically with additional ornaments and symbols framing the Jina. In the thirteenth century, this ensemble of figures was canonized and an early serial production of similar bronze altarpieces with a fixed pictorial program in almost identical form began (Fig. 12.3).

Through the encounter with Islam, however, Jainism also experienced positive impulses that stimulated new trends in art and religion. Thus, the already existing appreciation of books and writing increased to a veritable book cult, which resulted in the replacement of the cult of images by book worship in some Jain communities.

[21] The destruction of Hindu and Jain temples is often cited as an example for the violence used to spread Islam in South Asia (Durant 1954: 459f.). In fact, however, the devastations were not so much directed against the indigenous religions, but were primarily aimed at weakening the local authorities, to which the founders of the temples also belonged (Eaton 2021: 107).

Fig. 12.3 Jain bronze altarpiece, Gujarat or Rajasthan, dated VS 1472/1415 AD (private collection)

While western India developed into a center of the Shvetambaras, the school of the Digambaras was predominant in southern India. In Karnataka and Tamil Nadu, important pilgrimage centers emerged from the eighth century onward, and the construction of temples with attached libraries was also introduced here in the Middle Ages. Among the oldest surviving sites is the cave temple of Sittanavasal in Tamil Nadu, which was probably constructed in the seventh century and whose ceiling frescoes in the antechamber of the temple in the ninth century are among the oldest evidence of Jain painting (see Longhurst, 1930 and Ramachandran, 1961).[22] In contrast to the wall paintings in the cave temple 32 ('Indrasabha') in Ellora, which were created at about the same time, the frescoes in Sittanavasal do not show an image of the Jina, despite certain stylistic similarities. The cave complex at Ellora

[22] The frescoes show a pond with lotus plants, fish and water birds as well as three people carrying lotus flowers. Presumably, the lotus pond here represents the place of Mahavira's enlightenment which, according to the tradition of the Digambaras, took place on a jewel pedestal in the middle of a pond in the Manohara Forest near Pavapura (Shah 1987: 190).

is one of the largest complexes of its kind in South Asia and was constructed during the reign of the Rashtrakuta (Rāṣṭrakūṭa) in the eighth or ninth century; it includes Jain and Hindu cave temples. The Jain caves are of art historical importance not only because of the aforementioned wall paintings (see Qvarnström & Hammer, 2021) but also because of the stone sculptural images of the Jinas and nature spirits *(yakṣa)* (see Owen, 2012), showing a marked expansion of the pictorial program and a consolidation of iconography compared with older images. This expansion of the pictorial program of Jain sculpture is a key feature of medieval Jain art.

The wall paintings at Ellora depict the Jain saint Bahubali (Bāhubali) in addition to images of the Jinas. The worship of Bahubali, the son of the first Jina Rishabha (Ṛṣabha), is especially widespread among the south Indian Digambaras and is most pronounced in Karnataka, where numerous monumental figures were erected in his honor from the ninth century onwards. The most famous of them is probably the 'Lord of the Mountaintop' (*gommaṭeśvara*) or 'Saint of the Mountain' (*gommaṭasvāmī*) of Shravanabelgola.[23] These monumental stone sculptures show the saint standing and immersed in asceticism while his body is overgrown with creepers. Five of these statues have survived, of which the figure in Shravanabelgola, at about 17 m high, is not only the largest but also the most prominent effigy. It was donated in 981 by a ruler of the Ganga dynasty and is visible from afar because of its elevated position (see Del Bonta, 1981). Shravanabelgola is the most important Jain pilgrimage site in Karnataka and consists of two hills, Indragiri and Candragiri. An inscription at Candragiri describes the migration of Bhadrabahu, the leader of a group of Jain monks from northern India, who fled a famine with some followers; thus it connects the founding myth of the site to the narrative about the origins of the Digambaras (see Srinivasan, 1981). Commemorative monuments (*niṣidhi*) prove that since the seventh century, numerous ascetics fasted to death at this site. Since the tenth century, this has also been documented for lay devotees.

In terms of literary history, it is difficult to separate antiquity and the Middle Ages. The medieval literature of the Shvetambaras as a whole belongs to the post-canonical period, although the creation of numerous post-canonical works dates back to antiquity. In terms of content, the post-canonical writings follow on from the canon, but in terms of literary history, they cannot be regarded as a chronological continuation. On the contrary, commentaries on individual canonical writings emerged at a rather early point in time. It should be noted that the commentary on the canonical scriptures proceeded in quite different ways. Some books were supplemented with appropriate commentaries at an early stage, others only at a later date, and for some texts, no commentaries were written at all.[24] There also is no clear break between canonical

[23] Among the Shvetambaras, Bahubali is recognized as an important saint, but he does not receive special veneration. Although Bahubali was not given the status of a Jina, he is depicted as such in art. His distinctive identifying mark are the creepers that grow around his lower body up to the hips.

[24] Among the writings of the Shvetambaras with particularly extensive commentary is the canonical Avashyakasutra (Āvaśyakasūtra), which deals with the indispensable *(avaśyaka)* duties of monks in six sections. The extensive commentary on the Avashyakasutra eventually gave rise to a literary genre of its own, the so-called Avashyaka (Āvaśyaka) literature, of which the Avashyaka-Niryukti (Āvaśyakaniryukti), containing numerous legends about Mahavira's ascetic life, is of particular

and post-canonical literature. Both groups of works are chronologically interlocked at least at individual points. A large number of hierarchically ordered commentaries were written for the exegesis of the canonical writings. In the process, the canonical text was first annotated by the Niryukti commentary, which is said to go back to the learned monk Bhadrabahu and was later supplemented by another commentary, the so-called Bhashya *(bhāṣya)*; both genres are written in Prakrit. Finally, since the eleventh century, the exegetical system was supplemented by the Tika *(ṭīkā)* and Vritti *(vṛtti)* commentaries written in Sanskrit. As a means to explain the canonical doctrinal texts, such commentaries often use narratives and legends relating to the lives of the Jinas, which are intended to contribute to the understanding of the annotated scriptures.

In addition to folk tales, Jain authors also adapted the material of the two ancient Indian epics Ramayana (Rāmāyaṇa 'Rama's journey') and Mahabharata (Mahābhārata 'great [story of the] Bharata'), creating several versions in which mostly pious Jains act as main characters, thus linking Jain and Brahman mythology. In particular, the thirteenth century Harivamshapurana (Harivaṃśapurāṇa 'ancient [story] of Hari's genealogy') of Devaprabhasuri is considered a Jain counterpart to the Mahabharata; an older version of this story was written as early as the eighth century by the Digambara monk Jinasena.

Until the eighth century, the commentary literature of the Shvetambaras was written in the Prakrit language Maharashtri (Māhārāṣṭrī). Around the middle of this century, however, the commentaries of Haribhadra written in Sanskrit heralded the replacement of the Prakrit languages as the predominant literary language of the Shvetambaras; among the Digambaras, this process began significantly earlier. An example of this is the Tattvarthasutra (Tattvārthasūtra 'instruction on the nature of reality') of the learned monk Umasvati (also: Umasvamin) who probably lived in the fourth or fifth century. This work summarizes the extensive knowledge and doctrinal content of Jainism in a concise manner and is largely based on the doctrine that was handed down in the canonical scriptures (Tatia, 2007). Another important group of works are the Jain writings on world or universal history. Starting at the end of the Middle Ages numerous works were written, devoted to the life and work of the Jinas. From this abundance of poetry and narratives, a distinct literary genre eventually developed, known as Carita ('deeds' or 'experiences') or Caritra ('[right] conduct'), and usually translated as 'curriculum vitae' or 'biography'. The Caritas relate primarily to the activities of the Jinas as well as the mythical rulers and heroes of prehistoric times.

---

importance; to a lesser extent, this is also true of the Avashyaka-Churni (Āvaśyacūrṇi) commentaries of Jinadasa and Avashyaka-Tika (Āvaśyakaṭīkā) of Haribhadra. As a model for the legends contained therein, the commentators presumably used primarily the tales from ancient Indian folk literature, which were adapted to the Jain theme and thus preserved.

12.3 Early Modern Times (C. 1400–1850)

The history of Jainism during the modern period is characterized by a strong fragmentation into many different directions and schools (Sangave, 1980: 51–56). The reorganization of community structures that had begun in the Middle Ages was consolidated by the beginning of the modern era and, apart from further splits and new foundations, remained largely unchanged until today. In addition, reform movements increasingly divided Jainism into groups worshiping images and those who rejected image worship, in addition to the denominational split into Shvetambaras and Digambaras. Especially among the Shvetambaras numerous movements arose that replaced image worship with the study of scriptures and the instruction by teachers.

The Shvetambaras can be divided into three main movements, the image-worshipping Murtipujaka *(mūrtipūjaka* 'image worshiper'*)* communities and the Sthanakvasi *(sthānakvāsī* 'meetinghouse-dweller'[25]) and Terapanth (*terāpanthī* '13-fold path'), who both reject image worship. The image-worshiping Shvetambara communities are further subdivided according to a relatively uniform system: The smallest unit is the Sangha (*saṅgha* 'community'), although this term is also occasionally used to describe the community of all Jains ('assembly').

The next largest unit is the Kula (*kula* 'lineage' or 'spiritual family tree'), which groups together the members of a common doctrinal tradition. Several Kulas are grouped together in a Gana (*gaṇa* 'group' or 'flock') or Gaccha (*gaccha* 'itinerant[community]'). It seems that Gana is the older term, which is already mentioned in canonical literature.

In the Kalpasutra (chapter Sthavirāvalī 'list of elders', §1) it is noted that already the original Jain community, due to the large number of members, was divided into several Ganas, each led by one of Mahavira's closest confidants as Ganadhara (*gaṇadhāra* 'group leaders'). In the older literature, two Kulas always formed a Gana, but later the number of Kulas grouped in a Gana was not specified. In modern Jainism, the category Kula is hardly ever used. Between Kula and Gana/Gaccha, there also exists the category Shakha (*śākhā* 'branch'). Medieval literature of the Shvetambaras cites a fixed number of eighty-four Gacchas; their actual number always fluctuated. This categorization is applied in a similar way by the Digambaras.

Among the most important Gacchas of the image-worshiping Shvetambaras is the Kharatara Gaccha, founded by Vardhamanasuri in the eleventh century. Vardhamanasuri rejected the lifestyle of temple-dwelling ascetics common in his time and sought to reform monastic discipline in accordance with the original itinerant asceticism. The order he founded was initially called Vidhimarga (*vidhimārga* 'the

[25] The origin and meaning of the name of the order are uncertain. Possibly the name derives from the monks' lounges or the meetinghouse (*sthānaka*) of the community, which were frequented by lay followers for instruction and meditation. However, it seems that the name was commonly established only in the nineteenth century.

way of the [right] method') and was only later renamed Kharatara ('sharpness') Gaccha.[26] Today the Kharatara Gaccha is based mostly in Rajasthan and Mumbai.

Of similar importance is the Tapa Gaccha, founded in the thirteenth century by Jagatcandrasuri in the town of Chitor in southern Rajasthan. Lax monastic practice prompted the founding of this Gaccha, too; the stricter interpretation of which gave the Tapa (*tapā* 'asceticism') Gaccha its name. In the course of the sixteenth and seventeenth centuries, the Gaccha disintegrated into numerous smaller groups, but was reunited by reform movements in the nineteenth century, carried mainly by the laity, and is today the largest of all Gacchas in terms of followers.

Among the most important and lasting reformers was Lonka Shah, who probably lived around the middle of the fifteenth century. He was the founder of the Lonka Gaccha, a reform community named after him; the image-rejecting schools of the Sthanakvasi and Terapanth, founded in the seventeenth and eighteenth centuries respectively, both trace their origins back to this movement. Little is known about his life. He probably came from a wealthy merchant family in Rajasthan and had good relations with the Muslim court in Ahmedabad. Lumpaka, as he is also called, studied the scriptures of the Shvetambara canon and found its contents to be strongly at odds with the temple system and the common rituals of the Jain lay communities. Probably under the influence of Muslim adverseness to images, he founded a reform movement that renounced the construction of temples and sought to revive the tradition of the pure ascetic order. The Lonka Gaccha was later largely absorbed into the schools of the Sthanakvasi and the Terapanth, but a community of followers of Lonka Shah that traces its roots directly to his renewal movement exists to this day in the area around Vadodara.

The Sthanakvasi is one of the movements within the Shvetambaras that rejects image worship (see Flügel, 2000–12). The exact circumstances that led to the founding of this reform movement have not been handed down. However, it seems likely that the Sthanakvasi evolved in the seventeenth century from a group of the disintegrating Lonka Gaccha. Since the late nineteenth century, the order has focused particularly on charitable causes and the education of its followers. Apart from Gujarat, the Punjab is a traditional stronghold of the Sthanakvasi. The other major reform movement pushing back on image worship is the movement of the Shvetambara Terapanth, founded in 1760 by the Sthanakvasi monk Bhikhaji. Bhikhaji, who later became known as Acharya Bhikshu, had left the Sthanakvasi order along with four other monks after disputes over monastic discipline and the role of lay followers. The movement he founded was based on Mahavira's '13-fold path' (*terāpantha*), which became eponymous and consists of the five great monastic vows *(mahāvrata)*, the five rules of mindfulness (*samiti*), and the threefold self-restraint (*gupti*).

---

[26] A distinctive feature of this movement is the veneration of the Dadagurus (*dādāguru* 'grandfatherly teachers'), a group of four ascetics who lived between the eleventh and seventeenth centuries and are still held in high esteem today and are a major focus of lay piety. Although none of these ascetics attained omniscience, they veneration they receive resembles that of the Jinas. The Dadagurus are regarded as protectors of the religion. At the same time, they are said to perform miracles, which enabled them to convert numerous people to Jainism.

Regarding Jain literary history, the early modern period is characterized by the increasing importance of early regional languages, which gradually replaced Sanskrit. Probably under the influence of Islam, cosmological themes are treated more in Jain literature. In addition to numerous literary works on cosmology, the form and structure of the cosmos became an important subject of manuscript illustration in the seventeenth century (see Krüger, 2021).

One of the developments of modern Jainism significant also for the wider cultural history is its distinctive culture of manuscript production and book illumination (see Chandra, 1949, Doshi, 1985 and Andhare, 2020). The production of palm-leaf manuscripts can be traced back in Gujarat to about the mid-eleventh century, ending around 1400 after the introduction of paper. Both materials were used side by side only during a short transitional period between about 1375 and 1400.[27]

In contrast to the wooden book covers used to store the manuscripts, the palm-leaf miniatures have their own style and a separate pictorial program with motifs adapted to the rather small space allotted to each image.[28] The style in which the miniatures were executed is already fully developed in the oldest manuscripts known today. It is characterized by a hard drawing as well as pointed and angular forms. Instead of a spatial juxtaposition, individual figures and pictorial elements are arranged one above each other in a strictly two-dimensional manner. The color spectrum is initially very limited, but is quickly expanded. A characteristic feature of early Jain miniature painting is the red background against which the scenes are set; it was introduced in the thirteenth century at the latest. It is uncertain whether the red background is an Indian invention or whether the artists here drew on models from the Persian or Arabic cultural areas. It is well known that the Jain traders maintained close contact with these areas, and it can therefore not be ruled out that this also led to an exchange of artistic ideas.

With regard to the enormous number of illustrated manuscripts produced in Gujarat and parts of Rajasthan in the course of the fifteenth and sixteenth centuries, this period may rightly be regarded as the heyday of Jain book art. Most illuminated manuscripts of the fifteenth century are copies of the Kalpasutra, alone or in conjunction with the aforementioned 'Story of the Jain monk Kalaka', as well as of the 'Later Chapters' (Uttarādhyayanasūtra), one of the most important scriptures of the canon which describes aspects of the monastic behavior and discipline.

The style in which the miniatures are executed is most often referred to as the 'Western Indian style' (more rarely as the 'Jain style' or the 'Prakrit style') and probably originated from a combination of an ancient vernacular Indian imagery and an adoption of influences from the Islamic world (Fig. 12.4). The origins of this style

[27] The palm leaf manuscripts are characterized by their special format, which is due to the material. The individual leaves can be up to half a meter long and about 8 cm wide. The individual leaves are not bound, but laid loosely on top of each other as a collection of texts. Often the leaves are perforated in several places so that they can be bound together with a string.

[28] Until the twelfth century, the pictorial themes were limited to a depiction of various deities, presumably intended as guardian spirits of the manuscripts, and to colored diagrams. Only later were more complex scenes shown and the first miniatures depicting scenes from the Kalpasutra and other Jain legends were finally created in the second half of the thirteenth century.

Fig. 12.4 Folio from a Kalpasūtra-Manuscript depicting Mahavira and his entourage, Gujarat, c. fifteenth century (Berlin Museum of Asian Art)

of painting are obscure, but the Buddhist monk Taranatha reports in his History of Buddhism (written in Tibet in 1608) that the Western school of painting goes back to a tradition founded by the artist Shringadhara (Śṛṅgadhāra) in the seventh century (Chandra, 1949: 16f.). The style is manneristic and is defined by the repetition of fixed pictorial formulas. Miniatures of this style were produced mainly in Gujarat and Rajasthan.[29]

[29] In a few cases, manuscripts were also created in distant areas such as Jaunpur (see Khandalavala and Chandra, 1962 and Krüger, 2020) or Mandu (see Khandalavala and Chandra, 1959), where apparently Jain communities existed that sought demonstrate their link to the West Indian Jain culture by donating a manuscript in the respective style.

Around the turn of the fifteenth century, the red background was extended in some places by blue image areas, which were inserted in specially defined places in the picture. It is possible that the introduction of a second background color was intended to create an impression of spatial depth, as the Indian artists were probably familiar with this idea from Persian painting (see Krüger, 2020). However, this development quickly came to a halt, and instead of spatial depth, artists developed a peculiar play with backgrounds, where red and blue color areas alternated until a predominantly blue background finally prevailed. The influences of Islamic art in the Kalpasutra manuscripts are most evident in the decoration of the page borders and in the ornaments of borders. While the borders were mostly painted by hand, the marginal decoration was often applied by stencils. It can be assumed that the addition of decorative borders was an attempt to visually adapt the Jain manuscripts to the Islamic manuscripts thus marking them as objects of religious importance in a way recognizable to their Muslim contemporaries, too.

12.4 Modernity and Present-Day (Since 1850)

Due to British colonial rule, the Jains lost their connection to the political elites that had ensured the prosperity of the communities during the Sultanate and Mughal periods. However, the Jain communities were also not subject to any significant restrictions. Jainism in the nineteenth century is marked by its encounter with Western culture. This occurs first through the British colonial empire, but by the end of the century also through tentative missionary attempts in Europe and North America. These are not so much aimed at a conversion to the Jain religion, but can be understood as an early form of interreligious dialogue, the goal of which is above all a deeper knowledge of Jainism in the West.

Under the increasing pressure of Christian missionary activity in the British Indian colonial empire, new reform movements arose that sought to revitalize traditional beliefs through renewal. In 1893, for example, the 'All India Digambara Jain Conference' was founded; one of its goals was to unite the Jains, who were fragmented into countless sects and schools, in order to better assert themselves against competitive pressure and intellectual attacks from Hindus, Muslims, and Christian missionaries.

In the twentieth century, numerous Jain diaspora communities emerged in Africa, Europe, and North America (see Kumar, 1996 and Jain, 2020). Since Jain monks and nuns are only allowed to travel on foot, these communities, as purely lay groups, in the beginning, were largely cut off from the monastic order. For decades, the religious practice of the Jains in the diaspora was therefore largely upheld by the rituals of the lay community. To counteract this, the spiritual leader of the Shvetambara Terapanth founded the Terapanth Saman order in 1980; its members were allowed to use means of transportation and to travel. In this way, the predominantly female members of the order, known as Samanis, were able to visit those communities outside India and instruct and spiritually guide their members. At the same time, some Samanis taught at Western universities, thus increasing the visibility of Jainism in Europe and North America.

However, since conversion to Jainism is not usually envisaged, there are only isolated Western followers of Jainism. Jain centers and temple buildings in the West are therefore run almost exclusively by members of the diaspora communities. Since the second half of the twentieth century, fully-fledged Jain communities have been established outside India, with the largest communities in the United States (about 50,000). In Europe, most Jains live in Great Britain and Belgium (together about 30,000).

The changes brought about by the globalized and increasingly digitalized society of the early twenty-first century also affect Jainism. The use of the internet and here especially social networks leads to strong changes in the religious life and also in community structures (Vekemans, 2022). Networking occasionally weakens the ties of individual believers to the local community; at the same time, it gives diaspora communities the opportunity to build and maintain closer ties with Jain communities in India and enables Jainism as a minority religion to have a stronger public presence and perception overall.

References

Ācārāṅgasūtra. (Ed.) (1976). Muni Jambūvijaya, *Āyāraṅga-suttam*. Jaina-Āgama-Series No. 2, 1. Bombay: Shrī Mahāvīra Jaina Vidyālaya.

Andhare, S. (2020). *Calligraphy and art of writing in jain manuscripts*. Ahmedabad: Bhulabhai and Dhirajlal Desai Memorial Trust.

Armstrong, K. (2006). *The great transformation. The beginning of our religious traditions*. New York: Alfred A. Knopf.

Aupapātikasūtra. (Ed.) (1883). Ernst Leumann, *Das Aupapātika Sūtra, erstes Upāṅga der Jaina. I. Theil: Einleitung, Text und Glossar*. Leipzig: Brockhaus.

Barbier de Meynard, C. (1965). ***Maçoudi.** Les Prairies d'or. Textes et Traduction par Charles Barbier de Meynard et Pavet de Courteille, Tome 2*. Paris: Geuthner.

Basham, A. L. (2009). *History and Doctrines of the Ājīvikas. A Vanished Indian Religion*, Delhi: Motilal Banarsidass.

Brown, W. N. (1933). *The Story of Kālaka. Texts, History Legends and Miniature Paintings of the Śvetāmbara Jain Hagiographical Work the Kālakācāryakathā*. Washington: Smithsonian Institution.

Bruhn, K. (1987). Das Kanonproblem bei den Jainas. In A. Assmann & J. Assmann (Eds.), *Kanon und Zensur. Archäologie der literarischen Kommunikation II* (pp. 100–112). München: Fink.

Carrithers, M., & Humphrey, C. (1991). Jains as a community. A position paper. In M. Carrithers & C. Humphrey (Eds.) *The assembly of listeners. Jains in society* (pp. 5–12). Cambridge: Cambridge Universuty Press.

Chandra, M. (1949). *Jain miniature paintings*. Ahmedabad: Sarabhai Manilal Nawab.

Cort, J. E. (2010). *Framing the Jina. Narratives of icons and idols in Jain history*. Oxford: Oxford University Press.

Cort, J. E. (1991). The Svetambar Murtipujak Jain Mendicant. *Man* 26, 4 (New Series): 651–671.

Del Bonta, R. (1981). The temples and monuments of Shravana Belgola. In S. Doshi (Ed.), *Hommage to Shravana Belgola* (pp. 63–100). Bombay: Marg Publications.

DeCaroli, R. (2015). *Image problems. The origin and development of the Buddha's Image in Early South Asia*. Seattle: University of Washington Press.
Doshi, S. (1985). *Masterpieces of Jain painting*. Bombay: Marg Publications.
Dundas, P. (2002). *The Jains*. London: Routledge.
Durant, W. (1954). *Our oriental heritage*. New York: Simon and Schuster.
Eaton, R. M. (2021). Temple desecration in Pre-Modern India. In S. Kumar (Ed.), *Demolishing Myths or Mosques and Temples? Readings on History and Temple Desecration in Medieval India* (pp. 93–140). Gurgaon: Three Essays Collective.
Flügel, P. (2018). *Askese und Devotion. Das rituelle System der Terāpanth Śvetāmbara Jaina*. Dettelbach: Röll.
Flügel, P. (2000–12). Protestantische und Postprotestantische Jaina Reformbewegungen. Zur Geschichte und Organisation der Sthānakavāsī I-IV. *Berliner Indologische Studien* 13 (2000): 37–103; 15–17 (2003): 149–192; 18 (2007): 127–206; 20 (2012): 37–126.
Folkert, K. (1993). The 'Canons' of 'Scripture'. Text ritual and symbol. In J. E. Cort (Ed.), *Scripture and community. Collected essays of the Jains* (pp. 53–81). Atlanta: Scholars Press.
Gombrich, R. (2006). *Theravāda Buddhism. A social history from Ancient Benares to Modern Colombo*. London: Routledge.
Handa, D. (2002). *Jaina Bronzes from Hansi*. New Delhi: Aryan Books International.
Härtel, H. (1993). *Excavations at Sonkh. 2500 years of a town in Mathura District*. Berlin: Dietrich Reimer.
Jain, U. K. (1975). *Jaina sects and schools*. Delhi: Concept Publishing.
Jain, P. (2020). *Dharma in America. A short history of Hindu-Jain Diaspora*. New York: Routledge.
Jain, K. C. (1963). *Jainism in Rajasthan*. Sholapur: Jaina Saṃskṛti Saṃrakshaka Sangha.
Jain, K. C. (1991). *Lord Mahāvīra and his Times*. Delhi: Motilal Banarsidass.
Jain, K. C. (2010). *History of Jainism* (Vols. 1–3). New Delhi: D.K. Printworld.
Jain, S. (2017). *Identity, community and state. The Jains under the Mughals*. Delhi: Primus Books.
Jayaswal, K. P., & Banerji, R. D. (1929–30). The Hathigumpha Inscription of Kharavela. *Epigraphia Indica, 20*, 71–89.
Johnson, H. M. (1931–62). *Triṣaṣṭiśalākāpuruṣacaritra, or The Lives of the Sixty-Three Illustrious Persons, by Acarya Shri Hemacandra*, translated into English by Helen M. Johnson (Vols. 1–4). Baroda: Oriental Institute.
Kapadia, H. R. (1941). *A history of the canonical literature of the Jainas*. Bombay: Gujarati Print Press.
Khandalavala, K., & Chandra, M. (1959). A Consideration of an Illustrated Ms from Maṇḍapadurga (Mandu) dated 1439 A.D. *Lalit Kalā, 6*, 8–29.
Khandalavala, K., & Chandra, M. (1962). An Illustrated Kalpasūtra Painted at Jaunpur. *Lalit Kalā, 12*, 9–15.
Krüger, P. (2020). *Miniaturen mittelalterlicher Kalpasūtra-Handschriften. Eine ikonographische Betrachtung mit kultur- und religionsgeschichtlichen Anmerkungen*. Wiesbaden: Reichert.
Krüger, P. (2021). The Tangible Universe. Aspects of visualization and materiality of the Jain Cosmos. *Ancient Punjab, 9*, 20–44 (http://pu.edu.pk/images/journal/archaeological/PDF/3_V9_21.pdf)
Kulke, H., & Rothermund, D. (1998). *A History of India*. London: Routledge.
Kumar, B. (1996). *Jainism in America*. Mississauga: Jain Humanities Press.
Leumann, E. (1966). *Das Aupapātika Sūtra, erstes Upāṅga der Jaina. 1. Theil: Einleitung, Text und Glossar*. Nendeln: Kraus.
Longhurst, A. H. (1930). The Sittannavāsal Paintings, Pudukottai State. *Annual Bibliography of Indian Archaeology, 1930*, 9–11.
Majmudar, M. R. (1965). Cultural History of Gujarat (from early times to pre-British period). Bombay: Popular Prakashan.
Mette, A. (2010). *Die Erlösungslehre der Jaina. Legenden, Parabeln, Erzählungen*. Berlin: VWR.

Kalpasūtra. (Ed.) (1879). Hermann Jacobi, *The Kalpasūtra of Bhadrabāhu. Edited with an Introduction, Notes and a Prākṛit-Saṃskṛit Glossary.* Abhandlungen für die Kunde des Morgenlandes, VII. Band, No. 1. Leipzig: Brockhaus.

Ohira, S. (1994). *A study of the Bhagavatīsūtra. A chronological analysis.* Ahmedabad: Prakrit Text Society.

Owen, L. N. (2012). *Carving devotion in the Jain Caves at Ellora.* Leiden: Brill.

Quintanilla, S. R. (2000). Āyāgapaṭas. Characteristics, symbolism, and chronology. *Artibus Asiae, 60*, 79–137.

Quintanilla, S. R. (2007). *History of Early Stone Sculpture at Mathurā, ca. 150 BCE – 100 CE.* Leiden: Brill.

Qvarnström, O., & Hammer, N. (2021). Joyful celestials. Jain Murals of Ellora. *International Journal of Jaina Studies, 17*(1), 1–66.

Qvarnström, O. (2002). *The Yogaśāstra of Hemacandra. A Twelfth Century Handbook on Śvetāmbara Jainism. Edited and translated by Olle Qvarnström.* Cambridge: Harvard University Press.

Rahula, W. (1956). *History of Buddhism in Ceylon. The Anuradhapura Period 3rd Century BC – 10th Century AC.* Columbo: Gunasena & Co.

Ramachandran, T. N. (1961). Cave-temples and paintings of Sittanavasal. *Lalit Kalā, 9*, 30–54.

Sangave, V. (1980). *Jaina community. A social survey.* Bombay: Popular Prakashan.

Sawant, R., & Shete, G. (2016). A review of early historic urbanization in India. In G. R. Schug & S. R. Walimbe (Eds.), *A companion to South Asia in the past* (pp. 319–331). Chichester: Wiley.

Saxena, K. K. (2021). *Before Kṛṣṇa. Religious diversity in Ancient Mathura.* Oxford: Oxford University Press.

Schubring, W. (1962). *The doctrine of the Jainas. Described after the old sources.* Delhi: Motilal Banarsidass.

Shah, U. P. (1951). Age of differentiation of Śvetāmbara and Digambara Images and the earliest known Śvetāmbara Bronzes. *Bulletin of Prince of Wales Museum, Bombay, 1*, 1–11.

Shah, U. P. (1955–56). Bronze Hoard from Vasantagaḍh. *Lalit Kalā* 1–2, 55–65.

Shah, U. P. (1952–53). Seven Bronzes from Lilvā-Devā. *Bulletin of the Museum and Picture Gallery Baroda, 9*(1–2), 43–51.

Shah, U. P. (1959). *Akota Bronzes.* Bombay: Department of Archaeology, Government of Bombay.

Shah, U. P. (1987). Jaina-rūpa-maṇḍana. New Delhi: Abhinav.

Shah, N. (2004). *Jainism. The World of conquerors* (Vol. 1). Delhi: Motilal Banarsidass.

Singh, H. (1982). *Jaina temples of Western India.* Varanasi: Parshvanath Vidyashram Research Institute.

Smith, V. A. (1969). *The Jain-Stūpā and other Antiquities of Mathurā.* Varanasi: Indological Book House.

Srinivasan, L. K. (1981). Shravana Belgola in legend and history. In S. Doshi (Ed.), *Hommage to Shravana Belgola* (pp. 45–50). Bombay: Marg Publications.

Tatia, N. (2007). *Umāsvāti/Umāsvāmi's Tattvārtha Sūtra. That Which Is. With the combined commentaries of Umāsvāti/Umāsvāmi, Pujyapāda and Siddhasenagaṇi*, translated with an introduction by N. Tatia. Delhi: Motilal Banarsidass

Upadhye, A. N. (1933). Yāpanīya Saṅgha. A Jaina Sect. *Journal of the University of Bombay, 1*, 224–231.

Upadhye, A. N. (1975). More light on the Yāpanīya Saṅgha. A Jaina Sect. *Annals of the Bhandarkar Oriental Research Institute, 55*, 9–22.

Vekemans, T. (2022). *Digital and Diaspora. Intertwined Frontiers of Contemporary Jainism.* Baden-Baden: Ergon.

von Glasenapp, H. (1964). *Der Jainismus. Eine indische Erlösungsreligion.* Hildesheim: Olms.

Weber, M. (1921). *Gesammelte Aufsätze zur Religionssoziologie. II. Hinduismus und Buddhismus.* Tübingen: Mohr.

Williams, R. (1983). *Jaina yoga. A survey of the Mediaeval Śrāvakācāras.* Oxford: Oxford University Press.

Part III
India Through Colonization and Modernity

Chapter 13
Literary Exchange Between India and Sri Lanka

Justin W. Henry

Abstract This chapter explores points of contact between India and Sri Lanka with respect to the exchange of religious, poetic, narrative, and philological literature. I consider the initial transmission and translation of canonical and commentarial Pali works in Sri Lanka, the development of Pali literature under the influence of Sanskrit in "the long twelfth century," the prolific and religiously inclusive period of Sinhala literary production during the fifteenth century, concluding with reflections on avenues for future research to enhance our understanding of the influence of Tamil literature on Sinhala.

Key Terms Sri Lanka · Sanskrit literature · *Kāvya* · Pali · Sinhala · Tamil

13.1 Introduction

In 1887, in the midst of a thriving Colombo theater scene attracting Sinhala speaking audiences to dramatic renderings of such Sanskrit classics as "Shakuntala," "the story of Nala and Damayanti" and "the theft of Sita," Simon De Silva Seneviratne, Chief Translator to the British Government, produced a stage play entitled *Kālidās Nṛitya Pota, The Historical Tragedy Entitled Kalidas.* De Silva's drama recapitulates a centuries old legend wherein the famed poet Kalidasa, in exile in Sri Lanka following the sudden death of his young bride, the princess of Mathura, finds a place at the court of the king of Anuradhapura, only to himself fall victim there to the wiles of a courtesan, who exploits the poet for his intellectual labor before finally murdering him (Seneviratne, 1887). While clearly apocryphal in its provenance, this imaginative Sri Lankan rendering of the fate of Kalidasa evoked for its audience reminders of a real and intricate history of literary exchange between Sri Lanka and the Indian subcontinent. The king of Anuradhapura featured in De Silva's drama, Kumaradasa, was himself a real historical person, attributed with the authorship of a sixth century Sanskrit poetic rendering of the *Rāmāyaṇa*, the *Jānakīharaṇa*

J. W. Henry (✉)
University of South Florida, Tampa, FL, USA
e-mail: jwhenry@usf.edu

L. Vemsani (ed.), *Handbook of Indian History*,
https://doi.org/10.1007/978-981-97-6207-1_13

(Godakumbura, 1967). Kalidasa's own famed *Meghadūta* was known to Sri Lankans, with the genre that it inspired (*sandeśa kāvya*, "messenger poetry") supplying the format for the most celebrated Sinhala poems of the fifteenth century (Rhys Davids, 1894), a period regarded as the final flourishing of the classical literary tradition in advance of European colonial intrusion.

Indeed, syncretic results of centuries of migration, storytelling across languages, and multi-religious community are conspicuously discoverable in many aspects of Sri Lankan literature, culture, and ritual life. While the early Pali chronicles connect the earliest monarchs with the north Indian Shakya dynasty to which the Buddha Gautama himself belonged, the *praśasti*s and sponsored inscriptions of some of the greatest royal patrons of Buddhism of medieval Sri Lanka were equally concerned to highlight descent from the "Solar Dynasty" (*sūrya vaṃsa*) of Ikshvaku—progenitor of the royal lineage including Dasharatha and Rama according to the Sanskrit epics and Puranas. Shrines (*devālaya*s) to Hindu deities such as Vishnu, Parvati, Ganesha, and Skanda are found on the premises of nearly all of the island's Buddhist temples, both large and small. Some of Sri Lanka's most trafficked devotional sites—Sri Pada (Adam's Peak), Kataragama, Our Lady of Madhu Shrine in Mannar—attract Buddhist, Hindu, Muslim and Christian visitors (Sri Pada being a site of multi-religious pilgrimage on account of the polysemic significance of the "footprint" indited at its summit, with Buddhists understanding it to be the footprint of the Buddha Gautama, Hindus the footprint of Lord Shiva, and Muslims the footprint of the Biblical Adam).

This chapter considers the history of literary exchange between Sri Lanka and the Indian subcontinent, attending to the influence of both the "great tradition" of Sanskrit literature, grammar, and poetics on Sri Lankan literary culture, as well as to the more demotic exchange of folklore, legendary ancestries, and devotional cults at the level of translation between vernacular languages of the region.

13.2 Early Buddhist Literary Exchange

Sri Lanka's Pali Buddhist chronicles—noteworthy as the earliest documents of their kind in the region—articulate a succinct vision of the Buddhist religion as a civilizing force. The *Dīpavaṃsa* (3rd or fourth century) and *Māhavaṃsa* (c. fifth century) recall a series of visits by the Buddha Gautama to the island of Lanka, during which occasions he delivered sermons to the resident Nagas and Yakkhas (*yakṣa*s), ridding the island of these and other species of demon inhabitants in order to clear the way for the arrival of Sri Lanka's first human inhabitants, a band of castaways from the northeastern Indian kingdom of Lata led by a prince named Vijaya.

The Pali chronicles relate a dramatic story of the introduction of Buddhism to the island, in the context of a mission dispatched by the Indian king Ashoka. In this version of events, the mission to Sri Lanka was headed by Ashoka's own son, "the Arahant Mahinda," a renouncer in the Buddhist Sangha. Mahinda, on instruction from the god Indra, uses the power of his supernatural attainments to fly from his residence in north India and alight on Mt. Missaka (Mahintale), where he encountered King Devanampiya Tissa who was on a hunting excursion (lured to Mahinda's location by the god of the mountain who had taken the form of an elk-stag), and converted Devanampiya Tissa to the Buddhist path.[1] The earliest evidence for Buddhism in Sri Lanka (in the form of donative inscriptions and coinage) corresponds temporally to the periods of Ashoka and Devanampiya Tissa, dating to the third century BCE, though the distribution of donative inscriptions of the period (dispersed throughout almost the entire island), suggest a more diffuse introduction of Buddhism than does the Pali chronicle account of the sudden conversion of a single king of Anuradhapura (Coningham, 1995).

The traditional account has it that the Buddhist scriptures—the Pali Tipitaka—arrived in Sri Lanka by way of a mission dispatched by King Ashoka promptly after Mahinda's first contact. The Tipitaka along with its accompanying Pali commentaries (*aṭṭhakathā*) were in this version of events rendered into Sinhala during the reign of Vattagamani in the late first century BCE, with the commentaries finally rendered back again into Pali by the prolific commentator of the fifth–sixth century, Buddhaghosa.[2] In the absence of any evidence to confirm such a precise series of events prior to the time of Buddhaghosa, we can at least acknowledge that the account of an initial translation of a Pali Tipitaka into Sinhala conforms to the mandate of the Buddha himself regarding the necessity of teaching the Dhamma (Skt. *dharma*) in languages familiar to its audience, according to Pali canonical texts. The *Cullavagga* gives a story of Buddha being approached by two monks (Yamelu and Tekula) who ask about translating his teachings into Sanskrit for the sake of preserving their uniformity. Rebuking the two at the mere suggestion, Buddha insists that the Bhikkhus of his Order should be permitted to learn the Dhamma "each in their own dialect" (*sakāya niruttiyā*) (de Zilva Wickremasinghe, 1934). The mandate of comprehensibility of the Dhamma is again at play in Buddhaghosa's own justification for his project of re-translating the corpus of commentaries from Sinhala back into Pali,

[1] Devanampiya Tissa's conversion is narrated in this chapter and Chap. 14 of the *Dīpavaṃsa* (Dīpavaṃsa 1908).

[2] See Malalasekera (1928: 79–101). Ashoka's edicts themselves record allude to Dharma-bearing missions (the king's "conquest of Dharma") dispatched southward beyond the lands of the Cholas and Pandyas, "as far as Taṃbapamni," a likely reference to Sri Lanka (the island referred to in other sources from antiquity as "Tamraparṇi" in reference to the copper-colored soil of the north). See Sen (1956: 66f., 102f). Continental sources are silent on the specifics of Ashoka's mission outlined in the Pali chronicles, that is, we find no references in the Indian epigraphical or literary tradition confirming that Ashoka's son Mahinda led the mission to Sri Lanka, nor that Ashoka's daughter Sanghamitta introduced the Bhikkhuni Sangha as well as the first cutting of the sacred Bodhi Tree to the island. In the words of Robin Coningham, et al., the archaeological evidence available to us constitutes "physical evidence of links between the core of the Mauryan culture sphere and Sri Lanka," and, "although a link can be identified, its exact nature is less certain, as the ware predates the rule of Ashoka and may represent down-the-line trade rather than courtly exchange" (Coningham et al., 2017: 28).

as he declares his desire for these essential works to be broadly available to monks outside of Sri Lanka (who may know Pali but not Sinhala).[3]

While the vast majority of Pali canonical and commentarial literature is written in formulaic prose, Pali verse is also attested from early on in the tradition. The *Theragātha* and *Therīgātha* of the Khuddada Nikāya contain poems in Pali attributed to early monks and nuns of the tradition; the *Dīpavaṃsa* and *Mahāvaṃsa* give their accounts of the acts of kings in verse. The subject matter for much later Sinhala literature is established in early Pali texts, central among these being the chronicles of the acts of the kings of Sri Lanka, the biography of the Buddha Gotama, and the "birth stories" (Jātaka Kathā) of the Buddha in his former lifetimes on the path to enlightenment. Poetic formats, devices, and themes well known from continental Sanskrit and Prakrit *kāvya* also deeply inform Sinhala literature of Sri Lanka's medieval period.

From quite early on, Sinhala poets were experimenting with versification making use of the novel medium of etching onto the "mirror wall" at Sigiriya ("Lion Rock"), a plateau-top fortress in north-central Sri Lanka rendered into an elaborate palace complex by Kassapa I (r.c. 473–91 CE). The Sinhala graffiti verses adorning the famed Sigiriya mirror wall—composed by miscellaneous hands from the 6th to tenth centuries—sport puns, similes, and the theme of the intensification of erotic sentiment in the absence of one's lover (*vipralamba-sṛṅgāra*) familiar from continental *kāvya.* These amateur poets drew inspiration from the scenic environs of the ruined rock fortress along with the frescoes of nubile women adorning the passage to its summit, employing these "apsaras" as facsimiles for living objects of their own romantic affection:

> [She] who offers a coquettish smile [comparable to the rows of] seeds of a melon,
> Her pleasant speech as sweet as the marrow of that [fruit],
> Her long eye like a segment of the rind of that same [fruit],
> —she inflames my heart and leaves not my mind.[4]

> Ah! The golden-colored one on the mountain side, who entices one's eye and mind and whose breasts are delightful to look at, directed my mind to the intoxicated swans.[5]

> We peeped [to see] whether there was a streak of lightening above [and then] saw all that is worth seeing, [namely],
> the golden colored ones who stood on the mountain side [of the rock fortress], without speaking, in the manner of those separated from their lovers.[6]

The Sigiriya graffiti attests to a lively tradition of informal composition in Sinhala from a quite early period, with those poets who signed their work deriving from a

---

[3] See Malalasekera (1928: 79–101). For complications and uncertainties related to this traditional account of the transmission and translation of the Tipitaka and commentaries, see Collins (1990).

[4] *komuḷ amaḍ-leḍ lina sī | e bonda miyar yaha bäsī | e kapal-dala van digäsī | mana jal[va]yi [sit] no musī.* Adapted from Lokubandara's translation (2007: 84 (no.103)).

[5] *[nu]yun mana badnā piyavuru bälum-rusnā | a beyabahi ranvan mana mata-has yo my kaḷa tamā* (Lokubandara 2007: 77 (no.126)).

[6] *vidu-ki[da] mata [ä]ti da ebimo [di]si tak di[ṭi] vī | viyevun bandun beyadihi ran[vanu]n no [me vī] buṇa.* Adapted from Lokubandara's translation (2007: 50 (no. 555)).

broad cross-section of Sri Lankan society, both men and women. While the poetic figures of the graffiti are generally speaking fairly elementary, Jayadeva Tilakasiri notes affinities in other respects with an early (seventh century) Indian collection of Prakrit poems, Hala's *Sattasaī*, such as a rhythmic balance between couplets and end rhymes (Tilakasiri, 1986: 136f.).

13.3 Sri Lanka's Medieval Literary Tradition

A vast catalogue of works which might offer a proscenium view of the intellectual and religious milieu of Anuradhapura have been lost to the circumstances of history. Only the Mahavihara fraternity—one of three competing Buddhist schools of ancient Sri Lanka—survived beyond the eleventh century, with the liturgical texts, commentaries, chronicles of the Abhayagiri and Jetavana Viharas irrevocably lost. Archaeological and textual evidence gives us a sense of greater theological openness within the Mahavihara's competitor fraternities. The 9th or tenth century Chinese biography of Amoghavajra (d. 774) records that this Indian monk in the service of the T'ang emperor bypassed the famed university at Nalanda to travel directly to Sri Lanka in order to secure a cache of Tantric manuscripts (the crest-gem of which was the *Sarva Tathāgata Sattva Saṃgraha*). Abhayagiri monks appear to have been involved in transporting Yoga Tantras to Central Java in the eighth century.[7] The *Cūlavaṃsa* contains a possible reference to monastic quarters (the "Vīrankura Arama") constructed by King Sena I (r.c. 833–53 CE) on the premises of the Abhayagiri campus for the sake of monks of the Mahasanghika Order—Mahasanghikas being an Indian school understood to have developed initial doctrines of Mahayana and Vajrayana.[8]

The altered political landscape of Sri Lanka following the restoration of the northern portion of the island to local control by the twelfth century meant the loss of guaranteed large-scale royal patronage for Buddhist monastics. During this period—that of "the long twelfth century," to use Alastair Gornall's designation—Buddhist authors relied increasingly on the support of lesser nobility and local patrons to finance their work. Perhaps counterintuitively on the model established by Sheldon Pollock (which assumes consolidated royal patronage as a necessary condition for the development of robust vernacular literary traditions in premodern South Asia (Pollock, 2006)), the long twelfth century brought with it the intense flourishing of Pali and Sinhala tetxtual production. These works were modelled often on continental Indian literary fashions, including that time when technical literature in Sanskrit prosody, poetics, and grammar was highly developed.

---

[7] On epigraphic and archaeological evidence for the presence of Abhayagiri representatives in Java, see Sundberg (2004: 103f., 110–119).

[8] *Cūlavaṃsa* 50.68 (Cūlavaṃsa (1980 [1925, 1927]). On complications of the reading of the term *mahāsaṅghika* in this passage of the *Cūlavaṃsa*, see Gunawardana (1979: 247f.), Cousins (2012: 121f).

Buddhist authors were well informed of the literary landscape of India during this era, maintaining connections with intellectual centers in India including within the Bengal region. The grammars of Moggallana, Sariputta and Sangharakkhita endeavored to demonstrate that Pali grammar was every bit as refined as that of the Sanskrit language, while simultaneously exuding a concern to preserve the regularity of the grammar of Pali texts as they were transmitted, in an effort to ensure the integrity of the original meaning of the Buddha's teaching.[9] Dandin's seventh century *Kāvyadarśa*, "The Mirror of Poetry," was no less influential in Sri Lanka than it was elsewhere in the region as a foundational text on literary devices and the ideal structure of epic poetry. Sri Lankan authors drew heavily from Dandin's *Mirror* in rendering the *Siyabas Lakara* ("The Ornament of our Own Language"), a tenth century Sinhala work on poetic figures, as well as two centuries later (in Pali) the *Subodhālaṃkāra* ("Lucid Poetics") of Sangharakkhita. Trepidatious towards the martial and erotic subject matter of so much continental *kavya*, the authors of these two treatises encourage poets instead to take the narration of the virtues of the Buddha as their subject matter and inspiration. Congruent with a long-established attitude among Indian literary commentators, however, the authors of these Sri Lankan poetic manuals understood the process of becoming a competent and refined reader (a *sahṛdaya*, "[one who apprehends] with the heart") of poetry as one intimately related to the development of moral character. The author of the *Siyabas Lakara* closely follows Dandin's language in the introductory portion of the *Mirror* to admonish their audience that:

> Language is like a wish-conferring cow that gives what is desirable to those who can use it in the proper manner, but for others it will only impart bovine qualities.
>
> How can those who have not studied the Shastras distinguish between what is excellent (*guṇa*) and what is a blemish (*doṣa*); does the blind person have the capacity to perceive the differences in visual objects?
>
> Therefore the learned men of old who were driven by the desire to enlighten the world composed treatises for those who were entering the beautiful path (*visituru magga*; Skt. *vicitra mārga*).[10]

What was in the Sanskrit poetical tradition a generalized, Aristotelian perception that "good readers" made for good citizens who had internalized norms of good behavior through the study positive and negative literary characters, becomes in the *Siyabas Lakara* (and also in parallel language in the *Subodhālaṃkāra*) a more specific insistence that is a careful study of literature of the appropriate type—literature exemplifying Buddhist virtue, we assume—precipitates one's journey on "the beautiful path" to enlightenment. With respect to Lankan contributions to Indic literature during this prolific age of Buddhist scholasticism on the island, Sri Lankan Buddhist monks wrote the earliest attested Sanskrit grammatical handbook (the *Rūpāvatara* of Dharmakirti) as well as the first attested astrological digest the (*Daivajñakāmadhenu* of Anavamadarshin) in the early second millennium (Gornall, 2020: 121).

---

[9] See Chap. 4 of Gornall (2020).

[10] Translation in Hallisey (2003: 701f.), corresponding to *Siyabas Lakara* I.8–10. Cf. *Kāvyadarśa* vv.4–9.

Works on Buddhist historical themes of this golden era of Pali *kāvya* were also rendered into Sinhala for the sake of presentation to a broader audience, including the *Dāṭhavaṃsa* on the history of Buddha's tooth relic and its transportation to Sri Lanka, along with the *Thūpavaṃsa*, the account of Dutthagamini's construction of the great reliquary at Anuradhapura. Medhankara's thirteenth century *Jinacarita* on the life of the Buddha exemplifies Sri Lankan Pali *kāvya* of the period, juxtaposing ornamental description of the opulence of Siddhartha's young adult palace life with the urgency of renunciation and bliss of escape from worldly life (Duroiselle, 1906).

13.4 Cosmopolitan Literary Idiom in the Kotte Period

Two experimental Pali poems anticipate what would by the fifteenth century become a format of first resort for Sinhala authors: the thirteenth century *Mahanagakula Sandesa*, relating a letter of correspondence from the prelate of the Mahanagakula Temple (in Sri Lanka's central highlands) to one Mahathera Kassapa Sangharakkhita of the city of Arimaddanapura in Pagan (modern Burma); and the other the *Vuttamala Sandesa Sataka*, written sometime around the 1340s by a resident of the Gatara monastic college, describing instructions given to a messenger bird concerning who is told to fly from Dedigama to the temple to Vibhishana at Kelaniya, in order to request that the god ensure the safety of King Parakramabahu V (Barnett, 1905).

The numerous messenger poems written during the reign of Parakramabahu VI (c. 1410–1467) at Kotte (on the outskirts of modern Colombo) offer a glimpse of a remarkably cosmopolitan literary and religious milieu. Sinhala messenger poems of this period uniformly involve the conceit of a poet conveying a message to be delivered by a bird, instructing their avian envoy on the route to take along the way. While Indian Sanskrit *sandeśa*s (following Kalidasa's *Meghadūta*) in most cases involve a message dispatched from a man to his beloved residing some distance away, Sinhala *sandeśa*s of the late medieval period take the form of requests to a god for the welfare of the royal sponsor of the author (involving flight paths to or from the temple to Vibhishana at Kelaniya or the temple to Upulvan at Dondra). These Sinhala poems share titles with a number of Keralan Sanskrit *sandesha*s composed several centuries prior (e.g. *Haṃsa*, *Mayūra* and *Kōkila*), and are also stylistically similar to Keralan examples in their attention to detail with respect to the cadastral specificity of the routes dictated to the messenger birds.[11]

Although the authors of the Sinhala *sandeśa* poems were in most instances Buddhist monks, in addition to the temples to Vibhishana and Upulvan (who is a local

[11] Stephen Berkwitz observes another probable source of influence of South Asian *sandeśa kāvya* in Sri Lanka given the preference for the term "*sandeśa*" over "*dūta*" in titling the poems (2017: 269 n. 73). On Kerala as a center for Sanskrit literary production and preservation from the seventh century, see Kunjunni Raja (1980 [1958]). On the specificity of the geography of southwest India outlined in the *Śuka Sandeśa* of Lakṣmīdāsa and the *Kokila Sandeśa* of Uddaṇḍa, see Unni (1985: 10).

version of Vishnu, in fact[12]) messenger birds are *en route* directed to visit various temples to Shiva, Ganesha, Kali, Aiyanar, and other Hindu gods, exemplary of the high level of religious inclusivism of the period.[13] The destinations of the cuckoo bird of the *Kokila Sandeśaya* (composed c.1450)—showcasing the longest flight path of any Sri Lankan messenger poem—offer a prime illustration of this phenomenon. The poet, a resident monk of a monastic college near Dondra on the southern coast, instructs his Kokila bird to traverse the entire western seaboard of the island, in order to deliver a congratulations to Prince Sapumal, Parakramabahu VI's adopted son, who had just secured victory in his campaign against the northern kingdom of Jaffna. Along the way the bird is instructed to visit: Devinuvara, with its temple to Vishnu-Upulvan; a Naga Kovil in the vicinity of Vellemadama (v.45); Weligama, where "Tamil songs are recited" (v.57); Totagamuva near Hikkaduwa, where the famed scholar-monk Sri Rahula is called "the very manifestation of Skanda upon the earth" (v.84); Paiyagala Vihara, a Buddhist temple with resident Tamil poets and grammarians of different schools (v.97); the Ganesha Kovil near Potupitiya (v.103); the Pattini Shrine near Kotte (vv.115–120); the temple at Munneswaram, where Shiva ("the Moon-turbaned One") resides (v.188); and the temple of Aiyanar ("Ariyan Kovila") at Mavatu-patuna (Mantai) (v.208).[14]

Sri Rahula, the above mentioned "very manifestation of Skanda upon the earth," was a towering scholastic figure of the Kotte period. Another adopted son of Parakramabahu VI, Sri Rahula renounced within the Buddhist Sangha to become principal of the Vijayabahu Pirivena, the Buddhist college at Totagamuwa, a lively center of higher education for both monks and laypeople. In addition to "wearing the Tipitaka around his neck," the author of the *Kōkila Sandeśaya* boasts that Sri Rahula "composes poems in the six languages,"[15] gesturing to the prolific body of poetry and scholarship attributed to him. Legends of this scholar-monk of royal extraction endure to the present day in southwestern Sri Lanka, where he is remembered as having translated the "Yak Tovil" (Yaksha propitiation) ritual corpus from Sanskrit, Telegu, Tamil, Malayaam and other Indian languages into Sinhala (Larsen, 2009: 433), and to have extracted the procedural knowledge of *mantra*s and medicine (*vedakama*) from a visiting cohort of Rishis and Munis from India, rendering it into Sinhala for free distribution in Sri Lanka (Scott, 1994: 199–201). The *Girā Sandeśaya* ("The Parrot's Message"), written at some point between 1450 and 1460, features

[12] On the historical identification of Upulvan (*utpala varṇa*, "the lotus-hued one") with Vishnu, see Holt (2004).

[13] This is again another shared feature between Sinhala *sandeśa* poems and South Indian messenger poems, such as the *Śuka Sandeśa* of Lakṣmīdāsa, *Mayūra Sandeśa* of Udaya, and *Kokila Sandeśa* of Uddaṇḍa, which instruct their messengers to visit major temples at Trivandrum, Calicut, Shrirangam, Kañcipuram, and elsewhere.

[14] The author of the *Kōkila Sandeśaya* remains anonymous, but notably claims to be "deeply learned in the Sinhala and Tamil languages" (*dasana matin däna heḷu demaḷa baṇa tatu*, v.290). Text and translations in Sumanasuriya (1958).

[15] *Kōkila Sandeśaya* v.84. Cf. *Girā Sandeśaya*, v.245. The *Kōkila Sandeśaya* does not tell us which "six languages" are meant, thought traditionally the title of *ṣaḍbhāṣā-parameśvara* designated knowledge of Sanskrit, Prakrit, Magadhi (i.e. Pali), Sauraseni̅, Apabhraṃsa and Paiśāci̅.

Sri Rahula as the recipient of an avian telegram, giving us a sense of the curriculum at the Vijayabahu Pirivena. The anonymous author claims that, in addition to Pali, metrics, grammar Sanskrit poetics, and Tamil poetry and drama were also taught at the college.[16] Setting the scene, the reader is informed that, as the elders of the monastery vigorously discuss the Eighteen Puranas:

> A cohort of Brahmins train there—seated throughout the monastery they dispel intellectual uncertainty with their discriminating acumen, memorizing the meaning of the Vedas while ordering them as is fitting.[17]

It is difficult to know whether or not the author of the *Gira Sandeśaya* is relating their own eye-witness testimony, or reproducing stock descriptive conventions for the sake of poetic embellishment. Collating the references to individuals learned in Sanskrit and Tamil within the Buddhist scholastic milieu of the day (as for example the references from the *Kōkila Sandeśaya* quoted above), we do in any case get a sense of the openness of monastic authors towards literary and scholastic traditions beyond the narrow purview of Pali Buddhist orthodoxy.

Furthermore, little question remains concerning the erudition of Sri Rahula himself: his Sinhala commentary on the twelfth century Pali grammar of Moggallana quotes from no less than fifty-nine Sanskrit texts, most of them grammars and lexicographies.[18] Sri Rahula in his *Pancikāpradīpaya* also imparts to us an intriguing referent to a reference work he calls the *Demala Jātaka Gätapadaya*, a Tamil commentary on the stories of the former lives of the Buddha Gautama, we must assume on the basis of the title (Godakumbura, 1955: 37). Sanctioning the worship of Hindu gods and confirming his affection for Tamil poetic composition, Sri Rahula in his own *Parevi Sandeśaya* ("The Dove's Message") instructs his messenger bird halfway along the journey to Devinuvara to:

> Rest at the temple to Kāli in Bentota and gaze upon those youths—who won't see you upon your perch—where the dancing women arouse the mind, their ample breasts shining like golden plates.[19]

Before finally reaching the temple to Upulvan on the southern tip of the island, Sri Rahula tells his dove to stop off at a Naga Kovil where "vibrant young people gather like a ring of bees set upon a red lotus" (v.133), and afterwards at a Ganesha temple at Velle Madama, where:

> Morning drums sound at the temple to Ganesh—famously named after [its patron] the great merchant Rama Candra—where proficient Tamil poets (*pubudu demaḷa kivi*) sing songs of praise resembling the tender cries of the peacocks.[20]

---

[16] These subjects in addition to poetry and drama in Sanskrit, Pali and Sinhala (*saku magada eḷu demaḷa kav naḷu*) (Girā Sandēśaya (1985), v.227).

[17] *Tiyuṇu näṇin keremin säka nivāraṇa | pamuṇu vamin ekineka samaya kāraṇa | dämuṇu sitin iṅda kara vehera pūraṇa | bamuṇu räsek veda'rut karati dāraṇa* (v.223).

[18] The work is Sri Rahula's *Moggallānapañcikā*, written in 1458, Gornall (2020: 71).

[19] *Rantäṭi ayuru tuṅgu pin piyayuru udala | manaṭi karana aṅganan raṅga dena ipila | unsäṭi balā un salaḷun no pä äla | bentoṭi ne' tera sätapeva kāli kōvilā* (Parevi Sandeśaya (2008), v.72).

[20] *Pasiṅdu rāmasandara vesiṅduge namina | gaṇiṅdu vimana aluyam bera gana gosina | pubudu demaḷa kivi miyuran saha tosina | siniṅdu kekā nada van tiyu gī kiyana* (v.145).

Another work attributed to famed scholar monk, the *Sälalihiṇi Sandeśaya*,[21] reaffirms the cosmopolitan disposition of the court of Parakramabahu VI, telling us that in addition to the temple enshrining the Tooth Relic of the Buddha at Kotte, there was nearby a great temple to Shiva:

> Stop to rest at the charming temple of Ishvara [Shiva],
> Where the smoke of the black aloe and camphor
> Rises to meet the rows of fluttering flags,
> Where the resounding beat of the Mridangam drum
> And the blowing of the conch shells
> Meets the sound of the ringing bells,
> Where Tamil songs of praise are sung
> By the ecstatic throng of devotees.[22]

The transition from the conservative tenor of the monks composing in the twelfth and thirteenth centuries to the conspicuous liberalism of Sri Rahula's day was surely in no small part effected by the broad demographic trends (involving immigration from southern India), as well as the ascension of several families of Tamil and Malayalam extraction to the courts of Sri Lanka's southwest. The courtly bilingualism and religious inclusivism suggested in the poetry of the period is furthermore expressed in the alliances which took place at Kotte, where marriages between members of the royal family with southern Indian princes and princesses were a regular affair, as well as in temple architecture, which conformed to southern Indian tastes.[23]

13.5 The "Little Tradition" of Sinhala Literature

What became of this vibrant, cosmopolitan cultural landscape of southwestern Sri Lanka depicted in Sinhala *sandeśa kāvya* of the fifteenth century? Sri Rahula and his fellow scholar monks stood at the precipice of a transformative and turbulent era of European colonial incursion upon the island, inaugurated by the Portuguese with their arrival in 1506, followed a century and a half later by the Dutch. Much was lost amid the campaign of destruction of religious property throughout coastal Sri

[21] While regarded as an exemplary token of Sinhala poetry of the Kotte period, the attribution of the *Sälalihiṇi Sandeśaya* to Sri Rahula remains tenuous on the basis of the textual record available.

[22] *Kaḷu väl kapurudum atuḷa leḷena dada peḷa* | *suvisal mihiṅgusaksan miṇihaṇḍa pataḷa* | *kärä lol satan pavasana tiyu gī demaḷa* | *manakal isutu kōvilä laginẹ̄ lakaḷa* (Säḷalihiṇi Sandēśaya (1999), v.22).

[23] For a survey of sources and evidence on migration to Sri Lanka from Kerala, see Pathmanathan (2015: 427–449). In his study of the emergence of the goddess Pattini (who derives from Kannagi of the *Cilappatikāram*) at Parakramabahu VI's court at Kotte, Gananath Obeyesekere recovers evidence for the probable of Buddhists from Kerala and other Buddhist centers in South India from the 8th to eleventh centuries, many of whom found a new home in Sri Lanka (see summary at Obeyesekere 1984: 528).

Lanka carried out by the Portuguese, who razed Buddhist and Hindu temples indiscriminately.[24] Additional loss occurred when the Buddhist Sangha itself underwent a fissiparous period of reorganization in the years leading up to and following the British annexation of Sri Lanka in 1815, during which time the major ordination lineages which endure to the present day in Sri Lanka were imported from Siam and Burma.[25]

While a record of most of the scholastic works and *kavya* which we presume to have populated the library shelves of the Vijayabahu Pirivena is no longer available to us, the legacy of the domestication of Indian literature into Sinhala is still present in more demotic forms—in ritual texts, folk drama, popular poetry, and in oral tradition. Beyond the continental Sanskrit *sandeśa* format, which remained a favorite among Sri Lankan poets for centuries,[26] Tamil genres such as *viruttam* and *paraṇi* informed Sinhala "war poetry" (*haṭan kavi*) and erotic verse (Dharmadasa, 1995). Kandyan period Sinhala poets found inspiration in the Hindu epics, popular Indian stories and story collections such as the *Pañcatantra*, the life of king Harishchandra, and the Tamil *Cilappatikāram* (de Silva, 1917; Obeyesekere, 1984). Each using similar phrasing, the authors of three c. seventeenth century Sinhala poems explicitly acknowledge their indebtedness to Tamil sources, these being the *Rāvaṇa Katāva* (a Sinhala *Rāmāyaṇa* emphasizing the tragedy of the war with Rama from the Lankan perspective), the *Mahāpadaraṅga Jātakaya* (an apocryphal Jataka story in which the Buddha-to-be is born as Yuddhisthira (in this version named "Dharmabuddhi")), and the *Vetālan Katāva* (an adaptation of the *Vetāla-pañcavimśatika* or "The twenty-five stories of the goblin") (Godakumbura 1946 and 1955: 178–82). The author of the *Rāvaṇa Katāva* offers this statement of attribution at the outset of their poem:

> Regarding the close of the great era [in which transpired] the war
> involving prosperous Ravana—
> Since we now know very little of what the Tamil teachers (*demala äduru*) knew,
> Unable to give a full account of the story,
> I will narrate an abridged version in Sinhala verse.[27]

The poem goes on to incorporate an episode in which Hanuman is captured and offered as a sacrifice to a subterranean temple of the goddess Kali, incorporating the premise of a well-known supplement to a number of vernacular Indian *Rāmāyaṇa*s in which other of Ravana's brothers—Mahiravana or Ahiravana—draw Hanuman to

[24] For a study of the social dynamics of the period of Portuguese involvement in Sri Lanka, see Strathern (2008).

[25] On the state of monastic education in Sri Lanka in the eighteenth century, see Blackburn (2001).

[26] In his 1949 study of Sinhala *sandeśa*-s (1962 [1949]), P.B. Sannasgala names 114 Sinhala messenger poems, beginning with the late fourteenth century *Mayura Sandeśaya* through to a number of titles published in print in the nineteenth and twentieth centuries (Sannasgala 1962 [1949]).

[27] *Rāvaṇa Katāva*, v.3. For complete text and translation, see appendix to Henry (2023).

the underground realm of "Pātāla Lanka."[28] Other Sinhala works of the Kandyan period reproduce popular Indian variations on the *Rāmāyaṇa* in their domestication of the epic to Lankan soil. The *Sītāvaka Haṭana* (c. 1585), a poem commemorating a battle between the kingdom of Sitavaka and the Portuguese, describes the discovery of baby Sita born out of a pot buried in a farmers field—the pot had initially been filled with the blood of one hundred feudal lords of the island on by the forces of Ravana, in a vicious coup to consolidate power on the part of the ancient demon-king.[29] The introduction of the Freudian complication that Sita is in some sense Ravana's "daughter" (adopted or born of Ravana's wife, Mandodari) is also found in throughout the Indian tradition.[30]

Several variations of Sinhala dance-drama which developed into full expression during the Kandyan period also bear evidence of Indian influence in their themes, technical execution, and ritual dress. The myriad ornaments and waist garment (*inahediya*) of the Kandyan dance costume bear striking visual similarity to those of Kathakali performers of South India. The Kolam dance of southwestern Sri Lanka, a largely impromptu performance structured around a plot concerning the efforts of a king to satisfy the cravings of his pregnant queen, involve ecstatic performances and invocations to Bhadra Kali clearly reminiscence of the "Kolam Tullal" apotropaic rite performed in Kerala (Raghavan, 1967: 77–84) (Sinhala *kolam* itself derives from a Tamil/Malayalam term, in this context referring to someone wearing a distinctive costume).

Vannam, a class of solo dances enacted by a single performer, take inspiration from Hindu themes, including the "Ganesha Vannama," an invocation to the god Ganesh, the "Ishvara Vannama," a reenactment of Shiva's search for Parvati in the Himalaya mountains, and the "Hanuman Vannama," in which the actor masquerades as a monkey (in a performance bearing strong affinities to the dance of the Pandaram or Sadhus of South Travancore who would traditionally go on alms rounds similarly attired (Raghavan, 1969: 131–33)). "Nāḍagam" or Sinhala folk plays, with origins probably in the eighteenth century, developed on the basis of Sri Lankan Tamil models, themselves inspired by continental performance styles (Pieris, 1974).

[28] For a study of *Rāmāyaṇa* stories involving Hanuman's rescue of Rama and Lakshmana from the subterranean kingdom of "Peacock Ravana," see Lutgendorf (2004). For a translation of the Tamil version of the story, the *Mayil Irāvaṇaṉ Katai*, see Zvelebil (1987).

[29] *Sītāvaka Haṭana*, vv.125–32.

[30] In several north Indian versions Sita is conceived by Ravana's wife, Mandodari; in one Kannada folk version Sita is born out of a sneeze of Mandodari; in Telugu folk songs Sita is discovered as an infant in a pond and brought to Ravana by his servants, and elsewhere (Ramanujan, 1986: 65, 1991: 147; Shulman, 1986: 118).

13.6 The Tamil Literary Milieu and Desiderata for Future Research

While I have throughout this essay gestured to the probable points of contact with Tamil and Malayalam speakers which informed Sinhala literary tradition, I have said relatively little about Sri Lankan Tamil literature itself. There is a substantial corpus of Sri Lankan Tamil works, most of it dating from the sixteenth century onwards, including legendary histories (*tala-purāṇams*) of several of the island's most significant Shaiva temples, secular and religious poetry, and lexical and grammatical works. Very little of this corpus is available in translation, with a good deal of more scholarly study on the subject yet to be undertaken. Motivated by the tragic destruction of the Jaffna Library its archive of rare books and manuscripts in 1983, the Noolaham Foundation has recent years undertaken to make out-of-print Tamil books available through open-access, as well as to digitize Tamil manuscripts in private Sri Lankan collections for scholarly use. Further exploration of Sri Lankan Tamil literature would serve to enhance our understanding of the circulation of works and persons between Sri Lanka and the subcontinent, as it is clear that the authors of many of these compositions had regular contact with the Indian mainland.[31] Additional comparative work on the Tamil source materials at play in Kandyan period Sinhala poems on Indian Hindu themes could furthermore offer a more defined sense of the body of Tamil works circulating in Sri Lanka from the early modern period, especially those which enjoyed a bilingual readership.

There is in addition a story to be told concerning the transmission of literary works from Sri Lanka *to* India, as Tamil authors (unlike Sinhala authors) had a potential continental audience for their compositions. One recognized example is the history of the reception of the *Kaṇṭirācaṉ Oppāri* ("The Lamentation of the King of Kandy"), an early nineteenth century Tamil poem recalling the tragedy of the disinheritance of Sri Vikrama Rajasinha, the last sovereign monarch of Sri Lanka deposed by the British in collaboration with a group of disaffected Lankan noblemen. The subject of the tragedy of the fall of the Sri Vikrama Rajasinha endured as a subject of literary and dramatic interest in Thanjur—where the king and his surviving family ultimately found themselves in exile—with stage adaptations of "Kaṇṭi Nāṭakam" performed there into the 1960s (Nataṉ, 2012: 39).

This example reinforces the principle theme of this essay: the fact that Sri Lanka was never "islanded" with respect to the broader literary cultural and scholastic trends of the greater South Asian region, as Sri Lankan authors have for over two millennia labored to domesticate Indian literature and literary theory in conformity with local customs, tastes, and theological concerns. Sri Lankan authors made valuable contributions in Sanskrit, Pali and Tamil to be received in India, while others simultaneously developed Sinhala literature under the inspiration of continental models giving rise to unique and intricate forms of poetic expression.

---

[31] On continental Tamil models for the *Taṭcaṇa Kayilāca Purāṇam*, a c. fifteenth century *tala-purāṇam* of the Koneswaram Shiva Temple, see McKinley (2020).

References

Primary Sources

Cūlavaṃsa, being the more recent part of the Mahāvaṃsa. (1980 [1925, 1927]). (Wilhelm Geiger, Ed.). Pali Text Society.
Dīpavaṃsa: The Dipavamsa. (1908). (W. Geiger, Ed.). Pali Text Society.
Girā Sandēśaya. (1985). (Nanadasēna Ratnapāla, Ed.). Ratna Pot Prakāśayō.
Haṃsa Sandeśaya. (2005). (Kristi Da Silva, Ed.). Ratna Pot Prakāśayō.
Parevi Sandeśaya of Śrī Rāhula. (2008). *R.A. Liyana Āracci.* Samayavardhana Pothala.
Sälalihiṇi Sandēśaya: purāṇa sannaya saha artha pradīpikā. (1999). (Bandusēna Guṇasēkara, Ed.). Sarasvatī Prakāśana.

Secondary Sources

Barnett, L. (1905). The Manavulu-Sandesaya: Text and translation. *The Journal of the Royal Asiatic Society of Great Britain and Ireland* [no issue no.], 265–283.
Berkwitz, S. (2017). Sinhala sandēśa poetry in a cosmopolitan context. In Z. Biedermann & A. Strathern (Eds.), *Sri Lanka at the crossroads of history* (pp. 94–112). University College London Press.
Blackburn, A. (2001). *Buddhist learning and textual practice in eighteenth-century Lankan Monastic culture.* Princeton University Press.
Collins, S. (1990). On the very idea of a Pāli Canon. *Journal of the Pali Text Society, 15*, 89–126.
Coninghan, R. (1995). Monks, Caves and Kings: A reassessment of the nature of early Buddhism in Sri Lanka. *World Archaeology, 27*(2), 222–242.
Coninghan, R., Manuel, M., Davis, C., & Gunawardhana, P. (2017). Archaeology and cosmopolitanism in early historic and medieval Sri Lanka. In Z. Biedermann & A. Strathern (Eds.), *Sri Lanka at the crossroads of history.* University College London Press.
Cousins, L. (2012). The teachings of the Abhayagiri School. In P. Skilling, et al. (Eds.), *How Theravāda is Theravāda? Exploring Buddhist identities* (pp. 67–128). Silkworm Books.
de Silva, W. A. (1917). The popular poetry of the Sinhalese. *Journal of the Ceylon Branch of the Royal Asiatic Society, 24.1*(68), 27–66.
de Zilva Wickremasinghe, D. M. (1934). The evolution of the language of the Pāli Canon. *The Journal of the Ceylon Branch of the Royal Asiatic Society of Great Britain & Ireland, 33*(87), 18–33.
Dharmadasa, K. N. O. (1995). Literature in Sri Lanka: The sixteenth, seventeenth and eighteenth centuries. In K. M de Silva (Ed.), *University of Peradeniya, history of Sri Lanka* (Vol. 2, pp. 471–490). Sridevi.
Duroiselle, C. (1906). *Jinacarita or "The Career of the Conqueror"* British Burma Press.
Godakumbura, C. E. (1946). The Dravidian element in Sinhalese. *Bulletin of the School of Oriental and African Studies, University of London, 11*(4), 837–841.
Godakumbura, C. E. (1955). *Sinhalese literature.* The Colombo Apothecaries' Company.
Godakumbura, C. E. (1967). A note on the Jānakīharaṇa. *The Journal of the Ceylon Branch of the Royal Asiatic Society of Great Britain & Ireland [new Series], 11*, 93–98.
Gornall, A. (2020). *Rewriting Buddhism: Pali literature and monastic reform in Sri Lanka, 1157–1270.* University College London Press.
Gunawardana, R. A. L. H. (1979). *Robe and plough: Monasticism and economic interest in early Medieval Sri Lanka.* The Association for Asian Studies/University of Arizona Press.

Hallisey, C. (2003). Works and Persons in Sinhala literary culture. In S. Pollock (Ed.), *Literary cultures in history: Reconstructions from South Asia* (pp. 689-746). University of California Press.
Henry, J. W. (2023). *Ravana's Kingdom: The Ramayana and Sri Lankan history from below*. Oxford University Press.
Holt, J. C. (2004). *The Buddhist Viṣṇu: Religious transformation, politics, and culture*. Colombia University Press.
Kunjunni Raja, K. (1980 [1958]). *The Contribution of Kerala to Sanskrit Literature*. University of Madras.
Lokubandara, W. J. M. (2007). *The Mystique of Sigiriya: Whispers of the mirror wall*. Godage International Publishers.
Larsen, H. M. (2009). *Buddhism in popular culture: The case of Sri Lankan "Tovil Dance"*. Ph.D., dissertation, University of Bergen, Norway.
Lutgendorf, P. (2004). "Hanumān's adventures underground: The narrative logic of a *Rāmāyaṇa* 'Interpolation". In M. Bose (Ed.), *The Ramayana Revisited*. Oxford University Press.
Malalasekera, G. P. (1928). *The Pali Literature of Ceylon*. M.D. Gunasena.
McKinley, A. (2020). Making Lanka the Tamil way: A temple history at the crossroads of landscapes & watersheds. *South Asian History and Culture, 11*(3), 254–276.
Nāṭaṉ, C. (2012). *Kaṇṭirācaṉ Katai*. New Century Book House.
Obeyesekere, G. (1984). *Cult of the Goddess Pattini*. University of Chicago Press.
Pathmanathan, S. (2015). *Facets of Sri Lankan history and culture*. Kumaran Book House.
Pieris, E. (1974). The origin and development of Simhala Nādagam. *Journal of the Sri Lanka Branch of the Royal Asiatic Society [new Series], 18*, 27–40.
Pollock, S. (2006). *The language of the gods in the world of men: Sanskrit, culture, and power in Premodern India*. University of California Press.
Raghavan, M. D. (1967). *Siṅhala Näṭum: Dances of the Sinhalese*. M.D. Gunasena & Co.
Raghavan, M. D. (1969). *India in Ceylonese history, society and culture*. Indian Council for Cultural Relations/Asia Publishing House.
Ramanujan, A. K. (1991). Three hundred Rāmāyaṇas: Five examples and three thoughts on translation. In P. Richman (Ed.), *Many Rāmāyaṇas: The diversity of narrative tradition in South Asia*. University of California Press.
Ramanujan, A. K. (1986). Two Realms of Kannada Folklore. In S. Blackburn & A. K. Ramanujan (Eds.), *Another harmony: New essays on the Folklore of India* (pp. 41–75). Oxford University Press.
Rhys Davids, C. W. (1894), Review of T.B. Pāṇabokke's 'The Megha Dūta by Kālidāsa with a Sinhalese Paraphrase'. *Journal of the Royal Asiatic Society of Great Britain and Ireland* [no issue no.], 632–633.
Sannasgala, P. B. (1962 [1949]). *Sinhala Sandēśa Sāhityaya*. Lake House Press.
Scott, D. (1994). *Formations of ritual: Colonial and anthropological discourses on the Sinhala Yaktovil*. University of Minnesota Press.
Sen, A. (1956). *Asoka's edicts*. Published for the Institute of Indology by the Indian Publicity Society.
Seneviratne, S. D. S. (1887). *Kālidāsa Nṛtya Pota, the historical tragedy entitled Kalidas*. F. Cooray.
Shulman, D. (1986). Battle as metaphor in Tamil folk and classical traditions. In S. Blackburn & A. K. Ramanujan (Eds.), *Another harmony: New essays on the folklore of India* (pp. 105–130). Oxford University Press.
Sumanasuriya, E. T. W. (1958). *A critical edition of the Kōkilasandēśaya with an introduction*. Ph.D., dissertation, University of London.
Sundberg, J. R. (2004). The wilderness monks of the Abhayagirivihara and the origins of Sino-Javanese esoteric Buddhism. *Bijdragen Tot De Taal-, Land- En Volkenkunde, 160*(1), 95–123.
Strathern, A. (2008). *Kingship and conversion in sixteenth-century Sri Lanka: Portuguese imperialism in a Buddhist land*. Cambridge University Press.

Tilakasiri, J. (1986). The influence of Sanskrit Poetical Motifs and technique on Sinhala Poetry. In W. Morgenroth (Ed.), *Sanskrit and World Culture: Proceedings from the Fourth World Sanskrit Conference of the International Association of Sanskrit Studies* (pp. 136–142). Akademie Verlag Berlin.

Unni, N. P. (1985). *Śukasandeśa of Lakṣmīdāsa.* Nag Publishers.

Zvelebil, K. (1987). *Two Tamil Folktales: The story of King Mataṉakāma; The story of Peacock Rāvaṇa.* Motilal Banarsidass.

Chapter 14
Devotionalism in the Cultural and Social Spheres of India: Popular and Monastic Aspects of Hinduism in History

Nalini Rao

Abstract Popular Hinduism can be understood by examining into the institution of the Guru, name the Hindu monastery or *matha*. Gurus are held in great respect due to their wisdom, exemplary behavior, and spiritual knowledge. The gurus as heads of Hindu monasteries are ascetics and are considered to have performed miracles With the growth of Hindu monasteries during the medieval period, particularly of Vedanta *mathas* in South India, *bhakti* (devotion) began to grow among the populace as a major attitude towards the guru as well as towards God. Vaisnavite Vedanta monastic establishments, particularly of Ramanuja and Madhwacharya redefined as devotion towards the guru whose spiritual stature was similar to that of God. This article investigates into the reconciliation of two opposing concepts, asceticism and *bhakti*. It queries into the phenomenon of the ways the ascetic head of Vaisnavite Vedanta monastery redefined, redirected or re-intepreted *bhakti* into the monastic norms of asceticism, teaching and spirituality. What were the changes in doctrine, worship, and imagery within the monastery that attracted numerous devotees? What were the reasons for *bhakti* to become an intrinsic part of the religious doctrine of the guru and of his institution, the *matha*?

Keywords *Bhakti* · Guru · Matha · Vedanta · Vrndavana · Vaisnavism · Monasticism

14.1 Introduction

Religious devotionalism has been recognized by Hinduism as intense love for God, an experience, and a path. It is known as *bhakti* and its cultural and religious role has been tremendous. During the medieval period, its social impact led to the rise of saints, sages, and social reformers whose musical compositions inspired popular devotion. Although there has been significant research on the history of the saints of

---

N. Rao (✉)
Soka University of America, CA Aliso Viejo, USA
e-mail: nrao@soka.edu

L. Vemsani (ed.), *Handbook of Indian History*,
https://doi.org/10.1007/978-981-97-6207-1_14

the *bhakti* movement and their poetry, there have been few research on the influence of devotionalism on Hindu monasteries. This paper examines the influence of *bhakti* on Hindu monastic organizations and the mode of popularization on the Indian monastic system. *Bhakti* as a popular element within Hinduism arose almost at the same time when monasteries emerged and developed; there appears to be an inexplicable relationship between the two. The Hindu monastery is an institution of the ascetic or *sannyasin* who has renounced the world, while *bhakti* is a subjective experience of intense devotion. The two ideologies appear to be in conflict and a conundrum. It raises questions regarding the method and path of *bhakti* yoga as a means for the popularity of the monastic system. How did the ascetic head redefine, redirect, or re-interpret *bhakti* into the monastic norms of asceticism, teaching, and spirituality? What were the significant changes in doctrine, worship, ritual, or imagery within the monastery that attracted the populace? Was it the charisma of the ascetic head (Guru) who weaved the philosophical concepts and *bhakti* poetry or were there other social influences.

14.2 *Bhakti* as Popular Devotionalism

Bhakti meant a simple, sincere devotion to a deity. It encompasses a range of meanings—it is a subjective experience of sincere, intense devotion, a yogic path for God realization as well as a rasa or aesthetic delight (Frazier, 2013). It has deep roots in Indian culture and associated with First Millennial texts such as the *Sveteshvara Upanishad* and the *Bhagavad Gita* (Robinson, 2005, 28–30; Pechilis Prentiss, 1999, 26–32, 217). With the composition of the *Bhagvata Purana* around 10th C C.E., a new theory of devotional aesthetics arose, the *bhakti rasa* that was incorporated into dramatics, poetics and philosophy. Followers of Basava, Vallabha Caitanya, Ramananda, Kabir, Tulsidas, Surdas, Mirabai recited and sang the poetic compositions of their saints. However, the beginnings of devotion may be said to have begun by the Nayanars in South India who sang emotionally about Siva. These were paralleled by the Alvar saints (seventh–eighth century CE) who preached loving adoration towards Vishnu (Bhandarkar, 1929).[1] They were known for their love and pleasure over the physical form of *sat, chit, ananda* (truth, consciousness and bliss) and based their philosophy and spirituality on the *Bhāgavad Gītā* and the *Upanishads*. The earliest three of the traditional list of Alvars (Saroyogin, Bhutoyogin and Mahadyogin) were ascetics as well as lovers of God.[2] Saints, such as Srinathmuni composed verses which was later transformed into a path (*Prapati marga)* of *bhakti*

---

[1] Permission has been granted non exclusive and no fee by the publisher of my book *The Hindu Monastery: Social, Religious and artistic Traditions* 2020 by Rowman & Littlefield "all rights reserved". Few parts of this article have been published in the book.

Alvar means the person that has dived deep in the ocean of spirituality.

[2] The 12 famous Alwar saints were Visnu Chitta, Andala, Kulashekar, Vipra Narayan, Munwahan, Poyagai, Bhutatta, Peya, Bhaktisar, Neelan, Madhur, Namma. They were superior to ordinary folks and wandered from place to place addressing songs of love.

by Ramanujacharya. Later in the thirteenth century CE, Maharashtra produced the remarkable *Bhakti* saint, Jnanesvar. While Jnanesvar was a brahmin, his contemporary Namdev, who addressed his songs to a Nirguna (formless God) belonged to the low caste. Other saint poets of Maharasthra include Eknath, Tukaram, and Ramdas. In northern India Ramanand collected a remarkable band of disciples including Kabir, the weaver, Raidas the cobbler, Dhanna the Jat farmer, Sena the barber and Pipa the Rajput. These disciples who had broken the caste barrier, wrote and sang poetry that moved the heart. In North India, Nimbarka in eleventh century CE was also a leader of the *bhakti* movement and stressed self-surrender to God and devotion to the Guru. In their songs of *bhakti* God *(saguna* or God with attributes) was called Rama or Krishna in the Hindu fashion or Rahim or Karim.

After the death of Kabir (who had been raised by a Muslim weaver in Varanasi) in 1518 CE disciples of the *bhakti* saints in turn, who composed poetry helped the process of co-existence. Other *bhakti* poets who sang about the attributes of a God (*saguna*) were Surdas (1483–1563 C.E.), Mirabai (1498–1546), Chaitanya (1486–1533), Sankkaradev (1449–1569) and Tulsidas (1532–1623). In northwestern and eastern India, people gave their hearts to Tulsidas's magnificent rendering of the *Ramayana* in folk verse. In southern India, it was captured in Tamil by Kamban. On the other hand, love for Krishna formed the themes for the verses of Surdas, Mirabai and Chaitanya. Chaitanya Mahaprabhu's movement in the sixteenth century CE and that of the Goswamies provided a detailed explanation of *bhakti rasa* that transferred it to theology and religious consciousness.[3] *Vaisnava* devotionalism found the emotion of *sringara* in the love of Krishna and the *gopis* as symbols of union of God and human souls which took many forms. It included the form of friendship, *sakhya* as in the case of Arjun and Krishna, the tender fondness of parents for their children, *vatsalya*, as in the love for Krishna of his parents, servitude, *dasya* of devotees to Krishna and *santa rasa* as fulfilled love with an intensity *ujjvala*.[4] All *bhakti* poets propagated tolerance, whether taking a *saguna* or *nirguna* stance.

In addition, *bhakti* songs might have been influenced by Sufi saints for mutual accommodation. Sufi doctrine particularly of Wahadat-ul-wujud's concepts of God may have played a part in the rediscovery of the God of the *bhakti* poets. However one should also note that Abu Yazid–al-Bistami who lived in the ninth century C.E. had access to the Advaita stand in Hindu philosophy. Hindu poets recognized and accepted the influence of Sufism, as God was loving in both the religious sects. The religious divide between the two had been crossed, although in Sufism God was not portrayed with forms or attributes, but the God of all the poets offered mercy and grace.

While *Bhakti* became popular due to the compositions and followers of Vallabhacharya, Chaitanya, Ramananda, Kabir, Tulsidas, Surdas, and Mirabai in North India, in the South, monasteries and ascetic heads of monasteries incorporated them and provided *bhakti* with a philosophical basis and directed it towards the Guru. *Bhakti* is an attitude which a disciple/devotee shows to his Guru as the personal

[3] Prabhupāda, (1975).

[4] Rupagoswami, (1975).

manifestation of the deity (Mlecko, 1982).[5] The *Bhagavad Gita* introduced *bhakti yoga* and asserted devotion shown to God (1 V. 8), as well as towards the Guru. It states "Give me your mind and give me your heart, give me your offerings and your adoration; and with your soul in harmony, and making me your goal supreme, you shall in truth come to me (IX, 34). In the Gita, Krishna is both Lord and Guru (XVIII, 75). The ascendancy of both *bhakti* and the guru occurred during the 7th C C.E. after the decline of Buddhism. In the *Narada Bhakti Sutras* a systematic account of *bhakti* philosophy is described, called affection and submission. The *Puranas*, such as the *Visnu and Padma Puarans*, as well as the *Tantras* all gave importance to the Guru, who could be within an institution of the monastery or outside the organization.

14.3 The Hindu Monastery

Hindu monasteries have not been popular and a brief introduction about the Guru, the institution, and the relationship between the God and Guru will provide the rationale for the link between popular devotion and the monastery. Although Hindu monasteries have been popular for the past seven hundred years particularly in South India, scholars have not paid sufficient attention in comparison to Hindu temples (Granoff & Shinohara, 1994). While numerous studies on Buddhist monasteries have been published, Hindu monasteries remain nearly as obscure to the western scholar today as they did years ago (Schopen, 1997). Studies on the monastery have tended to focus merely on the philosophical commentaries written by monastic heads of *Vedanta mathas*, namely the *Advaita, Visithadvaita* and *Dvaita mathas.* Among them, are some significant publications such as by Cenkner (1983), *The Teaching Tradition* which focuses on Adi Sankaracarya (Cenkner, 1983). In 1992 Yoshitsugu Sawai elaborated on the doctrines of Adi Sankaracharya in his book, *The Faith of Ascetics and Lay Smartas*, I.S. Madugula, G.C. Pande (Mudugula, 1985) Pavan Varma; Harold Coward (Coward, 2008). B.N.K Sharma, in his *History of the Dvaita School of Vedanta and its Literature* (Sharma, 1961), and Philosophy *of Sri Madhvacarya in 1962* (Sharma, 1962). Subsequent publications include those by C.M. Padmanabhachar, Hayavadana Rao, and Acharya Bannanje Govindacarya (Padmanabhacharya, 1983). The role of the monastery in relation to *bhakti* in a historical context is a complex topic and is replete with varied problems, especially in terms of literary and historical evidences. Books have been written from the standpoint of extolling the Guru in a monastery and more importance has been given to Hindu temples while the monastery has been relegated to the background despite the living Guru is still very popular, powerful, and revered.

The term for a Hindu monastery is *matha.* The Hindu *matha* has a more expansive function and a more flexible organizational structure than a Christian monastery (Leclercq & Misrahi, 1961). Apart from being a place of residence for the ascetic (Sawai, 1992), it is a rest house for travelers, a religious, and educational institution

[5] Mlecko (p. 42, 46)—Year not given.

a monastic school. In the late medieval period, grew to be a center of philosophy (Cenkner, 1983), as well as a place of worship headed by an ascetic (*sanyasin*) who has renounced worldly life (Yocum, 1990).The *matha* may be defined as an organized integral system of education, worship, feeding, and lodging, consisting of a community of disciples and headed by a Guru, who is normally an ascetic (Rao, 2020). Although evidences about the existence of *mathas* go back to 2nd BCE, It was only after the decline of Buddhist *saṅgha* that Hindu monasticism arose as an institution with an ascetic as the head of the order. After the gradual waning of Buddhist *sanghas*, various types of educational institutions arose. Hindu education was in the ascendancy around 7th C C.E. and many Hindus consecrated their lives to a life of celibate study. The *matha* appears to have been an amalgamtion of functions of some of the existing educational institutions, such as *gurukulas, aśramas, ghaṭikas, vidyalayas, vidyapitahas, brahmapuris* and *agraharas* in South India but due to historical circumstances, it was adapted by wandering ascetics with an organizational structure, norms and principles (8th C C.E.) and later in the 9th c as full-fledged institutions.

The head of a monastery is often a celibate (called here Guru). The term Guru means a teacher, in the narrow sense of the term, but a Guru within the institution of a *matha*, is an ascetic, a celibate, philosopher-monk.[6] He follows specific rules and norms, beliefs and practices affiliated to the original founder of the organization of a particular *matha*. He maintains the *guruparampara* (lineage of Gurus) and is responsible for the interpretation of religious doctrines. Often, the Guru solves disputes, and even functions as a fund raiser. His learning, and charismatic leadership elicits admiration and respect from the community. Today, an additional function of the Guru is proper guidance in matters of religious issues at various levels. His learning elicits admiration and respect from the community. Although known by various terms, such as *jagadguru* or world teacher, *swami*, *ananda* and *tirtha*, the most common epithet is *acharya* or simply Guru. The chief aim of the Hindu monastery is to preserve the body of religious doctrine composed by its founder (or later Gurus), and to transmit these traditions for an ordered society. This determines the teachings, beliefs and practices of the disciples, students, and lay followers (or devotees). The contributions of a monastery to philosophical literature have been extraordinary, particularly those of *Vedanta mathas* whose heads have compiled numerous commentaries on the sacred scriptures, *Vedas* and *Upanisads*.[7] The ultimate religious purpose of the *matha* is to help the individual to attain *moksa* (liberation) from *samsara* (bondage through attachment). The aim of the Guru is to help his disciples to discover the "self" which is hidden beneath layers of ignorance, through a discipline of the mind and body, spiritual precepts, and worship. The practices might range from pure meditation to physical rigors, prayer, *mantra* (chants), and forms of worship. At a collective

---

[6] There are approximately 95 monastic orders in Hinduism, and about 75 adhere to celibacy.

[7] *Vedanta mathas* are the *Advaita, Visisthadvaita* and *Dvaita mathas* that uphold the authority of the *Vedas* and *Upanisads*. *Vedanta* developed into a major philosophical system in the medieval period. They consist of *Advaita* (monistic) order, the *Visithadvaita* (qualified monistic) and *Dvaita* (dualist) systems all of which believed in the concepts of *Brahman* (God), *Atma* (soul), *Dharma, Karma*, and other *tattvas* (realities) and adhered to the *Vedas* and *Upanishads*.

level, within the monastery and community at large, there is a pervading emphasis on the Guru who has attained liberation through renunciation and who has realized God. Thus, *mathas* with the leadership of the Guru, have preserved and helped in the transmission of religious and philosophical traditions thereby playing an important socio-religious role. It was the pivotal role of the Guru that would bring him to the forefront from twelfth century CE onwards till today.

Mathas went through a long trajectory of growth till it developed to be of seminal importance to the community. Between the seventh and twelfth centuries CE they went through an evolutionary period when they grew to be semi-independent institutions, in three different regions. They developed as independent institutions in three major areas: (a) Shaiva *mathas* in Central India, under the Kalachuris, (b) in Tamilnadu in Chola and Pandyan domains in Tamilnadu, (c) Andhra (under the Kakatiyas) and Karnataka under the Chalukyas of Badami, Chalukyas of Kalyani, Rashtrakutas and Hoysalas. At the same time was the growth of Lingayat *mathas* founded by Basaveshvara, who believed in the supreme all loving God opposed the caste system. Thus, the growth of Shaiva *mathas* as formidable centers of both secular and religious education laid a solid foundation for the growth of Vedanta *mathas* that institutionalized the system of monasticism.

14.4 Vedanta *Mathas*

With the rise of the Vedanta *mathas* that spread from Karnataka to all parts of South India, *bhakti* received a new impetus. The importance and popularity of the Vedanta *mathas* was their philosophical orientation. The basis of their doctrines was the Upanishadic theistic philosophy, rooted in the authority of the *Vedas*.[8] The Vedanta *mathas* include: the Advaita Vedānta *mathas* (that arose in the 9th C C.E.) founded by Adi Sankaracharya (788–820 CE), Vishishtadvaita *mathas* (between eleventh and twelfth centuries CE.) founded by Ramanujacharya (1017–1137 CE.); and Dvaita *mathas* (thirteenth and fourteenth centuries CE) founded by Madhwacharya (1199–1278 C C.E.)[9] The growth of *Vedanta mathas* was largely due to their systematization of Vedic philosophy, royal patronage and individual identity. They were headed by charismatic ascetic Gurus whose lineage, ideology and practice of *bhakti* has continued to play a key role in socio-religious matters. They institutionalized the

[8] The *Prasthānatrayī* consists of the *Brahma Sūtras*, known as *Nyāya Prasthāna* (that included Badrayana's systematic commentary on the *Upanishads*, fifth century BCE), the *Upaniṣads*, known as Upadesha Prasthana, and the Bhagavad Gita, known as *Sādhana Prasthāna*. Cenkner, 1981 p. 19 Cenkner, William. *A Tradition of Teacher:* Shankara *and the Jagadgurus Today*. Columbia, Mo.: South Asia Books, 1983.

[9] Other Vedanta organizations include the *Dvaitadvaita Darshan* of Nimbarka (12 or 13th century CE), The Shuddha-advaita of Vallabhacharya (15–16th C), the *Achintya-bhedabheda* of Chaitanya Mahaprabhu (16th century CE), and *Akshar-Puroshottam* of Bhagwan Swaminarayan (19th century CE). The Ramakrishna Vedanta Society (*Ashram/Matha)* founded by Swami Vivekananda (19th century CE) belongs to the *Advaita* tradition of Shankaracharya.

monastic system, developed a deep symbolic relation between the Guru and God, and used visual symbols on the physical body, worship along with the incorporation of *bhakti*.

14.5 Advaita Vedanta *Mathas*

Adi Sankaracharya is known for his philosophy of *Advaita* (non-dualism/monism), the essence of which is the union of the *Atman* (individual soul) with the *Brahmaṇ* (universal soul). His noble achievement was the founding of four *mathas*, each headed by an ascetic philosopher (Cenkner, 2001, 110). *Advaita* monasteries were established in four different zones of the subcontinent: Sringeri (Sawai, 1992), Dwaraka, Puri, Badrinath (and in addition, Kanchipuram) as principal seats of learning. Each *matha* was headed by an *acharya*, titled *Saṅkaracharya*, and recognized as a *Jagadguru* (Sawai, 1992) or world teacher who claimed direct lineage from the founder.[10] Under the leadership of the 'Guru-*sanyasins,*' *mathas* became educational and philosophical institutions with their own system of pilgrimage sites, organization, ritual, and philosophy. During the post-Sankaracharya period, *Advaita* became a form of personal religion and philosophy, and institutional aspects of monasteries took place in an unprecedented fashion. The *Advaita* monasteries became a *vyakhyanasimhasana* (throne of exposition) and it developed into a *samsthana* (region under its jurisdiction, resembled kingdoms of royalty) in Sringeri where it held lands as a trust (Shankara *pitha.* Sawai, 1992). Although Shankara worshipped (five gods) personal gods in temples and within the premises of the *matha*, the philosophy of Advaita was idealistic, with an emphasis on *jnana* (knowledge) than *bhakti*.

14.6 Vaishnava Vedanta Monasteries

About four hundred years after Sahnkaracharya organized the monastic order, Ramanujacharya (1017–1137 CE) formulated the philosophy of qualified monism, by which he refuted Shankaracharya's doctrine of *maya* (illusion) and incorporated the concept of *bhakti* (devotion) turning to Vaishnavism. Vaishnavism had emerged by 750 CE as a popular religion in North India, particularly with the gradual decline of Buddhism and Jainism (Bhandarkar, 1929). It had incorporated various religious streams of thought and centered around the cults of Viṣhṇu, Narayaṇa and Krishna-Vasudeva, as well as mythical and historical heroes. The composition of *Puraṇas*, such as *Viṣhṇu Puraṇa, Padma Puraṇa, Harivamsha*, and the *Bhagavad Gita*, had a

---

[10] Jyotir *matha* at Badri in the North, Sarada *pitha* at Dvaravati (Dwarka) in the west, Govardhan-*matha* at Puri in the east.

mass appeal (Bhagowalia, 1980). The flexibility and assimilative character of Vaishnavism and its popularity, contrasted with the rigidity of Vedic fire-worship. This was due to the *avatara* (incarnation) theory that assimilated various local gods/cults such as Narasimha, Varaha, Rama, Krishna, Buddha that narrowed the gulf between followers of Buddhism and orthodox Hinduism.[11] The divine appearance of God in the form of living beings, became a central feature of the Vaishnava tradtion. In addition, the doctrine of the Bhagavata cult with Krishna–Vasudeava held a unique place within *bhakti* (yoga and *rasa*) and *marga* in the Gita (Gonda, 1977).[12] However, the philosophical and rational basis for the basis of *bhakti* were the teachings of Ramanujacharya who held that liberation was attained mainly through *bhakti* (Mlecko, 1982, 47).

Ramanujacharya refuted Sankaracharya's doctrine of spiritual monism which had negated *bhaktivada*, the doctrine of love and faith. He argued that if there is only one universal sprit, there is no scope for love or devotion which necessarily postulated two separate entities—the lover and the beloved. Liberation can be attained mainly through *bhakti*. He placed the *bhakti* cult on a firm philosophical basis by expounding the doctrine of qualified monism or *Vishishtadvaita* which recognized three eternal principles, individual soul, the insensate world and the supreme soul (the creator), thereby reconciling his philosophy of qualified non-dualism with *bhakti*. He also elaborated the system of worship in temples and propagated sixteen modes of worship to be practiced by the devotees of *Viṣhṇu*, stressing *bhakti, karmayoga*, worship, pilgrimage, charity, and *jnanayoga*. He established about seventy centers of teaching of Visishthadvaita philosophy and method of worship in Vaishnava temples, amalgamating the functions of the temple and monastery, as in Melkote and Srirangam (Kumara, 2015).

After the death of Ramanujacharya, the Vishishṭadvaita school divided into Vadakalia (Northern school) and Tenkalai (Southern school) in the sixteenth century CE.[13] The essential difference between the two is the connection between God's grace and man's effort in bringing about final deliverance. Some of the important Visisthadvaita *mathas* are the Ahobala *matha* with its center in Andhra (founded in 1398 CE), Parakala *matha* in Mysore (patronized by the Wodeyar dynasty), Melkote *matha* (Tirunarayanapuram), all belonging to the *Vadakalia* denomination; while the Vanamamalai and the Yadugiri Yaturaja *matha* (established in 1103 C.E. by Ramanujacarya) belongs to the *Tenkalai* school.

In the meantime, in the twelfth century CE. Basava, the founder of Virashaivite monastery had reformed Shaivism, by freeing it from the caste system. He gave the devotee eight shields, to be given by the Guru. These were the *linga, padodaka* (water sanctified by the guru), *prasada* (food), *bhasma* (sacred ashes), *rudraksa*

---

[11] The ten *avataras* of Viṣṇhu are Matsya (fish), Kurma (tortoise), Varaha (boar), Narasimha (man-lion), Vamana (dwarf), Rama, Krishna Buddha and Kalki, among which Krishna was the most complete, convincing and emotionally satisfying of all the incarnations.

[12] Its practical teachings and doctrine of *karma yoga*, the theory of detachment bridged the gap between *sanyasin* (giving up all action—as a *sanyasi*) and living a materialist life.

[13] The Tenkalis recognized Pillai Lokācārya and gave importance to *Divya Prabandhams*, while the Vadagalis followed *Vedānta* Desikachar and gave preference to the *Vedas*.

(rosary) and *mantra*. The Guru was given an important place due to his knowledge and was worthy of more reverence than Lord Shiva. Thus both Ramanuja and Basava played a significant role in the transformation of Vaishnavism and Shaivism from a ritualistic and intellectual 'Hinduism' to a highly devotional tradition around 12th and 13th C C.E (Sangari, 1990).[14] They synthesized *bhakti* tradition with Vedanta philosophy, and provided a rational basis for devotionalism. While in North India, *Vaishnavism* became more secularized, due to assimilation of immigrants and the Islamic community, the South hardened the tenets and principles. It became more conservative and distinct from Shaivism, as reflected in the doctrines of Vishishtad-vaita (and later *Dvaita*). In southern India, Vaishnavism that centered around *bhakti* and *puja* (worship), stories, deeds of gods, and older Vedic mythology were expanded to a popular level (and articulated in the *Purāṇas*), while the Upanishadic philosophy and commentaries continued to be learnt by merely a section of the population.

14.7 Dvaita Monasteries: Rise of Madhwacharya

With the coming of Madhwacharya (1238–1317 CE), the historical founder of the *Dvaita* or dualist system of philosophy, the trajectory of *mathas* takes a different turn.[15] His school of thought is also known as *tattvavada* or realism. He postulated that Viṣhṇu as *paramatma* (supreme soul) and *jivatma* (individual soul) are independent realities, but the latter is dependent on the former.[16] In the post Madhwacharya period, a voluminous literature grew around his works. Later exponents of this school as Madhvatirtha, Jayatirtha, Vyasatirtha, Vadiraja, and Vijayindra were interpreters, commentators, dialecticians and philosophers (Sharma, 1961). In addition, due to certain negligible philosophical differences between his disciples, the Dualist *maṭhas* began to get divided when ascetic disciples set up their own *maṭha*. This led to the emergence of secondary (or branch) *maṭhas*. They formed two main groups, namely, *Asthamathas* and *Desasthamathas*. In Udipi, the eight *matha*s are: *Palimar Matha, Admar Matha, Krishnapur Matha, Puttigea Matha Sirur Matha, Sode Matha, Kaniyoor Matha*, and Pejawar *Matha*. While the *Asthamathas* were located on the west coast at Udipi, below the Western Ghats, the early *Desastha Matha*s were based in Northern Karnataka (over the Western Ghats). The *mathas* that they established came to be known by their names: Vyasaraya *Matha*, the Raghavendra Svami *matha,*

[14] *Bhakti* has been defined as "a structure of personal devotion which hegemonic groups as well as into the redefining of dominant classes, and is also central to the production of a syncretic vocabulary in accessible vernacular languages" (Sangari, 1990, 25, 27).

[15] Sharma, B. N. K. (2008). *History of the Dvaita School of Vedanta and its Literature.* First Edition, Bombay: Motilal Banarsidass, 1961, reprint Delhi, 2008.

[16] According to Madhvacharya's *siddhanta* (philosophy), *Jagat* (world) is real; it is dependent and the only independent entity is *paramatma* or *brahmaṇ*. Every *jiva* (individual) is inherently different or *svarupatha*. God impels each *jiva* into activity and converges benefits in conformity to the *karma* performed by the *jiva*. God is the creator of *Jivas*, he grants sorrow and joy, and discrimination between *jivas* is due to one's *karmas*.

Uttaradi matha, Vyasaraya *matha*, Kundapur Vyasa Raja *matha* the Sosale Vyasa Raja *matha*, Raghvendra Swamy *matha*,[17] Sripadaraja *matha*, Majjigehalli *matha*, Kudli *matha*, Balegaru *matha*, Subrahmanya *matha*, Bhandarkeri *matha* Bhimana—katte *matha*, Citrapura *matha*, Gokarna-Partagali—Jivottama *matha*, and Kasi *matha*, with each pontiff setting his own *matha* with its own lineage.[18]

*Vedanta matha*s, while continuing the self- defining ways as individual philosophical centers, also saw a need for individual identity that manifested in various ways, such as body marks, lineage, organization, and worship. They functioned as centers of learning, taught disciples in their respective doctrines, were *chattras* (charitable feeding houses) for devotees observed the practice of initiation (*diksha*), and erected temples (Pandey, 1976). They were headed by ascetic philosophers whose commentaries on the Vedas became scriptures. The commentaries on the *Vedas* eventually became scriptures.

Identity of *mathas* in the form of body markings of disciples was a natural growth from Shaiva and Vaisnava religious movements. Followers of *Advaita*, worship Siva and are distinguished by horizontal marks (Sawai, 1992). They characteristically wear on their forehead, triple white *vibhuti* or *tripundra* (formed from ashes). The Virashaiva *matha* disciples identify themselves with a *linga* tied around their neck. Vedanta Sri Vaishnavites (followers of Ramanujacarya's Vishisthadvaita *matha*) wear *tilakas* which are vertical markings worn by Vaishnavites. The followers of Madhwacharya adopt the marks worn by Vaishnavites, namely a mark on their forehead composed of two white perpendicular lines made with *gopicandana* (white or yellow clay) and a dark line in the middle with a spot in the center (Rao & Vasudeva, 2002, 54–55). Followers of Madhva Siddhanta also receive *mudradharane* (sort of tattoo, symbolic of fire ordeal). There were differences between *mathas* in the ritual worship of gods as well. Advaita *matha*s worshipped five deities, of the *panchayana* namely Ganesa, Śiva, Vishnu, Subramanya and Devi with Śiva being regarded as *parabrāhmaṇa*. In Śringeri, there is a temple for Chandramoulishvara (Śiva Liṇga) and a temple for Śrī Saradamba (Sarasvati) (Sawai, 1992). *Dvaita matha*s were worshippers of Viṣṇu and his *avataras*, Narasimha, Janardana, Venkataramanan and gave importance to Krshna. Regarding the performance of rituals, all *mathas* performed the death ceremonies of the founder Gurus.[19] Thus ceremonial worship

---

[17] Raghavendra Swamy, was the 17th pontiff of *Śrī Madhvācārya Peetha* (1623–71).

[18] While *Advaita* heads of *matha*s or *jagadgurus* do not have various denominations, and are known *Śaṅkara matha*s while the heads of four (or 5) branches are called *saṅkarācārya*s, *Dvaita Matha*s, came to be known by various names, depending on the site or founder.

[19] The *punyatithi* (annual death ceremony) of Raghavendra Swamy is performed for three days in all Raghavendra Swamy mathas, both in the original *matha* and its numerous branch *mathas*, and is termed *aradhana* in Kannada.

Dvaita mathas perform the following festivals as well: *Ugadi* (new year), *Matsay Jayanti, Rama Navami, Hanuman Jayanti, Akshay Tritiya, Vasant utsava, Vasant Dvadasi, Narasimha Jayanti, Prathama Ekadashi, Jayatīrthas punyatiti, Upakarma, Hayagriva Jayanti, Anniversary of Raghvendra Swamy, Krishna Jayanti, Ganesh Chaturthi, Vamna Jayanti, Anata chaturashi*, and *Navaratri*.

of numerous gods within the monastery, similar to those in Hindu temples, the philosophical explanation and importance given to *bhakti* led to the popularization of the monastery. In addition, were the provisions of boarding and lodging to pilgrims in the monasteries, providing traditional education and the charismatic leadership of the ascetic Guru, all of which contributed to the rise of Hindu monasteries in South India. Furthermore, the interpretive teachings of the living Guru, his guidance to his devotees led to the veneration of the Guru who came be considered as God.

14.8 Icons of the Guru in the Monastery

Today, Gurus (who wears the orange robe) are popular largely due to their ascetic qualities, spiritual knowledge and wisdom. People desire to listen to their interpretations of scriptures, doctrines. Examples of such great ascetics in modern times are Swami Prabhupada, Sri Chandraskhearan Sarasvati, Raman Maharshi, Ramakrishna Pramahamsa, Swami Vivekananda, Satya Sai Baba, Dayananda Sarasvati, and Sri Bala Sivayogi. As mentioned above, the Guru within a monastery, is an ascetic, who preserves the body of religious doctrine formulated by the founder of the monastery and transmits the traditions for an ordered society. With the growth of the Vedanta *mathas* and the importance and sacredness attributed to him, the Dvaita *mathas* reinvented an icon of the Guru, which provided a tangible object of worship within the monastery. The icon of popular worship in *Dvaita* monasteries is the *vrndavana.* This icon is in the form of a massive rectangular non-figural stone sculpture that contains the entire embalmed whole-body relic of the deceased Guru. *Vṛndāvanas* are sacred, immovable non- figural stone structures and hence may be called sepulchral and mortuary icons. Interestingly the relics within could be multiplied, as was the practice in Buddhism. A particle of soil (*mritige)* or deposit from the original (*moola*) *vṛndāvana* can be reinstalled to create secondary *vṛndāvanas* (*mritige vṛndāvanas*) and thereby a new branch monastery (Flügel, 2010). Hence, each Dvaita monastery that has a *moola vṛndāvana* (with the deceased body) is known as a *moola maṭha*, and each original monastery (*moola maṭha)* can have various branches in different geographical areas, called secondary monasteries (*mritige maṭhas).* The division or re-installation of the relics (rather a symbolic division through the soil) led to the proliferation of these *mathas* along with their secondary *vrndavanas.* Such a transformation of the profane remains of a past *guru* into a sacred death marker, developed into icons of extreme devotion and intense worship that led to admiration and demand.

Etymologically, *vrindavana* means the garden (or orchard) of Vrinda, the wife of Vishnu. In this garden of Vrinda, Krishna, the main deity of Vaishnavitesis said to have danced with his female devotees, *gopis.* The *vrndavana* meant different to different groups—to the devotees of Krishna, the *vrndavan* on this 'earth' was a manifestation of the original *gokula vrindavan,* site of Lord Krishna. It is possible that while Krishna lived in *vrindavana,* by analogy, worship to the *vrindavana* meant worship to Lord Krishna. Indirectly, the *vrindavana* acquired a powerful symbolism and meaning to the devotee. It established a triangular relationship between the

Guru, God and the *bhakta* (devotee). With the growth of sectarian Dvaita *maṭhas*, *vṛndāvanas* in the sanctum, came to play a seminal role in the popularizing the *bhakti* to the past Guru as well as the living one within the monastery. Such a popular term was further enhanced in imagery and ritual by the introduction of practices, such as offering flowers, lights, incense, saffron colored robes, food, mantras and music similar to the worship of a deity in a Hindu temple. Furthermore, Gurus within the monastery, such as Narahari Tirtha 14th C, Padaraj Tirtha, and other saint poets as Purandardasa and Kanakadasa popularized the *bhakti* movement. The musical compositions of these Dasakutas propagated *bhakti* through the message of Dvaita philosophy, worship of Vishnu and rememberance of the Guru. Guru Stotras (such as those for Raghavendra Swamy) were composed that describe the miracles and powers of the Guru. The Guru could provide all material and spiritual benefits, attain liberation and shower divine grace upon the devotee. The interaction between *bhakti* and the Gurus led to an altered and expanded meaning of *bhakti* that was inclusive of all layers of society. Vaishnavite monasteries added a new dimension to *bhakti* experience, towards the Guru and God. It reminded the devotee of the life of the Guru—his biography, renunciation, knowledge, and a performer of miracles. The Guru is also similar to a God, but is not equivalent to a God. The Dvaita *mathas* did not adhere to the *Advaita* philosophy of *Aham Brahmasmi* (I am *Brahman*), instead they took care to negate the idea by placing an image of a god above the *vrndavana* and making sure that there were no stone portraits of the Guru in a *matha* (where a stone image of a God could be housed). The Guru in a *matha* was equal in status and sacredness to that of God. Madhwacharya was said to be an *avatara* of Hanuman and Bhima.

The efficacy of the *vrndavana* was not in the connotations of death or the embalmed body or relic, but in the life within the Guru as well as in each of the devotees. Here the boundaries between the dead and living, sacred and unholy, aniconic, and iconic, relic and icon, were crossed and where the boundaries between the Guru and God, were not defined. It revealed the religious exchanges between the dynamic traditions of asceticism and *bhakti* with extraordinary efficacy.

14.9 Conclusion

The idea of popular Hinduism can be better understood by what is not popular. The latter is largely the Sanskrit recitations of Vedas, the Upanishads, the *mantras*, *Puranas* and meditation. More popular are the epics, rituals at home and in the Hindu temples and talks by the Gurus. Gurus are popular largely due to their spiritual knowledge, wisdom, exemplary behavior, and ascetic qualities; it is believed that he can liberate the individual. He is treated as a supernatural human who can perform miracles and regarded to have a divine origin. With the growth of Hindu Saiva Siddhanta monasteries in Central India and in Tamilnadu, and the compositions of the Alvar saints, *bhakti* began to grow among the populace as a major attitude towards God as well as towards saints and Gurus. Vaisnavite monastic establishments, particularly Ramanuja and Madhvacharya redefined *bhakti* as devotion towards the Guru whose spiritual stature was similar to that of God. As a result of *bhakti*-infused popular Hinduism preached by Saiva *bhakti* Tamil and Vaisnava *bhakti* saints, monasteries incorporated this simple form of pure love. Influenced by the devotional movements, the monastic and philosophical schools of Hinduism imbibed the devotional content and achieved a new doctrinal synthesis. Visisthadvaita and Dvaita schools reinterpreted Vedic ideas to incorporate the *bhakti* philosophy. Thus, *bhakti* infused Hinduism through doctrinal re-interpretation and integration with Vedic and Upanishadic ideologies, showed a remarkable capacity for generating religious movements, which served to meet the challenge of Shankara's metaphysical theory. Ramanujacharya, and Madhwacharya became heroes as popular as Rama and Krishna in the epics. Other factors played a role, such as the organizational abilities of the head of the monastery, the Guru who was a personal teacher of spirituality. In addition, due to the lack of a unified hierarchical organization the religious teacher played an important role (Mlecko, 1982, 33–61). With the incorporation of *bhakti*, a new dimension was added to the religious doctrines, imagery, narrative of gods, musical compositions and temple worship. During the Vijayanagara period, the kings patronized saints, such as Purundaradasa and Kanakadasa, whose influence largely spread through devotional poetry and music and were effective religious propagation. The genres of *bhakti* expanded in various forms in space and time. Rituals, portraits, icons, relics within a monastery added to the authoritative position of the Guru within a monastery that contained an established staff, disciples, *shastras* and functioned as teaching, boarding, learning institutions. The growth of Vaishnava monasteries and worship of the *vrndavana* led to the spread of pilgrimage sites. Mass religion depended on monasteries with its adopted devices of beliefs and practices, thereby fulfilling a socio-religious function. Whether within or outside the institution, the disciple came to be bound closely to the Guru in a personalized way. Whether it is the icon of *vrndavana* or Sai Baba or the portrait of Ramakrishna or Vivekananda, God and Guru have become interchangeable.

Popular Hindu doctrine of *bhakti* with its broad umbrella of meanings, affiliations, and practices, (and with no one ecclesiastical authority to administer and regulate the boundaries of its tradition) provided a unifying religious force. Monasteries rephrased the devotional traditions, interpreted the iconography, enacted temple rituals while the Gurus maintained the philosophical traditions, providing a sense of continuity with earlier concept of devotions and echoing *Vedic* and *Upanashadic* thoughts. Within a complex tradition of devotion, spirituality, education, asceticism and sacredness Hinduism connected seemingly disparate genres. Organized centers of socio religious power and the idea of devotion to God and Guru provided a structure and sustained the growth of popular Hinduism.

References

Bhagowalia, U. (1980) *Vaiṣṇavism and society in Northern India: 700–1200*. Intellectual Book Corner.
Bhandarkar, R. G. (1929) *Vaiṣṇavism, Saivism and minor religious systems* (N. B. Utgikar, Ed.). Bhandarkar Oriental Research Institute.
Cenkner, W. (2001). *A Tradition of Teachers: Sankara and the Jagadgurus Today*. Columbia, MO: South Asia Books, Delhi: Motilal Banarsidass, 1983. Reprint, 1995.
Coward, H. G. (2008). *The perfectibility of human nature in eastern and Western thought*. State University of New York Press.
Flügel, P. (2010). The jaina cult of Relic Stūpas. *Numen, 57*(3–4), 389–504.
Frazier, J. (2013). Bhakti in Hindu cultures. *The Journal of Hindu Studies, 6*(2), 101–113.
Gonda, J. (1977). *Visnuism and sivaism: A comparison*. Munshiram Manoharlal Publishers.
Granoff, P. E., & Shinohara, K. (1994). *Monks and magicians: Religious biographies in Asia*. Motilal Banarsidass Publishers.
Leclercq, J. (1961). *The love of learning and the desire for god: A study of monastic culture*. Translated by C. Misrahi. New York: Fordham University Press.
Mlecko, J. D. (1982). *The Guru in Hindu tradition* (Vol. XXXIX). Numen, Fasc. 1.
Mudugula, I. S. (1985). *The Acarya: Sankara of Kaladi*. Motilal Banarsidass.
Padmanabhacharya, C. M. (1983). *Life and teachings of sri madhvachariar*. C.A. Pattabiraman and C.A.P. Vittal.
Pechilis Prentiss, K. (1999). *The embodiment of Bhakti*. Oxford University Press.
Prabhupāda, A. B. S. (1975). *Sri Caitanya-Caritamrta of Krsnadasa Kaviraja Gosvami*. The Bhaktivedanta Book Trust. Mumbai.
Rupagoswami. (1975). Laghu-bhagavatamrta. Bhaktivedanta Book Trust. Mumbai.
Robinson, C. (2005). *Interpretations of the Bhagavad-Gita and images of the Hindu tradition*. Routledge.
Rao, V. (2002). *Living traditions in contemporary contexts: The madhva matha of Udupi*. Orient Longman, New Delhi.
Rao, N. (2020). *The Hindu monastery in South India: social, religious, and artistic traditions*. Lexington Books. Rowman and Littlefield. Maryland. https://www.amazon.com/Hindu-Monastery-South-India-Traditions/dp/179362237X
Sawai, Y. (1992). The faith of ascetics and lay Smārtas: A study of the śaṅkaran tradition of śṛṅgeri. *The Journal of Asian Studies* (G. Oberhammer, Ed.), XIX.
Sharma, B. N. K. (1961). *History of the Dvaita school of Vedānta and its literature: From the earliest beginnings to our own times* (1st ed.). Motilal Banarsidass.
Sharma, B. N. K. (1962). *Philosophy of śrī madhvācārya*. Motilal Banarsidass.
Schopen, G. (1997). *Bones, stones, and Buddhist monks: collected papers on the archaeology, epigraphy, and texts of monastic Buddhism in India*. University of Hawaii Press.
Yocum, G. E. (1990). *Monastic life in the Christian and Hindu traditions: A comparative study* (A. B. Creel & V. Narayanan). Edwin Mellen Press.

Chapter 15
Hinduism in the New Millennium: History, Tradition, and Practice in the Goddess Festival

Lavanya Vemsani

Abstract This chapter examines the intersection of History, society, and religion in one of the most disturbing periods of Indian history in the region of Deccan. Ruled by Kakatiya Dynasty Deccan emerged as one of the wealthy, largest and strongest empires of Deccan region between eleventh and thirteenth centuries C.E. However, from 1295 C.E. onwards this empire is subjected to numerous raids from the Sultanate, which was newly established in Delhi at the turn of the twelfth century, which was trying to gain a strong foothold by destroying as many empires as possible as quickly as possible. The southern strategy of the Sultanate brought about 11–12 quick invasions towards Deccan. These quick succession of battles brought utter destruction to the Deccan including the empires of Yadavas, Kakatiyas, and Hoyasalas. The Kakatiya empire included a number of local rulers called Nayakas, some of which are also tribal chiefs including Koya, Chenchu, and other tribes. The tribes contributed military support to the empires they were part of and fostered alliance. Hence, Kakatiya armies are supported by large contingent of Koya archery contingent and Vijayanagara contained contingents of Chenchu archers. Destruction of Kakatiya empire also brought destruction to the Koya society and way of life. Destroyed Koya temples such as Koyilakuntla Narasimha temple and numerous other goddesses' temples stand as mute witnesses to this destruction at the turn of the second millennium. However, from this destruction also rose festival of goddesses which memorializes this trauma yet indicates the arrival of new life. The goddesses Sammakka and Sarakka festival incorporates this historical background and social life of Deccan experienced in the thirteenth century. The festival of Sammakka and Sarakka is examined to help elucidate the history, memory, and practice in an effort to understand the social and religious history of the Deccan in the second millennium.

Keywords Telangana · Sammakka and Sarakka · Medaram · Jatara · Shakti · Durga · Koya · Sumangali · Kakatiyas · Malik Kafur · Feminine divine ·

L. Vemsani (✉)
Shawnee State University, Portsmouth, OH 45662, USA
e-mail: lvemsani@shawnee.edu

School of Historical Studies, Jawaharlal Nehru University, New Delhi, India

L. Vemsani (ed.), *Handbook of Indian History*,
https://doi.org/10.1007/978-981-97-6207-1_15

Sthalavriksha · Krishna · Harivamsapurana · Rudrama Devi · Pratapa Rudra · Tughlaq · Kumkuma Bharina · Jaggery/bellam

15.1 Introduction

Second Millennium brought new political and religious upheavals throughout India. The prevalent political and religious modes of life came under attack from invading conquerors, which brought Hindu temples and institutions under attack. Hinduism especially that which is associated with goddess worship is recorded in India since the Upper Paleolithic Era (Chakrabarti, 1999: 24–36; Kenoyer et al., 1983: 88–94). However, academic study of religious practices associated with the goddesses are one of the most confused subjects of study in the academic study of Hinduism (Vemsani, 2021: 1–23). The festival of Goddesses Sammakka and Sarakka is the best representative of primeval (prehistoric) goddess faith continuing within Hinduism with overarching religious practices evolving over the centuries showing variations due to regional and social background. The goddess's festival of Medaram is a blend of tradition and modernity resulting in a modern Hindu goddess festival of immense popularity.

Examination of Sammakka and Sarakka festival helps understand the historical religion of India and popular practice within society unhampered by the narrow divisions of society imposed later during the colonial era. While being centrally associated with the family and clan of Koya tribe the festival of Sammakka and Sarakka is unmistakably connected to Hinduism, which forms part of Koya traditional religion. Koyas are one of the traditional tribes of Deccan spread between Orissa, Chhattisgarh, Madhya Pradesh, and Maharashtra.

The Sammakka and Sarakka Jatara emerged in this disturbed historical era of thirteenth–fourteenth centuries. Hence, it incorporates the historically scarring memory of war, blood, and gory within the central sacred story of the festival. The Sammakka and Sarakka *Jātara*, is a biannual festival celebrated in veneration of the mother and daughter goddess pair of Andhra Pradesh, initially venerated for their selfless sacrifice, mainly by her clan of Koya tribe, but clearly emerged as a minstream festival with Sammakka recognized as an amsa of goddess Durga Mahishamardini. Stories of female tribal leaders are abound in Indian history. Some of them are celebrated with folk festivals such as *jani shikar*, which is celebrated every 12 years in the memory of two female Oraon heroines, Singi Dai and Killi Dai, although none of the festivals have reached the epic proportion in popularity as the festival of Sammakka and Sarakka (Singh, 2002). Koya's practice a variety of early Hinduism, with animistic beliefs and cosmogony similar to Hinduism, while the clan elders act as pradhans and priests of the community (Heimendorf, 1948a, 1948b; Murty, 1991; Pannala, 1981).

On account of Sammakka and Sarakka *Jātara*'s exceptional popularity, the state government of Andhra Pradesh has declared it as the state festival of Andhra Pradesh in the 1980s. As a state festival the Andhra Pradesh state and currently the Telangana state make arrangements for the celebration of the festival as well as construction and maintenance to temples for Sammakka and Sarakka with grants from Endowments Board of Andhra Pradesh State Government previously and now from the Telangana State Endowments Board. Strangely, the state governments manage Hindu religious places (temples and institutions) through a government appointed Endowments Board in a strange arrangement not common to a modern democracy anywhere in the world. This recognition as a state festival of Andhra Pradesh brings forward an important development in the popular Hinduism of Andhra Pradesh in the recent years: popular religion acquiring the status of traditional religion and recognition.

Even though the Sammakka and Sarakka Jatara maintains a blend of rituals derived from Koya traditional practice, which also contains elements of ancient Hinduism, along with regional elements of practice, which form part of traditional religion in Deccan. Veneration of *kunkuma* (vermillion dot) is derived from regional practice of Hinduism. The five elements associated with sumangali (married woman) are *kumkuma* (vermillion), *katuka* (black eye liner), *pasupu* (turmeric powder), *gajulu* (bangles), and *poolu* (flowers). All these elements form part of the festival celebration to be discussed below following the discussion on history of the festival.

However, due to the historical development of religious practice in the Deccan region it is not unusual to notice the tribal practices within Hinduism and Hindu temples. Telugu region spreads from the eastern Deccan region up to the East Coast of India is known for such primeval practices of early Hinduism which are preserved in some tribal practices.

Hinduism is a diffuse and multifaceted religious faith, with numerous regional practices along with many communities practicing Hinduism while also venerating their own clan gods/goddesses (kula devata). Therefore, in the following chapter as the Sammakka and Sarakka festival is examined to an understanding of how the Koya tradition maintains its distinct strand of faith while also following overarching Hinduism, while adapting to modernity. The Koya religious doctrine includes elements of ancient Hinduism, which are typical of Koya life and traditions (Murty, 1991). Hence the festival has a mass appeal to the Hindu community in general, of which Koyas are considered a distinct part with ancient traditions. Blend of tribal and Hindu practice is commonly noticed in the Deccan in Hindu festivals and Hindu tradition in the Narasimha temples (Vemsani, 2022: 97–99; Vemsani 2009:35–52) Rama temples, and Goddess temples. Hence, the blend of tribal and Hindu tradition only shows the common origins of the populations living in this region, whose lifestyles and religious traditions may have diverged over centuries of practice.

Hinduism evades classification, definition, and categorization as a religion in the western sense of the term, while it survives as the third largest religion of the world and enters the new millennium as the only predominantly polytheistic religion in the world. Hinduism also differs from almost all the other world religions in having a dynamic and ritualistic popular religious practice apart from the highly developed esoteric philosophical, and metaphysical religious compendium. Although it seems as though a dichotomy exists between the philosophical Hinduism and popular strands of Hinduism, which is superficial, since practice defies these classifications, it only indicates the continuous layers of religious convention accrued over time around the Vedic core according to the changing social and religious circumstances. Numerous gurus, festivals, and rituals, and groups continue to evolve in various places, and are celebrated every day throughout India.

Twelfth century of India is religiously very dynamic and gave rise to numerous popular religious practices, popularly categorized as Shaiva traditions (Fisher, 2018: 1–28) and Vaishnava traditions (Bryant & Ekstrand, 2004: 1–36), shakti (Spina, 2018: 137–147) and Vedanta religion (see Chap. 19). Popular Saiva traditions have grown beyond their regional origins. Some may survive and continue to be practiced by the posterity, while some may not. It is this dynamic religious practice which distinguishes Hinduism from other major world religions. While the philosophical and meditative Hinduism is mainly confined to the ascetics and monasterics, it acts as a compendium of unifying framework of variety of themes encountered in the popular religious practices such as festivals, pilgrimages, and rituals. Influence of Vedic structure on the Mahabharata rituals is examined in detail (Austin, 2008: 283–308; van Buitenen, 1988: 305–321), as well as Vedic symbols and classical purana story elements are observed in the temple tales (sthalapuaranas) of various local temples in Andhra Pradesh (Vemsani, 2009: 35–52). Even though there is a great variety and divergence in Hinduism, a continuity can be noticed from the Vedic structure to Hindu rituals to regional tales and festivals in Practice (Smith, 1998: 86–99). Therefore, even though it is not apparent at the first glance closer examination reveals unmistakable connections between Vedic philosophy and popular religion of India (Nicholson, 2010). In fact, the popular religion of India is an expression of the central belief of the philosophy of the *Vedas* and the *Upanishads* that the universe is part of the formless supreme absolute *Brahma* (Universal Self), who also is formless, hence inconceivable, and incomprehensible. However, the absolutely formless divine can be experienced, imagined, and expressed in a symbolic (pratika) form in anything and any form to be felt approachable by the devotee within the manifest universe, since everything and every being in the universe originates from *brahma*. Hence, the universal divine appears in a variety of forms to different people as representation of the divine spirit, through their perceived experience. Based on this philosophy, an elaborate system of popular devotional theology evolved symbolizing historical instances or persons, as representation of immense shakti (divine energy) and this symbolism may also be reflected in the reverence of such mundane materials as waters of the rivers, trees, stones, or other everyday objects in India (Coomaraswamy, 1971; Cutler et al., 1985; Eck, 1981; Feldhaus, 1995; Haberman, 1994). Unlike the institutionalized religious traditions, in which organic growth is restricted or limited by the institutional control, Indian religious traditions, especially Hinduism, has a wider dynamic religious practice, apart from the overarching textual theology and philosophy, which work in tandem. Role of common people, in shaping the religion through practice in the way it suites the changing times (although the central philosophy and theology may not differ greatly) and circumstances is a notable feature of the religion in South Asia, especially, the goddess religion (goddess Leela). Therefore, in this chapter I examine the popular festival of goddesses, Sammakka and Sarakka Jatara of Telugu region, which illustrates this all-embracing aspects of popular and classical Hinduism succinctly. The Sammakka and Sarakka festival of Medaram, incorporates the symbolism classical tradition as well as the numerous materials and instances of everyday life, nature, and the shakti (feminine divine), in a single festival, which propels it to the status of the most popular festival of India, next only to *Kumbhmela*.[1] It is therefore important to study the festival of Sammakka and Sarakka to understand the intersection of history, tradition, and practice, a spontaneous phenomenon of popular religion rooted in Hinduism, yet, reflecting history, tradition, practice, and continuity of the religion of India. The classical symbolism and popular nature of this festival is striking and points to the historical evolution of Hinduism over the centuries, which will be discussed in detail in the following pages.

Colonial scholarship produced during the colonial period depicts India as a land inhabited by numerous races, which are not cognate but rivals. Colonial concepts, especially the concepts of "indigenous," versus "invader," effectively pitting some groups of Indians against the other groups of Indians occupies constant usage in the academic literature about India during the early eighteenth and nineteenth centuries (Trautman, 1997: 190–216). It is not far from truth to say that none of the research work and texts produced on India during colonial era are devoid of the Aryan theory and racialization of India even though no race called Aryan exists in India. The tribal groups, often termed indigenous are further classified as Negrito, Australoid, Austronesian, or Mongoloid mostly based on language and to some extend based on their physical features and appearances, while it is entirely presented as linguistic difference, even though the so-called tribal dialects do not differentiate sufficiently from the local languages used by others around them. The tribes of central India, such as Chenchus, Koyas and Sabaras are described as Austroloid races although they do not differ physically or linguistically from their neighbors, called variously as Aryan or Dravidian. The perceived minor physical differences might be the result of lifestyle rather than racial differences as shown by the genetic heritage, which was similar. However, this festival is celebrated by the people of Madhya Pradesh, Chhattisgarh, Maharashtra, Orissa, and Telugu states of Andhra Pradesh and Telangana regardless of social and linguistic differences. The Koya (Khond) tribes use a variety of language influenced by the regional Prakrit of this region, but not Austroloid or Austronesian languages and do not have anything in common with Austroloid or Austronesian tribes found in other areas of the world. Racial designations imposed on Indians demonstrates oppression of the natives through haphazard use of racial designations in the early scholarship based on spurious physical characteristics or languages. British administration used such racial designations many tribes and castes of Peninsular India are designated as Criminal Castes and Tribes. This confused jumble of races and artificial designations coined to reinforce perceived differences during the colonial rule only shows the colonial administrative policy of 'divide and rule' rather than existence of any legitimate races. Recent genetic research also showed that the

[1] Kumbhamela is a classical festival celebrated in veneration of the river Ganga, symbolized as the goddess Ganga, and the stellar phenomenon, the Makara Sankranti (the entering of Sun into the constellation of Aries. This festival attracts the largest gathering of pilgrims to celebrate the festival (mela) of Kumbh.

Koyas and Chenchus do not differ much from the other Hindus in their genetic make-up. This helps us deduce that it is the Hindus that changed their lifestyle while the Hindu tribes, namely, the Koyas and Chenchus adhered to the prehistoric lifestyle and preserving the earlier religion (Vemsani, 2022: 8–11; 59–68; 151–167).

Popular practice of Hinduism displays a group dynamic involving massive celebrations usually noticed in the major festivals such as Kumbahmela, Ramleela and, Dasara, the ten-day celebration of the goddess in her multiple forms evokes this group dynamism in its popular religious practice. It is also noted in the earlier religion as the Vedas describe massive attendance of Jana at the yagnas. All social groups regardless of social distinctions whether caste or tribe have rich comprehensive ritual practice, which also intersects in festivals at sacred centers such as Narasimha temple of Ahobilam and Srirama temple of Bhadrachalam. The temple of Narasimha at Koilkuntla was built and maintained by Koyas until they were killed and the temple was destroyed during one of Aurangzeb's raids in the Deccan in seventeenth century (Vemsani, 2022: 161). However, the roots of Hinduism are notable in the popular practices that remain grounded in mass participation erasing any distinctions between various social groups. Hinduism is traditionally connected to tribal faith since the Vedas and incorporation of tribal beliefs in Hinduism is noticed across India, but more prominently in the middle India (Vemsani, 2022). Numerous temples in Orissa also show an affinity with tribes, including the Jagannatha temple in Puri and Nrusimhanatha temple on Gandhamadhana hill near Paikmal, Bargarh. The tribe of Konds associated with Nrusimhanatha temple at Paikmal are a cognate tribe of Koyas. Koyas are a subclan of the Gond (Kond) tribes of Central India and show early Hindu practices. This demonstrates that Tribes are also Hindus practicing a mixture of early Hindu and local beliefs. This affinity is much more intimate in some cases where the castes and tribes share ritual structure in the well-known temples of Andhra Pradesh, as seen in the case of Narasimha temple in Ahobilam, Shiva temple in Srisailam, Sri Rama temple in Bhadrachalam, where the tribes participate and perform some of the central rituals offered to the central deity.

Unlike the institutionalized religious traditions, in which change is restricted or limited by the institutional control, Indian religious traditions, especially Hinduism, has a wider practice-based religion, apart from the central textual theology and philosophy, which serves as the central core. Role of common people, in shaping the religious practice in the way that evolves in tandem with the changing times (although the central philosophy and theology may not differ greatly) and circumstances is a notable feature of the religion in India, especially, the goddess religion.

Previous scholarship divided and labeled goddesses variously. Therefore, my approach to the study of goddesses Sammakka and Sarakka festival is twofold. On the one hand I would examine the historical origin, nature and religious symbolism in the festival of goddesses Sammakka and Sarakka in detail. On the other hand, I will examine the universal principles of divinity underlying their veneration and connect my research on the current theories on goddesses in India and propose that the goddesses must be understood from their dynamic role in the broad context of the society in which they are revered, but not from their marital status. Context can be used to understand the divinity but it should not be used to bestow narrow identities and derogatory labels. The marital status is marginal to their pivotal role, as goddesses (Micheals et al., 1996: 2021; Pinchman, 1994; Vemsani, 2022: 7–9). Goddesses are generally studied in opposition based on their marital status as spouse goddesses or wild goddesses (Vemsani, 2022: 9–11). Another way the goddesses were studied was imposing a hierarchy of Sanskritic goddess and village goddesses (Pinchman, 1994) which was not conceptually noticed in India as all goddesses are considered to be forms of the universal great goddess, the Mahadevi.

The first goal of this paper therefore is to study the central features that contributed to such meteoric rise in the popularity of the goddesses, during the past 700 years, which I will undertake in the first three sections of this paper. This then leads us to the second goal of this paper, the tradition, classical concepts of feminine divine in relation to the goddess and the status and nature of goddesses Sammakka and Sarakka in the established goddess religion of India in the fourth section (15.3) of this paper. An examination of Sammakka and Sarakka as popular goddesses reveals both similarities and differences with other village and Sanskritic goddesses of India (Pinchman, 1994) and contributes to our understanding of goddesses in Hinduism. The goddesses Sammakka and Sarakka defy all classifications and labels.

Therefore, the secondary goal of this paper is to bring into light, the broad spectrum of religious practices in relation to the goddesses of India and show the futility of imposing categorizations on the religion of India in general and goddesses in particular. It is not only pertinent to investigate this festival closely to understand the popular religion in Andhra Pradesh, but an examination of this festival also helps us in understanding the nature of goddesses and contribute to the current theories on goddesses.

15.2 Traditions of the Feminine Divine in Classical and Popular Traditions

15.2.1 Feminine Divine

Hindu religion, especially that of the goddess-centered (Shakti) religion is not static but dynamic and representative of the society, in which they are revered. However, the special place attached to goddesses isn't only their flexibility but their capacity to appeal to a number of universal human feelings: love, aspirations such as wealth and victory as well as avoiding fear, anxiety, sickness, danger, or poverty etc. Since most human feelings are universal, it is not surprising that goddesses often defy limitations of class, religion, race, and caste in attracting a mass following. Goddesses of India play a major role in Hinduism, but elucidate being categorized into a neat typology, although they are accorded a special place in the minds of their devotees. Scholars have proposed various typological categories, but none of them satisfactorily explain the status or nature of the goddesses, since early scholarship attempted to understand goddesses from patriarchal perspective, placing marriage at the center of their theoretical analysis while studying these categorizations and their application to goddess and women in India, which academic authors have noted to be futile (Gatewood, 1985: 15; Vemsani, 2021: 7–13). Another danger in erasing the line between the human and divine realms through applying such designations is that sometimes it devolves into derogatory terminology such as "tooth goddess" and "breast goddess" (Ramanujan, 1986). It also leads to the slanted phenomena that the societal ills are blamed on the devotional practice as inconsistent with society even though it can be argued that the criminal elements of a society might not have much to do with the devotional traditions of a society. Hence, a society might have many reasons for its social evils including crimes against women unrelated to devotional traditions centered on goddesses. Strangely, such incongruity is never proposed in the case of high number of crimes and devotion to gods. Males and male gods escape such censure. In a similar vein it might not be out of place to notice here that such criticisms do not find any parallels between crime rates of a society and devotion to male divinity or gods. Hence, it is completely out of context to look towards devotion to goddesses to provide clues for the life of women. The human errors are blamed on devotional practices centered on goddesses as if that should explain the social status of women in a society. Strangely, such connections are never explored in the case of men and gods. Goddesses are seen as an extension of women, however impossible that connection might seem. Research in the areas of religious traditions in connection with goddesses should take a new direction in evaluating the goddess traditions of India in order to escape this male fixation with marriage and their relation to male counterparts as a central feature to understand the nature of goddesses and their manifold roles. Instead, it would be rewarding to understand the goddesses from the role they play in society and the human concerns and social issues that they represent.

Research devoted to goddesses or the study of festivals especially devoted to goddesses is limited when compared with the studies on the gods of major religions such as Christianity, Judaism, and Hinduism, the amount of research done on the popular goddesses of oral tradition is even more limited. Although the Tamil region of Southern India has recently received scholarly attention focusing on the goddess traditions and practice it has been sparse in the case of the Andhra Pradesh, Telangana, and other states of southern India (Hendelman & Shulman, 1995; Narayana Rao, 1989; Younger, 2002).

Therefore, studying the popular goddesses is beneficial to understand the religious life of Andhra Pradesh in two ways: On the one hand, popular tradition provides the underlying concepts to understand the cultural evolution that may have missed the textualization and normalization tendencies. On the other hand, it helps in understanding the goddess traditions in a new light.

Earlier studies of the popular goddesses of India have attempted to understand the goddess traditions by placing them into two categories based on their marital status. Many of the popular goddesses are angry, violent, mothers of disease and also both protectors and violators of territorial boundaries (Beck, 2015). Descriptions of any Indian goddess attribute their violence to the absence of a consort (Babb, 2020). Many of these goddesses are ferocious conqueresses until tamed, married and made docile or passive in relation to their husbands (Fuller, 1980; Ramanujan, 1986; Shulman, 1980). For popular epic goddesses such as Sita and Draupadi, violence and marriage are central to their story. Marriage is not central to their divinity. By contrast, the marital status of Sammakka and Sārakka is clear. Their marriage is never in question and it does not form part of the celebration. Analysis of gender in the Sammakka-Sārakka festival will demonstrate that earlier androcentric analyses of goddesses simply do not apply here. In this paper, I argue that anger, ferociousness and violence can be part of the natural personality of a goddess, just as much as fertility and domesticity can be part of the personality of a god. This paper also questions the appropriateness of applying concepts such as marriage and domesticity i.e. assumed feminine characteristics, to all goddesses regardless of their historical, geographical, and societal context.

In particular, Hinduism is living religion of India, which adopts to change and appears in new forms and expressions as the society adopts and experiences new modes of life. Goddess religion is especially noted for such adoption and change. With the changing society the goddesses acquire new forms and function or new goddesses emerge from the old ones (Hawley & Wulff, 1998). For example, fertility and life is one of the earliest features associated with goddesses since prehistoric era (Sree Padma, 2013: 46–70). When life was uncertain and diseases and death ravaged life, the goddesses of plague, chickenpox, and other diseases, offering protection and hope for life are worshipped (Stewart, 1995: 389–397; Wadley, 1980: 33–60). It is also not unusual that some of the goddesses change their nature and acquire a new purpose, as the society changes (Hawley, 1998). Therefore, it is obvious that the goddess religion needs a special model that takes into account the special characteristics, nature, and function, to move away from the model based on marital status or functionality such as auspiciousness, wealth or poverty and disease to understand the divine nature of goddesses in Indian society. I propose that such categorization and labels must be discontinued, especially those terms that are derogatory labels such as "tooth goddess" or "wild goddess" (Vemsani, 2022: 7–9). These categorizations and labels display entrenched patriarchy and the dominance imposed on the academia by the male scholars of an earlier era, which was followed by female scholars knowingly or unknowingly, but certainly an aspect that needs to be changed immediately.

Their function might be derived from the context of the society in which they are revered, but their divinity is beyond the human realm. Therefore, the goddesses should be understood from their overarching role, not divorced from the context of society and culture in which they are revered. This aspect of goddess religion is aptly represented by the festival processes and rituals in the Sammakka and Sarakka festival discussed in the later sections of this paper. Therefore, through a study of Sammakka and Sarakka Jātara, I demonstrate below, classification of the goddesses from the perspective of their overarching role rather than marital status or location.

The Sammakka and Sarakka festival has two distinct dynamics: individual as well as group. For the individual, the mother and daughter goddess pair reiterate the value of family and self-sacrifice. For the community that attends this festival it represents a return to the roots, an escape from the hustle and bustle of city life to the pristine forests, where the inequalities of the society are no longer valid.

The origin of this festival is as much rooted in the historical circumstances of this region as much in the socio-cultural background of the Deccan. Koyas are one of the well-known and well studied progressive tribes of India (Aggarwal et al., 1990). The Koyas are one of the most ancient tribes of the Gondwana region. The Gond Empire[2] of the Central India functioned as an umbrella state of the tribes spread across Madhya Pradesh, Orissa, Andhra Pradesh, and Maharashtra states of modern republic of India (Mohapra, 1992). The Koyas are organized into endogamous patriarchal clans, which are loosely organized into related clans living in a geographically close region, but each clan is politically and socially independent. What unites all these tribes is uniformity of language, religion, and culture, and the Koyas of this region speak a dialect of Koya language known as Gommu dialect, which is heavily influenced by Telugu (Tyler, 1969). Koyas follow early ritualistic Hinduism with similar beliefs in cosmogony and polytheism as Hinduism. Koyas are one of the economically well-adjusted tribes of central India, who practice stable agriculture, although, a clan known as kondadoras/kondareddys or kondakoyas (also known as Hill Reddies) still practice limited *podu*, a type of slash and burn agriculture, which requires burning of forests every few years to bring land into cultivation (Pannala, 1981: 31–66). Due to this reason, the type of agriculture Koyas practice is called "shifting agriculture". Under this type of agriculture, known as 'slash and burn' agriculture, new tracts of land is brought into cultivation every few years by burning and clearing the forests. Large tracts of forestland has been brought into cultivation and made habitable in this region by the pioneering agricultural activity of the Koyas during the past 2000 years. The Podu agriculture is banned by the Government of Andhra Pradesh/Telangana, and the Koyas have been forced to look for work elsewhere, resulting in large scale migrations to nearby towns. Koyas follow clan system with a patriarchal family system. Average household acreage of Koya households is about two and a half acres and collection of forest products forms a large part of the economic sustenance (Pannala, 1981: 81–100). Therefore, the Koyas have a close relationship with the forest. This relationship is intricately woven into the festival processes in the Sammakka and Sarakka Jatara (*Jātara*), as the forest forms the central setting of the festival. Sammakka and Sarakka Jatara (festival) is held during the spring season every two years, in the forest near the village of Medaram located in Warangal district of Andhra Pradesh. Although the festivities continue for numerous days, the actual festival is conducted for three days before the *Māgha-Purnima* (full moon). The month of Magha (*Māgha)* roughly corresponds to February–March of

[2] Although not much information is known about this empire before sixteenth century, its existence if acknowledged by a number of oral stories and folk tales. The queen of Gondwana Empire Rani Durgavathi, Rajput princess of Chandela lineage is said to have married the Gond prince Dalpat Sahi and became a Gond by marriage. While she refused marriage proposal from Timurid (Mughal) Akbar, which resulted in anger in the emperor which lead to the emperor leading an unsuccessful military expedition to the Gondwana region. Abul Fazl, *Akbarnama* Vol. II. Trans. Beveridge (Delhi:1972): 323–331. The Koyas faced numerous raids from the Delhi Sultanate and the Timurids (Mughals) between the thirteenth and the seventeenth centuries, which resulted in destruction of tribal hamlets across Telangana in addition to their sacred centers and temples.

the English calendar, a very pleasant time of the year in Medaram. It is the flowering season in this region, and many forest trees bloom during this time and fill the area with colorful flowers, especially the Mahua, popularly known as the fire of the forest. The temperatures are not too high. During this period people from the state of Andhra Pradesh, as well as its neighbouring states of Andhra Pradesh, such as Orissa, Madhya Pradesh and Maharashtra gather here on this little forest town to remember and recount the stories, catch a glimpse of the goddesses; to participate in the worship of the goddesses.

Although the tremendous popularity of this festival might be the result of fourteenth century phenomenon, its celebration and popularity among the Gonds cannot be denied in the long established tradition of goddess worship. The Sammakka and Sarakka festival has been noted to have originated over 7 centuries ago around early fourteenth century as a traditional festival of the rural communities. The festival in fact begins with a boy wandering off into the forest to find the symbolic memoir of the goddess, the bottu pette/kumkuma bharina(vermillion box). Popular folk legend commonly known among the people of the region narrates that the heroic self-sacrifice of Sammakka and Sarakka of Koya tribe against battles and raids of Andhra Pradesh. Malik Kafur's raids brought the armies of Sultanate and ruthless warfare to the south between 1303 and 1323. Kafur defeated Kakatiyas and others in his numerous raids defeated the Kakatiyas and his armies looted the countryside ruthlessly. Tribal warriors formed along with important part of Kakatiya armies in this area thus receiving ruthless attacks from Kafur's raids. The Sultanate armies looted any material goods and precious metals, but they also captured and took away young male and females above the age of 5 years to be sold in the slave markets from Delhi to Multan in northern and northwestern India. The largest slave market of the world of this era was located in Multan. I include a brief summary of the legend as recollected in the festival lore below:

> The Koya ruler, Medaraja of the forest kingdom, Medaram, was killed by the invading forces. The invading forces then started raiding the forest kingdom demanding tribute, and they were then opposed by the local people under the leadership of Sammakka and Sarakka the wife and daughter of the dead king. The invading forces had to retreat and eventually turned away from Medaram due to the stiff resistance offered by Sammakka. As the invading forces and tribal armies were retreating, one of their soldiers had stabbed Sammakka from behind. Legend has it that Sammakka then disappeared into the forest and was never seen again. Her family and followers had searched the forest and found a kumkuma bharina (vermillion container), precisely at the place where she disappeared in the forest. Considering the Kumkuma bharina as her last remaining possession they performed her last rites and memorial service to it which continues to this day at the interval of two years.

In order to remember the heroic sacrifice of Sammakka and Sarakka and to honor their sacrifice for the protection of community this festival was began to be celebrated every two years in Medaram the place of their death. This annual festival still marks the heroic self-sacrifice and reveres them as savior goddesses.

Throughout Telangana, one can witness hero stones (vīra gal) or memorial stones of heroes in almost every village, especially belonging to the Kakatiya era. Although Sammakka and Sarakka worship follows from the same local tradition of worshipping the martyrs, it differs from this tradition in many ways. The foremost of the differences is the status and significance of this festival. The tradition of worshipping the local heroes even female warriors is not unusual as memorials sometimes housed in mandapas are noticed (https://web.archive.org/web/20171026053901/http://www.dtnext.in/News/TamilNadu/2017/04/03005110/1030460/Hero-stones-of-women-warriors-found-in-Krishnagiri.vpf?TId=112131). Their worship has not attained the status and significance that the festival of Sammakka and Sarakka has achieved. This might be due to the major wars that Sammakka and Sarakka had lead.

Suffering and untimely death have been noted to be one of the explanations for the reverence of heroic goddesses. Although these features form part of deification of the Sammakka and Sarakka; another feature of their deification is central to their festival, the aspect of sumangali (auspicious woman). Therefore, family ties are at the center of this festival. I will examine parallels between the story of goddess Sammakka and classical goddess Nidra and Durga Mahishamardini in the following pages. The goddess Sammakka is firmly connected to the Shakti through her symbolic identification with goddess Durga.

15.2.2 Goddess Traditions: Historic Precendents

Memorialization and inception of the worship of Sammakka and Sarakka closely resembles the tradition of worshiping heroes is noticed in the Hindu Epics, the Ramayana and the Mahabharata, which is ubiquitous across India including the Deccan region. However, being feminine divine, their worship differs from the usual. Thus, the festival of Sammakka and Sarakka assimilates qualities and practices associated with epic goddesses and local memorials. It is celebrated in a way similar to the existing tradition with the addition of innovations of its own. In its evolution as the most popular festival of Andhra Pradesh, and central India, the story of the goddesses resembles features of the classical Hindu goddesses of the Puranas. Hence, I consider below, some of the epic parallels of the goddesses.

The goddesses, Sammakka and Sarakka are associated with village goddesses and with the great goddess, the Śakti. They are not in any way connected to the Saptamatrikas (the 7 mother goddesses) or any of the village goddesses commonly worshipped in the villages. Nonetheless, for the people who attend the Jātara, benevolent qualities, spirituality and divinity of Sammakka and Sarakka are manifested in the same way as any other Hindu goddess. They are no less than the Śakti or Mahādevi or no more than the popular village goddesses. They embody the popular and dynamic nature of the goddesses. The specific heroism and strength of these goddesses is not obliterated by this ritual projection, but their superior efficacy is indicated by the undifferentiated devotion. In fact, by this process, Sammakka and Sarakka became members of the huge group of goddesses who are born whenever it is necessary to alleviate the fears of the struggling devotees.

Prakriti (nature) is symbolic of the feminine divine. The trees themselves are also considered divine and worshipped as goddesses. neem, pipal or banyan tree are especially noted for such worship. Almost all the major temples have a tree in the temple compound known as the "*sthala vriksa*". This tree is offered worship as sacred in the usual procedure as the divine icons in the temple, with offerings of flowers, incense, turmeric, sandal, fruits, food and red *kumkuma*. This shows the Telugu cultural fabric, which celebrates the woman with five simple symbols for her auspiciousness as sumangali: flowers, turmeric, bangles, kumkuma (red dot adorning the forehead), katuka (eyeliner). Exchanging these or at least the kumkuma if nothing else is available is common practice among Telugu women. Giving bottu (bottu pettatam) is the most common tradition of women honoring their relationship or friendship. Bottu is the most central practice of the festival and closely connected with Telugu regional culture. Women exchange bottu when they meet and depart, it is considered inauspicious if someone is not honored with bottu upon arrival or leaving. The festival begins with finding bottu pette (vermillion box) and kumkuma/bottu also forms central part of offerings in a symbolic gesture of embodying the local culture. Therefore, the festival is Hindu in nature while also incorporating regional Telugu and Koya cultural practices.

The devotees also tie small pieces of cloth or strands of thread to the branches of the tree expressing their wishes, which they hope will be fulfilled as they express them in this way to the trees. Early cults of the sacred groves and wish granting trees are known from Buddhist texts, Jain sources, and the Hindu *puranas*. The trees are worshipped in India as abodes of gods, yaksas and other spirits. Trees are closely connected with a number of deities in devotional Hinduism especially, in relation to Krishna and Balarama. The popularity of tree worship is also indicated in an event narrated in the Harivamsa, when Krishna felled two Ashoka trees in Vraj, which are known as "wish granting trees" from which two *Yaksas* emerged. The stories of Balarama from the *puranas* indicate absorption of several such tree cults into the devotional Hinduism.

Paleolithic goddess and Indus valley goddess set apt precedent for long established goddess worship in India. Early art of India from Mathura (100–300) yielded a number of images depicting woman and a tree or woman embracing a tree. The women in these images are considered to represent female deities, *yaksinis*, who later emerged as the numerous goddesses in Hinduism, while the trees are considered to represent fertility. In fact, the *Dasara Navaratras*, includes the worship of goddess Durga adorned with vegetables representing *Sakambari Devi* (Leaf and Vegetable clad goddess representing Prakriti), as a goddess of vegetation. Ancient trees are regarded as sacred and worshipped as deities. Pillalamarri, in Mahabubnagar district of Andhra Pradesh is a holy site with a seven hundred year old banyan tree (extends almost up to three miles), as the central deity of worship. Another large banyan tree, recorded as the world's the largest banyan tree in the Guinness book of world records, known as Thimmamma Marrimanu considered to be sacred and worshipped (Vemsani, 2006: 76). Modugu tree forms the central part of celebration in the festival of goddesses Sammaka and Sarakka. Modugu tree is also known as Palash tree, referred to as the flame of the forest for the bright red flowers it bears in spring. Its scientific name is Butea Monosperma, one of the widely growing trees in Deccan region. This tree produces red colored flowers in the Spring, hence known as fire of the forest. This is the season the Sammakka and Sarakka festival generally takes place.

In her depiction as the ultimate goddess, Sammakka shares many features of classical Hindu goddesses. I will examine below similarities between the images of Sammakka and epic goddesses Nidra and Durga Mahisamardini of the epics (Kinsely, 1998). Goddess Durga is depicted with tiger or lion. She is the tiger riding goddess. Legend has it that Sammakka was found by her adoptive parents and fellow tribesmen returning from a hunting expedition in the forest of Dandakaranya. The Koya hunters were awestruck upon seeing a young girl child playing with the tigers in the wild forest and the Koya chief Medaraja has decided immediately to adopt her and brought her home right away. The unmistakable symbolism of tigers and the goddesses are immediately clear. Sammakka plays with the tigers, while Durga rides the tiger. This legend portrays her as equally ferocious and fearless as the goddess Durga Mahisamardini. The memory also depicts her sharing one of the central features of the goddess Durga through her symbolic playing with the tiger. Hence, she shares the central feature of *Leela* as that of playful relationship with tigers. This episode depicts goddess Sammakka as an amsa of goddess Durga.

Another similar epic precedent can be found in the story of the birth of Krishna (Vemsani, 2006). According to this story Kamsa (a demon king) pledges to kill Krishna as soon as he is born. Thus, Krishna was transferred to a cowherd village and was replaced with a girlchild born to Yaśoda, in the cowherd village (Gokula). The goddess Nidra, in the form of the girl child was brought back to Kamsa. She was killed by Kamsa, mistaking her for Krishna, the 8th child of Devaki and Vasudeva. This event is indicative of the motif of self-sacrifice and suffering associated with the goddesses (Vemsani, 2006: 68–71). Nidra underwent this sacrifice in order to save Krisna and the Yadavas, from the atrocities of Kamsa.

The goddess Nidra differs from all the other goddesses and gods in the sense that she faced suffering and sacrifice in order to bring an end to the suffering of others, while Durga Mahishamardini, slays the demon, Mahisha, due to his atrocities. This is one of the features that set her apart from all the other goddesses, so also the goddesses Sammakka and Sarakka in this tribal legend. The suffering and sacrifice is for the others, Koyas this case. It is this feature of rushing into danger without fearing for life and rescuing the others, that is the central feature that unites the goddesses in our story with goddess Nidra of *Harivamsapurana* 45 (Vemsani, 2006: 68–71; 2022: 162). However, for the people who attend the Jātara, they are just goddesses and the questions of identification do not matter. They attend the festival in order to find solutions (answers) for their own concerns and anxieties that the goddess may help alleviate. Numerous stories of the goddesses' miracles in helping with alleviating the daily concerns are recounted during the Jatara by the devotees.

During the past three decades the erstwhile Andhra Pradesh, currently Telangana state, is subjected to an unprecedented and sudden industrialization and now a computerized modernity. This has brought about urbanization and changes in the life of the common people. Life in the city is characterized by intensified sensory stimulation, depersonalized relationships, brutal competition for economic gain and the atrophy of individual culture. Now with the emergence of mini-Jātaras all over the state of Andhra Pradesh, it is easier than ever to attend the festival and regain and regenerate the spirit of life.

The festival has survived the ravages of time through minimal adaptations. It is a peaceful pilgrimage for the people tired and confused with their modern existence. These goddesses are believed to come down to earth every other year to receive worship and bless the people.

Participation in this festival is now an escape from this modern life. Many people make preparations to stay at the place of the festival for a period ranging from 3 days to more than a week. Participation in this festival marks remembering one's roots: roots in tribal life in an agriculture based society, and in the mother.

In the following section I will examine the rituals associated with the goddesses Sammakka and Sarakka Jātara in order to understand their symbolic meaning and discuss how they are connected to the anxieties of modern life.

15.3 Feminine Heroic to Feminine Divine: Goddesses Sammakka and Sarakka in Historic Memory

The second millennium brought sudden upheavals as former political, social, and religious structures faced sudden destruction from invading forces completely alien to the established structures. Deccan region underwent numerous raids between thirteenth and fourteenth centuries. The Yadava, Kakatiya, and Hoyasala empires faced incessant destructive wars. Sammakka and Sarakka Jātara originated during a very tumultous period in the history of Andhra Pradesh and Telangana. The period between 1300 and 1450 C.E represents a time of tremendous upheaval resulting in changes in the socio-economic, cultural, religious, and political life of Andhra Pradesh. Religious conflicts between the followers of Hinduism, and the new Muslim invaders, are common during this period (Parabrahma Sastry, 1978). Andhra Pradesh was also affected by the arrival of an important new religious movement with the migration of Sufi saints to this region (Deccan area) from occupied Islamic states of northern India. Incessant wars that looted and captured young men and women weakened the region and destroyed the hamlets and temples leading to sorrow. But this also leads to the establishment of new memorials for the departed heroes among which Sammakka and Sarakka festival is ranked at the top.

The Deccan region suffered from political unrest and instability during the early stages of establishment of Sultanate in Delhi due to the Muslim raids they sent into the Deccan conquering the Yadava and Kakatiya empires. The state was divided into numerous minor principalities ruled by the local Nayakas. Although the Nayaks were subject to superior order overlords, the local rulers were independent in their own areas and ruled without much intervention from the above. Because of the existence of numerous small kingdoms, power struggles were common and battles were frequent. The forest kingdom where this festival is held now was ruled by Medaraja during 1036 C.E, who in turn was subject to a local kingdom Vemulawāda Chālukyas (Vemsani, 1993) who were defeated and subjugated to the rule of the Kākatiya rulers of Warangal during 1100 C.E. Thus Medaram, a part of Polavasa principality, was part of Kakatiya empire since the eleventh century.

With the foundation of the Kakatiya empire in the Deccan region between tenth and eleventh Century C.E. the region experienced unprecedented economic prosperity. The status of women improved significantly during this time in the Telugu region. Women seem to have participated in public affairs during this period, while one of the rulers of Kakatiya empire is a strong woman, Rudrama Devi. From 1000 C.E onwards, names of women appear in temple inscriptions of this region, as donors and active participants of temple activities. This was less common prior to the tenth century in this region (Vemsani, 1993). Women also appear in various capacities as participants in various ceremonies and the rituals of temples. The new economic activity and donations made by women might suggest that women were involved in other economic and political roles, which might have allowed them the freedom to donate to religious organizations and were less confined to their domestic roles.

It is in this society that during the late 1100 C.E two heroic women, Sammakka and Sarakka came to be worshipped. At that time the Koyas were undergoing great hardships, and these women came to be revered for their heroic sacrifice. This festival, established in their honour celebrates marginality as its central focus in two ways. Firstly, it honors the Koya tribal community, which is one of the forest communities existing on the margins of society, and secondly it gives central place to the women, who form the oppressed section part of the society. This festival, by placing marginality at the center of the celebration, has come to acquire a central place in the hearts of the common people to Andhra Pradesh. In its historical evolution, the festival has overcome the sectarian identities and acquired popular reverence regardless of caste, creed, community and gender.

Mulugu region was part of the Kakatiya empire ruled by Kakatiya emperors Rudrama Devi (1262–1289) and Pratapa Rudra (1289–1323). Especially, the reign of Kakatiya emperor Pratapa Rudra is subjected to numerous Islamic raids. During the late thirteenth century 7 raids were launched on the Kakatiyas weakening the state ruled by the emperor Pratapa rudra. Every section of Telugu society suffered the ravages of incessant Islamic invaders' raids from Delhi.

Sammakka and Sarakka festival originated in the forest kingdom of Medaram during the Kakatiya empire (1100 C.E–1324 C.E) among the Koya tribal community of Andhra Pradesh. The turn of the millennium brought a violent war-torn period in the history of Andhra Pradesh. Each of the Kakatiya emperors fought successive battles with neighbors as well as with the occupied Islamic state of the Delhi Sultanate, the first occupied Islamic state in India. Small wars on the country-side ensued as a result of these wars, since the invading armied raided the countryside, capturing treasure and slaves. In the case of the last two Kakatiya wars with the Delhi Sultanate these raids resulted in immense devastation and loss of life.

Kakatiya inscriptions record wars with two Medarajas, one during the military expedition of Gangadhara in 1117 C.E. (Gangaraja in some inscriptions HAS No. 19. P. 129), a military general of Kakatiya Emperor Prolaraja II (1117–1150) and another Medaraja during the rule of the Kakatiya Emperor Rudradeva (1150–1195). The Medaraja who was defeated by Prolaraja II is a Mandaleswara (ruler of Mandala) of the Polavasa region. Polavasa included parts of Karimnagar and Warangal districts of Modern Andhra Pradesh, which includes the Mulugu region. Another Medaraja was defeated by the Kakatiya emperor Rudradeva in 1182 C.E., who occupied the Polavasa region. Two Medarajas (dated 1117 C.E. and 1182 C.E) are said to have been defeated by two Kakatiya emperors successively according to the inscriptions, which indicates that the second might be a repetition or might have been another expedition, and scholars have guessed that the second Medaraja might have been a grandson of the first Medaraja defeated earlier (Khandavalli, 1975: 18–23). Whatever might have been the historical events of this region, it can be understood that the tribal region of Mulugu spread between Warangal, Karimnagar and Khammam districts was successively included in the Kakatiya empire before 1200 C.E., which serves as a historical backdrop to the events connected to the festival of Sammakka and Sarakka. However, the Kakatiya empire faced wars from neighbors and Delhi Sultanate since 1295, the year Prataparudra, the last emperor of the Kakatiya state took over the empire, unfortunately, the same year also marked the beginning of Khilji rule in Delhi Sultanate. Close to 7 wars were recorded between Delhi Sultanate and Kakatiya State between 1303 and 1323 C.E. These led to immense loss of life, wealth and economic strife on the countryside. The Kakatiya emperor surrendered immense wealth, horses, and elephants as tributes to the Delhi Sultanate, including the Koh-i-noo diamond. However, it only increased the thirst of the Sultanate for more wealth leading to more wars. The first two Tugluq rulers were responsible for the 7 raids into the Kakatiya empire (Parabrahma Sastry, 2005: 131–137). Therefore, the historical events connected to the festival of Sammakka and Sarakka can be placed in early 1300 C.E. in the destructive period of Islamic raids approximately 700 years ago.

15.4 Modern Practice in the Goddess Festival

Indian religious traditions, especially Hinduism has a wider practice-based religion, apart from the traditional textual religion. Role of common people, in shaping the religious practice in the way that suites the changing times and circumstances is a notable feature of religion in the Indian Subcontinent, especially the goddess religion. The popularity of the festival of Sammakka and Sarakka should be understood as a social phenomenon in this aspect, but should not be considered in isolation. Therefore, the broad goal of this paper is to bring into light, the broad spectrum of religious practices in relation to goddesses of India, and the futility of imposing categorizations on the religion of South Asia in general. It is not only pertinent to investigate this festival closely to understand the popular religion in Andhra Pradesh, but an examination of this festival also helps us in understanding the nature of goddesses and contribute to the current understanding of goddesses, and Hinduism in India in general.

Sammakka and Sarakka *Jātara* originated in the of the forests of Mulugu area as a small Koya *Jātara* during 1323 C.E. on the eve of the fall of Kakatiya empire, even though it has come to be regarded as the people's festival of modern Andhra Pradesh surpassing the limitations of class, creed and gender. In the recent years, the biannual festival celebrated in reverence of Sammakka and Sarakka has acquired tremendous popularity, attracting devotees of all religious backgrounds from far and wide. Even though Heimerndorf seems to have studied certain clans of Koyas of Adilabad, it is doubtful if he has visited the Mulugu area, although he undertook an extensive ethnographic research in the Nizam's dominions (Heimendorf, 1948a, 1948b), he does not record Sammakka and Sarakka *Jātara*. Hemindorf's work is mostly focused on Adilabad district and Rajgonds and Kondareddys of that area. Although for reasons that remain mysterious, this led to the surmise by some people that, the festival might not have been as popular during that time (1945), which seems far from the truth. It should be noted that, Heimendorf's research is sketchy on the Koyas of Warangal and Khammam districts. This might be due to two reasons: First, he might not have had closer relations with Koyas of this region as other areas and secondly, that he might not have spent enough time in this region to know the social and religious practices as the Sammakka and Sarakka Jatara is celebrated once in two years, he might have missed it.

It would be interesting to study what features have contributed to such meteoric rise in the popularity of the goddesses, during the past 700 years. Sammakka and Sarakka festival then brings forward a new phenomenon in Hinduism and this is also characteristic of goddess religion, which is fluid and popular based naturally. Popular religion based on such goddesses is indicative of the transformative nature of Hinduism.

This popular worship of Hinduism depicts worldly objects as symbols and images of the other world (divine sphere) and provides a sense of profound meaning to the everyday life. Life becomes a burden if it is seen as an end in itself. By providing sacred meanings and symbolic connections to everyday life, the popular religion provides a fulfillment and meaning to life and living itself.

More than two million people were recorded as having attended this festival last time it was celebrated in 2022. For the people who travel far and wide to take part in this festival and for the others who participate and facilitate the organization of the festival in various other ways, this festival represents a journey to the roots to the forest and to their origins. The festival in the forest kingdom is reminiscent of life of the centuries past, and is in total contrast to the busy, modern lives of the urban centers. Participation in this festival now provides people with a renewed sense of their roots and enables them to return to their modern lives with a new sense of belonging and strength. Therefore, the festival of Sammakka and Sarakka is as much a tribute to the goddesses as that of the nature in the form of forest, and life of previous era.

The popular nature of Sammakka and Sarakka festival is also indicated by the dramatic contrast in naming between the traditional festivals associated with temples and popular festivals in the terminology used to designate the festival. The festival of Sammakka and Sarakka is a bienniel festival called "Jātara," while a festival associated with a temple of a Hindu god or Goddess is more likely to be called as "Tirunāl". "Tirunāl" means "holy day," while Jātara would closely correspond to the idea of Carnival [3]. Another contrast is that there is no permanent structure such as a temple at Medaram, although a temple and numerous shrines are built across Andhra Pradesh now under the supervision of the Andhra Pradesh State Endowments Board (see Sect. 4 below). Devotees and followers of Sammakka and Sarakka return to this place at the time of the festival every two years and construct the required structures. The survival and popularity of this festival among tribal and non-tribal communities in Andhra Pradesh signals that progress is being made in both directions, in that of Koyas opening to the outside world and that of the outside world to the Koyas and their culture through reception and participation in their festivals. This festival has become a symbol of resistance, cultural transformation and adoptation, which is why it has acquired the status of state festival of Andhra Pradesh. I discuss below, the celebration of Sammakka and Sarakka Jatara in detail.

I discuss below the sacred narrative of Sammakka and Sarakka to understand, how it connects with traditional symbols and myths while evoking a new tradition in itself.

15.5 Festival Processes: Clan Traditions and Modern Adaptations

The festival begins with a unique procedure of its own, which connects the memory to the present. The goddess is said to appear in a dream vision to a tribal boy of Koya tribe. Then this boy leaves for the forest in search of the goddess and returns with a casket of vermillion (*kumkuma bharina*) known in Telugu as *Bottu pette* (vermillion box), which is then taken in procession and installed on the *gaddelu* (earthern platform) specially prepared for this occasion, at the precise spot where she disappeared almost 700 years ago. The *kumkuma bharina* is then set on the bamboo poles after initiatory ritual and offerings of *bali* (sacrifice) start with descendants of her family acting as the officiating priests.

The memory is awakened in the vision of a young boy who then wanders in the forests, enacting the final event (scene) in the life of Sammakka, thus awakening the memory in the onlookers and the whole community gathered to remember and celebrate her heroic self-sacrifice. Thus the memory of her life is etched on the hearts of the devotees gathered as it is etched on the landscape of the forest and carries on to the future generations.

Memory and memorialization happens in a different way among the people unlike the museums where articles act as remnants of bygone era, the memory is enlivened here symbolically through the boy and imprinted on the hearts of the people.

Traditionally fowls and sheep or goat are sacrificed along with an offering of gur (brown sugar). Offering of gur is common and continues throughout the duration of the Jātara.

I will consider below, the symbolism of these three processes noticed here, namely, the search and finding of the Kumkuma bharina, sacrifice of goats and fowls, offering of Gur.

Kumkuma bharina is one of the five symbols of *sumangali* (married woman). The central place given to the kumkuma bharina as symbolic representation of reappearance of the goddess stresses the importance of marital status in this Jātara. In light of the prevalent symbolism associated with marriage, it can be assumed that kumkuma bharina in this festival indicates the status of sumangali in the case of the goddess Sammakka. The officiating priests are the descendants of the family of Sammakka and Sarakka. This festival therefore represents the femininity, motherhood, and centrality of the family. A pilgrimage to this Jatara is like a journey to the mother and roots of one's origin. In fact, Sammakka and Sarakka festival symbolically begins with the journey of a young boy (about 10 years of age generally) deep into the forests in search of kumkuma bharina. The status of the mother and the return to the roots is represented here. The symbolism in this forest region represents the centrality of woman at the base of the family at the same time stresses the central role of males in their role as officiating role seen at every stage of the Jātara.

The ritual of "sacrifice" represents the violence that the goddesses had undergone as human beings. Sacrifice also represents the principle of regeneration. The goddesses are auspicious because of the regenerative power that the female represents. Here the sacrifice represents the battle, when these people have heroically defended their kingdom under the leadership of Sammakka and Sarakka. The sacrificial animals represent the suffering that the innocent people had faced during the time of the battle, while the offerings of jaggery/gur (known as, bellam, in the local language, Telugu, is solidified Sugarcane juice) represents the swetness and ever continuing life.

The jaggery/gur represents the eternal cycle of life and regeneration. Sugarcane plants never lose their life totally. New plants grow from the left over shoots after each crop season. While the animal sacrifices represent the battle or violence in the death of Sammakka and the battle, where numerous people have lost their lives, the offerings of brown sugar denote the renewal of life, as derivative of sugar cane, which regenerates each season from the remaining stalks. This renewing life from the old remaining stalks represents life and regeneration. Its sweetness also represents the sweetness of sharing with the community and happy life.

People throng to this festival and pray to the goddesses seeking favors in mundane matters such as seeking offspring, economic welfare, relief from illness, trouble etc. The power of the goddesses deriving from their self-sacrifice is evident in these prayers. I consider below some of the modern meanings. Modern conveyances such as buses, cars, and helicopters are employed to travel to the temple of Sammakka and Sarakka for this festival. A permanent temple is constructed by the State Endowments Board here. Political leaders including the Chief Minister of the state undertake the festival pilgrimage to the Sammakka and Sarakka temple.

15.6 Memory, Nature, and Tradition in Goddess Festival

It is hard to isolate myth from the memory of public history in the festival of Sammakka and Sarakka. The myth and memory are so closely fused together that it is impossible to understand when memory turns into myth.

Memory, especially public memory of historical figures of significant nature is a ubiquitous part of Hindu popular religious practice. Popular saints themselves are memorialized through narratives, performances and festivals (Novazke). Although the process of memorialization in the festival of Sammakka and Sarakka is similar to that noticed in the sacred hagiographies of saints, and the regional tradition of revering the heroes with viragal. Therefore, Sammakka and Sarakka festival is typical in its popular nature for its reverence of heroic sacrifice, although heroic identity or a savior motif is usually associated with male deities, from time to time, Indian tradition attributes a goddess with the heroic role as savior as noted in this festival. It is in the heroic and savior role that, the goddesses Sammakka and Sarakka are remembered and worshipped in Medāram village in Andhra Pradesh.

Memory plays a central role in this festival. In fact, Sammakka and Sarakka festival incorporated the collective memory of the life and death of the goddesses, now symbolized in the festival for the people of India. Other traditions of memory are also noticed in Andhra Pradesh as noted above including the Viragal (memorial stones). Memorial stones erected in memory of the departed heroes are noted in the countryside of Andhra Pradesh in almost every village. But they differ in several respects from the Sammakka and Sarakka Jatara. Firstly, Viragals are marked by permanent memorials (memorial stones with or without structural construction), while Sammakka and Sarakka Jatara uses temporary materials and structures (wooden pole), as the Jatara is based on reconstruction of memory rather than the memorials. The festival of Sammakka and Sarakka thrives on the enactment of memory, but not the memorial itself in the festival. Secondly, Sammakka and Sarakka festival honors female heroines similar to the *viragals*, which are erected in memory of male or female heroes across southern India. This difference separates Sammakka and Sarakka from folk festivals of Andhra Pradesh and places her securely in the center. However, Sammakka is in a different league identified with other Hindu goddesses, who are attributed the heroic savior role from time to time. It is in the heroic and savior role that, but as the goddesses Sammakka and Sarakka are remembered similar to the other Hindu goddesses.

I will examine below how the goddesses Sammakka and Sarakka are connected theologically to the Epic goddesses of Hinduism.

Sammakka and Sarakka festival has attracted unprecedented following in the Telangana, Andhra Pradesh, and its neighboring states, Orissa, Madhya Pradesh, Chhattisgarh, and Maharashtra. This has prompted some modern adaptations to take place in the celebration of Sammakka and Sarakka Jātara.

Modern meanings have projected this festival to be declared as the state festival of Andhra Pradesh, which is a major step in attributing centrality to the goddesses Sammakka and Sarakka in the mainstream religious practices of Telugu region.

These goddesses are now honored and celebrated regardless of gender, caste, creed, community, and religion. This modern recognition has resulted in replication and multiplicity of the festival. This phenomenon has led to the creation of what is termed as mini-Sammakka jātaras taking place at various places all over the Telangana region of Andhra Pradesh. The mini-jātaras are miniature replicas of the central jātara that takes place in Medaram, and takes place where the devotees decide to congregate during the same time that the Jātara takes place in Medaram. A number of towns such as Manugururu and other towns in Warangal and Khammam district also constructed permanent shrines and hold the biennial festival with help from the Endowments Board of Andhra Pradesh State Government. Koya tribal head of such a new sacred place acts as the officiating priest in establishing the bamboo replicas of the goddesses at the selected place and officiating in a way similar to the ritual of the Medaram Jātara. Although it is not the same place, as Medaram, the place in the forests where the goddess disappeared or the officiating priests are not the descendants of her family, the festival is celebrated with the same fervor and enthusiasm by the enthusiastic devotees with similar rituals including sacrifice, procession, as noted above in the Medaram Jātara making it clear that it is for the values that they represent are projected to central status. With this development, the goddesses Sammakka and Sarakka have completed the full circle in their meteoric rise to the status of the most popular goddesses of Andhra Pradesh. Similar to goddess Durga, their replicas can be established anywhere people find it is necessary to worship.

Private airlines offer festival trip on helicopters to Medaram Jatara from cities such as Hyderabad at minimal costs, which show the immense popularity of the festival and its socio-economic consequences in a fast paced modern Indian society. Such services are very rarely offered in the case of numerous other temples or sacred places in India.

Recently, the Endowment Board of the Andhra Pradesh State Government tried to incorporate cultural events (Banjara dance etc.) from other tribals groups into this Jatara in 2012 as part of the festival, which were strongly opposed by the Koya tribal elders, who closely guard the festival as a traditional festival representing the Koya traditions, not to be diluted by incorporating other tribal traditions. This shows how the tribe is committed to protecting the clan identity and authenticity of the festival, although Hinduism runs as an overarching theme in the festival. Koyas were not ready to compromise the clan and ritual authenticity of the festival.

This is one of the most colorful and passion filled goddess festivals of Andhra Pradesh. Due to the historic antecedents connected to this festival, people participate in the festival with a spirit of nostalgia. Old stories are recounted, new ones are added. It is the protective and beneficent power of the goddess that brings people here. Now the Government of Andhra Pradesh has recognized the ancient spirit represented by this festival and is the official sponsor of the festival. This festival has come a long way from being a local tribal festival to being recognized as an official state festival of Andhra Pradesh.

15.7 Conclusion

This study shows that the goddesses are not limited by any of the known normative structures or principles of society. I argue here that the role of religion, caste, class or language in the worship of goddesses are minimal. The major goddess Durga Mahishamardini depicted as riding tiger is symbolically connected to Sammakka and worshipped as a representation of goddess Durga by one and all. This paper represents one of the directions that the study on goddesses requires to work beyond the barriers of definition and function. Patriarchal norms of gender analysis is secondary to the Sammakka and Sarakka festival. Therefore, this paper adopts such gender inclusive analysis in the study of goddesses and adopts the analysis of historical society by understanding the symbolism associated with this festival.

Although this paper does not provide answers for all the questions raised in the study of goddesses, women, and religion it offers some of the methods and widens the field of study by attempting to study a festival of goddesses that originated on the margins of society during one of the most violent periods of history acquired centrality. This study also indicates that the previous labels or traditional models of the academic study of goddesses are not useful in understanding the implications of gender in goddess tradition. This paper also questions the application a single model approach regardless of the context and individual attributes of each goddess. In addition, the study of Sammakka and Sarakka Jatara shows that it is the central concepts associated with the goddesses that have projected them to the central status and understanding these concepts would be fruitful to understanding the nature of a popular religion. Labeling the goddesses as spouse goddesses or wild goddesses is derogatory while imposing patriarchal normativity.

My research presented in this chapter challenges contemporary academic research on goddess-worship to rethink the categories of definition based on patriarchal notions of womanly function and questions the validity of applying a single model regardless of cultural and social context and individual attributes of each goddess. The goddess festival that originated on the margins of society and yet acquired centrality as a state festival flouts norms of hierarchy and gendered classification imposed on the goddesses.

The survival and popularity of this state festival among tribal and non-tribal communities in Andhra Pradesh and Telangana is significant. This festival has become a symbol of cultural transformation and adaptation, and careful analysis reveals that the role of religion, caste or creed is minimal. Put differently, the goddess worship in this festival appears to transcend the boundaries of religion, and gender. Similarly, my analysis of this popular, modern state festival seeks to transcend the boundaries of gender bias that has dominated goddess research in the past.

References

Aggarwal, J. C., Raza, M., Ahmad, A., & Aggarwal, S. (1990). *An atlas of tribal India: With computed table of district level data and its geographical interpretation.* Concept Publishing House.

Austin, C. A. (2008). The Sarasvata Yatsattra in the Mahabharata 17 and 18. *International Journal of Hindu Studies, 12*(3), 283–308.

Babb, L. L. (2020). *Religion in India: Past and present.* Dunedin Academic Press (DAP).

Beck, B. (2015). *The legend of Ponnivala. Graphic work.* University of Toronto.

Bhattacharyya, N. N. (1977). *The Indian mother goddess,* (2nd rev. ed.). Manohar. First ed. 1970.

Bryant, E. F., & Ekstrand, M. (Eds.). (2004). *The Hare Krishna movement: The postcharismatic fate of a religious transplant.* Columbia University Press.

Chakrabarti, D. 2010 [1999]. *India: An archaeological history.* Oxford University Press.

Coomaraswamy, A. K. (1971). *Yaksas.* 2 vols. 1928 and 1931; repr. Munshiram Manoharlal.

Cutler, N., & Narayanan, V. (Eds.) (1985). *Gods of flesh and gods of stone: The embodiment of divinity in India.* Anima Books.

Eck, D. L. (1981). *Darsan: Seeing the divine in India.* Harvard University Press.

Feldhaus, A. (1995). *Water and womanhood: Religious meanings of rivers in Maharashtra.* Oxford.

Fisher, E. (2018). Multi-regional and multi-linguistic Virasaivism: Change and continuity in early devotional tradition. In L. Vemsani (Ed.), *Modern Hinduism in text and context.* Bloomsbury.

Fuller, C. J. (1980). *The camphor flame.* Princeton Univerrsity Press.

Gatewood, L. (1985). *Devi and spouse goddesses.* Manohar.

Haberman, D. (1994). *Journey through the twelve forests: An encounter with Krishna.* Oxford University Press.

Hawley, J. S., & Wulff, D. M. (Eds.) (1998). *Devī: Goddesses of India.* Motilal Banarsidass.

Hawley, J. S. (1998). The Goddess in India: One goddess and many, new and old. In J. S. Hawley & D. M. Wulff (Eds.), *Devī: Goddesses of India.* Motilal Banarsidass.

Heimendorf. (1948a). *The Raj Gonds of Adilibad.* Oxford University Press.

Heimendorf. (1948b). *The Reddis of the Bison Hills.* Oxford University Press.

Hendelman, D., & Shulman, D. (1995). *God inside out.* Oxford University Press.

Kenoyer, J. M., Clark, J. D., Pal, J. N., & Sharman, G. R. (1983). An upper paleolithic shrine in India. *Antiquity, 57*, 88–94.

Kinsley, D. (1998) [First published 1986]. *Hindu goddesses: Visions of the divine feminine in the Hindu religious tradition.* Motilal Banarsidass.

Micheals, A., Vogelsanger, C., & Wilke, A. (1996). *Wild goddesses in India and Nepal.* Peter Lang.

Mohapatra, Ch. P. K. (1992). *The Koya.* Tribal and Harijan Research cum Training Institute.

Murthy, S. A. (1991). *Religion and society: A study of Koyas.* Discovery Publishing House.

Murty, M. L. K., & Sudhakar Reddy, Y. A. (2004). *Studies in Indian folk culture.* Centre for Folk Culture Studies.

Nicholson, A. (2010). *Unifying Hinduism: Philosophy and identity in Indian intellectual history.* Columbia University Press.

Padma, S. (2013). *Vicissitudes of the goddess: Reconstruction of the Gramadevata in India's religious traditions.* Oxford Scholarship Online.

Pannala, R. (1981). *Tribal economy of India (A case study of Koyas of Andhra Pradesh).* Light & Life Publishers.

Parabrahma Sastry, P. V. 2005 (1978). Telugu translation. In *Kakatiyulu.* Media House Publications.

Pinchman, T. (1994). *The rise of the goddess in Hindu tradition.* SUNY Press.

Ramanujan, A. K. (1986). Two realms of Kannada Folklore. In S. A. Blackburn & A. K. Ramanujan (Ed.), *Another harmony: New essays on the Folklore of India.* University of California Press.

Rao, N. (1989). *Text and tradition in South India.* Princeton University Press.

Shulman, D. D. (1980). *Tamil temple myths: Sacrifice and divine marriage in Tamil temple myths.* Princeton University Press.

Singh, K. S. (2002). Tribal women: Resurrection, demystification, and gender struggle. In A. Basu & K. Singari (Eds.), *Breaking out of invisibility*. ICHR, Northern Book Center.
Smith, K. B. (1998). *Reflections on resemblance, ritual, and religion*. Motilal Banarsidass.
Spina, N. (2018). In relationship with the goddess: Women interpreting leadership roles and shaping diasporic identities. In L. Vemsani (Ed.), *Modern Hinduism in text and context*. Bloomsbury.
Stewart, T. K. (1995). Encountering the smallpox goddess: The auspicious song of Śītalā. In D. S. Lopez (Ed.), *Religious of India in practice* (pp. 389–397). Princeton.
Trautman, R. T. (1997). *Aryans and British India*. University of California Press.
Tyler, S. (1969). *Koya, an outline Grammar: Gommu dialect*. University of California Press.
Van Buitenen, J. A. B. 1988 (1972). On the structure of the Sabhaparvan of the Mahabharata. In L. Rocher (Ed.), *Studies in Indian literature and philosophy: Collected articles of J.A.B. van Buitenen*, (pp. 305–321). Motilal Banarsidass.
Vemsani, L. (1993). *Inscriptions of Karimnagar district*. M.Phil. Thesis, University of Hyderabad.
Vemsani, L. (2006). *Hindu and Jain mythology of Balarama*. Edwin Mellen Press.
Vemsani, L. (2009). Narasimha, the Supreme Deity of Andhra Pradesh: Tradition and innovation in Hinduism—An examination of local mythology, folk stories and popular culture. *Journal of Contemporary Religion, 24*(1), 35–52.
Vemsani, L. (2016). *Balarama in Hindu and Jain texts*. Amazon.
Vemsani, L. (2018). *Modern Hinduism in text and context*. Bloomsbury Academic.
Vemsani, L. (2021). *Feminine journeys of the Mahabharata*. Palgrave McMilan/Springer Nature.
Vemsani, L. (2022). *Hinduism in middle India: Narasima, The Lord of the middle*. Bloomsbury Academic.
Wadley, S. S. (1980). Śītalā: The cool one. *Asian Folklore Studies, 39*, 33–62.
Younger, P. (2002). *Playing host to the god*. Oxford University Press.

Chapter 16
Legacies of Colonial Rule in India: How Race and Caste Continue to Divide Modern India

Jyoti Mohan

Abstract The use of the word 'race' in the Nineteenth century came to be harnessed to the colonial expansion of European powers, to justify and explain why certain nations were able to conquer large parts of the world. In India, French and German Indologists created a hierarchy of races to argue that while India was originally the home of the Indo-European or Aryan people, explaining the great cultural achievements of Ancient India, the racial intermixing over centuries with inferior races had caused the degeneration and decline of Indian civilization in the present time. The British harnessed these theories to argue that Indians needed to be governed based on their racial heritage, and created further categories of 'martial' races, and 'criminal' races. They also used the Indian system of social ordering (the caste system) to create concrete, unchangeable categories of hierarchy and power. This chapter looks at the manner in which these categories were created, and the results of such categories in terms of actual colonial rule. It provides correctives to the colonial studies which justified such divisions and examines the legacy of such categories in contemporary India.

Keywords Caste · Race · Racial hierarchy · Criminal castes and tribes · Thuggee · Martial races · Valandai · Idangai

16.1 Creating Racial Hierarchies

The modern meaning of the word 'race' came from the development of the Nineteenth century social science of Anthropology. Prior to this mid-Nineteenth century understanding, 'race' was a loosely used term that could indicate ethnic, linguistic, geographical, religious, or even culturally similar groups. The development of anthropology as a social science itself was a result of the rapidly expanding colonial regimes of European nations in the world. Having annexed large parts of the world that did

J. Mohan (✉)
Independent Historian, Baltimore, USA
e-mail: jyoti_mohan@hotmail.com

L. Vemsani (ed.), *Handbook of Indian History*,
https://doi.org/10.1007/978-981-97-6207-1_16

not belong to them, they needed a justification for their continued presence in these colonies—not only to convince the inhabitants of these colonies of their own importance, but also to justify their presence to other colonial empires and White nations. Anthropology, or the scientific study of man, became rapidly popular; in particular the branch of anthropology dealing with race, race theories and racial hierarchies, became convenient explanations for the colonial empires.[1]

Anne Maxwell notes that by the middle of the nineteenth century the idea that race (defined in physiological rather than linguistic or cultural terms) was a determining factor in the capacity of people to progress was established (Maxwell, 2000). Studies on race provided validation to the colonial civilizing mission since the white race was now indubitably superior to other races. In the case of India, ethnographic accounts describing the religion, customs, rituals, language and history of different ethnic, regional and caste groups, placed the various races on a hierarchical ladder which was based on parallel anthropological studies which focused on categorizing human races on a civilizational and developmental hierarchy based on race. Martin Staum points out that physical criteria for classifying men had triumphed over cultural criteria by 1850 (Staum, 2003). These physical criteria included anthropometric measurements like cranial and nasal indices, height and limb length to compare different races with the 'norm' or dominant group of Europeans.

India first caught the attention of French anthropologists due to its diverse racial composition. Nearly every pure (three pure races present in India were the Caucasoid, Mongoloid and Negroid) and mixed race (which included the Turanian and Dravidian races in the Indian context) was represented in the larger sub-continent. Therefore comparisons between races and studies in relative intelligence, ability, and civilization of races were made easy in India since there were so many races existing side by side. Unlike other comparisons of races where climate, language and even history were variables and therefore could be cited as the cause of difference, racial hierarchy could clearly be proved by studying India, since Aryans (representative of the Caucasoids), Mongoloids, Dravidians and Negrito races had developed their different cultures and civilizations within the same climatic and historical conditions. By studying India, anthropologists tried to prove that the crucial element in determining the physical and intellectual ability of people was not their history or climate, but their racial make-up.[2]

[1] In the early years of the Nineteenth century, theories of race were dominated by Jean-Baptiste de Lamarck and Geoffroy Saint-Hilaire, who were more or less in agreement that racial differences sprang from evolutionary needs, be it environmental, or climatic; in opposition to Georges Cuvier, who insisted that race was a reflection of intellectual and physical development, thus providing an early justification for apologists of racial hierarchies.

[2] It is important to recognize the fundamental flaw in this argument- 'India' itself was an artificial construct of the European colonizers. The boundaries of 'India' were recognizable as the boundaries of the British Indian Empire, and not an organic national entity. The cultures, religions, languages, climate and even history of the peoples contained within the geographical construct of 'India' were diverse. As a point of reference India is as large, geographically, as Europe, without Russia. If even all Europeans could not be classified as purely of one race, how could the people of India be ranked based on assumptions of commonality?

An example of the means by which 'race' was constructed can be seen in the description of the 'Dravidian' case. In an article published in the *Nouveau Journal Asiatique* in 1828 (before the craze with racial hierarchies took center stage) the pre-eminent French philologist Eugene Burnouf examined the context of the usage of the words *Drâvida* and Tamil and concluded that the variety of meanings ascribed to the words made it impossible to make any conclusive statement about whether they implied a linguistic, geographical, or racial sense. It was certainly wrong to ascribe the word 'Dravida' or the word 'Tamil' to any particular race. Yet, as Thomas Trauttman had demonstrated in his work on Languages and Nations, the 'Dravidian proof' which was elaborated by F W Ellis in 1816 suggested that Southern languages[3] like Telugu did not have Aryan antecedents. i.e. they were not part of the Indo-European group of languages associated with the Indo-European or Caucasoid group (Trauttman, 2006). While Burnouf had pointed out that the geographical boundaries of what constituted 'Tamil' had constantly shifted over the centuries, Ellis assigned his assertions to a defined geographical area. The Asiatick Society of Calcutta, under the leadership of William Jones[4] had presented major languages in the Indian subcontinent as being derived from Sanskrit, which was Indo-European; Ellis was now suggesting that the languages of the Southern peninsula owed their existence to a 'Dravidian' kinship rather than an 'Indo-Aryan' kinship.

Ellis' argument was made in the context of an administrative decision to train young Englishmen coming to India. Working from Madras in Southern India, he anticipated that Englishmen with no prior exposure to Indic languages, would have a better chance of success if the College in Hayleybury in England, which trained all English administrators shipping out to India, were to break down its linguistic offerings into an 'Indo-European' one consisting of Persian and Sanskrit roots which could ostensibly make some sense of most of the Northern Indian languages, since they were derived from Sanskrit (as in the case of Bengali) or Persian (as in the case of Urdu) or a combination of both (as in the case for Hindustani or Hindi and its multiple dialects and cognates); and a Dravidian language offering (focusing on the root words common to Tamil, Telegu, Kannada and Malayalam).

While neither Ellis nor William Jones engaged in speculations about race, the category of 'Dravidian' was quickly co-opted into a non-Aryan racial category. By the middle of the Nineteenth-century Paul Topinard, a prominent French anthropologist, who categorized the Dravidians as part of the Mongoloid races, noted in his book *Science and Faith*, that they were capable of relatively high civilizational attainment, due to their sharpness of mind, but ultimately, they were preoccupied with the material things of life, and lacked the aspiration to a higher moral, aesthetic and ethical achievement that was the hallmark of the white races (Topinard, 1899).

[3] The Southern group of languages in India consist of Tamil, Telugu, Kannada and Malayalam, corresponding to the states of Tamil Nadu, erstwhile Andhra Pradesh (now divided into Andhra Pradesh and Telangana), Karnataka and Kerala.

[4] The Asiatick Society of Calcutta was the earliest organized group of Indologists founded in 1784, who studied Indian literature and culture. Many were Indophiles like Sir William Jones, Charles Wilkins and Alexander Hamilton (not the American statesman!) and eventually the society began to admit Indians as well.

Topinard's application of racial principles to define progress was clear in the Indian context in his work, *L'Anthropologie* (Topinard, 1876). In this work, he defined the Hindu type as best represented by the Rajputs and most of all by the brahmins of Mathura, Thaneswar, and Benaras. This 'Hindu type' was a new variation on the racial types of the anthropologists. If any more proof was needed that despite their protestations about relying on hard data, and having a scientific basis of their pronouncements on race, most anthropologists continued to use terms haphazardly.

Among the most visible works on racial theory in the nineteenth century was the Comte de Gobineau's *Essai sur l'inégalité des races humaines* (Gobineau, 1967 transl). Fascinated by the varying accomplishments of different civilizations, Gobineau concluded that the only variable to explain the differing levels of achievement was race. There was a fundamental, *measurable* intellectual and moral capacity for each race that determined civilizational development which only miscegenation could alter. This scale, based on cranial measurement and moral and material achievement of races in their purest form, proceeded with the whites declining to the yellow race and finally the blacks at the bottom. Translated to the Indian case, Gobineau described the Hindus as having reached great heights of intellectual and metaphysical achievement but fundamentally lacking in material desire and therefore material accomplishment. Gobineau divided races into those dominated by the 'male' principle of material desire (*purusha*) and headed by the Chinese civilization; and those dominated by the female principle (*prakriti*) of 'intellectual current' and headed by the Hindus who chose to focus their entire energy on philosophical and theological ideas to the detriment of material progress. Moreover, this achievement had been accomplished in the early stage of the development of Hindu civilization, when the Aryan race was at its purest. Gobineau argued that a civilization was strongest when the blood or race of its founders was purest, and that degeneration occurred with inter-racial unions and the weakening of inherent racial qualities. To Gobineau race mixing was the cause for the downfall of Indian civilization. When the conquering Aryans decided to mix with the indigenous blacks, they allowed the many characteristics of the blacks, including their lack of judgment and reason to cloud the naturally intelligent Aryan mentality. In the present day and despite its noble origins Brahminism was in complete decline and decadence, riddled with absurd superstitions, theological complications and a lack of great men to guide it. This was solely a result of the influx of black and yellow blood into the original Aryan blood, to such an extent that it was impossible to tell a high caste brahmin from a lower caste anymore.

16.2 What Was the Reality?

The reality is that the Aryan invasion theory has been questioned by most modern historians because it contains too many contradictions (Thapar, 2015). What we do know about the period of time around which the Aryans supposedly entered India, is that there was a thriving, urban, highly developed civilization called the Indus Valley Civilization. The people of this civilization were certainly not of Aryan origin, but were indigenous to the subcontinent. The technological, architectural, economic, legislative, religious and philosophical accomplishments of this civilization are still being discovered, but the people of the Indus Valley seem to have created and sustained a Bronze Age civilization that was larger in scope than Mesopotamia, Egypt and the Andean civilizations.

The history of the Aryans, so far as historians are able to trace them, indicate on the other hand, that they were pastoral, nomadic people, considerably less accomplished in all walks of life than the Indus Valley people, except in their militarism. This fact in itself turns the idea that the Aryans were the most advanced race on its head. Furthermore, there is evidence that it was the Indus people who taught the Aryan nomads metallurgy and technology.

The French and German schools of Indology did have a vested interest in promoting the notion of a common origin race for most of the world's great civilizations; for the French the idea of a French racial unity which lay in their Gallic heritage; for the Germans their Indo-European roots. These schools therefore promoted the notion of an Aryan race in India which had accomplished its greatest feats in the Vedic age. The British did not benefit from promoting any notion of Indians having the capability of a superior civilization, nor did they rally around a common racial identity in the Nineteenth century. As Joan Leopold notes, the British being more interested in ruling India had little to say about India's Aryan past (Leopold, 1974). British explanations of India's inferiority were based on Lamarckian notions of the environment, which in India were considered physically enervating and morally sapping; the admixture of Dravidian blood and institutions, history and the influx of Mongoloids, Muslims, and Dravidians into pure Aryan blood and the notion that, in India, the Aryans exhibited an arrested growth. The combination of these factors was applied in theories of rule to justify British rule which would provide Indians with the necessary institutions and civilization needed to develop. On the other hand, the essentially Aryan roots of India also meant that a combined Orientalist and Anglicist method be used in the Indian government and reform.

Thus, the modification of the theory that Indo-Aryans were the originators of the Indo-Europeans argued that the historical inferiority of India validated British colonial rule. Nevertheless, the British used racial categories to sow dissension in India in keeping with their classic 'divide and rule' policy. For instance, after the Revolt of 1857,[5] Indian Muslims fell out of favor with the British since many of

[5] The East India Company had created an Empire in India. Until 1857, it was Company Rule. In 1857, a combination of factors, including a disregard for traditional laws concerning succession among native kingdoms, economic exploitation and high taxes, indiscriminate territorial annexations as well as social tensions within the Company's own army which was dominated by Indian soldiers, led to a Revolt. Far from remaining a minor military mutiny, the Revolt grew in size until it threatened to unseat the Company itself. It was eventually suppressed but the British government had learned that India was too economically valuable to risk. In 1858, the Government took over the official rule of India. Queen Victoria was declared Empress of India and the era of the Raj (rule) began. The Revolt of 1857 continued to serve as a warning to the British to never allow the kind of unity that had come close to overthrowing British power, to resurface. Administrative policies always emphasized the idea of 'divide and rule' to avoid creating unity among large sections of the Indian population by pitting them against each other.

their leaders had led the Revolt. The British also created the idea that the period of time from the 11th to the fourteenth centuries was a 'dark age' for India because large Indian/ Hindu empires had collapsed and were taken over by invading Islamic dynasties like the Khiljis, and the Tughlaqs (Wilson, 1858).[6] Respite for India arrived only with the Mughals, and even then, the more Islamic the ruler (like Aurangazeb) the more Indians had suffered.[7] They therefore offered up this idea, that based on the historic invasions which had occurred in the subcontinent, from the invading Aryans themselves, all the way to the Mughals, India had been taken to new heights of civilization and glory by specific invaders. The British positioned themselves as the natural heirs to the Mughals in this cyclical theory of Indian history and emphasized that the only invaders who had failed to raise Indian civilization to a higher level were the Turkish invaders who reigned during the 'dark ages'.

16.3 Creating a Nexus of Race and Caste

Related to the idea of race was the idea of caste. If the white races were superior, then the upper castes of India must be descended from them, while the lower castes would have originated in the indigenous Dravidian and mixtures of Dravidian and Negroid peoples. Gobineau for instance, pointed out, that the Indian notion of beauty was described in terms of the typical Aryan physiognomy—fair skin, oval face, and muscular and graceful appearance. The descriptions of great heroes and Gods in Indian literature always conformed to this ideal of beauty, which in turn was the

---

[6] The largely indigenous empires and kingdoms in the subcontinent of India were challenged by a series of invasions as the Islamic empires began expanding. From the invasions of Mahmud of Ghazni in the Eleventh century to the empires of subsequent conquerors like the Khiljis and the Tughlaqs, these invaders originated in Central Asia but eventually settled in India. While the period was certainly a tumultuous one, it was by no means the 'dark ages'- Southern Empires flourished and even established colonies of their own in South East Asia, while the economy flourished, technological innovations and social movements also continued unabated. The equation of the medieval period of Indian history with the 'dark ages' of the European medieval era was motivated in part by a desire to divide Hindus and Muslims.

[7] While the founder of the Mughal Empire in India, Babur, was an outsider from Central Asia, all the subsequent rulers were Indian-born, making it hard to argue that outside Muslim invasions were continuing to cause India to decline. Furthermore, the extraordinary period of peace and prosperity created by the Mughal Empire, as a result of its policies of tolerance and coexistence made it hard to sustain any argument against Muslims. Much of the British narrative focused on the rule of Aurangazeb in the Seventeenth-century, who was a devout Muslim, and more of a zealot than his predecessors, to push the narrative that Islamic bigots had always caused havoc in India. The controversy over Aurangazeb continues with historians like Audrey Truschke arguing that Aurangazeb was not harsher on non-Muslims than other Mughal Emperors, while others have argued that Aurangazeb was considered a bigot even by his contemporaries. In terms of the larger argument about Medieval India constituting a Dark Age however, evidence indicates that economic prosperity and technological progress continued; only slowing down and eventually reversing under British rule.

appearance of the higher castes, which were more Aryan than the lower castes.[8] The Indian term for caste, 'varna' also meant color.

The need for an overview of Indians was considered necessary in order to strengthen rule, and particularly to avoid a repeat of the 1857 Rebellion. The government instituted a decennial Census, which collected information relating to race. The Census Commissioner, Herbert Risley was profoundly influenced by Topinard's anthropometric method and instructed his juniors to collect data about the nasal and cranial indices of different groups in India. The result of this process was the institutionalization of the caste system.

Caste, while initially defined as a typically Hindu institution, soon came to define Indian life in general. Hindus, Muslims and even native Christians were so deeply entrenched in forming social identities around the institution of caste, that it cut across religious barriers and was a universal aspect of Indian life. Caste thus embraced the diverse races of India—the Aryan, Dravidian and the various sub-races springing from these two primary components of India's racial make-up. Caste also encompassed the diverse religions—Hindus, Muslims, native Christians. Even Parsis, who were relatively recent arrivals to the subcontinent had recourse to the hierarchy of caste in order to define an individual's rights, duties and place in society! Ultimately however, as Nicholas Dirks noted, in his book *Castes of Mind* (Dirks, 2000), caste as it was defined and written and discussed, was the result of a long colonial encounter wherein an attempt to understand the colonized for purposes of colonial rule and legitimation evolved into a project of classifying and organizing the native into a single, identifying entity.

The study of the constructions of caste in colonial India also provides us with a valuable window into the exigencies of colonial rule; the manner in which this all—encompassing category of caste, successively defined over almost three centuries of colonial rule, was an expression of the political needs of the rulers. The definition of caste thus changed dramatically from the eighteenth century to the early nineteenth century when efforts at social reform were made, and again recast in the aftermath of 1857. The eighteenth century Indological and Oriental pursuit of Hindu greatness threw caste into the role of a unique method of social hierarchy and stratification, which precluded any social upheavals in the backwash of economic or political developments. In effect, the caste system was seen as India's answer to the rapidly

[8] Gobineau's pronouncement was typical of the simplification of Indian religion. In reality the Gods of the pantheon were different colors, which may have represented their affiliation to the natural elements or to other aspects of their personalities. For example, while Indra the God of lightning was fair, Agni, the God of fire was described as being of a reddish hue. The God Vishnu, who is touted as being representative of the original 'Aryan' race is dark blue and is described as being handsome but exceedingly dark in the most human of his avatars- that of Rama and of Krishna. This aspect of his color is often overlooked by those who, like Gobineau, looked for references to race in the Hindu pantheon, and pointed to the existence of the dark Shiva, who represented the expansion of Aryan religion to include elements of the indigenous, tribal beliefs. In fact, of the Trinity in Hinduism, only Brahma who is not actively worshipped, is presented as fair. Both Vishnu the preserver and Shiva the destroyer, are dark. The fact that their consorts are fair and in fact all Goddesses in Hinduism, except for Kali, are fair, speaks more to a gender basis for the equation of fairness with beauty than with race.

changing society of the industrial and politically prolific West. The works of William Jones, Halhed and other Orientalists all highlighted the positive effects of the caste system upon the nature of the Indian.

By the early Nineteenth century, colonial rule was truly evolving into a mature system of administration and rule. The efforts of William Bentinck[9] and social reformers like Ram Mohun Roy[10] came from an understanding that while the caste system had provided an efficient social system in the past, it was now obsolete and no longer a positive influence, having degenerated into a morass of blind traditions and adherence to heinous customs like sati, female infanticide, the blind insistence on rituals etc. In effect the caste system was identified with the superior castes, now in the role of villains who had formulated and enforced a loyalty to outdated and cruel customs. The works of J. S. Mill, Wilks and other historians painted caste as the black specter, which had prevented India from progressing in any way. Missionaries like J. Peggs wrote pleading tracts, describing the horrors which the caste system had wrought, including sati, female infanticide, slavery and untouchability and concluded that it was Britain's burden to help civilize India and break her from the evil shackles of caste beliefs. Missionaries were at the forefront of denouncing the caste system, believing it to be the greatest impediment to conversion and emancipation of their Indian flock.

The government soon became involved in the issue of caste, with the introduction of the Census. The first India Census of 1871–72 was meant to catalogue every aspect of Indian life, and the development brought about by British rule. It included statistics on roads and rails, on agricultural and commercial production, on education, of hospitals and medical facilities, on sanitation, on jails etc. In the process, statistics were compiled also of the sections of the native population actively involved in these activities—natives involved in agriculture, manual labor, trade and commercial activity were catalogued as well as castes that seemed to have a high percentage of criminal members. This project snowballed into an official ethnographic project cataloging the castes and tribes of India. As Gloria Goodwin Raheja suggests, the exercise also utilized discourses of consent by cataloguing the languages, castes, and ethnic divisions in India, the official enterprise was portrayed as one which was being carried out with the consent and participation of the subjects, even though the writings of Edgar Thurston and other ethnographers clearly stated otherwise (Raheja, 1999). The Decennial Census of 1881 continued this system. The total population of British India was divided into three broad categories of brahmins, Rajputs and 'other castes', which included agricultural castes, artisans and village servants, merchants etc.

Under the influence of a growing proliferation of views about the origin and nature of the caste system among Western scholars, the 1891 Census gave up caste-based

---

[9] William Bentinck was the first Governor General of India from 1834–1835. He was a reformist minded administrator, who wanted to end the burning of widows (sati), female infanticide and other social evils.

[10] Ram Mohun Roy was an early reformist minded Indian, who believed that the social ills of Indian society were preventing progress towards independence and development. He launched a movement to eschew organized religion, caste barriers and gender restrictions.

classifications. The nature of caste as a social or religious institution was questioned in favor of a theory of occupationally based caste. The case for this classification had been strengthened by writers like William Crooke, Denzil Ibbetson and John Nesfield, whose researches in the Punjab and North West Provinces had concluded with the theory that caste had originated as an occupational division of the population. The 1891 Census accordingly divided 60 subgroups of the Indian population into 6 occupational categories: agricultural and pastoral, professional, commercial, artisans and village servants, vagrants and other races and indefinite titles. Caste was used only to explain long-term changes for an occupational group. The succeeding confusion was immense. The clear dichotomy between a caste and its occupation, even of various occupations within a single caste, made for some very mixed and inaccurate results.

The Census Commissioner for the 1901 Census, Herbert Risley, was a firm believer in anthropometry as an indicator of race, human development and social status. Caste, which had been increasingly conflated with race theories in the past few decades, was now made the basis of the census. Higher castes were presumed to be descended from Indo-Aryans and therefore their anthropometric measurements were correspondingly more developed. The downward scale of race followed the pattern of the Aryan at the top, followed by the Dravidian, Mongoloid and African. The anthropometric measurements of nasal and cephalic measurements of different castes were now correlated with the race that they were shown to originate from. The result was shown to be the present social hierarchy of India, whereby the Aryan and Aryan-descended castes were the highest castes followed by the Dravidian, Mongoloid and African castes, in that order.

Risley was simultaneously denying that India had progressed beyond a primitive form of social organization, and attributing to the prevalence of caste, the widespread belief in superstitions, and outdated rituals. Here was the height of the colonial construction of caste as proven beyond doubt, to demonstrate India's backward social development and corresponding lack of infrastructure to survive in a modern world, without the tutelage of a Western power.

Risley's conclusions about the nature of caste prompted him to comment on the role of caste in the social and political life of India. Contrary to European notions that caste was breaking up, he pointed out that caste ties in India remained as strong as ever. It prevented the formation of a unified nationalism and democracy. Factors prompting a nationalistic feeling, like a community of origin, common language, common political history, common religion or ties by intermarriage being lacking due to caste divisions, national sentiment in India tended wither to be lacking or to produce dissension rather than cohesion. According to Risley, the existence of whatever little national feeling in India, was due to the common intellectual tradition and communication caused by the introduction of English, and the unity provided by a single colonial government and common system of laws. While Risley acknowledged that it was not impossible for a number of castes to form a common national attitude, citing the Marathas as an example, he also claimed that this was a long and frustrating process, which would constantly be impeded by caste.

Caste was then introduced as the fundamental basis of organizing colonial government. For instance, it was understood that the brahmins were naturally intellectual, so they were given clerical, secretarial, judicial and administrative jobs. Warrior castes were recruited into the army, making it almost impossible for other castes to be recruited. Lower castes were recruited for labor and blue-collar jobs. Laws were reconfigured based on the colonial understanding of caste. A brahmin committing the same crime as an untouchable would get a lesser punishment. Entire castes were castigated as possessing criminal tendencies, or sexual deviancies and were rounded by, surveilled and otherwise punished by the government. Local administrators were hyper-vigilant about the caste composition of the areas under their governance, and took pains to ensure that caste-based tensions did not arise due to the legal structure. The government even stepped in when it perceived, for instance, that an 'agricultural caste' was selling too much land to a 'merchant caste'.

16.4 What Was the Reality?

Extensive studies of castes in different parts of the subcontinent in the late Twentieth century exposed the varying uses, hierarchies and peculiarities of caste. Far from being the monolithic system officially sanctioned by the British as a hallmark of Indian civilization, the importance of caste itself varied by region and according to circumstance. It was a fluid category, meant to provide a sense of community while acknowledging that other ties of community could also co-exist and even supersede the tie of caste.

For instance, in Southern India, the distinction between Right-Hand (*valangai*) and Left-Hand (*idangai*) castes was far more important than the racial hierarchy of caste. Virtually all castes were further divided into Right-Hand castes and Left-Hand castes from the highest to the lowest, and the rights and privileges claimed by either side was greater than any single caste demand. The records of the local courts in both British and French colonies in southern India record the conflict between Right and Left-handed castes as most frequent of all caste conflicts.

Other studies, like Karen Leonard's study of Kayasths (Leonard, 1978), and Mattison Mines' (Mines, 1984) study of the Kaikkoolar weavers in Tamil Nadu have demonstrated the initiative and enterprise taken by castes who were in danger of losing their livelihood, to re-invent themselves into another profession, questioning the view that caste-occupation was permanent and could not be changed. The dominance of the four-fold caste hierarchy has also been questioned by studies like Gloria Goodwin Raheja's study of Pahansu (Raheja, 1999), Harold Gould's study of caste hierarchy (Gould, 1958) and Janet Benson's study of Medak district (Benson, 1976) which indicate that the highest caste of brahmins, being primarily recipients of other castes' generosity (in that they received payment for ritual services performed) often in practice were subservient to the economically dominant caste in the village. Irawati Karve notes that the role of caste in determining power, ritual purity, occupation and privileges has constantly shifted as a result of local and supra-local politics, changing economic environments, new occupations, and other variables (Karve, 1968). While caste as an identity has existed in India for centuries, it was certainly not a mono-dimensional, four-fold division with set expectations and privileges.

According to Padmanabh Samarendra, what is likely is that the British, in their eagerness to categorize and compile, put people who described themselves as belonging to certain occupational or linguistic or ethnic groups into the same caste, thus blurring the distinction between them (Samarendra, 2011). The hierarchy of caste, also based primarily on the reporting of the interviewee, would have varied enormously, so the same occupation may have reported different caste hierarchies in different regions. Falling back upon their tried and tested method of the four-fold classification of castes, the Census officials thus inadvertently created the 'Caste System' as it came to be known.

16.5 Implications of Race in Caste: Two Examples.

Martial races Theory: The British initially did not use Indians in their military. During the seventeenth century, as their trading interests in India expanded, the British noted the success with which the French East India Company had recruited local Indian troops into their military. Subsequently, they too adopted this practice of recruiting local Indian troops. Throughout the seventeenth and eighteenth centuries the East India Company maintained local Indians in the positions of privates, or *sipahis* (sepoys), while allocating positions in the Officer Corps to British and European soldiers. Terrified of dying from tropical malaises a reduction in the number of common soldiers who were European meant that white soldiers were paid better than local Indians, and had more comfortable lodgings, better food and drink and less exposure to the elements, which in turn led to a better chance of survival in the tropical climate.

At the time of the Great Revolt of 1857, the army of the East India Company consisted mostly of local soldiers, drawn from all castes, but primarily hailing from Bengal, Bihar and Awadh since that was the largest Company territory at the time. They were mostly from the higher castes since the British assumed that the higher castes would be more loyal to them. After the Revolt, when theories about why and how the sepoys had turned disloyal and revolted were rife, attention was paid to the sections of the army which had revolted against Company rule, primarily in Northern India, and sections of the army which had remained loyal to the Company and had helped to quell the revolt. Historian Pradeep Barua, who had studied the process by which the theory of 'martial races' came into play, noted that the Peel Commission which was established to determine the causes of the Revolt concluded that the British had failed to recognize that certain races were 'martial' in nature, meaning that they were good fighters, disciplined and loyal (Barua, 1995). This last quality was the most important in identifying martial races, beginning with groups of Indian soldiers who had stayed loyal to the British during the Revolt—the Sikhs, Rajputs, and Marathas. Eventually other groups like the Pathans, Dogras, and Gurkhas were added to the ranks of the martial races. The theory of certain races possessing intrinsic 'martial' qualities was buttressed by anthropometry or physical measurements like height, weight, and facial measurements, as well as folklore which supported the martial narrative. Similarly, areas with cooler climates were preferred for recruitment since the inhabitants of such climates were likely to be harder, and more physically fit than the inhabitants of the enervating, hot plains of India. Areas further south in the Indian subcontinent, which had been relatively peaceful for over a century, were non-martial since the inhabitants of such areas had no incentive to battle, while the northern states, particularly those that were frontier states to Afghanistan were used to frequent border skirmishes and prepared for battle. And finally, urban life had an emasculating effect on men. As Kaushik Roy notes, martial stock was more likely to be found among hardy, rural folk, who performed daily physical labor, and by virtue of their location, were unlikely to be intellectual, or highly educated, or likely to question authority (Roy, 2021). By the 1930s Maj-Gen MacMunn wrote his magnum opus, 'The Martial Races of India', which was based not only on field reports but also on similar ethnographic reports of individual groups like the Sikhs, Gurkhas and Rajputs by British administrators (MacMunn, 1933).

Impact of the theory of Martial Races on Army Recruitment: In their indoctrination as 'martial races' the defining feature of loyalty to the British was always highlighted. Not surprisingly in the study of Heather Streets on *Martial Races* indicates that the bulk of the British Indian army was recruited from these ethnic groups. Also unsurprisingly, these groups were at the forefront of battle, whether it was at the frontier in India, or the conquest of new colonies like Burma, or even in the World Wars (Streets, 2004). Most importantly, these groups were at the frontlines of troops used to quell nationalistic demonstrations. For instance, the troops commanded by Gen Dwyer at Jallianwala Bagh in Amritsar,[11] who opened fire on their fellow country men and women, were themselves Gurkha, Sikh and Rajput. As Kaushik Roy notes, the typical Indian soldier was a career soldier, serving at 25 years before becoming eligible for a pension. Desertions were rare and discipline was good. Since recruitment was heavily from the same communities, the men were often connected by bonds of family or village, making any infraction by one an embarrassment for all.

Criminal Castes and Tribes: William Sleeman, a British solider and administrator in India during the first half of the nineteenth century, 'discovered' the existence of organized gangs of criminals, whose modus operandi, was death by strangulation.

[11] In 1919, a large group of Indians gathered for a peaceful protest against British rule in general and against the declaration of martial law and a curfew in Punjab. The garden or bagh in Amritsar was surrounded by high walls and had only one narrow exit. Even though the organizers of the meeting had emphasized the peaceful nature of the protest, General Dwyer gathered a number of troops and blocked the only exit to the garden. After a couple of verbal warnings to disperse, which could not be heeded because the troops had blocked the exit, he ordered the troops to shoot into the crowd until their ammunition was exhausted. Hundreds, possibly thousands were killed and the same number injured. The event caused shock waves even in Britain and further galvanized the movement for Indian Independence.

While mention of criminal gangs had been made as early in Company rule as 1810, no organized action had been taken to deal with them until Sleeman's efforts in the 1830s. Sleeman's actions corresponded with the Governor-Generalship of William Bentinck, a devoted social reformer, who was determined to 'improve' India. Among the actions taken under his rule were the abolition of Sati, the establishment of English as the medium of instruction in all educational institutions supported by the British Indian government as well as the suppression of female infanticide and human sacrifice. Sleeman was an able subordinate to Bentinck in his efforts to eradicate Thuggee. In 1836 the Thuggee and Dacoity Suppression Act was passed, with several modifications made to the Act until 1848.

Take this introduction to the semi-fictional Confessions of a Thug, by Philip Meadows Taylor. Published in 1839, this tale, based on the real 'discoveries' of William Sleeman caused a sensation in England, and cemented the fear of the 'Oriental' in English minds. The protagonist of the story, Ameer Ali, is said to be based upon Sleeman's informant, 'Feringhea'.

> 'The tale of crime which forms the subject of the following pages is, alas! almost all true; what there is of fiction has been supplied only to connect the events, and make the adventures of Ameer Ali as interesting as the nature of his horrible profession would permit me.
>
> I became acquainted with this person in 1832. He was one of the approvers or informers...whose appalling disclosures caused an excitement in the country which can never be forgotten. I have listened to them with fearful interest, such as I can scarcely hope to excite in the minds of my readers; and I can only add, in corroboration of the ensuing story, that, by his own confessions, which were in every particular confirmed by those of his brother informers, and are upon official record, he had been directly concerned in the murder of seven hundred and nineteen persons. He once said to me, "Ah! Sir, if I had not been in prison twelve years, the number would have been a thousand!"
>
> How the system of Thuggee could have become so prevalent,—remain unknown to, and unsuspected by, the people of India, among whom the professors of it were living in constant association,—must, to the majority of the English public, who are not conversant with the peculiar construction of Oriental society, be a subject of extreme wonder. It will be difficult to make this understood within my present limits, and yet it is so necessary that I cannot pass it by...'

Sleeman, acting with Bentinck's approval, launched an organized attempt to suppress the Thugs. Since the Thugs were active all over India, military measures were taken to arrest adult men who were suspected of being Thugs. Sleeman himself wrote manuals on how to recognize Thugs by their distinctive speech, clothing and customs. As a result thousands of adult men who were suspected by Thuggee by virtue of their clothing, language, and even interior decoration of their homes, were arrested and jailed.

What was the reality of Thuggee? The work of several modern historians has exposed the fallacy of the British construction of Thuggee. Sleeman's own exposé of Feringhea is suspected of being a work of semi-fiction, probably a compilation of crimes from several different individuals rather than the murder of hundreds by one single individual. As Kim Wagner, who has worked extensively on uncovering the truth of thuggee writes, 'Today it is obvious to anybody that Sleeman's account of thuggee is full of inconsistencies and exaggerations and that by presenting it as a serious obstacle to the introduction of law and order all over India he was in fact furthering his own position within the British administration' (Wagner, 2007). Importantly, from the early instances of dacoity and robbery being recorded as disparate instances from 1800–1830, the narrative became more cohesive once Sleeman became involved. As Wagner points out, the information was solely based on the narrative of the thug-turned-informant. Often these men were given the opportunity to be released if they agreed to provide information about their fellow criminals. By the 1830s however, the informant had to follow a set narrative in order to be believed and granted pardon, thus tainting the archive with bias. In particular, the interrogator, primarily Sleeman, was obsessed with the aspect of Kali worship of all thugs. Yet the archive clearly states that different individuals provided evidence of belief in various goddesses, and their criminal activities were not all performed as a 'religious sacrifice' to the Goddess. This is an example where Sleeman so badly wanted to create a religious narrative for thuggee that he closely questioned informers until their answers corresponded with his beliefs.

Furthermore, the existence of criminal activity was not particular to India. From time immemorial criminals—petty robbers, dacoits, bandits—have enlivened the annals of human history. India was no different. What is interesting is that in times of economic distress, the amount of criminal activity increased, indicating that the poorer people, marginalized communities, and particularly non-sedentary communities, who were hardest hit, may have resorted to crime in order to sustain themselves. A sort of social Robin Hood movement if one likes. These were also the communities who were vilified by British brahmin interlocuters, so the British had a natural suspicion of them. Furthermore the fact that these communities, in times of distress, tended to move around as itinerants also made it harder to police and surveil them. As a result entire communities were castigated as thugs or hereditary robbers and stranglers.

Once the process of constructing these communities as criminals began, the British colonial engine created a cohesive narrative around them. Wagner has demonstrated how the skulls of seven Indians, called 'thugs' by the British were carefully analyzed and documented (Wagner, 2010). With the progress of racial theories, similarities in the skulls were cast as evidence that there was a racial factor in determining criminals in India. By 1871, the concerted campaign to arrest, jail and hang people suspected of being thugs or dacoits was so successful that the British concluded that Thuggee had been virtually eradicated in India. But instead, as Radhika Singha has noted in her study on law and crime, they put forward the idea that certain castes were so hereditarily inclined to criminal activity that they would be categorized as Criminal Castes and Tribes (Singha, 1998). The Criminal Tribes Act (CTA) of 1871 castigated entire communities as 'criminal'. The people marked by this act were restricted in their movement as well as whom they could socialize with. Adult males had to report to the local police weekly. Not surprisingly, most the so-called criminal tribes and castes were low-caste communities who lived on the margins of society, as well a forest and hill tribes who were difficult to police due to their nomadic lifestyles. Members of these groups could be arrested with little to no evidence, children separated from their parents, adults sent to penal colonies or jailed. The list of these groups was so extensive that in 1931, the colonial government listed 237 criminal castes and tribes in the Madras Presidency alone! The numbers of people listed under the CTA at one point equaled 30% of the total population! Most of these groups form the core of the Dalit Society[12] in modern India. Since the movement of these castes and tribes was severely curtailed, they could not avail themselves of higher education or better job opportunities thereby perpetuating the cycle of their poverty and helplessness.

16.6 Legacies

Of Race: Theories of racial hierarchy were internalized by Indian writers, especially the indigenous elite. Even in the colonial period, several Indian leaders wove in the narrative of Indian civilization being descended from Aryan roots in order to challenge British colonial legitimacy, i.e. if India was indeed of Aryan heritage, then she came from the most superior race and therefore had no need for the 'colonizing mission' which the British insisted was their main motive for continuing to remain in India. A corollary to this idea of the Aryan past was the notion that the greatest accomplishments of Indian civilization had occurred during Vedic times, when the Aryan blood was most pure. One school of Indian leaders, from Ram Mohun Roy to Nehru and Gandhi adhered to this belief of the greatness of the Aryan/ Indian race and the Vedic golden age. Ram Mohun Roy even attempted to appeal to a kindred spirit in England when he visited and spoke of 'our common Aryan ancestors'. Most cited French anthropologists and Indologists as their source for this understanding. The majority of leaders who spoke publicly about India's Aryan ancestry did so to claim the right to belong to a superior race which did not require or indeed tolerate colonialism in the form of the White Man's Burden. The echo of Risley, Thurston and Crooke is clear in the works of B. S. Guha, Ramaprasad Chanda and M. M. Kunte who were writing under the Raj. In addition the application of these theories skewed accounts of legendary and heroic origins of races, in terms of clashes between Aryans and indigenous peoples, the description of tribals as jungle peoples, semi-savages appears in the works of early post-independence historians like V. Raghaviah and D. D. Kosambi, who used the racial hierarchy to argue for the technological development in pre-historic India, and even the doyenne of ancient Indian history, Romila Thapar, who classified the 'Aryan invasion' as the last in a series of racial influxes in India. She has subsequently changed her views. This construction of the *adivasis*—tribals and aborigines—has been attacked by G. S. Ghurye, Andre Beteille, Binay B. Chaudhuri, K. Sivaramakrishnan, and others. As Sumit Guha points out, 'the archaeological record offers little support for the mythic history of clashing races that took shape when the brown sahibs and white sahibs sought to escape their fears

[12] The Dalits was the lowest strata of Indian society, forming the bulk of Untouchables or Pariahs.

about the instability of social hierarchy by giving it a biological basis and projecting it into the past…' (Guha, 1998).

Of caste: The nineteenth century saw the involvement of several men in Indian public life, in matters of caste—whether it was as social evil or progressive and dynamic, whether brahmanical claims to unique sacred knowledge were justified, the origin and meaning of untouchability and issues of the corporate nature of caste. The participants in this debate supported three theories of caste. The first was to view caste as a divisive, social evil, a negation of Indian nationhood. This was the 'incubus theory', and was popularized by social reformers like M. G. Ranade, R. Raghunatha Rao, T. V. Vaswani, Rao Bahadur M. Audinarayana Iyer, C. Sankaran Nair and other members of the National Social Conference. These men recognized the importance of caste in Indian life but pushed for radical reforms within the system. A more extreme version of the reform movements came with the anti-brahmin movements of the early twentieth century, like E. V. Ramaswamy Naicker's Self-Respect movement, founded in 1925. Naicker called for a repudiation of all Aryan values and organizations, including the caste system, as a manifestation of brahmin tyranny. While some of the reformers visualized a casteless, egalitarian society in India's future, most of them pressed for immediate social reforms especially with regard to educational opportunities, social restrictions of caste and political representation.

In discussing the nature of caste, it is impossible to ignore B. R. Ambedkar's indictment of the caste system as an oppressive, exploitative regime, which needed to be wiped out from India. Well known for his efforts to uplift the Untouchable castes and his disapprobation of the *chaturvarna*, as it was understood in India, Ambedkar described caste in scathing terms:

> Hindu society as such does not exist. It is only a collection of castes. Each caste is conscious of its existence. Its survival is the be-all and end-all of its existence. Castes do not even form a federation. A caste has no feeling that it is affiliated to other castes except when there is a Hindu- Moslem riot. On all other occasions each caste endeavors to segregate itself and distinguish itself from other castes. Each caste not only dines among itself and marries among itself but each caste prescribes its own distinctive dress.

Ambedkar accused higher castes of deliberately keeping lower castes economically and culturally deprived. Demonstrating that caste sanctions were imposed by appeals to religious scriptures, he called for an entire overhaul of the religious and social system of India.

> The effects of caste on the ethics of the Hindus is simply deplorable. Caste has killed public spirit. Caste has destroyed the sense of public charity. Caste has made public opinion impossible. A Hindu's public is his caste. His responsibility is only to his caste. His loyalty is restricted only to his caste. Virtue has become caste-ridden and morality has become caste-bound. There is no sympathy for the deserving. There is no appreciation of the meritorious. There is no charity to the needy. Suffering as such calls for no response. There is charity but it begins with the caste and ends with the caste. There is sympathy but not for men of other castes.

The second theory regarding caste was the 'golden chain view' which regarded caste as varna, an ideology of spiritual order and moral affinity and a rallying point for the regeneration of the nation. Proponents of this view included Dayanand Saraswati and Tilak. Tilak saw caste standards as divinely mandated, while Saraswati saw caste as the basis for an ordered Hindu society, while simultaneously allowing for spiritual and sacral access to all. The theory that caste was a means of ordering Hindu society was also popularized by members of societies like the Manava Dharam Sabha and the Prarthana Samaj. While the members of these groups pressed for social reform within the caste system, they nevertheless saw the institution as essential to Indian nationhood.

The third view was of caste as an 'idealized corporation', where caste equated with occupation, was a concrete ethnographic fact of Indian life. The proponents of this view included the organizers of Maratha and Rajput movements, valorizing kshatriya values, and extolling the 'natural' attributes of courage, strength and character of kshatriyas. They essentially equated caste with racial identity, taking their cue from British ethnographies which defined the castes in terms of belonging to Aryan, Dravidian and aboriginal races. From the writings of Dayanand Saraswati, V. D. Sarvarkar and B. G. Tilak came the intersection of 'Vedic' with 'Hindu'. They insisted that Hindu India had always been peopled by a great race. Degeneration of culture, racial ability and accomplishment occurred from the time of the Islamic invasions. According to these leaders, the downfall of Indic/ Hindu civilization was due to the influx of invading Islamic hordes and their intermixing with the indigenous 'Hindu' people. This idea had been seized upon, in the Twentieth and the Twenty-First centuries, by both the Rashtriya Swayamsewak Sabha or RSS and the Bharatiya Janata Party or BJP, to argue for the elimination of certain minority protections enshrined in the Constitution for Muslims in India, as well as soft attempts to intimidate and threaten Muslim communities in India.[13]

Another way in which the legacy of colonial theories about race can be seen in contemporary India is the deep divide between Aryan and Dravidian. The emphasis on Northern India being of Aryan stock and India south of the Vindhya mountains coming from Dravidian stock, coupled with the notion that the Aryan race was the superior one, and led to the development of the Dravidian movement in Southern India. The leaders of this movement praised Ellis for his contribution in highlighting the Dravidian people. The division of Tamil society into brahmin, non-brahmin middle classes and Untouchables led to the formation, by the second group, of the Justice Party in 1917, which was meant to act as the political voice of the non-brahmins who saw the nationalist movement and the congress party as being dominated by brahmins. The Untouchables played little or no role in the Justice Party while certain castes, like the *Valangai* or Right-Hand castes, played a dominant role. The Justice Party, reformed by E. V. Ramaswamy who launched the Self Respect Movement, eventually became the *Dravidar Kazhagam* which aimed to establish a state for the Dravidas. After Independence the movement evolved into political

[13] Anti-Muslim rhetoric has taken the form of campaign speeches, exhortations of violence against Muslim communities, the outbreak of religious riots in various cities in India and the BJP led government's attempt to ban beef (commonly consumed by Muslims), and pass other anti-Muslim legislations.

parties like *Dravida Munnetra Kazhagam* (DMK) and All Indian *Anna Dravida Munnetra Kazhagam* (AIADMK) which have dominated politics in Tamil Nadu.

Caste politics has become an intrinsic part of the Indian political system in other ways as well. Several caste associations sprang up to support their members in the Nineteenth and Twentieth centuries, like numerous associations for Kayasths, the Chitrapur Saraswat Brahmin Association, the Sengutha Mahajana Sangam of the Sengunthar Mudaliars or Kaikkoolars. Some advocated for their members and provided networks of community. Others acted as guilds, becoming the political spokesperson of their caste. Under British rule, when law was based on 'accepted caste dogma' several castes lobbied and petitioned over the course of the Censuses to be accorded a higher caste status. For instance, the several Sengunthar Mudaliars, originally a weaving caste (therefore somewhere in between the 3rd and 4th castes) by the Twentieth century, were claiming a kshatriya heritage. Similarly the Nadars, who were originally toddy tappers and a low caste, by 1891 were claiming a kshatriya status in the Census. The Nadar Mahajam Sabha, formed in 1910, focused on officially in making the Nadars a kshatriya caste in the Census. But by 1935, when the notion of affirmative action was suggested for lower castes, the Sabha did an about turn and requested to be included as a Backward Caste. A caste movement, led by Shri Narayana Guru in Kerala, centered on the Iravas, who were toddy tappers in Kerala. Guru urged his followers to sanskritize themselves, by eschewing alcohol, meat, and stressing the importance of sexual restraint and personal hygiene. He also encouraged them to educate themselves and adopt many professional vocations like medicine, education and law. The result for the Iravas, was the creation of a movement spearheaded by highly educated and influential Iravas, who were able to succeed in the political sphere far beyond the Nadars of Tamil Nadu. The caste continues to be socially and politically prominent in Kerala even today. In the report of the Mandal Commission, the status of Other Backward Castes was established as castes which were not necessarily the lowest caste or untouchables but had been marginalized nevertheless. Other Backward Castes were to be included in the program of affirmative action, particularly in education seats in Colleges and Universities, as well as mandated quotas in Government jobs. Caste associations became very active in advocating the OBC mantle for themselves to avail of affirmative action, in what has become known as the 'Mandalization of Indian politics'. What seems clear is that there is no clear path ahead in the fragmented ethnic politics in India without first reckoning with and understanding the implications of the colonial heritage of caste.

Of Martial Races: After Independence in 1947, the Indian army continues to be dominated by recruitment from the erstwhile 'martial races'—it would appear that generations of military service and the belief that they are 'martial' has been internalized and continues to play a role in the identity of groups like the Sikhs, Gurkhas, and Rajputs. The modern Indian army is disproportionately dominated by the Sikhs, Gurkhas and Rajputs, not only in terms of volunteers to the army, but also in terms of targeted army recruitment. Despite disavowing the belief in martial races, the military continues to be staffed primarily by certain groups, which have created their own ethnic power structures and coteries within the military. This has famously created impossible situations, such as Indira Gandhi's use of the Sikhs to storm the Golden Temple in Amritsar during Operation Blue Star in 1984. Shocked by this outright attack on their most holy ground, Gandhi's own bodyguards, also Sikh, assassinated her. Similar ethnic tensions have arisen due to the composition of the Indian army in Kashmir, among the Naxalite regions and the North Western States.

Of Criminal Castes and Tribes: The CTA was repealed after the Independence of India in 1947. This was followed by what the press reported as a huge increase in petty crime, leading many to advocate for the re-institution of the CTA in the form of a new law, the Habitual Offenders' Act or HOA. This Act aimed to punish frequent law breaker more severely, but without taking the socio-economic circumstances which had created the grounds for the CTA itself, the HOA re-stigmatized these groups as possessing criminal traits and tendencies. Significantly, it also led to the cementing of popular beliefs regarding the 'criminal' tendencies of certain castes and tribes. Despite the HOA being dismantled and the groups that were formerly labelled Criminal Castes and Tribes now being labelled 'denotified castes and tribes' there is still substantial popular suspicion of them. Due to the systemic oppression they have faced, these groups continue to be poor and subsist on the margins of society, making them more culpable for petty crime. Several groups have since advocated to be included in the list of social groups in India which benefit from affirmative action, but until there is significant grass roots mobilization and change, these castes will continue to be poor, and therefore more likely to fall prey to crime.

Conclusion: India continues to grow and flourish despite the many challenges left behind by the colonial past. Yet in some matters, such as caste and race, the colonial imprint is too deep, and too divisive to ignore. India cannot continue to build a political, social, economic and legal structure upon this inherited, but utterly artificial foundation provided by colonial rule. Only by reckoning with this past, and recognizing and reorganizing thought and education will modern India be able to overcome these divisions and thrive.

References

Ambedkar, B R. (1936). The Annihilation of caste. New Delhi.

Ambedkar, B R. (1948). The Untouchables: Who were they? And why they became untouchables. New Delhi.

Barua, P. (1995). Inventing Race: The British and India's Martial Races. *In the Historian, 58*, 1.

Benson, J (1976). A South Indian Jajmani System. In Ethnology 15.

Beteille, A. (1986). The concept of tribe with special reference to India. *European Journal of Sociology, 27*(2).

Burnouf, E. (Oct. 1828). Seconde lettre à M. le Rédacteur du Journal Asiatique, sur quelques dénominations géographiques du Drâvida ou pays des Tamouls, Nouveau Journal Asiatique, Vol 2

Chanda, R. (1916). *The Indo- Aryan races. A study of the origin of Indo- Aryan people and institutions.* Rajshahi.

Chaudhuri, B. B. (1994). The myth of the tribe. *Calcutta Historical Journal, 16*.

Conlon, F. (1977). *A Caste in a changing world. The Chitrapur Saraswat Brahmans, 1700-1935.* Berkeley.
Crooke, W. (1896). *The tribes and castes of the North-Western Provinces and Oudh.* Four vols.
Dirks, N. (2000). *Castes of mind.* Univresity of Princeton Press, Princeton.
Ghurye, G. S. (1932). *Caste and race in India.* Bombay.
Ghurye, G. S. (1963). *The scheduled tribes.* Bombay.
Gobineau, A. (translation, 1967). *The Inequality of Human Races. Translated by Adrian Collins.* New York, H. Fertig.
Gough, K. (1955). The social structure of a Tanjore Village. In Marriot, McKim (Ed.) *Village India.* Chicago.
Gould, H. (1958). The Hindu Jajmani system. *Southwestern Journal of Anthropology, 14.*
Guha, B. S. (1937). *An outline of the racial ethnology of India.*
Guha, S. (1998). Lower strata, older races, and aboriginal peoples: Racial anthropology and mythical history past and present. *In JAS, 57*, 2.
Hardgrave, R. (1965). *The Dravidian Movement.* Bombay.
Hardgrave, R. (1969). *The Nadars of Tamilnad. The political culture of a community in change.* Berkeley.
Ibbetson, S. D. (1883). Punjab castes.
Karve, I. (1968). *Hindu society: An interpretation.* Poona.
Kosambi, D. D. (1956). *An introduction to the study of Ancient Indian history.* Bombay.
Kunte, M. M. (1880). *Vicissitudes of Aryan civilization in India.* Bombay.
Leonard, K. (1978). *Social history of an Indian caste: The Kayasths of Hyderabad.* Delhi.
Leopold, J. (1974). British application of the Aryan theory of race to India. *English Historical Review, 89*, 3.
MacMunn, Major, G. F. (1933). The martial races of India.
Maxwell, A. (2000). *Colonial photography and exhibitions. Representations of the 'Native' and the making of European identities.* University of Leicester Press, London and New York.
Mines, M. (1984). *The Warrior Merchants: textiles, trade and territory in South India.* Cambridge
Peggs, J. (1830). *India's cries to British humanity.* London.
Raghaviah, V. (1968). Nomads. Secunderabad.
Raheja, G. G. (1988). *The poison in the gift: Ritual.* Prestation and the Dominant Caste in a North Indian Village.
Raheja, G. G. (1999). The illusion of consent. Language, caste and colonial rule in India. In P. Pels & O. Salemik (Eds.) *Colonial subjects. Essays on the practical history of anthropology.* Ann Arbor: University of Michigan Press.
Ranade, M. G. (1915). The miscellaneous writings of the late Hon'ble Mr. Justice M.G. Ranade.
Risley, H. (1915). *The People of India* (2nd edn.).
Roy, K. (2021). Martial races and recruitment in the Indian Army during the Two World Wars. In D. Delaney, M. Frost, A. Brown (Eds.) Manpower and the armies of the British Empire in the two world wars. Ithaca: Cornell University Press.
Samarendra, P. (2011). Census in colonial India and the Birth of caste. *EPW, 46*(33).
Saraswati, D. (1884). Satyarth Prakash.
Sarvarkar, V. D. (1928). *Hindutva: Who is a Hindu?*
Singha, R. (1998). *A despotism of law: Crime and justice in early colonial India.* Oxford University Press.
Sivaramakrishnan, K. (1993). Unpacking colonial discourse: notes on using the anthropology of tribal India or an ethnography of the State. *Yale Graduate Journal of Anthropology, 5.*
Staum, M. (2003). *Labeling people. French Scholars on society, race and Empire, 1815–1848.* Mc-Gill's-Queen's University Press, Montreal and Kingston.
Streets, H. (2004). *Martial races, the military, race and masculinity in British Imperial Culture, 1857–1914.* Manchester University Press.
Meadows Taylor, C. (1839). *Confessions of a thug.* Richard Bentley, London. https://www.gutenberg.org/cache/epub/44881/pg44881.txt

Thapar, R. (2015). 'Fallacies of Hindutva historiography', EPW, January 3.
Thurston, E. (1909). *Castes and tribes of Southern India.* Madras.
Topinard, P. (1876). *L'Anthropologie.* Reinwald and Cie.
Topinard, P. (1899). *Science and faith.* Free Press, Chicago.
Trautmann, T. (2006). *Languages and nations: The Dravidian proof in colonial Madras.* University of California Press.
Wagner, K. (2010). Confessions of a skull: Phrenology and colonial knowledge in early nineteenth-century India. *History Workshop Journal, 69*, 28–51.
Wagner, K. (2007). *Thuggee: Banditry and the British in early nineteenth century India.* Palgrave Macmillan.
Wilson, H. H. (Ed.). (1858). *The history of India by James Mill* (10 vols.). London: Piper, Stephenson and Spence.

Chapter 17
Indian Indepentism: Networks Abroad

Mathieu Gotteland

Abstract A fair assessment of the Indian independentist movement abroad, of its strengths and its shortcomings, of its short- and long-term consequences is difficult to reach to this day. Certainly, the international and transnational nature of the nationalist movement cannot be ignored. Foreign events and remote revolutions helped embolden the movement and give impetus to the cause, while inspiration had been found in the–sometimes revisited–history of the West and Asia. Early alliances with anti-British anticolonial parties helped forge from the onset the conscience that the fate of Indian independence was linked to that of oppressed people everywhere. Exposure to foreign ideas and conditions gave shape to a national Indian consciousness shared by Muslims and Hindus, Sikhs and Bengalis. The mobilization of the Indian diaspora of all classes, students and workers, bourgeois and farmers, and their enlistment behind a common ideal is certainly a notable feat, not least because it had preceded the politization of the masses in India proper. In Punjab especially, the Ghadr movement is certainly to credit for the widespread rejection of British rule among a population that had been considered a pillar of the empire since the Sepoy Mutiny. Naturally, Indian revolutionaries abroad did not obtain by themselves the independence of India. The latter is the consequence of a number of factors, which included Bengali terrorism, Gandhi's campaigns and generally speaking the gradual loss of support to British rule within India, as well as the rising cost of the colony to the British crown. Nevertheless, they participated mightily in the support and provision of this movement in India, as well as to the politization of the masses, either through Ghadarite returnees, former jihadists, or simply the publicity given by the British themselves to the numerous trials linked to the activities of political exiles.

Keywords Bal Gangadhar Tilak · Anusilan Samiti · Yugantar · Shyamji Krishnavarma · The Indian sociologist · Vikaji Rustomji Cama · India house · Ghadr · SS Komagata Maru · Taraknath Das · Indian independence league · Free Hindusthan · Har Dayal · Lala Lajpat Rai · M.N.Roy · Indian independentism

M. Gotteland (✉)
Universite Paris- Partheon-Sorbonne, Paris, France
e-mail: mathieu.gotteland@gmail.com

L. Vemsani (ed.), *Handbook of Indian History*,
https://doi.org/10.1007/978-981-97-6207-1_17

Until several praiseworthy recent attempts, a diligent and global study of Indian independentism outside of India's borders has been lacking. The portion of either Indian or foreign historiography that took a sporadic interest in Indian revolutionary movements abroad, political exiles or foreign patrons has long stayed partially blind. "The suddenness and surety with which India achieved independence in 1947 has led scholars of the subject to passively accept the simplified narrative of the Indian nationalist movement's origins" (Jain, 2022, p. 45). The creation and diffusion of a national myth have been a natural by-product of the heavy emphasis on nation-building–and thus on nationalism–during the leadership of Jawaharlal Nehru (1947–1967), the first prime minister of India (Singh & Arya, 2006), as well as in British India's other successor states, which pursued similar policies after their independence, albeit with a different emphasis (Faheem et al., 2021). Apart from Indo-centrism, studies of Indian independentism have also suffered from several prejudices, including the perception of political exiles as "anticolonialists on a global map", obscuring the contribution of the Indian diaspora (Bhatte, 2013, p. 157), but also transnational solidarities and political exchanges with other revolutionary and anticolonial movements (Fischer-Tiné, 2007, p. 327). Historians need to widen the lens and decentralize their gaze to get a fair understanding of the global and interactive network of "world forces", as well as the organization, strategy and ideology of Indian nationalists, abroad and at home.

The Indian National Congress (INC), founded in 1885, first championed reformism and dialogue with the British in order to achieve autonomy. This moderate course of action was opposed notably by Bal Gangadhar Tilak, in Maharashtra (Bhagwat & Pradhan, 2008). The first political assassination was committed in Poona in 1897. From 1901 onwards, terrorist secret societies were created in Bengal, most notably Anusilan Samiti, founded in 1902 in Kolkata, declared illegal in 1909, and Yugantar, from 1906 onwards (Heehs, 1993). But these developments did not unfold in a vacuum. The influence of such European movements as Italian carbonari and Russian anarchists, the publications and visits to Calcutta (1900–1901) of Okakura Kakuzō, a Japanese promoter of pan-asianism, and the example of similar terrorist anticolonial or revolutionary movements across Asia (most notably in China, Korea and Vietnam) have been paramount in the inspiration, organization and preferred means of those Bengali secret societies (Heehs, 1994).

Naturally, the movement was first encouraged and strengthened by local frustrations and hardships, such as outbreaks of plague, recurring famines, inadequate response from the authorities, as well as the attempt at a partition of Bengal, in 1905, ironically decided to contain independentism spreading at the heart of British India. Nevertheless, either through their education, the medium of books or journals, Indian intellectuals were keenly aware of any event that would hint at a weakening of the Western grip on the world and of Britain especially. Such events as the failed Italian invasion of Ethiopia (1895–1896), the Boer war (1899–1902), the international repression of the Boxers in Northern China (1900–1901) and more strikingly the Japanese victory over Russia (1904–1905) provided impetus to the nationalist movement, while cementing from the onset the belief that the fate of India would be linked to that of the non-Western world (Bose, 1971, pp. 8–9, Deepak, 2012, p. 148).

17.1 From India House to Ghadr, 1905–1913

In 1897, the year Tilak began to lead the so-called extremists in India (as opposed to the moderates of the INC), Shyamji Krishnavarma, a lawyer, formerly council member to the maharaja of Udaipur and diwan of Junagadh (1893–1897), moved to London. His house quickly became the meeting place of the nationalist Indians in the capital of the empire, where they enjoyed more liberty than they did at home. A friend of his and one of the staunchest advocates of Indian independence, likewise led to political activism by the experience of the plague in Bengal and its handling by British authorities, Vikaji Rustomji Cama, set shop in Paris as a jeweller in 1901 while continuing her political activities. Both cities thus became the prototypes of later more important "hubs" or "nodal points" of a soon-to-be global network of Indian revolutionaries.

It took however the British decision to divide Bengal on religious lines, first made public in December 1903, for Krishnavarma to take further decisive steps: the publications of a journal for independentist propaganda, *The Indian Sociologist*, in January 1905; the foundation of the Indian Home Rule Association, in February; and finally the creation of an India House, meant as a boarding house and a training centre for Indian students in London, on 63, Cromwell Avenue, in Highgate, along that of five fellowships to bring Indian students to British universities, in July of the same year (Bose, 1971, pp. 13–17; Sareen, 1979; pp. 2–11, Fischer-Tiné, 2007, p. 328).

From the onset, the new organization developed links both with Yugantar and with non-Indian anticolonial, revolutionary or otherwise subversive movements. Indians rejoined Bengal from Paris, providing arms, propaganda, and a new-found expertise in the manufacture of explosives, as they had been taught by Russian maximalist Nicolas Safranski. All the while Krishnavarma weaved bonds with the Irish independentists in Britain and in North America, who in turn served as intermediaries with Egyptian pan-islamists and nationalists. From 1906, *The Indian Sociologist* published articles of the Republican (Sinn Féin) *Gaelic American*, and vice versa. On the same year and during the visit of Mustafa Kamil Pasha, head of the Egyptian National Party, Krishnavarma gave a speech demonstrating the Indian solidarity with the struggle of the Egyptian people. An Indo-Egyptian Club was founded by the group from India House in 1909 to allow for closer cooperation. Members of the India House tried to rejoin the Rif rebellion in January 1909, both as a gesture of anti-imperial solidarity and to gain experience in the use of arms and in guerrilla warfare. They had to turn back in Tangiers however, for they lacked the proper travel documents. Internal dissensions due to Krishnavarma's caution, interest from the British and French authorities and press, the use of agents provocateurs, several arrests, the death of some of the guests at India House either as a result of their terrorist actions in India or sentences in British courts of law and finally a ban on an Indo-Egyptian joint conference to be held in Paris prompted the sale of the Highgate mansion and the effective end of all nationalist activities in either Western European capital from

1911 onwards (Bose, 1971, pp. 19–33; Sareen, 1979, pp. 37–48; Fischer-Tiné, 2007, pp. 330–333; Laursen, 2021a, 2021b).

North America also proved a fertile ground for nationalist propaganda and organization at about the same time. Unlike in London, home to a large Indian community (Bhatte, 2013, p. 159), hardly any Indians inhabited New York until the early 1900's. Indian nationalists enjoyed nevertheless both a greater degree of freedom than in Western Europe to carry on their political activities and the amity of most Irish-Americans, allowing the city to momentarily become another major node. Attempts to organize, carried by the Clan-Na-Gael with the help of Indian students and activists, notably the editor George Freeman of *The Gaelic American* and the lawyer Myron H. Phelps, were short-lived (Bose, 1971, pp. 38–41; Sareen, 1979, pp. 53–56; Fischer-Tiné, 2007, pp. 333–335).

Indian immigration in significant numbers to the Pacific coast of Canada and the United States began in 1904. It swelled to several thousands a year from 1906 onwards. Most immigrants were Sikhs and had been formerly employed in the police or the army. In their new homes, they became acquainted with liberal political ideas, while meeting with widespread hostility. Resented by the working class because they were often paid less to work longer hours and were employed as strikebreakers, they were perceived as socialists and anarchists by employers.

The continuous journey regulation, adopted by the Canadian government in January 1908, was thus meant to indirectly prevent any further Indian immigration. As a challenge to this exclusion law, on April 4th 1914 the SS Komagata Maru was chartered for a special voyage from Hongkong to Vancouver, via Shanghai, Moji and Yokohama. While in Japan, the ship was visited by revolutionaries Bhagwan Singh and Barkatullah. The attitude of the Canadian government, which refused for the ship to dock in Vancouver, first sent the police and then a war ship, before forcing the steamship and nearly all of its 375 passengers to turn around, gave the Indian cause a publicity that played a large part in furthering the cause of independentism in the diaspora (Bose, 1971, pp. 62–65; Sareen, 1979, pp. 77–83; Johnston, 1989).

While the United States did not resort to law, Asian exclusion leagues flourished, and the authorities did their utmost to curb Indian immigration. It is in this context that Taraknath Das founded the Indian Independence League in San Francisco in 1907, before moving to Vancouver where he momentarily opened a school for Indians (later closed on order of the government) and first published an English-speaking journal, *Free Hindusthan*, with the help of George Freeman. Persecuted and prosecuted, he moved to Seattle and New York in 1909–1910, where he founded short-lived organizations (Bose, 1971, pp. 48–51; Fischer-Tiné, 2007, pp. 333–335).

17.2 The Ghadr Movement in North America

It took the arrival to the United States of Har Dayal from India House to make the independentist organization in the country one of the most serious threats to the British hold on India. A professor of Indian philosophy for a short while at Stanford

University, Har Dayal resigned in September 1911 and devoted himself to nationalist propaganda. In May 1913, he founded the Hindi Association of the Pacific Coast, and in November of the same year, created in San Francisco a newspaper, *Ghadr*, published in several South Asian languages, English, Gorkhali, Gurmukhi, Gujarati, Hindi, Urdu and Pashtu. It was distributed all over the empire and to other countries hosting Indian communities, most notably China, Japan and Southeast Asia (Bains, 1962, pp. 48–49; Bhatte, 2013, p. 166; Sohal, 2019, p. 132). Its name, meaning "mutiny", served as an echo to the Sepoy Mutiny of 1857, celebrated as the First War of Independence since Savarkar's *Indian War of Independence*, published in 1909 (Puri, 2008, p. 72).

The pupil of both India House and Russian revolutionaries (Oberoi, 2009; Bhat, 2019b, p. 2359) Har Dayal became associated with the International Workers of the World. His arrestation on the ground of his anarchist sympathies and subsequent flight to Switzerland did not smother the movement but, much like the Komagata Maru incident, galvanized Ghadr sympathizers in North America (Johnston, 2010, pp. 15–17). Inspired and influenced by the values of the French and American revolutions, anarchist and socialist methods and ideals, faced with racial discrimination in their new homes and let down by the empire (Ramnath, 2011, p. 6), supported by a large community of mainly Punjabi ex-soldiers (Sohal, 2019, p. 128) and Irish(-American) revolutionists (Ramnath, 2011, p. 5), the arrestation of a prominent figure of the movement could not suffice to weaken the movement. The latter was not indeed an organized party but a "body of people bound by a collective spirit" and "committed to shared objectives and norms of behaviour and loyalty" (Bhat, 2019a, p. 2131). The movement instead initiated the "political and social transformation of a large section of hitherto politically innocent people" both at home and abroad (Bhat, 2019a, p. 2127).

A combination of wishful thinking and careful analysis of anti-British trends had helped Indian nationalists identify Germany as a potential ally and expect a war between her and Britain since at least 1908. Ghadar publications regularly called for sympathizers to prepare for such an event. Friedrich von Bernhardi's *Germany and the Next War*, published on October 1912 and immediately translated in English, was widely acclaimed by independentists (Bose, 1971, pp. 82–83; Sareen, 1979, pp. 116–118). Indian independentists in New York went as far as looking to ally themselves to German socialists (Sareen, 1979, p. 118). It was therefore only natural that as soon as the news of the outbreak of war in Europe reached them, they would decide to return *en masse* to India to carry out the revolution, either directly aided by Germany or in a view to profit from England's momentary weakness (Bose, 1971, pp. 64–65).

It is estimated that around 8,000 Indians returned home in the beginning of the war, 2,000 of which under Ghadar's influence (Jensen, 1979, p. 73; Puri, 2008, p. 74). They left all countries touched by Ghadr propaganda, most notably North American, East and Southeast Asian countries (Brown, 1948, p. 301). German consulates in America, and central government, indeed seeked to aid with arms and ammunition, but returnees were beyond any possible assistance before the German consul in San Francisco could contact Ram Chandra, editor of the *Ghadr* since Har Dayal's flight to Europe (Fraser, 1977, p. 258; Sareen, 1979, p. 123). They still received aid and support from the German diplomatic network in Neutral Asia (see infra). The famous Singapore Mutiny was in fact largely the result of the exposure of a Sikh contingent to Ghadarite(-jihadist) propaganda, as well as to the encouragement of the German prisoners of war (POW) they were guarding (Streets-Salter, 2017, pp. 117–141; Malhi, 2021; Jain, 2022, p. 56).

Most of them were arrested on arrival, and either put on house arrest or tried. Ghadr's greatest strength was to be its fatal weakness. A mutiny did occur, on February 1915, although not simultaneously across the Indian territory. The Singapore Mutiny, having occurred on February 15th, could legitimately be understood as a part of this wider scheme. It was doomed to failure, however. A proto-mass movement with no clearly established hierarchy, it did not allow for proper organization or co-ordination. Their exodus was "rash and ill-concealed", but remained nevertheless the most menacing threat to Britain's rule on India during the war (Johnston, 2010, p. 24).

The movement survived the exodus and the mutiny of February 1915, and remained very active during the war, in coordination with both Yugantar and Germany. Constantly evolving strategically and ideologically to better fit is aims, it did not officially dissolve before 1948. It helped shape an Indian and a Sikh national consciousness, in the diaspora and at home, producing offshoots as diverse as the Indian Workers Association in the United Kingdom, Santokh Singh's Kirti or Bhagat Singh's Hindustan Socialist Republican Association in Punjab (Puri, 2008, pp. 75–76; Raza, 2011; Kalra, 2017; Jain, 2022, p. 46). Its networks extended from Germany to Brazil and China and became the main link between Indian independentists abroad. It borrowed from political libertarianism, economic socialism, romantic revolutionism, was patriotic and internationalist, anarchist and republican. With no official party line and a great ideological flexibility, Ghadarites have actively supported Hindu nationalism, marxism, pan-islamism, and it has been convincingly argued that the Ghadr network "overlapped at some point, at no more than a degree of separation, with every radical tendency of its time" (Ramnath, 2011, pp. 2–7).

17.3 Indian Independentism and the German-Turkish Call for Jihad

In 1912, plans for German support to Indian independence were elaborated by Chempakaraman Pillai's International Pro-India Committee, in Zürich. The organization also produced propaganda articles in the German and Swiss press and published the magazine *Pro-India*. Krishnavarma participated in the effort, and Har Dayal, fleeing from the United States, joined in March 1914. The latter also actively worked for the coordination of Indo-Egyptian revolutionary activities (Bose, 1971, p. 83; Fraser, 1977, p. 256). As soon as 1911, Yugantar as well reached out to Germany. At the outbreak of war in 1914 and in line with his *Weltpolitik* vision, the German emperor Wilhelm II himself was enthusiastic about collaborating with nationalists and pan-islamists to dismantle the British, French and Russian empires. His view was shared by a circle of German industrialists and intellectuals, most notably Albert Ballin, general director of the Hamburg-America Line, and Max von Oppenheim, a German archaeologist and former diplomat (Bose, 1971, p. 84).

The sultan-caliph of the Ottoman empire, Abdülhamid II, promoted pan-islamism as a means of soft power in the Muslim world and diplomatic leverage vis-à-vis European powers since the 1880's. It was helped in that endeavour by emperor Wilhelm II. In a much-commented speech, given in Damascus in 1898, the latter declared himself to be the eternal friend of the sultan and 300 millions of muslims (Lüdke, 2005, pp. 35 and 48). The emperor's *Islampolitik* and the argument of a global jihad against Britain, France and Russia weighed heavily in the German acceptance of an alliance with Turkey, despite skepticism on the part of the German foreign office. Finalized as early as August 2nd, 1914, it allowed for a formal call to jihad to be formulated on November 14th of the same year, and directed to Muslims of all nationalities (Lüdke, 2005, pp. 43–46).

While Pillai approached the German consul in Zürich to implement wide-ranging plans for German assistance, Har Dayal had been travelling to Istanbul to enquire about Turkish willingness to support Indian plans; on the German side, Oppenheim and Ballin had set up an agency tasked with intelligence and propaganda operations in order, first and foremost, to use this German-Turkish call for jihad, the *Nachrichtenstelle für den Orient* (NFO). As soon as September 1914 and as a counterpart to the German NFO was established the *Indisches Unabhängigkeitskommittee* (IUK) or India Independence Committee to coordinate Indo-German subversive activities worldwide. The creation of other national committees of nationalities aided by the Germans in their revolutionary activities helped further transnational solidarity and establish a sort of "anticolonial international" in Berlin (Jenkins, 2013; Zetterberg, 1978). A large amount of propaganda was to be produced, including the journals *Der neue Orient* and *El Dschihad* by the NFO and *Hindostan* distributed to Indian POW by the IUK. Subsidiary centres of the IUK were created across Europe and the Middle East (Bose, 1971; Sareen, 1979, pp. 120–122; Oesterheld, 2004).

Despite persistent tensions between Hindu, Sikh and Muslim nationalists, the Indo-German-Turkish alliance and the pan-islamist stance were not altogether new to Indian independentists. The early rapprochement with Egyptian nationalists, as well as the presence of pan-islamist propagandists in the ranks of Indian activists, made it a natural argument. Muhammad Barkatullah, who sat on the IUK, collaborated with Krishnavarma's *Indian Sociologist*, was one of the co-founders of the Pan-Aryan Association in New York and the Ghadr movement, while editing in Tōkyō from 1909 to 1914 the pan-islamist, Ottoman-funded journal *Islamic Fraternity*, in which columns he also called for the India's national liberation, with the support of the (Muslim) Chinese minister as well as influential Japanese characters (Bose, 1971, pp. 66–70; Siddiqui, 2017). Wahhabis, in the North West Frontier Province (NWFP, now a region of Pakistan), resisted the British in the name of jihad since 1824 (Baha, 1979; Rauf, 2005, 2007).

17.4 Indo-German Operations on the Northwestern Border

The IUK as well as the German consular network have actively aided German-Turkish jihadist efforts during the war, propaganda and secret war operations in Mesopotamia and in Palestine, in Persia and in Afghanistan, or active preaching of the Muslim holy war by nationalists of any religion or by Turkish, Chinese, Japanese or Christian German agents. Taraknath Das, a co-founder of the Ghadr party, was sent to Palestine by the IUK to spread independentist and jihadist propaganda in the Indian troops stationed in Egypt and serve as liaison with Bedouin tribes and Egyptian nationalists. Others were sent to Mesopotamia to convert Indian troops to their cause (Mukherjee, 1966, pp. 79–91; Sareen pp. 164–165, 171).

Both Turks and Indians participated in the German expedition of Wilhelm Waßmuß, nicknamed the “German Lawrence”, to Southwestern Persia, where he had been a consul before the war. There they led guerrilla operations against the British along with Tangestani tribes (Crouzet, 2017, pp. 85–103; Göttrup, 2013). Meanwhile Lieutenant Oskar von Niedermayer headed a German diplomatic mission to Persia. Travelling alongside Waßmuß up to Bagdad, he reached Tehran in April 1915. His presence in the Persian capital momentarily served German influence, with a support base made of the Persian democrats, the IUK- supported nationalists and even the Swedish gendarmerie corps, powerfully aided by a parallel shi’i jihad declaration made by Iraqi religious leaders (Seidt, 2002; Hanioğlu, 2015).

Those initial German successes prompted another diplomatic expedition, this time headed to Afghanistan. Although we know both Waßmuß and Turkish strongman Enver were at the initiative, the part of the IUK in the inception of such a plan is unclear. It is known, however, that the country, on the Northwestern border of British India, was deemed by them a priority on equal terms with Siam. It was therefore only natural that the expedition, although headed by German diplomat Otto von Hentig, included as IUK agents Raja Mahendra Pratap Singh as well as Muhammad Barkatullah, the latter a pan-islamist columnist and co-founder of Ghadr. Conceived in January 1915, it reached Kermanshah and Esfahan in June. Niedermayer, by then disillusioned on the intentions of the Persian government—a pro-German coup was attempted in November of the same year—joined the Hentig-Pratap expedition and helped it escape Russian scrutiny while crossing the Afghan border. When it reached Kabul in October 1915, the party comprised 6 Germans, 2 Indians, 2 Turks, 1 Persian, 60 Arabs and a number of Afridi deserters from the NWFP (Bose, 1971, pp. 103–109; Sareen, 1979, pp. 172–174; Hugues, 2004).

The Indo-Germans had a number of strong arguments, the first of which was the global jihad, which helped gather support in the general population, as well as the token British army then present in India, the prospect of a German-Ottoman(-Persian) alliance, the support of the wahhabites in the NWFP, the promise of weapons delivery and a project of reorganization of the Afghan army. Austro-Hungarian POW came to Kabul from POW camps in Russian Turkestan, while 15 *mujahirin*, Indian Muslim students from Lahore, also crossed the Indo-Afghan border. A treaty of friendship was even signed on January 29th 1916. Indo-German sympathies among

Afghan nobles, including the emir's brother, allowed for Pratap, Barkatullah, and newly arrived Ubaidullah Sindhi (also through the Indo-Afghan border) to form a Provisional Government of India (PGI), as well as an "army of God". Another formal treaty was signed between the Afghan government and the PGI (Pratap, 1947, p. 52). Neither these arguments however, nor the promise of extending Afghan territory from Bombay to Samarkand, nor Pratap's offer to the emir of being crowned emperor of India could sway the latter, who appears to have been financially compensated by the British. By April, both the Germans, through China and Persia, and the Indians, through Russian Turkestan, had left Kabul (Mukherjee, 1966, pp. 89–91; Sareen, 1979, pp. 176–180, Hughes, 2004; Anjum, 2013).

Although considered as a failure by historiography and by Oppenheim himself (Lüdke, 2005, p. 186), this call for jihad—and its conjunction with Indian nationalism—had wide-reaching consequences for India and its immediate neighbourhood, from the independence of Afghanistan in 1919 to the Khilafat movement in 1923 (Qureshi, 1973, p. 36; Wasti, 2006; Gotteland, 2021, pp. 287–318), as well as, later on, Muslim Indian socialist activism, both in India and in the USSR (Ansari, 1986).

17.5 Indo-German Organization in East and Southeast Asia

Rapidly after the creation of the IUK under German patronage, agents from Berlin not only left for the Ottoman Empire but also established contacts and co-ordinated the efforts of the two other major nationalist organizations: Yugantar, in Bengal, and Ghadr in the United States. Herambra Lal Gupta was sent as the IUK liaison to the Ghadr in the United States, while Bhagwan Singh, who assumed control of the Californian Ghadr since the flight of Har Dayal to Europe, toured Asia to create subsidiary centres of the Ghadr in a number of East and Southeast Asian cities, most notably in Bangkok, Manila, Shanghai, Singapore and Tōkyō. He was helped in this enormous task by earlier Ghadr attempts, his own earlier travels across the region and sympathies with local political movements (Deepak, 1999, p. 440; Ramnath, 2011, p. 75; Cao, 2017, p. 153; Gotteland, 2021, p. 265). Mathra Singh, who had fought alongside Chinese republicans in the revolution of 1911, had begun Ghadr work in Shanghai as early as 1913 (Deepak, 1999, pp. 440–442).

While Germans were unable to aid Ghadr returnees either from Europe or North America, Ghadr-German efforts were paramount in helping them reach India from China, whether they came from that country or stopped in Chinese ports on their way from the United States (Bose, 1971, p. 128; Gotteland, 2021, pp. 265–266). Despite some reluctances on the part of several diplomats and most notably the ambassador in Washington—but accounts on the issue are contradictory—the German diplomatic network was essential to the structure and functioning of the Ghadr network as well as German secret war efforts in America and Asia. In those efforts, the Indian or Indo-jihadist stake was primordial, while Indian agents were also used to carry on operations wholly irrelevent to the cause of India's independence. Difficulty in communicating with Berlin in times of war often meant important decisions had to be taken at a local level, although a loose hierarchy meant the German consulate in Shanghai—and its intelligence branch, the *neue Abteilung* or New Section (NA) —were in charge of Indian and German operations across the Asia–Pacific, its reach extending from Manchuria and Siberia in the North to Siam and the Dutch Indies in the South (Gotteland, 2021, pp. 215–254). Bhagwan Singh, as the Ghadr contact of the NA, had stayed in Shanghai from October 1915 to May 1916, had been directly funded by it and participated in important decisions (Gotteland, 2021, p. 266).

17.6 German Attempts at Arms Delivery from the Philippines, the United States and China

Apart from funding, organization, propaganda, as well as the manufacture of explosives, the primary aim of German aid in North America and East Asia was the delivery of arms and ammunition to India properly. The best known and much publicized in contemporary press articles are the attempts to make such delivery across the Pacific Ocean either from the Philippines or from the United States, as they constituted the main argument of the so-called "Hindu-German conspiracy trial", which extended from November 1917 to April 1918 and put an end to most German-Ghadarite activities in North America during the war.

Albert Wehde and George Paul Boehm, both born German and naturalized American, were recruited by Herambra Lal Gupta, then liaison agent of the IUK, through the intermediary of the German consul in Chicago in March 1915. It seems that Boehm's mission may have been to train Ghadarites in Siam, although Boehm itself, Sukumar Chatterji, arrested in Bangkok, and Chandra Kanta Chakravarty, the successor of Gupta, arrested in New York, gave consistent reports pointing to a much more ambitious mission to reach Nepal through Siam, Burma and Northeastern India, capture the expedition of explorer Friedrick Cook to assume his identity, bribe Gorkha soldiers and offer the trone of India to the king of Nepal.

In any case, the mission of both German-Americans changed when they arrived in Manila in May 1915. They were to find a way to bring those arms and ammunition kept on board two interned German ships, the SMS Sachsen and SMS Suevia, to Indian activists in Siam and in India. Due to the interference of American customs they failed however, and sailed instead to the Dutch Indies in order to try their luck with such arms and ammunition as were kept on German interned ships there. Having reached Paleleh, in Borneo, they had to go back to Jolo and Manila because of engine failure, maybe due to sabotage. Boehm, sick, tried to reach Bangkok through the Dutch Indies in order to go back to America, but was arrested in Singapore. Wehde managed, however, to reach China were he served German interests as a propaganda columnist and intelligence agent (Wehde, 1923; Ramnath, 2011, p. 88; Streets-Salter, pp. 111–141; Gotteland, 2021, pp. 276–280).

Another attempt stemmed from a decision taken in Berlin, on October 1914, in conjunction between the German marine ministry and the newly founded IUK, to bring 10 to 20 thousand rifles directly from the United States to Indian independentists in Siam or in India. The plan was however convoluted and poorly executed. Franz von Papen, head of the German Military Information Bureau in New York, managed to gather thousands of rifles, pistols and cartridges, thanks to the help of the Krupp agent in the city in December 1914. The cargo reached San Diego in January 1915. Loaded on an old schooner, the Annie Larsen, their alleged Mexican destination is credible enough for the American customs to take the sea. Such a ship could not reach Asian shores, however, which justified the purchase of an oil tanker, the SS Maverick, in March 1915. In need of repair, the Maverick failed to meet the Annie Larsen on Socorro island in April 1915, arriving one day after the latter left for Hoquiam, Washington. Interned on arrival, the arms were confiscated by the American customs. The Maverick first returned to San Diego–although in Mexican waters, where it was ordered to reach Hawai'i, and from there Java, Siam or directly Karachi. It was also interned on arrival in the Dutch Indies, despite not carrying any contraband (Brown, 1948; Fraser, 1977; Hoover, 1985; Ramnath, 2011, p. 79; Streets-Salter, 2017, p. 115; Gotteland, 2021, pp. 283–286) Papen tried to redress the situation by loading another cargo on a Dutch steamship bound from New York to either Java or Sumatra, the SS Djember. The Holland America Line refused to load it however, having been informed by the British general consul on the nature of said cargo (Fraser, 1977).

Less known are the German attempts to reach the same shores from the much closer and more convenient Chinese ports. In September 1915, Adolf Nielsen, a chemist and prominent NA agent, convinced Chinese boatsmen to bring several crates of contraband "medicine" to India, being in fact pistols and cartridges. While Nielsen was protected by extraterritoriality, the Chinese involved in the trafficking of "medicine" were still brought to trial for the edification of Chinese and international public opinion, exposing the NA, and diminishing its capabilities for the rest of the war. Further attempts were discovered, including Nielsen's attempt to buy a Japanese steamer in Shanghai, the SS Shinten Maru, and the interception by the French navy in Indochinese waters of the SS Iro Maru, both on November 1915. On the latter case, crates were thrown over board but the German former consul in Mukden, a passenger, confirmed having carried a—lost—confidential letter he was to open on arrival in Bangkok and being entrusted with an important and secret mission. Some sources suggest those attempts might have been part of a larger plan to send no less than five ships with instructors, funds, arms, ammunition and explosives to Bengal. Given the help given by the NA to Ghadarite returnees at the beginning of the war, it is plausible that other ships may have reached Indian shores in such a manner (Gotteland, 2021, pp. 216–218 and 219–220).

17.7 Indo-German Operations on the Northeastern Border

The oddity of German attempts to bring such funds, instructors, arms, ammunition and explosives to Siam rather than directly to India is explained by the set up in that country of a large Ghadr operation, the so-called "Siam-Burma plan", made known to the general public at the Mandalay trial. This Ghadarite appetite for a Siamese base of operation seems to have been made known to the NFO in January 1915 by Har Dayal and Barkatullah, and then sanctioned by Oppenheim. German consul in Hankou Dr Ernst-Arthur Voretzsch, however, traveled to Bangkok from October to December 1914, ostensibly to set up German-Ghadarite operations in the country. Santokh Singh, who founded the Ghadar branch in Bangkok, co-ordinated with the German minister in the Siamese capital, while the German consulate in Shanghai provided explosives, arms, ammunition, funding and oversight. 600 to 700 Ghadarites are estimated to have emigrated to Siam either from North America or China, while a small Indian community existed on site, notably thanks to the building of a railway involving Indian workers and German engineers. The British learned about the plan from March to June 1915. When they informed the Siamese government in July of the same year, triggering a wave of arrests among the revolutionaries, the Indo-German operation counted a press in Pakoh, a training camp in Bandon and another at the Burmese border, as well as a factory of explosives in Paknampho. A Ghadar branch had been created in Rangoon. At the time they sounded the alarm in Bangkok, the British captured a party of 6 Ghadarite "invaders", tried at Mandalay and hanged. Interestingly, the plan seems to have had an important jihadist component, both in terms of propaganda and recruits (Bose, 1971, pp. 72–73, 133–134; Fraser, 1977; Deepak, 1999, p. 443; Ramnath, 2011, pp. 81–82; Streets-Salter, 2017, pp. 155–157; Gotteland, 2021, pp. 272–275).

Burma had been the target of Turkish pan-islamist propaganda since 1913, and the proximity with Bengal meant Yugantar extended there its operations, at least in terms of propaganda. Early and persistent Indo-German interest in Burma and Northeastern India is also explained by the very long border with neutral China and Siam as well as the relative proximity of neutral Sumatra and Java. In the Spring of 1915, two Chinese agents of Dr Voretzsch approached Burmese prince Myngoon-Min in Saigon (Bose, 1971, pp. 137–138; Streets-Salter, pp. 332–335) All the while, plans were drawn up for either a Chinese or a regional (Yunnanese) invasion of Burma as soon as December 1914 (Gotteland, 2021, p. 269), while the later "Pawelka mission", likely carrying funds, arms and ammunition, meant to incite more localized invasions by lesser warlords along the Sino-Burmese borders, while preaching jihad and attempting to meet Ghadarites from Siam (Bose, 1971, pp. 136, 141; Gotteland, pp. 269–270, 338–340). Failing any invasion of Burma of any extension, either from the east or the north, it seems Yugantar lobbied the Germans to fund and support a rebellion of the "Abors" (Indian first nations of the Northeast) and to deliver arms and ammunition through the Sino-Indian border in 1915 and 1916, although with little success (Roy 1964, 4–5, 12; Bose, 1971, p. 172; Gotteland, 2021, pp. 270–271). Taraknath Das tried to build a pan-asianist organization in China with this very aim in 1916 and 1917, until the declaration of war of his host country to Germany and Austria-Hungary (Gotteland, 2021, p. 300).

Plans were simultaneously drawn up to take Rangoon from the south. Vincent Kraft, before the war a planter in the Dutch Indies, injured on the Western front, wrote in early 1915 to the German foreign ministry about plans to help Indian revolutionaries from Java and Sumatra while selling the information to the British. After meeting Wesendonck on April, his plan is sanctioned by both the ministry and the IUK on May 4th. The German minister in Beijing sent him a Chinese agent in May, while he met with the German consul in Shanghai in August. He then had under his command around a hundred German volunteers, and reported the support of Indonesian nationalist organization Sarikut islam. With his "liberation army" and the arms that were to be sent by the SS Djember, he was to reach the Andaman islands on the German warships interned in the Dutch Indies, seize Port Blair and liberate the Ghadarite and Yugantar prisoners. Sources are contradictory however as to the next step of his plan, which may have been to deliver arms to Bengal and Odisha, to capture Rangoon, or both simultaneously. The plan was called off partly because of suspicions on the presence of a British spy in Kraft's ranks, and partly because of the affair "Medicine for India" in Shanghai; Kraft himself does not seem to have been suspected and pursued a career as a double agent in Mexico and Japan until the end of the war (Roy 1964, p. 3–5; Bose, 1971, p. 142–143; Fraser, 1977; Ramnath, 2011, p. 81; Gotteland, 2021, pp. 272–275).

17.8 The Chinese Nexus

India's immense Northern border was naturally also a priority for Indian activists, although apart from the borderline extending from Bhutan to Burma and inhabited by the "Abors", the Himalayan kingdoms neighbouring British India were difficult to access, and harder still to sway. Nevertheless, while Boehm's mission very probably extended to Nepal, Pratap, then out of favour in the Afghan capital, but still enjoying the support of the governor of Khanabad, managed to send an emissary to the king of that same country with a letter from the German foreign minister and a letter of his own, in the summer of 1917 (Pratap, 1947, pp. 56–57). At a time when Tibet declared independence from China (since 1913), was forbidden to foreigners and in fact still very rarely entered by them, he organized an expedition to Tibet from China in 1925, with Ghadr support, funding and accompanied by 7 Ghadarite volunteers (Pratap, 1947, pp. 101–128; Bose, 1971, pp. 114–115).

The 1911–1912 Republican revolution was a source of inspiration to Indian independentists, although contacts had already been established as soon as 1905, and some Indians actually participated in the Chinese revolution (Deepak, 2012; Thampi, 2021). Sun Yat-Sen found himself courted by prominent Indian revolutionaries in 1915–1916. Sun's writings, as well as Sun-friendly columnists could be said to show sympathy for the cause of Indian independence. Both Bengali Rash Behari Bose and Ghadarite leader Bhagwan Singh had stayed in Japan under the protection of Sun as well as Japanese influent personalities. Barkatullah, who was in Japan for some years, met with Sun in 1913 and kept cordial relations with the Chinese revolutionary leader, while Lala Lajpat Rai, although he opposed the idea of co-ordination with Germany during the First World War, also met with Sun in 1915 (Deepak, 2012, pp. 152–155).

Roy, then agent of the Yugantar, also met Sun in 1915, although he reported being disappointed by the encounter, Sun refusing to oppose Britain because the latter needed Hongkong as a base of operations in Southern China. Nevertheless Sun was also reported by Roy to have conceived a plan to allow for arms delivery across the Sino-Indian border either at the end of 1915 or the beginning of 1916. His plan was too elaborate, however, to be taken seriously by the German legation in Beijing, which was tasked by Sun to buy the arms from him for 5 million dollars, while they actually were in the custody of Tang Jiyao, governor of Yunnan. The agreement reached between Roy and Tang's envoy in Hankou, under the auspices of Dr Voretzsch, was not enough to obtain such an important payment from the Germans, which was the reason Roy then reached the United States, with the idea of asking for payment directly in Berlin (Roy, 1964, pp. 5–13).

Sun professed his "admiration" for the IUK, which itself cared much for China, either under the leadership of Bhagwan Singh, who established a number of Ghadr centres in the wider region (1914–1915), or later through IUK agents in America. Taraknath Das, acting as an agent of the IUK, again negotiated with Sun to buy weapons in 1916 (Brown, 1948, p. 301, Bose, 1971, p. 147, Ramnath, 2011, p. 117). Surprisingly, Sun is also reported to have vetoed the conclusion of a Sino-Indian alliance after Li Yuanhong became president of China, in June 1916. The alliance project, negotiated between Li's secretary Wang, then in the United States, and Chandra Kanta Chakravarty, IUK liaison in America from February 1916 to March 1917, included German support to Li's presidency, German protection granted China up to 5 years after the end of the war, and the delivery of arms and ammunition through the Chinese border (Brown, 1948, pp. 306–307).

What is certain is the interest taken by the IUK and by Chakravarty specifically for China herself. The latter not only prefered Chinese or Japanese agents to Indians, as they were less likely to be suspected by the British, but also believed, at a time when arms deliveries could hardly be attempted by sea, in the strategic value of the Chinese territory. In the autumn of 1916, he visited the Prime Minister of Japan Terauchi Masatake and asked for Japan's benevolent neutrality in case China could be used as the rear basis for an invasion of India. According to him, Terauchi did not seem opposed to the idea (Tenney, 1919, p. 97, Bose, 1971, pp. 153–154, Schuler, 2010, p. 137, Gotteland, 2021, pp. 196–198).

A last IUK agent, a Japanese Muslim, sent to Mexico in January 1917, was to carry a plan which carried Chakravarty's trademark: the setting up of clandestine presses and of a trading company in India to carry out the trafficking of arms, ammunition and intelligence with Berlin, supported by the Chinese community and Japanese consuls in India, the setting up of an intelligence network in Japan, focusing on swaying Japanese social political leaders in the favour of Germany and India, as well as the organization of sabotage expeditions along the Transsiberian. Such a late and grandiose plan was however doomed to failure (Bose, 1971, p. 157, Schuler, 2010, p. 138, Gotteland, 2021, pp. 301–302).

17.9 All Roads Lead to Moscow

While the entry of the United States in the war was followed by a series of repressive measures against Ghadarites (1917–1924, Ramnath, 2011, pp. 127–128), Germany's defeat also meant the dissolution of the IUK (in November 1918) and a much more difficult situation for Indian revolutionaries in Afghanistan and in China. While disgust at the conditions of German patronage made a loyalist out of Har Dayal—his war memoirs, published in 1920, resounding as a warning for other revolutionaries—the defeat also prompted in all independentist factions a reflexion on the underlying causes thereof. Along with the acknowledgement of widespread corruption, treachery, and otherwise obtrusive personal rivalries, the main lesson was a failure to convert and raise the masses (Ramnath, 2011, p. 125). This, along with geopolitical considerations, helped many Indian revolutionaries, whether romantic revolutionaries and/or pan-islamists to convert to communism and seek the patronage of the emerging subversive power that was revolutionary Russia. The alignment with Moscow was the result of several disconnected attempts, inherited from the battered Indo-German global network.

Pratap and his Kabul PGI had played with the idea of Russian support since 1916, but he was sidelined in 1917. Faced with difficulties either in Afghanistan, across the Persian or the Chinese border, he then opted to travel to Russia through Central Asia, and managed to meet Trotsky in Petrograd in March 1918. Regaining Berlin and Constantinople, he met one last time with the German emperor and Ottoman sultan before temporarily settling in Central Europa, all the while championing the idea of an "international socialist army" comprising the Russians, Germans, Austrians, Bulgarians and the Turks. Crossing the frontline of the Russian civil war in a German aeroplane, he met with Lenin in Moscow in 1919, before heading another mission to Afghanistan, this time in the name of Soviet Russia. Open to socialist ideas but an Indian patriot and a humanist first and foremost, his amities will allow him to cross Russia from east to west in 1923, from there to Kabul and back to Europe through Russian Turkestan in 1924 (Pratap, 1947, pp. 57–61, 81–96, Bose, 1971, p. 115).

While passing through Tashkent, on the way back from his 1919 Soviet mission to Afghanistan, Pratap met both Roy and Barkatullah, which he left in Kabul in 1916. Both the latter and Ubeidullah had also become seduced by communism and the prospect of a Russian alliance (Pratap, 1947, pp. 71–72, Ramnath, 2011, pp. 219–232). Roy, who had been first a Yugantar agent who travelled to the Dutch Indies and China to gather German support (1915) and eventually reached American shores (1916), was exposed there to anarcho-syndicalism, socialism and pacifism. Having fled to Mexico to escape arrest (1917), and while still funded and supported by Germany, he became an internationalist and communist revolutionary. With the support of Mikhail Borodin, he co-founded the communist Party of Mexico and was elected secretary-general (1919). He represented the American country at the 2nd International in 1920. There he presented his "supplementary theses on the national and colonial question", which helped set Comintern policy on whether to support bourgeois-nationalist anticolonial movements. The resulting compromise allowed to assist middle-class nationalist revolutionaries while also founding orthodox communist parties to convert the masses. A rising star within the organization, he had founded in Tashkent a Communist Party of India (1921). The latter relied heavily on Indian *mujahirin* come from India to Kabul, as well as later khilafatists come to defend Turkey's caliphate and independence. His star faded, however, after 1928 and a mission to China which could not avoid nationalist Guomindang turning on the Chinese communist party. Formally expelled from the Comintern in 1929, he focused thereafter on anti-fascism (Bose, 1971, pp. 197–213, Sareen, 1979, pp. 231–236, Goebel, 2014, Ramnath, 2011, pp. 123–125, 201–202).

As soon as December 1916-January 1917, Virendranath Chattopadhyaya left Berlin to take charge of affairs at the IUK subsidiary in Stockholm. There he met Troianovski, which he converted to the Indian cause. Carrying in his cases books and pamphlets provided by Chattopadhyaya, Troianovski left for Petrograd on November 1917. His return to his home country was probably one of the main causes for the publication in June 1918 of a Blue Book on India by Soviet Russia made of secret documents extracted from the archives of the Russian foreign ministry. The German connexion was not severed by Indian nationalists however, either in 1917–1918 or after German defeat. The German foreign ministry was informed of Chattopadhyaya's Bolshevik contacts and had funded Troianovski during his stay in Sweden (Bose, 1971, p. 98; Sareen, 1979, pp. 217–221; Aspengren, 2014).

At the end of the war, the IUK was dissolved. Berlin remained a major hub for Indian political exiles. The promise of a Soviet patronage, as well as Chattopadhyaya's efforts in Stockholm and Barkatullah's activism in Moscow allowed for a secret meeting to take place in Berlin as soon as May 1919. America's Ghadr was beginning to disperse between Bhagwan Singh's dissident faction in New York as well as Taraknath Das' Friends of Freedom for India. All European and American factions managed to gather within a new Indian Revolutionary Society (IRS), their representatives forming a Central Executive Committee. Chattopadhyaya had thus managed to keep the semblance of unity and global co-ordination that German patronage and the IUK had permitted during the war while providing the Soviets with a single interlocutor. In 1921, representatives of the new Committee gathered in Moscow to present their plans and their requests.

Three obstacles temporarily doomed any prospect for a Soviet patronage of Berlin's IRS: First, Chattopadhyaya seems to have been an active proponent of an invasion from Afghanistan and an arming of the tribes of the NWFP, then in line with Soviet policy. He rejected however vehemently—and surprisingly—any support to further pan-islamist propaganda. Secondly, the window for an Indo-Soviet and an Indo-Afghan alliance was closing on account of the normalization of relations between those countries and the United Kingdom in 1922. Finally, Roy gave Chattopadhyaya and the IRS an ultimatum: embrace communism, work to spread the new doctrine across the globe and accept him as a leader. Its rejection meant Soviet patronage would focus on Roy and his Bengali contacts until his fall from grace. Only in 1927 did Chattopadhyaya actively seek Soviet support, once again, through the League against imperialism. Having moved to Moscow in 1931, he was arrested and shot in 1937, a victim of Stalin's purges (Sareen, 1979, pp. 228–229, 237–243, Aspengren, 2014).

Santokh Singh, who set up the Ghadr branch in Bangkok in 1914–1915, had been arrested and sentenced to jail at the "Hindu-German conspiracy trial" held in San Francisco in 1917. His conversion to communism was the result to a chance encounter with Russian agents at the San Quentin prison. While the Ghadr hailed the Russian revolution as soon as 1917, Santokh Singh was instrumental in convincing Ghadarites to join hands with Russia and in converting the masses in his home region. He attended the 4th world congress of the Communist International in 1922, after which he returned to India through Afghanistan and created a socialist journal, named *Kirti*, in Punjab. The grassroots movement he managed to lead there is however beyond the scope of this short summary of Indian revolutionary activities abroad (Bains, 1962, pp. 53–54; Ramnath, 2011, pp. 123–125, 144–145).

17.10 Engaging with Racist but Subversive Powers: Fascist Italy and Nazi Germany, 1922–1939

Following the dispute between Chattopadhyaya and Roy, a vast number of Indian independentist activists were left without a patron and in need of foreign support. The revolution that was the march on Rome was not lost on them. When Muhammad Iqbal Shedai, a pan-islamist Ghadarite, arrived in Italy in 1923, he met with another jihadist nationalist: Barkatullah. From 1922 to 1939, Fascist Italy had no Indian policy and had no appetite for antagonizing Britain. This did not prevent Indian efforts from harvesting some—meager—results, in the form of contacts with Italian intelligence and financiers. Although Mussolini himself seems to have taken an early interest in India's fate, the visits of Rabindranath Tagore in 1926 and Gandhi in 1931—and their talks with Mussolini—were rather the result of a fascination for a revolutionary, subversive and modern regime than a reciprocal and genuine Italian interest. They do not seem to have borne much fruit, either in the form of Indian sympathy or Italian influence. Taraknath Das did write in the Italian journal *Asiatica* in 1935, but as an appeal for Italian support to pan-asianist Japan and its programme of "Asia to the Asians" and "India to the Indians". Shedai remained faithful to the regime up to the war years, when an India Office was created at the foreign ministry he managed a a regular radio broadcasting service in Hindustani and in English directed at an Indian audience. A military centre was established in Rome to train Indian POW; but the latter were never deployed, either in the Italian or the German army. Much more significant are the numerous meetings of Subhas Chandra Bose with Mussolini in 1934, 1935 and 1936. Shedai mistrusted Bose, an attitude which reflected negatively on the whole Italian foreign ministry, despite Mussolini's sympathies (Prayer, 1991).

Relations with Germans and the German state were, as we have seen, pivotal to the Indian independence movement abroad from 1914 onwards. For a time however, the main point of contact would not be in Berlin, as it was the case until Chattopadhyaya's departure for Moscow, but Münich. There, geographer and geopolitician Karl Haushofer had founded in 1925 the *Deutsche Akademie* (or German Academy), an organization dedicated to German soft power. Haushofer, whose later relations with the nazi regime remain controversial, had visited India in 1908–1909 and met Chattopadhyaya in Berlin during the war years. As soon as 1928, an *Indisches Ausschuss* (or India Institute) was set up within the Academy by Taraknath Das and Haushofer. The Institute would later accomodate and after 1939 identify with the regime (Roy, 2021).

Abdulrahman Saif Razad, an Iranian nationalist, close to Bose, who had taken part in the 1915 expedition to Kabul and continued his jihadist activities in Kabul under the patronage of the Soviets, styled himself as a "National Socialist Aryan" and served as a German spy in Bombay. He would be arrested and interned by the British from 1939 to 1944. He had also been the editor of the pro-nazi Tehran-based journal *Tehran-e Bastan* from 1933 to 1935 (Marashi, 2020).

The European travels of Subhas Chandra Bose, who would head the INC from 1938 to 1939, brought him to Italy, as well as Austria, Czechoslovakia and Germany. His attitude towards fascism and nazism was more ambiguous than that of Saif Razad, and bore much resemblance with that of other Indian nationalists towards the ideology of their foreign patrons since 1914. There is no doubt however, that they, along with communism, influenced Bose's own political views (Motadel, 2019, p. 871, Tumiotto, 2020).

17.11 The Height of Indo-Nazi Collaboration, 1941–1943

Initially, the nazi leadership showed no similar appetite for an alliance with the Indian cause. The reasons were partly of a geopolitical nature. Germany stood little to gain and much to lose, politically and commercially, from openly antagonizing Britain on account of a revolution she had few means to encourage. Racism naturally played a part. The early exemption of Indians, along with (non-Jewish) Arabs, Iranians and Turks from racial policies was the result of diplomatic pressure. Colonial people were considered racially inferior and vexations on this account during the stay of Indians in Germany were not unusual. Hitler himself had been enthusiastic about the British empire and conversely did not hide his contempt for these "bumptious Orientals" which were mere "garrulous posers", as he wrote in *Mein Kampf* (Motadel, 2019, pp. 855–856, 861, 893).

The war did not generate a renewed interest for the anticolonial struggle. Memoranda submitted in 1939 which advocated German support for Indian independence, penned by Hentig, former leader of the 1915 expedition to Afghanistan, Niedermayer, former leader of the 1915 expedition to Persia, and Oppenheim, founder of the NFO, found no echo at first. Only with the unfavourable turn of the war in 1941 did the German foreign ministry become more pragmatic and reach out to anticolonial movements. In Bose's memoranda of the same year, he took aim at the treaty of Versailles, painted the British empire as the one obstacle to the establishment of a new world order and called for solidarity with colonial peoples under the British yoke.

The new policy was coordinated by diplomats of the Political Department, organized in an India Section, an Orient Section and a Russia Section with Hentig being in charge of Central Asia. A large propaganda campaign was launched, with Radio Berlin broadcasting in South Asian language since 1942. The Wehrmacht, and later the Waffen-SS, began recruiting an Indian Legion or Azad Hind Fauj (meaning: Indian National Army, INA) in 1941, its batallions named after Gandhi, Nehru, Saif Razad and Bose himself, and its numbers growing to more than 3,000. More importantly, the German legation in Kabul would send arms and ammunition to NWFP rebels. An official recognition of India's independence on Germany's part only came at the very end of the war, however.

Still, once again, Berlin had been the stage of a "nationalist international against empire" characterized by a "reactionary cosmopolitanism" (Motadel, 2019, pp. 853–854). Along Bose's Free India Committee (FIC) were created smaller national committees under German patronage such as the National Turkestani National Committee, the Volga Tatar Fighting League and other smaller groups of Arab, Georgian, Armenian, Azerbaijani and Chechen activists. The FIC held congresses, displayed national flags and emblems, published a journal (*Azad Hind*) and interacted extensively with anticolonialists of other nationalities. Disagreements did appear however and the German regime, while offering them with ample resources, always remained cautious, submitting them to surveillance, detention and censorship (Hartog, 2001; Motadel, 2019).

17.12 Pan-Asianism: Reconciling Indian Anticolonialism with Japanese Imperialism

One of few still independent countries in Asia, Japan had been since the early days of Indian independentism a major focus, a symbol of modernity, a guide to follow and a model to emulate. Conversely Japanese interest for the movement, although not always and not at first emanating from the government, went as far back as Okakura Kakuzō's visits to Calcutta in 1900–1901. After the modernization of the Meiji era, the victory over China and the annexation of Taiwan (1895), the revision of bilateral "unequal treaties" (1899) and finally the victory over Russia and protectorate over Korea (1905) did much to nourish Japanese nationalism. The latter, in turn, translated into either critical discussion or appropriation of Western paradigms such as "race" and "civilization". The resulting pan-asianism often tended, in Japan, India and elsewhere, to equate Asian solidarity against Western imperialism with the acceptation or request of Japanese leadership and protection (Bose, 1971, p. 67, Gates, 2011, Solte and Fischer-Tiné, 2012).

The Japanese resounding victory in 1905, which in India coincided with plans for a partition of Bengal, led many Asian and Indian students to leave for Japan, and there plead for assistance in the anticolonial struggle. Over the course of a few years, several hundreds of Indian students attended Japanese universities. The political climate was not favourable yet, notably thanks to the recently renewed Anglo-Japanese alliance (1905), as exemplified by the short sojourn of Taraknath Das (1905–1906), the ban on the Association for Asian Harmony after only a few months of existence (1907), the difficulties opposed to the propaganda activities of Barkatullah (1909–1914) (Fischer-Tiné, 2007, pp. 328–329, Ramnath, 2011, pp. 115–118, Deepak, 2012, Siddiqui, 2017, Wang, 2019).

Pan-asianist ideology would however gradually hold more sway over Japanese policy, when early supporters such as Gotō Shinpei (minister for foreign affairs in 1918), Tōyama Mitsuru (founder of the Black Ocean Society) and Inukai Tsuyoshi (prime minister from 1931 to 1932) rose to power. As we have seen, Japan featured heavily in the plans of Indian independentists during the First World War, including Bhagwan Singh and Rash Behari Bose. Both Taraknath Das and Herambra Lal Gupta found shelter there from deportation thanks to Tōyama and carried on pan-asianist activities in the name of the Ghadr and the IUK (1916–1917). Das would go on to write pro-Japanese pamphlets, while pan-asianism would come at the forefront of his political thought (Ramnath, 2011, pp. 118–119). Rash Behari Bose, who arrived in the country in 1915, married in Japan and became a Japanese citizen in 1923. Bose was involved in a scheme to ship arms to Bengal in 1924–1925 (McQuade, 2016). Both he and Das wrote in *Nihon* from 1925 to 1932, the journal of prominent pan-asianist theorist Ōkawa Shūmei (Ramnath, 2011, p. 116).

17.13 Japan and the INA, 1942–1945

Raja Mahendra Pratap, who had extensively toured Europe, Western and Central Asia during and after the First World War stayed in Japan from 1922 to 1923, and visited Tōkyō and Kōbe on his way from California to Tibet in 1925. On both occasions he met Bose, and also Inukai and Tōyama. He finally settled there in 1929. There he would articulate his pan-asian and pan-aryan plans, plead for a "world federation" and preach his "religion of love", ideas matured since his first travel to Afghanistan in 1915, with the support of Japanese nationalists. He did not see at first any contradiction between his pacifist conception and his travels to and praise of Manchukuo. Forced to silence by the war and his subsequent loss of faith in Japanese benevolence, Pratap was briefly interned as a war criminal before rejoining India in 1946 and serving as a member of parliament (1957–1962) (Stolte, 2012).

Bose, who likewise hailed Japan's rise during the 1930s, aligned with the Japanese war effort, calling for the inclusion of India in the Greater East Asian Prosperity Sphere (GEAPS) (McQuade, 2016). Japan, however, does not seem to have at any moment considered a full-fledged invasion or the incorporation of India within her GEAPS. The anti-Japanese stance of the INC, the lack of means to control India and establish a stable state there, the distance from the actual theatres of war were major reasons for this disinterest. The aim of the Imphal offensive (March 1944) in North-eastern India was to secure Japanese hold on Burma and to cut the air liaison between Chongqing and India rather than use the region as a door to India's heartland. All things considered, the independentist movement from far-flung India proved to be of little concern in Japanese policy circles until overt anti-British hostilities in late 1941 (Lebra, 1969 and 2008).

This should not obscure however the continued presence, propaganda and terrorist operations of the Sikhs in Thailand, in direct continuity with Indo-German operations in Siam. Bhagwan Singh, who then supervised the setting up of Ghadr subsidiaries across the Asia–Pacific, remains in the late 1930s one of the leaders of its Bangkok centre, now called the Indian Independence League (IIL). The IIL seems to have collaborated with the Japanese diplomatic representation in Bangkok long before 1941, making the Thai capital once again a major centre of propaganda and espionage. It established offshoots across the country, including on the Malayan and Burmese borders, across which parties of volunteers have been sent. The IIL went on to become the skeleton of the INA in 1942 (Dali, 2008).

This second INA, distinct from the one established in Germany in 1941, but operating along similar principles, was a Japanese-IIL initiative meant to recruit Indian volunteers, either still serving in the British-Indian army or held in POW camps. Captain Mohan Singh, at the head of one of the first British-Indian batallions, became one of the main INA activists after meeting with Major Fujiwara of Japanese intelligence. The latter, arrived in Bangkok in October 1941, was the liaison with the IIL and the INA, all the while heading plans for Malaya, Sumatra and the overseas Chinese, in which Indian agents participated. Branches of the Fujiwara organization were established in Rangoon, Saigon, Singapore, Penang and Hongkong. The objectives of this Indo-Japanese alliance would be to encourage anti-British sentiment across Southeast Asia, to develop an intelligence network within India and to defend the Western flank of the GEAPS.

In early 1942, representatives of the IIL and the INA had been invited to a conference of Indians from Southeast Asia held in Tōkyō, while Subhas Chandra Bose, then in Berlin, was invited to Japan. Surprisingly and despite the latter attempt at catching Japanese attention, Fujiwara first heard of Bose from Mohan Singh. While Rash Behari Bose had been briefly involved with the INA and was already in Japan, he does not seem to have had much influence on Japanese policy; Bose, who managed to gain such an influence–although perhaps in part because of Japan's difficult position at the time, could not arrive in Japan before May 1943. In March 1943, Major Fujiwara, who had proven his sincerity and enthusiasm for the Indian cause, was replaced by Colonel Iwakuro, a seasoned intelligence officer. Shortly after, a leadership crisis opposing Bose and Mohan Singh led to the incarceration of the latter.

Those events exemplified the relative lack of interest of Japan's leadership before early 1943, but also the growing support for Fujiwara's organization and the simultaneous suspicion on the part of the Indian revolutionaries in Southeast Asia. Japan provided arms and support, but with reluctance. Fujiwara's activism was clearly not shared in Tōkyō. The IIL remained confined to propaganda, espionage and sabotage purposes. The lack of trust in the INA's ultimate goals and capabilities meant it was kept as a guerrilla fighting unit. Finally, the recognition of the Free India Provisional Government and the transfer to it of the Andaman and Nicobar islands in November 1943, although earlier than that of Nazi Germany, served mainly propaganda purposes and did not translate to shared control on the ground. Neither these reasons nor dwindling Japanese capacities convinced Bose to turn his back on the Japanese however, as he probably remained convinced of the necessity of a foreign patron for the revolution. He met his death on August 18th 1945, shortly after Japan's capitulation, while trying to reach Manchuria from Taiwan and plead the case of India's independence with the Soviets.

17.14 Conclusion: Preparing the Nation for Ultimate Success

A fair assessment of the Indian independentist movement abroad, of its strengths and its shortcomings, of its short- and long-term consequences is difficult to reach to this day. Certainly, the international and transnational nature of the nationalist movement cannot be ignored. Foreign events and remote revolutions helped embolden the movement and give impetus to the cause, while inspiration had been found in the—sometimes revisited—history of the West and Asia. Early alliances with anti-British anticolonial parties helped forge from the onset the conscience that the fate of Indian independence was linked to that of oppressed people everywhere. Exposure to foreign ideas and conditions gave shape to a national Indian consciousness shared by Muslims and Hindus, Sikhs and Bengalis. The mobilization of the Indian diaspora of all classes, students and workers, bourgeois and farmers, and their enlistment behind a common ideal is certainly a notable feat, not least because it had preceded the politization of the masses in India proper. In Punjab especially, the Ghadr movement is certainly to credit for the widespread rejection of British rule among a population that had been considered a pillar of the empire since the Sepoy Mutiny.

On the other hand, their romantic revolutionism proved as much a weakness as it was a strength. Rivalries and competition, lack of co-ordination, enthusiasm and trust in the moral standing of Indian leaders, as well as brazen defiance paved the way for failure, most notably in February 1915, but also in smaller schemes. Those defects allowed for widespread and harsh repression on the part of the British empire and its allies, in a series of trials in India, Burma, China, Singapore and the United States. Although certainly convinced of the righteousness and necessity of their efforts, corruption was widespread among revolutionary leaders. The revelations of the San Francisco trial led to the murder of Ram Chandra. Roy in Mexico, Chakravarty in New York, Bose in Berlin have without a doubt benefitted financially either from the naivety of fellow revolutionaries or from the generosity of their patrons. Their actions as well as their writings, nevertheless, leave no doubt as to their utmost sincerity. It is perhaps hardest to establish the character of each prominent personality within such a diverse and pliable movement, for personal animosities had been frequent and the resulting rifts irreparable. Such difficulties as the split between the California and the New York Ghadr or the confrontation between Roy's jihado-communists and Chattopadhyaya's Euramerican parties in Moscow have had the most serious consequences on the overall prospects of success. Frequent betrayals, not always financially motivated, allowed for intelligence services to stay well informed of the most important schemes.

The great ideological flexibility underlying the movement allowed to seek the simultaneous support of imperial Germany, feodal Afghanistan and Bolshevik Russia; to identify as "Ghadarites" not only Indian, Egyptian or Irish, but also Chinese, Mexican and Russian revolutionaries; to support without contradiction anarchism and authoritarianism, pacifism and colonial wars. The claim to transnational identities, based on race, religion or geography, such as pan-aryanism, pan-asianism and pan-islamism, the revisiting of history to claim an equality of rights on the basis of an Indian colonialism or of a superior Indian/Asian civilization were routinely merged and used in the name of furthering the overarching cause of Indian independence. Tactics naturally played an important role in the defence of such apparently volatile and flexible ideals. Adhesion to radical tendencies of the time as well as national ideologies of subversive powers, which as such were potential allies, were not entirely foreign to such attitudes. It would be a mistake however to write them off as mere posturing. The influence of solidary transnational networks, the admiration for successful revolutionaries and friendship with objective allies had a deep influence on their ideologies and worldviews. Bose's attempted synthesis between communism and fascism, to which were opposed such radical humanists as Roy or Pratap, is a case in point.

The foreign patrons they sought from 1914 onwards naturally raise the question of their autonomy, especially in time of war. Certainly the IUK served German interests worldwide, Roy the Comintern's, and the missions of the IIL- INA were as often of a nature to support Japanese rule and influence as to further the cause of Indian independence. It would be another mistake to consider the necessarily asymmetrical relationship between infra-state groups and their foreign patrons as being a mere instrumentalization of the independentist cause. They always kept a large autonomy and often managed to influence their protectors' programmes while courting them and pleading their case. The wedding of the pan-islamist and Indian cause at the NFO, the 1919 coup in Afghanistan, the presentation of Roy's theses on the colonial question on par with Lenin's, the invitation of Bose to Japan in 1942 all testify to such influence on the part of Indian political exiles.

Another striking point, as opposed to the ideological votality of the movement, is the strategic continuity. Although, like all strategic thinking, it is in part linked to the geography of India, it is nevertheless surprising to see Afghanistan so prominently featured in Indian operations, from 1914 and the convergence with the German NFO and the German-Turkish call for global jihad to the Soviet missions of the 1920s. Likewise, the Indo-Japanese operations from Bangkok in 1942–1945 were for a part reminiscent of the German-Ghadarite so-called Siam-Burma plan. This is explained by the survival of the Ghadr cell in Bangkok for a quarter of a century, despite heavy British-Thai repression in 1915, as well as the involvement of Bhagwan Singh. The Ghadr itself, although always evolving, only dissolved in 1948, a year after India became independent, despite the San Francisco trial in 1917. Berlin remained a revolutionary hub long after the end of the First World War, thanks to Chattopadhyaya's efforts. A mere student in Halle before the war, he had led the IUK from 1914 to 1916 and regrouped most of the Indo-German network from 1919 onwards.

Naturally, Indian revolutionaries abroad did not obtain the independence of India by themselves. The latter is the consequence of a number of factors, which included Bengali terrorism, Gandhi's campaigns and generally speaking the gradual loss of support to British rule within India, as well as the rising cost of the colony to the British crown. Nevertheless, they participated mightily in the support and provision of this movement in India, as well as to the politization of the masses, either through Ghadarite returnees, former jihadists, or simply the publicity given by the British themselves to the numerous trials linked to the activities of political exiles. Finally, they kept the British security apparatus on high alert across the empire, not least during the two world wars. As one of the pioneers of their historiography Arun Coomer Bose put it himself: "In a nation's fight for freedom a determined effort itself is half the achievement, and repeated efforts by a resolute group prepare the nation for ultimate success". (p. 226).

References

Published Documents and Testimonies

Har Dayal, L. (1920). *Fourty-four months in Germany and Turkey*. P.S. King & Son.

Isemonger, F. C., & Slattery, J. (1919). *An account of the Ghadr conspiracy, 1913–1915*. Superintendent Government Printing.

Ker, J. C. (1917). *Political trouble in India*. Superintendent Government Printing.

von Papen, F. (1952). *Der Wahrheit eine Gasse*. P. List.

Papers Related to the Foreign Relations of the United States: The Lansing Papers, 1914–1920. (1939). United States Government Printing Office.

Petrie, D. (1958). *Communism in India, 1924–1927*. In M. Saha (Ed.), Indian.

Pratap, M. (1947). *My life story of fifty-five years (December 1886 to December 1941)*. World Federation.

Rai, L. L. (1917). *Young India, an interpretation and history of the nationalist movement from within*. Home Rule for India League.

Rai, L. L. (1965). *Autobiographical writings*. Servants of the People Society.

Roy, M. N. (1964). *Memoirs*. Allied Publishers.

Rowlatt, S. A. T. (1918). *Sedition committee, report*. Superintendent Government Printing.

Sperry, E. E. (1918). *German plots and intrigues in the United States during the period of our neutrality*. The Committee on Public Information.

Tunney, T. J., & Hollister, P. M. (1919). *Throttled!, The detection of the German and anarchist bomb plotters in the United States*. Small, Maynard & Company.

Wehde, A. (1923). *Since leaving home*. Tremonia.

Bibliography

Anjum, T. (2013). A voice from the margins: An appraisal of Ubaid-Allah Sindhi's Mahabharat Sarvrajia party and its constitution. *Journal of Political Studies, 20*(1), 159–177.

Ansari, K. H. (1986). Pan-Islam and the making of the early Indian Muslim socialists. *Modern Asian Studies, 20*(3), 509–537.

Aspengren, H. C. (2014). Indian revolutionaries Abroad: Revisiting their silent moments. *Journal of Colonialism and Colonial History, 15*(3).

Baha, L. (1979). The activities of the Mujahidin 1900–1936. *Islamic Studies, 18*(2), 97–168.

Bains, J. S. (1962). The Ghadr movement: A golden chapter of Indian nationalism. *The Indian Journal of Political Science, 23*(1/4), 48–59.

Bhagwat, A. K., & Pradhan, G. P. (2008). *Lokmanya Tilak: A biography*. Jaico Pub. House.

Bhat, R. M. (2019a). Ghadar movement: Distortions and its role in India's struggle for freedom. *History Research Journal, 5*(6), 2121–2135.

Bhat, R. M. (2019b). Ghadar movement: Har Dayal and his ideological formulations. *Think India Journal, 22*(14), 2353–2362.

Bhatte, P. (2013). Transnational Ghadr movement: A disaporic dimension. 歴史文化社会論講座紀要, *10*, 157–173.

Bose, A. C. (1971). *Indian revolutionaries Abroad, 1905–1922: In the background of international developments*. Bharati Bhawan.

Brown, G. T. (1948). The Hindu conspiracy, 1914–1917. *Pacific Historical Review, 17*(3), 299–310.

Cao, Y. (2017). *From policemen to revolutionaries: A Sikh Diaspora in global Shanghai, 1885–1945*. Brill (Studies in global social history, volume 30).

Costanzo, T. D. (2017). Memory and history of the great(er) war and India: From a national-imperial to a more global perspective. *E-rea, 14*(2).

Crouzet, G. (2017). «For England everything centres round India and Arabia»: La guerre anglo-allemande dans le golfe Persique: Impérialismes, politique tribale et jihad (1914–1915). *Revue Des Mondes Musulmans Et De La Méditerranée, 141*, 85–102.

Dali, A. M. (2008). The INA's secret war and the Sikhs in Southeast Asia during World War II. *Sarjana, 23*(1), 38–51.

Deepak, B. R. (1999). Revolutionary activities of the Ghadar party in China. *China Report, 35*(4), 439–456.

Deepak, B. R. (2012). The colonial connections: Indian and Chinese nationalists in Japan and China. *China Report, 48*(1–2), 147–170.

Esenbel, S. (2004). Japan's global claim to Asia and the World of Islam: Transnational nationalism and world power, 1900–1945. *The American Historical Review, 109*(4), 1140–1170.

Faheem, F., et al. (2021). Identity and interests: History of Pakistan's foreign policy and the middle eastern Muslim states, 1947 to 1956. *Cogent Social Sciences, 7*(1).

Fischer-Tiné, H. (2007). Indian nationalism and the "world forces": Transnational and diasporic dimensions of the Indian freedom movement on the eve of the first world war. *Journal of Global History, 2*(3), 325–344.

Fraser, T. G. (1977). Germany and Indian revolution, 1914–18. *Journal of Contemporary History, 12*(2), 255–272.

Gates, R. B. (2011). Pan-Asianism in Prewar Japanese foreign affaris: The curious case of Uchida Yasuya. *The Journal for Japanese Studies, 37*(1), 1–27.

Goebel, M. (2014). Geopolitics, transnational solidarity or diaspora nationalism? The global career of M.N. Roy, 1915–1930. *European Review of History: Revue Européenne D'histoire, 21*(4), 485–499.

Gotteland, M. (2021). *L'Allemagne et l'Autriche-Hongrie en Chine, 1895–1918*. Université Paris I Panthéon-Sorbonne.

Göttrup, H. (2013). *Wilhelm Wassmuss: Der deutsche Lawrence*. Metropol Verlag.

Gould, H. A. (2006). *Sikhs, swamis, students, and spies: The India lobby in the United States, 1900–1946*. Thousand Oaks, Sage Publications.

Hanioğlu, Ş. (2015). Ottoman Jihad or Jihads: The Ottoman Shīī Jihad, the successful one. In E. J. Zürcher, *Jihad and Islam in World War I* (pp. 117–134). Leiden University Press.
Hartog, R. (2001). *The sign of the Tiger: Subhas Chandra Bose and his Indian legion in Germany, 1941–45*. Rupa & Co.
Heehs, P. (1993). *The bomb in Bengal: The rise of revolutionary terrorism in India, 1900–1910*. Oxford University Press.
Heehs, P. (1994). Foreign influences on Bengali revolutionary terrorism 1902–1908. *Modern Asian Studies, 28*(3), 533–556.
Hoover, K. (1985). The Hindu conspiracy in California, 1913–1918. *German Studies Review, 8*(2), 245.
Hugues, T. L. (2004). The German mission to Afghanistan 1915–1916. In W. G. Schwanitz (Ed.), *Germany and the middle east 1871–1945* (pp. 25–64). Vervuert Verlagsgesellschaft.
Jain, M. (2022). A forgotten revolution: Understanding the Ghadar movement's Impact on Indian nationalism, castes, and martial troops during world war I.
Jani, D. K. (2017). The concept of fascism in colonial India: M.N. Roy and the problem of freedom. *Global Histories, 3*(2), 121–138.
Jenkins, J. (2013). Fritz Fischer's "programme for revolution": Implications for a global history of Germany in the first world war. *Journal of Contemporary History, 48*(2), 397–417.
Jensen, J. M. (1979). The "Hindu conspiracy": A reassessment. *Pacific Historical Review, 48*(1), 65–83.
Johnston, H. J. M. (1989). *The voyage of the Komagata Maru: The Sikh challenge to Canada's colour bar* (2nd ed.). University of British Columbia Press.
Johnston, H. (2010). The surveillance of Indian nationalists in North America, 1908–1918. *BC Studies: The British Columbian Quarterly*, 3–27.
Kalra, V. S. (2017). 'From Ghadar to the Indian workers association. In R. Hegde, & A. Sahoo (Eds.), *Routledge Handbook of the Indian Disapora*. Routledge.
Kent Carrasco, D. (2020). Breath of revolution: Ghadar anti-colonial radicalism in North America and the Mexican revolution. *South Asia: Journal of South Asian Studies, 43*(6), 1077–1092.
Krása, M. (1972). The idea of Pan-Asianism and the nationalist movement in India. *Archiv Orientálni, 40*, 38–60.
Laursen, O. B. (2021a). "I have only one country, it is the World": Madame Cama, Anticolonialism, and Indian-Russian revolutionary networks in Paris, 1907–17. *History Workshop Journal, 90*, 96–114.
Laursen, O. B. (2021b). Spaces of Indian anti-colonialism in early twentieth-century London and Paris. *South Asia: Journal of South Asian Studies, 44*(4), 634–650.
Lebra, J. (1969). Japanese policy and the Indian national army. *Asian Studies, 7*(1), 31–49.
Lebra, J. (2008) *The Indian national army and Japan*. Institute of Southeast Asian Studies.
Lüdke, T. (2005) *Jihad made in Germany: Ottoman and German propaganda and intelligence operations in the First World War*. Lit.
Malhi, R. S. (2021). Malayan Sikhs' participation in the Ghadar movement: From loyal British subjects to ardent revolutionaries. *Sikh Formations, 17*(4), 435–449.
Manjapra, K. K. (2006). The illusions of encounter: Muslim "minds" and Hindu revolutionaries in first world war Germany and after. *Journal of Global History, 1*(3), 363–382.
Marashi, A. (2020). *Exile and the nation: The Parsi community of India and the making of modern Iran* (1st ed.). University of Texas Press.
McQuade, J. (2016). The new Asia of Rash Behari Bose: India, Japan, and the limits of the international, 1912–1945. *Journal of World History, 27*(4), 641–667.
Mishra, P. (2013). *From the ruins of empire: The revolt against the West and the remaking of Asia*. Penguin books.
Motadel, D. (2019). The global authoritarian moment and the revolt against empire. *The American Historical Review, 124*(3), 843–877.
Mukherjee, U. (1966). *Two great Indian revolutionaries, Rash Behari Bose & Jyotindra Nath Mukherjee*. K.L. Mukhpadyay.

Oberoi, H. (2009). Ghadar movement and its anarchist genealogy. *Economic and Political Weekly, 44*(50), 40–46.

Oesterheld, F. (2004). *"Der Feind meines Feindes ist mein Freund"-Zur Tätigkeit des Indian independence committee (IIC) während des Ersten Weltkrieges in Berlin.* Humboldt-Universität zu Berlin.

Plowman, M. (2003). Irish republicans and the Indo-German conspiracy of world war I. *New Hibernia Review, 7*(3), 81–105.

Plowman, M. E. (2013). The British intelligence station in San Francisco during the first world war. *Journal of Intelligence History, 12*(1), 1–20.

Prayer, M. (1991). Italian fascist Regime and Nationalist India, 1921–45. *International Studies, 28*(3), 249–271.

Puri, H. K. (1980). Revolutionary organization: A study of the Ghadar movement. *Social Scientist, 9*(2/3), 53.

Puri, H. K. (2008). The influence of Ghadar movement on Bhagat Singh's thought and action. *Pakistan Vision, 9*(2), 70–84.

Qureshi, M. N. (1973). *The Khilafat movement in India, 1919–1924.* University of London.

Ramnath, M. (2011). *Haj to Utopia: How the Ghadar movement charted global radicalism and attempted to overthrow the British empire.* University of California Press: Berkeley (The California world history library, no. 19).

Rauf, A. (2005). The British empire and the Mujāhidīn movement in the N.W.F.P. of India, 1914–1934. *Islamic Studies, 44*(3), 409–439.

Rauf, A. (2007). Pan-Islamism and the North West frontier province of British India (1897–1918). *Perceptions*, 21–42.

Raza, M. A. (2011). *Interrogating provincial politics: The leftist movement in British Punjab, c. 1914–1950.* St Anthony's College.

Sareen, T. R. (1979). *Indian revolutionary movement Abroad (1905–1921).* Sterling.

Sengupta, S. (2013). Indian independence committee: Some aspects on different schemes and group rivalries. *Proceedings of the Indian History Congress, 74*, 532–538.

Siddiqui, S. N. (2017). *The Career of Mohammad Barkatullah (1864–1927).* M.A. Thesis. University of North Carolina at Chapel Hill.

Singh, R., & Arya, A. (2006). Nehru's strategy of national integration. *The Indian Journal of Political Science, 47*(4), 919–926.

Sohal, S. S. (2019). The salience and silence of Har Dayal in the Ghadar movement: A critical appraisal. *Journal of Sikh & Punjab Studies, 26*(1–2), 127–154.

Sohi, S. (2014). *Echoes of mutiny: Race, surveillance, and Indian anticolonialism in North America.* Oxford University Press.

Stolte, C. (2012). "Enough of the great Napoleons!" Raja Mahendra Pratap's Pan-Asian projects (1929–1939). *Modern Asian Studies, 46*(2), 403–423.

Stolte, C., & Fischer-Tiné, H. (2012). Imagining Asia in India: Nationalism and internationalism (ca. 1905–1940). *Comparative Studies in Society and History, 54*(1), 65–92.

Streets-Salter, H. (2017) *World war one in Southeast Asia: colonialism and anticolonialism in an era of global conflict.* Cambridge University Press.

Thampi, M. (2021). Indian political activism in republican China. In M. Thampi, *Beyond Pan-Asianism* (pp. 329–349). Oxford University Press.

Tumiotto, M. (2020). *I soggiorni in Italia e Germania di Subhas Chandra Bose: Un leader politico indiano tra fascismo, nazismo e comunismo.* San Lazzaro di Savena: Bonomo.

Wang, C.-M. (2019). Towards Asian independence: The transpacific and inter-Asian trajectories of Taraknath Das. In *Trans-Asia as Method* (pp. 79–98).

Wasti, S. T. (2006). The political aspirations of Indian Muslims and the Ottoman nexus. *Middle Eastern Studies, 42*(5), 709–722.

Zetterberg, S. (1978). *Die Liga der Fremdvölker Russlands, 1916–1918: Ein Beitrag zu Deutschlands antirussischem Propagandakrieg unter den Fremdvölkern Russlands im Ersten Weltkrieg.* Helsinki.

Chapter 18
Independent India: Hawkish Neighbors and Few Friends

Marc Reyes

Abstract What follows is an examination of independent India under its first three leaders. All three Prime Ministers dealt with hawkish neighbors and found few friends, both in the decolonizing world and elsewhere. From its 1947 founding, India strived to be an immediate player in global affairs. Its size (a population of 350 million), storied fight for freedom, and later competition with China, attracted the attention of countless people. Because its fight for independence became a global story and foreshadowed the end of British colonialism, Indian leaders like Gandhi and Nehru wanted their nation to handle more than national issues and emerge beyond regional powerhouse; both believed India had a great deal to teach the world and lead it into a freer and more democratic age. The heart of this chapter profiles the first three Indian heads of state and the foreign policy challenges that each encountered. While no Prime Ministers' tenure was the same, all three faced problems with Pakistan and China. All three battled poverty and famine. The three rulers wrestled with the weight of inheriting the Gandhian mantle and showing that India could offer the world something different; that the violent ways of the past were just that, the past, and that independent India would chart a new path of nonalignment and nonviolence. But all three would have to resort to violence to solve problems. The world may have changed, but how it operated stayed the same.

Keywords India Foreign Relations · JL Nehru · Gandhi · Commonwealth · Partition of India · India-US relations · Panchasheel · LB Shastri · Indira Gandhi · Bangladesh liberation · 1971 War

---

M. Reyes (✉)
University of Connecticut, Storrs, USA
e-mail: marc.reyes@uconn.edu

L. Vemsani (ed.), *Handbook of Indian History*,
https://doi.org/10.1007/978-981-97-6207-1_18

18.1 Introduction

18.1.1 India Before Independence

1947, understandably, is an important year in Indian history. Like 1776 in U.S. history, the year is often used as a starting point, whether events were already ongoing. 1947 saw the British officially leave the Indian subcontinent and both India and Pakistan declaring independence that summer. With the British departure came Partition and before 1947's end, the first India-Pakistan War over the Kashmir portion of the then-state Jammu & Kashmir. It is easy to see the year as one of the most monumental in South Asian history. But there was another event in 1947, one that is under-examined but reveals not just how India saw itself pre-independence but what future role it sought to play in international affairs. At this critical juncture, most countries, before independence, are consumed with nationalism and focused primarily on their domestic agenda like building an economy or writing a constitution. But India was different. It discussed those lofty matters too, but its leading figures were global thinkers who understood the links between the international as well as the national. These leaders demanded an Indian voice in debates over global issues.

In late March 1947, representatives from over a dozen Asian countries, arrived in New Delhi, India for a ten-day conference about what the future of Asia would look like in the post-World War II era. Hosted by the soon-to-be Indian Prime Minister, Jawaharlal Nehru, and held at the Indian Council of World Affairs, the conference aimed to showcase and strengthen the bonds of Asian solidarity. Countries such as the Philippines and Indonesia had received independence only a year or two earlier. Some were still under the boot of colonialism (Indochina) or from disputed areas (Tibet). A few countries sent delegations as small as one or two people. Whatever the size of the delegation or the status of the country, what mattered was that these nations were envisioning what became what is now called the Global South. This was one of the first meetings, in the postwar era, where a bloc of developing nations were envisioning their own future and one outside the current system of superpower contest between the U.S. and the U.S.S.R. This was the Bandung nonaligned conference before Bandung.

In his welcoming address, Nehru spoke several times about his belief that the world was in an era of transition. Nehru argued that the past two centuries had been dominated by Western imperialism and a reduction of Asian power. Now the old methods of imperialism were washing away, and that Asia would play a vital role in the world affairs to come. He envisioned the conference, and its results, would mean no leaders and no followers, only Asian countries working together on an equal basis toward shared goals. He concluded his speech by saying, "There is a new vitality and powerful creative impulse in all the peoples of Asia. The masses are awake and demand their heritage. Strong winds are blowing all over Asia. Let us not be afraid of them but rather welcome them for only with their help can we build the new Asia of our dreams."[1]

After ten days of committee meetings and working groups, the conference concluded with an address by the leader of the Indian independence movement, Mahatma Gandhi. Speaking in a larger venue than most of the conference proceedings, before 20,000 visitors and delegates, Gandhi delivered a short address comparing the positions of the East and the West. Instead of speaking in Hindi or his first language, Gujarati, Gandhi's closing remarks were in English to emphasize the international aims of his address. He stressed that the messages of the East, of Asia needed to be love and truth. Gandhi asserted that the West wrestled with carnage and fears of destruction, the epitome, to him, being the proliferation of the atomic bomb. Gandhi, like Nehru, believed that a new age had dawned, an age of democracy and that Asia would lead a new movement built on knowledge and wisdom.[2]

Less than a year after his address, Gandhi was dead. Assassinated by a follower of India's far-right, the leading figure of India's successful independence movement and a global figure in the fight for freedom, was murdered by a fellow countryman who recoiled at Gandhi's message of Hindu and Muslim unity. With Gandhi gone, India needed leaders to step up and not only fight for domestic issues like the protection of minorities and eradicating caste discrimination, but ensure India had a voice in global matters such as the end of colonialism and the emerging Cold War. For the next quarter of a century, there were three Indian leaders—Jawaharlal Nehru, Lal Bahadur Shastri, and Indira Gandhi—who picked up the mantle of Indian leader and wrestled with the national and international issues India faced in its first decades of self-rule.

Gaining independence the same year or taking power shortly after were the two nations that dominated India's foreign affairs in its first few decades: Pakistan and the People's Republic of China (PRC). In the subsequent three decades, India would fight four wars with these two countries. Two were stalemates, one was a resounding defeat, and one was an overwhelmingly victory. As much as India hoped to shape world events and influence the actions of nations like the U.S. and U.K., it often had to tangle with its fellow Asian nations, and both would become enemies before too long. After their independence, the three nations garnered the fascination of the leading world powers. Nations like the U.S. and the U.S.S.R. wondered which country would breakout and become the next economic powerhouse or demonstrate to the developing world which path would be the fastest and most effective for national development. Whenever Pakistan or China achieved some success, India looked to be behind but under its leaders, especially Nehru, stressed its democratic nature unlike its rivals and that if it succeeded, the nation showed the decolonizing world that countries could thrive with both democracy and capitalism.

What follows is an examination of independent India under its first three leaders. All three Prime Ministers dealt with hawkish neighbors and found few friends, both in the decolonizing world and elsewhere. From its 1947 founding, India strived to be an immediate player in global affairs. Its size (a population of 350 million), storied fight for freedom, and later competition with China, attracted the attention of countless people. Because its fight for independence became a global story and foreshadowed the end of British colonialism, Indian leaders like Gandhi and Nehru wanted their nation to handle more than national issues and emerge beyond regional powerhouse; both believed India had a great deal to teach the world and lead it into a freer and more democratic age. The heart of this chapter profiles the first three Indian heads of state and the foreign policy challenges that each encountered. While no Prime Ministers' tenure was the same, all three faced problems with Pakistan and China. All three battled poverty and famine. The three rulers wrestled with the weight of inheriting the Gandhian mantle and showing that India could offer the world something different; that the violent ways of the past were just that, the past, and that independent India would chart a new path of nonalignment and nonviolence. But all three would have to resort to violence to solve problems. The world may have changed, but how it operated stayed the same.

As modern day India struggles with its democratic experiment, now in its seventh decade, it is urgent to revisit the nation at its founding. When its faith in democracy was as strong as ever. The combination of Gandhi's moral leadership and Nehru's political leadership stressed that independent India would never forget what it had labored decades to achieve. Its fight for freedom went mainstream and evolved from its elite origins to become a true grassroots movement defeating the largest imperial power without a full-scale war. It is often said India achieved freedom without having to fire a single shot. That's not true; there were many shots fired, but from the British on Indian bodies over many decades. There were massacres, mass shootings, and everyday violence visited upon Indians in the years up until August 15, 1947. What its first generation of leaders never forgot was all the blood and bullets spilled to achieve independence. Even as some leaders failed up to live up the promise of democratic rule, particularly Indira Gandhi, all three knew deep down that the fight for freedom was long and hard and their highest duty was to ensure its survival. Where India stood, both democratically and its place in foreign affairs, are where we begin our story.

18.2 The Nehruvian Era 1947–1964

Few countries have a beginning as poetic as India's. As the final minutes of August 14, 1947, ticked away, at the stroke of midnight, the new nation of India would come into existence, finally free after centuries of the terror of British imperialism. By now, students of Indian history are familiar with the images of India's first Prime Minister, Jawaharlal Nehru, clad in white and speaking to a packed Parliament, referencing India's "tryst with destiny" and challenging his countrymen to "accept the challenge of the future."[3]

After Mahatma Gandhi, there is no individual more identifiable with the cause of Indian freedom than Nehru. The first child of a prominent Allahabad lawyer, Nehru grew up in privilege, educated at the finest schools in Europe, and protected by his family's wealth and status. Yet, as Nehru became his own man, he grew indifferent to wealth and even disdainful of such extravagant displays.[4] Law may have been the Nehru family's original business, but in time it became politics. The family patriarch, Motilal, served in and even lead the Indian National Congress (INC), the premier organization advocating for Indian nationalism and later independence. Certainly, the son of a successful lawyer and politician, Nehru had access and benefitted in ways few younger INC members could have dreamed of, but his rise in Indian politics was not solely nepotism or luck. After his formal education, Nehru's outlook on the world was further forged by World War I and the interwar period where his nationalism collided with anti-imperialist ideology. For the young Nehru, his nationalism and internationalism were not in opposition to each other, in fact, they strengthened each other and feed off each's desire for freedom.[5]

Over time, Nehru's anti-imperialism worldview would change focus, even narrow, to defeating fascism or finding alternative methods for national progress but his faith in internationalism would never waver even as the world struggled through depression and an even more brutal world war. By the 1940s, in the final years of British rule, the Nehru who had worked alongside Mahatma Gandhi to make the dream of Indian independence a reality was far different from the young man who had joined the independence movement three decades earlier. As Nehru prepared to take up the mantle of head-of-state, he was more concerned with safety and stability. After what his country had endured at the hands of the British and as the world realized the true horrors of World War II, Nehru sought order in a time of chaos. The new Prime Minister never lost his idealism or ability to think big, but as a new India prepared to "awake to life and freedom," Nehru had to immediately work to reverse the centuries of British oppression and chart a better path for him and the 350 million citizens of the nascent nation. If Gandhi was the father of India as a nation, Nehru would have to be the father of India as a functioning state. Even as he asked his fellow citizens to envision India's future, he was already hard at work at conceptualizing his country's place in the world and role in international affairs.

In the run-up to its 1947 independence, future Indians leaders gathered for the Constituent Assembly of India to outline its eventual constitution and government. Foreign affairs were also on the agenda and the focus of debate over Article 51. The proposed article sought to "promote international peace and security;" "maintain just and honorable relations between nations;" foster respect for international law and treaty obligations in the dealings of organized people with one another..." "encourage settlement of international disputes by arbitration."[6] What was clear from these discussions was the influence of Gandhian thought and that if Gandhi had been the glue for a diverse nationalist movement, then perhaps his way of thinking could guide India's interactions with the world. Some participants wanted firmer moral commitments or stronger language condemning capitalism and warfare. Nehru charted a middle ground between those who believed India's mission to the world was peace and those who argued that the more powerful nations would ignore calls for arbitration or the peaceful resolution of matters.[7] Furthermore, there was the open question of how prepared India would be to use force when necessary. With debates like these, what animated Nehru was the role of international organizations in mediating conflicts. In the interwar period, Nehru had been a member of the League Against Imperialism and even as India prepared to throw off the chains of British colonialism, he advocated India's membership in the Commonwealth of Nations, a body of former English colonies. The future PM saw the Commonwealth as a venue for resolving differences peacefully but with the benefits of autonomy meaning India would not have to defend and could freely criticize apartheid South Africa or the still-colonizing England.[8]

But more than membership in the Commonwealth, it was the founding of the United Nations that gave Nehru hope for the future. In June 1947, Nehru offered his full support for the United Nations Organization (UNO).[9] He noted its progress since the 1945 signing of its charter and swore that any weakness of the UNO was due to the member states. Nehru, after seeing the crash and burn of the League of Nations, promised that India would be a strong pillar of the young enterprise.[10] Under Nehru's leadership, India would find numerous ways to work within the UNO even play a defining role in UNO peacekeeping missions.[11]

At the time of India's founding, Nehru knew he had to chart the precise course for the new nation. Although a follower of Gandhi and a close friend, Nehru was not a strict pacifist like his mentor. He reserved the right to use force and his 1948 annexation of the princely state of Hyderabad showed he would exercise that right. Yet Nehru did not want India to have a large army and he abhorred the weapons of mass destruction that threatened the world, speaking out forcefully against the atomic bomb.[12] Instead what Nehru began to formulate was a new approach, a new way of thinking that would challenge the status of democracy versus authoritarianism, and capitalism or communism. Nehru's lasting contribution to international affairs is the concept on nonalignment. A practice that one that would give India the freedom of independence in foreign affairs while also letting it develop as a potential great power. To implement his foreign policy vision, in 1947, he established the Ministry of External Affairs and Commonwealth Relations, serving as both the Prime Minister and Foreign Minister.[13] For Nehru, it was a natural extension of his longtime interest in international affairs and his belief that foreign affairs *were* the primary work of the Prime Minister.

Demonstrating his enthusiasm for nonalignment, in his September 1946 address, the first as the leader of India's interim government, Nehru advocated that, "We propose, so far as possible, to keep away from the power politics of groups aligned against one another, which have led in the past to world wars and which may again lead to disasters on an even vaster scale."[14] Only a few months after independence, Nehru and his new nation were about to experience their first foreign policy crisis: war in Kashmir.

Since their 1947 founding, India and Pakistan have fought three wars over Kashmir. None of the wars have been decisive, for either side. Little territory changed between the two countries, instead it is the people of the former princely state of Jammu and Kashmir that have suffered the most. India and Pakistan's obsessions with Kashmir is less about the strategic necessity of the area or a priceless resource that neither side can go without, but more about the lingering consequences of the Partition of British India and the role religious violence plays among Hindus and Muslims in the subcontinent. Explanations for why India and Pakistan have fought over Kashmir are nuanced and require a strong understanding of the context of the moment. With the 1947 war, it is crucial to remember that the princely state was ruled a by Hindu ruler, Maharaja Hari Singh, but the people were majority Muslim.

Before Singh were two options and a hope: either join India, or Pakistan, or neither and rule Kashmir as an independent state.[15]

With the help of the British, Singh's family had ruled the state since the mid-nineteenth century and hoped little would change with their leaving. Singh tried to delay and buy time; he worked both sides against each other and even wanted India to think, in order to stay in power, that he was prepared to accede to Pakistan, a self-declared Islamic state. The Maharaja's plan did buy time but not enough; on October 22, 1947, nearly five thousand tribesmen, including some raiders and bandits, seized towns in the Kashmir valley and began a march toward the state's largest city, Srinagar. Singh was out of time and options; with his hand forced, he formally acceded to India and requested Indian military assistance. The Indian Army ultimately repelled the invading tribesmen while India and Pakistan negotiated an end to the conflict and path forward for Kashmir. India's offer was a plebiscite that would decide Kashmir's fate. The people of the area would vote for their future. But Nehru had conditions, mainly that the Indian Army would only leave once Pakistan had pulled all of the invading tribesmen out of the state, something Pakistan claimed they had no control over, and that the plebiscite be supervised by the United Nations. To prevent a resuming and broadening of war, Nehru went to the United Nations to resolve the conflict and made the case that Pakistan, not India, were the true aggressors, India acted only in self-defense.[16]

India and Pakistan's first war over Kashmir ended with a ceasefire but no meaningful plebiscite ever occurred. Nehru became convinced Pakistan would never completely pull out its troops or the tribesmen acting as Pakistani agents so a plebiscite could never occur under Nehru's preferred conditions. Kashmiri self-determination remains a dream long deferred. Yet the fight over Kashmir, and India and Pakistan's willingness to go to war over it, did shift Cold War thinking. When the ceasefire went into effect on January 1, 1949, the Cold War was mostly seen as a European fight, with the countries of Europe rebuilding after the widespread devastation of World War II. In addition, U.S. leaders were more familiar with European countries, people, and languages, and far less knowledgeable of the newly decolonizing areas of Africa and Asia. For the U.S. to better manage the postwar order, it could no longer focus its attention solely on Europe and its reconstruction and future security situation. Kashmir, along with Communist China's 1949 victory in the Chinese Civil War and the Korean War (1950–1953), would be some of the international events that made the Cold War a global conflict. To better understand the new world the Cold War helped usher in, the United States needed to better know and understand figures like Nehru. What better way than through an official state visit.

On November 11, 1949, the world traveler Nehru arrived in a place he had never visited before, the United States. Flying in from London, aboard President Truman's personal plane, *The Independence*, Nehru touched down in Washington, D.C. on a cloudless, unseasonably warm fall afternoon. Nehru's first U.S. trip was a three-week odyssey through America, visiting California, cities such as New York and Chicago, and trips to the Tennessee Valley Authority and Niagara Falls. But Nehru's sojourn was not about sightseeing or showing him much of what the U.S. had to offer. Nehru's arrival in the U.S. occurred less than two weeks after the Chinese Communist party's victory over Chiang Kai-shek's Nationalists and the founding of the People's Republic of China.[17] The U.S. had supported the Nationalists for years, spending whatever it took to keep them from losing. Truman had presided over "the loss" of China and one of the largest countries in the world was now a communist government. For Nehru though, his visit allowed him to make the case for his nonaligned foreign policy. He explained his thinking on Kashmir and told the Secretary of State Dean Acheson that France's effort to wrestle back control of Indochina would fail. With President Truman, Nehru stressed that the U.S. needed to embrace the anticolonial cause in Asia and elsewhere and that the two nations, both democracies, had emerged from the struggles of colonialism.[18] It is difficult to find accounts of Truman and Nehru personally hitting it off, enjoying the other's company or making a new friend but the visit did have a practical benefit: securing emergency wheat for India.[19] In their conversations, Nehru spoke of India's fears of famine and his belief that U.S. wheat surpluses could alleviate such concerns. Although Truman would have to navigate a U.S. Congress skeptical of any foreign aid, especially to a nonaligned nation like India, eventually an Emergency Indian Wheat Bill passed the legislature and Truman signed it into law in June 1951. A modest bill, it played a role in keeping famine away and became the first exchange of aid to India from the United States. From these humble beginnings, a new era in U.S-Indian relations was forged.

As much as China loomed in the minds of U.S. policymakers, it dominated the thinking of Nehru. Indian-Chinese relations would define Indian foreign relations throughout the 1950s. For Nehru, China and his dealing with the country would be his lasting foreign policy issue, one that has come to define his legacy. After Nehru's 1949 U.S. visit, American policymakers began to see democratic India competing against communist China in a battle of newly independent nations. Each side made the case for their respective ideologies and governing philosophies. Whichever country could demonstrate genuine economic and political success would surely serve as a model for many of the other decolonizing or recently free countries. Assistant U.S. Secretary of State George McGhee subscribed to the thinking that India and China were in an economic competition and argued the consequences would be catastrophic if China advanced but if India faltered, it would mean not just economic turmoil, but the country could lose its hard-fought democracy too. Showing that India's success would reverberate through the decolonizing world, U.S. Ambassador to India, Chester Bowles, told President Truman, "If India…under democratic government grows stronger, all of the free nations of South Asia and the Middle East will be buttressed."[20]

With the world, including both the U.S. and U.S.S.R, seeing India and China representing two competing visions of governing, it is crucial to consider how Nehru saw his northern neighbor and its role in the international system. Nehru knew foreigners would quickly default to this easy binary of India versus China but like his embrace of nonalignment, Nehru's nuanced thinking offered clues to how he would deal with China. Despite being pitted each other, Nehru saw the People's Republic of China (PRC) as the true rulers of China, not the Nationalists who had decamped off the mainland to Taiwan. He urged world leaders to recognize this China and establish formal diplomatic relations. Furthermore, Nehru saw the PRC as a great power and advocated their seating, and not Taiwan's, at the United Nations' Security Council.[21] Only by treating the PRC as the great power it was, would it then take its proper role as a stabilizing force in international relations and thus bring order to a chaotic world order. Nehru's deference to China on the United Nations Security Council, and his rejection of calls for India to replace China and be the Asian voice on the council, reveal his later-in-life desire for stability and order rather than change and reform. In dealing with the PRC directly, Nehru made the decision to embrace the PRC through the idea of a shared Asian solidarity.

Even though Nehru believed fears of a spreading communism were overhyped and that the type of rapid progress U.S. policymakers feared from China were simply not possible, India's Prime Minister had his own China worries. First and foremost was the lack of a defined Himalayan border between the two countries. While India recognized the 1914 McMahon Line, drawn by the British to delineate British India from Tibet, China refused to recognize such a border, one drawn by imperialists. With the death of Stalin and end of the Korean War in 1953, Nehru believed this was a good time to reengage with China and proposed negotiating on Tibet.[22] By April 1954, Indian and Chinese discussions had paid off with Panchsheel, a five-point agreement between the two nations that called for mutual respect between the two nations, no meddling in the other's internal affairs, and a declaration of peaceful co-existence. To get to those proclamations, India recognized Chinese sovereignty over Tibet, forfeiting its own claims, ones they inherited from the British. In return, China agreed to respect India's northern border.[23] The legacy of Panchsheel and Nehru's effort for Sino-Indian rapprochement remain a fiery debate many decades later. Did Nehru squander Indian territory in a vain grasp for peace? Was this the best deal Nehru could get especially since Indian claims to Tibet were thin to begin with? Or did Nehru simply buy time before an eventual India-China war? His outreach appears genuine in that he saw the PRC as a great power but one that could be a stabilizing and productive member of the international community if treated that way. Plus, there was his hope to pull the PRC away from its alliance with the USSR and deal with them on a more one-on-one basis. Nehru did worry that Sino-Indian relations could worsen, but at least in 1954, the issue of Tibet was addressed. With an agreement with China in hand, Nehru continued to make his case for diplomacy and international cooperation, he would do so next at a summit in Bandung, Indonesia.

In April 1955, the developing world had its coming out moment. Twenty-nine countries, all with independent governments, sent delegations to Bandung for a conference promoting African-Asian unity. The assembled nations pledged economic and cultural cooperation and a continued push to rid the world of colonial rule.[24] Nehru saw the conference as a historic moment, where countries that had long suffered under colonialism, could demonstrate their hard-fought freedom and serve as a beacon to other African and Asian countries still under the yoke of imperialism. Despite the many offerings of cooperation and understanding, the Bandung conference did not yield many concrete results. No trade pacts or treaties or formal alliances were announced; even if there was interest in a developing world bloc, Nehru's strict adherence to nonaligned would have made short use of it. Instead, what Nehru offered was more symbolism than specifics. The presence of nearly thirty new countries, in the developing world, was, and to be honest, a triumph itself but these leaders were very different. All were nationalists and fought for independence, but some presided over democracies while others ran dictatorships. Some countries were aligned with the United States, and others the Soviet Union. There was unity but it was fairly shallow and not enough to build a counterforce to the U.S.-U.S.S.R. superpower binary. Nehru though, a believer in great power politics and the need to engage the world's great powers, was about to be reminded that the superpowers still dominated international affairs, even if the world had changed since the end of World War II.

What reinforced the great power order was the Egyptian leader, Gamal Abdel Nasser's 1956 attempted nationalization of the Suez Canal. Although the canal ran through Egypt, the actual country had seen little personal economic success from it, most of the spoils belonged to the canal's British and French shareholders. Nasser's nationalization attempt was a clear sign that the new nations of the developing world sought not just political sovereignty, but economic rights too. Since Nehru knew the leaders of Egypt and Britain well, he offered his services as a mediator. Months after the nationalization, Britain and France, with the help of Israel, launched an invasion of Egypt to wrest back control of the canal. The naked colonial aggression shocked the world community and led to condemnation even from allies the U.S.[25] Reeling from the blowback, the invading trio withdrew. Nehru was heartened to see the U.S., under President Dwight Eisenhower, not back its allies and instead uphold the sovereignty of Nasser's Egypt. Although Nehru and Eisenhower were very different world leaders, one forged by nationalism, the other by war, the two men had seen the worst of the twentieth century, and both became leaders of their respective countries in their 60 s. When Nehru visited the U.S. again in late 1956, the two men held deep discussions about international affairs, with Nehru more successful in making his case for India's nuanced thinking and actions in international affairs. Unlike Truman, Nehru made a connection with Eisenhower and found a greater respect for his leadership.[26] To build on their new relationship, Eisenhower would make his own journey to India in December 1959. During his four-day trip, the U.S. President addressed the Indian Parliament, spoke with the local press, and delivered a speech before half-a-million Indians. He offered his support of Nehru's China policy and gave the impression that if India and China ever went to war, the U.S. would help India.[27] Nehru greatly appreciated Eisenhower's support especially on China matters, but only a few years after Panchsheel and the proclamations of Sino-Indian peaceful co-existence, the Indian Prime Minister must have hoped it would never come to that.

As the 1950s concluded, Nehru was personally at a crossroads. Historian Ramachandra Guha often tells a story of a Nehru holiday to Kashmir in 1958. While on vacation, Nehru decided to retire and make way for a new generation of Indian leadership. But on his way home, he reconsidered and stayed in office.[28] At this point in his tenure, Nehru was often asked about retirement and succession and increasingly brushed off both topics.[29] Had Nehru retired at the end of 1950s, his legacy, both in India and internationally, would be very different. With the hindsight of decades, scholars can argue his decision to stay in office, and guide India into the

1960s, was a disaster. In Nehru's defense, there is a good argument that he wanted to finally resolve India's China issues and not bequeath them to his successor who would not have the same long tenure in foreign affairs or personal relationships with the PRC's leaders like him. But the decision to not retire put Nehru and his country on a collision course with its northern neighbor. Another round of negotiations was the first attempt but in time, war became the only option.

Even after the promises of Panchsheel and calls for Hindi-Chini-bhai-bhai – Indo-Chinese brotherhood – Indian-Chinese relations were running aground. Immediately after their 1954 agreement, India and China began contesting the ownership of a grazing ground near the Uttar Pradesh-Tibet border. Shortly after that, rumors increasingly grew that the Chinese were constructing roads on their side of the India-Tibet frontier.[30] Word of Indian roads and other construction projects popped up too. Both sides tried to show the other not to encroach on the other's territory. Nehru believed that India and China's 1954 agreement had established clear boundaries between the two nations, but now Chinese Premier, Zhou Enlai, told Nehru that China was printing older maps and had not conducted any surveys to make permanent the proposed borders. Nehru told Zhou he was not worried about old maps, but he tried to emphasize that China would feel a great sense of unease if India started printing maps showing Tibet as part of India.[31]

It is crucial to remember where the PRC was at this moment. Domestically, the country was embarking on the Great Leap Forward and in just a few years, tens of millions of Chinese citizens will die of hunger and starvation. Also at this time, the Tibetan uprising was happening with the PRC regularly accusing India of aiding the Tibetan rebels, even sneaking in U.S.-made weapons to fight the Chinese. For all of Nehru's desires to see stability in the international order, and his hope that treating China like a great power would make it act like one, this was increasingly not the case. Nehru's agreement with China was unraveling and both sides worked to fortify their positions and establish military posts.[32] Areas around the McMahon Line were becoming active conflicts with Chinese troops firing on Indian soldiers. Indian fighters would soon return the favor and what had started as border disputes was quickly becoming a hot war. Before the conflict could spread further, Nehu and Zhou made one more attempt at diplomacy.

Zhou accepted Nehru's invitation to visit Delhi and discuss border issues. Nehru wanted Zhou's China to respect the McMahon Line. Zhou proposed more land be debated and bargained with. Nehru was moderately comfortable discussing small or limited amounts of the Himalayan borders, whereas Zhou was fine haggling over a lot more. As historian Lorenz M. Luthi wisely points out, Nehru conducted his diplomacy with "a vibrant public discourse and a rigid constitutional framework" unlike Zhou who could make decisions without worrying too much about public perception or how to get his plans approved by Parliament.[33] This final diplomatic push did not produce any breakthroughs, only more general statements to keep talking and break the impasse in the future. Both leaders would not say yes or trusted the other to stick to their agreements. With no peaceful solution in hand, military posts proliferated as did low-level skirmishes. Nehru tried to simmer down the tensions saying that beyond "shouting at each other, not much would happen" in the Himalayas.[34] He was about to be proven dead wrong.

The summer and fall of 1962 saw Chinese and Indian troops exchange fire, including the Chinese Army, the People's Liberation Army (PLA), surrounded Dhola, an Indian outpost below the Thagla Ridge. The Indian government asserted that their army would launch a counterattack and expel the Chinese soldiers. The former did happen, but not the latter. On October 20, 1962, as the world endured the Cuban Missile Crisis between the United States, the Soviet Union, and Cuba, the PLA began bombing the Thagla Ridge area. By night's end, Dhola and two other Indian outposts were lost; on the opposite end of the Himalayas, the Chinese army attacked Ladakh, on the edge of the Aksai Chin.[35] The time for negotiations was over, a war between India and China had broken out. One side was fighting it, the other was fleeing it.

Far away in the capitol of New Delhi, Indian newspapers proclaimed the country at war, while members of the Indian Parliament began calling for severing diplomatic ties with Beijing. Nehru did not initially receive blame for the attack, most of that went to his Defense Minister, Krishna Menon. Menon, a close confidant of Nehru and one of his loyal enforcers of India's nonaligned foreign policy, ultimately would lose his Defense position, even though Nehru tried to place him in another Cabinet position.[36] As Indian lost more outposts, as the counterattacks failed to turn the tide, as India appeared unable to make a stand, dread turned to despair. Was India about to lose a war with its neighbor that seemed years, if not decades in the making?

After a week of fighting, China controlled significant parts of what had been Indian-controlled Himalayan territory. India's friendship with the Soviet Union, it found, had not mattered in getting the U.S.S.R to stop the Chinese excursion or slow it down.[37] Even India's friends in the nonaligned world were no help, with some buying the Chinese propaganda that China was simply defending itself from Indian aggression.[38] To save itself, Nehru knew he had one last option left: the United States.

On October 26, Nehru wrote President Kennedy asking for "sympathy and support." India needed aid but with the U.S. in particular, it needed a country to restrain Pakistan in case the country opened a second front. The country had been making "pro-Chinese noises" and was eager to support the enemy of its enemy.[39] Two days later, Kennedy sent Nehru a personal letter offering such sympathy and support, in the forms of light weapons, mortars, and ammunition.[40] For years, India had accepted food and economic aid, but waved away military aid, especially from the U.S., for fears that this type of aid would more likely suck them into an alliance that threatened their nonaligned status. As the aid worked its way to India, even requiring the U.S. to get Pakistan's cooperation, on November 22, Beijing declared a cease-fire.[41] The war was over; the conflict simmered for years and within a flash, was over after a month of fighting. With some wars, it can be difficult to ascertain who really won or made gains. In this particular conflict, it was clear: China won, India lost.

The consequences of the 1962 war were immediate and long-lasting. In the short-term, the competency Nehru projected in international affairs was gone. His China policy had gone up in smoke, and it was apparent he had lost face in the area of foreign affairs. The loss to China gave way to challenges to his leadership at home, skirmishes he had largely avoided during his then-fifteen-year tenure. His Congress Party lost seats in the summer 1963 elections, but more than anything, Nehru looked and acted like a leader who had stayed on too long. Even as he retained the nation's top job, he physically looked weak and frail.[42] The succession talk gained more currency as it appeared Nehru' health had worsened. Now Indians were seeing lists of possible successors including Nehru's daughter, Indira Gandhi. Nehru was implored to rest, but as both head of state and top diplomat, that was simply not possible.

In January 1964, Nehru suffered a mild stroke. Only then did he start reassigning some of duties to Lal Bahadur Shastri who in time would become a de facto deputy prime minister or prime minister in waiting. Shastri would not wait long; Nehru died of a heart attack on May 27, 1964. The Nehruvian era was over, and India would have its first new leader in nearly seventeen years.

In the decades since his death, there have been endless discussions of Nehru and his policies as they guided India in the years following independence. His immediate successors—Lal Bahadur Shastri and Indira Gandhi—tried to stick to Nehruvian ideas especially in the realm of foreign affairs, continuing a form of his nonaligned policy. But in time, starting with his own daughter, Indira Gandhi, there were breaks from Nehruvian thinking and today in India, there is an aggressive campaign to relitigate Nehru and his tenure. Some of these debates are fair, while others are less so and some are bad-faith polemics masquerading as legitimate debates. As long as there is an India, there will be debates about Nehru and how it led it pre- and post-independence. Certainly, China dominates the later years of his tenure, but Nehru's triumph at securing India much-needed development aid and organizing a nonaligned movement are major successes of his tenure. Perhaps most important was articulating another foreign policy for nations, especially in the developing world. Nonalignment, essentially an independent foreign policy free of coercion from the two reigning superpowers, was both Nehru's gift to India and the world. He offered a break from the binary of us versus them or East versus West. Nehru showed another way was possible, one that would give India and nations like it something that Western democracies had taken for granted: time to grow. If Gandhi had been the founder of the Indian nation, Nehru was the father of the Indian state. And once India finished mourning its first leader, it fell upon a new Prime Minister to keep the state growing and demonstrate that Indian progress was not tied to one particular leader. The Nehru era gave way to the Shastri era.

18.3 Shastri Takes the Helm 1964–1966

Because of his brief tenure (June 1964 to January 1966) there unfortunately is a tendency to treat the government of Indian Prime Minister Lal Bahadur Shastri as simply an interregnum between two of India's longest rulers, Jawaharlal Nehru and Indira Gandhi. Seeing Shastri as simply the Prime Minister between Nehru and Gandhi fails to comprehend how crucial this eighteen-month moment was for India.

Shastri emerged as the most popular choice of Congress Party officials especially members of Parliament who would be running with Shastri as the head of the party. Like Nehru, he had decades of experience in the Indian National Congress fighting for independence. He had served as both a State Minister and Cabinet Minister. Furthermore, he was seen as more accessible than Nehru had been, came from the Hindi heartland, and governing-wise represented a continuation of Nehru-like policies, not a break from them.[43] When Soviet leader Anastas I. Mikoyan visited India shortly after the new prime minister took power, Shastri vowed that his India would stick to Nehru's polices, not deviate from them.[44]

Shastri was the consensus choice at a time when India lacked consensus on a lot of issues. Yet even as took the helm and prepared to lead India, he acknowledged the large shoes he had to fill. In a June 11, 1964 broadcast to the nation, Shastri told his fellow Indians that he was conscious of the responsibilities placed on his shoulders. To approach his new duties, he vowed to serve "in a spirit of humility and with love and respect for all my countrymen." Shastri, a devoted Gandhian, argued that he and his fellow citizens must build upon the firm foundation left behind by Gandhi and Nehru. He promised to continue their work that India would be "free, prosperous, strong and a world at peace and without war."[45] India's new prime minister was about to find out that even as he hoped for peace, the world, especially India's neighbors, Pakistan and China, had other ideas.

Even before Nehru's May 1964 death and Shastri's June 1964 election as Congress Party leader, Pakistan was already testing India's resolve along its western border. As Nehru convalesced from his January stroke, Pakistan launched miliary probes in the disputed areas of the Rann of Kutch, a salt marsh in the western Indian state of Gujarat.[46] Since Partition, the area had been the site of border disputes between Indian and Pakistan. Even though the area offers little material or strategic value to either India or Pakistan, the fact that there are competing border claims between the two countries is sufficient casus belli.[47] The start of the Rann of Kutch affair also happened with the issue of Kashmir still simmering in the background, unresolved and neither side ready to compromise. For Pakistan, their probes and ventures into this particular India-occupied territory represented little investment of troops and resources. Neither side was prepared to go to war over salt marshes, but Pakistan could needle an India undergoing a major political succession while also distracted by the actions of another neighbor, China.

In 1956, India became the first Asian nation to launch a research reactor achieving criticality. It was heralded a testament to Indian science that a country not even ten years old had the atomic technology only wielded by members of the United Nations Security Council. Furthermore, in local media, the reactor was described as a product of Indian expertise and ingenuity.[48] But besides getting their first, India had beaten the People's Republic of China to a reactor. The PRC was the only other Asian country with a nuclear program and could have given Indian competition in the race for a reactor.[49]

From 1955 to 1958, Mao's China practiced what political scientist Vipin Narang calls "sheltered pursuit." The PRC sought both shelter (protection of their activities) and support (expertise, even bomb plans) from their Soviet Union ally. Although Mao had once publicly called nuclear weapons "paper tigers," privately he recognized them as something the PRC must have.[50] Years of pleading with the U.S.S.R. to aid the PRC's nuclear program with technical data or bomb blueprints, and even after Soviet promises to do so, Moscow officially notified Chinese leadership that it would not supply such material. The Sino-Soviet split was in process and PRC leaders did not believe the U.S.S.R. would come to their aid if the U.S. attacked them. Even as the Great Leap Forward shook and devastated the Chinese economy and society, Mao accelerated the PRC's nuclear weapons program and in Narang's words, "dared both the Americans and Soviets to stop it."[51]

China transformed from a position of "sheltered pursuit" (1955–1958) to "sprinting" (1958–1964) toward a bomb. Once a country decides to sprint, Narang estimates that the process can take between 5–8 years, longer if sanctions or military action are involved. Right in that range, China, on October 16, 1964, tested its first nuclear device, a uranium bomb.[52] Only six months into his tenure, Shastri now had to consider India's response to China's bomb. Like Nehru, Shastri opposed atomic weapons and called for disarmament of such weapons. In order to preempt national calls for India's bomb, or at least a reconsidering of India's no-nukes position, Shastri began speaking of nuclear security guarantees. U.S. President Lyndon Johnson had promised to "help the nations of Asia to defend themselves" and that nonnuclear nations needed protection to prevent nuclear blackmail.[53]

The United Kingdom was another nation seen as a possible protector of nonnuclear nations. Having tested their own bomb in 1952, and with little American help after aiding the U.S. in the Manhattan Project, British Prime Minister Harold Wilson invited Shastri to visit London in December 1964 to take nuclear security guarantees. On one hand, Shastri and his Ministry of External Affairs opposed such guarantees. Shastri feared such protections would limit India's freedom of action and mean a loss of its economic and political independence. In London, however, Shastri offered a nuance interpretation of Johnson's offer and called for "nuclear security guarantees from countries with nuclear weapons to all countries without nuclear weapons, including India."[54] Shastri had a careful balancing act to perform. He needed to offer a greater protection for his country but was opposed to nuclear weapons, as was much of his party and nation. Even though there were opposition party members of Parliament, as well as more bellicose Congress Party officials, in favor of an Indian bomb, Shastri did not want to grant them legitimacy or elevate their status in the debate. Shastri sought to continue the Nehruvian policy of nonalignment and ensure nothing or no one impeded India's actions. He did this while the negotiations for the Non-Proliferation Treaty (1965–1968) began so whatever options he had, would not last long since the treaty aimed to go into effect on July 1, 1968. It's important to remember though, that even if Shastri had completely reversed his position and became pro-bomb to counter China's nuke, the Indian nuclear program was years aways from a functioning bomb. There was still certainly Indian atomic expertise and resources available, but even if India sprinted like China, it would not have the bomb until the late 1960s. If China had weighed on Shastri's fall and winter 1964, by spring 1965, issues with Pakistan would come roaring back to life.

Just days into 1965, Pakistan crossed into Indian-claimed territory at the Rann of Kutch. Indian efforts at diplomacy or bringing the issue to the international community had stalled. By April, Indian and Pakistan troops were fighting and Pakistan notched some military successes. As the two countries fought over a marshland of little strategic value, Pakistani President Mohammad Ayub Khan showed his hand: to end the fighting in the Rann of Kutch, India needs to settle the Kashmir issue. Shastri said no, refusing to negotiate with a gun to his nation's head and on an issue that was supposed to be settled through democratic means, not military ones.[55] Pakistan was not willing to wage a wider war over the Rann of Kutch and if India would not bargain over Kashmir, Pakistan decided to take its success and agree to a ceasefire which occurred on June 30, 1965. For a few months, tensions in South Asia had lessened. The fighting did not lead to the loss of much territory but it damaged India and Pakistan in the eyes of the international community, especially the U.S. Both countries received aid from the U.S. and when President Johnson saw two aid recipients going to war with each other again, he shocked his advisors by withdrawing the invitation to President Ayub Khan just nine days before his Washington arrival.[56] To maintain an equal treatment and show his deep disapproval of both countries, Johnson also postponed a planned U.S. visit by Shastri. While Johnson saw Pakistan as the aggressor in the Rann of Kutch skirmish, and mostly blamed Ayub Khan, he also chaffed at Shastri's intransigence on the Kashmir issue, proving himself to be another Nehru on an issue the U.S. wanted to see resolved once and for all.[57]

With the Rann of Kutch ceasefire in effect, Indian and Pakistani tension moved back to the familiar territory: Kashmir. In August, Pakistani border-crossing excursions were regular occurrences. U.S. Ambassador to India, Chester Bowles, put the U.S. Embassy in New Delhi on high alert. His superiors at the State Department believed the excursions signaled more fighting was imminent; the CIA, on August 31, predicted a Pakistani attack on Indian Kashmir.[58] A day later, Pakistan invaded Indian Kashmir but unlike India's 1962 fight with China, Pakistan was met with massive resistance and counterattacks. India and Pakistan traded blows back and forth for much of the month. Its Russian-made MiG-21 s battled against Pakistan's U.S.-made F-84 s and F-104 s. The tide turned for India and the country mounted a drive toward Lahore. To break India's concentration, and keep Lahore out of Indian hands, Beijing threatened to enter the war on Pakistan's side. U.S. officials were unsure how serious the PRC was, especially to fight a war on behalf of a fairly recent ally.[59] But when the U.S. detected heavy radio traffic out of western China, the U.S. warned India that the PRC might be serious and urged them to stay away from Lahore and conclude the war quickly.[60]

When the war started, the Johnson administration had announced an embargo on American weapons, spare parts, and ammunition to both parties. Pakistan had received U.S. military aid for years and India became a recipient after their China war. The Pentagon had designed their aid programs in a way to prevent stockpiling of more than three weeks' worth of ammunition. Sure enough, by September 23, both sides were at a standstill and accepted a ceasefire.[61] India and Pakistan had now fought a second war over Kashmir and like the first conflict, neither side emerged as victorious. For the Kashmiris who live in perpetual warzone, it was more gridlock, more indecision, more delay on the question of what to do about Kashmir.

In such a short tenure, Shastri had dealt with a war, a limited skirmish, and a recent foe detonating a nuclear device. It can be easy to see the brief Shastri government as one bad story after another. But in all three instances, Shastri held his and his country's own. Although Shastri came to the Prime Minister's office with experience as a State and Cabinet Minister, most of his experience was in domestic issues, not foreign affairs. He was also a devout follower of Gandhi yet meetingt Pakistani aggression with Indian resolve. He waged war when needed and sought ceasefires to bring about peace. With China, he sought nuclear security guarantees but refused to accept any that would compromise Indian sovereignty and challenged the world's nuclear powers to provide nonnuclear nations the safety and security they took for granted. These are accomplishments worth celebrating, but it is another moment that should define the Shastri era.

Among the many challenges Shastri inherited upon becoming India's Prime Minister was the nation's perpetual fear of famine. Histories of eighteenth and nineteenth-century British India are replete with famines and the resulting mass starvation. Even as millions of Indians starved, wheat grown on the subcontinent was shipped to England to feed an already developed nation. The final indignity was the 1943 Bengal famine where as many as three million Indians perished due to malnutrition and disease. As the famine worsened, British officials denied it and then downplayed it. When they set up to commission to investigate the causes of the famine, they exonerated themselves and blamed Indians for their own starvation. The historian Benjamin Siegel has argued that in the aftermath of the final famine suffered by a colonized India, Indian nationalists tied the promise of independence with a right to food. Food and access to it became a part of Indian nationhood and citizenship, similar to voting or civil liberties. The 1943 famine came at a time of mass media like newspapers and telegraphs as well as transportation methods that could carry Indians from one part of the subcontinent to another far away. The famine helped Indians see that starvation was not just in some areas, but all areas of India. This new consciousness of the severity of the famine problem and that all subcontinent inhabitants could suffer contributed to Indian thinking of how an independent India would feed its future citizens and ensure sustenance for years to come.[62]

As Shastri battled external threats like a nuclear China and a bellicose Pakistan, he and his government waged a war over internal forces like hunger and famine. While his predecessor had tried growing more food and asking his fellow citizens to skip meals or change their diets, Shastri did something different, something that connected one fight with another. Shastri, in an explicit way, linked the fight in Kashmir with the battle against hunger. He popularized the slogan, *Jai Jawan! Jai Kisan! (Hail soldiers! Hail farmers!)* For the Prime Minister, India's survival depended not only on soldiers but farmers who kept their soldiers and civilians well fed. He rallied his people to ensure everyone had a part in their country's survival, not just the soldiers in the Rann of Kutch or Kashmir or the Himalayas. In an October 10 radio address, before the nation, Shastri told his fellows Indians to "consider self-sufficiency in food to be no less important than an impregnable defense system for the preservation of our freedom and independence."[63] Besides drafting everyday Indians into the nation's struggle against hunger and changing the perspective of how the government battled famine, it was Shastri, who undertook and began the agricultural reforms that would become the Green Revolution.[64] It was Shastri's government that made famine prevention a national emergency and worked to improve relations with the U.S. to resume American food aid.

As 1965 came to close, Lal Bahadur Shastri prepared to travel to Tashkent, Uzbekistan. The ceasefire between India and Pakistan in September 1965 had only stopped the fighting. The Tashkent Agreement, brokered by the Soviet Prime Minister Aleksei N. Kosygin, would restore the August 1965 borders between the two countries, condemn efforts for the other to interfere in the internal affairs of the area, a transfer of prisoners of war, and a pledge to work toward improved bilateral relations.[65] Despite little experience with foreign affairs, in his short tenure, Shastri had repelled an invading army and helped stop the fighting that plagued the subcontinent. But in a shocking turn of events, on January 10, 1966, only hours after signing a peace accord, Lal Bahadur Shastri suffered a heart attack and died.[66] India had lost its second leader in as many years. The county again plunged into confusion and began another transition period where Congress party leaders would find and pick the next Indian Prime Minister. In the last succession battle, Nehru's only child, Indira Gandhi, had been on the list but not far up on the list. Now, she was the favorite to be India's third head-of-state.

18.4 India's First Female Leader 1966–1977

Similar to the events that followed Nehru's death, with the passing of Lal Bahadur Shastri, Congress Party officials picked his replacement and like last time, many of the same names were bandied about. When Nehru died, his daughter, Indira Gandhi, made the list but was not the obvious choice. Before becoming Prime Minister, she had held less high-profile posts or important positions but only for a short time such as Congress Party President (1959) or Minister of Information and Broadcasting (1964–1966). To both domestic and international observers, Gandhi was her father's companion on international trips, his hostess at formal events, and an advisor on all matters of state business. This time though, she rocketed to the top of the list because of party thinking that saw her as a steady and reassuring choice following the two quick losses of popular leaders. Furthermore, she was young (forty-eight), known to many world leaders, and the daughter of a beloved Indian leader. She was also a woman, only one of two female heads of states at the time. All these reasons aside, the top brass of the Congress Party—dubbed the "Syndicate" —believed that because Gandhi had little administrative or leadership experience, she would rely on them to help run the country. The Syndicate envisioned collective rule and that Gandhi would defer to them on many matters as long as she retained the title of Prime Minister.[67] They would soon find out that would not be the case.

Like her father, Indira Gandhi put her focus into foreign affairs and immediately went to work on issues related to Indian diplomacy. As previously mentioned, the planned visit of Shastri to the United States had been postponed due to the 1965 Kashmir war. Once the fighting stopped and the Tashkent agreement signed, the expectation was that Shastri would eventually visit the U.S. His unexpected death, however, threatened to permanently cancel the visit but once Indira Gandhi took the helm, the Johnson administration urged her to come to Washington and make her case for continued U.S. support to India, especially food aid.

Less than three months after taking office, Indian Prime Minister Indira Gandhi ventured to the U.S. for a week-long visit in late March 1966. Gandhi's state visit, the first by a female prime minister captivated Washington and cast her as a heroic figure, saving her country one aid package at a time. In D.C., Gandhi made the in-person case to President Johnson and the U.S. Congress to resume monthly shipments of surplus wheat and the development dollars that had been flowing to India for over a decade. Gandhi promised to continue the agricultural reforms initiated by Shastri and then some. On top of devoting more acreage to wheat and less on cotton, Gandhi agreed to implement a devaluation of the Indian rupee, relax private sector regulations, and open more state industries, including on fertilizer, to foreign investors.[68] She, in effect, agreed to make Indian agriculture more like American agriculture, permitting a larger role for Indian agribusiness to shape national food and farming policies. The agricultural reforms were one thing, but on devaluation, Gandhi had not consulted Congress Party officials.[69] She believed, correctly, that aid would not be forthcoming unless fiscal reforms were paired with assistance. From both the Indian left and right, there were howls of protests and a complaint that in exchange for aid, Indira Gandhi had traded away Indian sovereignty and accepted the demands of the Western powers. Pretty soon, she would have the same powers furious at her.

After visiting the U.S., Gandhi made a point to visit Moscow and secure a Soviet aid deal too. In Gandhi's thinking, domestic issues, especially the economy, had boxed her in somewhat. The fiscally-conservative economic reforms she had agreed to had given the perception that Nehru's daughter was a closet-conservative and not at all like the Fabian socialist her father was. To get back in balance, she needed to move to her left and her best option was in the realm of foreign affairs. Similar to other countries, the Indian Prime Minister possesses greater leeway in handling diplomatic and defense matters. Plus, Gandhi's years of accompanying her father on foreign trips and meeting with world leaders well prepared her to make big diplomatic moves. First, she started by sending birthday wishes to Vietnamese leader Ho Chi Minh. Although India had sent perfunctory remarks acknowledging the anniversary of Ho's birth before, Gandhi's congratulations came as the U.S. began suffering setbacks in Vietnam and their policy was increasingly under attack, especially from countries in the Global South.[70] Second, she accepted invitations to meet with nonaligned figures like Josip Broz Tito of Yugoslavia and Gamal Abdel Nasser of Egypt.[71] Even though Gandhi did not want to be seen as nonaligned as them, she wanted to project an interest in Nehru's top policy and warn her American friends that she too could go nonaligned if they pushed her too hard. But what got the U.S.'s attention was more accident than intentional provocation. In July 1966, Gandhi left India for a state visit to Moscow.

The trip was designed to balance the trip she had taken that spring to Washington. The visit was a success for Gandhi as she secured Soviet promises of a billion dollars in development aid. In the joint communiqué announcing the deal and success of the visit, the statement also called for an end of the U.S. bombing of North Vietnam and referred to the war as the work of "imperialistic powers." U.S. officials, starting with President Johnson, were flabbergasted that Gandhi, who had visited the U.S. just months earlier and came seeking American aid, had condemned their war and referred to them as imperialists.[72] In the aftermath of the joint communiqué, cables from Washington characterized the Indians as ungrateful and official Washington went looking for ways to punish them without getting too much blowback.[73] In his 1971 memoir, former U.S Ambassador to India, Chester Bowles, theorized that the joint communiqué may have been more accident than intentional act. In his telling, the Soviets drafted the statement with a relatively low-level member of the Indian mission in Moscow and the press release was shown to Prime Minister Gandhi during a particular hectic moment of her visit. With little time or a seasoned advisor with her, she signed off on the damning document. In Bowles' estimation, whatever the true origin of the communiqué, it "demolished much of the goodwill in Washington" she had received earlier that year.[74]

Domestic politics would define much of the Indira Gandhi's first term as Prime Minister. In 1967, the first national elections with her as the head of the party occurred and even though Congress retained their parliamentary majority, they lost nearly eighty seats.[75] If the party had not had such massive parliamentary majorities and that there was no dominant opposition party, then the results would have been worse. As Gandhi mostly handled domestic issues during this period, some international issues did come to the forefront. Although the U.S. was furious at Gandhi's comments in Moscow, her follow up negotiations with American officials ensured U.S. food aid continued. Even though the U.S. suspended military aid to India, they also did so to Pakistan which relied much more on American military assistance. If India was not going to get U.S. military help, the only silver lining was that Pakistan was not going to get it either. As the 1960s ended, India stood out by not signing onto the Non-Proliferation Treaty (NPT). India would describe the treaty as "nuclear apartheid" as it did not require the five current nuclear powers—U.S., U.S.S.R, U.K. France, and PRC—to relinquish their weapons. Instead, the five nations would essentially be grandfathered in and there would be no efforts to slow down or stop their existing weapons programs. Any country that did not have bombs, would be forever locked out. India, not knowing if they would ever need a bomb deterrent, could not take that option off the table permanently and decided to stand outside the treaty. It could appear an odd fit for India, a country that had called for universal disarmament and spent much of the early Cold War criticizing the existence of such weapons of mass destruction. But what trumped those stances was India keeping as many options as possible available to them. In the late 1960s, the PRC tested many bombs including thermonuclear devices and India knew they would have to build a bomb if Pakistan ever got close to obtaining one. Lurking in the back of Indian policymakers' minds were the fears that the PRC could help or provide cover to Pakistan if they wanted to build a bomb. As the decade concluded, Indira Gandhi became a more frequent and strident critic of the American war effort in Vietnam. The war came to engulf U.S.-Indian relations as it did with other aspects of American foreign policy. Gandhi thought she and her country were patient and more restrained on American policy in Vietnam, but by this time, President Johnson saw even the slightest criticism as a moral affront. The prime minister felt freer to express criticism because her patience with U.S. policy had not yielded any benefits, just India becoming the U.S.'s "favorite whipping boy."[76] What would change the dynamics completely, for India, South Asia, and the world, was the year 1971 and what it would bring.

Few leaders have had a year that brought the type of successes that Indira Gandhi experienced in 1971. In the span of twelve months, she experienced overwhelming political triumphs and impressive military victories. Her first success that year was her smashing electoral success in the 1971 general election. After the disappointing 1967 elections, Gandhi undertook populist reforms to end poverty and aid the Indian poor, with the largest actions being the nationalization of several Indian banks and ending the privy purses of formerly princely states that had joined the Indian Union.[77] Gandhi called elections early and wanted an agenda that matched her priorities, not those of the Congress Party Syndicate. After years of their attempted control, Gandhi sought to break free, even if it meant cracking the party in half. Such was the case when the Congress Party split in two. There was Indira Gandhi's Congress (R) with R meaning requisition and Congress (O) for organization, which was led by the older, more conservative faction of the party. In the runup to the March 1971 elections, Congress (O) made the mistake of the personalizing the election and running in opposition to Gandhi, not in favor of any of the type of major reforms she was undertaking. Gandhi had positioned herself as a tireless advocate for India's poor and best fighter of corruption.[78] Congress (O) appeared to oppose everything she stood for and had nothing to offer the vast majority of Indian voters. Plus, Gandhi out hustled her opponents, traveling all over the country, holding rallies and meetings and making the case she was fighting against the special interests (banks, landowners, businesses) and that her opponents were too in hock to them to deliver for India's poor. The prime minister's political gamble paid off immensely as her party won 352 of 518 seats.[79] Congress (O) finished fifth, winning only 16 seats. It was a clear and total victory for Indira Gandhi who had come to office without a popular mandate. Now she had it and was prepared to use it.

With her domestic political standing much more secure, Gandhi flexed her diplomatic muscles and offered the biggest break from Nehruvian nonalignment. As the U.S. and China began rapprochement, aided in part by Pakistan, India moved closer to the Soviet Union and in August 1971, signed the Indo-Soviet Treaty of Peace, Friendship, and Cooperation.[80] Nehru had kept such treaties at arm's length to preserve India's independence and not get dragged into someone else's fight. But Nehru's daughter governed in a different time and needed a partner to both guarantee military supplies and help India fight China if the two went to war again.[81] While Gandhi never declared a death of nonalignment, her father's guiding foreign policy idea, she clearly did not see a need to continue it in the way he practiced it and after seeing the nonaligned world not come to India's aid in their 1962 and 1965 wars, she had little desire to lead a movement that was increasingly looking like a relic of the early part of the Cold War. With Gandhi's political and diplomatic standings at all-time highs, there came one more success. In its then-twenty-four-year history, India had fought two wars with Pakistan. Both were stalemates with no clear winners, each side gaining a meager amount of territory but nothing decisive. That would change in December 1971 and shift the balance of power in South Asia, a change that reverberates today.

When discussing the East Pakistan Crisis, which later became the India-Pakistan War of 1971 and ended with the birth of Bangladesh, it can be difficult identifying a starting point. Did it begin with the November 1970 Bhola cyclone that took over half a million lives and left millions more homeless? The incompetency of the then-ruling government of General Mohammad Yahya Khan in the aftermath of the disaster galvanized millions of East Pakistanis to vote against Yahya's party in the December 1970 parliamentary elections.[82] Or was it the student protests of late 1968 and early 1969 that help form the Awami League and greater calls for Bengali nationalism? For years there were growing calls for more autonomy for East Pakistan and that the western wing of the nation took advantage of the eastern wings' economic resources.[83] One could even go further back to the 1947 partition. British India was carved up into two states, India and Pakistan, but only the latter would exist with two halves and the former and a thousand miles of it in the middle of the two pieces that made up of newly independent Pakistan. Both sides shared the same religion but not the same language or culture or other senses of shared identity. There was bound to be a confrontation, but few expected war and secession.

What was probably the beginning of the end of a united Pakistan was the December 1970 elections that saw the Awami League win nearly all the seats in the country's eastern half (160 of 162 seats) and obtain a parliamentary majority. West Pakistan was shocked at their loss of power and having to surrender control of the country to their eastern counterparts. After three months of political negotiations, Yahya Khan decided that only force could resolve their internal dilemma. On March 25, 1971, Yahya launched Operation Searchlight to "save" Pakistan, but in reality, it was overturning an election, a crackdown on political dissent, and a campaign of genocide to rid West Pakistan of government critics and possible future leaders.[84]

As the violence unfolded, millions were forcibly expelled or fled and became refugees in neighboring India. Within months, India had become a safe haven to nearly ten million former East Pakistanis. Prime Minister Indira Gandhi had difficult decisions to make. On the one hand, she was outraged by news and refugee accounts of massacres and rapes committed by Pakistani armed forces. But she was not prepared to fight a war with Pakistan over it, especially as the country had gotten closer to both the U.S. and the PRC.[85] One wrong move and either or both countries could come to Pakistan's defenses and India could barely fight a war with Pakistan, let alone three including two great powers. Their new treaty with the U.S.S.R. offered some support but India knew if it went to war, it would be doing the bulk, if not all of the fighting.

Over spring and summer 1971, Indira Gandhi's government requested humanitarian assistance from the U.S. and U.N. to handle the influx of East Pakistani refugees, highlighted the atrocities of the Pakistani army, and allowed a "government of exile," led by the Awami League to be established in Calcutta (now called

Kolkata). But if war did come, India had to be better prepared than they were in 1962 or 1965. To that end, the Awami League recruited a liberation force, working with India's Border Security Force, called the Mukti Bahini.[86] They would bring the fight to the Pakistani army for now unless Pakistan attacked India.

As 1971 came to close, so did the East Pakistan Crisis. In October and November, Pakistan moved troops to India's western border. Sino-Pakistani talks ended in early November 1971 with India beginning to expect that despite their closeness, Beijing would not intervene in the war. With the U.S. still working to conclude the Vietnam War, Delhi suspected any U.S. role would be even more restrained than China's. As India prepared to strike Pakistani targets in early December, their archrival did them a favor and bombed Indian airfields on December 3, 1971.[87] Now India could claim they were not the aggressors, but their persistent foe, the one who had spent the year butchering and torturing their own people.

The following day India recognized Bangladesh and launched a military campaign in East Bengal. Neither India nor Pakistan could wage a long war. Both countries only had the resources for a two-to-three-week conflict. That worked out well for India as within two weeks, the Indian Army victoriously entered Dhaka and its commanders accepted the complete surrender of over 90,000 Pakistan armed forces in Bangladesh. Gandhi quickly declared a ceasefire and by July 1972, India and Pakistan had signed the Simla Agreement to formally end the war. The U.S. did order their naval fleet to the Bay of Bengal, but the *Enterprise* ended up being a witness to Pakistan's disintegration, not stopper of it. U.S. fears of India marching further into Pakistan and conquering the entire country were incorrect, more the frantic fears of the losing side. The American appearance in the Bay of Bengal only hurt the U.S. as India still won and other countries moved to recognize independent Bangladesh. As the war moved into the distant past, it was clear that India had dealt with the refugee crisis, acted in self-defense, and waged war as a last resort. They had won both the moral high ground and a decisive victory against their longtime foe. Furthermore, with Pakistan's loss of its eastern wing, it no longer had the economic engine that had propelled its growth through the 1950s and 1960s. While the legacy of the 1971 war is still a rich topic for discussion, what is not up for debate, is that India, not Pakistan, emerged the dominant power in South Asia. India's stature would continue to grow as Pakistan fell into a revolving cycle of democracy and authoritarianism as well as frequent economic turmoil. With India having finally won a clear military victory and its longtime foe on the ropes, India entered a new age, one where it increasingly stood among the world's great powers.

18.5 Conclusion

18.5.1 India Since the 1971 War

The India that emerged from the 1971 war was, as expected, more confident about its place in South Asia and the larger world community. In May 1974, India tested a nuclear device or what they dubbed, a "peaceful nuclear explosion," demonstrating their atomic expertise and being the only country, outside of the five permanent members of the U.N. Security Council, to deploy such a power. But as the military and scientific accomplishments added up, it faced more fundamental challenges. High inflation and later skyrocketing oil prices slowed an already weak Indian economy. Persistent strikes and vicious crackdowns on labor hobbled Indian industries and revealed the tyrannical nature of its prime minister. Even Indira Gandhi faced her own existential crisis: an election fraud case that threatened to remove her from office. It finally reached its crescendo in June 1975 when a court ruled against her, found she has used state resources in her election campaign, and voided her election. She was suddenly a prime minister without a seat in parliament, an office holder with no duties. When Gandhi declared a state of emergency and ruled by decree for 21 months, it was a radical break from the democratic tradition figures like her father had fought for and died in the decades before its 1947 independence. Emergency rule would end, and Indian voters would both reject and return Gandhi to power. Ultimately, it was assassins' bullets in 1984 that ended her tenure as Prime Minister. The India since the end of the Nehru-Shastri-Gandhi era, the first thirty-seven years of the country, spent the next few decades defined by coalition governments and economic liberalization to undo the regulatory regime established by Nehru and his generation of state planners. As the world turned to free trade and the privatization of state industries, India did too but to a far lesser extent. For all the proclamations about the end of "License Raj" or the "Second Indian Independence" (its 1991 economic liberalization reforms), India's economy is still tightly regulated especially to foreign investments.

Where India stood at the end of the twentieth century was a unique spot. The country had survived the Cold War, but its longtime ally, the Soviet Union, did not. India would continue its strong ties to the new Russian Federation, but it also turned to the West, and that meant the United States. Like other developing nations that liberalized its economies in the 1990s, India saw a rapid rise in its GDP. Fast enough to herald it as a future economic powerhouse but also strong enough to withstand economic sanctions once India, in 1998, decided to test another nuclear device, but this time declare it a weapon and announce themselves as a nuclear weapon state. India's nuclear euphoria was a longtime coming but short-lived: Pakistan tested its own bomb two weeks later. Suddenly South Asia was a nuclear proliferation hotspot and when India and Pakistan fought a fourth war, the nearly three-month long 1999 Kargil War, the world feared this war would be a nuclear one. After the 9/11 terrorist attacks and the world's greater focus on international terrorism, India, like many countries, adopted a more counterinsurgency strategy and is less likely to fight another conflict with a large army. Its economic success has continued into the twenty-first century as India has become a three trillion-dollar economy and the fifth largest economy in the world.

Even with its impressive economy and compared to much of the world, especially other Asian countries, its young population, India today is in a complex place, even a difficult spot. Similar to where it stood after its triumphant 1971 war, the India of the 2010s and now 2020s is becoming more and more a country of democratic backsliding. Its economic success is happening alongside erosions in civil liberties, a stronger, more repressive role for the state, and intentional sectarian strife between the country's large Hindu population and much smaller Muslim minority. Jawaharlal Nehru and Mahatma Gandhi would recognize some of modern India but would be dismayed at the weakening of India as a secular state and not just lack of efforts at Hindu-Muslim unity, but politically-calculated conflict. With developing nations, the thinking was that economic reforms would lead to political reforms. As countries embraced liberal economic reforms, in time they would pair them with liberal political actions. India is different though. What is occurring now, and throughout the world, are erosions in democracy and increasing authoritarianism. But this is not a new development in India. The Emergency of Indira Gandhi revealed that Indian democracy is fragile and can go up in flames in one night. Since the 1970s, India has been backsliding in democracy and failing to live up to the ideals of global leadership that figures likes Nehru and Gandhi fought for during the struggle for independence. As India's global stature grows, its economic success cannot be its only success. What the world needs now and will need for the future is democratic success. India should use its economic progress and voice in global affairs to lead a worldwide revival of democratic rule. That should be its legacy to the future global order, that should be its place in the twenty-first century and beyond.

Notes

1. Jawaharlal Nehru, Asian Relations Conference speech, March 24, 1947. https://www.tibetsun.com/news/1947/03/24/pt-jawaharlal-nehrus-speech-at-asian-relations-conference-1947
2. Mahatma Gandhi, Asian Relations Conference speech, April 2, 1947. https://www.icwa.in/Speechs/Gandhispeech/
3. Jawaharlal Nehru, Tryst with Destiny speech, August 15, 1947. https://www.theguardian.com/theguardian/2007/may/01/greatspeeches
4. Katherine Frank, *Indira: The Life of Indira Gandhi*, 6; Dennis Merrill, *Bread and the Ballot*, 41.
5. Michele L. Louro, *Comrades Against Imperialism: Nehru, India, and Interwar Internationalism*, 4.
6. Rahul Sagar, *The Oxford Handbook of Indian Foreign Policy*, 74.
7. Sagar, *Handbook of Indian Foreign Policy*, 75.
8. Ibid.
9. For more on Nehru and his thoughts on the UN and its role in the postwar order, see Manu Bhagavan's *The Peacemakers: India and the Quest for One World* (2012).
10. *Selected Works of Jawaharlal Nehru*, Series II, Vol. 3, 336.

11. Waheguru Pal Singh Sidhu, "The Accidental Global Peacekeeper" in *India and the Cold War*, 79.
12. Lorenz M. Luthi, *Cold War: Asia, The Middle East, Europe*, 167.
13. Pallavi Raghavan, *Handbook of Indian Foreign Policy*, 80.
14. Srinath Raghavan, *The Most Dangerous Place: A History of the United States in South Asia*, 124.
15. Srinath Raghavan, *The Most Dangerous Place*, 125; Srinath Raghavan, *War and Peace in Modern India*, 101–102.
16. Raghavan, *The Most Dangerous Place*, 125–128; Raghavan, *War and Peace in Modern India*, 107–130.
17. H.W. Brands, *India and the United States: The Cold Peace*, 48–50.
18. Merrill, *Bread and the Ballot*, 41–45, 69–74; Tanvi Madan, *Fateful Triangle: How China Shaped U.S.-India Relations During the Cold War*, 19–20.
19. For more on India and fears of famine after World War II, see works such as Kristin L. Ahlberg's *Transplanting the Great Society: Lyndon Johnson and Food for Peace* (2008) and Nick Cullather's *The Hungry World: America's Cold War Battle against Poverty in Asia* (2010). For a book solely on the role of famine and food, pre and post-independence, I strongly recommend Ben Siegel's 2018 publication, *Hungry Nation: Food, Famine, and the Making of Modern India* which examines how food and hunger helped shaped citizenship and the role of the state in independent India.
20. Merrill, *Bread and the Ballot*, 86.
21. Nabarun Roy, "In the Shadow of Great Power Politics: Why Nehu Supported PRC's Admission to the Security Council, *International History Review*, 1–22.
22. Luthi, 169.
23. Luthi, 169; Madan, 59.
24. Ramachandra Guha, *India After Gandhi: The History of the World's Largest Democracy*, 161–162.
25. Guha, 162.
26. Robert J. McMahon, *The Cold War on the Periphery: The United States, India, and Pakistan*, 229.
27. Madan, 124–125.
28. Guha, The Only Lesson That History Can Teach Us, *Hindustan Times*, August 2, 2015.
29. McGarr article.
30. Srinath Raghavan, "A Missed Opportunity? The Nehru-Zhou Enlai Summit of 1960," in *India and the Cold War*, 104–106.
31. Raghavan, "A Missed Opportunity," 105.
32. Luthi, *Cold Wars: Asia, The Middle East, Europe*, 171.
33. Luthi, *Cold Wars: Asia, The Middle East, Europe*, 171.
34. Luthi, *Cold Wars: Asia, The Middle East, Europe*, 171.
35. Berenice Guyot-Rechard, *Shadow States: India, China, and the Himalayas, 1910–1962*, 232–233.
36. Neville Maxwell, *India's China War*, 410–413.
37. Tanvi Madan, 143–153.
38. Maxwell, 423.
39. Madan, 143.
40. Merrill, 190.
41. Merrill, 191.
42. Guha, 340–342.
43. Guha, 386.
44. Luthi, 174.
45. *Speeches of Prime Minister Lal Bahadur Shastri*, "India Without Jawaharlal," June 11, 1964, 7.
46. Srinath Raghavan, *The Most Dangerous Place*, 230.
47. Robert J. McMahon, 324.

48. There certainly was Indian expertise involved but India also had atomic aid from France, the U.K., the International Atomic Energy Agency (IAEA) and U.S. support through the Atoms for Peace program.
49. Itty Abraham, *The Making of the Indian Atomic Bomb: Science, Secrecy, and the Postcolonial State*, 85.
50. Vipin Narang, *Seeking the Bomb: Strategies of Nuclear Proliferation*, 163.
51. Narang, 166–167.
52. Narang, 163. For more on China's nuclear weapons program, see John Lewis and Xue Litai's *China Builds the Bomb.*
53. Jayita Sarkar, *Ploughshares and Swords: India's Nuclear Program in the Global Cold War*, 101.
54. Sarkar, 101.
55. Sarkar, 102–103; Luthi, 175.
56. Ayub Khan had also gotten on Johnson's nerves by undertaking state visits to Moscow and Beijing. While in China, he praised Chinese leaders like Mao and pledged "lasting friendship and fruitful cooperation." Furthermore, Ayub Khan openly criticized the American escalation in Vietnam. Johnson would not tolerate any criticism of his Vietnam policy and India saw Ayub Khan as simply cozing closer to a fellow Indian enemy. No one would confuse or worry about Pakistan, a state with Islam as the official religion, "going Communist." Instead, it was one nation (Pakistan) poking the other (India) by befriending their enemy and recent combatant - McMahon, 321.
57. McMahon, 321–323.
58. Brands, 111.
59. Mohammed Ayoob, in his book *India and Southeast Asia: India Perceptions and Politics*, mentions a Pakistani Air Marshal who claimed that Indonesian President Sukarno offered to enter the war on Pakistan's side. They would do so by diverting India's attention by seizing the Andaman and Nicobar islands in the Bay of Bengal. If both China and Indonesia had entered the war, and on Pakistan's side, the war would have most likely had a much different ending and been a greater deal to international affairs and foreign relations history.
60. Brands, 112.
61. Brands, 113.
62. Siegel, 4–5.
63. Nick Cullather, *The Hungry World: America's Cold War Battle Against Poverty in Asia*, 215.
64. Guha, 399.
65. "The 1965 War." BBC News, http://news.bbc.co.uk/hi/english/static/in_depth/south_asia/2002/india_pakistan/timeline/1965.stm
66. Cullather, 222; Luthi, 176; Sarkar, 104.
67. Guha, 402; Sarkar, 104.
68. Cullather, 224–225; Frank, 296–298.
69. Before his death, Shastri had already begun negotiating a possible devaluation of the rupee with the U.S., International Monetary Fund and World Bank. Shastri would have probably gotten heat for these actions had he lived but because Gandhi was new to the job and a woman, she received harsh criticism for the decision and for much of spring 1966, was seen as weak and suspectable to Western pressure.
70. P.N. Haksar Paper, finish citation.
71. Brands, 121.
72. Merrill, 208; Surjit Mansingh, "Indira Gandhi's Foreign Policy," *The Oxford Handbook of Indian Foreign Policy*, 106.
73. McPherson to Johnson – LBJL – see footnote 83 in MA thesis.
74. Chester Bowles, *Promises to Keep: My Years in Public Life, 1941–1969*, 515.
75. Guha, 414–426.
76. Brands, 122.
77. Guha, 445.
78. Sarkar, 144.

79. Guha, 445–446.
80. Sarkar, 149.
81. Mansingh, 107.
82. Sarkar, 141.
83. Srinath Raghavan, *1971: A Global History of the Creation of Bangladesh*, 20–23.
84. Raghavan, 51; Luthi, 178.
85. A large reason being Yahya Khan serving as a secret go-between for the two countries as they prepared to resume diplomatic relations. Yahya had also gotten close to the U.S. President Richard Nixon. Henry Kissinger even considered Yahya one of Nixon's real friends, not just a yes-man or leader who was nice to Nixon for U.S. aid. This increasing closeness resulted in the U.S. lifting their arms embargo on Pakistan and refusing to criticize their atrocious actions in East Pakistan.
86. Mansingh, 107.
87. Luthi, 179.

Chapter 19
A Living Legacy: The Continuing Influence of Swami Vivekananda in the Western World

Jeffery D. Long

Abstract This chapter will explore the background, life, and teachings of Swami Vivekananda and trace his continuing influence in the Western world. Whether it is in the existence of Vedanta Societies in just about every major American city, the presence of Hindu themes in the music and lyrics of popular American and British artists, or the teachings of the Jedi master Yoda, the imprint of the life and work of Swami Vivekananda can be discerned in a variety of often surprising places in the culture of the contemporary West.

Keywords Vivekananda · Swami (1863–1902) · Sri Ramakrishna Paramahamsa (1836–1886) · Sarada Devi · Holy Mother (1853–1920) · Ramakrishna Mission · Vedanta society · Vedanta · Advaita Vedanta · Yoga · Prabhavananda · Swami (1893–1976) · Isherwood · Christopher (1904–1986) · Huxley · Aldous (1894–1963) · Harrison · George (1943–2001)

19.1 Introduction: A Guru to the World

Viewed by his many followers as, in the words of the title of his recent biography by Ruth Harris, a "Guru to the World" (Harris 2022), Swami Vivekananda (1863–1902) is easily one of the most important figures of the modern Hindu tradition. His importance rests in no small part with his international reputation and influence. He has certainly been a significant figure within India, both during his lifetime as well as continuously to the present day, playing a major role in inspiring the Indian independence movement (although he did not participate in it, or in any political activity, directly) and in making it respectable for Hindu renouncers to be actively

Portions of this chapter draw upon my article "The Impact of Swami Vivekananda in the West," published in 2014 in *The Vedanta Kesari*. These have been included with permission from the Ramakrishna Order, who are the publishers of *The Vedanta Kesari*.

J. D. Long (✉)
Elizabethtown College, Elizabethtown, PA, USA
e-mail: longjd@etown.edu

L. Vemsani (ed.), *Handbook of Indian History*,
https://doi.org/10.1007/978-981-97-6207-1_19

involved in *karma yoga*, or *seva*: that is, selfless service to suffering living beings. His legacy in India, in the form of the Ramakrishna Mission and the relief work that it continues to perform, is massive, and he is widely seen, by Hindus and non-Hindus alike, as a national hero.[1]

Beyond India, however, Swami Vivekananda has enjoyed a global influence, most of all in the Western world. Whether it is in the existence of Vedanta Societies in just about every major American city, the presence of Hindu themes in the music and the lyrics of popular American and British artists, or the teachings of the Jedi master Yoda, the imprint of the life and work of Swami Vivekananda can be discerned in a variety of often surprising places in the contemporary culture of the West.

In order to understand Swami Vivekananda and his ongoing appeal and influence, the first step is to get an understanding of just who he was within his original historical context. Who were the people and what were the cultural movements which shaped this important Hindu figure?

19.2 Swami Vivekananda's Historical Context: Colonial Bengal and the Hindu Renaissance

Born Narendranath Datta on January 12, 1863, in Calcutta, Swami Vivekananda was the son of Vishwanath Datta, "an attorney in the Calcutta High Court," and Bhuvaneshwari Devi, who was a devoutly religious traditional Hindu housewife. (Harris 2022, 22) Calcutta, during this time, was the capital of the British Empire in India.[2] Indeed, as one of the first places in India to have been colonized by Europeans, European, and particularly British, influence was especially strong in Calcutta, and in the region of Bengal more broadly. Many middle- and upper-class Bengalis in Calcutta were civil servants who worked for the British government. They were often the recipients of an English education, alongside whatever traditional Indian systems of learning they might have experienced through their families. Young Narendranath Datta was no exception in this regard. He received his formal education first at the Metropolitan Institution, then at Presidency, and then at "the General Assembly Institution (now known as the Scottish Church College), the oldest liberal arts and sciences college in India" (Harris 2022, 28).

The arrival of the British in India sparked a great deal of intellectual and religious ferment, particularly in Bengal, and particularly within the Hindu tradition. The nineteenth century saw the rise of what has come to be known as a "Hindu Renaissance," as Hindu intellectuals came to grips with the various challenges presented by Western thought. These challenges included the teachings of European Christianity, with its

[1] At an interfaith gathering held in New Delhi in March of 2013, in honor of the 150th birth anniversary of Swami Vivekananda, I heard a highly renowned Islamic leader and scholar, the late Maulana Wahiduddin Khan (1925–2021), describe Swami Vivekananda as his guru. Khan was the founder of the Centre for Peace and Spirituality and a major voice for inter-religious harmony.

[2] The capital would be moved from Calcutta (now Kolkata) to Delhi by royal decree in 1911.

affirmation of Christ as the one true light of the world, as well as the skepticism of Enlightenment thinkers and the growing successes of the scientific method, which challenged the validity of all claims based upon faith–Hindu or Christian–and unsupportable by observation and reason. This Hindu Renaissance was centered primarily in Bengal (and is thus also known as the Bengal or Bengali Renaissance) and saw the rise of new organizations intended to reform Hindu thought and practice in response to the challenges raised by the West.

The first such Hindu reform organization was the Brahmo Samaj, established by a major Bengali intellectual named Ram Mohan Roy (1772–1833). Roy is widely known as "the father of modern India" (Richards 1985, 1). His response to criticisms of Hinduism by both skeptics and Christian missionaries was neither to retreat into simply reaffirming the tradition nor to renounce it. Rather, he put forth the idea of an original Hinduism, to be found in the Vedanta philosophy of the *Upanishads*, which he claimed had been corrupted during later stages of history. This original Hinduism, as understood by Roy, was a monistic doctrine which taught the inherent dignity and the ultimate divinity of all people. He thus combated skeptical and Christian critiques of Hinduism by claiming that those elements which the skeptics and the Christians found objectionable–such as caste prejudice and unequal relations between men and women, as well as the use of images in worship, or "idolatry"–did not actually reflect authentic Hindu philosophy. He was also critical of those elements of Christianity which he claimed did not reflect the authentic teachings of Jesus, as he understood them, going on the offense against what he saw as irrational and superstitious in the Christian religion as well as seeking the reform of his own Hindu tradition.

Roy saw the reform of Hinduism as essential for improving the lives of Hindus in India. In the words of a letter dated January 18, 1828:

> I agree with you that in point of vices the Hindus are not worse than the generality of Christians in Europe and America; but I regret to say that the present system of religion adhered to by the Hindus is not well calculated to promote their political interest. The distinction of castes, introducing innumerable divisions and sub-divisions among them, has entirely deprived them of patriotic feeling, and the multitude of religious rites and ceremonies and the laws of purification have totally disqualified them from undertaking any difficult enterprise…It is, I think, necessary that some changes should take place in their religion, at least for the sake of their political advantage and social comfort. (Richards 1985, 8–9)

Roy's Brahmo Samaj was dedicated to carrying out the kinds of reforms that Roy believed to be necessary for the Hindus of his time to incorporate into their traditions. During his lifetime, he was a prolific writer and deeply committed activist, most famously working to bring an end to sati, or "suttee," the practice of the immolation of widows which was at that time prominent amongst some upper caste Bengali families.

Although the Brahmo Samaj never became a mass movement, attracting followers mainly from the English-educated middle and upper classes of Bengal, like Roy himself, its ideals would end up having a massive impact on the practice and self-understanding of Hindus throughout India, and eventually, globally, through the teachings of Swami Vivekananda, who, early in his life, was a member of this organization and a follower of the Brahmo leader Keshub Chunder Sen (1838–1884).

The first president of the Brahmo Samaj after the passing of Ram Mohan Roy was the well-known essayist and intellectual, Devendranath Tagore (1817–1905), father of the renowned Nobel laureate, playwright, poet, songwriter, essayist, and icon of Bengali culture, Rabindranath Tagore (1861–1941). The elder Tagore had a profound inclination toward spirituality. Having absorbed the widespread skepticism of the era, he longed to have a direct experience of the divine reality, which could dispel his doubts and place his religious faith on the firm footing of personal awareness. This theme of spiritual longing, as we shall see, is a predominant trait of Bengali Renaissance thought. It is beautifully articulated in this passage from one of Tagore's many essays:

> Then I went out and sat underneath an ashvattha tree and according to the teaching of the saints began meditating on the Spirit of God dwelling in my soul. My mind was flooded with emotion, my eyes were filled with tears. All at once I saw the shining vision of Brahma in the lotus core of my heart. A thrill passed through my whole body, I felt a joy beyond all measure. But the next moment I could see Him no more. On losing sight of that beatific vision which destroys all sorrow, I suddenly rose from the ground. A great sadness came over my spirit. Then I tried to see Him again by force of contemplation, and found Him not. I became as one stricken with disease, and would not be comforted. Meanwhile, I suddenly heard a voice in the air, 'In this life thou shalt see Me no more. Those whose hearts have not been purified, who have not attained the highest Yoga, cannot see Me. It was only to stimulate they love that I once appeared before thee.' (Richards 1985, 27)

Keshub Chunder Sen (1838–1884) was another important leader within the Brahmo Samaj, and one with whom the young Narendranath Datta had a great deal of interaction as, beginning in 1880, he began to frequent Brahmo Samaj gatherings in Sen's home.

A major theme, as we shall see, of Swami Vivekananda's teaching is the ideal of a harmony underlying the world's religions. This ideal was also a central teaching of Keshub Chunder Sen as well, who proclaimed the idea of a "New Dispensation" (or *Nava Vidhan* in Bengali) consisting of the unification of Hinduism and Christianity, and ultimately, of all religions. He describes this New Dispensation as:

> …the harmony of all scriptures and prophets and dispensations. It is not an isolated creed, but the science which binds and explains and harmonizes all religions. It gives history a meaning, to the action of Providence a consistency, to quarrelling churches a common bond, and to successive dispensations a continuity. It shows marvelous synthesis how the different rainbow colours are one in the light of heaven. (Richards 1985, 33)

Sen then shifts metaphors, making the concept of *harmony* explicit in comparing the religions of the world to musical instruments:

> The New Dispensation is the sweet music of diverse instruments. It is the precious necklace in which are strung together the rubies and pearls of all ages and climes. It is the celestial court where around enthroned Divinity shines the light of all heavenly saints and prophets. It is the wonderful solvent, which fuses all dispensations into a new chemical compound. It is the mighty absorbent, which absorbs all that is true and good and beautiful in the objective world. Before the flag of the New Dispensation bow ye nations, and proclaim the Brotherhood of God and the Brotherhood of man. (Richards 1985, 33–34)

19.3 From Narendranath Datta to Swami Vivekananda

Narendranath Datta absorbed many of the teachings and much of the sensibility of the Brahmo Samaj, particularly through his interactions with Sen. From his English education, Datta had developed a skeptical bent of mind. At the same time, chiefly from his devout mother, he had also absorbed a deep knowledge of Hindu practices and beliefs. One can easily see the attraction of the Brahmo Samaj for someone who, on one level, valued the traditions he had received from his family, but on the other, saw the force of the logical arguments presented by modern thinkers, as well as the power which Europe's knowledge enabled it to wield over the rest of the world. The Brahmo Samaj was, again, a response to the crisis provoked by the encounter of Hindu thought and practice with the philosophy of the modern West. This response consisted essentially of an affirmation of a core of truth at the heart of Hinduism, or at least of what was taken to be its original philosophy–the Vedanta tradition founded on the *Upanishads*–while at the same time rejecting all in both Hindu and Christian practice that was seen as deviating from this rational and ethical center.

Datta's skepticism, however, prompted him to question even the theistic philosophy of the Brahmo Samaj. It is said that the young skeptic set about asking many of the intellectual leaders of Calcutta, including Keshub Chunder Sen, the simple question, "Have you seen God?" This was in 1881, when he would have been eighteen years old. Until the end of his life, Datta–Swami Vivekananda–held that it was vital to spiritual life not simply to believe in God with the intellect, on the basis of the testimony of others, but to have a direct experience–a direct awareness–of the ultimate reality for oneself in order to affirm its existence in an authentic way. In his own words:

> …religion itself consists in *realization*. We all say, "There is a God." Have you seen God? That is the question. You hear a man say, "There is a God in heaven." You ask him if he has seen Him, and if he says he has, you would laugh at him and say he is a maniac. With most people religion is a sort of intellectual assent and goes no further than a document. I would not call it religion. It is better to be an atheist than to have that sort of religion. (Vivekananda 1979, Volume 4, 34)

Datta's quest for someone who had seen God directly–who had *realized* God–eventually led him to the meeting that would transform his life and set him on the path to becoming Swami Vivekananda, world teacher: his meeting with Sri Ramakrishna Paramahamsa (1836–1886).

After asking one of his teachers at the Scottish Church College, a Reverend William Hastie (1842–1903), his question—"Have you seen God?"—Reverend Hastie, interestingly, directed young Datta to pay a visit to the temple of the Goddess Kali in Dakshineshwar, north of Calcutta. There, Hastie said, he would meet "a true man of God" in the form of the priest, Sri Ramakrishna.

Datta and Ramakrishna actually had already met briefly at this point, at the home of Keshub Chunder Sen. Sen became close to Ramakrishna, despite the rather dramatic differences between them and their respective approaches to spirituality. Keshub was the rationalist, the Brahmo Samaj leader deeply engaged with reforming society and saving the world from inter-religious conflict. Sri Ramakrishna was a semi-literate Hindu priest from a highly traditional Brahmin family hailing from the small Bengali village of Kamarpukur and serving as a priest of the Mother Goddess. As a member of the Brahmo Samaj, Sen did not believe in the use of images in worship. Ramakrishna, on the other hand, conducted the ritualistic worship of an image of the Mother Goddess for a living. Keshub, however, was so deeply impressed with Sri Ramakrishna that his views on image worship softened in his later years. Indeed, in 1878, Sen split from the Brahmo Samaj and formed a new organization, the Sadharan Brahmo Samaj (or universal Brahmo Samaj), in part on the basis of his evolving views, though also partly due to his having arranged the marriage of his young daughter, contrary to Brahmo Samaj teaching which sought to reform Hindu society partly by moving away from such customs.

Sri Ramakrishna is a central figure in the history of modern Hinduism, known mostly for the powerful visionary experiences which formed the basis of his teachings. At the age of nineteen, he was hired, along with his elder brother, to serve as a priest at the newly constructed temple of the Goddess Kali in Dakshineshwar. From his childhood, Sri Ramakrishna was known to fall into ecstatic trances, into a state of consciousness which Ramakrishna characterized as *samadhi*, which is the highest stage of yogic attainment in the eight-limbed or *ashtanga* system of practice outlined in the *Yoga Sutras* of Patañjali. Skeptics, including his own concerned family members, feared that Ramakrishna was suffering from a neurological disorder, such as epilepsy. Ramakrishna, however, saw his trance states as experiences of God-consciousness, and on their basis, he exhibited a deep knowledge of many topics discussed in Hindu scriptures (despite the fact that he had not formally studied these texts). The Kali temple at Dakshineshwar, due to its being situated on a very popular pilgrimage route, was a frequent stopping place for holy persons representing a variety of diverse traditions, many of whom engaged in conversation with Ramakrishna on spiritual topics. Some of these holy persons were so deeply impressed with him that they regarded him as an *avatar*, or a divine incarnation. (Nikhilananda 1942, 19).

Ramakrishna is best known for the wide variety of spiritual practices, or *sadhanas*, which he pursued, from an array of diverse religious traditions. Initially, after becoming a priest of Kali, and soon after the death of his elder brother, with whom he had come to Dakshineshwar, he felt a great longing to see the Mother Goddess: to experience her presence directly. This longing was so great that those who knew him feared for his mental health.

Eventually, however, this intense longing culminated in a powerful experience in which the Goddess, Ramakrishna believed, appeared to him, not in her iconographic form, but as waves of light and love:

> It was as if the houses, doors, temples and all other things vanished altogether; as if there was nothing anywhere! And what I saw was a boundless infinite Conscious Sea of Light! However far and in whatever direction I looked, I found a continuous succession of Effulgent Waves coming forward. (Saradananda 1952, 163)

After this powerful and transformative vision, Sri Ramakrishna felt drawn to the practice of various traditions in the hope of having the experience of the divinity reality in the varied ways that these traditions might make available to their sincere practitioners. His diverse sadhanas all led to experiences of the kind he had experienced with the Goddess Kali of *samadhi*, or complete absorption. Based on these experiences, he affirmed that all religions are paths to the same goal, or ways of experiencing the same infinite reality in myriad ways:

> 'I have practiced,' said he, 'all religions–Hinduism, Islam, Christianity–and I have also followed the paths of the different Hindu sects. I have found that it is the same God toward whom all are directing their steps, though along different paths… The substance is One under different names, and everyone is seeking the same substance; only climate, temperament, and name create differences. Let each man follow his own path. If he sincerely and ardently wishes to know God, peace be unto him! He will surely realize Him. (Nikhilananda 1942, 35)

Given this background, it should come as no great surprise that when Narendranath Datta, heeding the advice of Reverend Hastie, went to Dakshineshwar to meet Sri Ramakrishna and asked him his question—"Have you seen God?"–that Ramakrishna responded, "Yes, I have seen God. I see Him as I see you here, only more clearly" (Nikhilananda 1942, 15).

As Datta himself would later note, if most of us were to ask a person if he had seen God, we "would laugh at him and say he is a maniac." This, in fact, was also Datta's initial reaction to Sri Ramakrishna. He thought that Ramakrishna must be a madman. This reaction was exacerbated by his general behavior towards Datta, according to whom Ramakrishna "folded his palms together and began addressing me as if I was some divine being, 'I know who you are, My Lord. You are Nara, the ancient sage, the incarnation of Narayana. You have come to earth to take away the sufferings and sorrows of mankind" (Isherwood 1965, 195).

At the same time, though, Datta, according to his own account, also found something to be strangely compelling, and even impressive, about this odd and eccentric priest, who was strikingly different from the intellectuals and thought leaders of Calcutta to whom he had taken his question. "'Here is a true man of renunciation,' I said to myself; 'he practises what he preaches; he has given up everything for God'" (Isherwood 1965, 195).

In the weeks that followed, Datta resisted his impulse to make a return visit to learn more from this strange teacher. Christopher Isherwood vividly recounts the deep struggle that occurred in Narendranath Datta's mind between what Sri Ramakrishna represented and everything that he had learned from the Brahmo Samaj and from his Western education:

> One can't become the disciple of a madman. And Ramakrishna *must* be mad. He *had* to be mad. Because if–terrible thought!–he was sane, then John Stuart Mill and Herbert Spencer were mad, the Brahmo reformers were mad, the whole rest of the world was mad. If Ramakrishna was sane, then everything that the world believed in and taught must be turned inside out and upside down. And Naren would have to turn himself inside out, too. (Isherwood 1965, 196)

This, in effect, is what happened. From this initial 1881 meeting until Sri Ramakrishna's death due to throat cancer in 1886, Datta, along with other young seekers, visited Dakshineshwar regularly, gradually becoming devout followers of the priest of Kali whose teachings had changed their lives.

Shortly before he passed away, Sri Ramakrishna gave a select group of his disciples, Datta among them, orange robes, thus initiating them into *sannyasa*: that is, renunciation, the life of the Hindu monastic practitioner. He thus laid the foundation for the Ramakrishna Order. Ramakrishna himself, during his practice in the Advaita Vedanta tradition, was ordained by the teacher Totapuri.

After their master's passing, his disciples began living together as a monastic community, forming the nucleus of what would eventually become Belur Math, the central headquarters of the Ramakrishna Order, in modern Kolkata, just across the Hooghly River and slightly to the south of Dakshineshwar.

Datta, however–henceforth known by his monastic name of Swami Vivekananda–felt a calling to live for a time as a wandering sannyasin. He traveled the length and breadth of India, visiting such cities as Banaras and Baroda, spending time in solitary meditation in the Himalayas, and famously journeying to Kanyakumari, the southernmost tip of India, in late 1892 and receiving a vision on Christmas Day while meditating on a rock off the coast–a rock which today bears his name. Encouraged by a local ruler, the Raja of Ramnad, who had become one of his disciples, Swami Vivekananda resolved to undertake the trip that would make him a teacher to the world: to be a Hindu representative at the first World Parliament of Religions. This event, which would mark a major turning point in his life, was held in Chicago in September of 1893.

19.4 Swami Vivekananda's Teaching in the West

During his lifetime, Swami Vivekananda traveled twice to America. The first journey was in 1893, from which he would return to India in 1897. The second journey was in 1899. He returned to India from this voyage in 1902. This is the same year that he passed away, on the fourth of July, at the young age of thirty-nine.

Swami Vivekananda's welcome address at the World Parliament of Religions has become a highly renowned document. It is depicted in colored lights on the staircase which leads into the main portion of the Museum of the Art Institute of Chicago, which is in the same building where Vivekananda spoke. The portion of Michigan Avenue on which the museum is located has also been named the Honorary Vivekananda Way, after the famous swami.

Swami Vivekananda's welcome address can be seen as marking the moment that Hinduism arrived on the world stage. The ideals expressed in this speech have come to define, in the minds of many, the ethos of the Hindu tradition. They have also helped to inspire the interfaith movement, and the hope among adherents of many religions that a way might be found for people with diverse worldviews to live together: not merely in a state of co-existence, but of mutual appreciation and respect. It was given on September 11, 1893, and begins with the words, "Sisters and Brothers of America." Considering that India was still under European colonial domination at this point, that non-white people had still been slaves in America, there is a beautiful audacity in Vivekananda's choice to address his mostly white and Christian audience as equals. He speaks, not with arrogance, but with dignity, and with great pride in his Hindu heritage. By all accounts, including his own, his audience reacted with great warmth to these words, and applauded for a considerable length of time in response. After this, Vivekananda continued:

> It fills my heart with joy unspeakable to rise in response to the warm and cordial welcome which you have given us. I thank you in the name of the most ancient order of monks in the world; I thank you in the name of the mother of religions; and I thank you in the name of millions and millions of Hindu people of all classes and sects. (Vivekananda 1979, Volume One, 3)

Some readers may be puzzled by Vivekananda's reference to "the most ancient order of monks in the world," given that the Ramakrishna Order had been established only about seven years prior to the Parliament. One must bear in mind, though, that the Ramakrishna Order is itself part of the much older Dashanami Order established by the Hindu sage Shankara, to which Ramakrishna's teacher, Totapuri, had belonged. Even this is not, however, "the most ancient order of monks in the world," given that both the Buddha and Mahavira, for example, established their respective orders of monks many centuries before Shankara.

Shankara himself, however, in establishing his order, was in fact re-organizing an already existing monastic lineage, of which he was himself a member. It seems that it is this order, tracing itself back to the sages of the *Upanishads*, to which Swami Vivekananda is referring.

Vivekananda then refers to his fellow delegates from Asia, which included, among others, Pratap Chandra Majumdar, of the Brahmo Samaj, Virchand Gandhi, representing the Jain tradition, and Anagarika Dharmapala, who represented the Theravada Buddhist tradition of Sri Lanka:

> My thanks, also, to some of the speakers on this platform who, referring to the delegates from the Orient, have told you that these men from far-off nations may well claim the honor of bearing to different lands the idea of toleration. (Vivekananda 1979, Volume One, 3)

This brings us to the central theme of the welcome address: a rejection of the intolerance that is so often associated with religion. Vivekananda goes on to characterize Hinduism as a tradition not only of tolerance, but of acceptance:

> I am proud to belong to a religion which has taught the world both tolerance and universal acceptance. We believe not only in universal toleration, but we accept all religions as true. I am proud to belong to a nation which has sheltered the persecuted and the refugees of all religions and all nations of the earth. I am proud to tell you that we have gathered in our bosom the purest remnant of the Israelites, who came to Southern India and took refuge with us in the very year in which their holy temple was shattered to pieces by Roman tyranny. I am proud to belong to the religion which has sheltered and is still fostering the remnant of the grand Zoroastrian nation. (Vivekananda 1979, Volume One, 3–4)

What, precisely, does Swami Vivekananda mean when he says that "we accept all religions as true"? The world's religions are, of course, greatly varied in their teachings. Some religions claim, for example, that after one lifetime, the soul dwells eternally in either heaven or hell, while religions teach the existence of a cycle of rebirth which lasts for eons, until the soul becomes liberated from it. Vivekananda clarifies this in a later lecture, presented in 1900 in Pasadena, California:

> I believe that they [the world's religions] are not contradictory; they are supplementary. Each religion, as it were, takes up one part of the great universal truth, and spends its whole force in embodying and typifying that part of the great truth. It is addition, not exclusion. That is the idea. System after system arises, embodying a great idea, and ideals must be added to ideals. And this is the march of humanity. Man never progresses from error to truth, but from truth to truth, from lesser truth to higher truth–but it is never from error to truth. The child may develop more than the father, but was the father inane? The child is the father plus something else. (Vivekananda 1979, Volume Two, 365)

Swami Vivekananda, much like Keshub Chunder Sen and Sri Ramakrishna, thus sees the core ideals of the world's religions as being in harmony, despite whatever differences may exist amongst them in regard to specific doctrines. He also has an idea of a hierarchy of truth–of "higher" truth and "lesser" truth–which suggests a standard in terms of which the relative truth of different religions might be measured. For him, this standard is provided by the Vedas:

> [T]he fourfold scripture known…as the Vedas being the first, the most complete, and the most undistorted collection of spiritual truths, deserve to occupy the highest place among all scriptures, command the respect of all nations of the earth, and furnish the rationale of all their respective scriptures. (Vivekananda 1979, Volume Six, 182)

Apart from "truth" in the literal sense of the correspondence of its teachings with reality, the idea of a religion being "true" can also, in popular usage, refer to its salvific efficacy: the ability of a religious practice or faith to lead to the ultimate goal of human existence, however that might be seen in the religion in question. As his welcome address continues, we can see that Swami Vivekananda is speaking of this as well when he refers to accepting "all religions as true":

> I will quote to you, brethren, a few lines from a hymn which I remember to have repeated from my earliest boyhood, which is every day repeated by millions of human beings: "*As the different streams having their sources in different places all mingle their water in the sea, so, O Lord, the different paths which men take through different tendencies, various though they appear, crooked or straight, all lead to Thee.*" (Vivekananda 1979, Volume One, 4)

This verse, from the *Shiva Mahimna Stotra*, affirms an ancient Hindu ideal: that many religions, even if they are not all equally "true" in the literal sense, are capable of leading their adherents to the ultimate goal. Vivekananda continues this line of thinking as the welcome address continues, turning now from the *Shiva Mahimna Stotra* to the *Bhagavad Gita*:

> The present convention, which is one of the most august assemblies ever held, is in itself a vindication, a declaration to the world of the wonderful doctrine preached in the Gita: "*Whosoever comes to Me, through whatsoever form, I reach him; all men are struggling through paths which in the end lead to me.*" (Vivekananda 1979, Volume One, 3)

This is Vivekananda's gloss on the eleventh verse of the fourth chapter of the *Bhagavad Gita*, in which Krishna teaches Arjuna that the many forms of the ultimate reality presented in the different systems of religious practice can all act as ways of reaching Krishna himself. As I have argued elsewhere, if one thinks in terms of the tripartite model developed by theologian Alan Race of exclusivism, inclusivism, and pluralism, Swami Vivekananda is inclusivistic with regard to truth (taking one's own tradition as the measure by which truth is known, but seeing truth in many traditions) and pluralistic with regard to salvation (seeing many religions as leading to the ultimate goal) (Long, 2023; Race, 1982).

As Swami Vivekananda's welcome address reaches its climax, it becomes evident that there is a third 'axis' along which his philosophy of religion can be categorized as well: with regard to how the adherents of traditions other than one's own ought to be treated. In this regard, he is a thoroughgoing pluralist:

> Sectarianism, bigotry, and its horrible descendant, fanaticism, have long possessed this beautiful earth. They have filled the earth with violence, drenched it often and often with human blood, destroyed civilization and sent whole nations to despair. Had it not been for these horrible demons, human society would be far more advanced than it is now. But their time is come; and I fervently hope that the bell that tolled this morning in honor of this convention may be the death-knell of all fanaticism, of all persecutions with the sword or with the pen, and of all uncharitable feelings between persons wending their way to the same goal. (Vivekananda 1979, Volume One, 3–4)

He further elaborates upon this pluralism with regard to social interaction in the same lecture, cited earlier, from 1900, delivered in Pasadena, California, and titled, "The Way to the Realisation of a Universal Religion":

> Our watchword, then, will be acceptance and not exclusion. Not only toleration, for so-called toleration is often blasphemy, and I do not believe in it. I believe in acceptance. Why should I tolerate? Toleration means that I think that you are wrong and I am just allowing you to live. Is it not a blasphemy to think that you and I are allowing others to live? I accept all religions that were in the past, and worship with them all; I worship God with every one of them, in whatever form they worship Him…Not only shall I do all these, but I shall keep my heart open for all that may come in the future. Is God's book finished? Or is it still a continuing revelation going on? It is a marvellous book–these spiritual revelations of the world. The Bible, the Vedas, the Koran, and all other sacred books are but so many pages, and an infinite number of pages yet to be unfolded. (Vivekananda 1979, Volume Two, 373–374)

Contrary to the idea that he supported any kind of religious nationalism, passages affirming a practice of acceptance toward the adherents of diverse religions can be found throughout Swami Vivekananda's *Complete Works*. For example:

> All narrow, limited, fighting ideas of religion have to go. All sect ideas and tribal or national ideas of religion must be given up. That each tribe or nation should have its own particular God and think that every other is wrong is a superstition that should belong to the past. All such ideas must be abandoned. (Vivekananda 1979, Volume Two, 67)

In a similar vein, he cites his teacher, Sri Ramakrishna:

> My master used to say that these names, [such] as Hindu, Christian, etc., stand as great bars to all brotherly feelings between man and man. We must try to break them down first. They have lost all their good powers and now stand as baneful influences under whose black magic even the best of us behave like demons. (Vivekananda 1979, Volume Six, 302)

After the Chicago Parliament, where he, by all accounts, made a major impression, Swami Vivekananda toured the United States, remaining until 1897. In 1894, he established the Vedanta Society of New York. This would be the first of many such centers established by Vivekananda and his followers. Many of these centers would be staffed by swamis of the Ramakrishna Order. New Vedanta Societies continue to emerge in America today. These typically consist, initially, of gatherings of devotees and people interested in learning more about Vedanta philosophy. As each group becomes large enough to buy a property, a formal center is established and, if a live-in swami can be sustained, one is assigned from the headquarters of the Ramakrishna Order at Belur Math. Large centers, like the Vedanta Society of Southern California and the Greater DC Vedanta Society, may house multiple swamis. Some centers, such as the Vedanta Society of Dallas, are run not by swamis, but by pravrajikas–woman ascetics, who, though fewer in number than the swamis, are nonetheless important leaders in the movement.

19.5 The Influence of Swami Vivekananda in the Western World

There was certainly sufficient interest among Americans in Indian thought during Swami Vivekananda's time, and a spiritual hunger sufficiently profound, to enable him to find a ready and willing audience and abundant support for the founding of the first Vedanta Societies, and also for the ventures that he pursued upon his return to India, such as the establishment of the Ramakrishna Mission and Belur Math. Though his role in spreading awareness of Hindu traditions in America is considerable, Swami Vivekananda was not the first person to do so, though he was the first guru to come from India and develop a large following. Earlier in the nineteenth century, there were, of course, the Transcendentalists, as well as the Theosophical Society. Even as early as the eighteenth century, John Adams, who would become the second president of the United States, showed a very strong interest in India and in Hindu thought (Goldberg 2010, 30).

Once the first Vedanta Societies were established, they soon became a magnet for important intellectual and literary figures–what might today be called cultural influencers–who have played a major role in disseminating the Vedantic teachings of Swami Vivekananda throughout American culture. These figures, shaped by the thought of Swami Vivekananda, have done much to shape present-day spiritual development in the West.

Christopher Isherwood, a famed novelist and an associate of such literary figures as W.H. Auden, E.M. Forster, and Somerset Maugham–as well as Jiddu Krishnamurti–assisted Swami Prabhavananda, the founder of the Vedanta Society of Southern California, in his translations of such important Indian philosophical works as the *Bhagavad Gita*, the *Yoga Sutras* of Patañjali, and the *Viveka Chudamani* of Shankara. Finally, drawing upon his considerable literary talents, Isherwood wrote what is probably the most popular biography of Sri Ramakrishna in the English language: *Ramakrishna and His Disciples* (cited earlier in this chapter).

Aldous Huxley, also affiliated with the California center, was an essayist and a novelist who wove Vedantic themes through his fictional and non-fictional works. His well-known essay, *The Perennial Philosophy*, outlines Swami Vivekananda's ideal of a universal religion that underlies all existing religions through a common core of direct mystical realization. A major theme of his novels is the expansion of consciousness, and one of his most provocative works, *The Doors of Perception*, is the source from which the popular California-based band, the Doors, took their name.

Shifting from the west coast to the east coast, author J.D. Salinger was associated with the New York Ramakrishna Vivekananda Center. Salinger was a disciple of Swami Nikhilananda, and is best known in America as the author of *The Catcher in the Rye*, a novel of youthful alienation and protest against the norms of conventional western society. Salinger's later works, though, such as *Frannie and Zooey*, are replete with Vedantic themes and references. Salinger abruptly withdrew from society at the height of his fame–a retreat that was the source of much speculation until after his death, in 2010, when it came to light that he spent the last five decades of his life practicing meditation and studying the *Bhagavad Gita*.

Two very prominent scholars of religion, Huston Smith and Joseph Campbell, were deeply influenced by Indian values and philosophies, especially Vedanta. Smith almost singlehandedly transformed the study of the world's religions into a popular discipline, in demand on nearly every college campus in the United States. Campbell also popularized the comparative study of religion and mythology, partially through his own work, such as the celebrated *The Hero with a Thousand Faces*, on the theme of mythic archetypes, but also indirectly, through the influence he exerted on filmmaker George Lucas.

Lucas, inspired by the work of Campbell, dreamed of developing a distinctively American mythology drawing upon Indian, Japanese, and other world spiritual traditions. This vision took the form of the wildly popular *Star Wars* films. Indeed, *Star Wars* has today expanded into other media as well, such as streaming television series, video games, and books. In the philosophy of Lucas's Jedi Knights, one can discern numerous elements of Asian philosophy. Even the clothing of the Jedi is clearly modeled upon the kimonos traditionally worn by Japanese samurai when not in battle.

Especially in the teaching of the Jedi Master Yoda, one can hear echoes of Vedanta in the *Star Wars* universe. "Luminous beings are we," Master Yoda tells his disciple, Luke Skywalker, "not this crude matter." This reflects the teaching of the *Bhagavad Gita* that the true Self is beyond the realm of the body and the senses. "As the embodied soul continuously passes, in this body, from boyhood to youth to old age, the soul similarly passes into another body at death. A sober person is not bewildered by such a change" (*Bhagavad Gita* 2:13, Prabhupada 2020, 75). Even the first meeting between the initially doubting and scornful Luke Skywalker and his eccentric, seemingly mad master, as depicted in *The Empire Strikes Back*, reflects the first encounter between the young Narendranath Datta and the divine madman, Sri Ramakrishna.

Finally, yet another major disseminator of what has emerged as the contemporary global spiritual movement, has been George Harrison, lead guitarist from easily the most popular rock band of all time: the Beatles. Harrison's initial attraction to Indian spiritual thought was, not surprisingly for a musician, through the medium of Indian music, as it was presented to him by his friend and mentor, Ravi Shankar. But it was not long before Harrison would immerse himself fully into Hindu thought and practice. His first visit to India, in 1966, was spent for the most part doing contemplative reading in a houseboat in Kashmir. The two books Harrison took with him, which he quickly absorbed during this time, were *Autobiography of a Yogi*, by Paramahamsa Yogananda, and *Raja Yoga*, by Swami Vivekananda. Vedantic and Yogic themes would continue to pervade both the lyrics and the music of George Harrison until his passing in November of 2001.

Through the works of the various scholars, authors, and artists who received the influence of Swami Vivekananda, either through his writings or through the Vedanta Society, and through the various spiritual teachers who came to the West following his example, Vedantic thought now pervades America, despite there being relatively few Americans who actually know Vivekananda's name or are directly familiar with his teachings. In a 2009 *Newsweek* editorial with the provocative title "We Are All Hindus Now," journalist Lisa Miller cites polling data indicating that a majority of Americans–65%–believe "many religions can lead to eternal life." This number includes a surprising 37% of white evangelical Christians. This survey also indicates that 24% of Americans believe in reincarnation, and that 30%–almost a third–identify themselves as "spiritual but not religious" (Miller, 2009), and thus choose not to identify truth narrowly with any single culture or tradition. Other reputable polls have yielded comparable numbers in response to similar questions.

If one takes a stroll through an American shopping mall and browses through the various stores, one increasingly finds clothing and home decorations adorned with images of Lord Ganesha and other Hindu deities. Popular musical artists also express Hindu themes in their works, such as the British band Kula Shaker, as well as the American band Greta Van Fleet, whose song "Trip the Light Fantastic" includes an invocation of the Hindu deity Rama.

In 2011, an international super group, SuperHeavy, with an all-star membership including Mick Jagger and A.R. Rahman, had a hit with their song, "Satyameva Jayate." Actress Julia Roberts "came out" as a Hindu in 2010 after having starred in the film *Eat, Pray, Love*, which includes a pilgrimage to India as a prominent chapter in the life journey of its protagonist. Other Western celebrities wear *Om* jewelry and sport Sanskrit tattoos, as do growing numbers of young people. One of the biggest hit films of 2012, a film that won multiple academy awards, was the beautiful and profound, Vedanta-infused *Life of Pi*.

If one digs beneath the surface of this outward veneer of appreciation for Indian culture among Americans, and a widespread acceptance of Vedantic beliefs (though, again, without very widespread awareness of or acknowledgement of the source of these beliefs), one can see that the West today bears the imprint of Swami

Vivekananda's thought and that of the wider Hindu tradition of which he was part. In the words of religion scholar Vasudha Narayanan, "Americans may not know it, but they've long been embracing Hindu philosophy" (Narayanan 2019).

One important imprint that Swami Vivekananda has left on the West has been his emphasis on concrete action for the relief of human suffering as a spiritual path: that is, karma yoga. Beyond the important and vital relief work of the Ramakrishna Mission that he established in 1897, another major figure on whom he had an enormous influence was Mohandas K. Gandhi. Gandhi actually sought to meet Swami Vivekananda when the Indian National Congress was meeting in Calcutta in 1902, but Vivekananda was unfortunately on his deathbed at that point, and unable to receive visitors. Many of Gandhi's ideals about education and social upliftment were drawn almost word for word from the teachings of Swami Vivekananda. Gandhi has in turn influenced movements for a peaceful transformation of society across the globe, shaping the thought of such Western figures as Martin Luther King and Nelson Mandela.

In the realm of the intellect as well, Swami Vivekananda has also had influence on global spirituality. Among the prominent intellectuals who came into direct contact with him during his time in America was William James, a Harvard professor of psychology and philosophy who, though somewhat of skeptic about aspects of Vedanta, was open to the wider realm of experience reflected in Vivekananda's thought and in the life of Ramakrishna. James would have tremendous influence upon the thought of Alfred North Whitehead, the father of the system of philosophy known as *process thought*. Process thought shares many strong affinities with both Vedanta and Buddhism, as well as Jain philosophy. Whitehead's thought also bears the imprint, via William James, of Swami Vivekananda's influence.

In terms of bhakti yoga, the path of devotion, Swami Vivekananda's greatest influential contribution has been in promoting the idea of the *ishtadevata*, or chosen form of divinity. The radical spiritual freedom that this idea implies is the essence of his teaching: that whatever form of the divine reality attracts us, whether it be a Hindu deity, a Buddha, a Jina, Allah, Jesus Christ, or any of the great manifestations celebrated in the world's religions and philosophies, may serve as the vehicle by which our devotion can carry us to the infinite. The infinite truth cannot be bound to any one form or tradition. With this understanding, and his teachings of universal acceptance and the harmony of religions, Swami Vivekananda revolutionized the interfaith movement.

Finally, the popularization of meditation and the practice of Hatha Yoga (known simply as "Yoga" in the west) is similarly hard to conceive of without the influence of Swami Vivekananda: particularly his treatise on Raja Yoga, which is his commentary on the *Yoga Sutras* of Patañjali. Again, outside the Vedanta Society and Ramakrishna Mission which he instituted, his influence in this regard has probably been felt most deeply through the work of Sri Aurobindo, who explicitly attributes his own profound yogic transformation to a spiritual encounter with Swami Vivekananda in a series of meditative visions. Although Vivekananda would no doubt have been critical of the use of yoga purely as a form of physical exercise, those systems of yoga which emphasize the centrality of the practice of meditation are in harmony with the spirit of his teaching.

These are just a few samples of the ways in which Swami Vivekananda has had an impact in the West: Gandhi-inspired movements for social justice, the movements of religious pluralism and process thought within the realms of philosophy and theology, the interfaith movement in the area of religious devotion, and the popularization of meditation and other yogic practices. The genealogies of all these movements converge in the life and teachings of Swami Vivekananda.

Vivekananda once said that, "It may be that I shall find it good to get outside of my body–to cast it off like a disused garment. But I shall not cease my work! I shall inspire men everywhere, until the world shall know that it is one with God" (Vivekananda, Volume Five, 414). This would seem to be an accurate description of what has been happening since Swami Vivekananda his passing on the 4th of July 1902. And this work continues even today.

19.6 Conclusion: Why Swami Vivekananda's Influence is Important

Swami Vivekananda's impact in the West is even more important today than it was when he lived and walked the earth over a century ago. The destructive capacities that human beings have developed are a danger to all life on this planet. Humanity stands at a crossroads from which we can either make this world into a heaven or a hell. It is within our power either to continue on a path to destruction, or to transform ourselves. The teachings of Swami Vivekananda hold the key to this transformation. This key is the idea of universal acceptance and the perception of the divinity of all beings that is at its heart. In the words of Swami Medhananda:

> …[I]n our contemporary climate of religious strife and violence, Vivekananda's Vedantic religious cosmopolitanism is not merely of academic interest, as it can play a vital role in fostering mutual respect–and mutual learning–among the world's religious practitioners. (Medhananda, 138)

As we have seen, Swami Vivekananda says, in his welcome address to the Parliament of the World's Religions in Chicago in 1893, "I am proud to belong to a religion which has taught the world both tolerance and universal acceptance. We believe not only in universal toleration, but we accept all religions as true." (Vivekananda 1979, Volume One, 3) And in a later lecture, he says, "I accept all religions that were in the past, and worship with them all; I worship God with every one of them, in whatever form they worship Him." (Vivekananda 1979, Volume Two, 374) This is not mere tolerance–an aversion to the other concealed beneath a polite veneer–but a true acceptance.

In concluding his welcome address, Vivekananda says, "Sectarianism, bigotry, and its horrible descendant, fanaticism, have long possessed this beautiful earth. They have filled the earth with violence, drenched it often and often with human blood, destroyed civilization and sent whole nations to despair. Had it not been for these horrible demons, human society would be far more advanced than it is now" (Vivekananda 1979, Volume One, 4). Echoing Vivekananda, Carl Sagan similarly speculates that had the great library of Alexandria not been destroyed by a fanatical mob in 391 AD, humanity might already be traveling to the stars (Sagan, 1980).

"But," Vivekananda concludes, on a note of hope, "their time is come; and I fervently hope that the bell that tolled this morning in honor of this convention may be the death-knell of all fanaticism, of all persecutions with the sword or with the pen, and of all uncharitable feelings between persons wending their way to the same goal" (Vivekananda 1979, Volume One, 4). This hope is Swami Vivekananda's greatest legacy.

References

Goldberg, P. (2010). *American Veda: From Emerson and the beatles to Yoga and Meditation—How Indian spirituality changed the West*. Three Rivers Press.

Harris, R. (2022). *Guru to the world: The life and legacy of Vivekananda*. Harvard University Press.

Isherwood, C. (1965). *Ramakrishna and his disciples*. Vedanta Press.

Long, J. D. (2023, April). Religions as Yogas: How reflection on Swami Vivekananda's theology of religions can clarify the threefold model of exclusivism, inclusivism, and pluralism. *International Journal of Hindu Studies, 27*(1)

Miller, L. (2009, August 31). We are all Hindus now. *Newsweek*.

Narayanan, V. (2019, February 6). Americans may not know it, but they've long been embracing Hindu philosophy. Retrieved February 9, 2019, from https://qz.com/india/1199543/americas-long-and-complex-relationship-with-hinduism/

Nikhilananda, S. (1942). *The Gospel of Sri Ramakrishna*. Ramakrishna Vivekananda Center.

Prabhupada, A. C. Bhaktivedanta Swami. (2020). *Bhagavad Gita as it is*. Bhaktivedanta Book Trust.

Race, A. (1982). *Christians and religious pluralism*. Orbis Books.

Richards, G. (Ed.). (1985). *A source-book of modern Hinduism*. Curzon Press.

Sagan, C. (1980). *Cosmos*. Ballantine Books.

Saradananda, S. (1952). *Sri Ramakrishna: The great master* (S. Jagadananda, Trans.). Sri Ramkrishna Math.

Vivekananda, S. (1979). *Complete works*. Advaita Ashrama.

Chapter 20
How Becoming a Myth Leads to History: A Modern Embodiment of the Goddess Durga as the Female Shankaracarya in Hindu Society

Antoinette DeNapoli

Freedom is Women's Most Precious Possession
—Mataji Trikal Bhavanta Saraswati, 2019.

Abstract Women's access to leadership as monastic heads (i.e., Śaṅkarācāryas) in India has been restricted by enduring patriarchal structures for twelve centuries. Until the female guru named Trikal Bhavanta Saraswati ("Mataji"), who resides in the politically right-leaning northern state of Uttar Pradesh and leads an ascetic women's order, appointed herself the title in 2008, the status has been subject to the sole control of Brahmin men. Modern contexts, however, present unique opportunities for women to reinterpret conventional religious ideals that restrict feminine virtue to the realm of domesticity. This essay shows that Mataji's leadership asserts an alternative narrative of women's monastic authority as institutionally normative. By using her status, she is promoting a new Hindu identity that contests Brahmanical hegemony as a structural outsider. Grounded in ethnographic fieldwork conducted from 2014 to 2019, the essay illuminates Mataji's performance of personal narrative to rectify gender inequities and restructure power hierarchies by affirming the normative status of the female ascetic (sādhu). A key part of this analysis relates to how she elucidates the feminine symbolism portrayed by the heroic goddess Durga to sanction female *sadhus*' institutional autonomy as a normative right. Through performance, Mataji engenders her identification with the goddess as she acts in myth and in history, empowering women with a localized conception of autonomy as the emanation of Durga in worldly affairs and the female Shankaracharya as an incarnation of Durga. The essay applies insights drawn from feminist studies, performance studies, and fieldwork observations toward the development of a hermeneutical approach to understanding the roles of religion and gender in Mataji's process of revising perceptions of autonomy as a threat to respectable womanhood. It argues

A. DeNapoli (✉)
Texas Christian University, Fort Worth, TX, USA
e-mail: a.denapoli@tcu.edu

L. Vemsani (ed.), *Handbook of Indian History*,
https://doi.org/10.1007/978-981-97-6207-1_20

that Mataji constructs autonomy as an aspect of female virtue by correlating women's self-asserting capacities with Durga's agentive power while dismantling the patriarchal right to control women. Thus, the essay extends feminist perspectives on what autonomy can mean to ascetic women in accordance with Mataji's teachings, and explores Mataji's practices that enable women's greater freedom and parity of status in Hindu society.

Keywords Gurus · Goddesses · Hindu women · *Sadhus* · *Sannyas* · Renunciation · Monasticism · Autonomy · Gender equality · Women's rights · Performance · Hinduism · India · South Asia · Modernity

20.1 Introduction: A Self-appointed Female Guru and the Innovation of Monastic Leadership

On a characteristically rainy afternoon of the monsoon season in July 2019, hundreds of people make their way into a Hindu temple located in southern Delhi, where three female gurus are sitting on a stage and preparing to address the public. The temple is sponsoring a "*nārī dharm saṅsad*," or women's religious parliament, during which these gurus will speak about women's rights issues from Hindu perspectives. Many of the attendees have come to hear the teachings of a guru representing herself as the "first" female Śaṅkarācāryā of India (a monastic head in the lineage of the ninth-century male guru Ādi Śaṅkarācārya), who is named Trikal Bhavanta Saraswati (hereafter, "Mataji" or "Respected Mother") (see Fig. 20.1). With the support of the other gurus and the temple's trustees, Mataji has agreed to participate in this event in order to raise awareness of the flouting of women's rights in patriarchal monastic society.

As soon as she takes the microphone, Mataji says that "The *Śāstras* [religious texts] tell us that women are the form of Mother Shakti." After a brief pause, she says, "Whenever there is a loss of truth [*dharm*], Shakti appears as Durga. She has given me this charge of rescuing our *sanātan dharm* [Hindu teachings based on Vedic and other literature] through my leadership as the Shankaracharya. My trident will rise whenever there is a need to fight for truth." People clap their hands so loudly that Mataji has to raise her voice to speak, and soon enough, she, too, is speaking with such force that her words resound from every corner of the temple:

> Whenever our culture, our nation, and our religion are in trouble, women take the form of Durga…We have to choose *dharmācāryas* [religious leaders] who will work for our society, our country, and our religion. Today's *dharmacaryas* are not giving women the rights they deserve. They tell women to have ten sons, but these women don't have the money to feed their children or educate them…There are thousands of female ascetics [*sādhus*] who are qualified to lead our religion. When the gods [*devtās*] were in trouble, they gave their weapons to Mother Durga to fight the demons. Our *dharmacaryas* should do the same. They should fight [for women's rights] or give us the support to fight.

Fig. 20.1 Mataji at her ashram in 2019. Author's collection

Women's access to religious leadership as monastic heads (i.e., Shankaracharyas) in India has been restricted by enduring patriarchal structures for twelve centuries. Until Mataji, who appointed herself the title in 2008, the Shankaracharya status has been subject to the sole control of Brahmin men. While the Shankaracharya represents the highest authority within an orthoprax branch of Brahmanical (Sanskritic) Hinduism, other parallel lineages refuse to accept the headship of women. The mainstream tradition has construed high-caste maleness as normative for institutional control, and has thus failed to appoint female Shankaracharyas, Rāmānujācāryās, or Madhvācāryās.[1] Modern contexts, however, present unique opportunities for women

[1] There are different institutions within diverse expressions of Brahmanical Hinduism that attribute the origins of their lineages to guru-founders (*ācāryas*), such as Adi Shankaracharya (ca. ninth century), and Ramanujacarya (ca. twelfth century), and Madhvacarya (ca. fourteenth century). These religious leaders have organized and, through the establishment of monastic centers, institutionalized

to reinterpret and revise conventional religious ideals and values that restrict feminine virtue to the realm of domesticity. As I will show, Mataji's leadership asserts an alternative narrative of women's monastic authority as institutionally normative. By using her status, she is promoting a new Hindu identity that contests Brahmanical hegemony as a structural outsider.

Despite being outside the mainstream monastic system,[2] through her relationship with the goddess Durga, whom Mataji claims "called" her to lead in the role, Mataji is maneuvering her outsider status to change the tradition from the inside. By claiming the title (Mataji's self-appointment is based on revelatory experiences of the goddess), as a female Shankaracharya, she has mobilized women and other historically underserved identities to throw off the shackles of centuries of religious patriarchy and caste hierarchies and demand their right to leadership. Mataji and her constituency across multiple lines of difference are fighting for social equality within a domain of Hindu monastic life that has hitherto been a bastion for the Brahmin class.

Female ascetics (*sadhus*) and monastics (i.e., *sadhus* initiated into ascetic orders known as *akhāṛās*) must contend with sexism and misogyny that, like caste discrimination, is endemic to the monastic culture. However, ascetic female gurus such as Mataji have devised innovative strategies for bucking the religious convention and breaking into institutional roles that are engendering a new normativity for women's monastic leadership in patriarchal Hindu society.

This article focuses on an intrepid female guru who has taken on the challenge of pressing traditional Hindu monastic communities and leaders to recognize the religious potential for rethinking how gender and power structures can or should coordinate in the context of an increasingly modern set of values about freedom, selfhood, and community in India. As the female Shankaracharya and leader of an ascetic women's order, Mataji is rectifying gender inequities and reversing gender hierarchies that subordinate women by affirming the normative status of the female *sadhu*. Her leadership sanctions the legitimacy of autonomous, women-led orders created by and for women, and connects modernist notions of women's equal rights with traditional Hindu views of women's roles, empowering them to act to change their lives and destinies. Thus, the article illuminates the intersectionality of religion and modernity, tradition and innovation, through Mataji's quest for ascetic women's institutional autonomy.

---

theological systems, such as the school of non-dualism, Advaita Vedanta, the school of qualified dualism, Vishistadvaita Vedanta, and the school of dualism, Dvaita Vedanta, based on competing interpretations of Vedic literature. See Long (2018).

[2] Mataji's Shankaracharya status has been repudiated by the established Shankaracharyas and the leaders of the All India Akhara Parishad. Thus, Mataji relies on charismatic authority to sanction her alternative authority and challenge traditional authority. See DeNapoli (2019, 2022, 2023a, 2023b).

20.2 The Contexts of the Field Study: Methods, Theoretical Frameworks, and Hypothesis

Grounded in ethnographic fieldwork conducted from 2014 to 2019 in the northern state of Uttar Pradesh with Mataji and her community, this essay analyzes Mataji's performance of religious discourses (*pravacan*) and personal narratives to unravel systemic gender- and caste-motivated oppression, discrimination, and exploitation within the Hindu monastic orders (*akharas*). I examine the discourses Mataji gave in public devotional contexts, such as the *nari sansads*, which she began sponsoring in 2015. Apart from the *sansads*, Mataji delivered stories about her life and work to female devotees and me in the more personal setting of her temple and ashram. These narratives comprise fifty hours of narrative told over five years of collaboration, and provide the primary source material for my analysis of Mataji's teachings and practices.

Examining the dynamics of a female guru's authority in monastic culture has drawn my attention to an under-researched dimension in Hindu studies scholarship concerning "autonomy." As I listened to Mataji speak about "women's power" (*matṛ-śakti*), and analyzed my data transcriptions and field notes for content and patterns, "autonomy" surfaced as a salient theme in her teachings. For years, I have wrestled with the question of how such a presumably liberal western concept relates to women's social realities in the Global South. Although I was wary of viewing Indian women through "western eyes" (Mohanty, 2003) and of translating Mataji through my own values as a white American woman and western-educated feminist scholar, I nonetheless followed my hunch. I am now convinced that the study of women's shifting relationships to the local structures of caste, gender, and religion would be incomplete without exploring the forms and capacities for female autonomy as they manifest within such arenas.[3]

Some western feminist scholars studying the congruence between modernist, rights-based ideologies and 'traditional' religious worldviews have questioned the utility of the concept of autonomy (i.e., the right of citizens of secular democracies to exercise personal freedom and choice) to interpret women's status and subjectivities in non-Western societies. In this regard, Alison L. Boden has argued that, based on anthropological research conducted in India, women in the northern states do not desire autonomy. She has said that, in the localized cultures that they inhabit, the women view it negatively. They find autonomy 'unattractive and frightening,' and do not want it (2007, 135). Accordingly, for a woman to exercise autonomy by going to the market to buy herself clothes, food, and so forth brings to mind cultural associations related to "a loss of prestige, status, influence, or caring. What is understood by others to be a gain in terms of independence is experienced by [the women] as a real social loss" (Boden, 2007, Ibid).

Even if some women's relationship to the concept reveals interpretive fault lines, Boden's observations nonetheless relate to rural Indic society and not to *Hindu*

[3] See also Richa Nagar/Sangtin Writers (2006).

monastic culture. Scholars cannot assume that the norms of Hindu culture are reducible to or interchangeable with those of the wider Indic society since the latter consists of a diverse mix of local, regional, national, as well as urban and rural viewpoints and traditions. Moreover, as the work of other anthropologists in India has shown, women are not a homogenous group that affirms the same visions or experiences of womanhood. Their sense of self and personhood shape, and are shaped by, different constituent social elements and relationships (Raheja, 2003; Sangtin Writers, 2006). It feels shortsighted to close the door on the explanatory potential of autonomy for Indic women's self-representations without consideration of the perspectives of ascetically-oriented women.

Besides vowing celibacy, devotion, and simplicity, what distinguishes female *sadhus* from householders has to do with the freedom of movement and personal autonomy afforded by an ascetic way of life. In the popular religious imagination, *sadhus* are expected to be perpetual wanderers who, having rejected norms and caste- and gender-based responsibilities, live on the periphery of the Hindu social world. Autonomy and being a *sadhu* are thus tacitly connected.

My use of "autonomy" as the label for a basic principle of Mataji's teachings to and for women, emerges from her use of Indic terminology. 'Autonomy' as a term may be foreign, but the concept crosses cultural boundaries. Mataji's emphasis on women's right to develop their talents and her association of self-asserting behaviors with the feminine principle called *śakti* ("power") inform my classification of her teachings under the rubric of autonomy. She uses the term 'svayambhū,' which denotes the 'self-manifesting' agency of a divinity that emerges in the natural world and is activated within human beings through inspiration, dreams, and visions. It is equivalent to natural life-force. As such, the essay extends feminist perspectives on what autonomy can mean for ascetic women through Mataji's eyes, and explores the practices of a guru by which she advances a view of the concept otherwise eclipsed by Euro-American models.

A key part of this analysis relates to how Mataji elucidates the feminine symbolism portrayed by the heroic goddess Durga to construct autonomy as the female birthright. Through storytelling, Mataji performs her identification with the goddess as she acts in myth and history, empowering women with a localized conception of autonomy as the emanation of Durga in worldly affairs and the female Shankaracharya as Durga's incarnation. Since Mataji performs an oral version of the Durga myth[4] based on the *Devī-Māhātmya*'s (ca. sixth–eighth century CE) textual representation of the goddess fighting against the sexual advances of male demons to protect her bodily integrity and freedom, I limit my analysis to this episode. Mataji's narrative performance promulgates a Hindu feminist theology of the righteousness of women's insubordination against the male sex right (i.e., male supremacy over women). This

[4] There are many versions of the Durga myth (i.e., the story of Durga's battle against the demons threatening cosmic balance) as featured in the Brahmanical Sanskritic literature, such as the *Devī Bhāgavatā Purāṇa* (ca. ninth–fourteenth century and the *Devi Mahatmya* (ca. sixth–eighth century CE), as well as localized oral traditions (see Menon and Shweder 2000; see also Humes 2000).

theology connects female *sadhus*' autonomy to their basic human right to live free of male domination, predation, and control.

I argue furthermore that Mataji performs Durga's myth to sanction women's institutional autonomy as a normative right and their resistance against patriarchal privilege as respectable femininity. In this way, she creates unique opportunities for women's greater freedom in Hindu society. Her style of leadership enacts a female grassroots, which I have termed "grassroots religious feminism," that is spearheading a transformative social vision of ascetic (or monastic) women's and men's parity of status. Her feminism aligns with the Black American journalist Isabel Wilkerson's claim that freedom is fundamentally a universal human good (2020, 77).

Thus, the essay unites ideas drawn from feminist critical theory, performance-centered studies, and fieldwork observations toward the development of a hermeneutical approach to understanding the roles of religion and gender in Mataji's process of revising perceptions of autonomy as a threat to female virtue. By telling stories to (re)interpret Hindu thinking about what being a woman means and how human/divine women can protect themselves against male sexual hegemony, Mataji asserts female *sadhus*' equality to male *sadhus*. Storytelling performs one way, among others, for Mataji to raise the status of monastic women in the patriarchal *akhara* culture; thus her goals are practical, tangible, and social (i.e., they are not just symbolic).

20.3 "Women Should Be Shankaracharyas!": Mataji's Forming an Ascetic Women's Order

Born in 1965 to a lower-middle-class family of peanut farmers in a village, and the third of four children, Mataji comes from a subordinated caste (see Fig. 20.1). She considers her leadership to be a "vehicle" for the deities Shiva and Shakti (and Durga) to establish the religious equality of monastic women and men (see Fig. 20.2). Mataji's quest began in the early 2000s while organizing camps for female *sadhus* at the Kumbh Melā fair. She wanted to provide women pilgrims an alternate option for temporary housing to the camps run by the *akharas*.

Female *sadhus* constitute a class of Hindu practitioners who may be viewed as extraordinary and unusual women because of the intensity of their devotional and moral commitments. *Sadhus* are traditionally respected, and sometimes feared, in Hindu society. They relinquish ordinary expectations, such as marriage and family, wage labor, and other caste- and gender-related duties, dedicating themselves to the divine and offering selfless service (*sevā*) to society. To become a *sadhu*, initiates take ritual vows of celibacy and voluntary poverty and strive to cultivate detachment and equanimity in their relationships. *Sadhus* follow a path called renunciation (*sannyās*) to escape infinite rebirths *(sansār)*. An uncommon way of life,[5] *sannyas* represents

[5] According to the statistics given by scholars, there are approximately 150 million *sadhus* in a population of 1.3 billion people. They comprise 10–15% of the Indian population. See Hausner (2006), Narayan (1989), Gross (2001), Khandelwal (2004).

Fig. 20.2 A poster displayed at the Prayagraj Kumbh Melā featuring male monastics from different *akharas* taking a ritual bath in the Triveni Sangam, 2019. Author's collection

an alternative to the Hindu ideal of family and householding (*grihasth*); as many of the *sadhus* I worked with have said, being a *sadhu* is difficult and not for the faint of heart.

To give some context for the relationship of *sadhus* to the *akhara* system, following their initiation, *sadhus* will usually join an order. Loosely defined as 'gymnasium' or 'wrestling ring,' an *akhara* represents a religious association through which *sadhus* receive religious training, education, and initiations. Credentialed gurus that have been ordained with titles, such as Mahāmandaleśwar ('Lord of the Great Circle'), which authorizes them to teach a knowledge tradition and initiate others, have received ordination through their *akhara*. Some orders operate as residential monasteries where *sadhus* receive room and board. But the orders that function in this capacity restrict residency to male practitioners. Female *sadhus* cannot live in the male-led *akharas* (Dasgupta, 2021; Jha, 2019); based on what some *sadhus* have told me, they do not want to live in them because of the sexual harassment and exploitation of women that happen there.

As with many social organizations, becoming a member of an *akhara* imparts benefits, such as instilling for *sadhus* a sense of pride in and connection to a monastic lineage and, for the more influential *akharas*, perpetuation of a monastic legacy. Many of the *sadhus* with whom I worked referred to *akharas* as a "house," suggesting shared views that *akharas* provide shelter and kinship structures in the metaphorical sense.

That *sadhus* would join an *akhara* to feel a sense of belonging to a fictive family may seem incongruent with their way of life. However, it speaks to the social role of monastic institutions in offering a source of cultural legitimacy and institutional protection for people who, despite having cut their ties, inhabit a society that strongly values family and ancestral lineage, and may judge them based on those expectations.

Furthermore, *akharas* elevate their members' religious status. An *akhara*'s status varies, with the Niranjani and Juna *akharas* claiming the highest status (these are also two of the orders that accept women), depending on a constellation of factors, such as its history, membership numbers, economic capital, outreach, and leadership. Concerns with status indicate an aspect of *akharas*' appeal, because *sadhus* can be accused of predatory fraud (Bloomfield, 1924; Gross, 2001; Narayan, 1989). Hence, aligning with an *akhara* can be a way to claim legitimacy and lessen suspicion.[6] *Akharas* provide the symbolic power of association that may act as a shield against scrutiny and criticism. At the Kumbh Mela, *akharas* perform their status through ritual bathing, with the most respected of the orders taking a holy bath in the Ganges river before all the other *akharas*, and before the general public, at the most astrologically auspicious times (see Fig. 20.2).

As of this writing (2023), the Hindu monastic society consists of thirteen established associations (*akharas*), which are male-led and dominated. The mainstream *akharas* refuse to grant institutional legitimacy to any *akhara* that does not operate within its pyramidal power structure and by its rules. This is not to say that the leadership structure excludes female *sadhus* from its ranks. Female monastics occupying positions of authority hold a subordinate status to that of male leaders, and the power they exercise is largely derivative of male monastic authority.

However, by appointing herself as a Shankaracharya (she extends the pronunciation of the final 'a' vowel to amplify the newness of her female leadership), Mataji repurposes traditional structures to provide women the legitimacy of formal institutional status that elevates the normativity of female authority to the level of critical insight. This modern innovation in the leadership structure taps into the symbolic significance of Hindu religious conceptions of ascetic women as a form of the goddess Durga and feminine creative power (*shakti*), aligning the ideology with concrete outcomes to reinforce female *sadhus* and male *sadhus*' equal status.

Because monastic women comprise a minority population, Mataji founded a women's *akhara* in 2014 in order to reduce gender disparities (see Fig. 20.3). Reportedly, the order is the first of its kind and works to uplift *sadhus* at the margins of Hindu society by providing them shelter, training, education, skills, and an autonomous female lineage that parallels the male orders. She has named it Pari Akhara, which I have translated as the 'Society of the Free Birds'. Residing in Uttar Pradesh, a northern state known for its religious orthodoxy, and governed by a Hindu nationalist government under the current Chief Minister Yogi Adityanath, Mataji leads a small, but demographically diverse, religious community in Prayagraj (formerly Allahabad).

---

[6] Many of the *sadhus* with whom I worked in the northern states of Rajasthan and Uttar Pradesh showed me their *akhara*-granted certificates as proof of their being authentic practitioners.

आस्था

महिला शंकराचार्य के पट्टाभिषेक में नहीं पहुंचे किसी अखाड़े के शंकराचार्य

त्रिकाल भवंता के पट्टाभिषेक से बना इतिहास

मीनाक्षी कुशवाहा

इलाहाबाद। अखाड़ों के इतिहास को चुनौती देते हुये इस माघ मेले से शुरू हुई एक क्रान्ति की महाशिवरात्रि के पर्व पर एक सफल परिणति हो गयी। अरैल स्थित श्री सर्वेश्वर बैकुण्ठ धाम मुक्ति द्वार अखाड़ा 'परी' की कार्यकारिणी का गठन विवादों को दरकिनार करते हुए हो ही गया। पूरे विधि-विधान के साथ वैदिक मन्त्रोचार के बीच गायत्री त्रिवेणी तीर्थ प्रयाग पीठाधीश्वर जगतगुरु शंकराचार्य श्री सद्गुरु त्रिकाल भवन्ता का पट्टाभिषेक किया गया। साथ ही पदाधिकारियों को शपथ दिलाई गई। हालांकि इस आयोजन में कोई शंकराचार्य नहीं शामिल हुआ।

शंकराचार्य त्रिकाल भवंता के पट्टाभिषेक के बाद आरती पूजन करतीं महिला भक्त

महाशिवरात्रि पर्व के शुभ अवसर पर गुरुवार को नैनी स्थित अरैल में विधि-विधान से वैदिक मन्त्रोचार के बीच शंकराचार्य त्रिकाल भवन्ता का पट्टाभिषेक किया गया। इस अवसर पर उन्होंने कहा कि स्वतंत्र महिला अखाड़े के गठन के साथ ही आधी आबादी की दुनिया में एक नये युग की शुरुआत हुई। कार्यकारिणी में प्रमुख रूप से रमता पंच

शुरुआत

विवादों को दरकिनार कर महाशिवरात्रि पर्व पर 14वें अखाड़े की कार्यकारिणी गठित

परमेश्वर में साध्वी गौरी परी, साध्वी मीरा परी, साध्वी गीता परी, साध्वी तारा परी रहीं।

वहीं सचिव पद के लिए साध्वी सरस्वती परी, कोठारी पद के लिए साध्वी भैरवी परी, भण्डारी पद के लिए साध्वी श्यामा परी और कोतवाल के लिए साध्वी सबरी परी ने शपथ ग्रहण कर कार्यकारिणी में शामिल हुई। इस मौके पर प्रमुख लोगों में डॉ. तरुण पाठक, पण्डित अनुज त्रिपाठी, नागेश्वर मिश्र, भागीरथी यादव, रूबी यादव, संयोगिता, अन्जू द्विवेदी, रुचि मिश्रा आदि उपस्थित रहीं।

Fig. 20.3 A local newspaper article about Mataji's consecration as a Shankaracharya by the devotees of her women's ascetic order, Pari Akhara, 2014. Author's collection. Article written by Meenakshi Kushwaha. Used with permission of the article's author

Before becoming a *sadhu*, Mataji was a married householder with two children, a boy and a girl. She worked in Benares at a women's NGO from 1998 to 2000. She held the positions of General Secretary and Assistant Director. During this time, Mataji received leadership training for teaching women from urban slums in the region about their constitutional rights. In 2007, Mataji left her family and took initiation into renunciation from a guru in the Saraswati lineage. The ritual happened on the banks of Prayagraj's Triveni Sangam. This marks the location where, according to Hindu imagination, the Ganga, Jamuna, and (hidden) Saraswati rivers converge. "I promised my guru to improve women's lives," Mataji said in her first interview with me in 2014:

> At the NGO, I saw firsthand the abuse which women endure in this country. It's everywhere. In the home, the school, the bazaar, the workplace, and even in the ashram. Our female *sadhus* are being abused in many ways. They are being exploited, discriminated against, and raped by their gurus in our temples and ashrams. Our *sadhus* are suffering. They bear their pain alone. Some kill themselves. The shame and humiliation become too much…In our religion, women have all the power [*shakti*]…Our *Shastras* say that 'where women are worshipped, there the gods are happy.' Today's *dharmacaryas* preach these words from their mouths but do not follow these teachings in daily life. I have plunged the depths of *sannyas* and I have seen it all…We need a *dharmacarya* who will protect the rights of the female *sadhus*. That is why I am here.

From her standpoint, rights-based norms are not a modern invention of what reactionary Hindu nationalist discourse often labels the political left.[7] Rather, they designate basic Hindu religious principles as much as the fundamental priorities of the secular Indian state. Mataji says that Hindu notions of "rights" predate liberal western formulations delineated in India's Constitution. The term she uses to denote "rights" relates to the polyvalent Hindi term "adhikār," which may be translated as "authority," "eligibility," and "privilege." As Mataji explains,

> Hindu *sanatana dharm* recognizes the rights [*adhikar*] and equality [*samāntā*] of all humans, regardless of sex, caste, age, and class. *Dharm* policy informs every policy. Our Constitution is based on equality as revealed by God [Bhagvan] and the sages [*ṛṣis*]. In our Hindu *sanatan dharm*, men and women are equal [*barābar*]. God made men and women equal [*samān*], not superior and inferior. If God made them equal, then, as per my thinking, there should be a [female] Shankaracharya. Women [*sadhus*] have as much right to leadership as [male] *sadhus*.[8]

She attributes the source of her alternative authority to the power of divine intervention. She told me that in 2008, she had a religious vision (*darśan*) at an annual regional fair (*magh mela*) in which Shiva and Shakti (Durga) called her to the leadership and empowered her in the role. Mataji considers that vision to be her ritual initiation (*dīkṣā*) as a Shankaracharya by the gods. Following the revelation and with increasing community support, Mataji claimed the status in the same year. Her audacious self-appointment happened without the "official" recognition of the mainstream *akhara* leaders or formal Vedic training and initiations required for the position.

Mataji's struggle for women's institutional autonomy unsettles Brahmin supremacy as culturally normative. What is more, her leadership highlights that structural inequality is related to ingrained societal perceptions of female *sadhus* as having a lower status than male *sadhus*. Their presumed inferiority stems from the birth-ascribed status of the female sex associated with customary cultural ideas of gender difference and from menstrual blood as a polluting contagion.[9] Sex and

[7] Right-wing Hindu nationalist discourse tends to portray rights-informed visionaries as "leftists" in the mainstream and populist news media.

[8] June 8, 2018.

[9] Hindu orthodox teachings indicate that menstruant women between the ages of ten and fifty embody ritual impurity, and some temples ascribing to this view restrict women's entry into the space.

social status are, therefore, intertwined in Hindu monastic society and impact women in tangible ways.[10] Similarly, the *sadhus*' imposed secondary position justifies religious patriarchy's default rationale for an unequal culture (i.e., women's subordinate status is the supposed result of biological traits rather than an outcome of widespread exploitative structures). Female *sadhus*' perceived inferiority renders legitimate the cultural system designed to reward men because of the normative biological status ascribed to the male sex and further entrenches structures of male dominance over women (Narayan, 2019, 173).[11]

Mataji's leadership provides a public platform to advance female *sadhus*' equal status and right to lead monastic institutions independently of male control.[12] She says that women should practice their religion as they see fit. In this vein, she reframes the dominant gender discourse of Brahmanical Hinduism by advancing the notion that autonomy is as normative to the female *sadhu* as it is to the male *sadhu.*[13] Upending orthodox prescriptions of female obedience, submission, and dependence as the ideal qualities of virtuous womanhood, Mataji teaches ascetic women that "freedom is [their] most precious possession." Here, Mataji's idea of "freedom" concerns women's capacity for self-expression, self-determination, and self-regulation—that is, personal autonomy (Boden, 2007; Krishnan, 2019; Tomm, 1991, 77).

Just as significantly, Mataji considers these competencies to be intrinsic to the female sex as one type of "normative humanity" (Bhasin, 2019; Gross, 2000, 107; Tomm, 1991, 78). She stresses that autonomy enacts the agentive power, or *shakti*, of the goddess Durga, a force that she says awakens ("comes to life") in the bodies and through the actions of women. By this reasoning, women's exercise of autonomy accomplishes not only Durga's "self-manifesting" power (*svayambhū*) in the temporal sphere but also women's duty (*svadharm*) to become divine. Mataji's use of Durga's symbolism reconfigures patriarchal models of desirable womanhood by correlating the goddess's "self-manifesting" in female *sadhus* and other women with feminine respectability. Thus, Mataji constructs female autonomy as beneficial to Hindu monastic society.

[10] See Boursier (2021, pp. 3, 231–232).

[11] In *Chup: Breaking the Silence about India's Women* (2019), Deepa Narayan labels power structures based on gender/sex, and other markers of identity, the "cultural design" of patriarchal Indic society; see p. 245 for her discussion of bias against less powerful groups and how that justifies the dominant system of male privilege. See also DiAngelo (2018) on race as a system of cultural advantage.

[12] Mataji argues that women-led organizations such as Akhara Pari should, at least initially, be funded by the male mainstream tradition and the state and central governments of India, to equalize monastic women's chances for education, training, and leadership representation.

[13] In making this argument, I draw on the insights of the feminist philosopher Tomm (1991).

20.4 A Female Shankaracharya's Religious Grammar of Autonomy as "Leaking" from Women

Before we move any further, it will be helpful to take a deep dive into the metaphorical sea of Hindi terminology that Mataji uses to conceptualize what I am denoting by the term "autonomy." To a large extent, Mataji models through her leadership the normativity of female autonomy that she envisages for women, and particularly, for female *sadhus*.[14] In speaking about autonomy, Mataji sometimes uses the Sanskritic term *svatantratā* (translated as "freedom" or "liberation"). Mostly, though, she refers to the intertwined, self-constituting aspects of thinking, feeling, and doing so, she underscores that "women themselves" can and should develop these competencies to advance their equality in religion and other social spheres in which they are oppressed. More often than not, Mataji peppers her statements on "equality" with the personal pronoun "svayam." It means "oneself," "by oneself," "on one's own," and "of one's own accord." It is a term from which the Indic language concept of *svayambhu* is derived.[15]

In the Sanskrit language, the word *svayambhu* comes from the verbal root *bhū*, which means "to be," "to arise," and "to exist." It is used in Hindi language religious discourse to refer to a deity who "manifests" in acts of creation. As a "self-born" life force, a *svayambhu* god acts of its own desire and freedom and, thus, wills its existence in the universe. For instance, stones, rocks, and other formations that resemble the phallic-like symbol of the lingam, an aniconic image connected with the god Shiva, are called "svayambhu" by Hindus in northern India and elsewhere. Such naturally occurring objects are said to represent the "self-manifesting" presence and power of the deity—in this case, Shiva (Rao, 2019, 113–114).[16] Hence, *svayambhu* (i.e., the impulse for the divine to self-emerge) is thought to be a constitutive attribute of divinity in Hindu cultures. It represents an agentive principle (and life potential) immanent in the world of creation. The god appears by virtue of the authority of its own "wish" (*icchā*). It is the god's "right" as the ultimate absolute that is understood in Hindu tradition to create, sustain, and destroy the world (Fig. 20.4). The application of *svayambhu* to material objects not only implies the notion of divine intentionality at work in the manifest world, but also spotlights a linguistic context for imagining the autonomous (self-asserting) capacities of divinity in Hindu society (see Fig. 20.5).

For Mataji, *svayambhu* characterizes an agentive capacity mediated by divinity. However, because, as she also says, the world is born of the combination of divine love (*prem*) and desire (*iccha*), it inherits divinity's "self-manifesting" potential, which I have denoted as "autonomy." According to Mataji, *svayambhu* represents the dynamic, self-determining principle of life, and is sacred. Exercising that power enables living creatures to experience love for an interdependent creation. It discloses an embodied modality through which life manifests its inherent sacrality.

---

[14] See Khandelwal et al. (2006).

[15] McGregor, editor (2002).

[16] The *svayambhu* principle is not limited to Śiva but is understood as intrinsic to the great gods, such as Vishnu. See Lucia (2021).

Fig. 20.4 Images of the monkey-god Hanuman (left), the goddess Gayatri (represented in a three-dimensional form between main images and in a poster image at the back), and the goddess Durga (right) enshrined at Mataji's temple, 2014. Author's collection

Fig. 20.5 Mataji narrates her life story to the author, 2018. Author's collection

Thus, as Mataji reasons, autonomy is crucial to normative human development, and especially to women's personal and social development within oppressive structures.[17]

In this framework, *svayambhu* power underlies and drives the process of autonomy.[18] A metaphor may help to clarify Mataji's idea of how autonomy works in practice. *Svayambhu* power operates like the flow of electrical current present in the cosmos that is channeled into humans by means of their creation and, like switching on the light, activates their innate aptitude to act and function independently. Humans, like other life forms, are "wired into" the cosmic "circuit." That connection allows for *svayambhu* power to manifest within them. While human affect, aspiration, and activity quicken that power-flow, *svayambhu* is generated automatically in the natural world and can be accessed by humans. As a quotidian trait, autonomy comes as naturally as breathing or blinking. For Mataji, it *is* life. We might say, as she has suggested, that autonomy "leaks" out of humans such that constricting its expression denies their right to life.

Although the term *svayambhu* is used in reference to Shiva, Mataji applies it both to Shakti and Shiva. This is noteworthy, because Mataji's association of self-assertion with female divinity alludes to a concept of feminine potential that recognizes autonomy as essential to women's health and well-being. Her discourses heighten the legitimacy of independent feminine power to exist and act for and by itself.[19] She affirms the righteousness of women realizing their full potential without perceiving themselves as violating virtuous womanhood.[20] From this angle, *sadhus*' actualizing autonomy depicts at the levels of personal and collective transformation, the divine "manifesting of self" which Mataji's *svayambhu* status underscores *par excellence.*

According to Mataji, the idea of the "self" designates two interlinked meanings. The first involves Mataji's correlation of "self" with the divine inner self (*ātmā*), which she suggests autonomy brings forth through people's purposeful engagement with others. To be clear, "self" does not reference the ego-self (*ahaṅkār*) that Hindu discourse equates with a person's insatiable material nature and temporal desires that must be subdued to achieve self-realization (*mokṣa*).

Another meaning implied in Mataji's use of "self-manifesting" to support female autonomy is this: Knowing the "self" involves knowing oneself to be Śakti, the Goddess (*devī*), incarnate—that one's freedom to be, think, act, move, and be in ways that honor the integrity of the divine feminine materializes Shakti's "self-manifesting" power in the temporal sphere. To that extent, autonomy and Shakti represent equivalent life forces of independent female power for Mataji. She teaches

[17] I am referencing Nita Kumar's writing on the formation of female subjectivity as being shaped by "parallel discourses." See Kumar, editor (1994).

[18] Mataji's understanding of autonomy extends to all life forms, but for the sake of simplicity, I'll limit my discussion to human autonomy.

[19] See also Tomm (1991, pp. 91–99).

[20] Ibid, p. 95.

this theology of woman-goddess equation in the *sansads* in which she participates.[21] For instance, in the *sansad* cited earlier, Mataji says that "In India, we worship the feminine principle as *shakti*. We say that Mother is supreme; She is the first teacher and supreme life-giver, because She is *shakti*. But how can we worship Shakti if we suppress women's power? My thinking is that we worship Śakti by respecting women's freedom. This is the right [*adhikar*] of women who are Shakti."

From the perspective of Mataji's theology, a *sadhu* can neither know the "self" nor recognize Shakti as the active potentiality of the "self" unless she is determined to "meet the self." This requires the *sadhu* to make a relationship with herself. Mataji says that the *sadhu*'s self-relationship impacts her life and overall health as significantly as her relationship with divinity. It generates feminine self-love (i.e., love precisely for those qualities that Hindu orthodoxy reviles) and the deep sense of the woman's dignity and authority. Through it, the *sadhu* learns to see herself as a person worthy of her own affection and respect; as valuable as those to whom Hindu society accords normative status. Mataji's prescription for fashioning feminine self-love does not diminish the value of interpersonal relationships but focuses *sadhus*' vision toward an alternate horizon that illuminates the ontological parity of women's and men's status. For *sadhus* to realize that they participate in Shakti's independent nature because of their female sex inspires an understanding of autonomy as normative for women. Exercising autonomy accomplishes Shakti's "self-manifesting" in, through, and with female bodies in action. Let us turn now to Mataji's personal stories as a householder and an ascetic to consider how narrative practice promotes the institutional and personal autonomy of female monastics as a normative right.

20.5 "I Showed My Durga *Rūp*!": The Righteous Insubordination of a Householder Woman

Over the years, Mataji's relationship with Durga has been a source of her charismatic authority. It inspired her mobilization of the "first" women's monastic order of India. Since its formation in 2014, Pari Akhara has evolved into a women's liberation movement. Its creation gives form and purpose to the awesome female potential that Mataji associates with Durga, showing women and girls what autonomy, as the agentive power of the goddess, makes possible.

Many of my interactions with Mataji consist of her attributing the indefatigable spirit of religious change that she claims to embody in her ability to confront and eradicate oppression, to Durga's power and love for her (see Fig. 20.6). "Who can do what I have done?" Mataji asks me. Her statement comes in response to my question about how she is able to persevere in her quest, despite the coordinated resistance from the Hindu nationalist state government and religious orthodoxy. "Who can live like me? Who can face what I have? This is all Durga's blessings (*āśirvād*). Mother's

[21] The phrase "woman-goddess equation" is drawn from the work of Madhu Khanna. See Khanna (2002).

power is functioning through me." Durga's symbolism supplies the mythic matrix for Mataji to make meaning of her life in contexts of personal narrative performance.

In narrating her experiences as a married householder, Mataji emphasizes specific dramatic moments in which she "showed her Durga form [*rup*]" to men who acted inappropriately with her or tried to harm her. The phrase "to show Durga's form" illustrates a pervasive cultural idiom in India. It articulates Mataji's understanding that she became the human form of Durga's ferocity to defend herself against unwanted male attention and behavior. We could say that, in "showing [her] Durga *rup*," Mataji went into her "warrior goddess mode."

Fig. 20.6 Temple image of the ferocious goddess Kali (who is a *shakti* that emerges from Durga's body during the battle), placing her right foot on top of Shiva's torso at the Shri Camunda Nandikeshwar Mandir, Dharmasala, India, 2018. Author's collection

It is common to hear Hindu women in India make explicit reference to "putting on" the Durga *rup* (McDaniel, 2004, 222).[22] According to the scholar of Indian religions June McDaniel, "the Durga *rupa*...represents Durga's personality, strength, and virtue" (ibid). This aspect of Durga's power gives expression to a heroic form of femininity that women can evoke for self-protection. It emerges when women feel enraged, threatened, misunderstood, cheated, and violated (Kishwar n.d., 18). The Indian scholar-activist, Madhu Kishwar has talked about "playing Durga" many times in her life. Kishwar has written, "Even without being a Durga devotee, I unconsciously began to successfully 'play Durga' in dealing with a whole range of situations, from sexual harassment to...bringing under control neighborhood drunkards and wife beaters" (ibid).

To be clear, English translations such as "putting on," "showing" or "playing" Durga can be misleading, implying that Durga acts as a persona for protection (that she does not enter into the bodies of the women invoking her). McDaniel clarifies that such phrases in Indic contexts "mean taking on an emanation body. Durga does not put on a mask when she takes an embodied form, she enters into it fully."[23] Hence, my use of the phrase "showed her Durga form" to describe Mataji's experience underscores Mataji's view that Durga enters into her body and acts through her. In fact, so interwoven into the "habitus" of Indic cultures is the notion that the Durga *rup* emanates from women in real or perceived danger (notice that Kishwar does not identify as Durga's devotee) that it also appears in contexts of Mataji's talking about her life.[24]

One time, Mataji was walking to the local bazaar, and a man driving a car stopped and asked her where she was headed. He offered to take Mataji to her destination. "Let me help you," he pleaded. Despite her intentionally ignoring him, the man would not leave Mataji alone and continued to follow her. Fed up with what she calls the man's "harassment" (*śosan*), Mataji says, "I made my face cruel [like Durga's] and thought now he will leave me alone." He did.

On another occasion, a married friend of her (former) husband came to the home Mataji and her spouse shared in Prayagraj. I will call this friend "Raj." As Mataji describes him, Raj was a lively person and "joked around a lot." He often brought gifts and other goods for Mataji's family. One day, as Mataji remembers the incident, Raj violated the customary codes of conduct in his behavior with Mataji as the wife of another man (Raj's friend). She says,

> We were all sitting together, and he [Raj] poked me. He poked me like this [Mataji pokes herself with her index finger on her midsection]. I immediately showed him my Durga *rup*. I scolded him for this act. I warned him, "Listen, never touch me again! You talk to me from

[22] Many of the female *sādhus* with whom I worked in Rajasthan and Uttar Pradesh made reference to this idiom in their interactions with me. For example, a *sādhu* named Maya Nath shared a harrowing story of becoming Durga when she heard thieves trying to break into her ashram in the middle of the night.

[23] June McDaniel, Personal Communication via email, May 19, 2023.

[24] We could look to the example of women, gurus and householders, from the Hindu nationalist front who have invoked Durga's image to mobilize women's participation in movements against Indian minorities, such as Muslims.

> a distance. If you have something to say to me, say it from a distance. If you want to joke, that's fine, but don't touch me again!" [Raj] told me, "Your elder sister-in-law [*bhābī*] is better than you." He pointed towards her. I told him, "Let her be. If I am bad, then let me be bad."

No relationship caused Mataji more anguish (*duhkh*) than that of her marital bond. After her father died in the 1980s, Mataji's elder brother and eldest sister arranged Mataji's and her youngest sister's marriages in order to fulfill the deceased father's paternal duty. Mataji was twenty years old, and her sister was eighteen years old. From the beginning, Mataji's marriage was troubled. As she soon learned, everything that Mataji's family had been told about her husband was a lie. He was not a doctor but rather a compounder[25] who worked for a doctor in a hospital in Prayagraj; he did not own a home but instead lived rent free in a room at the hospital. The man could barely support himself, let alone Mataji. But the hardest blow for Mataji was discovering the serial infidelity of her philandering spouse. Mataji's confronting him about his intolerable behavior did not change the situation. He did not seem to care about her feelings.

Theirs was a volatile relationship. Many of their quarrels involved Mataji's wanting to study nursing and naturopathic medicine and work outside the home in order that she could support their family and send their children to good schools. She pursued her postsecondary education, but not without constant opposition from her husband and his family (Mataji worked as a midwife for nearly a decade and received the highest level of Ayurvedic medicine training before she became employed as a social worker with the NGO in Benares, as mentioned earlier).

What Mataji and her husband fought over has to do with Mataji's exercising of female autonomy. This is the leitmotif of her stories around which she performs her sense of self. Mataji conceives of autonomy as her birthright. It accomplishes her right to be free of male domination. In the light of her narratives, autonomy is akin to being alive. It's as integral to life as breath itself. Mataji's husband sought to repress her autonomy by restricting her movements within and beyond the domicile. Mataji describes the mental "torture" and the physical and financial abuse that she endured from her husband, because she refused to submit to his control. Mataji's Durga *rup* emanates when her husband interferes with her exercising that birthright. She says,

> My husband tortured me so much. I felt that he liked to tease me. He laughed when I cried or when I scolded him. I thought what type of man is he that he enjoys irritating me? Slowly, I tried to leave him. He came to know of my intentions. This next incident happened on the morning that I was to go to Benares. There were two doors in our house. When I approached one door, he blocked my path. When I moved my body, he shifted his body to stop me from leaving the house. Now, this happened for ten minutes and I became really upset. I got so angry that I slapped him. I told him, "You [expletive], you don't let me live! When I am going you are not letting me go." When I was standing near the door, my elder-brother-in-law was standing at this distance and my elder sister-in-law was standing at that distance. They blocked both of the entrances so that I couldn't leave. I slapped my husband twice really hard on the cheeks. He grabbed me and held me so tightly that I couldn't move. He would not let me leave. I spit on his face without realizing it. Yeah, I became really angry.

[25] A compounder characterizes a person who mixes medicines and works under a pharmacist.

Mataji's anger explodes to epic proportions in her last confrontation with her soon to be ex-husband. By this point in her life, she is living alone in Benares, and her children are staying in a boarding school in Benares that she has been paying for with the earnings from her NGO work. Her salary was good enough that Mataji could also afford to build a house in the city. She returns to Prayagraj to file divorce papers. To her horror, she hears by way of local gossip that her husband is telling people that she left him for another man. On her way to the court, Mataji runs into her husband and his lawyer in front of the court building. Her advocate, whom Mataji has informed of her spouse's alleged rumors about her infidelity, turns to her and says, "You want to beat him? Go ahead, beat him." Then, tucking the part of her sari that was draped over her shoulders into her blouse, Mataji removes her slipper and approaches her husband. She says,

> With the slipper in my hand, I hit him here and there. I abused him [verbally]. Am I a prostitute [*raṇḍī*]? Am I a prostitute? Take this. All of this happened in front of the court. It was summertime. After I beat him, I took my seat at the stall [where divorce papers are prepared]. I didn't run. The person whom I never called "tum"[26] [second-person pronoun for "you"] in front of anyone, I raised my hand on him that day and called him "tum," not "ap." Everybody scolded him for letting his wife beat him. They said he brought the name of menfolk to shame. Even the lawyers who were standing around were instigating him. I saw him coming at me with his shoe in his hand. He held it in the same style that I held my slipper. I was watching him coming. I took my slipper and hit him as hard as I could. I hit him so hard that he had to run away from there. Those who were watching me said that I became the incarnation [*avatar*] of Durga. When I started beating him, he had to release himself and run. I had decided that if anytime in the future he will come in front of me, I will pierce his chest [with a weapon] just like Devi Durga pierced the chest of the demon Mahisha. I thought I will make him remember everything. He then removed himself from my hold. I decided that day that I will never live with him again…I had decided on that day that I will never let him hurt me again.

Every time Mataji acts in her Durga *rup*, whether to confront, chastise, or clobber the men whom she perceives as violating her, she feels morally right in her actions. Recall her words to "Raj," her husband's friend, "If I am bad, then let me be bad." If being a "good woman" means allowing a man, a relative and otherwise, to touch her inappropriately, then Mataji would rather be a "bad" woman and keep her self-respect intact. Rejecting Hindu orthodoxy's concept of the *pativratā*, Mataji refuses to accept that her husband, or any man, is superior to her and that his male sex grants him ownership of her body. In Brahmanical Hinduism, the concept of the *pativrata* describes the ideal wife who vows (*vrat*) to treat her husband (*pati*) as her Lord. She defers to his authority and serves her conjugal family with obedience. The *pativrata* symbolizes what Deepa Narayan terms the "compulsive pleaser" (2018, 97). The woman whose existence is validated by pleasing others while denying herself. She

[26] In the Hindi language, "tum" refers to the second-person pronoun used for people of the same rank. Hindi recognizes three forms of the second-person pronoun, namely *ap*, *tum*, and *tu*. Whereas "ap" denotes a respectful way of speaking to someone or to one's superior (e.g., a boss, a teacher, a guru, etc.), 'tu' is used for subordinates. Traditionally, wives are expected to call their husbands "ap" in public. By calling her husband "tum," Mataji signals her loss of respect for him (and his demotion of status).

lives to please and is pleased to serve others. The *pativrata* is selfless. She reveals Hindu orthodoxy's exemplar of ideal femininity.

But *pativrata* womanhood—deferential, selfless womanhood—is not the feminine identity endorsed by Mataji. For her, respectable femininity extends beyond the dominant male imaginary. Her narratives encourage the uncommon view that women who respect themselves *are*, in fact, "good"; that women who stand up to and spurn the cultural expectation for women to please men, along with the larger cultural system of male entitlement, *are*, in fact, virtuous. By equating her behavior with Durga's, Mataji's narratives perform what Durga's myth makes apparent: the idea of the righteousness of female insubordination against the male sex right.

Drawing on the critical insights of feminist theorists, I use the concept of "the male sex right" to designate the socially sanctioned right of men to dominate women. Narayan implies this idea in her deft observation that Indian culture trains women to think that men, and in reality patriarchal society, own and control women's bodies (2019, 40–42). She says that this "deep training" teaches women to become invisible (102). Beginning in childhood, and continuing throughout their lives, women learn from their families, teachers, bosses, the police, the media, and the society to 'stay put,' 'speak little,' 'hide their bodies,' 'want less,' and 'adapt more.' These culturally desirable behaviors epitomize the patriarchal ideal of "womanly goodness" (78).

From a feminist critical perspective, the male sex right cashes in on this training. It renders explicit the unspoken "cultural arrangement" that makes it socially acceptable for some men to feel entitled to women's bodies and expect sex from them (Narayan, 2019, 148).[27] Historian Carole Pateman has written that the male sex right constitutes "the power that men exercise over women" (cited from Tomm, 1991, 85), but also signals the 'original social contract…which explains why [that] right is legitimate' (Ibid). Winnie Tomm has extended Pateman's theory to elucidate that "[The social] contract initiates the patriarchal right…[T]he assumed natural male sex right [grants] access to women's bodies…giving power to men over women's bodies in a way that women do not have over men's bodies" (88). Tomm has said:

> If we look at the structuring of social relations throughout history (whether in social contracts, such as marriage or employer-worker arrangements, or informal social relations between the sexes) with the idea that they were shaped by the sexual contract, then we perceive the social relations between the sexes to be fundamentally characterized by dominance-subordination. A woman who enters into social relations between the sexes and who does not accept that hierarchical relation (either implicitly or explicitly) commits an act of insubordination. Feminist theory and the women's social movement constitute a collective act of insubordination (Tomm, 1991, 85).

To that extent, the feminist concept of the "male sex right" magnifies the deep structures of prevailing attitudes of male superiority and female inferiority, and the customary practices indoctrinating women into the moral authority of male privilege by surveilling their bodies, muffling their voices, and punishing them with violence. But this right shows up in other, more subtle ways, too. From another

[27] See also Manne (2018), who critiques patriarchal systems that entitle men, as a dominant status group, to feel that they are owed women's bodies and sex, for their attention, protection, and support.

angle, it valorizes the socially ascribed powers of women correlated with marriage and reproduction. As Kathleen Erndl has argued in her scholarship:

> [T]he Hindu patriarchal impulse to subordinate women is rooted in the acknowledgement that women are powerful...[It] glorifies women, celebrating their auspiciousness and life-giving powers...[O]n the other hand, [it] prescribes women's dependence upon male protectors. These [views] are not at all contradictory. They recognize women's power and propose to control it for patriarchal purposes" (Erndl, 2000, 96).

Mataji's insubordination against men's attempts to control and harass her resists more than a nebulous "patriarchy." It opposes the underlying cultural double-standard that renders acceptable the systemic oppression, exploitation, silencing, demeaning of and violence against women across social spectra (Narayan, 2019; Nagar/Sangtin Writers, 2006). Such "Durgafied" resistance, as I shall characterize this alternative embodiment of righteous femininity, models Mataji's view of the sanctity of female insubordination against the patriarchal right. In her view, Durgafied womanhood represents Durga herself stepping forth to punish the men who harm them. Similarly, Mataji's righteous insubordination suggests her perception that the materializing of Durga's presence through the bodies and behaviors of women enacts on the mundane plane of existence Durga's refusal to relinquish her autonomy to any form of male control. From Mataji's standpoint, male control over female autonomy is tantamount to quashing the independent female power that *is* Durga. To protect the female birthright to "self-manifest," Durga appears when she feels threatened. Every time. Thus, the epiphany of Durga happens immediately and automatically. It is emotional, physical, and *violent*, acting at once to rectify gender injustice.

After narrating the stories featured earlier, Mataji commented that she "always acted with dignity." The term that she used for "dignity" was "maryādā." Also a polyvalent concept, *maryada* denotes a "limit," "correct behavior," "self-respect," and "dignity; honour."[28] For Mataji, showing her Durga *rup* inhabits the parameters of desirable femininity. By this logic, I suggest that the behaviors that Mataji exhibits to protect her right to what the feminist philosopher Martha Nussbaum has termed "bodily integrity" (1999, 41) expand the feminine ideal in a generative way. Her "becoming Durga" actualizes a liberating vision of womanhood, according to which autonomy and dignity operate as co-constitutive elements of women's status, respect, and authority. By emphasizing the righteousness of female insubordination against the male sex right, Mataji advances that autonomy as Durga's "self-manifesting" through women *is* virtuous. It exacts that which Mataji's Hinduism recognizes as fundamental—their right to exist.

[28] McGregor (2002, 794).

20.6 "No God Has the Right to Control Durga!": The Righteous Insubordination of a Goddess

Let me clarify: Durga's symbolism derives from the textual and ritualistic resources associated with Brahmanical Hinduism (Bose, 2018; Coburn, 1991; Erndl, 1993; Humes, 2000; Kinsley, 1988). Hindu orthodoxy conceives of a supreme, independent power in the anthropomorphized image of a woman who makes life and its becoming possible and who possesses the attributes of omniscience and omnipresence. But the formidable personality of the goddess appearing as the invincible warrior queen Durga arises *only* in times of crisis. She shows up insofar as *dharm* (cosmic order, balance, and virtue) has become threatened by malevolent powers, whose lust for power, greed, and selfishness have turned the normal order of the universe upside-down.[29] This reversal of *dharm* renders the gods powerless against the demons.

Indeed, Durga arrives when the world is in shambles. Her presence illustrates a response to an unusual cosmic situation (Kinsley, 1988, 97). The gods themselves do not interact with Durga regularly or to the extent that they interact with other females like the milder Parvati, from whose skin, in some of the myths,[30] Durga emerges, and who is Shiva's consort (Dimmitt & van Buitenen, 1978). Not only their impotence, but their anger triggers the supernova of Durga's brilliant manifestation. Once she appears, the gods offer her their praises and their weapons.[31] After Durga completes her task of vanquishing evil, the gods once again glorify Durga through paeans and then bid her farewell (she returns to the Vindhya mountains where she is said to dwell and where she lives in isolation from other cosmic forces). The gods know who and what Durga is. They recognize the awesome, and yet, intimidating power that is Durga and do not interfere in her business (instead, they watch her battle the demons from afar). They know that this goddess can wipe out evil all by herself. This is why they have summoned Durga.

Dharm's reversal releases a magnificent female force, unlike any other in the pantheon, that restores the natural order of the universe that was there before the calamity began. But this cosmic U-turn of *dharm*, as some scholars have argued, also leads to the reversal of ideal femininity by the goddess. Durga steps forward in this transitional, but nonetheless temporary, moment of chaos and demonstrates the salvific purpose of her divine existence. Perhaps there is no better time than a crisis situation for women to step out of conventional gender molds and assert themselves in ways that the dominant discourse on womanhood has otherwise suppressed. As the historian of religion David Kinsley has said, Durga "is created because the situation calls for a woman" (1988, 97). The male gods want to subdue and destroy the demons, but they simply cannot. Durga, however, has all the power now, and she battles

---

[29] See Kinsley (1988, pp. 95–113).

[30] This is a version of Durga's "creation" story featured in the third chapter of the *Devi-Mahatmya*. See Coburn's (1991).

[31] An observant male colleague pointed out that perhaps the gods "do this [give their weapons to the goddess] to make sure she knows they are not enemy combatants." Matt Calhoun, Personal Communication, March 29, 2023.

against evil with aplomb. According to Kinsley, Durga's behavior on the battlefield amplifies this reversal of the ideal woman to cosmic heights. He has observed that, "Durga violates the model of the Hindu woman. She is not submissive, she is not subordinated to a male deity, she does not fulfill household duties, and she excels at what is traditionally a male function, fighting in battle...she reverses the normal role for females...Unlike the normal female, Durga...takes power from the male gods in order to perform her own heroic exploits" (Ibid; see also Sugirtharajah, 2002, 6).[32]

However, I want to nuance Kinsley's deft observation and propose another interpretation based on Mataji's performance of the myth. Although Durga's strong, independent nature would appear to reverse the gender order, she does not violate the universal order (*dharm*). Rather, she reverses cosmic disorder to revive *dharm*. She does not violate the power of good over evil. Nor does she defy the divine *stri svadharm* to which she is beholden and which she embodies "[a]s an independent warrior who can hold her own against any male on the battlefield" (Kinsley, 1998, 97).

Moreover, if, as the Brahmanical version of the myth and the epithets used by the gods for the goddess suggest, Durga represents the divine mother, it would seem that she acts as a mother (or guardian) might given the situation. Does a mother breach her femininity by protecting those she loves from harm even if her actions are violent? Arguably, it comes with the territory of being a responsible parent. As the universal mother, Durga conducts herself in accordance with the specificity of her role. She becomes aggressive toward the aggressors who deliberately wreak havoc on the gods and world of creation, which doubly signify the children of the goddess. Even the cosmos symbolically designates the goddess' body such that an attack on it is equivalent to an attack on Durga. This is not an acceptable outcome to the goddess. Durga's violent behavior enacts *righteous feminine behavior*; conceived by a patriarchal logic, it depicts an intensification of maternal femininity, which she hoists to a ferocious level in the battle.

Thus, Mataji's interpretation of the myth counters Kinsley's claim that Durga "violates" ideal gender norms. Her performance *reverses the patriarchal femininity of Brahmanical Hinduism by representing Durga's womanhood as normative for female self-actualization and virtue*. Using Mataji's feminist hermeneutics, I would argue that Durga's conduct is gender appropriate for righteous motherhood and *for a goddess of her class*. It is not a violation of *her* feminine *dharm as a martial* deity. In other words, though Durga is a mother goddess, she is also a female warrior divinity; in this way, she is different from the other female divinities (and divine mothers) who are married householders and whose power is derived from their mates.

To judge Durga by the standards appropriate for the other goddesses is like comparing apples and oranges. As the divine protectress, Durga illustrates the womanly virtue that distinguishes the key elements of her heroic personality and warrior goddess *dharm*. This reading intersects with Kinsley's insight that what appears to be Durga's "violation" of patriarchal femininity is necessary, because the

---

[32] Sugirtharajah (2002) talks about gender reversals in the context of *bhakti* saints, but the comparison with unconventional goddesses such as Durga can be made as well.

rules of the cosmos have changed. She only fights against the demons who disrupt *dharm*'s normal flow, not all men (see Fig. 20.8). Durga's unfettered and liberated behavior stands to magnify her beneficent relationship to *dharm* as the force of cosmic good but also to the expectations according to which *a female* may exist righteously. Because she is Durga, she has the right to live in accordance with her dharmic *raison d'être*, which is, as Mataji interprets Durga's symbolism, to live on her own terms and free of the male sex right.

Although Brahmanical patriarchy's vision of divine femininity accords pride of place to the independent female power that Durga's myth renders transparent, it is a liminal and temporary one, nevertheless. To cite Kinsley, "In her role reversal, Durga exists outside normal structures" (1988, 99). Durga occupies a "betwixt and between" status.[33] Because Durga's symbolism—or, in my terms, "Durgafied femininity"—holds an ambivalent status within the sacred canopy of Brahmanical patriarchy, it is virtuous as long as *dharm* is disabled. Once *dharm* returns to its original state through Durga's heroic actions, the value, necessity, and *presence* of Durgafied womanhood decreases in a rehabilitated cosmos. During the period that she inhabits the universe, Durga achieves the level of transformation that only a goddess of her order can effect. But Durga embodies too potent, and by implication, too potentially subversive, a (female) presence for a cosmos wherein *dharm* (order; harmony) has been recuperated (see Fig. 20.7). As the Sanskritic tradition would have it, Durga does not overstay her welcome. Rather, the goddess takes off immediately after the deed is done, making sure to live far away from everyone else.

Received understandings that women's showing of their Durga *rup* occurs as a direct response to their experiences of being harmed allude not only to the idea of Durga's liminality, but also to the potentially subversive aspect of the goddess's power after it has emerged. On the one hand, Durga's challenging the sex right of the demons implies that no male has the authority to obstruct and imprison female autonomy. They intend to capture Durga and make her their lover by treating her as if she exists to satisfy their male fantasies. On the other hand, Durga's righteous insubordination portends the fate that awaits the man (divine or demonic) who tries. Durga's autonomy, therefore, inextricably interfaces with her *svadharm* and enacts a function of who she is as a female who "exists independent[ly] from male protection or guidance" (Kinsley, 1988, 99). But since Durga's autonomy is neither governed nor controlled by male power, it poses the risk for getting out-of-control and, consequentially, for destroying the natural order.[34]

Mataji's story about beating her husband with her slipper while in her Durga *rup* cues inherited cultural fears of the dangers associated with independent female power (i.e., women whose movements, bodies, and lives elude male control), and illuminates why it is perceived as threatening to the patriarchal order. The autonomy evidenced

---

[33] Interestingly, there are few Durga temples in India, meaning temples dedicated to Durga. Personal communication with June McDaniel, AAR, San Diego, November 25, 2019.

[34] In the *Devi-Mahatmya*'s representation of the goddess, Kali represents the manifestation of Durga's rage against the male demons who have sexually objectified and humiliated her; thus, Kali's emanation signifies the unleashing of raw feminine power against evil.

through means of Mataji's actions dramatically dislodges the male sex right by both claiming women's right to be treated with dignity and respect and interrogating the oppressive logic underlying patriarchal womanhood.[35] Her increasing autonomy to control her affairs parallels her husband's loss of control and power over her. By losing control, the husband forfeits his social contract of sexual power over Mataji. This is unacceptable to the crowd of men, many of whom are attorneys, and who as bystanders witness this incredible manifestation of heroic femininity. They shame the husband for what they consider a humiliating blow to some imagined notion of Indian manhood and proceed to wound his ego further by calling him a disgrace to "menfolk." More troubling is their goading him to reclaim his right to bring his woman under his control by inflicting on Mataji a beating worse than the one she gave him. For these men, a "real" man dominates his woman into submission.

Try as he might, the husband fails to subordinate Mataji. Instead, scared by the impressive force standing before him, which through Mataji's narration, performatively becomes the Durga power appearing through Mataji, or perhaps being unleashed by her, he loses courage and runs away. He has to free himself of Mataji's grip, otherwise Mataji acting in her Durga "avatar" may kill him (see Figs. 20.7 and 20.8). In the eyes of the passersby, Mataji's unleashed rage transforms into the magnificently fierce form of Durga (also called Kali/Camunda) who slays the half man, half buffalo demon named Mahishasura (literally, "the demon [*asura*] Mahisha").

This version of Durga is glorified as *Mahishasuramardini*, the "slayer of Mahisha," in various forms of Hinduism, and the *Devi-Mahatmya* describes her as "Death enraged" (4.2.13; see Fig. 20.8).[36] Maybe, as with Mahisha, this is the terrible face of death that Mataji's husband sees and from which he flees. Like the passersby in Mataji's story, the gods also witness the annihilatory force of Durga's anger and tremble with "ecstasy" at its valor (4.1.2).[37] Mahisha's shape-shifting power (he turns into a lion, then an elephant, and then resumes his buffalo form) raises Durga's hackles. She becomes so "angry"[38] by the demon's imbecile games (he has to use trickery to defeat her) that, "quaff[ing] a superior beverage, [a]nd...with reddened eyes," Durga exhorts:

> Roar, roar for a moment, O fool, while I drink (this) nectar! When you are slain here by me, it is the gods who soon will roar! (3.36.38)...Having spoken thus and springing up, she mounted the great Asura. Having struck him with her foot, she beat him with her spear (3.37.40). Then he, struck with her foot, came forth out of his own mouth, [c]ompletely hemmed by the valor of the Goddess (3.38.41). That great Asura...was felled by the Goddess, Who had cut off his head with a great sword (3.39.42) (*Devi-Mahatmya*, Coburn translation 1991, 47).

After Mahisha's defeat, the gods "graciously" solicit Durga for boons relating to their own and the world's welfare; she agrees (or "consents") and then "disappear[s]" (4.33.39). Likewise, after beating her husband in public, Mataji, too, leaves the scene.

[35] See Manne (2018, pp. 84–91).

[36] Coburn translation (1991, p. 49).

[37] Ibid, p. 46.

[38] Ibid. 3.33, p. 47.

Fig. 20.7 Gouache painting depicting Durga Mahishasuramardini in battle with the buffalo-demon. The goddess Kali, who is shown seated on the battlefield behind Durga absorbs drops of the demon's blood with her tongue while Durga slays the demon[39]

She decides to permanently cut ties with the man and his family, promising herself never to let him harm her again. Mataji knows, in fact, that she can never "live with" him again, not without endangering herself, and that is not an option for her. She says, "I knew he would kill me because I insulted him a lot."

While the Durga of Hindu orthodoxy retreats from the world, Mataji does not. This incident would have occurred in 2000, while Mataji was working for the women's and children's development NGO in Benares. Her daughter would have been preparing for post-secondary school, and her son would have been enrolled in college. Long before joining the NGO, however, Mataji had dedicated herself to working on increasing and improving women's welfare (recall the promise she made to her guru), and that journey began by changing the conditions and quality of her own life. Years before she separated from her husband and family, Mataji, under the guidance of a family guru, started reading the *Bhagavad Gītā*. Mataji's study of the text deepened her understanding that "no one belongs to me and no one is mine." In 2018 she said,

[39] Mahisauramardini; Durga slaying the buffalo demon, Mahishasura. Gouache painting by an Indian painter. Gouaches. Place: <A HREF = https://wellcomecollection.org/>Wellcome Collection </A>. https://library-artstor-org.ezproxy.tcu.edu/asset/24902975.

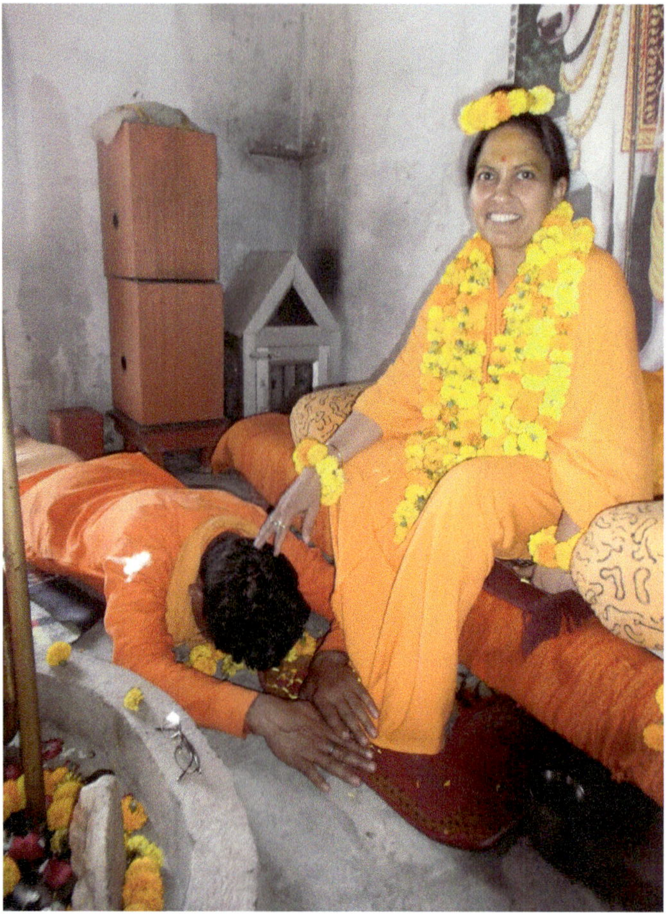

Fig. 20.8 Mataji blesses a male disciple at her temple, 2014. Author's collection

> When I started reading the *Gita*, I got detached from the materialistic world. And, equally important was that I recited prayers and performed rituals daily to reduce the suffering of others. The first spiritual vow (*vrat*) I ever took was to work on my spiritual life. I learned that whatever I have received in life, I should accept it with love. When you no longer have the things that have moved away from you [e.g., a loyal husband and a happy marriage], you should accept that from today it doesn't belong to you. I started believing this. Till then I struggled a lot. I filed for divorce. I got into fights. I faced many pressures. There was the pressure of my family and my children. I endured it, because I became detached. By 2000, I had taken a mental vow of *sannyas* [i.e., Mataji had chosen to renounce without taking formal ritual initiation from a guru]. I thought, I am ready to become a *sadhu*. I am ready to do this for the entire society. I am part of this society.[40]

[40] Personal interview with Mataji, June 8, 2018.

Family troubles may have precipitated Mataji's decision to renounce householding (which is not to suggest that she sees them as the cause for her becoming a *sadhu*), but her vow of "mental sannyas" does not cut her off from the world. Her relationship to the society, and especially to its underserved women and girls, strengthens because of her detachment (*vairāg*).[41] Detached from the sorrows of householding life occasioned by her husband's deception, Mataji gives her spouse the house that they shared in Prayagraj, refusing to battle him over property she has no use for. In this way, she frees herself from the ties which trapped her in the endless cycle of pain and suffering. She understands now the deeper meaning and purpose of her life. By cultivating detachment through ritual, dietary, and other practices, Mataji becomes immersed in the world in a way that she could not as a householder, and she becomes convinced of her role (*svadharm*) to help others. This is the duty for which, according to Mataji, she "was born [to do]." Mataji says, "I've never felt that I was born to do housework or ordinary things. God put me on this earth to reduce the suffering of humanity. To reduce people's despair and troubles."

Through narrative performance, Mataji interweaves her feminine identity with Durga's to heighten her alternative authority as the female Shankaracharya. Her interpretation of the myth locates Durga's symbolism within a potent religious feminist hermeneutic by ascribing female autonomy normative value (i.e., it is not simply an attribute that appears only in response to women's being endangered; it *is* Durga emanating from them for their self-actualization). Additionally, Mataji constructs Durgafied femininity as the *restoration* of the natural gender and moral order rather than a gender role reversal. Her representation effects a repositioning of independent female power at the apex of the divine hierarchy that not only reverses the patriarchal feminine ideal but as significantly proposes a new normativity for respectable womanhood, thereby sanctioning female monastic authority. In effect, she condemns religious patriarchy's repression of women's autonomy as a violation of *dharm*, by assimilating her role with Durga's, and female monastics' role with that of the *shaktis* that help Durga on the battlefield of *dharm*. Just as Durga battles against demonic forces, fortified by the army of *shaktis* that arise out of her body, Mataji sees herself as a warrior queen who, assisted by her army (*akhara*) of female *sadhus*, fights against the ruinous forces of sexual discrimination, inequality, and violence.

Thus, Mataji interprets Durga to be a goddess of a different order than Lakshmi, Parvati, and Saraswati, as householder goddesses. Similarly, because they are ascetics, female *sadhus* represent women of a different order than householders. To Mataji, the former group constitutes heroic women devoted to protecting *dharm* on the mundane plane. They function as Durga's earthly representatives, the human *shaktis* who, by leaving worldly life, dedicate themselves to *dharm*. For Mataji, different classes of women, divine and human, should live by a different set of *dharmas* and gender norms. It would appear that Mataji's interpretation of *dharm* is attuned to the specificities of its function among different classes of Hindu women.

---

[41] This attitude is not unique to Mataji but rather surfaces as a common theme in the lives of female *sannyasinīs* (renouncers) as described in the ethnographic studies of female asceticism in South Asia (Khandelwal et al., 2006).

Through this reasoning, she understands *sadhus*' feminine duty to work by different norms than the ones governing householders that nonetheless work to invert the standard patriarchal logic. In Mataji's reading of the myth, Durga's femininity establishes the sanctity of monastic women to live as they see fit.

Mataji stresses that she and her female "army of the free birds" (i.e., Pari Akhara) will "save society" by returning *dharm* to its "normal functioning."[42] To hold *sadhus* accountable to the gender norms of householders would interfere with their *dharm.* Like Durga who comes to rescue *dharm* in a disordered cosmos, Mataji says, "I have come forward to stop those who are looting the religion. I, the female Shankaracharya, will stop evil."[43] Thus, I argue that her reversal of patriarchal femininity through the normalization of Durgafied womanhood promotes the inversion of gender hierarchies within the monastic society to achieve greater gender parity.

20.7 A Lone *Shakti* in the Jungle: The Righteous Insubordination of a Female Guru

For Mataji, the problem is not female autonomy but religious patriarchy's suspicion and repression of it. This theme is clear in the next series of stories, which bring to the fore the interplay of interpersonal and institutional challenges with which ascetic women contend. From the perspective of Mataji's teachings, female autonomy, to use Erndl's language, "rescues *śakti* from its patriarchal prison" (2000, 96). Without autonomy, ascetic women's fulfillment of their religious callings and concerns would be difficult. The relationship that Mataji creates with Durga through a religious feminist reading of her myth serves as a reminder to female monastics to "'remember' [themselves] as [women] with normative ontological status" (Tomm, 1991, 78).

I begin with scene 1, which represents an episode extracted from a larger narrative account. Here, she speaks about a male leader (*bābā*) of an influential *akhara.* They met each other at the Kumbh Melā that occurred in Prayagraj in 2013. Like Mataji, the *baba* was also attending the fair, and having heard about her intention to make a separate *akhara* for female *sadhus*, he decided to pay Mataji a visit at her temple, to talk her out of that decision (see Fig. 20.9). Their meeting makes her aware of religious patriarchy's problem with female autonomy, whether it is realized by *sadhus* or by the founding of an ascetic order. This is her story:

> The *baba* came to my temple in 2013. He said that I was like Sati Anusuya in that I was doing *tapasyā* [penance] alone in the jungle. He asked me, "how will you be able to survive in the jungle by yourself?" He said that I was "powerful and great," but he kept asking me how would I live in the jungle where it is dangerous [for women to live alone]. He told me, "By doing all this *tapasya*, who can be a greater *sadhu* than you, Mataji? He asked me to join his *akhara.* He said that if I join, he'll make me a *mahāmandaleśwar* [leader] of his

[42] Mataji, June 9, 2018.

[43] Mataji, June 9, 2018.

> *akhara*. He promised me a big title. Being a *mahamandaleshwar* is no small thing. The *baba* said that if I join his order, he would do whatever I wanted. I said, "Mahraj-ji, I need to raise money to become a *mahamandaleshwar*." He said, "No, no, Mataji. I have the money. I will organize a *rath yātrā* [formal procession in which Mataji would be paraded in a chariot to honor her new status] for you. I will arrange a feast for you. I will give you a great name."
>
> At that time, I had struggled a lot. I wondered if I could handle everything on my own. I thought that maybe I should become a member of his *akhara*. You know, become a member of his group. I figured that if I join his *akhara*, that I would have protection against my enemies, and I had a lot of them. I felt that I would not have to fight the corruption of these religious leaders all by myself.

On the condition of joining his *akhara*, the baba vows the promise of male protection to Mataji. But he does not stop there. The *baba* not only offers to bestow on Mataji the "big title" of *mahamandaleshwar*, which entails a leadership role within the *akharas*, but also boasts about the wealth and status that come with such a title. He seems to know the ins and outs related to the *akhara*'s power structures, for he himself holds the title of *mahamandaleshwar*. Bragging about his lordship over a seemingly infinite supply of wealth, he assures Mataji that he can be her cash source without incurring any financial loss to himself. These goods become the carrot and stick that the *baba* waves in her face to persuade her to become a member of his *akhara*. The baba, as the story suggests, possesses the power to give Mataji the world. His use of saccharine speech is meant, perhaps, to soften her heart and seal the deal. He

Fig. 20.9 A poster of Mataji at her ashram showcasing her Shankaracharya title, 2014. Author's collection

showers Mataji with compliments about her asceticism (*tapasya*) to suggest being impressed with her superior spiritual attainment. "Who can be a greater *sadhu* than you?," he says. He compares Mataji with the mythic figure named Sati Anusuya, who epitomizes female virtue, power, and devotion in the Hindu imagination.

With sweet words, lofty promises, and magnanimous gestures befitting erstwhile kings and lords, implying his royal-like power, the *baba* pulls out all the stops in seducing Mataji into leaving her jungle-style living, where, in his eyes, she is barely surviving, and takes shelter with him in his *akhara* where she can thrive like the divine queen of the world. Hence, the *sadhu*-king desires to make Mataji, the glory of virtuous women such as Sati Anusuya who performed asceticism in the jungle, his *sadhu*-queen. His offer strikes this author as a marriage proposal.[44]

In being propositioned by powerful male monastic with possibly questionable intentions, Mataji is not alone. Even Durga, to which Mataji compares herself, is no stranger to the "trickery" of sexual seduction used by cosmic powers to woo her into accepting marriage. As taken from an episode of the *Devi-Mahatmya*, Shumbha, a demon-king, is alerted by his two generals about an unattached and glorious goddess dwelling in the Himalayas. Their description of Durga enchants Shumbha to the point that he becomes consumed by the thought of seizing her. To that end, he sends a messenger to Durga with this proposal. On behalf of Shumbha, the messenger says:

> Śumbha is the lord of the demons, the supreme lord in the three worlds…
>
> He whose command is always obeyed where celestials dwell, he has conquered all the enemies of the demons. Hear what he says: All the three worlds are mine; all the gods have come under my sway…All the finest jewels in the triple world have come into my power, with no exceptions. Similarly, the jewel of elephants, the very mount of the lord of gods, has been taken away. The jewel of horses, born from the churning of the ocean…And whatever valuable things exist among gods…All these things are mine, O Fair One. We regard you as the jewel among women in the world, O Goddess. You should come to us, for we are the enjoyer of jewels…By taking me, you will acquire supreme, unparalleled domination. Having reflected on this with your keen intellect, come be my wife (Coburn translation, 1991, 57).

In response, Durga says: "What you say is true; there is no falsehood in what you have said uttered?" (5.67, Coburn translation, 57). But there is more in store for Shumbha, not to mention the *baba*.

Let us now move into scene 2 of Mataji's story. Here, she weighs the various options that the *baba* has laid out for her but with the caveat of her joining his *akhara*. Having struggled alone for so long, the idea of having the *baba* as a potential ally and the support of an influential *akhara* behind her seems irresistible to Mataji, titles and wealth notwithstanding. She considers becoming a member of his *akhara*. However, realizing that what is being wagered and is at stake in her interactions with the *baba* concern independent female power, Mataji responds as follows:

> That baba told me that he would give me whatever I wanted. He promised me an air-conditioned car, elephants, horses, a comfortable bed, jewelry, money. He promised me everything. Clothing, silks, ashrams, temples, and even a chariot. All I had to do was become

[44] Indeed, in Hindu mythology, Sati Anusuya is a married woman.

> his disciple and give him control of my ashram. But I thought why should I do that? This is my property. This place is my entire savings. I do not have any house. I have sold my house, and all the money I had, I invested in my children's education. Whatever money was left was spent on my spiritual life…I asked the *baba* to explain what he intended to do for female *sadhus* in his *akhara*? Was he going to improve their situation, by giving them full rights [to leadership]? I wanted to know what his exact intention was for the women of his *akhara*? I told him that I wanted to see the constitution of his *akhara*, to see what kinds of facilities and provisions were made for women. But he wouldn't give it to me. I asked him if I could work independently for women in his *akhara*? I asked him if he would object if I tried to do something for the women. I explained that I do not like to be told what to do and that if he objects, I will not join him. I said that I did not become a *sadhu* so that his *akhara* could put rules on my head.
>
> I said, "Maharaj-ji, if you will not show me the way, it will be difficult for me to join." I told him, "Both of us are *sadhus*. Both of us wear *bhagva* [ochre robes]. If you ever require support, do come to me, I will help you." He shouted, "No! I will not come. I was thinking of your development. But if you are not ready to become my disciple, then I cannot help you. Whatever happens, I cannot help you." I became confused. I said, "But we are *sadhus*, right? As a *sadhu*, as a human, if I will face any problem in the future, then you should help." "No," he shouted. "I will not help." I said, "So be it. If you do not want to help, it's o.k. But I will not become your disciple. I will face everything alone."

For her own self-preservation, Mataji declines the *baba's* offer. Agreeing to his hard and fast terms for male protection comes with the condition of surrendering her will, her choices, her autonomy, and even her ashram to the *baba*, by making him her guru. As her guru, the *baba* would be entitled to Mataji's obedience, humility, and submission. His superior status would give the *baba* the upper hand in this spiritual partnership, and Mataji knows it. As his disciple, Mataji would be obliged to give the *baba* whatever he asks of her. As Mataji has told me, "the disciple is expected to give her *tan* [body], *man* [mind], and *dhan* [wealth] to the guru. She is expected to obey the guru's orders." The asymmetrical structure of the relationship between guru and disciple may create a disadvantage for the female disciples of male gurus with less-than-noble intentions.

To his credit, the *baba* lays it all out on the table for Mataji: give him her personal freedom and property in exchange for his support and his *akhara*'s protection. Claiming ownership of her ashram would, in effect, give him financial control over Mataji's temple resources. She depends on the donations made to the temple for her daily sustenance. They are her bread and butter. By taking control of the temple she heads, the *baba* would make Mataji dependent on him for her survival. His protection would be a function of her dependence on him.

She is keen to recognize that his offer comes at too high a cost to herself. Sensing a conflict between the *baba's* desire to possess her, in this case by vowing her luxuries, and her aspiration to govern her affairs independently of male control, Mataji asks herself, "Why should I do that?" Why should she hand over the powerful capacities which connect her to the primordial *shaktis* of will (Lakshmi), activity (Durga), and wisdom (Saraswati)? Relinquishing her autonomy negates Mataji's conception of her infinite human potential at the level of her soul (*atma*). No *baba* is worth such a price. Mataji was seeking an alliance with him, not a sentence of life imprisonment in his sticky web of power and control. In the end, she rejects his proposal.

As Mataji tells the story, the *baba* sees her as an object, which he can add to his other possessions, and increase his status and sense of masculine virility. His behavior as reconstructed through her memory of the event in connection with the *baba's* trading a life of detachment and poverty for that of luxury, comfort, and the company of women, suggests that the conventional ascetic ideal has lost its luster in modern times. Name, fame, and wealth have replaced the traditional ideal. But why would a *sadhu* offer another *sadhu* what she has given up, if not to impress her with cars—air-conditioned ones!—elephants and parades, and to subject her to his will. The items offered set a trap to ensnare Mataji in the thralls of attachment, and this is unacceptable for a person who has achieved the level of detachment required to sever one's ties to the world, including creature comforts worthy of religious royalty. As significantly, attached to the *baba*'s terms is the incipient expectation that Mataji will blithely surrender her autonomy and allow herself to become his handmaiden. But to do that would violate her feminine *sadhu dharm.*

Mataji's refusal to become the baba's disciple, however, amounts to shirking the virtues exemplary of the ideal devotee and respectable woman, as seen through a patriarchal lens. It commits an act of female insubordination against his male sex right to Mataji's body, mind, and assets. Expecting her obedience, humility, and submission to his authority as feminine devotion, the baba does not take her rejection well. In point of fact, he shouts at her and declines her offer to help each other down the line. But before departing, he leaves her with an ominous warning concerning her personal safety: "Whatever happens, I cannot help you." "So be it," she says. Female autonomy, which the baba's seems to conflate with female disobedience against the monastic patriarchy, brings multiple punishments on women, especially female *sadhus*: social ostracism and the risk of sexual violence, to name two of them. Thus, the price Mataji has to pay for denying the *baba* the normative sexual right to which he feels entitled, despite his renunciant status, is heavy. He burdens her with the notion that she is responsible for what happens to her.

Shumbha, too, expects Durga's obedience without argument, but she refuses to let him have it. Her body, her autonomy, and her righteousness (virtue, goodness, power) belong to her. Rejecting his proposal of marriage, Durga tells the demon-king through his messenger:

> Let me tell you of the promise I once dim-wittedly made: He who conquers me in battle, he who overcomes my pride, he whose strength is comparable to mine in the world, just he will be my husband. Therefore let Shumbha come here…Having conquered me, he will (then) readily take my hand in marriage. Why delay?

Breaking sex-specific stereotypes even for goddesses (after all, Hindu orthodoxy views Durga as dangerous), Durga brazenly refuses to submit herself to male control. Her rejection of Shumbha's offer commits a divine act of insubordination against the demon's (self-assumed) patriarchal right over her body, freedom, and life. The messenger's reaction to Durga's response is comparable to the *baba's.* He did not expect the goddess to disobey Shumbha, "the lord of the triple world." Hearing Durga's words, the messenger says, "You are a haughty one, O Goddess! You should not speak in this fashion in front of me!" As if this were not enough, the messenger disrespects the goddess by telling her that she is nothing in front of Shumbha, that she is stupid to think she can overcome the demon-king. Drunk on his power over the gods and an inflated sense of his grandiosity, Shumbha did not consider the possibility that a female could defeat him and bring him and his minions under her authority by being a better warrior than he thinks she is.

Of course, the messenger's reaction ranks second only to Shumbha's. Upon receiving the news of Durga's insolence, he shouts at the two generals who brought her to his attention:

> Damn it, Caṇḍa! Damn it, Muṇḍa! You two go there, surrounded with many forces, and bring her here quickly. Seizing her by the hair or trussing her up. But if you have any doubt about being able to do this, Then let her be assailed in battle by all the Asuras with their various weapons. When that *wicked* woman has been assaulted and her lion slain, Then seizing and binding this [Goddess], let her be brought here!" (italics by the author).

Knowing that Shumbha will not take her insubordination favorably, Durga, smiling resplendently, waits for the demon army to arrive, poised to assail her foes. Perhaps she feels the way Mataji felt when Raj scolded her for rejecting him: "If I am bad, then let me be bad." What the demons call a "wicked" goddess, Mataji would appear to call a "wise" woman based on Mataji's understanding that a woman's-goddess's-guru's body belongs to her and no one else.

In the last episode of Mataji's story, she issues a spectacular challenge to the religious patriarchy like Durga does to Shumbha through his messenger. Mataji summons the monastic leaders to compete with her in a 24-hour event of yoga, meditation, and debate. In return, she promises to make the leader who defeats her in the competition her guru. In her words,

> I say to all the religious leaders that I am ready to stand in a competition with you. I challenge you to come and sit in front of me in your loin cloths. If you will be able to sit, speak, and meditate with me for hours, I will believe in you (i.e., that you are my true guru). You people ask me about my guru. I say nobody is worth making a guru. If anybody is more equipped in his behavior and knowledge than I am, then I will make *him* my guru. I say to all of the leaders out there, there is no one whom I can call a guru. Come and do *sādhanā* [religious practice] with me for twenty-four hours. If you can sit with me for that long, if you can defeat me in *sadhana,* I will accept you as my guru. Let us see who is more powerful. My name, Trikal Bhavanta, means Shakti. This is why no one is accepting my challenge. These monastic people have confirmed that I am the real Shankaracharya!

Contrary to dominant Sanskritic representations of idealized womanhood, Mataji revises an orthodox Hindu view of Durga's liminality (and gender role reversal) as readily as she promotes the institutional autonomy of female *sadhus* as normative. Durga hardly constitutes a temporary, remote, or threatening, presence that appears, disappears, and reappears to Mataji during life's trying moments. Rather, Durga's presence is alive and continually present with and palpable to Mataji. Refusing to capitulate to the monastic society's oppressive institutional patriarchy has enlarged Mataji's awareness of Durga as a normative presence, enabling her to embody this fierce feminine force as the female Shankaracharya of a women's lineage. Unlike Brahmanical patriarchy, Mataji has given Durga a permanent place at the table of respectable womanhood. Her practices underscore that the Durga power "self-manifesting" in Mataji is a "part of the society," not an outlier to it. Through Mataji's alternative authority, Durga makes her presence known and claims space, a process by which the goddess moves from the margins of existence to its center, like Mataji and the people on whose behalf she works in Hindu society.

In this respect, Mataji's telling of personal narratives forwards the dual insight that Durga belongs in the world as much as female *sadhus* belong in the Shankaracharya lineage. They are neither liminal to the monastic culture, nor transgressing feminine virtue *for their class*. Along parallel lines, Mataji teaches that Hindu society needs female *sadhus*' presence and participation to reverse an uneven, and unjust, gender-caste system back to the dharmic state of equality. Without them, according to Mataji, the society would collapse like the cosmos without Durga would fall asunder. Mataji represents her struggle for women's institutional autonomy using the language of "reviving *dharm*." Of her leadership role, she says, "I am reviving the old naturalist system [*purātan vyāvasthā*]…I talk of natural things. Women want to be free, because this is the natural order [*dharm*] of life…Women and men are equal, because nature makes everyone equal,[45] and nature never makes a mistake. Nature made everyone equal, but people have destroyed the natural system. Nature wants me to unite everyone under the old system."[46]

However, people's cultural training installs potent gender imaginaries that enclose feminine virtue within the legitimating structures of prescribed norms and reduce women who embody alternative ideals to the status of transgressive subjects. This socialization obscures the surface and deep structures of inequality that barricade female *sadhus*' access to institutional control as well as conceals the mechanisms of their oppression. Consequently, their exclusion elicits an outcome that is as punitive as it is marginalizing: it punishes women, including the *sadhus* with preceding education in the system and with the buy-in of institutional stakeholders, which qualify them for the leadership, for presumably usurping the roles intended for men of the dominant castes. To keep female *sadhus* out of the leadership through customary means, or by fiat, ensures that they do not cross sacrosanct gender-caste lines and defile ritual purity.[47] More pointedly, it keeps women in their assigned place—below men and invariably inferior to them.

Mataji's struggle for institutional autonomy blurs these lines of high and low, deserving and undeserving, virtue and contagion.[48] Her alternative authority not only disturbs culturally dominant narratives about women's and subordinate identities' "proper" place in Hindu society. It also turns the mainstream tradition on its head, by disrupting received understandings of male superiority and Brahmin supremacy. How could it not? After all, Mataji operates from a different set of normative religious commitments than those enforced by the monastic patriarchy.

---

[45] In Hindi: "*prakritī ne sabhī ko samān banāyā hai, par logon ne vyavasthā ko barbād kar diyā.*"

[46] Interview with Mataji, January 27, 2019.

[47] My argument has been influenced by Isabel Wilkerson's claims as featured in her book (2020), *Caste: The Origins of Our Discontents.*

[48] Ibid.

To her, Hindu society's gender and caste imbalances are no more the result of divine will than they are the outcome of the laws of nature.[49] Rather, they attest to the real and damaging material effects of the dominant religious culture of prejudice against oppressed subjectivities that Brahmanical patriarchy has camouflaged for millennia by theologizing a person's birth-ascribed status as inviolable. Mataji condemns institutionalized gender inequities and reorients the discourse on feminine moral goodness to advocate the normativity of female autonomy.

For example, on March 8, 2018, International Women's Day, she explained in a video uploaded to her Facebook page that "women should be determined enough to believe in who they are and work for society. Our society blocks women a lot and treats them unfairly. It differentiates between men and women, and, per my thinking, they get less than what the men get, from food to education to religion. I worked for the society for many years, and have seen all this with my own eyes. Women are denied equality. They must come out of the ill-minded thoughts that harm them. They must remember the personalities of all the *shaktis* on this day."

From the feminist perspective of Mataji's teachings, Durga's myth makes visible the heights to which monastic women can "fly" as they develop the consciousness of themselves as *shaktis* "self-manifesting" in a world where they are seen, heard, and respected; where, through the formation of Pari Akhara, the *sadhus* gain access to resources, opportunities, and networks for exploring themselves and their worlds.[50] For Mataji, the exercise of autonomy asserts their feminine worth and enhances their sense of being alive to life, by embodying a divine female force that is as virtuous as it is fierce. Mataji's interpretation of Durga's myth stands to inform women of their ontological birthright to flourish in institutions that historically have resisted change and define their priorities independently of what mainstream society imposes on them.

What distinguishes the emancipatory potential of Mataji's leadership within a deeply stratified Hindu monastic society is that, through it, Mataji dares to encourage women as a class to release themselves from the imprisoning patriarchal narratives of who they are, where they belong, and what they ought to do with their lives. As her teachings free women from stultifying prescriptions of patriarchal femininity, the institution that she has organized in order that women actualize their autonomy provides them the tools to take their rightful place as monastic heads.

Let us recall the image of Durga taking her weapons (or powers) from the gods that Mataji summons in the *nari dharm sansads* that she leads, which we encountered in the essay's opening vignette. It portrays what I suggest autonomy means to Mataji: the interactive socio-spiritual process of women awakening to the fullness of their humanity and aptitudes through the intentional support and encouragement of the community. She advises the people attending her *dharm sansads* that "You must support women and girls. You don't have the right to dominate them. Even the gods don't have the right to control Durga. Freedom is everyone's right."

---

[49] Ibid, pp. 101–114.

[50] Part of the power and impact of female autonomy, as Tomm (1991) has explained, is that it enables women to grow their consciousness of themselves as embodiments of the Goddess.

This counsel is usually well-received by the audience. For Mataji, autonomy does not refer to the individualistic viewpoint that women should become "islands" unto themselves and abandon their relationships and responsibilities. It feels ridiculous to propose such an idea, considering that, as a *sadhu* herself, Mataji relies on the generosity of her supporters to sustain her life and that of the ashram. Her temple provides food, shelter, clothing, and other resources for the women and children living there. As *brahmacārinīs* (female spiritual seekers who have vowed to abstain from meat, alcohol, intoxicants, and sex, and live a life of purity), these women perform different tasks at Mataji's ashram. Everyday life in this devotional ecosystem unfolds within collaborative structures consisting of relationships of reciprocity and interdependence, countering the "survival of the fittest" mentality associated with hegemonic masculinity.

Mataji's self-appointed status affirms an *interdependently relational* vision of autonomy in the spirit of that which has been discussed by scholars such as Anderson (2014), Friedman (2014), Feder Kittay (1999), and Tomm (1991). Her theology raises from within the depths of women and girls the wherewithal to "strive…against patriarchal constraints" (Friedman, 2000, 37), and enhance their sense of self and interconnectedness with others (Barclay, 2000, 52).

20.8 Conclusion: The Shankaracharya as an Indic Feminist Model for Female Monastics' Lives

In the *Devi-Mahatmya*, as Durga combats Shumbha on the cosmic battlefield, using every weapon and every *shakti* she has available, the demon-king insults her one last time by saying, "O Durga, puffed up with misplaced pride in your own strength of arms, don't be so haughty" (10.2, Coburn translation, 1991, 71). Like the so-called "haughty" goddess with whom she identifies, and whose power she says motivates her leadership, Mataji has been on the receiving end of vicious insults. The leaders whom she has affected through her fiery rhetoric have labelled Mataji a "fraud," accusing her of acts of disrepute, including the running of a "home for prostitutes." She has also been attacked twice with a knife by masked individuals at her temple.

Despite the threats to ostracize her from the larger monastic community, Mataji proceeds valiantly in her quest for women's institutional autonomy and, as she says, without concern for retaliation. In my observation, her confidence in the goddess outweighs her fear of upsetting the religious status quo. Frankly, Mataji is a "badass"; as such, she will not compromise herself to please a patriarchal establishment that would otherwise grant her the status of institutional legitimacy in exchange for her freedom. Like vital breath, it is her human birthright, not a commodity to be bought and sold in the monastic marketplace. Mataji sees her leadership as far more than a public platform and plea for increasing women's rights in Hindu society. Her *grass-roots religious feminism* resonates on a deeply personal and potentially universal level. Much like Durga, not only is Mataji involved in the fight of her life, battling against shape-shifting social demons like gender inequality, discrimination, sexism, and misogyny. As the female Shankaracharya of India (see Fig. 20.9), she is also fighting to affirm and protect fundamental human freedoms, which, to her, enrich human life and ignite the fires of human creativity.

One of those priceless freedoms involves the right of female *sadhus* to be religious in a manner that makes sense to them, or in a way that divine forces compel them to be. In her view, to diminish independent female power in the field of religion corresponds to killing *shakti*, the ultimate source of vigor and life. Her leadership aspires to reawaken and revitalize *shakti* by turning on the light of knowledge concerning autonomy as the female birthright. As Mataji explains, "I am the light that removes the darkness. A small bulb can light up the entire room."

Perhaps there is no female more formidable than a woman/goddess/guru on a mission to wipe out injustice. Mataji's righteous insubordination against the patriarchal right of the traditional authority may have set off a firestorm of controversy among the gatekeepers of institutionalized Brahmanism in India. Her leadership as the Shankaracharya has been a riptide in the ocean of Hindu monastic society. But this is why Mataji's presence is provocative and of great consequence, *because of its message for women in the wider Indic culture.* Her leadership formally sanctions monastic women's institutional autonomy. Just as importantly, it dramatically prioritizes monastic women's freedom as a normative right, enlarging the frontiers of respectable womanhood to include the independent female power characteristic of female *sadhus*/monastics.

Like the global #MeToo movement in modern times, Mataji's leadership gives women devotees religiously sanctioned permission to say 'no' to male supremacy and to take control over their lives and become the protectors of their bodies. She teaches women across the spectra of class, caste, education, ethnicity, language, citizenship, sexual orientation, and age that their right to repudiate forms of male sexual privilege within and beyond the sphere of religion exceeds any freedom enshrined in the Indian Constitution and mandated by law. From where she stands, women's resistance against male hegemony and chauvinism achieves the birthright of monastic and householder women to flourish of their own accord and for their own benefit.

In sum, by applying a grassroots feminist hermeneutics to interpret Mataji's life, leadership, and life narratives, this essay has shown the interpersonal and institutional challenges that ascetic women have to deal with and overcome to exercise autonomy and realize monastic headship. To be seen and treated as "real" *sadhus* on par with male *sadhus* and of superior spiritual achievement would appear to be one of them. Ascetic women, such as Mataji, are viewed by their male counterparts as if they are still married householders (e.g., Sati Anusuya) devoted to their husbands and families and, hence, entangled in worldly life. This would imply that women are incapable of renunciation and hold an inferior status in the monastic society.

At the same time, the essay has made clear that Mataji's telling of Durga's myth is not a symbolic response to gender problems. Rather, it performs Mataji's practice of accessing and relating to the potency of a deity that legitimates Durgafied femininity as a normative element of ascetic womanhood—and an honorable quality of heroic women defending themselves *and others* against harm—to teach the ontological primacy of the female sex and personal freedom as a normative right. To Mataji, Durga is *real*, she has *chosen* Mataji, and she provides *real power* to Mataji to do the goddess's work. Because autonomy makes possible the flight of the human spirit toward transformation and, by implication, *shakti*'s emancipation from the prison of repressive attitudes, Mataji emphasizes that women's realization of autonomy represents their "most precious possession." She equates autonomy with the weapons Durga uses to defeat evil. Like the *shaktis* that emerge from Durga's divine body to assist her on the battlefield, autonomy gives expression to Durga's martial *shakti* emerging from the human bodies of female *sadhus* as their superpower weapon to protect and increase their rights on the battlefield of the Hindu religion.

If we think about it, Durga's battle with the demons and Mataji's battle with the monastic leaders ensue because of their insubordination to patriarchy. Perhaps because Mataji and Durga refuse to be controlled, the patriarchal forces are keen to subdue them, whatever the cost to 'right order' and gender relations. And patriarchy is tricky. Like the demon Raktā-bījā ("blood seed"), whose blood that is shed on the battlefield assumes the form of new demons (see Fig. 20.8), patriarchy can assume many forms and be difficult to defeat. What better way, then, to teach *sadhus* about the virtue of female autonomy and that of self-respect and human dignity than to arm them with the salvific wisdom that refusing the legitimacy of male control over their lives exacts a divine imperative as manifestations of *shakti* incarnate. By modeling her life and religious feminism on the heroic symbolism imaged in the Durga myth, Mataji, as the leader of the female *sadhu* army (i.e., Shankaracharya), is etching into an evolving Indic consciousness a culturally potent, local Hindu feminist model of the virtue of independent female power for our times.

References

Anderson, J. (2014). Autonomy and vulnerability entwined. In C. Mackenzie, W. Rogers, & S. Dodds (Eds.), *Vulnerability: New essays in ethics and feminist philosophy* (pp. 134–161).

Barclay, L. (2000). Autonomy and the social self. In C. Mackenzie & N. Stoljar (Eds.), *Relational autonomy: Feminist perspectives on autonomy, agency, and the social self* (pp. 52–71). Oxford University Press.

Bhasin, K. (2019). What is feminism? Kamla Bhasin's key note speech at the International Seminar Interpreting Feminism *vis-à-vis* Activism. *Sangat Blog*. 23 July. Retrieved June 9, 2022, from https://sangatnetwork.org/blogs/

Bloomfield, M. (1924). On false ascetics and nuns in Hindu fiction. *Journal of the American Oriental Society*, *44*(no issue number), 202–242.

Boden, A. (2007). *Women's rights and religious practice: Claims in conflict*. Palgrave Macmillan.

Bose, M. (Ed.). (2018). *The goddess: The Oxford history of Hinduism*. Oxford University Press.

Boursier, H. (Ed.) (2021). Introduction. In H. Boursier (Ed.), *The Rowman and Littlefield handbook of women's studies in religion* (pp. 1–10). Rowman and Littlefield Publishers.

Coburn, T. (Trans.) (1991). *Encountering the goddess: A translation of the Devī-Māhātmya and a study of its interpretation*. SUNY Press.

Dasgupta, K. (2021). *Sadhus in Indian politics*. Sage Publications.

DeNapoli, A. (2019). A female Shankaracharya? The alternative authority of a feminist Hindu guru in North India. *Religion and Gender, 9*(1), 27–49.

DeNapoli, A. (2022). 'I will be the Shankaracharya for women': Gender, agency, and a guru's quest for equality in Hinduism. In U. Hüsken (Ed.), *Laughter, creativity, and perseverance: Female agency in Hinduism and Buddhism* (pp. 75–102). Oxford University Press.

DeNapoli, A. (2023a). Can a woman be a true guru?: Female gurus' grassroots religious gender activism, and the performativity of saintliness at the Kumbh Mela. In M. Cheema (Ed.), *Feminist encounters: A journal of critical studies in culture and politics, special issue on gender activism in South Asia* (Vol. 7, No. 1). https://doi.org/10.20897/femenc/12884

DeNapoli, A. (2023b). "*Everyone drinks from the same well*": Charismatic female gurus as feminist influencers' in South Asian Hinduism. In A. DeNapoli & J. McDaniel (Eds.), *The religions (MDPI) special issue, gurus, priestesses, saints, mediums, and yoginis: Holy women as 'influencers' in Hindu culture. Religions, 14*(6), 785. https://doi.org/10.3390/rel14060785

DiAngelo, R. (2018). *White fragility: Why it's so hard for white people to talk about racism.* Beacon Press.

Dimmit, C., & Van Buitenen, J. A. B. (Trans./Eds.) (1978). *Classical Hindu mythology: A reader in the Sanskrit Purāṇas.* Temple University Press.

Erndl, K. M. (1993). *Victory to the mother: The Hindu goddess of Northwest India in myth, ritual, and symbol.* Oxford University Press.

Erndl, K. M. (2000). Is shakti empowering for women: Reflections on feminism and the Hindu goddess. In K. Erndl & A. Hiltebeitel (Eds.), *Is the goddess a feminist* (pp. 91–103). New York University Press.

Friedman, M. (2000). Autonomy, social disruption, and women. In C. Mackenzie & N. Stoljar (Eds.), *Relational autonomy: Feminist perspectives on autonomy, agency, and the social self* (pp. 35–51). Oxford University Press.

Friedman, M. (2014). Relational autonomy and independence. In A. Veltman & M. Piper (Eds.), *Autonomy, oppression, and gender* (pp. 42–60). Oxford University Press.

Gross, R. (2000). Is the goddess a feminist? In K. Erndl & A. Hiltebeitel (Eds.), *Is the goddess a feminist: The politics of South Asian goddesses* (pp. 104–112). New York University Press.

Gross, R. L. (2001). *The sadhus of India.* Rawat Publishers.

Haunser, S. (2006). *Wandering with sadhus.* University of Indiana Press.

Humes, C. (2000). Is the *Devi-Mahatmya* a feminist scripture? In K. Erndl & A. Hiltebeitel (Eds.), *Is the goddess a feminist* (pp. 123–150). New York University Press.

Khandelwal, M. (2004). *Women in ochre robes: Gendering Hindu renunciation.* SUNY Press.

Khandelwal, M., Hausner, S., & Gold, A. (Eds.) (2006). *Nuns: Yoginis, saints, and singers: Women's renunciation in South Asia.* Palgrave Macmillan.

Khanna, M. (2002). The goddess-woman equation in Shakta Tantras. In D. S. Ahmed (Ed.), *Gendering the spirit: women, religion, and the post colonial response* (pp. 35–59). Zed Books.

Kishwar, M. (n.d.). Of humans and divines: Feminine role models in Hindu tradition. *Manushi, 136*, 17–30.

Kinsley, D. (1988). *Hindu goddesses: Visions of the divine feminine in the Hindu religious tradition.* University of California Press.

Kittay, E. F. (1999). *Love's labor: Essays on women, equality, and dependency.* Routledge.

Krishnan, K. (2019). *Fearless freedom.* Penguin Books.

Kumar, N. (Ed.) (1994). Introduction. In N. Kumar (Ed.), *Women as subjects: South Asian histories* (pp. 1–25). University of Virginia Press.

Jha, D. K. (2019). *Ascetic games: Sadhus, Akharas, and the Making of the Hindu vote.* Context Publishers.

Long, J. D. (2018). *Discovering Indian philosophy: An introduction to Hindu, Jain, and Buddhist thought.* Bloomsbury Publishers.

Lucia, A. (2021). Charisma in Hinduism. In J. P. Zúquete (Ed.), *Routledge international handbook of Charisma* (pp. 175–185). Routledge.

Manne, K. (2018). *Down girl: The logic of misogyny.* Oxford University Press.

McDaniel, J. (2004). *Offering flowers, feeding skulls: Popular goddess worship in West Bengal.* Oxford University Press.

McGregor, R. S. (Ed.) (2002). *Oxford Hindi-English dictionary*. Oxford University Press.
Menon, U., & Shweder, R. (2000). Power in its place: Is the great goddess of Hinduism a feminist? In K. Erndl & A. Hiltebeitel (Eds.), *Is the goddess a feminist* (pp. 151–165). New York University Press.
Mohanty, C. T. (2003). Under western eyes: Feminist scholarship and colonial discourses. In C. T. Mohanty (Ed.), *Feminism without borders: Decolonizing theory, practicing solidarity* (pp. 17–42). Duke University Press.
Narayan, D. (2019). *Chup: Breaking the silence about India's women*. Juggernaut.
Narayan, K. (1989). *Storytellers, saints, and scoundrels: Folk narrative in Hindu religious teaching*. University of Pennsylvania Press.
Nussbaum, M. (1999). *Sex and social justice*. Oxford University Press.
Raheja, G. G. (Ed.) (2003). *Songs, stories, lives: Gendered dialogues and cultural critique*. Kali for Women Press.
Rao, M. (2019). *Living mantra: Mantra, deity, and visionary experience today*. Palgrave Macmillan.
Sugirtharajah, S. (2002). Hinduism and feminism: Some concerns. *Journal of Feminist Studies in Religion., 18*(2), 97–104.
Tomm, W. (1991). Goddess consciousness and social realities. In A. Sharma & K. K. Young (Eds.), *The annual review of women in world religions* (Vol. I, pp. 71–104). SUNY Press.
Wilkerson, I. (2020). *Caste: The origins of our discontents*. Random House Trade Paperbacks.
Writers, S., & Nagar, R. (2006). *Playing with fire: Feminist thought and activism through seven lives*. University of Minnesota Press.

Chapter 21
Conclusion

Lavanya Vemsani

Abstract This chapter discusses the unique contribution of the foregoing chapters included in this volume Handbook of Indian History to the understanding of Indian history and its role in the world history.

The *Handbook of Indian history* brings together recent research on special topics of Indian history frequently overlooked. The present chapter undertakes the difficult task of attempting the survey of the contributions of each of the foregoing chapters of the book here, since it is impossible to appreciate the full contribution of each chapter through a short survey.

The book is organized into three sections chronologically bringing together pre-first millennium subjects in **Part I. The Beginnings of Indian Civilization**, while subjects of history of the first millennium India are included in **Part II. India Beyond the Borders**, and the subjects of second millennium are organized into **Part III. India through Colonization and Modernity**.

21.1 Part I The Beginnings of Indian Civilization

The first part of the book, Handbook of Indian History, examines subjects of early history of India until the turn of the first millennium. Articles included in this part of the book might be the most controversial of all the three parts of Handbook of Indian History due to the previous colonialist theories prevalent in Indian history narratives earlier. However, it is important to bring out the data-driven analyses to understand the early beginnings of Indian history. Chaps. 2–7 included in the first section address subjects of genetic history (Chap. 2), prehistory (Chaps. 3, 4,), prehistoric art history (Chap. 5), textual studies focusing on linguistics (Chap. 6) and gender (Chap. 7).

L. Vemsani (✉)
Shawnee State University, Portsmouth, USA
e-mail: lvemsani@shawnee.edu

School of Historical Studies, Jawaharlal Nehru University, New Delhi, India

L. Vemsani (ed.), *Handbook of Indian History*,
https://doi.org/10.1007/978-981-97-6207-1_21

Although these chapters focus on India they also venture beyond the borders of modern India to contextualize the history of India. Chapters included in this section establish the absence of large population migrations or invasions into India, instead demonstrating through genetic and archeological evidence the indigenous evolution of Indian civilization.

The Chap. 2 **The Beginnings of India's History: Archeological and Genetic History** by Lavanya Vemsani brings together recent research in archeological and genetic history to probe the beginnings of Indian history. The first strides of early humans, now established as two different genera known as Hominids (Anatomically Ancient Humans) and Hominins (Anatomically Modern Humans) left their traces in India. The early occurrence of first humans is traced to pre-Pleistocene era through the discovery of skeletal remains of Ramapithecus and Sivapithecus. However, these early Hominids may have been replaced by the late Pleistocene arrivals, the Hominins. This chapter illustrates the early settlements of humans in India from 500 million years ago to about 5 thousand years ago. This helps explain the early origins of Indian civilization which was shrouded in mystery due to the colonialist theories of twentieth century. This chapter helps establish the continuing civilization of India beginning with its early foundations earning it the epithet of Founders Zone.

The Chap. 3 **Palaeolithic Culture of Deccan in the Upper Krishna Basin of India with Special Reference to Recent Studies** by Jayendra Joglekar examines the Paleolithic Cultures of Deccan regions contributing to the understanding of early settlements of India. Paleolithic culture (Lower, Middle, and Upper) is noticed in all its three phases across India. Chap. 3 studies one of the earliest phases of Paleolithic culture in India classified as the Acheulian culture. This chapter focuses on Deccan region, part of the southern region of India. One of the significant aspects of this region is that the Bori archaeological site is covered in Toba volcanic ash from which the paleolithic handaxes are recovered. This establishes the devastating effects of Toba volcano and the slow recovery of prehistoric settlements across India. This chapter also establishes the spread of early stone age across India prior to the Toba volcano eruption about 74 KYA (Thousand Years Ago).

The Chap. 4 **Southern Neolithic Cutlure of India: People, Plants, and Animals** by R. Arjun examines one of the typical Neolithic Cultures of India, which are divided into eight types of Neolithic cultures mainly based on the regions in which they flourished. The diversity of these cultures is prompted by the availability of natural resources like metals and stone as well as clay which is used as a building material as well as material for fashioning pottery and cooking vessels. This helps understand the diversity of cultural practices in early settlements, as people began settling down practicing sustainable production along with domestication of plants and animals in this region. The Neolithic age in India demonstrated evolved civilization spreading across the subcontinent of India. This also shows the absence of new arrivals (knowns as Aryans) during the Neolithic phase of Indian history. Such well entrenched neolithic phases across India and their continuity and evolution helps understand the indigenous development of Indian civilization. No large invasions or sudden destructions of habitation or any mass graves are notices across the thousands of prehistoric sites excavated in this region or across India, which supports the theory of indigenous and gradual evolution of Indian civilization.

The Chap. 5 **The Indus River Valley and Other Bronze Age Cultures** by Marie N. Pareja ventures beyond the borders of India examining the enduring motifs of Indus valley and other Bronze age cultures across the world. This chapter discusses Indus culture along with other Bronze age cultures as understood from their artistic contributions. This chapter provides the necessary world history context to Indian history even within the prehistoric context, since, each region developed its own culture, there are still enduring similarities with different cultures which indicate the oneness of humanity across the world.

The Chap. 6 **The Historical Reception of Panini's Sanskrit Grammar** by Rishi Rajpopat discusses the significant contribution of the earliest linguistic text of the world, Ashtadhyayi. The chapter discusses one of the important rules of the text to help contextualize the historical development of Sanskrit and its textual tradition. One of the oldest surviving languages of the world Sanskrit presents an important historical linguistic wonder. This chapter helps contextualize the evolution of complex civilization within India as its developed complex culture is demonstrated by the linguistic, artistic, and religious systems.

The Chap. 7 **Classical Understanding of Gender in Indian Texts** by Lavanya Vemsani examines the concept of gender through a study of classical texts. The story of Amba is examined who faces unimaginable struggles in her first life. She strives and reborn to transition to become a man in her next life to take revenge on her arch nemesis from her first life. Incorporation of stories demonstrating gender dysphoria and gender transition in the pre-first millennial C.E. society of India suggests the complex social understanding India might have possessed during that early historical era.

21.2 Part II India Beyond the Borders

The chapters included in this part of the Handbook of Indian History examine historical India during the chronological era of the first millennium C.E. The Chapters included in this part discuss the important development in technical progress as well as religion and culture. Expansion of trade and Indian culture beyond the borders of India, which gradually led to fostering the Indian Ocean trading system that experienced tremendous growth in the first millennium C.E. thrusting India to the center of Indian Ocean trading system. Chapters in this section discuss, Indian ocean trade and material and cultural relations on the Indian ocean (Chap. 8) and cultural relations that influenced religion (Chap. 9), evolution of religious practices in India (Chaps. 10, 12) and comparative analysis of Sanskrit and Tamil languages to understand the evolution of vernaculars of India (Chap. 11). History's focus has been on wars, heroes, and large constructions. However, cultural developments including language, religion, and the arts are important expressions of society. Therefore, examination of historical culture is important to understand the manner in which a society evolved and progressed.

The Chap. 8 **Sailing Ships and Seafaring Networks: The Indian Ocean and the Maritime Silk Road** by Himanshu Prabha Ray examines the Maritime history of India. Maritime history is one of the neglected fields of Indian history. Maritime travel on the West Coast and East Coast of India was brisk and its contribution to the emergence of first world trade system is immense. This chapter fills the lacuna within the understanding of the contribution of this network of trade systems frequently referred to as Maritime Silk Road invoking its immense contribution to world trade similar to the Silk Road network of trade conducted with China on land routes.

The Chap. 9 **Relations Between India and East Asia in Light of Buddhism** by Bradley S. Clough examines Buddhism and cultural relations between India and the East. This chapter offers an analytical examination of relations between India and the East Asia. This chapter examines the travel of Buddhism eastwards and the arrival of Chinese monks in India during the first millennium. This chapter also examines the recent relations between India and Japanese Buddhism in 19th and 20th Centuries.

The Chap. 10 **Shaiva Traditions of Southern India: Tamil Shaivism and Shaiva Siddhanta** by Michael A. Gollner offers contextual examination of Saiva traditions in Tamil Saivism. Spread of Saivism in Tamil region during the first millennium and its historical development in second millennium are examined in this chapter.

The Chap. 11 **The Reconstruction of the Early History of Tamil-speaking Southern India** by Herman Tieken examines the theories of Tamil language and its early history comparing it with Sanskrit literature. Examining the textual sources of multiple languages this chapter demonstrates that the poets of Sangam literature did not describe a contemporary society and that Sangam poetry was developed only in the 8th c. CE under the *aegis* of the Pandya kings, who wanted to present themselves as the rightful successors of the rulers of that same name of the earlier period and, like them, as patrons of Tamil literature. Therefore, even though this early Tamil literature is an unreliable source for the early history of southern India, it does provide an interesting example of a process taking place around the same time all over the subcontinent, namely the use of the regional languages for fictional literature, which before that was the exclusive domain of Sanskrit. Tamil is not only slightly earlier than the other regional languages but also provides insight into the ideas and successive steps involved in this process of development of vernacular languages of India. Therefore, this chapter provides crucial discussion on the sources for the history of southern India through an examination of its early sources in comparative perspective.

The Chap. 12 **Jainism in Indian History and Culture** by Patrick Felix Krüger examines the multiple strands of Jainism as it historically evolved in India. Through an examination of primary sources this chapter focuses on the history and culture of Jainism and its diversity of thought practice. Hence, Chap. 12 helps highlight the multiplicity of thought and practice within Indian religion.

21.3 Part III India Through Colonization and Modernity

Chapters included in Part III of Handbook of Indian History examine the history of India in the second millennium C.E. India experienced unprecedented growth, expansion, and unprecedented wars, invasions, as well as colonization. Therefore, the chapters included in this section examined a variety of subject focusing on the growth and colonial debacles of second millennium India. Examination of cultural developments within and beyond India (Chaps. 13, 14) as well as wars and colonialist administration (Chaps. 15, 16), and struggles for India's independence from outside India (Chap. 17), India's international policy after independence (Chap. 18) India's thought outside India (Chap. 19), and development of new religious thought led by women renunciants in twenty-first century India (Chap. 20). Overall, the chapters in this section contribute to understand the culture and struggles of India inside and outside of India.

The Chap. 13 **Literary Exchange between India and Sri Lanka** by Justin W. Henry examines the initial transmission and translation of canonical and commentarial Pali works in Sri Lanka, the development of Pali literature under the influence of Sanskrit in "the long twelfth century," the prolific and religiously inclusive period of Sinhala literary production during the fifteenth century, concluding with reflections on avenues for future research to enhance our understanding of the influence of Tamil literature on Sinhala. Chapter 13 shows the spread of literary cultures of India beyond the borders of India.

The Chap. 14 **Devotionalism in the Cultural and Social Spheres of India: Popular and Monastic Aspects of Hinduism in History** by Nalini Rao examines the historical development of devotionalism and its impact in cultural and social sphere of India. This chapter examines how the heads (Gurus) of ascetic centers (Mathas) redefine, redirect, or re-interpret *bhakti* into the monastic norms of asceticism, teaching, and spirituality. This chapter also addresses the questions of what were the significant changes in doctrine, worship, ritual, or imagery within the monastery that attracted the populace? Was it the charisma of the ascetic head (Guru) who weaved the philosophical concepts and *bhakti* poetry or were there other social influences. This chapter examines the interaction of ascetic religious centers and lay devotees.

The Chap. 15 **Hinduism in the New Millennium: History, Tradition, and Practice in a Goddess Festival** by Lavanya Vemsani discusses the formation of a goddess festival in thirteenth century Deccan from the experience of war and suffering due to the invading raids between 13th–fourteenth centuries. Focusing on the history and practices associated with the festival of goddesses this chapter contributes to the understanding of the tumultuous history of India at the turn of the Second Millennium of the Current Era. In addition, Chap. 15 also demonstrates that categorizations and labeling limits examination of feminine divine and displays entrenched patriarchy.

The Chap. 16 **Legacies of Colonial Rule in India: How Race and Caste Continue to Divide Modern India** by Jyoti Mohan examines the use of the word 'race' in the Nineteenth century during the colonial expansion of European powers, to justify and explain why certain nations were able to conquer large parts of the world. In India, French and German Indologists created a hierarchy of races to argue that while India was originally the home of the Indo-European or the so called Aryan people, explaining away the great cultural achievements of Ancient India as that of others, while its decline was attributed to the racial intermixing over centuries with inferior races. The British harnessed these theories to argue that Indians needed to be governed based on their racial heritage, and created further categories of 'martial' races, and 'criminal' races. They also used the Indian system of social ordering (the caste system) to create concrete, unchangeable categories of hierarchy and power. Chapter 16 helps elucidate the insidious nature of colonialist theoretical constructions of race and history that manipulated the public perceptions of Indians to turn them into malleable colonial subjects.

Chapter 17 **Indian Indepentism: Networks Abroad** by Mathieu Gotteland examines the activists and independent movements operated with support from outside of India. Revolutionary movements of Punjab, Bengal, and the southern India are examined demonstrate the multi-pronged nature of Indian independence movement, which is generally focused on the non-violent movement. Chapter 17 helps elucidate the lesser-known independent struggles of India that originated outside of India and contributed immensely for raising international awareness for the cause of India.

The **Chap.** 18 **Independent India: Hawkish Neighbors and Few Friends** by Marc Reyes examines the international relations of India while emerging as an independent nation. Although India faced hawkish neighbors and very little support in the international arena, it was able to foster balanced relations. The first three Prime Ministers of India tried to lead India into Non-Aligned relations to balance international concerns. However, this did not really help foster peace as the first three Prime Ministers were pushed into wars with the neighboring nations of India.

Chapter 19 **A Living Legacy: The Continuing Influence of Swami Vivekananda in the Western World** by Jeffery D. Long examines the impact and continuing legacy of Swami Vivekananda on the Western World. From Vedanta societies in most major cities of America to popular culture Vivekananda's legacy lives in America. Vedanta, the essential Hinduism reached the West through the teachings of Vivekananda thus one of the world's ancient teachings from India continue to inspire and spread in the West.

The Chap. 20 **How Becoming a Myth Leads to History: A Modern Embodiment of the Goddess Durga as the Female Shankaracarya in Hindu Society** by Antoinette DeNapoli argues that Mataji constructs autonomy as an aspect of female virtue by correlating women's self-asserting capacities with Durgā's agentive power while dismantling the patriarchal right to control women. Thus, the essay extends feminist perspectives on what autonomy can mean to *ascetic women* in accordance with Mataji's teachings and explores Mataji's practices that enable women's greater freedom and parity of status in Hindu society. The fact that Mataji is able to freely operate and spread her teachings is indicative of the women's autonomy and practice within the Hindu society. In addition, this chapter shows the enduring inspiration of ancient tales of Hindu goddesses which continues to inspire female religious leaders in the twenty-first century.

The foregoing chapters in this book *Handbook of Indian History* bring together unique subjects contributing to innovative understanding of Indian history.